A Social History of
Nineteenth-Century France

Hutchinson Social History of Europe:
series editor Richard Evans,
Professor of European History, University of East Anglia

A Social History of Nineteenth-Century France

Roger Price

HUTCHINSON

London   Melbourne   Sydney   Auckland   Johannesburg

Hutchinson Education

An imprint of Century Hutchinson Ltd

62–65 Chandos Place, London WC2N 4NW

Century Hutchinson Australia Pty Ltd
PO Box 496, 16–22 Church Street, Hawthorn,
Victoria 3122, Australia

Century Hutchinson New Zealand Ltd
PO Box 40–086, Glenfield, Auckland 10,
New Zealand

Century Hutchinson South Africa (Pty) Ltd
PO Box 337, Bergvlei 2012, South Africa

First published 1987

Set in 10 on 12pt VIP Bembo by
D P Media Limited, Hitchin, Hertfordshire

Printed and bound in Great Britain by
Anchor Brendon Ltd, Tiptree, Essex

British Library Cataloguing in Publication Data

Price, Roger, *1944–*
    A social history of nineteenth-century
    France, 1815–1914.——(Hutchinson social
    history of Europe; 1).
    1. France——Social conditions——19th
    century
    I. Title
    944.06   HN425

    ISBN 0 09 172930 0
    ISBN 0 09 173201 8 Pbk

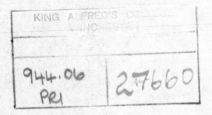

Contents

Acknowledgements

This book has been a long time in the making, and over the years I have benefited considerably from the stimulus afforded by students taking my course on nineteenth-century France. The University of East Anglia has also accorded me excellent library facilities and for these I am particularly grateful to Barry Taylor, Bill Marsh and Ann Wood.

Although it is largely based on secondary sources the book also represents the findings of research conducted over the past twenty years and I would like to acknowledge once again the financial support which made this possible, particularly from the British Academy, the Leverhulme Foundation, Twenty-Seven Foundation, the Wolfson Trust, and the School of Modern Languages and European History of the University of East Anglia.

I would also like to record my thanks to my colleague Richard Evans for first suggesting that I should contribute a volume to Hutchinson's Social History of Europe, and for his perceptive comments on earlier drafts. Extremely helpful advice also came from another colleague, David Barrass, from Colin Heywood of the University of Loughborough, and Roger Magraw of the University of Warwick. Sydney Thomas, the vicar of Pontyberem in Dyfed took time off from his parish duties to comment on the chapter on religion. I am grateful to all of them, but above all to Heather Price for the numerous improvements in content and style she has suggested.

Claire L'Enfant at Hutchinson has once again been a great encouragement, and Sarah Conibear has efficiently edited a manuscript which turned out to be a little longer than expected. As always I would like to express my gratitude to Robert and Jane Frugère of Bois Colombes for their many kindnesses.

Above all however I am grateful for the love and support – and all the fun – that comes from living with Heather, Richard, Siân, Emily and Hannah.

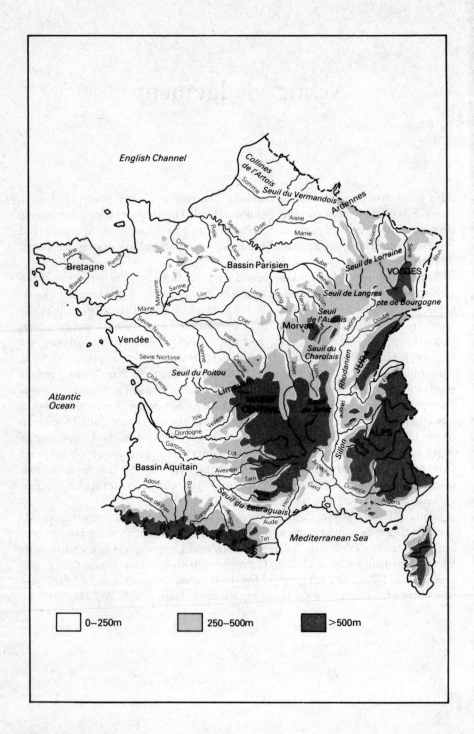

Figure 1 *Relief map*

Introduction

Nineteenth-century France, like other European nations, experienced a complex of changes involving industrialization, urbanization, the commercialization of agriculture, the greater cultural integration of provincial societies into the national whole, politicization and the growth of the modern bureaucratic state. Although this is not the place to discuss the economic changes in great detail, they were clearly of fundamental importance. France went through a period of transition from an economy dominated by agricultural and artisanal forms of industrial production, towards an economy in which – in spite of important continuities with the past – industrial production predominated in terms of the value of the physical product. The balance within the economy was significantly altered, although it must be stressed that agriculture retained its pre-eminence as a source of employment and incomes. A series of innovations occurred, at first gradually and then with increased rapidity from the 1830–40s, and most notably in transportation with railway construction, in the organization of commerce, in various branches of textiles and in metallurgy and engineering. The adaptation of steam as a relatively cheap and flexible source of power was a striking feature of these developments. In total they signified the transition from a civilization based upon wood and water as the primary source of fuel and energy, to one built upon iron and coal.

In many respects what Ernest Labrousse described decades ago as the *Ancien Régime économique et sociale* survived in France until the 1840s. The events of the revolution had done little to change an essentially pre-industrial economy and society based on small-scale workshops and farms, with low levels of productivity – a system which remained susceptible to frequent crises induced by poor harvests, the resultant substantial rise in food prices and decline in the demand for manufactured goods. The years 1846–7 saw the last major upheaval of this kind. The widespread misery and social tension which ensued, prolonged by the 1848 Revolution and the troubled period which followed it, combined to form a long and intense mid century crisis, brought to an end by the establishment of authoritarian government as a result of Louis-Napoléon Bonaparte's *coup d'état* in December 1851. Together with the re-establishment of business confidence and an international economic upturn, this created conditions favourable to a renewal of the economic growth so evident in the earlier 1840s. It might be suggested, in fact, that the social impact of the revolution of 1789, great as it was, has been exaggerated, and that a far more decisive turning point in French history was precisely this period of structural change in the economy and in society which began just before and continued after mid century, and which finally led to the disappearance of the age-old threat of famine and dearth.

Structural change in the economy together with the substantial growth in its productive capacity was bound to have significant effects upon the scale and distribution of wealth, of economic influence and social power. At another level, it affected the way in which people organized their lives – at work, and in the home and community. For society as a whole there were massive problems of adaptation. Housing and sanitary facilities had to be provided on a new scale. The very fabric of society appeared to be threatened by the tensions created or inflamed by the various challenges to traditional social relationships which increasingly seemed inappropriate in a world in flux. Whereas the 1789 Revolution can be set within a pre-industrial world, and explained largely in terms of the social tensions created within that world; those of 1830 and especially 1848 are explicable only within the context of a far more complex society. Yet, 1848 was to be the final revolution. The creation of a capitalist economic system, and gradually of a liberal-democratic polity, led to widespread improvements in living conditions, to opportunities for self-improvement for at least a significant minority, and through a complex of cultural and political institutions promoted more effective methods of socialization and social control, and means of institutionalized political protest which isolated potential revolutionaries on the fringes of society.

This then is the story we have to tell. It concerns the process of 'modernization', the emergence over a century (and longer) of the world in which we live.

Space inevitably imposes limits on the range of subjects to be considered, and indeed the historian's role is to select those features of a society which appear the most significant. To do this it is necessary to develop a conceptual *schema* which provides criteria of relevance. It is important, therefore, to make such 'presuppositions', or theories about the 'connections between things that are significant' (Beattie) explicit. Thus, in the case of the relationship between economic and social history, and the actual arrangement of the chapters in this book, the priority given to economics and to demography is based on a belief that this is the most effective means of understanding the structure of society, the division of property so essential to an understanding of social distinctions and relationships, and the material conditions of existence of the various social groups. It is not intended to imply, as Marxists inevitably do, that economic relationships *predetermine* social, nor that social history is a mere appendix of economic history. Rather, I would affirm, that social history, because of its comprehensive character, is the pre-eminent form of historical study. Only through study of social structure and of group dynamics within particular societies can economic, political or cultural forms be appreciated more fully.

The chapters which follow focus on particular problems, overall seeking to examine the interrelationship between four levels of historical reality – the

1 Pas-de-Calais
2 Nord
3 Somme
4 Aisne
5 Ardennes
6 Seine-Maritime
7 Oise
8 Marne
9 Meuse
10 Meurthe-et-Moselle
11 Moselle
12 Bas-Rhin
13 Vosges
14 Haut-Rhin

15 Terr de Belfort
16 Haute-Saône
17 Doubs
18 Haute-Marne
19 Cote-d'Or
20 Aube
21 Yonne
22 Nièvre
23 Seine-et-Marne
24 Loiret

25 Seine-et-Oise
26 Seine
27 Eure-et-Loir
28 Eure
29 Orne
30 Calvados
31 Manche
32 Mayenne
33 Ille-et-Vilaine

34 Côtes-du-Nord
35 Finistère
36 Morbihan
37 Loire-Inférieure
38 Vendée
39 Maine-et-Loire
40 Deux-Sèvres
41 Sarthe
42 Indre-et-Loire
43 Vienne
44 Loir-et-Cher
45 Indre
46 Cher

47 Allier
48 Saône-et-Loire
49 Jura
50 Ain
51 Haute-Savoie
52 Savoie
53 Isère
54 Hautes-Alpes
55 Drôme
56 Rhône
57 Ardèche
58 Loire
59 Haute-Loire
60 Puy-de-Dôme
61 Lozère

62 Aveyron
63 Cantal
64 Creuse
65 Corrèze
66 Lot
67 Haute-Vienne
68 Charente
69 Dordogne
70 Lot-et-Garonne
71 Charente Inférieure
72 Gironde
73 Landes
74 Basses-Pyrénées
75 Gers

76 Tarn-et-Garonne
77 Hautes-Pyrénées
78 Haute-Garonne
79 Tarn
80 Ariège
81 Aude
82 Pyrénées-Orientales
83 Hérault
84 Gard
85 Bouches-du-Rhône
86 Vaucluse
87 Basses-Alpes
88 Var
89 Alpes-Martimes

Figure 2 *Departments and their capitals*

economic, the social, the cultural and the political. The first examines and seeks to explain changes in the economy, the second considers the impact of this upon the material environment, the evolution of living standards, the changes in behaviour and attitudes signified by movements in birth rates, and the changing balance between urban and rural populations. It helps to illustrate the interrelationships between people and their environment, which is at one and the same time both destructive and creative; it also reveals the human significance of unequal shares in resources and in life's opportunities. From the perspective of the late twentieth century the developments evident especially from the 1840s might appear slow and discontinuous. What was novel about them in comparison with earlier epochs was the fact that they were sustained, and that the cumulative effect was to create a very different type of society. The examination of changing societies is again taken up in the second part of the book, which is concerned with the identification of the major social groups which made up French society, with their internal structures and life-styles, with relationships between social groups, and the development of systems of control and subordination, of repression and resistance – in short of political activity. The third and final part analyses a set of institutions – religious, educational and political – of crucial importance in influencing people's perceptions of the world in which they lived, in promoting social integration, and as a means of social control. Inevitably one of the fundamental concerns of the book will be with the possession and use of power in its various forms – economic, social and political.

PART ONE

A Changing Environment

Population growth, industrial development, urbanization, rail, road and canal construction, together with changes in agricultural methods, had a marked impact upon the landscape, which it would be fascinating to examine. However, it is the interaction of people and their social environment which is the central concern of the following chapters – to define the main features of economic change and assess the impact of these changes on living standards, employing such demographic indicators as mortality rates; upon people's perceptions of their own and their children's life-chances, using the key indicator which is birth rate; and the responsiveness to changing opportunities indicated by the decision to migrate from country to town.

1

The economy: continuity and change

Introduction

The French economy underwent considerable change during the nineteenth century. At its beginning, a very high proportion of the population worked in agriculture, incomes were low and spent mostly on food and other necessities, demand for manufactured goods was limited, and poor communications further restricted the market. With low levels of demand, techniques in both agriculture and industry remained relatively primitive. From the 1840s the pace of economic change accelerated, with radical alterations to the structure of the economy. This affected the composition of total output and the distribution of employment, and had a profound impact upon society at large. The main problem is how best to describe, and then explain, this change. Economic relationships can only be understood as part of an overall social system. It is thus essential to attempt to understand the interaction of a multiplicity of variables of different types. The historian must, moreover, concern himself not only with change, but also with continuity. The two are interrelated and inseparable.

There is no simple explanation of the economic changes which occurred in France in the nineteenth century. The British example was, of course, an important stimulus due to the threat of competition and the simple desire to emulate, but economic change in France has to be explained primarily in terms of the specific French context – in relation to particular conditions of relief and climate, the structure of market demand, and the supply and cost of the factors of production.

Nineteenth-century economic growth differed from that of previous centuries in that it was sustained and involved major structural changes in both economy and society. The crucial characteristic of this growth was the increase in per capita production revealed in Table 1. The statistics should be treated with caution, due to the problems involved in their collection, but they can be regarded as indicators of general trends.

Demand might be regarded as the *initiating* force in the development of an economic system. Sustained growth meant breaking out of the vicious circle which in a traditional society resulted in low real income because of low per capita productivity, caused by low levels of investment in capital equipment, which in their turn were the result of low levels of demand due to low real

Table 1   *National income at constant prices (in 1905–13 francs)* [1]*

Years	Total national income (millions of francs)	Per capita national income (francs)
1825–34	10,606	325.6
1835–44	13,061	380.5
1845–54	15,866	443.0
1855–64	19,097	510.9
1865–74	22,327	602.0
1875–84	24,272	644.2
1885–94	26,713	696.6
1895–1904	30,965	794.7
1905–13	34,711	876.4

income. The problem was intensified by a tendency for population growth to accelerate in the early stages of development, at a time when industrial growth and the provision of employment opportunities outside the agricultural sector was slow. To a substantial extent per capita income and the whole cycle of economic growth depended upon rising agricultural productivity both to feed this population and provide resources for industry. A long period of increased demand was necessary to encourage economic innovation, the shape of which was determined by the range of techniques available and the capacity of potential innovators to make use of them – itself determined by the availability of capital and of labour equipped with the necessary skills.

Innovation must be considered within the context of established local and regional economic systems. New techniques tended to be more rapidly accepted the more easily they fitted into existing productive systems, the lower their capital cost and the greater the possibility of financing them through self-investment. In effect modernization involved not the substitution of 'modernity' for 'tradition' but the interpenetration of various attributes of both.

The structure of demand in the nineteenth century was decisively transformed by transport innovation, which increased the size of potential markets by reducing the cost of transporting commodities. There can be no doubt that the effectiveness of all forms of transport was substantially increased from the 1840s. The means were provided for the cheap and rapid movement of commodities, of people, and through the telegraph and press of information. Progress had undoubtedly been made before the railway spread, but the traditional forms of transport had constituted a major obstacle to the development of a more unified market and a major disincentive to increased production. Comparisons might be instructive. Britain, a much smaller country, possessed the advantages of a relatively dense waterway system which facilitated the easy

* Superior figures refer to the Notes and references beginning on p. 366.

Table 2   *Internal transport of merchandise (milliard tonnes/kilometre)* [2]

Years	Road	Canal	Rail	Sea (coaster)	Total
1830	2.0	0.5	—	0.6	3.1
1841–4	2.3	0.8	0.06	0.7	3.86
1845–54	2.6	1.2	0.46	0.7	4.96
1855–64	2.7	1.4	3.0	0.7	7.8
1865–74	2.8	1.3	6.3	0.6	11.0
1875–84	2.6	1.5	9.4	0.6	14.1
1885–94	2.7	2.3	10.9	0.8	16.7
1895–1904	2.8	3.2	14.9	1.1	22.0
1905–14	2.9	3.8	21.0	1.1	28.8

establishment of integrated markets. France had more in common with a large landmass like Germany, in which the railway played a major role in stimulating changes in market structures. It would be too much to describe the railways as a necessary precondition for the substantial extension of markets, but transport changes without doubt profoundly affected the spatial structures of economic activity. Table 2 reveals both the large increase in goods transported and the stimulating effect of the rail network. Large-scale production is dependent upon access to large markets. Prior to the development of the railway network, high transport costs made it difficult to break out of an economic system based upon small-scale production for localized markets. The exceptions were regions close to the sea or waterways, with relatively cheap access to markets. In such regions the techniques of production were determined primarily by the relative costs of the various factors of production. Everywhere in early nineteenth-century France the availability of abundant supplies of low-cost labour made large-scale capital investment seem unnecessary.

However, it is a mistake to assume new methods of transport wrought immediate transformation. They tended (as Figures 3 and 4 indicate) to favour the already more developed regions of plain and river valley, which offered profitable traffic and low costs of operation. These were already prosperous areas, more responsive to change given their relatively high per capita production, incomes and investment capacities. To a considerable extent the relative economic position of the various regions remained unchanged, save where previously isolated areas enjoying specific natural advantages were provided with better access to markets by the railway. For many individual producers and regions adaptation to the new markets created by the transport revolution was to be extremely difficult. At the same time, as some activities were stimulated by access to enlarged markets, others experienced a heightening of competitive pressures as markets previously protected by high transport costs were invaded by competitors.

Since certain parts of a developing country are more responsive to change than others it is essential to consider regional development and the relationships

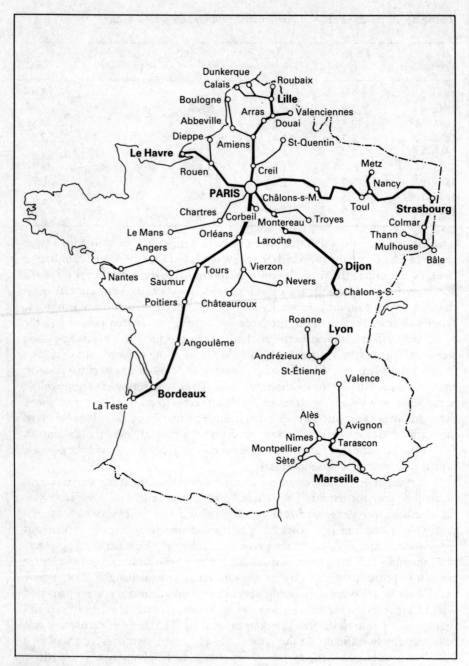

Figure 3   *Goods traffic by rail in 1854 (the line Paris–Rouen represents an annual traffic of 400,000 tonnes, that for Vierzon–Châteauroux represents 40,000 tonnes)*
    Source: *After D. Renouard*, Les Transports de marchandises par fer, route, eau depuis 1850   *Colin 1960*

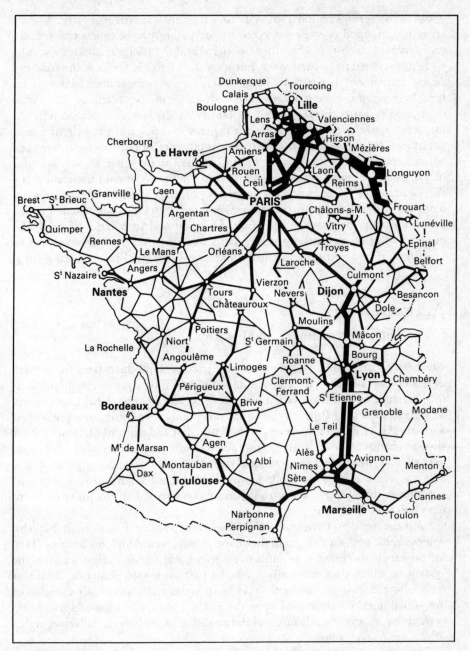

Figure 4 *Goods traffic by rail in 1913 (the line Mézières–Longuijon represents an annual traffic of 7,800,000 tonnes, that from Châteauroux to Limoges 1,400,000, and that from Cherbourg to Caen 300,000 tonnes)*

Source: *After D. Renouard*, Les Transports de marchandises par fer, route, eau depuis 1850   *Colin 1960*

between the various regional subsystems within the national economy. A 'dual' economy emerged as investments tended increasingly to be concentrated in the more dynamic centres. The more 'modern' and the more 'traditional' sectors were not isolated from each other, but were distinctive in terms of the scale and capital intensity of production. These differences were most marked in agriculture, between the more market-orientated capitalistic farms and peasant farms orientated towards the satisfaction of family needs. It is also vital to note the importance of the towns as economic centres – as poles of growth attracting enterprise, capital and labour and serving as markets for both manufactured and agricultural commodities – and among towns the existence of an economic hierarchy based upon location in relation to the means of communication and the significance of commercial functions. Primary railway networks were designed with urban–industrial interests in mind. Not only did particular towns act as initiators of growth, the same might be said to be true of particular industries during particular periods. Thus a succession of *leading sectors* can be identified – first agriculture and then subsequently various branches of industry.

Agriculture
Continuity with change *c.* 1800–*c.* 1850

The basic factors influencing demand for agricultural products were the growth of population and per capita demand. Individual food consumption, and thus the structure of demand, varied according to socio-professional groups, and also geographically. Prior to the communications revolution, in a predominantly rural society with low average incomes, diet and patterns of demand were slow to change. Subsequently change accelerated. The process of urbanization, in particular, meant that an increasingly small proportion of the population was able to produce its own food. Consumer demand in the growing towns, together with improved access to urban markets provided a major stimulus to innovation in agriculture.

Land use reflects a complex of factors, not only environmental, but also demographic and socio-legal in the shape of landownership and tenancy. Historical survivals continue to influence agricultural regions centuries after the system of which they originally formed a part came into existence. This was especially the case in northern areas with open fields in which exercise of individual initiative depended upon the gradual transformation of agricultural systems by means of enclosure and the abolition of traditional collective rights of pasture (*vaine pâture*).

Change was inevitably slow in traditional agricultural economies, based as they were on delicate internal balances. Groups of plants needed to be integrated in such a way as to facilitate the division of work throughout the agricultural year. Of even greater importance was the production of a range of commodities in a polycultural system. Plants with different vegetative cycles provided some guarantee against the failure of any one crop due to bad weather. Innovation, although never absent, normally depended upon almost certain confidence that the replacement of one element in the cultural system would not upset the equilibrium of the whole. The peasant cultivators who dominated much of French agriculture, concerned above all with family subsistence, required empirical proof of the value of innovation before engaging in it themselves. Such stability was intensified by isolation and by the absence of the stimuli afforded by large urban markets.

Attitudes towards innovation should be seen as part of a complex of social and mental attitudes in a community. The farmer who turned away from subsistence crops faced the risk of subsequently having to purchase food at inflated prices after a poor harvest. Prudence enjoined an effort to meet these needs as a first priority. The reduction of risks rather than profitability was of primary concern. Innovation occurred, normally by means of a slow accumulation of experience, usually gained in the first instance by the larger farmers who possessed sufficient land and capital to take risks. However, and in spite of poor access to markets, not even the most traditional of peasant families could isolate themselves entirely from commercial considerations. It was necessary for every peasant family to cultivate a cash crop or else to hire out labour, work in rural industry or have recourse to temporary migration, to obtain the cash resources vital for the payment of taxes or purchase of necessities which were not produced locally. Even the most isolated regions were engaged in trade.

The diversity of the products of French agriculture is partially revealed in the following estimates. Table 3 suggests that in the earlier part of the century

Table 3 *Production*

Years	Cereals[1]	Potatoes[1]	Wine[2]	Natural and cultivated pasture[1]	Roots[1]	Sugar beet[1]	Meat[3]	Milk[2]	Butter and cheese[3]	
1815–24	86.44	25.30	37.24	—	—	—	548	43	113	
1825–34	97.02	42.16	40.17	—	—	—	602	47	127	
1835–44	111.60	63.26	38.65	178	(50)	16	685	58	153	
1845–54	126.08	49.79	47.92	268	50	18	823	63	167	
1855–64	138.89	68.77	48.42	313	52	44	972	73	193	
1865–74	140.89	80.26	60.44	360	90	77	1091	74	200	
1875–84	142.92	92.99	46.01	408	128	78	1251	74	200	
1885–94	147.39	118.04	30.70	418	143	64	1374	87	132	137
1895–1904	153.73	106.22	45.05	458	250	75	1464	81	150	154
1905–14	154.92	117.35	52.79	604	370	77	1535	109	170	174

Notes:
[1] millions of quintals;
[2] millions of hectolitres;
[3] millions of tonnes.

Source: J. C. Toutain, *Le produit d'agriculture française, de 1700 à 1958*, T.II La Croissance, in Cahiers de l'Institut de Science Economique Appliques, Suppl. 115 (July 1961), pp. 13–14.

farmers' efforts continued to concentrate upon the production of basic food-stuffs. Only from mid century did their interest markedly shift towards the production of meat and dairy products or wine, something indicative of a growing responsiveness to changes in the structure of demand as living standards generally improved.

In most areas a subsistence polyculture prevailed, with cereals as a dominant element. Variations in physical conditions inevitably resulted in nuances and contrasts. These were infinitely varied and can be considered here only at the very broadest level. Thus, the polyculture of northern France tended to be typified by the triennial rotation of crops, with an autumn cereal such as winter wheat, followed by a spring-sown cereal such as oats, barley or rye, and this by a year of fallow. Spring cereals could be sown due to the relatively high humidity of early summer. A temperate climate and rich soil were the primary natural advantages of the north, along with access to major urban markets. The west, centre and south suffered contrasting disadvantages, save exceptionally in the broad river valleys and areas of plain. The polycultural systems of the south tended to include a greater variety of plants, but spring sowing was very risky due to the dryness of the summer months, so that in general only a biennial rotation, of wheat and fallow, was possible, although vegetables or fodder were often grown in the latter, particularly as population pressure grew. Practices varied with soils. On better soils in the south-west maize might be cultivated in what otherwise would have been the fallow year, or else a triennial rotation of wheat, maize and fallow was introduced. But on the acidic or granitic soils of much of the Massif Central or Breton interior low yields meant misery. Another major contrast was that in the north around three-quarters of the land was cultivable, in the south little over a quarter, the remainder providing a large area of poor-quality grazing and land for the cultivation of valuable supplementary foodstuffs like chestnuts. In spite of their relative technical backwardness southern polycultures, by their variety, provided a greater guarantee against crop failure.

If the two major causes of change within traditional agricultural systems were increasing population and growing participation in commerce, both stimuli were more effective in the north. Nothing indicates the overall contrast between agriculture in the north and south better than the difference between the net value of the product per hectare revealed by the agricultural census of 1852 – in the Nord 393 francs, Seine-et-Oise 302 francs, Seine-Inférieure and Pas-de-Calais 257 francs, and in the southern departments such as Landes 47 francs, Basses-Alpes 50 francs and Lozère 51 francs. In the first half of the nineteenth century there were clear signs in most regions that, in spite of improvements in agricultural productivity, populations remained extremely susceptible to food shortage in the event of a poor harvest. These caused repeated economic crises – in 1801–2, 1810–12, 1816–17, 1828–9, 1837–9, 1845–7 – with serious consequences for popular living standards. Low productivity, technically backward agricultural systems were especially liable to yield fluctuation.

The increasing cultivation of marginal land and the use of a growing proportion of the land to produce basic foodstuffs were clear symptoms of relative overpopulation. Moreover, in a primarily subsistence economy price depression between 1817 and 1851 did little to alter the balance between products. The cultivation of fodder was increasing and allowed the maintenance of increased numbers of animals who provided more manure. But generally basic human subsistence needs continued to determine land use. Animals were often only tolerated as providers of draught power and manure, and because of inadequate care and feeding were inefficient at both. Another obvious symptom was the underemployment of rural populations as population densities reached historical maxima in most agricultural regions without a commensurate increase in employment opportunities in either town or country. The development of rural industry and of temporary migration, while alleviating misery, were evidence of a desperate struggle to make ends meet.

It does not appear as if anywhere in France the mass of the rural population had escaped from a situation in which misery was normal, intensifying to extreme distress during the frequent periods of crisis caused by poor harvests. Thus an undernourished and unproductive labour force sought to maintain the precarious balance between food resources and population, primarily by employing the most obvious means of increasing production. The cultivated area, which is believed to have been around 16 million hectares in 1789, increased to 20,590,000 by 1840 and to 22,340,000 by 1852. The alternative was to reduce the extent of fallow and diversify production, especially through the introduction of fodder crops providing animal feed and often retaining nitrogen in the soil. Only in the Paris basin and the north, where the existence of major urban centres and the more market-orientated systems which had developed gradually over centuries in response had permitted the establishment of relatively large-scale farms, whose occupiers and/or owners possessed the capital to finance technical innovation, did productivity increase substantially in the first half of the century and was population pressure on resources eased.

Innovation required capital, however limited, and a sense of future security. Thus the size of units of production and the characteristics of tenurial systems were of considerable importance in determining ability to innovate. Most of the land was farmed in small units by peasant proprietors or tenants and except for a small minority it appears as if large landowners usually had little interest in farming. Most behaved as *rentiers*, quite satisfied with the tendency for rents to increase as population pressure grew. Instead of encouraging innovation, leases tended to forbid the modification of established canons of good practice in case change caused impoverishment of the soil. This, together with capital shortage and social pressures for employment, generally made innovation labour – rather than capital – intensive. Rich and poor alike were aware of the need to avoid breaking the precarious social equilibrium by innovation which might threaten food supplies or else bring unemployment. Indeed, where there was a shortage of capital, labour intensive means of cultivation represented the 'appropriate technology'. The land and labour remained the principle inputs of a traditional agriculture. In such a situation the technical inferiority of the small peasant farm was compensated for by greater labour input and productivity levels per hectare were often superior to those of large farms.

The most optimistic estimates of progress in the first half of the nineteenth century are probably those of Lévy-Leboyer,[3] who calculates an increase in production between 1815 and 1852 of the order of 78 per cent, made up of a 72 per cent increase in the value of vegetable production and 131 per cent in that of animal production. In spite of this progress, the fragility of the system was clearly revealed by the crisis of 1845–7. Other than in the north, and even there progress was limited, innovation was localized and exceptional. The difficulty of access to urban markets meant limited revenue and capital for investment, and a lack of incentive. Some form of participation in production for the market was increasingly likely as communications improved, but the very limited degree to which regional specialization developed is indicative of the continued dominance of subsistence production. This often meant cultivation of basic foodstuffs in unsuitable natural locations, which combined with technical backwardness – insufficiently deep ploughing, poor aeration of soil and clearance of weeds, poor drainage, etc. – to result in a situation in which yields remained low and in many regions hardly increased at all. Morineau's maps based on the 1840 agricultural inquiry provide some indication of this general backwardness and of regional diversity.[4] Although farmers were to some extent responsive to the price differences between different crops, fear of food shortage limited the degree to which they were prepared to reduce the area under cereals. In Calvados, in spite of a fall in cereal prices of around 20 per cent in the first half of the century, the extension of pasture was slow. On the plains of Languedoc, the vine was excluded from the most suitable land by cereals, even though wheat yields were as low as 9.5 and 10 *quintaux* per hectare.

Economic systems engender a variety of goals. The foremost concern of the vast majority of peasant farmers remained the need to secure the subsistence of their families. Only when farmers felt certain that they could provide for family needs more effectively by specialized production would the balance in agriculture move more decisively towards production for the market. Relative isolation due to poor communications and the limited needs of urban markets severely limited the extent to which this could occur before the 1850s. The development of modern communications networks was the decisive factor stimulating innovation in agriculture in the second half of the nineteenth century. The changes in market structures which resulted provided both incentives and a threat of competition. In response farmers could seek to increase productivity – both of the land and of labour – by technical innovation or modification of their crop mix. Increased productivity and commercialization were the potential means of improving the living standards of individual farm families and factors of some significance in the context of overall economic development. The capacity to innovate was in large part determined by the structure of pre-existing agricultural and social systems – natural conditions, structure of land-holdings, access to capital, crop mix, social attitudes – and the spatial relationship with the new means of communications which provided improved

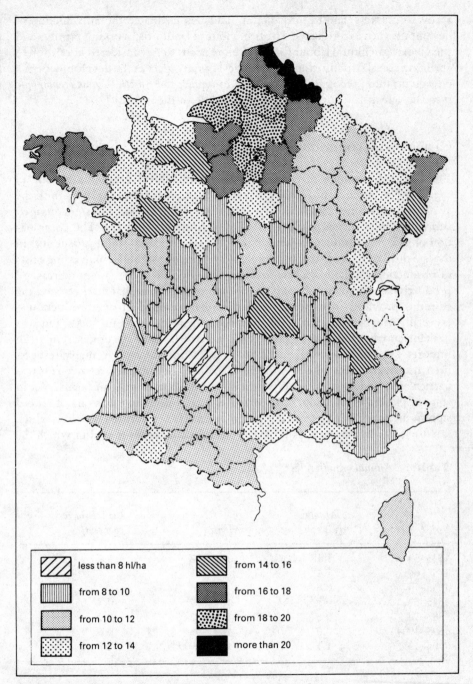

Figure 5 *Wheat yields in 1840 (hectolitres per hectare)*
Source: *After M. Morineau*, Les Faux – semblants d'un démarrage économique   *Colin 1970*

access to markets, and to information, and also facilitated the introduction of new inputs such as fertilizers. The behaviour of landlords, working farmers and the whole agricultural labour force therefore needs to be considered in relation to changing social structures and mentalities – as an aspect of the development of a new civilization, recognizably modern, to replace the *Ancien Régime économique et sociale* which had survived until the middle of the century.

Change with continuity, *c.* 1850–1914

The broad chronology of change suggested in Table 4 was the same for all regions. The initial improvement of access to markets from the 1840s until the 1870s and subsequent provision of secondary rail and road links encouraged substantial increases in productivity and in commercialization. The combination of growing production with high and rising prices brought prosperity. In the last third of the century, however, falling prices combined with rising costs of production resulted in a severe crisis and a decline in the rate of increase of productivity. The establishment of national and international markets, and the stimulus provided to increase production had resulted in overproduction – especially of wheat and wine. Recovery commenced in the mid 1890s, but was hesitant and limited. Tariff protection effectively limited competition from imports and substantially reduced the pressure to innovate. In many respects French agriculture on the eve of the First World War remained archaic. This was particularly evident in the survival of large numbers of peasant farms. Yet in spite of the limits to change, the period we are considering was one of crucial significance for the long-term evolution of French agriculture – a period which saw the final disappearance of the age-old subsistence crises, and in which the

Table 4   *Annual growth rates*[*][5]

Period	Toutain (per cent)	Period	Lévy-Leboyer (per cent)
1845–54	1.18	1847–72	1.8
1855–64	1.4		
1865–74	0.8		
1875–84	−0.5	1872–82	−0.7
1885–94	0.3	1882–92	−0.7
1895–1904	0.0	1892–98	0.65
1905–13	1.1	1898–1909	2.7

Note:
[*] Estimates of the annual growth of agricultural production vary according to the way in which the basic statistics have been 'corrected', definition of what precisely agricultural production includes, the period considered, etc.

operating context for farmers was transformed and more substantial innovation occurred in three or four decades than had previously occurred in as many centuries. Although one must stress the element of continuity with the past throughout and well beyond the period, it is difficult to deny that during it the markets for agricultural products, for labour and for capital were significantly transformed and productivity substantially increased. During these years, in spite of its continued relative backwardness compared with Britain, French agriculture made a decisive break with tradition.

Land and labour

Whereas the two prime inputs of traditional agriculture were land and labour, and productivity was thus limited by the quality of the land and the amount of labour, in a modern agriculture productivity is substantially increased by inputs of working capital in the form of fertilizers, improved hand tools, and mechanical power. This change appears to have been determined by the evolution of three basic groups of variables – product prices, the prices of the factors of production (land, labour and capital) and development of the economic infrastructure, i.e. of transport and marketing facilities – an evolution which intensified the commercialization of agriculture by means of a 'two-way tie' to the market economy, i.e. through the sale of products and the purchase of equipment and fertilizers.

The size of the active agricultural population is also an obvious influence on the calculation of productivity. In the period of transition from pre-industrial to industrial social structures, significant changes in labour supply–demand relationships were clearly taking place. Of especial importance was the fact that the rate of population growth was low – far below that of contemporary third world countries – and that agricultural productivity increased more rapidly than population. In 1852 there were 100 male agricultural workers for every 459 inhabitants. In 1882, in spite of improvements in diet, 100 were able to provide food for 590. Figures 6 and 7 illustrate both the increase in labour productivity and its regional variations. They reveal that the gross product per agricultural worker increased by something like two and a half times between 1852 and 1882, but also that the scale and rate of increase varied considerably between departments, and major existing regional differences in productivity were maintained with the basic contrast between France north and south of the line linking very roughly Saint-Malo and Geneva.

The question of farm size is of crucial importance to an understanding of the technical, financial and economic structure of farming in France. In effect the mix of the factors of production labour and capital *tended* to be determined by the size of the farm. Comparison between the statistics provided by the 1862 and 1882 agricultural censuses is possible because the categories used are relatively homogeneous (Table 5). These statistics combine to show a clear tendency towards parcellation, i.e. a decline in the number of large farms and an increase in the number of small-size units, which continued into the last decade of the century. Options varied between places and over time. Parcellation tended to be

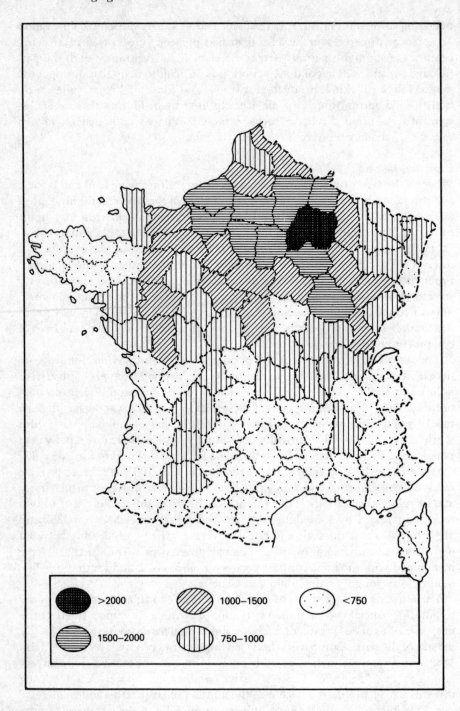

Figure 6 *Gross product per agricultural worker 1852*

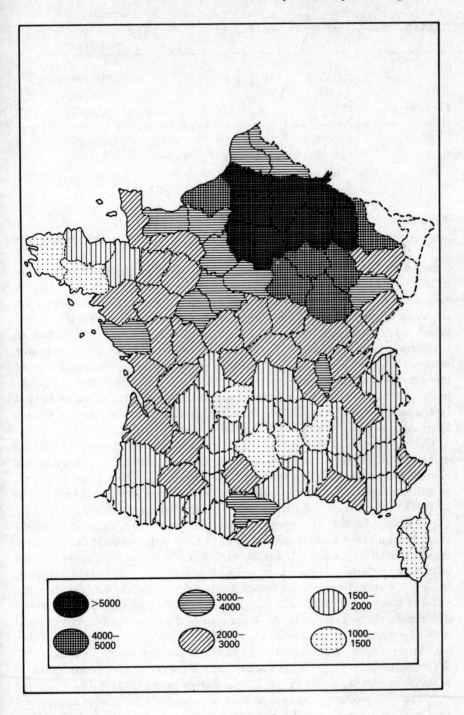

Figure 7 *Gross product per agricultural worker 1882*

Table 5   *Numbers of farms by size 1862–82*

Hectares	1862	1882	Change	1882 as percentage of 1862
1–5	1,815,558	1,865,878	50,320	103
5–10	619,843	769,152	149,309	124
10–20	363,769	431,335	67,556	119
20–30	176,744	198,041	21,297	112
30–40	95,796	97,828	2,032	102
40 and above	154,167	142,088	12,979	92

a particular characteristic of areas in the south and west, regions of polyculture or else vine cultivation and market gardening. In contrast in an area roughly north of the Loire subdivision of large farms was far less evident, with a clear tendency towards consolidation in the centre of the Paris basin and in lower Normandy. Large farms were the product of an old established orientation to the market, and the acceptance by both landowners and tenant farmers that income, whether in the form of rents or profit, could be maximized by an intensification of this capitalistic farming. Parcellation was the result of a growing tendency of large landowners in many areas to transfer capital out of the land into more profitable investments. Division into small plots maximized returns from sales to peasants anxious to fulfil their dreams of landownership.

The coexistence of both market-orientated producers and those with a fundamental orientation towards provision for the subsistence of the peasant family constitutes a major analytical problem. Holdings below 10 hectares represented an estimated 68 per cent of the total in 1852, 85 per cent in 1882 and 84 per cent in 1908. The existence of such a large number of small units, employing essentially family labour, would have significant consequences for farm technology. However, the number of small farms should not be allowed to obscure the economic importance of larger units. Thus, according to the decennial inquiry of 1892 (and now excluding holdings of below 1 hectare, i.e. effectively gardens), holdings of over 40 hectares represented only 4 per cent of the total number, but covered almost half of the land farmed, with an average size of 162 hectares; those under 10 hectares included 76 per cent of the total number, but covered only 23 per cent of the total area. The remaining 20 per cent of the total number and 30 per cent of area were held by medium farmers, with 10–40 hectares. Wage labour was employed essentially on the 24 per cent of farms above 10 hectares. In terms of tenure, in 1892 75 per cent of the farms were directly owned by those who worked them, but these covered only 53 per cent of agricultural land with an average size of 4.37 hectares; 6 per cent (mostly in the west and south) were sharecropped, covering 11 per cent of the farm land with an average size of 10.7 hectares; and 19 per cent were rented covering 36 per cent of the land, an average of 11.7 hectares.

Land use

Agricultural systems undergoing modernization required substantial capital inputs, in spite of the fact that change was limited and relatively slow. In this respect, the rate of innovation was partly determined by the availability of capital. Toutain has estimated that an increase in the value of capital investment in agriculture of between 34 and 41 per cent occurred between 1851–3 and 1873–82 (or of 14–26 per cent excluding land). Subsequently, levels fell due to economic recession. This vagueness is a mute comment on the shortcomings of agricultural statistics. While the value of buildings and of *materiel* inexplicably stagnated, investment in livestock increased by 107 per cent. But even in 1878–82 the value of livestock plus *materiel*, compared with land and buildings, was only about 9 per cent (9 milliard francs compared with 98 milliards). The distribution of capital between farm types and regions is an unknown.[6] Capital shortage, however, certainly confined the more expensive innovations to the minority of commercial farmers – to some of the 8–900,000 who in 1882 habitually had a surplus to sell in the market. This meant that the other three-quarters of all farmers who were less completely involved in commercial agriculture were likely to be restricted to the less capital-intensive forms of innovation.

Peasant farmers introduced new plants once their success had been empirically proven, either by someone better placed to take the risk, or on a small scale by the peasant himself, in his garden rather than fields. This was inevitably a slow, piecemeal process, but gradually brought into existence a new, more intensive *petite culture*. Together with the more decisive patterns of change evident on the larger farms of the northern plains, it represented increasing yields by means of modification of land use. This was the primary means of increasing productivity. Most simply, and thus most commonly, it was effected by improvements in existing polycultural systems rather than by their rapid transformation – by a process of selection between potential cash crops and a gradual transition towards specialization.

Replacement of fallow in rotation systems with cultivated grasses, nitrogen fixing plants which regenerated the soil, and cleaning plants which substantially reduced the number of weeds, all had the effect of directly increasing yields. They had the added advantage of permitting the retention of increasing numbers of livestock. These innovations spread rapidly in the Paris basin in the first half of the century and into other areas subsequently. Moreover, the cultivation of fodder in areas of the centre, south and west, allowed the clearance of wasteland which had formerly served as an essential source of pasture. The extension of the vine in southern France was more dramatic. Improved access to urban markets provided an immense stimulus to wine production. This was the essential causal factor. Production was increased by means of an extension of the area under vines, and by increasing yields through the introduction of higher yield plants and more intensive cultivation. An assured supply of wheat from other regions and, with free trade, from international suppliers, led to an acceleration in the replacement of cereals by vines. Change inevitably required capital and some assurance that perceived demand trends were more than short-term fluctuations. Nevertheless, the end of the need to assure self-subsistence in case of dearth allowed a wider margin for change. Relatively high wine prices until the late 1870s combined with barely profitable cereal prices in the south to make cultivation of the vine something of a craze even among peasants, who were able to ensure better living conditions for their families than the traditional polyculture had allowed.

This led to decisive shifts within polycultural systems, in the direction of increased dependence upon the market. Vine cultivation spread from the hill-sides on to the more fertile plains. At the same time cultivation of the vine declined rapidly in regions at the climatic margin – in Oise, Seine, Seine-et-Oise, and Aisne, for example – wherever low quality wine for popular consumption was now unable to compete with wine transported cheaply from the south. In much of the Midi, where soil and climate were unsuitable for cereal cultivation or for the introduction of fodder crops, the vine provided a means of modernization through better adaptation to the natural environment. Its extension was limited only by geographical conditions. Above 500 metres vine cultivation was impossible and extensive cereal cultivation survived, as it did in Upper Languedoc where high humidity caused the development of parasitic fungi on the vines which only expensive chemical treatment could prevent. While the economy of Upper Languedoc, formerly a region of commercial wheat production, contracted due to competitive pressures, that of Lower Languedoc turned, in contrast, from subsistence polyculture towards specialized wine production. New market conditions encouraged the rapid extension of regional specialization. Table 6 makes clear the declining relative importance of the departments of the Atlantic seaboard – Gironde, Charente-Inférieure, Loire-Inférieure, and Maine-et-Loire – which had previously possessed the advantage of easy access to the major markets by water.

Table 6   *Wine production, 1850–79*[7]

Region	1870–9 production in millions of hectolitres	1850–9 to 1870–9 increase in production (per cent)	1870–9 percentage of national production
Midi	16.3	152	31.4
South-west Aquitaine	8.0	89	15.4
Charentes	7.7	112	15.0
Middle Loire	4.3	137	8.3
Bourgogne-Lyonnais	2.8	94	5.5
France	51.7	71	—

The development of specialization was slowed by the phylloxera beetle, which appeared first of all in the south, in the Gard, in 1864. Its devastating effects restrained competitive pressures on more northerly producers and post-poned the demise of *vin ordinaire* production in departments like Côte-d'Or. In the south itself, some areas – like Aude and Pyrénées-Orientales affected only in the 1870s – were able to profit from high prices for a further decade as total production fell.

The subsequent reconstruction significantly changed the structure of the vineyards. The higher cost of production due to the need to give chemical protection to the plants, plus the capital costs of reconstituting the vineyards encouraged replanting on the plains where yields were high. Previous profitabil-ity had attracted some large investors – in part using capital transferred from the declining southern textile industry – reconstitution because of its cost, at perhaps 2,000f per hectare, plus the temporary immobilization of capital while the plants matured, increased the tendency towards concentration and accentu-ated the capitalist character of part of the wine industry, and the technical gulf between large-scale producers like the *Compagnie des Salines du Midi* and the mass of peasant farmers. Improved transport facilities also encouraged the commercial production of other products formerly of secondary importance in a polyculture – especially fruit and vegetables. The development of market gardening on the plains of the Lower Rhône valley was another example of the rapid transformation of agricultural structures due to the better access to mar-kets provided by rail.

The emergence in some regions of a new specialization more suited to natural conditions and to new market structures was accompanied by a reduction in cereals cultivation – replaced usually by pasture or vines. Productivity per worker increased as the product mix shifted in favour of those of higher value. However, natural caution and the force of tradition, plus continued market imperfection, slowed the process of change. Cereals continued to be grown at high cost in unsuitable physical conditions, particularly where no immediate alternatives were obvious. In the Midi the combination of high cost, low yields, increased competition and low price, with a growing demand for wine, created a situation favourable to innovation in crop patterns. Elsewhere, where negative factors were more evident, it took longer to realize that a fundamental transformation had occurred in the market for cereals.

The establishment of international and interregional markets had created a more competitive situation and one in which lower prices generally prevailed. In spite of this most farmers continued with cereal cultivation, innovated only very slowly and sought salvation through a return to the tariff protection which had been withdrawn in 1859. In 1882 France remained above all a cereals producer. However, the relative importance of cereals had declined – from 61 per cent of the arable in 1851–62 to 57 per cent in 1882 – marking the end of the age-old effort to extend the area of cultivation. Increased yields and interna-tional supplies and the disappearance of dearth meant that a smaller percentage of the land needed to be given over to cereals production for human subsistence.

If a more competitive market often resulted in the reduction of cereals cultivation in areas in which conditions were unsuitable, it also stimulated more efficient wheat production by means of more complex rotation systems and intensive farming, which both increased the fertility of the land and provided additional marketable products in the form of fodder for animals or sugar-beet, thus reducing the overall cost of production. As part of the development of regional specialization, a growing proportion of total production, and even more of the total volume of grain entering the market, tended to be produced in the regions of advanced agriculture in the north. With improved transport the farmers of the north were able to sell their grains more easily and to sustain local price levels. This tendency towards specialization in cereal production can be seen in the slow decline evident in the Mediterranean regions and in the north-east, and to a lesser extent in the east and in Normandy. Conversely, cereal cultivation increased in some thirteen departments, including the plains of the Brie and Beauce, and in Poitou–Limousin. Abandonment of marginal land, although evident in some regions as population declined – especially in the north-east and the south of the Massif Central – was slow.

The modifications so far considered constituted labour-intensive responses to new market conditions. Increased specialization in livestock was a response which economized on a resource becoming increasingly expensive. The increase in the number of cows and horses (the limits of which are revealed by Table 7) was advantageous in itself – providing increased supplies of manure and draught power, and also marketable products – and where pasture was extended to replace arable, it reduced farm labour needs. The motives for change were thus varied and their scale ranged from alterations in the polycultural balance to the development of a more specialized form of agriculture. The provision of better access to major urban markets was everywhere the factor of crucial importance. Estimates of per capita consumption of meat in the 1882 census indicate a Parisian average of 79.31 kg, a lower figure of 60.39 kg for other towns, and a minimal 21.89 kg for the rural population. The change in market conditions led, in many areas, to livestock being considered as a viable commercial proposition, where formerly they had been viewed merely as

Table 7   *Number of livestock (thousands)*

Year	Horses	Cows	Sheep and goats
1840	2,818	11,762	32,131
1852	2,866	11,911	33,282
1862	2,914	11,813	29,530
1882	2,838	12,997	23,809

Source: Annuaire statistique, **58**, 1951, *résumé rétrospectif*, pp. 119–20 (these are among the least reliable of statistics).

necessary auxiliaries to arable farming. This growing interest in the commercial potential of livestock led to efforts to improve feeding, stabling conditions and to increased selective breeding. Moreover, from the mid 1850s a significant change became evident in the relationship between cereal and meat prices. Particularly in the 1860s, as cereal prices platformed, it was realized in some regions that livestock or livestock products might be more profitable. From the 1870s, price depression was less marked for meat and dairy products than for cereals, a factor which accelerated the trend towards regional specialization.

The possibility of increased specialization in livestock was especially welcomed in upland areas, where natural conditions were unsuitable for arable farming, although its abandonment was relatively slow because of delays in improving communications in the mountains. Sheep were more easily integrated into mountain agriculture, with its thin pastures, or into poor quality pasture anywhere than were cows. Outside upland areas, and in spite of breeding intended to increase meat yields in order to compensate for low wool prices, a continuous decline in their numbers occurred. Thus as the number of cows increased, that of sheep declined due to the reduction of the area of pasture at fallow, the clearance of wasteland and especially to the decline in wool prices caused by imports.

Innovation in pastoral farming was slow and restricted to particular regions. It depended on natural conditions, supplies of fodder and access to markets. The statistics on land use indicate how gradual the extension of cultivated fodder was, in spite of substantial progress. By 1882 there were five main areas that were to a degree specializing in livestock – a block including the Charolais, Nivernais and Bourbonnais producing meat for Paris, Lyon, Dijon and the east; another composed of Maine, Poitou, Vendée and the Charentes, specializing both in the provision of young cattle for other regions and in fattening cattle for the Paris market; Brittany selling young cattle to other regions; and southwest Aquitaine. The degree of specialization reflected the scale of local markets and ease of access to other regions. Possession of milk cows was widespread, but specialization in dairy produce was more limited – to Brittany and Normandy and upland areas of the Franche-Comté – spreading into Poitou and the Saintonge in the 1880s.

The increase in the number of cows and the establishment of better land–animal relationships had significant effects on the supply of nutrients to the land. One major weakness of traditional cereal-based rotation systems had been their inability to maintain livestock adequate to the manure needs of the fields. Traditionally insufficiency of manure had been partially offset by the collection of dead leaves and other vegetable matter, of sand and of waste products from sugar beet refining etc. Lack of stabling, resulting in haphazard dispersal of manure in the fields and the creation of dungheaps exposed to wind and rain which dried and washed away nutrients, had led to considerable waste. Although in parts of the Paris region and Flanders farmers had been able to take advantage of urban manure, in most regions the normal insufficiency of natural fertilizer had made a period of fallow essential to avoid exhausting the soil.

Cultivation of fodder permitted an increase in the numbers and weight of animals, particularly on the larger farms which had the space and could afford the investment. Moreover, from the 1850s such farms were able to use commercial fertilizer – first guano, and then chemical phosphates from the 1870s. Of more widespread importance was the growing application of marl and lime. Most fodder crops depend on the presence of lime in the soil to do well, while its addition to acid soils permitted the cultivation of wheat in place of rye and encouraged land clearance. It could only be adopted gradually because of the cost of transport from lime deposits.

Given the significance of the cost of transport in the final price of fertilizing agents, it follows that their use in large part reflected the degree of development of communications and that isolated areas not only lacked the incentive of access to markets but also the ability to rapidly and substantially increase yields. Innovation tended to follow the railway, entering the plains first and spreading along the valleys and the coasts before penetrating the interior, the plateaux and mountains. Those areas in the centre, south and south-west, with some of the poorest soils, most in need of fertilizers, were least able to use them. In the 1860s it was estimated that marl cost 75–100f per hectare in Seine-et-Marne, 140–250 in the Ardennes, 250–300 in Doubs, and 300f in Basses-Pyrénées. Gradually, in the west and in the Massif Central, Gâtinais, Vosges, Bresse and Landes, improved communications and access to lime and marl resulted in substantial changes in agriculture, and, in particular, in reductions in the area of wasteland and in increased wheat production. Contemporary observers repeatedly associated agricultural progress with better transport and the improved access to markets and fertilizers this provided. Even though French agriculture continued to suffer from inadequate efforts to improve soil fertility, the increased application of fertilizing agents seems to have become fairly general. Fertilizers represented a relatively cheap means by which the productivity of the land could be increased. Otherwise the pace of technical innovation in agriculture can be linked to changing relationships between the cost of the various factors of production and their availability. While the cost of labour remained low, it was possible to use it intensively. As labour became more expensive and less available, due both to increased demand and migration, more capital was invested in items ranging from improved spades, scythes and ploughs to (much less frequently) reapers and threshers, all of which, in more or less dramatic fashion, increased labour productivity. Extension of market opportunities was the other major incentive, and increasingly so, even for the mass of peasant family farms. It encouraged efforts to increase production, and especially during the periods of rising prices increased revenue and provided the wherewithal for innovation. The importance of the period *c.* 1851–*c.* 1873 was that rising prices and the relative prosperity of the countryside accelerated the processes of capital accumulation, of investment, of increasing productivity and of participation in commercial agriculture, and as an aspect of this, the farmers' dependence on purchased goods and services.

Awareness of opportunities increased as communications improved. Access to new markets encouraged efforts to increase production and to modify its structure. The gradual and accumulative response, even of peasant farmers, to growing urban demand reflected an exposure to new networks of communication and mechanisms of decision-making external to the village community. A new, less fatalistic, mentality developed. This was promoted to an important degree by the rapid disappearance of the traditional subsistence crises after the early 1850s. Improved communications and market integration freed the peasant from fear of dearth, presented him with increasing opportunities for earning cash and also with new ways of spending it. The peasant became less concerned with subsistence and more with prices. The aims of the family farm underwent gradual revision. Peasants began to look favourably upon labour saving and cash earning innovations. The intensification of competitive pressures proved another vital stimulus.

Whatever the shape or scale of innovation, it was significant in that it involved the farmer in new economic relationships, in the purchase of tools or consumer goods which had to be paid for in cash. This had to be earned through the increased commercialization of the farm product. Commercial activity, whether as buyer or seller, made it essential to balance cash earnings and outlays. This enjoined constant caution upon the innovator and explains the attraction of gradual and low-cost innovation, allowing the slow accumulation of marginal increases in productivity. One can only presume that the majority of farmers followed innovators to the degree that their economic situation, their means and attitudes allowed, but that at a certain point particular innovations became the orthodox way of doing things. This helps to explain the time-lag between initial innovation, usually by the larger farmers, more aware of change, and for whom the penalty for introducing an uneconomic innovation was an acceptable risk, and its generalization among the less well-off. The large majority of peasant farmers only slowly extended their participation in commercial agriculture. Reliance on family labour, intensive cultivation and low living standards made economic survival possible, at least until the burden of labour became intolerable, or the capacity of the peasant farm to earn sufficient income to finance even minimal outgoings became insufficient. Price depression and the crises affecting particular crops would result in growing difficulties from the 1870s.

Moreover, although the income gap between rich and poor regions, measured by revenue per hectare, narrowed (see Table 8), it remained obviously true that varying geographical locations, natural conditions, farm structures and social structures and mentalities, produced extreme variety in the bases from which adaptation to changing market structures took place.

In the north, Flanders and Picardy, the Paris basin and Normandy retained the advantages of richer soils, larger farms, accumulated capital and access to major urban markets. Here agriculture had become a speculative activity requiring capital investment and attracting capital by success measured in terms of profitability. This had affected peasant family farmers as well as more obvious capitalists. Substantial improvements in productivity occurred in some areas of the west and centre-west, due to the application of lime and cultivation of wheat

Table 8   Net taxable revenue[8]

Region	Increase 1851–79 (per cent)	Revenue per hectare in 1879 (francs)
Brittany	60.9	49.3
Garonne region	59.1	63.3
Midi	56.0	58.3
North	45.7	114.5
Massif Central	41.4	33.0
Centre of Paris basin	23.8	77.0
East-north-east	18.0	42.4

in place of inferior cereals; and in some upland areas of the Doubs and Jura due to specialization in livestock. In these areas the handicaps imposed by natural environment were reduced by technical change. The poorest regions remained the upland zones of central France, the Aquitaine basin, the south-east and now also the north-east which had experienced relative decline. In the north-east and Aquitaine this was due to the maintenance of an especially traditionalist polyculture, in the absence of large population centres and in the latter also due to the loss of markets for cereals in the Midi as a more competitive grain market was established. In the south-east it was due to a series of crises affecting silk, madder, and the vine, and often leading to the temporary replanting of cereals in unfavourable geographical conditions. In all of these regions a far larger proportion of farmers than elsewhere remained fundamentally orientated towards family subsistence. From the 1880s, moreover, the onset of phylloxera throughout much of southern France and more generally of price depression had marked effects on incomes and attitudes.

The last third of the nineteenth century was a period of crisis for French agriculture – a crisis of transition to a new national and international economy. In effect development of the market not only represented opportunity but also a threat to existing regional economic structures. The consequences of changes in market structures were most strongly brought home to farmers by the clear tendency from the 1860s for agricultural prices to stagnate and by the complex effects this had on incomes. The period between 1874 and 1895, that of the 'great depression' in the agriculture, was to be particularly difficult because of the decline in the prices of most farm products. The crisis was especially marked for cereals, wine and wool producers, but also affected the producers of meat and dairy products. Farmers still producing primarily for subsistence were least affected; but even they needed to earn some cash.

Cereal prices began to decline in the 1870s and by 1895 were 27 per cent below the 1871–5 level. The decline was over 33 per cent in the case of wheat, 14 per cent for oats, 26 per cent for rye. The collapse of potato prices began later, reaching about 35 per cent from 1885. The decline in livestock prices was less

Table 9   *Growth rates of industry and agriculture*

Year	Agriculture (per cent)	Industry (per cent)
1824–59	1.15	2.30
1860–91	0.23	1.67
1892–1913	0.78	1.94

marked and less regular – by 1895 it amounted to 19 per cent for beef and 10 per cent for veal. Butter fell by about 7 per cent, cheese by 15 per cent, while milk prices remained stable. Only sugar beet prices continued to rise, but this was due to the substantial increase in the sugar content of the beet. Wine prices were affected by phylloxera and rose until about 1881–5, then fell as domestic production recovered and imports increased.[9] By the turn of the century a glut was evident. The problems this caused in the departments of Gard, Drôme, Ardèche and Vaucluse were intensified by the concurrent decline of silk production due to disease, and of that of madder due to the development of synthetic dyes.

In the face of repeated *crises d'adaptation*, due to the intensification of first national and then international competition, pressure built up for a return to tariff protection. This was accorded by a series of laws from 1881–97 designed to increase price stability and raise basic levels. These measures, together with the revival of urban markets, helped to stimulate limited recovery from the late 1890s. Without protection, the fall in the prices of agricultural products would certainly have been more marked, and the social and political crises which resulted even more intense. Politically there appeared to be no alternative to protection, but there can be no doubt that protection, together with government pressure on the railway companies to withdraw differential freight rates which favoured imports, had the effect of reducing competitive pressures and facilitated the survival of a large and technically backward sector of peasant farming.

This slowing of change in agriculture reinforced a century-long gulf in annual growth rates between agriculture and industry (see Table 9).[10] Development in these two sectors was obviously interdependent. While the rate and structure of industrial development influenced the scale and structure of the demand for agricultural produce and determined the level of employment opportunities outside agriculture and migration from the countryside, it is also evident that the survival of a large agricultural sector and the level of disposable income possessed by farmers had crucial effects upon industry.

Industry

Demand for industrial products

The structure of demand was complicated. It depended not only upon the size of population and its per capita income but upon a mass of decisions about expenditure, and upon personal taste. Poor communications had meant the survival of a decentralized market and thus the dispersal of production. The nineteenth century saw a rapid expansion of trade as part of a process of improved communications, market integration, and transition from relatively closed to far more open local communities. This had vital effects in terms of the creation of substantial homogeneous markets, high levels of demand for standardized products, and the promise of high profit levels. To a significant extent there was a direct correlation between the size of the market and the scale of industrial enterprise. However, the rate of increase of demand for industrial products continued to be influenced by the relatively slow increase in population (averaging 1.3 per cent per annum in 1820–65, and 0.6 per cent from 1865–95), by the predominance of a low productivity peasant agriculture, and by the immobility of population and the slow growth of towns. The situation was worsened by the depression of agricultural prices from 1817 to 1851 which caused a deterioration in the terms of exchange between agriculture and industry. Additionally, throughout the century the distribution of a very large part of the total income in the form of rents, interest and dividends and conversely the restraints imposed on the growth of earned income helped to preserve a highly individualized bourgeois demand for luxury products, which hindered the development of large-scale production.

To some extent export markets compensated for the limitations of internal demand. However, continuity with the rapid growth of exports in the eighteenth century was broken through the loss of markets during the revolutionary and imperial wars. After the disasters of this period exports increased primarily where they were not in competition with British factory production, i.e. particularly in the markets for high quality goods like silks and *articles de Paris*. Even so, France remained second in the world for exports of manufactured goods until 1870. Foreign trade is estimated to have represented 13 per cent of the gross national product in 1830, to have reached 19 per cent in 1850, 29 per cent in 1860 and a maximum of 41 per cent in 1870. Only after the 1870 war, with the loss of major industrial areas in Alsace, with growing protectionism and worldwide depression, and changes in fashion which affected the traditional export of goods like silk and gloves, did the French share in international trade decline. It fell from an estimated 16.2 per cent in 1876–80 to only 11.8 per cent in 1911–13. Rates of growth declined to 2.74 per cent between 1875 and 1913 in increasingly competitive world markets.[11] Industry, therefore, continued to depend primarily upon internal demand which grew from as early as the 1830s, as agricultural productivity increased. Technical innovation and reductions in the prices of industrial products further encouraged demand from the rural population for such things as iron tools and cotton garments. But in the absence of any fundamental changes in market structures, this growth in demand was met primarily by means of the extension of traditional forms of production. In general, artisans and merchants produced and redistributed goods to spatially limited hinterlands. Inefficient, high cost producers were protected from competition by high transport costs.

From the 1840s the pace of change accelerated. The progressive constitution of a national market had begun centuries earlier with the improvement of roads and waterways, but the railway – as can be seen from the massive increase in the volume of goods transported – profoundly transformed the system. Improvements in communications by breaking down isolation affected both the structure of demand and intensity of competition. Reductions in transport costs promoted market integration. The stimulus afforded to agriculture together with rising incomes led to improvements in living standards and to the growth of increasingly standardized patterns of consumption. This provided increased incentives to invest in large-scale production. Even if market imperfections remained and product innovation accelerated in a manner which allowed the survival of numerous small- and medium-sized producers, it might safely be asserted that, just as in agriculture, more profound structural changes occurred in the next three or four decades than had previously occurred in as many centuries. The process of change in markets and industrial structures brought both new opportunities and increased competitive pressures. The latter were evident in the contraction of artisanal production in textiles, and small-scale metallurgy, and in the commercial functions of a host of small towns as activity was increasingly concentrated in the larger towns which constituted bigger markets and provided better communications facilities.

The growth of the tertiary sector is an important characteristic of modern society, involving the concurrent development of communications, financial and commercial networks. Structures and habits changed as the volume of goods produced and marketed increased. The traditional fairs declined. That of Beaucaire, formerly so vital to the textile trade of the Dauphiné, had already suffered from the improvement of port facilities at Marseille, and of communications along the Rhône valley. Major commercial entrepôts like Orléans saw their importance decline due to the development of direct links between producers and consumers by post and telegraph and the possibility of transporting goods rapidly to their destinations. As the scale of production increased and the investment in plant and machinery grew, manufacturers adopted less passive attitudes towards their markets and began to escape from their previous dependence on wholesale merchants. They started to prospect for new customers – the commercial traveller appears in the 1820s – and to advertise their wares. The growth of a mass circulation press was vital in this latter respect. The retail trade, too, was transformed by the establishment of growing numbers of shops, including the first department stores, with their carefully arranged displays of goods with clearly marked prices. The small trader, however, revealed a striking capacity for survival. In spite of the development of some chain stores towards the end of the century the number of trading licenses issued increased from 1.7 million in 1872 to 2.33 million in 1913, reflecting 'the commercialisation of activities in even the smallest village'.[12] In 1913, even in Paris, only 17 per cent of trade (by value) was in the hands of the department stores.

The growth of demand stimulated industrial activity but the upward trend was subject to interruption. For much of the century – until at least the late 1860s – demand for industrial products fluctuated primarily with the state of the harvest. A poor harvest and rising food prices forced consumers to economize on such items as clothing. As demand for industrial products fell off, so the employment and incomes of industrial workers declined – at the same time as food prices rose – causing further reductions in mass purchasing power. Such crises, typical of the *Ancien Régime économique*, were frequent and had devastating effects upon popular living standards. However, the characteristics of economic crises changed with the structure of the economy. As manufacturing industry grew in importance, an associated economic cycle developed, and subsequently replaced the traditional crises. Industrial over-production and financial crises of confidence sparked off by a variety of causal factors, often international in character, affected the cycle of production. From the 1850s as rail and telegraph permitted the more effective adjustment of food supply to demand on an international scale – by means of the rapid transmission of market information and the reduction of overland and oceanic freight rates – the more purely commercial and financial causes of crises became dominant.

Nevertheless the agricultural depression of 1882–96, due both to internal market integration and to the growth of competition from the New World, and the resultant price depression had significant effects upon the demand for industrial products. A marked deceleration occurred in the growth of the French economy. However, this to an important extent pre-dated the agricultural crisis. It reflected the culmination of the investment in urban development and the major railway network which had provided such an important stimulus to economic activity in the previous two decades. Furthermore, overseas levels of demand had been substantially reduced by the consequences of the American Civil War and the destructive effects of the Franco-Prussian War of 1870. A decline in confidence and dynamism appears to have occurred due to this and to the political tensions and uncertainties of the last years of the Second Empire and the beginning of the Third Republic.

The subsequent recovery from crisis – with industrial growth rates calculated at 2.66 per cent per annum between 1885 and 1905, and 4.42 per cent between 1905 and 1913 – reflected greater political stability and confidence among entrepreneurs, but also changes in demand levels. For one thing, accelerating emigration from countryside to town, and a rise in real wages had substantially stimulated urban demand. Real wages appear to have fallen by 23 per cent from 1820 to 1855, then to have risen by 25 per cent from 1855 to 1875 and, more vigorously by 48 per cent between 1875 and 1905. This, together with a series of technical innovations, the so-called 'second industrialization' based on electricity, motor cars, aeroplanes, iron and steel, electro-chemistry, and electro-metallurgy, stimulated a new cycle of industrial and urban investment with cumulative effects on the structure and volume of demand. The market for industrial goods had changed decisively. The creation of a modern transport infrastructure had promoted market integration and large-scale production, and established a situation of overwhelming urban predominance over patterns of production and demand. Mass consumer demand from urban markets had taken over from a rural and localized demand for clothing and farm tools as the essential stimulus to industrial activity.

Industrial structures

Inevitably, given the importance of technological borrowing, French industry has been compared with British and found wanting. This approach does have its limits, however. It fails to take account of differences in social and economic structures leading to alternative, but equally rational types of industrial growth. Industrialization represented a response to changing market conditions, to new opportunities and competitive pressures which stimulated technical innovation. This encouraged transfers of capital and labour from the less productive sectors of the economy to the more profitable. In large part, too, the stimulus to growth was internal to industry in that the enlargement of one industrial sector promoted demand for the products of others.

Technological levels were thus determined by a complex of factors, including the scale of demand for the product, the comparative cost of labour and of machinery both as an initial investment and in operational terms, and the availability of capital. Until the very end of the century, with the development of electro-metallurgy and chemicals on a large-scale, technology was only marginally influenced by science. In practice it developed by means of the piecemeal application of new developments, and their adaptation to the particular circumstances of time and place. Once introduced, new equipment (such as steam engines) was employed for fifty years or more, although with occasional modifications. The major partial exceptions to these generalizations occurred with the construction of large-scale integrated metallurgical establishments, and the development of the railway network, in which advanced technology in the form of the steam engine was integrated into what was otherwise a labour-intensive form of transport. Technological changes in these two sectors had fundamental effects on the whole economy through the provision of large quantities of cheap iron and steel and the availability of a low cost means of bulk transport.

Nevertheless there was no abrupt change in the structure of French industry. The most obvious method of responding to increased demand is simply to produce more in the same old way. This is not necessarily perverse or lazy, but can represent an intelligent use of existing resources. In the French case this extension was stimulated by the availability of cheap labour, and the continued fragmentation of the market structure until at least the 1850s. The pre-rail economy was characterized by 'spatial dispersion, smallness of scale, integration with other sectors of local economies, and use of local sources of energy and also usually of raw materials'.[13] Moreover, innovation should not be expected to occur throughout industry at the same time. It tends to occur most rapidly in particular industries due to changes in demand, or in the relative cost of the various factors of production. Particular industries, in particular locations, were at various times especially responsive to pressures for change, and assumed a leading role in the industrialization process, with untypically high rates of growth in production. Until the 1860s industrial development in France might properly be described as 'dualistic' with various industries or sections of industries playing 'leading roles', and adopting new machine technologies, and alongside them a substantial growth of traditional household and artisanal production often located in the countryside and employing labour intensive forms of technology. It has been estimated that 58.9 per cent of the total industrial product in the period 1860–5 was still produced by craftsmen.[14]

In rural areas cheap labour was a major attraction. Moreover, very little capital was needed by the entrepreneur. The workers provided the basic equipment. As rural population densities grew until the middle of the century, wherever agriculture failed to provide for the subsistence of families some of their members were drawn into a complex of complementary activities including seasonal migration, wet nursing and above all rural industry. This was true, for example, in communities around the woollen centre of Reims, particularly where soils were poor and agricultural productivity low. Production was organized by urban merchants. In Picardy after 1830, wool and linen weaving took over from spinning, as that was mechanized, and they were in turn to be replaced by sugar refining. Numerous streams provided power for an infinite number of cloth mills, flour mills, saw mills, etc., while dispersed throughout the countryside were small-scale brickworks, lime kilns, quarries, coal mines, potteries, tanneries, etc., as well as the whole range of artisanal trades employing carpenters, masons, coopers, wheelwrights, tailors, shoe-makers, blacksmiths, etc., producing for essentially local needs.

From 1840–50 an acceleration occurred in a process of change which had commenced early in the eighteenth century. It was characterized by the growing predominance of factory production over artisanal forms and of the industrial economy over agriculture. This was a period of crisis and decline for many small scale producers, and saw the rapid spread of capital-intensive methods of production. T. J. Markovitch illustrates this by comparing the growth in production in large-scale mechanized industry (*industrie pure*) with that for industry as a whole. He found that the rate of growth in production of the former between 1835–44 and 1855–64 was twice as great as that for industry overall. In twenty years its share of the total industrial product rose from one-quarter to more than one-third, while that of artisanal production fell from around 69 to 59 per cent.[15] Small-scale enterprises were disadvantaged in an increasingly competitive market by their inability to enjoy economies of scale, their poor links to commercial networks, low profit margins and limited access to external credit which made innovations difficult and left them vulnerable to short-term fluctuations. The enlargement of markets and the growing complexity and cost of technology both favoured large enterprises, yet small-scale enterprises survived, in part by adapting to a more competitive environment. Even in the absence of technical innovation, forms of commercial concentration had already developed in which the various workshops supplying a particular merchant were pushed into increasing specialization of function, to supply only part of a product which they had formerly produced in its entirety. This form of division of labour was widespread in such trades as furniture, clothing and shoe production. It increased production, reduced costs and improved competitiveness, but at the price of simplifying the labour process and opening the way to dilution of the labour force with less skilled workers and of reinforcing the dependence of the workshop *patron* upon the merchant who controlled access to markets. Technical innovation threatened but also aided the survival of small workshops by establishing new needs and providing cheaper energy sources through gas and electricity. The introduction of the sewing machine, for example, was a major stimulus to both workshop and domestic production. By 1904 there were almost 800,000 domestic workers, 60 per cent of them women.

Thus throughout the century a multiplicity of small businesses existed, but with an accelerating tendency towards concentration which necessarily led to growth in the overall economic importance – as employer and producer – of large-scale entrerprise. In 1851, *grande industrie* was made up of 124,000 employers with 1.3 million workers, i.e. an average of eleven workers per unit, while *petite industrie* with its 1.55 million employers and 2.8 million workers represented a ratio of 1:2. Table 10 shows the situation in 1896. According to the 1906 census 71 per cent of all industrial establishments had no employees. Excluding the category of one-man businesses, 32 per cent of employees worked in establishments employing less than ten workers, 28 per cent in those with 10–100 people, 40 per cent in establishments with over 100 employees.

Clearly the size of the establishment varied according to the type of activity and the characteristics of the technical processes employed. Small-sized establishments were typical of food-processing, the building industry, and the clothing industries producing both high and especially low quality products, and the growing number of repair and service workshops – plumbers, electricians

Table 10 *Industry in 1896 (excluding transport)*

Size of establishment	No. of establishments	No. of workers	percentage of workers
1–4 employees	489,970	806,627	25.00
5–50 employees	78,105	913,976	29.34
Over 50 employees	7,456	1,392,603	44.75
Total	575,531	3,112,603	100.00

Table 11   *Industrial establishments categorized according to number of workers employed (1901)*

Number of workers	Number of establishments
1	309,658
1–50	278,978
51–100	4,377
101–200	2,310
201–500	1,315
501–1000	331
1001–2000	141
2001–5000	43
Over 5000	13
Total	597,166

and garages – created by the new economy and which tended to replace the traditional artisanate. Large-scale establishments were typical of the textiles, iron and steel, metal processing and mining industries using machinery and steam or electric power for mass production purposes. By 1906 factories employing over 500 workers each accounted for a total of some 680,000 people, while another 4000 factories, spread more widely over different industrial sectors, employed 101–500 people and 800,000 in all. Gille has identified the thirty largest businesses in 1881 in terms of their capital resources. Of these, nine were in transport (six rail, two shipping, one urban transport), five were coal-mining companies, six were gas and three water utilities, four were in metallurgy, one each in chemicals, electricity and food processing.[16]

The nature of the market appears to have been decisive. Small-scale enterprises survived and developed because of the social and geographical diversity of French markets and the demand for luxury goods and specialized services. Medium-sized enterprises, too, were a common feature of the French industrial scene, benefiting to a degree from economies of scale and also more responsive to changing patterns of demand than many large enterprises.

For these reasons the development of industrial concentration was slow and restrained. Nevertheless, decisive changes occurred in French industrial structures from the middle years of the nineteenth century. This can be further illustrated by consideration of patterns of investment and rates of growth.

Growth rates

Estimates of industrial growth rates vary.[17] Marczewski has calculated average annual growth rate of 2.73 per cent between 1815 and 1913. Markovitch's estimate is 2.9 per cent, Lévy-Leboyer's is 2.56 per cent. Crouzet goes for a somewhat lower rate of 1.8–2.0 per cent. The variations indicate how uncertain statistical calculation is on the basis of the information available to historians. Markovitch in his index of industrial production makes the significance of these gross estimates clearer. Using 1938 as equal to 100, he estimates production to have represented 9.4 in 1815–24, 19.5 in 1845–54 and 67.9 in 1913. Production sextupled over 100 years. The period 1815–46 appears to have been one of slow, regular growth in industrial production, interrupted by minor fluctuations; 1846–51 was a period of major political and economic crisis, followed, from 1852 to 1857, by a period of very rapid growth. 1858 and 1859 were years of depression, succeeded from 1860 to 1882 by slow growth interrupted by the war of 1870 and the resultant political crisis. 1882 to 1896 was another period of depression, ending in 1897 with a lengthy period of prosperity which continued until the First World War. The social significance of this growth can also be represented in terms of productivity, i.e. production per person (see Table 12, which is again based on Markovitch's estimates). Growth rates appear to have been particularly high around the middle of the nineteenth century. Maxima were achieved for short periods following political or military crises – an estimated 3.7 per cent per annum from 1815–20; 3.87 per cent from 1850–5 – and to have represented short-lived periods of recovery following periods with abnormally low rates of growth. 1905–13, with a rate of 4.42 per cent was exceptional in this respect. Over longer periods more modest rates were recorded. According to Lévy-Leboyer's relatively optimistic accounts: 2.98 per cent from 1815–45, 2.56 per cent from 1845–65, and 1.64 per cent between 1865 and 1890.

The main factor influencing growth rates appears to have been technical innovation, and the investment of capital, which brought about fundamental changes both in the structure of the economy and in productivity within particular industrial sectors. Investment in public works – in the development of the railway network and in urban reconstruction – appears to have been particularly important, with this form of basic investment being replaced by industrial innovation as the vital stimuli after the 1880s as new products like the motor car led to new patterns of production and consumption. Infra-structural investment had a stimulating effect on a whole range of industries both in terms of direct demand and the consequences for the formation of a more integrated national market. According to Caron's estimates the annual mean increase in capital invested was 200 million francs between 1830 and 1850; 1560 million

Table 12 *Production per person (gold-francs) 1781–1913*

Year	Production per person	Year	Production per person
1781–90	1059	1895–1904	2322
1835–44	1268	1905–13	2534
1855–94	2187		

francs between 1850 and 1880; and 2000 million between 1880 and 1913. He calculates that total investment rose from 5000 million francs in 1830 to 122,000 million in 1913, indicative both of a major switch of resources into productive investment and of the substantial growth in the volume of capital available.

The overall growth of industry obviously depended on that of its various sectors. Rates of growth varied between industries and parts of industries, and between regions. At particular times dynamic sectors can be identified which had important stimulating effects on particular branches of industry or, through interdependence with other industrial sectors and agriculture, on entire regions. Alongside the gradual and sustained growth of the textiles, clothing, building and foodstuffs industries throughout the century (and these it ought to be remembered were the major industries in terms of value of production and employment), the more spectacular achievement of industries such as coal, metallurgy, gas and later electricity and chemicals, ought to be noted. The relatively slow growth of the first group of more traditional industries inevitably imposed major restraints on the expansive capacity of the economy. According to Markovitch, until *c.* 1844 a fifth of the value added by industry was supplied by the textiles industries (or two-fifths including clothing). The annual average rates of growth for these industries were relatively low – at 1.77 per cent from 1831–5 to 1876–80, falling to 1.1 per cent between 1876–80 and 1909–13.[18] The growing significance of the second, more dynamic group of industries in the second half of the century reinforced the potential for change. Growth ceased to be 'dualistic' as capital intensive sectors experienced relatively rapid development, and traditional sectors, engaged in a more competitive market themselves, began to employ more capital in an effort to increase labour productivity. The process of structural change in the industrial, and indeed the overall, economy consequently accelerated from the 1840–50s through qualitative changes in productive techniques which growth rates do not clearly reveal.

Industrial geography

Obviously economic growth does not occur everywhere at the same time (see Figure 8). In any society particular places tend to be favoured due to a complex combination of circumstances. However, in the traditional society, characterized by poor communications and fragmented markets, which survived in its essentials until the middle of the nineteenth century, manufacture was dispersed. The typical enterprise produced on a small scale, for a localized market, using local sources of energy and of raw materials – running water, forests, small mineral outcrops, cereals, wool and leather from local farms.

According to a survey conducted as late as 1861–5, for 100,163 non-Parisian industrial establishments, power, measured in terms of horse-power was provided by water mills (60.0 per cent), windmills (8.1 per cent), horse-driven mills (0.9 per cent), steam engines (31.0 per cent). The predominance of hydraulic power meant dispersal of industrial plant. Water wheels usually generated

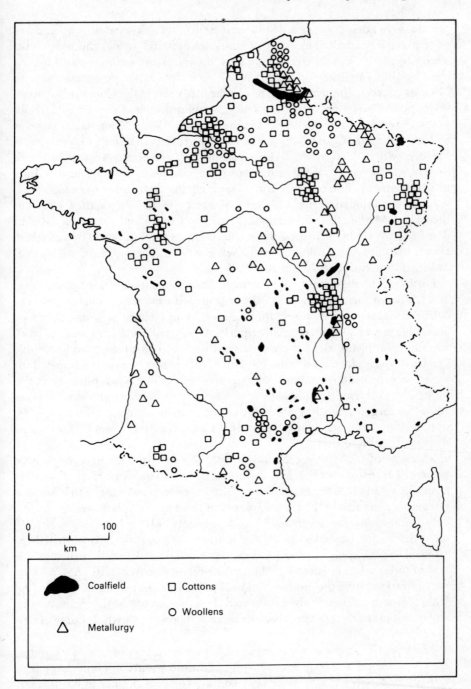

Figure 8 *Distribution of industry*
   Source: *After H. D. Clout*, Themes in the Historical Geography of France *Academic Press 1977*

around 3–10 horse power, and industrial establishments dependent upon them were inevitably small. The other obvious disadvantage of an otherwise cheap source of power was the irregular flow of the rivers and streams which turned the wheels. In conditions of either low or high water a loss of power ensued with obvious effects on industrial activity. In the first years of the nineteenth century water power was especially important to textiles. Much of the cotton and silk industry was localized along rivers in the Vosges, Alsace, Beaujolais, Lyonnais and in the Pays-de-Caux and *bocage* areas of Normandy. The only exception was Flanders where, due to the lack of fast flowing rivers, investment in steam power occurred at a relatively early date. The location of much of the metallurgical industry, and especially of forges applying the tilt hammer to fashion iron, was also conditioned by the availability of water – in the Vosges, the foothills of the Haute-Marne, the Châtillonnais. Franche-Comté and Dauphiné. Rising demand was met by increasing the density of mills and forges and by successful efforts to improve the efficiency of the water wheels. The apogee of this form of production occurred as late as the 1830–40s.

Furthermore, these numerous riverside establishments depended upon wood as a source of fuel. Significantly, the regions with the least industry were the Mediterranean south with few forests, the Massif Central in which the more accessible areas had already been stripped of trees, and the Paris basin. In 1850, metallurgical plants alone were estimated to have consumed 5 million cubic metres of wood. In areas like the Nivernais, where forge-masters competed for wood with demand from Paris, they temporarily closed when prices were too high. The problem of wood supply was becoming increasingly serious, especially for large establishments like that at Fourchambault producing 20,000 tonnes of pig-iron per annum in the 1850s and requiring around 40,000 cubic metres of wood to do so.

Shortage of coal and the peripheral location of coalfields have often been presented as reasons for the 'backwardness' of French industry. This should not be exaggerated given the existence of hydraulic power, and the fact that fuel was not a major element in the costs structure of most industries. Nevertheless coal consumption rose rapidly (from 7.5 million tonnes in 1851 to 21 million in 1869) once the major obstacles to its distribution, i.e. transport costs, had been reduced. As transport impoved and the cost of coal fell the traditional exploitation of forest resources declined. The reduction in the cost of coal was a decisive factor in stimulating the modernization of industries like metallurgy employing large amounts of fuel. It also stimulated the growing use of the steam engine, and by means of this, the provision of increased power to a whole range of new machinery.

The steam engine was not indispensable to the creation of large-scale industry, but beyond a certain stage further technical progress would have been difficult without it. There were only some 200 steam engines in use in 1810, mainly in coal mines. According to the official *Statistiques minérales* the numbers subsequently rose to 625 in 1830 (generating 10,000 horse power), to 1700 in 1836, 2800 by 1841, 3360 in 1843, 5200 by 1848, and 6000 in 1850 (producing

75,000 horse power). These were primarily small engines, often used to supplement water wheels in periods of low water. About a third were found in two major coal-mining departments – the Nord and the Loire. The steam engine remained primarily an adjunct to the coal-mine rather than a source of energy for industry. As transport costs for coal fell, however, the numbers of steam engines employed and the range of establishments using them rapidly increased. From 7739 in 1852, their number rose to 25,025 in 1864 and 32,006 in 1875. The 320,000 horse power installed in industry by 1869 would increase tenfold by 1913, and by 1906 only 22 per cent of this power was produced by water wheels. The growing availability of relatively cheap power in large quantities had significant effects on the process of concentration in industry (see Figures 9 and 10). It ended the phase of dispersal in such sectors as metallurgy and textiles and stimulated location in proximity to coal. (Only the development of electricity at the turn of the century – a more flexible energy source – would reduce this dependence. Electricity production increased rapidly from 340 million kilowatt hours in 1900 to 1800 million in 1913.)

Even prior to the development of the railway network the improvement of communications had increased competitive pressures. The southern woollens industry, for example, centred on such towns as Lodève and Montpellier, had faced growing competition from mechanized producers in the north. The railway brought collapse, and in this case a transfer of capital into more profitable areas like vine cultivation. In effect the railways transformed the character of the national market, i.e. the basis for industrial development. As competition increased it became more important than ever to make effective use of existing resources, but often these were inadequate. Where, for example, coke replaced wood for the smelting of iron, or steam engines proved more efficient than hydraulic power then traditonal methods of production and many centres of industry tended to decline. French industry was faced with a major *crise d'adaptation*. Successful change depended a great deal on location *vis-à-vis* the new means of communication, and the costs of access to major markets and sources of raw materials. A process of concentration of industrial activity occurred, influenced both by the structure of the new communications network, which clearly favoured Paris as the centre of the network, and by the freight tariffs charged by the railway companies, which because of their differential character tended to favour long-distance transport and to break the quasi-monopoly position of areas like Champagne which had previously benefited from close proximity to major urban centres. Furthermore, the reduction in transport costs, and the integration of markets this made possible stimulated production on a larger scale, in factories rather than in workshops. The face of France was profoundly transformed in the second half of the century.

Areas like the south-east experienced rapid de-industrialization. The textiles industries of Castres, Mazamet, Lavelamet, Foix and St-Gaudens and the Catalan forges in the Pyrenees declined quickly in the 1850s and 1860s. Their main problems were a lack of easy access to large quantities of raw materials, and

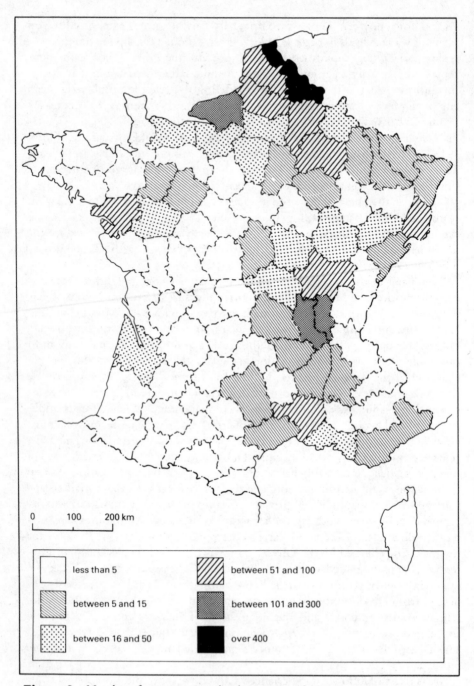

0   100   200 km

	less than 5		between 51 and 100
	between 5 and 15		between 101 and 300
	between 16 and 50		over 400

Figure 9 *Number of steam engines by department 1841*
Source: *After M. Lévy-Leboyer*, Les Banques européennes et l'industrialisation internationale dans la première moitié du XIXe siècle *P.U.F. 1964*

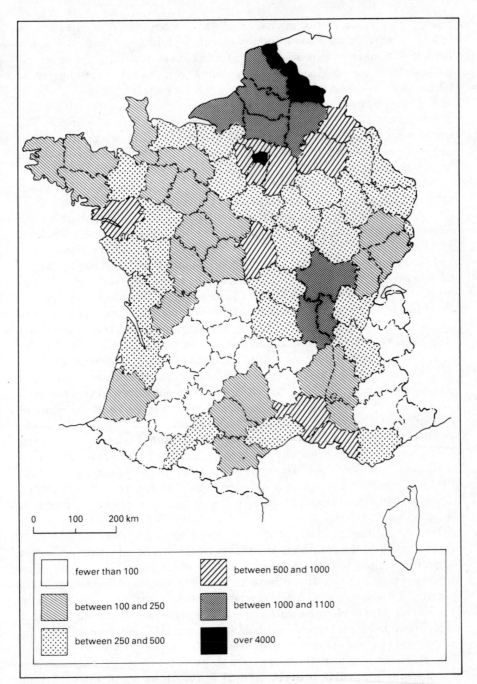

Figure 10 *Number of steam engines in 1878*
Source: *After* Atlas historique de la France contemporaine 1805–1965   *Colin 1966*

relative geographical isolation within the new communications network. A milieu favourable to traditional, small-scale industry was not necessarily favourable to modern industrialization. The decline of traditional industries was not always compensated for by the development of new forms of production. In Champagne, at a disadvantage in the production of basic metallurgical products and textiles due to the transport costs of coal from the Nord and relatively high labour costs, a reorientation in the direction of developing industries like engineering, chemicals or electricity was prevented by close proximity to Paris, a more dynamic centre because of its market potential and resources of skilled labour and capital.

Paris was an exceptional case. In the first half of the century the city was already the major industrial centre in terms both of the volume and value (about 40 per cent of the national product) of its production. By the end of the Second Empire in addition to the artisanal industries of the old city – cabinet-makers, jewellers, printers, etc. – there had occurred a multiplication of both small- and large-scale industry, most notably in chemicals and mechanical engineering in the suburbs and beyond, which was to continue to develop. Industrial location within the city was transformed as the luxury industrial producers of *articles de Paris* and precision engineering tended to concentrate in the north-eastern quarters, and printing and small-scale metallurgy moved from the centre, which was taken over by offices and shops, towards the periphery, which also saw, from the end of the century, the rapid development of new industries – electrical, automobiles and chemicals. The difficulties of transport in the city's narrow streets, the municipal tax (*octroi*) on raw materials and fuel entering its limits, the high cost of land and labour, as well as objections to the presence of industry from its better-off residents, all had the effect, from early in the century, of pushing industrial development towards the periphery. Already in 1810 measures had been introduced to prevent the instalment of insalubrious or dangerous industries. The stench from the tanneries concentrated along the banks of the little River Bièvre was an awful warning against unrestricted development. Both Paris and Lyon ceased to be workers' cities as their centres were de-industrialized.

Like Paris, Lyon owed its growth over the centuries to geographical location on crossroads in the communications system. Its privileged position was not preserved to the same extent within the new railway network. In terms of its functions as a commercial and financial centre its subordination to Paris was reinforced. Even its role as world capital of the silk industry was threatened by the development of international competition, but the previous accumulation of capital facilitated the development of new industries, and especially of the already existing chemicals and engineering, to compensate for the decline of silk. Even within industrial regions, such as that of the Nord, development was far from uniform, either between industries or localities. Particularly dynamic industries like coal-mining, or localities, like the textile complex of Lille–Roubaix–Tourcoing, attracted labour and capital, often at the expense of other industries or localities. On the other hand, they were also able to provide a

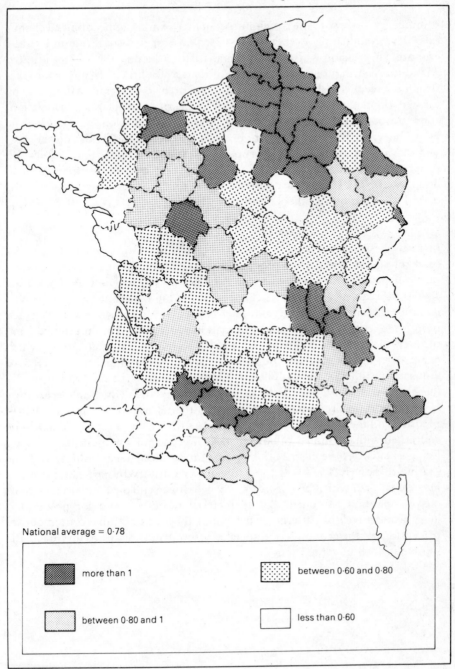

National average = 0·78

	more than 1		between 0·60 and 0·80
	between 0·80 and 1		less than 0·60

Figure 11 *Industrial production per inhabitant (by department) 1910–12 (in thousands of francs)*

Source: *After A. Armengaud*, La Population française au XIXe siècle   *P.U.F. 1971*

stimulus, in this case to the development of mechanical engineering and chemicals. The culminating event of the first wave of industrialization was the economic depression which affected France from the mid 1870s. This affected an industrial structure which, in spite of the acceleration of change as market structures were transformed, retained many archaic elements. The crisis, by further stimulating competition, intensified the trend towards mechanization, concentration of production and the disappearance of traditional producers. The prime beneficiaries were the more modern regions, in the north and the east, while industry in regions like the south-east experienced severe difficulties and sectors like the rural industry of lower Normandy and the Lyon area finally disappeared. The counterpart of industrialization in some regions was thus the de-industrialization of others (see Figure 11).

In many respects the economy of the eighteenth century, characterized by market fragmentation, a low productivity agriculture and small-scale manufacturing dependent on water and wood for power and fuel, survived until the 1840s. Subsequently, structural change occurred in the economy as improved communications improved access to markets and raw materials, but also created more competitive national and international markets. This promoted, and through heightened competition, forced technological innovation which resulted in higher rates of productivity and the growing concentration of industrial production. The result was a more prosperous, if still fundamentally inegalitarian, society, one free from subsistence crises, in which an increasingly large proportion of the population lived in towns and found employment in industry and the services. To a large extent, the chapters which follow will be concerned with the impact of both change and continuity in the economy upon living standards, the distribution of incomes, social relationships, and the sharing of power. They will constitute a social history by providing insights into the ways in which people lived, worked, loved and died, into the continuous competition to control scarce material resources, and for power and influence. As well as patterns of behaviour they will examine contemporary perceptions of the economic and social environment and seek to illuminate the motives which governed action.

2

The demographic indicators

Introduction

The nineteenth century saw the beginnings of a major social revolution. The transformation of economic structures made possible considerable improvements in human living conditions and changes in attitudes to life, the effects of which were clear in the decline in death and also in birth rates. In addition, the town replaced the village as the main place of residence. Figures 12 and 13 show where people lived at the beginning and towards the end of the century. Table 13 shows the manner in which the overall population is estimated to have increased. Clearly there was a tendency for the rate of population increase to decline almost continually. France was distinguished among the industrializing nations of the nineteenth century by its relatively low rate of population growth. This meant that in comparison with underdeveloped countries today population pressure on economic resources was far less intense.

Within the period 1815–1914 three major phases of evolution have been identified (see Figure 14). The first, from c. 1815 to c. 1848, was characterized by slow economic change. Although agricultural productivity rose, in many regions rapid population increase maintained dietary standards at low levels. This was essentially a period of continuity with the second half of the eighteenth century, with both high (although declining) death and birth rates. It was

Table 13 *Population increase (1750–1911)*

Year	Population (millions)	Year	Population (millions)
1750	21	1861	37.4*
1801	27.3	1872	36.1*
1821	30.5	1881	37.7
1831	32.6	1891	38.3
1841	34.2	1901	38.9
1851	35.8	1911	39.6

*Note: affected by territorial changes.

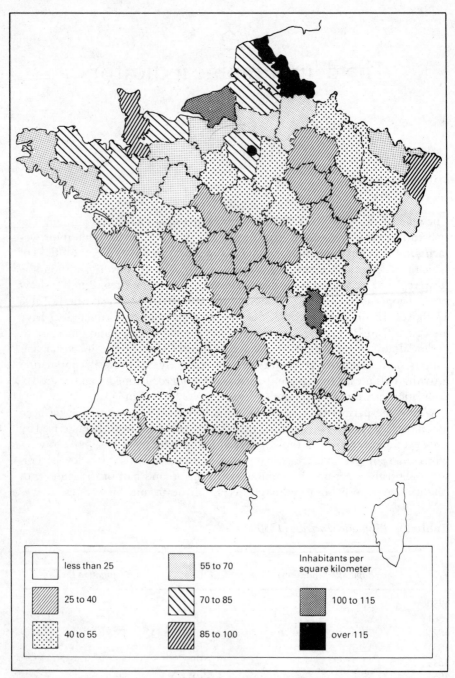

Figure 12   *Population density in 1801*
   Source: *After C. Pouthas*, Les Populations Françaises pendant la première
moitié du XIXe siècle   *P.U.F.*

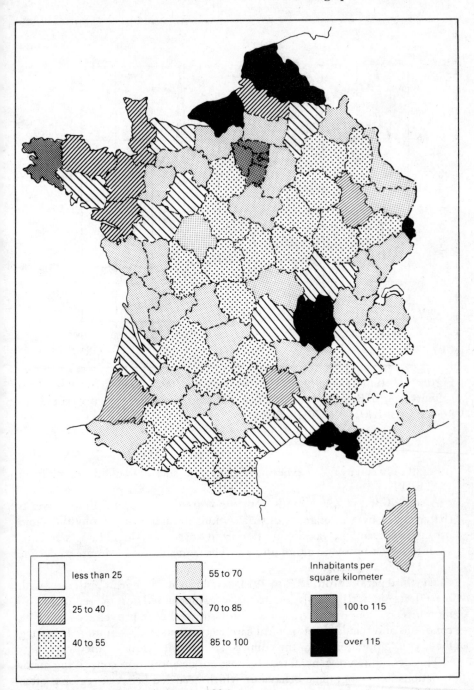

Figure 13 *Population density in 1886*
Source: *After F. Braudel, H. Labrousse (eds)*, Histoire économique et sociale de
la France   *Vol III/I   P.U.F. 1976*

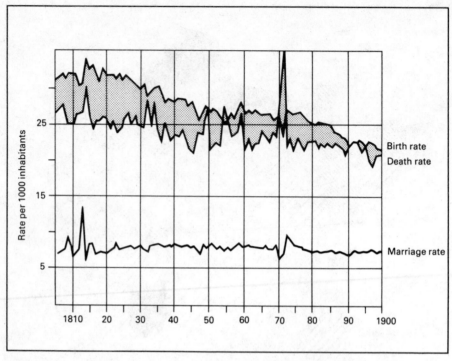

Figure 14　*Birth, mortality and marriage rates per 1000 inhabitants 1806–1900*
　　Source: *After Braudel, Labrousse (eds)*, Histoire économique et sociale de la
France　*Vol III/I　P.U.F. 1976*

brought to an end by the long period of economic, social and political crisis from
1846 to 1851.

A second period corresponds with the years of the Second Empire and is
characterized by accelerated industrialization, the transport revolution, rapid
urban growth and increased migration from the countryside. Living standards
seem to have improved, although an earlier tendency for birth rate to decline
appears to have levelled out.

The third period, from 1871 to 1914, saw a further decline in birth rate, with
the effects on total population partially compensated for by reductions in
mortality as economic development brought further improvements in living
conditons and standards of medical care were substantially improved. During
these years migration from the countryside became far more intense.

This description of general trends must not be allowed to conceal the major
variations in demographic behaviour which occurred between regions, often
small in size. The date and extent of transition from an eighteenth-century
pattern to a more modern pattern of behaviour varied significantly and was
influenced by a complex of factors in addition to economic change.

Mortality

Mortality rates showed a gradual although not a continuous tendency to decline
(Table 14). Particular crises like that of cholera in 1832, when the mortality rate
rose to 28.5 per 1000, or the effects of war and disease in 1870–1 had substantial
short-term effects on the statistics. The decline in mortality was translated into a
substantial increase in life expectancy (Table 15). The improvement was gradual
until the 1890s when they tended to accelerate. This process, occurring
throughout western Europe, was unprecedented in human history. The task of
the historian is to explain why it occurred, and this has to be done by means of an
examination of both the structure and causes of mortality.

The causes of death depended upon the specific living conditions of individual
people – their age, physical constitution, diet, working and living conditions.
The pathology of their entire society was determined by its material level of
development, the division of wealth between various social groups, and by the

Table 14   *Mortality per 1000 inhabitants (1816–1913)*

Year	Mortality (per 1000 people)	Year	Mortality (per 1000 people)
1816–20	25.3	1870–1	31.8
1821–5	24.7	1872–5	22.4
1826–30	25.5	1876–80	22.4
1831–5	26.0	1881–5	22.2
1836–40	23.7	1886–90	22.0
1841–5	22.7	1891–5	22.3
1846–50	23.9	1896–1900	20.6
1851–5	24.0	1901–5	19.6
1856–60	23.9	1906–10	19.2
1861–5	22.9	1911–13	18.3
1866–9	23.4		

Table 15   *Life expectancy at birth (in years)*[1]

Year	Men	Women
Eighteenth century	28.8	
1817–31	38.3	40.8
1840–59	39.3	41.0
1877–81	40.8	43.4
1898–1903	45.3	48.7
1908–13	48.5	52.4

complex of beliefs which helped decide both public and private attitudes towards hygiene. Over the course of the century the social environment and inevitably its pathology was subject to marked change. However, the maintenance of mortality levels above 20 per 1000 until the last decade of the nineteenth century is clear evidence of the persistence of poverty and of low standards of hygiene. Systematic statistics on the causes of death are available only for the towns. Even then, in the earlier part of the century, their collection was irregular. Comparison over time is rendered difficult by changing standards of medical diagnosis. However, according to inquiries made by the Paris Prefecture of Police in the 1820s in years free of major epidemics, the main cause of death was pulmonary consumption, which in 1823 accounted for 11.09 per cent of deaths, and in 1826 for 11.6 per cent. After this came other diseases affecting the respiratory system such as pneumonia (9.8 per cent) and pleurisy (12.7 per cent). Death caused by these varied annually according to climatic conditions, as did mortality due to intestinal complaints which accounted for 8.04 per cent of deaths in 1823, and 13.5 per cent in 1826. Diseases which today account for a large proportion of deaths, such as cardio-vascular complaints (1.83 per cent of deaths in 1823, 2.9 per cent in 1826) or cancer (2.27 and 2.47 per cent respectively), were far less significant. Among the most important factors affecting mortality rates were poverty and diet, housing, public hygiene and general standards of health and medical care.

Poverty

Poverty was the essential cause of high mortality. It resulted in a poor diet and inadequate accommodation with low standards of hygiene. It requires an imaginative leap for us to visualize the living conditions of the poor in the last century – the undernourishment and poor health, the overcrowded, humid, cold, insalubrious accommodation, the lack of water, the dirt and smells, the long working days, exhaustion and lack of leisure. It is difficult to comprehend the pressure of constant insecurity – the threat of unemployment, sickness and old age – in a society which had not yet advanced from charity to welfare as a basic right. Only a minority of well-paid workers were able to save and to afford the contributions to mutual aid societies which sought to provide some protection against these threats. The rest were forced to depend upon the help of families which could ill afford to provide it, and as a last resort upon the limited resources of public or private charity. Conditions in the countryside were particularly severe in the first half of the century when population densities were reaching their historical maxima. Poverty and misery were widespread due to the lack of work and inadequate remuneration. In many areas, only through an accumulation of tasks – on the land, in rural industry and through seasonal migration – could the poor make ends meet. Even in rich rural areas, like the Beauce plain close to Paris, major social contrasts existed between rich and poor. In the 1830s, day-labourers ate black bread, cheese and vegetables and drank only water. Conditions were at their worst in upland areas like the Pyrenees, where the introduction of the potato in the eighteenth century had permitted further subdivision of landholdings and the cultivation of marginal land up to 1400–1500 metres above sea level, and where, as in Ireland, the growing population desperately sought to secure enough food to eat, and was at the mercy of a poor harvest.

The 1850s saw the beginnings of improvement. This was made possible by increases in the productivity of agriculture and by favourable price-levels until the late 1870s. Furthermore, population pressure on resources in the countryside was eased considerably by increased migration towards the towns. All sections of the rural population shared in this prosperity. In the Pas-de-Calais, for example, the real incomes of agricultural labourers increased by 56 per cent between 1852 and 1882; fell by 5 per cent from 1882 to 1896; and then rose again by 6 per cent from 1896 to 1910.[2] The sources available make this a very rough estimate, but good enough to reveal the remarkable progress during the Second Empire and 1870s. It conceals, of course, variations due to the possession of a plot of land or the size of family and age of its members, and in spite of considerable improvements the worker remained at the mercy of unemployment and illness. Few were able to save. In 1913, 73 per cent of the families of agricultural labourers were still in receipt of some form of charity.

Living conditions in the towns were affected by the same kind of chronology of change. According to an official report on Paris in 1832 there were two classes of poor – those who by unceasing hard labour could normally provide for their own subsistence but constantly ran the risk of falling into extreme poverty due to some personal or social crisis, and below this 'useful and laborious class' another 'recognizable by its absolute destitution and profound degradation': a genuine *classe dangereuse*. 276,077 households (over two-thirds of the total) were so poor as to be exempt from taxes on their accommodation.[3] The influx of poor people into towns ill-prepared to receive them had had serious consequences for living conditions and save for the highly skilled contributed to the degradation of wages. Paris, and every other town in this first half of the century, was characterized by the immense weight of poverty and misery. The not infrequent economic crises, especially those caused by poor harvests, had disastrous consequences for already impoverished people. During the 1828–9 subsistence crisis 227,000 people needed assistance, while according to the official report on the distribution of subsidized bread in Paris during 1847 some 395,000 of a population of 945,000 needed aid, and in all three-quarters of the population were close to destitution. Similarly, in the south-west at Toulouse, 20,000 received gifts of bread, at Bordeaux 21,700 and at Montauban 6500 of a population of 17,000.[4]

In the second half of the century living conditions improved due to the slow increase in wages and fall in the price of some basic foodstuffs. The disappearance of traditional subsistence crises after 1853–6 removed one major cause of unemployment and expensive food. The development of the urban economy created new and more secure employment opportunities and helped to eliminate the *class dangereuse* as an identifiable social milieu. In all these respects the Second

Empire marked the beginnings of a social revolution. After a period of stability in the 1840s, male wages in Paris rose by 84.3 per cent between 1852 and 1882, and then far more slowly until 1905 when the rate of increase again accelerated. In France as a whole the improvement in real income was especially significant in the 1870s; it continued to rise, but less rapidly, from 1882 to 1905, and then stagnated due to rising prices in the period prior to 1914.

This catalogue of improvement is not presented in order to deny that many workers – particularly those with low wages and large families to support – continued to live in misery. In the poorest *arrondissement* of Paris in 1886 – the 20th – 12.89 per cent of the population were officially classified as 'indigents', in contrast with 5.91 per cent in the city as a whole and only 1.78 per cent in the 8th *arrondissement*.[5] Few workers had anything to leave when they died – some mediocre furniture or tools perhaps. Even if they could escape misery most lived in poverty. This was, however, a period which saw improvement in real wages and in diet as part of the general improvement in the standard of living.

Diet

In combination with infectious disorders, poor diet causing protein-calorie deficiencies was one of the main, even if indirect, causes of death and disease. Indirect because it determined a person's ability to resist disease and to survive a life of hard physical labour. Unfortunately the information available is very mixed in quality and difficult to use. It is clearly impossible to accurately calculate how much food was produced. The official statistics were affected by suspicions that they were designed to facilitate tax collection, while much of the food produced in countless smallholdings and gardens was consumed by the families without ever being recorded. The information on diet comes from a large number of contemporary observers who reveal little more than that there were countless variations between social groups, and between areas often small in size. Diet was closely related to the character of local agriculture, particularly before the development of rapid communications, but its evolution in turn was influenced by established dietary traditions. Income, taste and the organization of the food market were determining factors.

Urban diets tended to be better than rural because of higher incomes and access to a wider selection of foodstuffs. In particular, urban workers ate more meat. Even so, for most of the population the basis of the diet was bread. In Marseille, for example, average bread consumption was estimated at 613 grammes per day in 1822. In Grenoble and Perpignan bread consumption averaged 600 grammes; in Rouen 525; in Bordeaux 500 and in Paris 450. Taking the lower consumption of women, children, the aged and the wealthier classes into account it seems likely that the adult male worker ate 750–800 grammes per day,[6] a factor which explains why workers were so sensitive to fluctuations in bread prices. The lower levels of bread consumption in Paris reflected not only changing dietary habits but the relatively high levels of employment in the tertiary sector. However, for the poor the positive effects of a more diverse diet were often adversely affected by its qualitative shortcomings. Meat frequently came from animals which had been in poor health before slaughter. Fruit and vegetables past their prime might be purchased in order to save money. Moreover, cooking was difficult in overcrowded apartments, which meant that food was often poorly prepared.

In the countryside the basis of the diet was again either bread (particularly in the plains), or else some form of gruel or griddle-cake (in the Massif Central and Brittany) supplemented by chestnuts (Massif Central), potatoes and vegetables. Fat-stuffs were consumed in the form of butter in areas of cattle-breeding or a variety of animal fats or vegetable oil elsewhere. Most of the population subsisted on an austere diet – better in summer than in winter – with both meat and alcoholic drinks as luxuries, although in some cases, particularly during the long summer days, alcohol might serve as an important stimulant. The best produce of many smallholdings – poultry, eggs, butter, wine – was often sold rather than consumed, in order to accumulate the money essential to pay rents, taxes and to provide a small reserve in case of emergency or with which to purchase land.

Meat consumption is an important indicator of the evolution of living standards, in that consumption tended to reflect income. It was higher in towns than in the country, and in northern France than in the south. Even so, in this as in all aspects of diet, custom as well as cash was a major influence on eating habits. Moreover, there is no way in which one can accurately assess the contribution of the pigs and poultry which countless households kept, or that of hunting or fishing (frequently poaching). From early in the previous century the attenuation of subsistence crises had led to improvement in dietary standards, but for most of the population this tended to be a quantitative rather than a qualitative change. Diets continued to be dominated by carbohydrate intake and to lack nutritional balance. Thus Toutain has estimated that average daily food consumption rose from 1700 calories at the end of the eighteenth century to 2000 by about 1830, followed by a more rapid increase to around 3000 calories by about 1880. He further estimates that 80 per cent of this food intake was supplied by cereals in 1789 and 72 per cent in 1850 (30 per cent in 1960–4) while the contribution of meat was only 7 per cent in 1789 (15 per cent in 1960–4) and that of dairy production under 5 per cent from 1789 to 1880 (10 per cent in 1960–4).[7]

The quality of diet appears to have been particularly poor in Champagne, upper Poitou, the south of the Massif Central and the southern Alps. The physiological consequences of such diets are not easy to estimate. Calorific intake was normally adequate, but that of protein and vitamins (especially A and C) was grossly deficient. This had effects on the human organism at all stages of its development, including that within the womb. Even mild protein–calorie malnutrition was a cause of deficiencies in height and weight, while more severe deprivation could affect mental development and learning capacity, a condition which lack of stimulation from overburdened parents might aggravate. At all stages of life deficiencies caused a general debility and reduced resistance to disease and capacity for labour. The improvement of diet enabled the release of an enormous amount of human energy.

Conditions improved due to changes in the organization of commerce and in agricultural productivity, because of increased purchasing power and the complex evolution of taste. The date of change varied but everywhere it took the form of an increase in the consumption of meat, dairy products, fruit and vegetables, and a reduction in the dominant position of bread. Consumption of wine also increased. The first crucial manifestation of change was the disappearance of subsistence crises. Extreme deprivation became less common. This improvement in the regularity of supply, i.e. an essentially quantitative change, was followed by qualitative change, affecting first of all the towns from the 1850s, and from then spreading slowly out into the countryside. At a fairly early stage groups like the Limousin masons working in Paris returned home with a taste for meat, but in general the gradualness of the process of change needs to be stressed. It required the passing of generations. Improvements in purchasing power were not always accompanied by improvements in the quality of diet. Improvements in diet became general only from the 1890s, but even then dietary diversification did not go far enough, so that among lower income groups malnutrition remained a common problem.

Housing

At the beginning of the century the poor in town and country lived in overcrowded accommodation, poorly supplied with water or the means of disposing of human or household waste. Until the 1850s most of the housing stock in both town and countryside remained essentially medieval in appearance. New construction, mostly on the outskirts of town centres, was relatively limited. After the 1850s change was to occur at a much more rapid pace.

Generalizations about housing are difficult to make. Between the extremes – the grand mansion and luxurious apartment on the one hand, and the squalid furnished rooms, packed with desperately poor people on the other – there existed a great deal of variation. Adeline Daumard has distinguished three basic types in Paris. First, the lodgings of the popular classes – usually small apartments, overcrowded, poorly furnished, and with each of the rooms being used for a multiplicity of purposes; second, lower middle-class housing, with rooms allocated to precise functions, including dining and sitting rooms, bedrooms, a small room for a domestic, and in the closing decades of the century running water and toilets; and third, the spacious accommodation of the very rich, combining space, luxury and comfort, including rooms for large dinners and receptions, rooms for domestics, stables, and from the 1860–80s equipped with central heating, and by the end of the century a bathroom. For those who could afford them, prior to the introduction of running water, gas and electricity and the twentieth-century use of innumerable household gadgets, domestics were the vital means of easing the burden of maintaining a household.

Not surprisingly accommodation tended to serve as a symbol of social status. Even in the first part of the century this was reinforced by a growing social segregation. While not entirely mythical, the often repeated description of apartment blocks in old city centres sheltering diverse social groups from shopkeepers and artisans on the ground floor, to bourgeois professionals and rentiers above them, then successively clerks and workers on the higher floors, was not that common. Buildings generally accommodated a less diverse social mixture – rarely more than lower middle class and workers. The wealthy needed the attics of their buildings for their domestics. In Paris, even during the early part of the century, a clear opposition had developed between the west, favoured by the better-off, and the east, the Paris of artisans, manual labourers and the poor. Reconstruction of the city centre during the Second Empire intensified this, although even then, among the elegant streets of the west, there were still to be found narrow, sordid streets, and in the east, islands of comfortable life in the midst of misery. Moreover, large numbers of shopkeepers and merchants lived throughout the city.

The major problem faced in the capital and every other urban centre was the rapid influx of people. Paris and its inner suburbs (the present twenty *arrondissements*) had around 600,000 inhabitants in 1801; the population increase after this date is shown in Table 16. Population density in the city rose from 159 inhabitants per hectare in 1880 to 307 by 1846. In the old quarters of St-Honoré and les Halles there were more than 1000 people per hectare. In only six years from 1851 to 1856 the population increased by 20 per cent. Similarly, in Marseille the population rose from 195,000 in 1846 to 313,000 by 1872 (i.e. by 60 per cent). The situation was even worse in industrial Lille, which by 1858 had a density of 411 inhabitants per hectare. This growth created major problems in the spheres of housing, public hygiene, provisioning and the circulation of traffic. Municipal administrators were ill-prepared to cope with these problems. Prior to the economic boom of the Second Empire they were made all the more serious by an influx of people at a faster rate than jobs could be created for them. This more than anything else – the existence within the cities of large numbers of people existing from day to day, making ends meet by whatever means came to hand, often forced into petty or occasionally serious crime – created a feeling of crisis. Urban civilization appeared to be threatened.

Table 16 *Population of Paris (1836–1911)*

Year	Population	Year	Population
1836	1,002,633	1891	2,424,705
1851	1,277,064	1901	2,660,559
1872	1,851,792	1911	2,847,229
1881	2,239,928		

Most working-class families in the larger towns lived in one, two or three rooms. Much of the population was trapped in the poorest quality housing by low incomes. Rent was a major burden. In Lille, for example, in 1843 a single room cost 6–7 francs per month, a cellar 6 francs – a week's wage for the lowest paid textile workers. It has been estimated that in the 1880s the mass of working- and lower middle-class families paying rents up to a level of 1200–1500 francs per annum spent around one-quarter of their incomes on rent. Above this middle-class families spent only one-eighth to one-tenth. For an equivalent lodging, rents tended to be higher in Paris than in the provinces. In large cities, in particular, landlords needed to maintain rents at a high level in part to compensate themselves for loss of income caused by frequent 'moonlight flits' by people who could not afford to pay.

During the 1850s to 1860s, although wages tended to increase, rents rose more rapidly. Relationships between proprietors and tenants became very tense, often far worse than those between workers and their employers. Subsequently, rents fell or stagnated until around 1906, rising again throughout the pre-war years. Low incomes continued to force much of the population, particularly the least skilled and newcomers, to keep their rents to a minimum and resulted in inevitable overcrowding.

Lille, a rapidly developing industrial centre, frequently provided examples of atrocious urban living conditions. Of the 200 families visited by Dr Binaut in 1843, 106 lived in one room, forty-one in two, and only eleven in three. Overcrowding and lack of personal hygiene helped to make the interiors of these dwellings all the more nauseating. They had dirty walls, little furniture (a table and some chairs), beds with coverings of rags or old clothes and mattresses stuffed with straw which was rarely changed. Heat was supplied by a stove, light by a candle, or by the mid nineteenth century by an oil lamp. Sanitary facilities were little more than troughs, often shared by dozens of people, and inevitably infected. The lack of running water made cleanliness difficult. All this combined to create a smell of poverty and also its hubbub – the lack of privacy inevitable when so many people were crowded together. Frequently too, the buildings were packed together, separated only by narrow alleys which did not allow the sunlight to penetrate the windows of apartments on the first two floors. The result was high humidity, extremely damaging to health. Improvement was slow. In 1906 an inquiry among 900 families revealed that 75 per cent lived in one or two rooms.

At this time in Paris 26 per cent of the population had only one room, 30 per cent had two; at Bordeaux the figures were 20 per cent and 24 per cent respectively; at Brest 53 per cent and 24 per cent; at Fougères 50 per cent and 27 per cent; at Grenoble 21 per cent and 34 per cent; at Lyon 28 per cent and 22 per cent; at Rouen 25 per cent and 25 per cent; and at St-Etienne 28 per cent and 42 per cent. It appears that 80–90 per cent of workers dwellings lacked private sanitary facilities. According to an inquiry conducted into urban housing by Dr Bertillon, and published in 1908 in the *Revue d'hygiène et de police sanitaire*, of every 1000 inhabitants 260 lived in overcrowded conditions (defined as more than two per room including kitchens), 360 in 'inadequate conditions', 168 in adequate (one person per room), 167 in large accommodation, and forty-five in very large (more than two rooms per person). Although general housing conditions were poor, every large city had its *mauvais quartier*.[8] In the 1900s the Cité Napoléon in Lyon, and parts of the 13th, 19th and 20th *arrondissements* of Paris, together with areas of such north-western suburbs as Levallois, Asnières and Clichy were especially notorious. These were the product of the degradation of older buildings in which the larger apartments or rooms had been subdivided as demand for accommodation rose, and of the uncontrolled construction of jerry-built properties in the suburbs which were intended to pay for themselves very quickly by packing in as many people as possible, and spending little or nothing on maintenance. In the 1890s and 1900s it was the owners of this type of accommodation who were the last to equip their buildings with gas and electricity. The best working-class housing was probably to be found on the outskirts of cities, or in small towns where the better paid were sometimes able to purchase a plot of land and construct a simple wooden or brick structure surrounded by a garden.

In rural areas, according to a report presented by the geographer Jules Sion in 1938, the conditions of housing varied between three main geographical zones. The first, in the centre from Finistère to Cantal, and from Saône-et-Loire to Charentes, included twenty-eight departments in which an estimated 60 per cent of rural dwellings had one or two rooms. In the second, north and north-east of the Seine, three rooms was the norm; and in the third, in the south, four rooms were more usual. The poorest conditions were to be found in areas of high birth rate and of dispersed habitat (in which imitation was least likely). This was the result of low incomes, and also of attitudes which accorded low priority to the improvement of housing. It has to be recognized that above all the peasant cottage was a farm building and that its dimensions were closely related to the scale and character of agricultural activity.

Even so, significant improvement occurred from the prosperous years of the Second Empire onwards. Previously, high transport costs had enforced dependence on local building materials, and most rural housing had been characterized by small windows, earthen floors, poorly constructed chimneys, lack of water and sanitary facilities, and by overcrowding. The result had been high humidity, darkness, foul air and lack of cleanliness – ideal conditions for the spread of disease. From this period, in new construction, windows tended to become larger, floors were paved and the number of rooms increased, but the process of replacement or of improvement of existing houses was very slow. In 1913 in the Pas-de-Calais, for example, 65 per cent of households still inhabited one or two rooms with an average of 8 square metres per person.[9]

The bulk of new building inevitably occurred in the rapidly growing towns. In Paris, the most active periods of construction occurred between 1821 and 1826, 1837 and 1847, during the Second Empire, and from 1878 to 1885, followed by an especially long period of stagnation. Of greatest significance was the reconstruction of parts of central Paris associated with the Prefect Haussmann. This was the product of a complex of motives – the desire to create a fitting capital for the empire, to facilitate the movement of traffic, to make the preservation of public order easier, to improve living standards, and to provide employment. The scale of activity was unsurpassed. The normal problems of finance and expropriation were at least temporarily eased by government decision. At the same time development of lower cost housing on the periphery occurred, particularly towards the north and east, to absorb both people displaced by the demolition of inner-city slums and the waves of immigrants attracted by the opening of new factories on cheap land in the suburbs.

Housing construction was left essentially to private initiative. There were two main types of development – either high rent apartment blocks or else buildings which would maximize returns by taking in the largest possible number of tenants. The constant demand for relatively cheap accommodation allowed landlords to impose a heavy burden on poor tenants, while not bothering too much about repairs and maintenance. However, for reasons of prestige, and the desire to avoid the rapid deterioration of property associated with overcrowding, investors tended to prefer middle-class tenants. Moreover, during the 1860s, while it cost 700 francs per square metre to build housing for workers, rents averaged only 6f50–7f per square metre. In contrast, for bourgeois accommodation costing 1000 francs per square metre twice or three times as much could be charged. The housing market needs to be considered, therefore, in two parts – an upper and periodically oversupplied end, and a lower end, always undersupplied. Some model accommodation was provided for the poor. In Paris, for example, the Cité Napoléon was constructed on the rue Rochechouart between 1849 and 1853, with accommodation for 400 families; in Mulhouse between 1853 and 1867 manufacturers had constructed 800 houses for 6000 people, each with two living rooms, two bedrooms, a kitchen and cellar, with a latrine at the bottom of the garden. In addition large numbers of *pavillons* were constructed by or for those middle- or working-class families who had the capital.

Similar patterns of development occurred in all major towns – latest in the economically least active – as the constant accumulation of people in city centres caused growing alarm on grounds of both health and social order. In Lille from the 1840s, this forced the military authorities to allow the extension of the city outside its fortifications. The result was the rapid development of industry and working-class housing in the suburbs of Wazemmes, Moulins-Lille and Fives, which, even if they could not rival the old city centre quarter of St-Saveur in squalor, were soon overcrowded. Until the establishment of tramways in 1873 workers needed to live close to their places of work. Not until the 1894 Siegfried law (improved by the Strauss law of 12 April 1906) on low cost housing were efforts made to try to encourage the formation of companies to provide low cost housing (HBM) by means of tax exemptions and access to cheap credit. Progress in solving the enormous problem of inadequate housing was to be slow. By 1912 only 2725 apartments had been constructed for 11,969 people.

Public hygiene

In place of an interventionist role in the housing market, which would have been contrary to liberal economic principles, official bodies attempted to limit the effects of uncontrolled urban development upon public health. The various cholera epidemics were important stimuli for investigations into living conditions and action against the most degraded. A law of 13 April 1850 obliged each commune to create a commission to inspect unhealthy buildings and oblige their owners to carry out essential improvements. However, this applied only to rented accommodation and its effects were limited until the concentration of authority for matters of public hygiene at the Ministry of the Interior in 1889. This reflected a new will to act – seen in instructions to local councils requiring the analysis of drinking water and the closure of insalubrious establishments. Even so, the basic principles of hygiene continued to be ignored even in new buildings and only in 1902 was legislation introduced to establish basic standards. Until then local notables had tended to oppose intervention on principle, and because it was likely to lead to increased local taxes. Municipalities had largely restricted themselves to supervising the alignment of buildings in relation to the public highway. Public attitudes and the political will to increase expenditure changed only slowly. The growing concern of the press with questions of personal and public hygiene both reflected and stimulated this and in the 1870s and 1880s national and local *Sociétés d'hygiène* were established. More influential was the part played by primary education in inculcating basic concepts of hygiene. Substantial improvement in public hygiene required intervention by the state, to establish legally enforceable standards and help to finance improvements in water supply and sewerage disposal. On a large scale this was seen first with the work of Haussmann in Paris, but for most of France and indeed for substantial areas of the capital improvement came later.

Water supply was the crucial problem. For most of the nineteenth century water was inadequate in quantity and quality. Life without running water is difficult for us to imagine. Carrying water from wells or fountains, or from streams was an exhausting task, but essential for cooking, washing and for people and animals to drink. A great deal of the physical misery and poor health (most obviously endemic typhoid) which plagued the population in most areas until the twentieth century was due to poor water supply.

Improvements occurred first in the larger cities in the period 1800–50, but this provided running water only for the wealthy and in some cases the residents of barracks or hospitals. Although it had become technically possible to pump water to the upper floors of buildings at the end of the eighteenth century using the Périer Company's pumps, as late as 1850 in Paris there were only 358 kilometres of conduits, only one building in five was connected to the public water supply and a mere 150 buildings had water above the first floor. This was partly due to the unwillingness of landlords to pay for connection, but also because one-quarter of streets had no conduits. Most of the population obtained water from wells, but these were usually infected by infiltration and the water supply could only be used with safety for washing and cleaning. The poor obtained drinking water from the 1837 public fountains in the city, those who could afford to purchased it from water-sellers who themselves took their water from the fountains. The aim of Haussmann and his engineer Belgrand was to provide running water for every dwelling. Water from the polluted Seine was largely replaced – save in drought – by the resources of the Somme–Soucle valleys, by a reservoir at Chaumont and finally by the rivers Dhuis and of the Vanne – all linked to the city by lengthy tunnels and aquaducts. Within the city, the length of water-mains was increased to 1370 kilometres by 1874, while the number of buildings with running water rose from 6000 to 40,500 between 1854 and 1874. Many landlords, however, continued to avoid the expense – 20,000 buildings remained unconnected, mainly in the poorer northern, eastern and south-eastern areas of the city, while in many other apartment blocks only the ground floor was supplied. By the 1890s the supply had been further supplemented by drawing on the Avre, Loing and Lunain. This raised overall supply to an average of 150 litres per inhabitant per day, in marked contrast with the 6–7 litres which it was estimated were available in 1850.

In the provinces, towns were provided with improved water supplies from about 1860 to the 1900s, although the quality of the water often remained poor. In spite of efforts by government officials, elected councils and local notables remained reluctant to pay for improvements. Progress accelerated once such influential people changed their minds. Towards the turn of the century water supply became a matter of civic pride. At Nevers (Nièvre), for example, the town council assumed responsibility in place of a private company in 1909, and attempted to improve conditions. Previously only 1300 of 3620 buildings had had running water, and due to inadequate filtration the supply had been contaminated by sewage and industrial effluent.

A satisfactory water supply was essential to the proper working of the sewerage system. A decree of 1533 had obliged householders in Paris to provide *privés*. Another decree in 1809 reaffirmed this principle and indeed some progress was made, usually by means of the installation of a privy in the courtyard or under a stairway, often to serve large numbers of people. These were connected to foul smelling cesspits which were emptied periodically into the 2300 special carts which circulated through the city. Although there were significant improvements in the system of sewers in the first half of the century, by 1851 there were still only 132 km of underground sewers in 402 km of streets, and most of the sewage they collected poured into the Seine above the point from which the city's water supply was taken. Improvement accelerated so that by 1870 there were over 560 km of sewers of 805 km of streets, and by 1914 a network of 1227 km. These fed into a comprehensive system of collectors, the major sanitary achievement of the Second Empire, which joined the Seine well downriver of the capital, but with unfortunate consequences for towns like Mantes which suffered additionally from the attraction of the Seine for industries like chemicals and leather which needed to dispose of waste. A decree of March 1852 had given landlords in Paris ten years to build connections to the sewer network. Even then, however, cesspits remained common, particularly in the new suburbs, and in working class areas. Thus by 1894 only 4300 buildings had been connected and it required further legislation in 1889 and 1894 to increase the number rapidly to 23,000 in 1902 and 47,280 in 1910 (to 62.6 per cent of all dwellings). Again the poor *quartiers* were least well served and residents were often forced to share toilet facilities. [11]

As in the case of water supply, most towns only slowly followed where Paris led. Backward Limoges had no sewers before 1875. Until then sewerage and household refuse were simply thrown into central gutters in the streets which flowed into the River Vienne. The *rue de la boucherie* was notorious for the blood and guts with which it seemed to be paved. The smell was intolerable to visitors. Narrow, poorly paved, badly lit, evil smelling streets, awash with litter of all kinds were all too common features of France until at least the 1860–70s, when, again following the example of Paris, municipalities were increasingly active in paving and cleaning streets, and providing them with gas lighting. Industrial pollution contributed to the squalor. From early in the century the worst offenders in terms of pollution, such as tanneries, had been driven out of Paris itself, but not too far – in the west, for example, to the communes of Puteaux, Levallois and Clichy, in the north to St-Denis and Aubervilliers. The countryside was hardly more salubrious than the overcrowded quarters of the cities. Most small towns and villages were polluted by manure heaps and animal droppings as well as human faeces.

An improved water supply made it possible to flush human waste into and out of the sewers. It was also the essential prerequisite for better personal hygiene. There is not much information available on this question. However, before the advent of running water, bathing at home required considerable effort. In this respect domestics were invaluable, but even among the bourgeoisie – according to a *Manuel de civilité* published in the 1850s – women were expected to bathe just once a month. Middle-class men appear to have bathed even less often and usually, at least in towns, in public baths whose increasing numbers suggest a more positive attitude to water as the century progressed. Thus in Paris between 1817 and 1831 thirty-seven public baths were established, and between 1831 and 1840 a further twenty-three. By 1861 there were 107 and by 1900 some 500. These were not normally used by the poor, and their use could be counterproductive. Thus at Nevers the public baths gave access to the polluted waters of the River Nièvre. Further improvement depended on the spread of new attitudes and norms of behaviour promoted by medical science, by military service, which in the last decades of the nineteenth century imposed a daily wash and a weekly shower, and by education. This was part of a diffuse improvement in living standards and the development of less fatalistic attitudes to life. It occurred first among a relatively small urban élite. Among other social groups inertia was imposed by difficult living conditions and undemanding norms. In the 1830s workers at Lille were described as ignorant even of the most elementary hygiene. Their skin was covered with several layers of filth, while both adults and children frequently had hair full of vermin. At best the daily wash for most people for decades afterwards continued to amount to a rapid swilling of hands and face. The use of soap was limited by its cost. Clothes were normally dirty, especially among the poor. They were rarely washed, and then usually in streams and fountains of doubtful cleanliness. On the farm they were frequently impregnated with mud and manure. Underwear was rarely changed. People stank of sweat. Day clothes were in part worn in bed. Dwellings were equally unclean, and the general mediocrity of life did nothing to encourage improvement for much of the century. The poverty which forced large numbers of people to live in grossly overcrowded conditions, to work hard for most of the daylight hours just to survive, left little margin in terms either of cash or energy for better hygiene.

Health standards

Much of the population thus lived in a filthy, infected environment. Poor diet and germ-ridden surroundings inevitably caused poor health. Hard, and often dangerous work, frequently in the open, whatever the weather, compounded the damage – reducing much of the population to a state of physiological misery, made all the worse at the beginning of the century by the wars and subsistence crises of the closing years of the Napoleonic Empire. Conditions were slow to improve. According to a report on the ten most industrial departments made in 1840 to the Chamber of Peers by Charles Dupin, half of the potential conscripts were rejected as unfit for military service. This contrasted with only one-fifth in rural departments. An enquiry conducted by Binault among 200 working-class families at Lille in 1843 revealed that of the adult males 63.22 per cent were ill or infirm; the same was true of 47.66 per cent of the women and 24.9 per cent of the children.[12] This was a population of pale and thin people, in a poor state of health, with no alternative but to drag themselves off to work however ill they might feel. Social distinctions often seem to have been reinforced by the smell and appearance of the poor. They were dirtier, paler, often disfigured by skin diseases or industrial accidents, and generally of inferior stature to better-off people. Significantly, the poor themselves were particularly concerned about skin complaints which were likely to affect social relationships as well as with illnesses which might prevent them from working.

The conditions we have described were those in which diseases like tuberculosis flourished throughout the century. Although members of all social classes were liable to infection, it was poverty which above all explains its ravages. Individual genetic make-up was relevant, but the poor in general had lower resistance. Those engaged in hard physical labour for low wages were the worst affected, and particularly urban workers who lived and worked in poorly ventilated, overcrowded conditions. To contract the disease was almost certainly to be condemned to death. In a period in which – with the notable, but intermittent, exception of cholera – epidemic diseases substantially declined in intensity, tuberculosis appeared as man's worst scourge. In an industrial town like Fougères (Ille-et-Vilaine) even as late as 1908–10 it caused one-quarter of all deaths, and mainly among people in their 30s. In France as a whole in the period 1911–13 it killed 2136 per million inhabitants, substantially more than in Germany (1519) or Britain (1397), a comparison which is indicative of inferior living standards, the failure of the authorities to isolate its victims, or to institute tuberculosis testing of cows' milk. By 1911 the whole range of lung diseases accounted for an estimated 42.2 per cent of deaths, largely due to the increased prevalence of tuberculosis.

Even more frightening, because of their intensity, and the reminder of past pandemics, were the cholera epidemics of 1832, 1849, 1853–5, 1864–5, 1873 and 1884. In 1832 around 102,000 and in 1853–4 about 143,000 died of the disease. Again, although all social groups were affected, it was above all the poor, i.e. the weakest, who died. In Paris in 1832 the highest mortality rates were in the central, right-bank quarters, reaching 136 per 1000 in the Place de l'Hôtel de Ville, and 244 on the Quai de la Grève. It was in these areas, the most overcrowded and insalubrious of the capital, sheltering the poorest and most deprived, that contamination was most likely. After Haussmann's demolition of the old city, the 19th and 20th *arrondissements* became the primary centres of the disease.

In rural areas, too, it was the most impoverished who experienced the highest mortality rates. In the overpopulated Ariège in 1854, 11,256 people (4 per cent of the population) died, but the figure reached 20 per cent in five cantons in the Foix area, a level of mortality which inevitably caused considerable terror. In comparison, less densely populated and more prosperous departments in the same region suffered far less severely (2226 died in Haute-Garonne, 1241 in Tarn, seventeen in Tarn-et-Garonne).[13] These differences in mortality primarily reflect, however, the patterns of propagation of the disease, i.e. the movement of infected people, and also the receptivity of particular environments. Winter cold appears to have been unfavourable to propagation, which occurred primarily through infected water and overcrowded and insanitary living conditions. The diffusion of cholera corresponded essentially to the density of population. It spread most easily in the north and east and along the Rhône–Saône corridor. Areas of dispersed habitat in the west, centre and south-west were relatively spared in comparison with areas of higher population density.

Typhoid was another major killer. It was caused particularly by polluted water and, because of this, was a significant threat during the summer months – endemic normally, epidemic in some years. Boudin's *Trait de géographie et de statistique médicale et des maladies endémiques* (1857) attributed 9.1 per cent of Parisian deaths to typhoid between 1839 and 1850. Significantly, in Rennes the disease was blamed for 13.4 deaths per 10,000 inhabaitants per annum from 1870 to 1882 (5 per cent of total deaths), but this fell to 6.9 from 1883 to 1889 following only partial improvements in the water supplies.[14] The poor quality of water supplies was also largely to blame for a complex of intestinal complaints, including dysentery, easily recognizable from afar by its repugnant odour. In some areas poor drainage provided the marshland breeding grounds for mosquitoes, and malaria remained an important cause of death and debility in areas on the Mediterranean coast from the Camargue to Roussillon, on the Atlantic coast from the Landes to the Loire estuary, and on the Channel coast from Dol to the Somme. Inland, too, the Bresse, Sologne, Forez and Dombes areas were notorious, although the problem disappeared rapidly when marshes were drained from the 1850s.

Smallpox was another endemic disease which occasionally flared up into epidemics because of a widespread failure to take advantage of the vaccination which was only made compulsory in 1902. Another major cause of illness and death was venereal disease. Doctors in the last third of the century appear to have been especially concerned with what they saw as a rapid increase in the spread of syphilis, although medical statistics do not bear them out. Even so, this was the cause of 25–30,000 deaths a year by 1900. Its effects on the nervous system were particularly horrible and it was extremely contagious. Moreover, it affected the unborn, and was an important cause of stillbirths, miscarriages and infant mortality. As a result it came to be seen as a threat to the survival of the race, but it was difficult to treat because sufferers, from a sense of shame, were frequently reluctant to visit doctors.

Venereal disease was frequently linked in the public mind with another social scourge – alcoholism. Again, although all social groups suffered, a large part of the problem could be explained in terms of the misery and ignorance of the lower classes. Drunks were a common sight in the streets. Average annual consumption of wine was around 140 litres per adult in the period 1830–39, but this had risen to 208 litres by 1900–13. This obviously had dire consequences for their health, and also for their family life.

Explanations of mass poverty in terms of alcoholism and immorality had the additional effect of easing the consciences of the wealthy opponents of social reform. It was only from the 1880s, for example, that parliament began to show real concern with the industrial accidents and diseases which so often reduced poor families to penury. A law providing compensation for accidents at work was voted in April 1889, but industrial diseases were covered only in 1919. Even when they avoided accidents or disease masses of undernourished men and women often working in excessive hot, cold or damp conditions, unwilling to take time off work even when ill because of the consequences for family budgets, suffered deteriorating health and premature aging.

Medical care

Attitudes towards illness and death gradually changed as mortality rates declined. The frequency with which death traditionally had struck families meant that it had been received with sorrow but also with resignation, particularly among the poor who suffered most. Widowhood, becoming an orphan, the loss of children, were common. Fatalism was to some degree a means of psychological self-protection. It was intensified by the high cost and doubtful efficacy of medicine for much of the century, and by the teachings of the church. The clergy prepared the dying for a pious end, and provided a public celebration of their life, death and hope of eternal salvation. Even the poor were anxious to be buried with dignity. Many workers subscribed to mutual aid societies to make sure of this. In regions in which the faith remained strong and illness and death were believed to be God's judgement, intercession through the church and its saints often appeared to be the only effective means of avoiding illness. Only the better educated and those who could afford the doctor's fees and remedies were likely to place much hope in them.

How effective were these remedies? At the beginning of the century, following the disruption of medical services by the revolution, and judging by the poor training of many doctors and the scholastic debates among the élite of the profession, the standard of medical practice cannot have been very high. The point is reinforced by comparisons with the scientific medicine of the end of the century, following the discoveries of Pasteur, the modernization of training, the development of laboratories and reconstruction of hospitals. Even before Pasteur, the best doctors had already appreciated the importance of hygiene and the use of boiled water and soap, as well as the isolation of the contagious sick. The significance of this concern with hygiene and efforts to reduce the possibility of infection ought to be stressed. Its effects in terms of falling mortality rates were clear even before the development of bacteriological medicine. Furthermore, the introduction of anaesthesia in the 1840s revolutionized conditions for surgery.

Nevertheless, the effectiveness of combating contagious disease was limited until Pasteur's work in the 1860s and 1870s, which led to the use of antiseptics and sterilization and to a new concern with contagion and disinfection. The bacterial agents of most diseases were only identified from the 1880s, and only then were the first vaccines and serums developed. Previously doctors had been only too aware of the inadequacy of their treatments. During the cholera epidemics they had agonized over a variety of suggested remedies, including bleeding, steam baths and purgatives. Epidemics were frequently blamed on noxious miasma rising from stagnant water and transmitted by the prevailing winds. Not until 1887 was the link between water and typhoid firmly established and only then did adequate chemical analysis of water become possible. The most effective action doctors were able to take before this was to press for improvements in hygiene, a continual but slowly effective struggle against private and public ignorance and apathy. In this they drew obvious correlations between poverty, degraded living conditions and mortality.

That the 1890s constituted a major turning point can be seen from the growing confidence of doctors in the efficacy of their techniques, particularly in the sphere of preventive medicine, and the resultant increase in their prestige. One should take care, however, not to judge the state of medical practice by the achievements of its best trained and most eminent practitioners. In the provinces standards were often far inferior to those of Paris and other cities, which with their medical schools and wealthy patients were able to attract the services of many of the best doctors. Closeness to on-going research, membership of medical societies, subscription to medical journals, easier working conditions in comparison with colleagues bringing comfort to patients in the countryside, stimulated a greater interest in the new medicine. Differences between generations were also apparent, with the younger men emerging from the medical schools in the last three decades of the nineteenth century with a training superior to that of their elders. The accelerated pace of change – with the discovery in eighteen years of the pathogenic agents of nineteen diseases, including those of puerperal fever (1878), a major cause of death in childbed, typhoid (1880), pneumonia (1881), tuberculosis (1882), diphtheria, cholera (1884), meningitis, dysentery (1892) – must have been extremely disconcerting for the large number of doctors trained in less scientific periods.

The number of doctors did not significantly increase, but the improvement in the quality of their training was fairly continuous. This was particularly evident in the replacement of the poorly trained health officers by fully qualified personnel. The actual availability of doctors reflected a very unequal geographical distribution. They tended to concentrate where professional rewards were greatest, among the wealthy rather than the poor who were most in need of care but who could not pay as well. Paris, for example, had 1231 doctors in 1851, but 720 lived in three *arrondissements*, the 1st, 2nd and 10th. In the 8th (Faubourg St Antoine) there were only forty-six, and thirty-one of these lived in the Marais, its richest quarter. In Belleville in 1860 there were only three resident doctors per 20,000 inhabitants, compared with an average for the whole of Paris of 20 per 20,000. In 1912 the respective figures were still 6.2 and 27.2. Yet, Paris was much better off than other towns, and especially rural areas. In 1844 the department of the Seine had one doctor per 662 inhabitants, Morbihan had one per 5274. By the 1880s the disparities remained enormous – the Seine, due to an overall decline in the number of doctors, now had one per 1353 inhabitants; next best provided for were the Alpes-Maritimes with 1:1425, Hérault 1:1722, Gironde 1:2080. The worst off were the poorest of rural departments – Morbihan 1:9732, Côtes-du-Nord 1:8377, Hautes-Alpes 1:8195, Finistère 1:7825. Industrial areas like the Nord and Pas-de-Calais with large numbers of poor were not much better off.[15]

Along with that of doctors, but more slowly, the status of hospitals also began to improve. The hospitals inherited from the Ancien Régime were a means of coping with chronic misery, places of refuge rather than medical care. Hospitals were feared as places to which people were sent to die, and for most of the century only sick people without families or members of families without any resources were admitted to them. In Paris in 1817 they provided beds for 4700 people. In Marseille even in 1860 only 8.71 per cent of patients in hospital were native born *Marseillais*. Most were immigrants without families to care for them. 87.98 per cent were engaged in manual professions, 7.64 per cent were sailors, 1.32 per cent were shopkeepers, 3.06 per cent members of the liberal professions – evidence of the overwhelmingly lower-class character of patients.[16] In Paris during the period 1889–93 over 10,000 people were admitted to the city's hospitals each year with advanced tuberculosis. The wealthy sent their sick to sanatoria for medical care, proper diets, fresh air and rest. The poor coped with theirs for as long as possible, and then had them admitted to hospital to die.

Standards of care were miserable. During the 1832 cholera epidemic at Lille, patients at the St-Saveur hospital were crowded two to a bed; in the 1860s at Limoges it was still not the normal practice to isolate contagious cases. Gradually, however, medical care became more effective. Hygiene certainly improved from the 1860s, and new hospitals were gradually constructed. The popular fear of hospitals took much longer to decline.

The efficacy of medical care did not depend upon doctors alone. The attitude of potential patients was a factor of considerable importance. The poor were usually reluctant to call on the services of a doctor. In part this was because of the cost of fees and medicine – at Nevers in 1853 it cost a basic 1 franc to visit a doctor's surgery and 3 francs for a home call. The costs in terms of time or fees increased with distance. There were also often quite justified doubts about the effectiveness of medical care, which could be rather brutal with its bleedings and cauterizations, and among the masses, there was suspicion and hostility towards bourgeois practitioners. This was reinforced by a fatalism, the resigned acceptance of illness and discomfort as normal and providential. If it was God's will, what could the doctor do? An alternative medicine also existed, particularly in the countryside, which was often as effective as that of the physician, where the advice of neighbours and especially old women, of curers, quacks and charlatans, of wise men and women, was frequently sought, and a variety of magical/religious practices employed. In clerical areas like Brittany the influence of priests and of the nuns who frequently added medical care to sick visiting was often decisive. Here the cults of various saints remained strong. It was cheaper and perhaps personally more satisfying to appeal to them as intercessors between man and God, although the consequence of such traditional attitudes might be the survival of smallpox as an endemic disease, in places such as Caen where in 1881 twenty-three of sixty-nine victims died, because of prejudices against vaccination.

The better off and better educated were more likely to call in a doctor and to follow the advice he proferred. The poor tended to postpone seeking medical advice until an illness was advanced, while a variety of obstacles often prevented them from following a doctor's advice. These included an inability to comprehend his instructions, the strength of popular prejudices – in the Limousin, for example, against changing the underwear of a sick person – and the practical impossibility of paying for a medically recommended diet or improved hygiene. Attitudes did change. Gradually, as communications in the very widest sense improved, and the isolation of communities diminished, and as medical care grew more effective and the status of its practitioners rose, a desire to be treated *comme à Paris* spread down the social hierarchy. Real incomes increased; medical aid was provided for the poorest. In the Bas-Rhin a free

Table 17   *Mutual aid societies*

Year	No. of societies	No. of members
1851	2,237	255,472
1869	6,139	794,473
1902	15,572	2,073,787

medical service was introduced as early as 1810. Such schemes spread through-out eastern France in the first half of the century and elsewhere after 1850. In Lille in the 1850s there was a dispensary in each parish to which were attached several health officers and midwives. Free medical care was available for the poor in Paris from 1853, although it had been provided in some *arrondissements* from 1849. Already in 1854, 30,000 people were given free medical care at home. These new functions conferred growing prestige on the medical profession. Similar facilities were provided in many departments, although in some, such as the Corrèze, this was obstructed by the insistence of doctors upon their inde-pendence and, more generally, the network of medical institutions remained very diffuse. Opposition to their establishment was also based on a desire to maintain traditional forms of private charity and an unwillingness among notables to sanction increases in local taxes at a time when competing demands were being made to build schools, new churches and roads. Only in 1889 was a *Conseil Supèrieur de l'Assistance Publique* established at the Ministry of the Interior to co-ordinate and extend such activity, and only in 1893 was a law voted which recognized a right to medical care, although with strictly defined conditions of access. This was supplemented by charitable work by doctors and subscriptions to mutual aid societies which, however, only the better paid urban workers could afford (see Table 17). These were increasingly encouraged by government subsidies. This was further evidence of the development of more positive attitudes towards medical care as education increased awareness of the potential for improved health care particularly through better hygiene, and rising real incomes allowed more and more people to purchase the doctors' services and medicines. Significantly the prestige of the medical profession had already begun to rise even before the scientific discoveries of the last third of the century, as part of the development of a more positive and active attitude towards the environment seen in the work of urban renewal, and the process of economic growth.

Differential mortality

From everything we have said so far it should be clear that health standards and mortality rates varied considerably between social groups. Not surprisingly the poorest section of the community suffered most. The *arrondissements* of Paris

Table 18   *Parisian mortality rates, 1817*

	Rate of mortality per thousand	Corrected for hospitals
Group I		
(*arrondissements* 1–4)	16.7	23.2
Group II		
(*arrondissements* 5–7, 10–11)	25.3	26.5
Group III		
(*arrondissements* 8, 9 and 12)	29.6	37.5

have been divided into three groups, according to *degré d'aisance* in 1817, Table 18 shows the conclusions reached (with allowance made for the location of hospitals).[17] Subsequently, although there was a general decline in mortality, this was more marked in the richer quarters of the city, and inequality in the face of death tended to widen until towards the end of the century. By 1911–13 mortality rates varied between 11 per 1000 in the wealthiest *arrondissements* and 22.4 per 1000 in the poorest. Industrialization and urbanization, particularly in their earlier phases, had deleterious effects on the conditions of the poor. Whatever the shortcomings of their statistics the inquiries of people like Villermé and Guepin make it clear that in the first half of the century workers employed in the new factory industries experienced higher mortality than other professional groups. They identify major variations in mortality rates not only between social groups but also within the working class itself due to variations in income and working conditions. In addition there were differences between the sexes. Besides the greater genetic frailty of men, TB and respiratory diseases, harsher working conditions and heavier consumption of alcohol appear to have accounted for most of the excess male mortality. This was in spite of deaths in childbirth due to the poor health of many pregnant women, sanitary conditions and inadequate midwifery.

Important regional variations in mortality should also be noted. Urban mortality remained higher than rural (Table 19). This higher urban mortality was in spite of the more youthful age structure of urban populations. In the developing industrial towns in particular, deteriorating living and working conditions maintained high mortalities. In the Pas-de-Calais, for example, mortality rose from 20 per 1000 in 1851–61 to 38 per 1000 in the following decade, largely due to rapid industrialization.[18] Improvements in living and working conditions gradually reversed this as the decline in the proportion of conscripts exempted from military service for such shortcomings as hernia, scrofula, poor eyesight and inadequate height revealed. Indeed from the 1860s the physical appearance of young men seems to have changed significantly.

Age structure is clearly a factor in explaining variations in mortality rates between areas. Thus, over time migration had significant effects on rural

Table 19   *Mortality per 1000 inhabitants*

Year	Urban	Rural
1854–8	29.8	23.1
1859–63	26.0	21.9
1864–8	27.1	21.8
1871–3	30.2	24.9
1874–8	25.6	20.8
1879–83	25.2	20.8
1884–8	25.1	20.6
1889–93	25.1	20.9
1894–8	22.7	19.9
1899–1903	22.0	19.5
1904–8	24.8	19.0
1909–13	19.4	17.7

population structures, causing a relative ageing, which rather than the deterioration of living standards, often led to rising mortality rates. Age structure was also of some significance because of infant mortality. This remained high throughout the century with marked effects on general mortality rates. Until 1831–5 infantile mortality remained over 180 per 1000. After the first year only the most vigorous were left. It fell to 166 and 156 in the next quinquennia but this decline was not sustained. Infant mortality was 176 per 1000 in 1872–5 and remained around 170 per 1000 in 1891–5. A substantial and sustained decline occurred only from the closing years of the century – to 124 per 1000 by 1911–13 – and even then a summer epidemic of diarrhoea could push deaths up to 157 per 1000 in 1911. A similar decline occurred in the normally lower death rates among children aged 1 to 13.

The assumed causes of mortality in the early years of this century per 1000 infants under the age of 1 are shown in Table 20. For the age-group 1 to 4 years in Paris (per 10,000 children), the mortality rates and causes of death that were

Table 20   *Causes of mortality, 1900–13 (per 1000 infants)*

Cause	Number
Gastro-enteritis, diarrhoea	384.70
Respiratory infection	147.29
Congenital debility	170.76
Tuberculosis	24.70
Infectious diseases	49.61
Unknown	222.92

Table 21   *Infant mortality*

Cause of death	1886–9	1891–5	1896–1900	1901–5
Diphtheria	109	65	17	22
Measles	76	48	43	27
Scarlet fever	10	6	5	3
Whooping cough	20	17	13	15
Meningitis				
(non-tubercular)	74	54	37	26
Respiratory diseases	120	108	88	71
Diarrhoea	38	36	28	18
Tuberculosis	56	67	61	52
Other causes	23	25	28	23
All causes	526	426	320	257

recorded are shown in Table 21.[19] These older children were affected less by digestive illnesses and more by infectious complaints.

Infantile and child mortality was obviously influenced by the general evolution of living conditions and also by that of mentalities. Large families were particularly susceptible because of the greater difficulty they experienced in making ends meet, and also because, due to the greater length of the period of childbearing, they were more likely to be affected by the loss of a parent while there were still young children to care for. Mortality increased considerably with economic crises (at Rouen, for example, reaching 306 per 1000 between 1846 and 1848),[20] epidemics, cold winters and very hot summers. In this latter respect the significance of digestive complaints especially gastro-enteritis, and of bronchial illness should be stressed. Infant mortality tended to be higher in urban areas than in rural areas, particularly where large numbers of women were able to find work in the textiles trades, and often continued to work until an advanced stage of their pregnancy. Poorly fed, overworked women tended to give birth to babies with low birth weights and little resistance to infection. It was not until 1909 that a law allowed pregnant women to cease work for eight weeks in the period before and after delivery, and 1913 that another law established the principle of financial support to compensate for loss of earnings. The effectiveness of this legislation is difficult to judge. In any case hard physical labour and poor diets remained the causes of large numbers of premature and still births. In the industrial Nord, for example, still births were around 40 to 50 per 1000 from 1853 to 1912. The likelihood of this and also of continuing gynaecological problems for many women was increased by poor standards of midwifery, especially in isolated rural areas, and by the general lack of hygiene. Complications were frequent, especially haemorrhages and puerperal fever, and doctors normally called only in extremity. Hospitals, too, were usually avoided. In the Nord in 1857 only 1.5 per cent of legitimate births and 20 per cent of illegitimate took place in hospitals – reflecting a widespread judgement of their value. Even for wealthy women, who risked less because of more hygienic surroundings and better medical care, childbirth must have been a fearful prospect.

An early return to work following birth also had ill-effects. Mothers were unable to breastfeed and babies, cared for by relatives or child-minders, tended to receive poor quality milk from unsterilized or often unwashed bottles. According to a medical report from Caen in 1878, the mortality of bottle-fed children was 307 per 1000, contrasting with only 109 per 1000 among the breastfed. Significantly, there appear to have been two major zones of especially high infant mortality – one covering the north, from upper Normandy to Lorraine, the second the Midi. In the first, the availability of work for women and the transmission of feelings of repugnance towards breastfeeding down the social scale, together with the availability of wet nurses or else of cows' milk as substitutes, reduced the practice of breastfeeding. Moreover, babies were likely to be weaned too soon and fed on unsuitable solids which caused digestive illnesses and especially diarrhoea. In the Midi, in contrast, there were fewer opportunities for paid employment, and less animal milk. This meant that the infants were nursed at the breast for too long. The bulk of deaths occurred slightly later because of the growing nutritional inadequacy of mother's milk for older children, together with the consequences of gastro-enteritis in the hot summer months.

Wet nursing provided a useful supplement to incomes in rural areas close to major cities. The practice declined as sentiments towards children changed. Thus, whereas in 1896 some 110,000 legitimate children were boarded out, by 1913 the number had fallen to 92,000, although this still represented around one-tenth of new-born babies. Besides the children of working wives, many infants deposited at foundling hospitals, often by single parents unable to care for them, were sent on to wet nurses in rural areas, often to suffer the consequences of poverty and poor hygiene. Of 2400 infants sent from Paris to the *arrondissement* of Nogent-le-Rotrou in 1858–9, 35 per cent died in the first two years, compared with only 22 per cent of local children. Better medical supervision reduced mortality – but even in 1897–8, 15.1 per cent of those infants placed with wet nurses died, a rate higher than general infant mortality.[21]

Concern with depopulation aroused growing interest in the causes of infant mortality. As doctors began to understand the connection between micro-organisms and gastro-intestinal disorders an effort was made, especially from the 1890s, in collaboration with charitable societies and municipalities, to encourage breastfeeding, to improve the quality of purchased milk through pasteurization (from 1888), and hygienic bottle-feeding with sterilized glass bottles and rubber teats. Better public sanitation also had its effects. The consequences were dramatic – in the department of the Nord, for example, infant mortality fell from 194 per 1000 in 1900 to 128 per 1000 by 1914.

For as long as living standards for most of the population remained low, infant welfare had necessarily been subordinated to other objectives. Babies had been left unattended for long periods during both agricultural and industrial work. In especially difficult situations children sometimes had been murdered. Corbin has estimated on the basis of judicial trials, that between 1825 and 1859 one infanticide occurred per 583 births. In an impoverished region like the Limousin the figures were much higher – one for 232 in Corrèze, one for 252 in Creuse, and one for 320 in Haute-Vienne. It is likely that many more were undetected. These were usually the desperate acts of unmarried mothers. Many more children were abandoned – around the middle of the century some 33,000 per annum. In the period 1816–41 these accounted for one in twenty-four babies born in the department of Haute-Vienne, one in thirty in Creuse, one in forty-three in Corrèze. Foundling hospitals had traditionally been established to provide shelter, and from 1811 they had been provided with a turntable device so that babies could be abandoned without the parents being seen and embarrassed, in an effort to limit infanticide. Mortality in these institutions and with the wet nurses they employed was extremely high. In Paris, of 4779 babies taken in in 1818, 2370 died in their first three months, and another 956 within the first year. In Haute-Vienne of 9203 children abandoned between 1810 and 1842, 72 per cent died before the age of 10. Abandonment declined sharply, however, after mid century; the hospice at Limoges, for example, took in 305 babies in 1856, but only eight in 1860. This was indicative both of an improvement in living conditions and an increasingly critical public attitude towards the practice.[22] More generally, easier material circumstances permitted an improvement in the quality of mothering, while the tendency for family size to decline and the greater likelihood of infants surviving seems likely to have intensified the emotional links between parents and their children.

Thus attitudes to life were inevitably closely linked to those to death. The evolution of the birth rate provides an important indicator of the process of change.

Procreation

The nineteenth century saw the growing use of contraceptive techniques, and this occurred earlier in France than anywhere else. For the first time, on a mass scale, sexual activity and the conception of children became separate activities. This major change makes a discussion of sexuality particularly interesting. It is, however, a difficult subject. Demographers can measure birth rates, but judgements about the quality of sexual relationships are hampered by the unwillingness of contemporaries to discuss or write about their most intimate activities.

Marriage and the family

Most children were conceived within marriage, and the marriage rate was thus a key determinant of birth rate. Prior to marriage the behaviour of young people was in large part determined by local norms which defined the occasions for courting and imposed ritualized restraints on behaviour. In small communities these controls were effective. However, there does appear to have been considerable variation in the forms of behaviour tolerated. In Brittany pre-marital pregnancy resulted in life-long shame, in part due to the influence of the church. In the Basque country, pre-marital sex, or at least heavy petting, was tolerated between engaged couples, and where necessary pressure would be exerted to force the presumed father to marry a pregnant girl. Pre-marital sex might not be uncommon, but illegitimate births were comparatively rare. In general, societies which included families with marked differences in wealth, and in which family marriage strategies were crucial to economic and social status, are likely to have imposed far stricter restrictions than more egalitarian societies. In urban communities, especially where the young were able to earn their economic independence, greater sexual freedom resulted. Thus, in a community experiencing industrialization like Sainghin-en-Mélantois (Nord) a marked increase in the likelihood of pre-marital conception among women married before the age of 30 appears to have occurred (see Table 22). In contrast, in a rural community like Bilagrés-d'Ossau (Basses-Pyrénées) the rate of pre-marital conception fell from 7.76 per cent in 1740–9, to 2.8 per cent in 1820–59.[23]

Whether the absence of pre-marital conception meant continence before marriage, and the complete suppression of sexual desires are complex questions. Awareness of sex must have been intense given the crowded lodgings of most of the urban and rural populations and observation of the behaviour of animals. Since the Counter-Reformation the church had stressed the value of pre-marital chastity, and the constant reiteration of this ideal by priests and teachers must have influenced behaviour. The church had also traditionally denounced masturbation as a major sin, but from the eighteenth century confessors became much more concerned and condemnatory. In this they were influenced by medical opinion which saw the practice as a cause of madness or even death. This was perhaps symptomatic of the spread of repressive attitudes among the upper and middle classes, linked to a growing anxiety about immorality and the possibility of social disorder as the processes of social change accelerated.

Sexual activity within *marriage* was of course an entirely different question.

Table 22 *Pre-marital conception in Sainghin-en-Mélantois*

Year of marriage	Percentage of women pregnant before their weddings
Before 1769	15.2
1810–19	41.3
1820–9	58.2
1830–9	42.6
1840–9	54.8

Marriage was expected. Full adult status depended upon it. For the poor it was essential to the establishment of a 'family economy', outside which women, in particular, were extremely vulnerable given the low wages they received. On the peasant farm the normal sexual division of labour required collaboration between the sexes.

The statistics on nuptuality reveal that whatever the causes of falling birth-rates in the nineteenth century a declining propensity to marriage was not one of them. Marriage rates remained relatively stable (Table 23). The marriage rate varied with economic conditions – until 1860 it varied inversely with the price of cereals, the prime indicator of the overall economic situation in a pre-industrial economy. The political situation was also significant. However, the sharp decline at the time of the France-Prussian War was rapidly compensated for in the succeeding period.

Moving beyond measurement to a discussion of the quality of married life is complicated. The evidence, however, does suggest that among property-owners – from aristocratic landowners to peasants and artisans – marriage was about more than love. It also represented an attempt to secure the material interests of prospective partners and those of their families. Marriage settlements which involved a re-distribution of property concerned every member of a family group. The marriage strategy of a family was thus determined by three factors – the property it possessed, the number of children and their sex. Although pressure could be brought by parents in order to secure compliance, the upbringing of children involved the internalization of parental and community norms. They were socialized to want to marry a particular type of person. This was particularly evident among the wealthy for whom marriages were a means of extending networks of power and influence.

For a young man the ideal bride was drawn from a family roughly equivalent to his own in terms of status and wealth, with whatever culture, skills or

Table 23   *Marriage rate (per 1000 inhabitants)*[24]

Year	Rate (per 1000)	Year	Rate (per 1000)
1816–20	14.6	1866–9	16.0
1821–5	15.5	1870–1	13.3
1826–30	15.9	1872–5	17.6
1831–5	15.8	1876–80	15.2
1836–40	16.2	1881–5	15.0
1841–5	16.3	1886–90	14.4
1846–50	15.6	1891–5	14.9
1851–5	15.5	1896–1900	15.1
1856–60	16.2	1901–5	15.3
1861–5	16.0	1906–10	15.8
		1911–13	15.5

physical strength were necessary to perform the social or economic functions expected of her within her new family. This resulted in high levels of social endogamy. An analysis of marriage within the commune of Vraiville (Eure), a mixed community of farmers and weavers, has revealed that 72.46 per cent of marriages from 1803 to 1852 and 75 per cent between 1853 and 1902 were between couples originating in families of peasant proprietors. Agricultural day-labourers and weavers tended to intermarry, indicating the roughly equivalent status of those two impoverished groups. Exceptions to these tendencies were not uncommmon – promoted, for example, by the shortage of potential partners within a given socio-professional group or by the need to avoid marriage with close relatives. The ideal bride should bring a dowry which would improve or help preserve the economic position of her new family, and perhaps compensate it for providing a dowry for one of its own daughters. The choice of a marriage partner was a matter of concern to the family rather than simply the individual. Moreover, marriage, in as much as it represented an alliance between two families, was an important symbolic statement of the social status of each within the community. The marriage of siblings might in part depend upon this as well as on the economic arrangements.[25]

Marrying daughters tended to be far more difficult than marrying sons. They were marriageable for only a relatively short period and had to be provided with a dowry to make a reasonable marriage. To have too many daughters could represent economic disaster. Often girls had to leave home, or even migrate to work as agricultural labourers, in textiles or as domestics in order to save for a dowry. To have too many children of either sex inevitably meant parcellation of family property and the likely decline of members of the younger generation to a lower status in society than that possessed by their parents. Fertility strategy was of crucial importance if the family patrimony was to be preserved.

The choice of a marriage partner was traditionally regulated not only by the family but by other kin, peer groups and the whole process of community socialization and control. Most obviously the occasions for contact between men and women were determined by custom, usually in a very restrictive fashion. Geography was another major restraint. Not surprisingly, most marriages in town and country occurred between individuals resident within the same or nearby communities who might have met through friends or relatives, in the street or at work, at village festivals or nearby markets, and the reputation of whose families would either be known or could be traced easily. Considerable hostility was often shown by the young men of a village to the prospect of a local girl marrying a stranger. This threatened to reduce the stock of nubile females and transfer property to an outsider. Where a family possessed no property then obviously a freer choice of partner could be permitted. Earning a wage represented independence for young people. Even then, however, a partner needed to be selected with some care. It was only sensible to avoid the sickly and weak, those who might not be able to work and who would become a burden. Although physical attractiveness was valued, robustness and the ability to care for a household were regarded as of greater importance.

As socio-economic structures changed, so did the process of selecting a partner. With the creation of alternative economic opportunities and as the possibilities for migration increased, family controls were inevitably relaxed. Socializing and courtship were more likely to take place away from home. Parental approval continued to be sought, but more as a formality. Changes in socio-economic structures which affected the ways in which marriage partners were selected also had effects upon the structure of families and the quality of their inner relationships. The structure of any household was determined by a complex of factors including birth rate, family size, stage in the family cycle, the economic activity of the group concerned and prevailing attitudes towards family life. A great variety of situations was thus likely to exist even within one community. Indeed over time the members of a single family might experience a range of types. However, at any one time the prevailing form was the basic conjugal family, although stem families, i.e. with mother, father (perhaps children) and one set of grandparents were also common. Far less common were households composed of a number of families.

The link between economic activity and family structure was most clear among peasant farmers. The relationships between the availability of land, farm size and labour supply were crucial. Although the ideal was for marriage and access to land to coincide, frequently young couples were forced to live with parents. In order to avoid subdivision and maintain a viable holding, brothers and sisters might also live together, and in this case a high rate of celibacy was likely among younger siblings, although several families might on occasion cohabit. Inheritance custom was also a significant factor influencing the establishment of such multi-nuclear households. They were more likely in the south with its traditions of impartible inheritance than in the north where partibility prevailed. The Napoleonic Code, which from 1804 sought to enforce partibility, was one factor leading to a decline in complex household forms. However, the legal rules were not strictly applied where contrary to local custom. In Cantal and Aveyron, for example, to avoid excessive fragmentation of land-holdings, a single heir tended to be preferred over others. There were clearly complex interrelationships between demographic structures and inheritance systems. Nevertheless, possession of a farm increasingly frequently encouraged matrimonial and contraceptive strategies designed to limit its future subdivision. The organization of work on a farm was another important factor. In this respect the number of workers needed on a particular farm influenced the size of a household. If too many children were born, and survived infancy, those surplus to its labour needs were forced to find employment elsewhere, which often meant leaving home. This was always the situation for the children of farm labourers or industrial workers.

Whatever its size, the family was the basic social unit, within which new generations were socialized. By and large membership of a particular family, in a given social milieu, determined their future way of life.

Questions about the quality of family life are particularly difficult to answer. In appearance, at least, family groups were characterized by solidarity, a strong sense of interdependence and by subordination to paternal authority. The inferior position of women was enshrined in the law. Judging by the domestic upbringing of girls, which taught them to play the female roles the community expected of them, their subordinate position was a practical reality. On marriage, the husband was granted control of property, although in the case of the wealthier classes, safeguards were normally built into the marriage contract to protect the wife's ultimate rights over her contribution to their joint property. Similarly, control over children rested with the father. Even if women frequently possessed considerable practical authority within families, it was expected that they should accept their subordinate position in public or face ridicule. Divorce, which had become possible during the revolution, was abolished in 1816 and only restored in 1884, and even then the grounds were restricted largely to proven adultery, and it cost more than most people could afford. Significantly, a wife's adultery was regarded as more morally and legally reprehensible than a husband's, particularly because it might lead to her giving birth to a child (an heir) which was not his. In contrast, the wife of an adulterous husband was usually advised to be patient, forgiving and to find solace in religion.

Although upper-class women were not expected to engage in salaried employment outside the home, or in much else save charitable activities, it is obvious that many middle-class women helped to run family businesses, and that working-class and especially peasant women were often obliged to work. In the 1860s some 40 per cent of married women worked. By 1906 an estimated 68 per cent of single women over 16 were employed, and 56 per cent of married women. In the non-agricultural areas the proportion fell to 40.8 and 20.2 per cent respectively.[26] For the poor, exhausting work in factory, workshop or farm had to be combined with caring for the house and children. Among urban workers the ideal seems to have been that the wife should cease to work outside the home after marriage, or at least following the birth of the first child, but this was subject to the dictates of economic circumstances. The wife's responsibility for feeding the family and balancing its budget made her particularly aware of these circumstances. These varied female roles were essential to the survival of the family unit and must in practice have established husband/wife relationships on a basis of complementarity rather than male dominance.

It is difficult to judge how affectionate married couples were. Certainly a cult of sentimentality spread from the upper classes and affection seems to have been increasingly important both in the choice of a marriage partner and in marital life. It is even more difficult to consider how much pleasure couples, and particularly women, took in erotic activity. It was probably less central to most relationships than co-operation in making ends meet, partly no doubt as a result of the influence of the church which taught that sex was for procreation rather than mutual gratification. It has often been assumed, and no doubt with reason, that the lack of privacy in overcrowded dwellings (even allowing for a far less developed sense of privacy), and the overwhelming concern with material needs, as well as sheer physical exhaustion, must have reduced the emotional

The demographic indicators   79

and sexual content of many marriages. As a result many couples must have just coexisted with little time for sentiment. A Provençal proverb expressed the belief that 'when hunger is at the door, love goes out of the window'. However, different cultures have varying ways of expressing their emotions. Nineteenth-century folklorists who have provided us with most of the evidence on love and marriage were middle-class outsiders assuming that because peasants did not embrace in the same manner and use the same terms of endearment as the urban bourgeoisie, their lives must be bereft of all affection. However, the poor sharecropper from the Allier whose memoirs are recorded in Emile Guil-laumin's *La Vie d'un Simple* had no doubt about the place of love in rural life.

Birth rate

The statistics on birth rate – good quantitative history – provide little support for a discussion of the quality of marriage. Table 24 reveals a constant (save for a period of relative stability during the Second Empire) and substantial decline in the birth rate from an estimated 35–40 per 1000 towards the end of the eighteenth century. This began much earlier in France than elsewhere. In England and Wales the birth rate was still 35 per 1000 in the period 1871–5.

Within each quinquennia the influence of economic crises on marriage and contraception became progressively less marked. This was in marked contrast with the *ancien régime démographique* during which birth rate could be inversely correlated with grain prices, a relationship which disappeared from the 1850s.

A complex of factors affected birth rate, including diet and physical capacity to bear children, age at puberty and at the end of nubility, age at marriage, the length of the period of breastfeeding, calculation of individual and family interest, social pressures and religious beliefs, and inevitably there were significant social, geographical and chronological variations. General economic prosperity encouraged early marriage and larger families. Depression, the reverse. The practice of delaying marriage until a couple possessed resources

Table 24 *Birth rate per 1000 inhabitants*

Year	Birth rate (per 1000)	Year	Birth rate (per 1000)	Year	Birth rate (per 1000)
1816–20	32.9	1851–5	26.0	1881–5	24.7
1821–5	31.4	1856–60	26.6	1886–90	23.0
1826–30	30.5	1861–5	26.7	1891–5	22.3
1831–5	29.6	1866–9	26.1	1896–1900	21.9
1836–40	28.4	1870–1	24.2	1901–5	21.3
1841–5	28.1	1872–5	26.2	1906–10	19.9
1846–50	26.7	1876–80	25.3	1911–13	18.8

sufficient to allow it to assume the life-style normal for its particular social group survived most strongly among those who expected to inherit property, or groups like artisans or members of the bourgeois professions who needed to complete their professional training. Among the propertyless, the growing availability of wage labour reduced the need for delay. More or less deliberate decisions had to be taken by couples concerning the number of children they could maintain or otherwise needed to contribute to family income and to maintain the parents themselves in old age. How many live births were necessary to guarantee a completed family of the required size? Significantly, areas with high mortality rates tended to have high birth rates. Moreover, high infant mortality, which prematurely terminated breastfeeding, led women to ovulate and to conceive children sooner than would otherwise have been the case.

Decisions on family size appear to have varied, in large part in relation to the opportunities for employing children, whether on a family farm or in industry. Thus birth rate remained *relatively* high in the industrializing departments of the north and east. In the Pas-de-Calais, for example, the birth rate rose from an already high 45 per 1000 in the decade 1851–61, to 60 per 1000 in the following decade due to the influx of young people attracted by its coal-mines and factories, but also because of the susceptibility of much of the population to the influence of the church. Subsequently in-migration declined and as the population aged and attitudes changed, the birth rate fell. Industrial areas had higher birth rates than administrative or commercial centres, or their surrounding rural areas. They attracted young migrants who, because of the employment opportunities, felt able to marry early themselves and were reasonably confident that their children would, from an early age, be able to contribute to the family budget. Industrial areas also, significantly, had much higher illegitimacy rates, and only in part because of the presence of lying-in and foundling hospitals. At Lille, in the period 1851–6, 20.7 per cent of births were recorded as illegitimate, compared with a national average of 7.2 per cent; at Mulhouse 18 per cent of births between 1852 and 1870 were illegitimate; at St-Quentin 24 per cent; at Troyes 32 per cent. Conversely in the company town of Le Creusot the figure was only 4.2 per cent.[27] In general illegitimacy rates tended to rise until the end of the century, when the continuing spread of contraceptive techniques led to the beginning of a decline.

The status of unmarried monthers varied. Many illegitimate births were the product of more or less stable unions. For some couples the financial cost of marriage out-weighed the advantages, particularly where there was no property to protect. Often free union was the prelude to eventual marriage and legitimization of children. The ideal, even among the poorest, remained a stable family life. The stigma attached to illegitimacy appears to have been less strong in the industrial north, where the structures of the family had been to some degree weakened by industrialization and migration. In many cases, illegitimate births occurred where fathers had failed to keep a promise of marriage. Women workers or domestics, desperately anxious to find a husband because of loneliness or the difficulty of making ends meet, were especially liable to find themselves in this situation. In large towns, with mobile populations, the pressures for the enforcement of community norms were less intense. The Napoleonic Civil Code, by abolishing the *recherche de paternité*, had significantly reduced women's rights. In general the urban masses appear to have been more tolerant than the bourgeois administrators of *bureau de bienfaisance* and other charitable organizations who would provide help only to married mothers. In part, attitudes within communities depended upon a woman's previous reputation. Often unmarried mothers were, however, forced into prostitution – the last resort of many destitute women – a situation which led to further illegitimate births and, reflecting the misery of their mothers' lives, to particularly high infant mortality.

The crucial demographic question, however, concerns the fall in birth rate. In some areas this was at least partly due to the migration of the young and the ageing of the population, but in general the cause was a fall in marital fecundity. Previously, high and fairly constant levels of marital fertility had indicated the absence of birth control within marriage. Fertility had in effect been controlled through variation in the age of marriage. This, and such factors as celibacy rates and breastfeeding practices, had resulted in major variations in inter-genesic intervals, between social groups and regions, even where contraception had not developed. In the Limousin, for example, even in the 1870s, the normal period of breastfeeding varied between twelve and fifteen months in towns and at least fifteen to twenty months in the countryside.

Contraceptive techniques had been known since ancient times, but their use had normally been restricted to prostitutes. Only during the eighteenth century, when the upper classes began to practise contraception, did it begin to have demographic significance. This required a voluntary decision by at least one marriage partner to control the numbers of children. It seems to have been taken to limit the effect on a family's wealth of division among an excessive number of heirs. It also reflected a growing distaste among upper-class women for repeated pregnancies, and a desire to separate love-making from the conception of a child. This represented a major change in mentality and morality. The practice spread down the social hierarchy by a process of imitation, particularly as new aspirations and a more optimistic outlook developed among the poorer classes, as living standards began to improve noticeably. An explanation of the social and geographical diffusion of contraception is not easy. A variety of economic, social and cultural factors were significant. The revolution was one, accelerating diffusion by promoting the ambitions of many individuals, and through the effects of a period of disorder on traditional morality. Marcel Lachiver, studying the little town of Meulan (Seine-et-Oise), has concluded – after eliminating the involuntary sterile (about 18 per cent of all couples) – that some 8 per cent of couples married between 1760 and 1764 used contraception. The proportion increased to 16 per cent of those marrying between 1765 and 1789; 40 per cent of those marrying during the revolution and empire; and 55 per cent of those marrying during the restoration.[28] Some regions, and particular families and social groups within them, were affected before others. The effects of contraception on birth rates were certainly evident early in the century in the Paris basin, Aquitaine, Normandy and parts of Bourgogne, and in both town and country as middle classes, artisans and peasant property-owners devised strategies to restrict the dispersal of property often accumulated only as a result of a hard life of toil. In the Pays-d'Auge in Normandy birth rate fell substantially between 1820 and 1850 as a response to growing population pressure on resources and the desire to acquire a plot of land. In the Nièvre, and for much the same reason, they fell between 1840 and 1850. In the Limousin it appears that literacy, temporary migration to work in the cities, and lower birth rates were linked. The long absence of workers, but also the practice of birth control by families with wider mental horizons, distinguished areas of migration from those with more sedentary populations. In comparison with Britain, fewer urban employment opportunities and better hope of access to land provided stronger incentives for family limitation among the rural population. Once it had begun, development was self-sustaining. It became evident that children's futures would be fundamentally influenced by family size.

The spread of contraception was clearly evident in the decline of the numbers of large families. Families with five children or more constituted 14.2 per cent of the total in 1815–19, but only 6.7 per cent by 1870–4. It should be noted, however, that if among women born in 1881 only 24.2 per cent had four children or more, the offspring of these relatively large families made up over 50 per cent of the next generation.[29] Birth control was practised first and foremost by those with property and hopes of social promotion. As in the past high fertility continued to be related to high mortality. For these reasons among others, women in the poorest social groups continued to give birth to a relatively large number of children – many of whom would not survive infancy. Among the urban and rural poor there was little or no property to divide between heirs. There seemed little prospect of them being able to improve their situation and as long as children could be set to work at an early age there was little incentive to limit their numbers. Thus in Roubaix wives of textile workers averaged 4.8 live children in 1872. The subsequent decline in fertility there and in the mining centre of Anzin appears to have been linked to the reduction in the employment opportunities for children as industrial techniques changed and compulsory education was introduced. They remained at home longer and the financial and emotional investment in their futures increased. In many areas this did not occur until the beginning of the present century. It was at this stage that deliberate pro-contraceptive propaganda by the *Ligue de la Régénération* (1896) might have had some influence, although even at that late date the notion of limiting births appears to have spread primarily by informal means.

The adequacy of contraceptive techniques obviously had some effect on birth rate. The main means of contraception was the unreliable one of *coitus interruptus*, i.e. withdrawal, although a whole range of alternative practices such as the sheath (especially with the development of techniques for the vulcanization of rubber in the 1840s), diaphragm (1880s), rhythm method, douches, sponges and pessaries, were also employed. For much of the population, however, the sheath remained too expensive. The actual technique used depended upon knowledge of the various practices, which many, especially young couples, might not have possessed, and on their moral acceptability. As a last resort, the traditional techniques of abortion might be employed. This would either be self-induced by means of the infusion of traditional abortifacients such as ergot rye, or hot baths, violent exercise or whatever local gossip recommended, or require the help of a professional abortionist, often a midwife. Collective norms which stressed the desirability of a large family or the sinfulness of contraception clearly restricted its spread. In the latter respect the attitudes of the church were of great importance. Initially, because the notion of contraception spread orally, it did not provoke a firm reaction from the clergy. As late as 1842 Mgr Bouvier, Bishop of Le Mans, believed that most of the population were unaware of the views of the church. However, if the inhabitants of clerical regions do not appear to have rejected contraception, their populations employed it less systematically, and birth rates in these areas declined less rapidly than elsewhere. A hardening of the clergy's attitude was obvious from the 1850s. In particular, they sought to use the confessional to influence men, whom they held responsible for marital practices. This interference in the most intimate secrets of married life produced considerable hostility.

Age structure

The coincidence of an early reduction in birth rate, with the survival of high mortality throughout the century resulted not only in a relatively slow rate of growth of overall population, but in major changes in its age structure and vitality. The eighteenth and early nineteenth centuries were characterized by a large proportion of young people. According to the 1821 census 40.9 per cent of the population were aged between 0 and 19, 53 per cent between 20 and 64, and only 6.1 per cent were over 65 years of age.

Table 25 gives a clear picture of the evolution of age structure.[30] The relatively early adoption of birth control in France and the consequent effects on population growth and age structures meant that in 1914, in comparison with the period of the revolutionary and Napoleonic wars, a far smaller proportion of the men of military age in Europe were French.

Table 25 *Age structure per 1000 people*

Age	1778	1851	1881	1911
0–19	440	361	354	338
20–39	290	311	296	306
40–59	199	227	227	230
60 and over	71	101	123	126

Urbanization

The other major causes of social change were the interrelated processes of urbanization and migration from the countryside. The former was accompanied by the transformation of towns, which had remained almost medieval in character, to recognizably modern, urban centres. This was a complex development with the character and scale of growth depending upon pre-existing socio-economic structures, which were far from homogeneous, and the nature of economic change. Moreover, it was not only the size of towns which altered during these years, but also the age, sex and socio-professional structures of their populations.

While stressing the importance of urbanization, it is also important to remember its relative slowness in comparison with other west European countries, reflecting in large part the slow growth of overall population. The period of revolution and empire had been one of stagnation, and the growth rate of towns in the first half of the century was probably slower than it had been for much of the eighteenth. In 1821 there were only eight towns with more than 50,000 people, and only three – Paris (713,966), Lyon and Marseille – with over 100,000. By 1846 there were thirteen with over 50,000. The population of Paris was 1,054,000 (an increase of 47.6 per cent since 1821), and Marseille replaced Lyon as the second city, with 183,181 inhabitants. Even so, at the mid point of the century some three-quarters of the population could be classified as rural. Although some industrial centres had experienced significant growth – St Etienne, for example, from 16,300 to 56,000 between 1801 and 1851; Roubaix from 8000 to 34,700; and Mulhouse from 6600 to 29,600 – this was far from general. Industrial production continued, to a significant extent, to be dispersed throughout the countryside. Most provincial towns were small in size and closely linked to their rural hinterlands. Subsequently, urban population grew

Table 26   *Population (in 1000s) of major cities*

City	1851	1876	1902	1911
Marseille	195.3	318.9	491.2	550.6
Lyon	177.2	342.8	459.1	523.8
Toulouse	93.4	131.6	149.8	149.6
Nice	—	53.4	105.1	142.9
Bordeaux	130.9	215.1	256.6	261.7
St-Etienne	56.0	126.0	146.6	148.7
Lille	75.8	162.8	210.7	217.8
Roubaix	34.7	83.7	124.4	122.7
Tourcoing	27.6	48.6	79.2	82.6
Dijon	32.3	47.9	71.3	76.8

more rapidly as can be seen from the figures on the population of major provincial centres (Table 26).[31] The rising share of the urban sector (living in communes with a population of 2000 or over) in total population tells the same tale (Table 27).

While total population expanded by 34.8 per cent between 1806 and 1911, the urban population rose by 301 per cent from 1811 to 1911. Moreover, especially in the second part of the century, urbanization was not evenly spread. As Table 28 indicates it occurred through the growth of large and medium sized cities rather than small. The larger the city, the faster the growth.[32]

As Figure 15 shows some regions continued to experience a low rate of urbanization. In large part this was a reflection of the characteristics of regional economies. The growth of regional centres like Rennes, Toulouse, Bordeaux and Dijon, with mainly administrative and commercial functions, continued to be slower than that of industrial centres like Roubaix, Tourcoing and St-Etienne. Dijon, however, did benefit from its crossroads position in the new railway network, and this was one key factor influencing the range of possible economic activity in a given town. More clearly than before, a functional hierarchy was imposed on the urban network. Rapid communications permitted the concentration of economic and administrative activity in regional centres serving large areas – including their satellite towns – and a reduction in the dispersal of such activities between a large number of centres serving much smaller areas. In the Midi, for example, the devloping trade in *vins ordinaires* was

Table 27   *Urban population*

Year	Urban population (millions)	Percentage of total population
1851	9.1	25.5
1861	10.8	28.9
1872	11.2	31.1
1881	13.1	34.8
1891	14.3	37.4
1901	15.9	40.9
1911	17.5	44.2

Table 28

Percentage of total population in cities of	1801	1851	1872	1891
100,000 +	2.8	4.6	9.1	12.0
20,000–100,000	3.9	6.0	6.7	9.1
10,000–20,000	2.8	3.8	4.4	4.8
Total 10,000 +	9.5	14.4	20.2	25.9

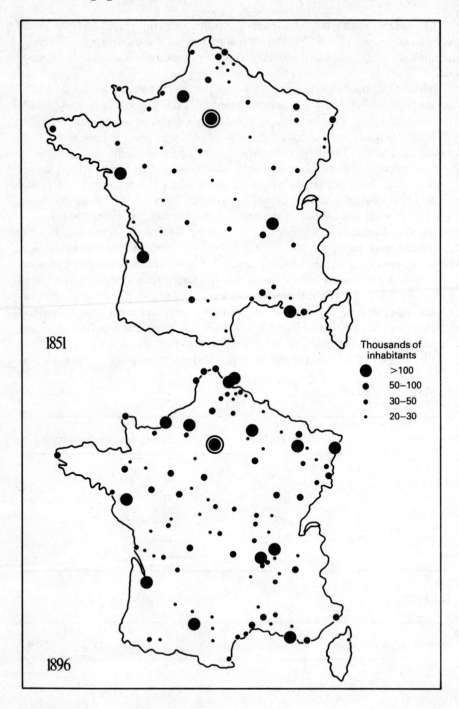

Figure 15   *Urban France 1851 and 1896*

increasingly concentrated at Béziers and Montpellier. Moreover, the growing concentration of textiles production in northern France caused the decline of southern centres of the industry. Even in rural areas activities and population tended increasingly to move from isolated farms and hamlets towards the larger villages and urban market centres.

Most notable, of course, was the growth of Paris. The city developed into a much larger agglomeration as its suburbs grew. In 1851, 3 per cent of the population of France lived in the department of the Seine, by 1911 10 per cent. The statistics tend to conceal this, as they do the numerous movements of people both within and between major urban centres in response to such diverse factors as changes in the location of specific industries, variations in employment or wages, or in rental levels between the *quartiers* of a city. During the course of the century the economic structure of the capital became increasingly complicated. In the early decades artisanal forms of production had been dominant. However, increasingly on the city's outskirts, especially to the north and east, heavy industry developed, particularly engineering and chemicals, while inner-city areas, although continuing to shelter the various artisanal trades, proved increasingly attractive to the development of administrative, financial and commercial enterprise. All these activities encouraged in-migration, although the cost of housing tended to force most low wage-earners into residence on the outskirts of the city. Only the development of mass urban transport facilities from the 1870s – suburban tramways, railway services and finally underground and bus services – made it feasible to live some distance from one's place of employment.

In terms of demographic growth, these large towns attracted people because of the range of employment opportunities and the higher wages they offered. Their growth was due much more to in-migration than natural increase. According to the 1861 census, 36.1 per cent of the population of Paris had been born in the city, 58.65 per cent in the provinces, while 5.92 per cent were foreigners. Migration to the towns had always occurred. Its primary cause had been poverty due to rural overpopulation resulting in increased parcellation of the land and underemployment. As late as the end of the July Monarchy, the French countryside, although to different degrees, was generally overpopulated given existing agricultural techniques. Much of the population depended upon earnings from a variety of activities in agriculture and rural industry, through seasonal migration, begging and poaching, to make ends meet. Rural societies remained extremely susceptible to crises caused by poor harvests, or the growing competitive pressures of urban industry. In many regions old traditions of temporary migration to work in both agriculture and urban industry were a vital means of attenuating rural poverty. This occurred especially from the Alps, Massif Central, Pyrenees, parts of the eastern Paris basin, Normandy and Brittany – essentially from areas of poor agriculture and an absence of alternative supplementary activities such as rural industry – and involved seasonal movements towards richer agricultural areas in the Paris basin or the Mediterranean plains, particularly to help with the harvest, or longer-term movements to the major cities, above all to work in the building industry. There were in addition a multiplicity of regular movements by pedlars and beggars. Abel Chatelain has estimated that during the First Empire these movements involved at least 200,000 people each year, and that by the middle of the century their number had risen to at least 500,000.[33] Considerable numbers of people circulated along the roads, often travelling quite long distances, as in the case of peasant-masons from the Limousin, who walked to Paris with the intention of earning money to supplement their meagre resources from farming and paying off debts, or even one day purchasing land. Their absence relieved the burden on scarce food resources. On their return they brought not only cash but also new ideas on diet, dress, agricultural techniques and even politics. Only after the middle of the century, as agricultural techniques changed, and the structure of urban employment was modified, did permanent migration tend to replace these temporary movements.

The date at which regions attained their maximum rural population varied. It was before 1860 in the south-west, southern Alps, Normandy, Picardy and much of the north-east, but later in the centre, Brittany, Vendée and some isolated departments like the Gironde and Seine-et-Oise (influenced by varying levels of marital fertility as well as by migration). A general decline in rural population appears to have occurred from around 1846, from 26,755,000 people to 22,000,096 by 1911, i.e. from 75.6 to 55.8 per cent of the total population (Table 29). Prior to the 1840s, although there had been extensive movements from the country to town, the net flow out of the countryside had been restricted by the lack of urban employment opportunities.

Subsequently, the character of migration began to change, stimulated by major alterations in urban–rural relationships, and particularly by the growing demand for labour in the towns. Industrial and commercial developments in the nineteenth century substantially increased urban labour needs, at the same time

Table 29   *Net decline of rural population*[34]

Year	Average annual decline	Decline per 100 of rural population
1856		
1861	−129,383	−0.50
1866	−132,232	−0.50
1872		
1876	−102,860	−0.41
1881	−165,950	−0.67
1886	− 99,313	−0.40
1891	−112,858	−0.46
1896	−116,553	−0.49
1901	−134,326	−0.58
1906	−111,222	−0.48
1911	−154,478	−0.69

as the transport revolution and changes in techniques promoted industrial concentration at the expense of the employment in rural industry on which so much of the population in the countryside had depended. The towns became more attractive because of employment opportunities which offered higher wages, greater security, less hard work (especially for women), and increased leisure. Their attractiveness grew especially from the 1850s, as the living standards of the urban population began to improve, and as improved communications made rural populations more aware of the contrasts between urban and rural life. Further stimulus was afforded between 1846 and 1856 by the harsh mid century crisis; and from 1876–81 by the concurrent crises caused by agricultural price depression and, in the south, by the effects of disease on silk cultivation and especially the phylloxera insect on the vineyards. By this time, however, migration was much less the result of a flight from misery than a positive action determined by the desire for a better life. People were less likely to accept poverty with resignation. An educational system orientated towards urban needs, the experience of conscripts, of relatives and friends who had migrated, all contributed to the creation of a sense of inferiority among the rural population and often of a psychological need to escape based less on pressing economic necessity than a desire for a different and easier way of life. In effect migration increased at the very time, from the 1850s, when agriculture was becoming more intensive and required more labour, when, as a result, higher wages were being offered and underemployment in the countryside was falling. The efforts by farmers to increase labour productivity by introducing better hand tools and, less commonly, by mechanization or replacement of arable by pasture, were a response to relative labour shortage rather than a cause of migration.

The first to leave the countryside were the poorest, the workers in declining rural industry, the agricultural labourers; then the small farmers and village artisans. Of the 4645 individuals recruited by the Marles mining company from the countryside of the Pas-de-Calais between 1853 and 1893, 73 per cent were day-labourers, 5 per cent farmers, 5 per cent farm domestics and 17 per cent artisans.[35] Those with a greater material stake in rural society were less likely to leave. In effect migration served as a safety valve, removing from the countryside its poorest elements, ending the threat of overpopulation, and permitting many of those who remained to acquire the small plots of land formerly farmed by migrants. The young predominated. Many were unmarried. Within the social groups affected by migration it tended to be the more dynamic and better educated who departed. However, most were unskilled in terms of industrial employment, so that the recent migrants tended to gravitate towards the poorest paid jobs – men as labourers or factory operatives, women as domestics. Only from the 1870s, particularly as the agricultural depression deepened, did migration become more general, and include many peasant proprietors and also landowners discouraged by the fall in revenue from rents. During the prosperous 1860s, expectations about living standards had risen. The depression came as a great shock and disappointment.

The scale and chronology of migration depended a great deal upon the socio-economic structure of a given locality, and upon the economic dynamism, proximity and attractive pull of urban centres. Such factors as the degree of intensification of agriculture, the fertility of the soil, the replacement of arable by pasture, the degree of rural de-industrialization, large-scale farming and the proletarianization of the labour force, were all significant causes of migration, while the survival of local industries and the availability of small farms to own or rent tended to restrain movement. Demographic pressures did not automatically result in the corrective action of migration. Large-scale movement was often slower to develop from the poorest upland areas. The most peripheral regions, isolated as they were from the competitive pressures and attractions of the modern economy, were not significantly affected until as late as 1900. During the decade 1852–62, which saw a substantial increase in migration, this occurred especially from the more prosperous rural areas, close to major urban centres, in spite of the relatively high wages of the agricultural labour force. Nevertheless, in the long term only relatively prosperous agricultural regions could hope to maintain high population densities. In the south, for example, the development of market gardening and fruit cultivation, and particularly of the vine, attracted labour, at least until the phylloxera crisis. In Picardy, although the rural population declined, this was largely due to the collapse of rural industry, so that the number of people actively engaged in agriculture often slowly increased in the period prior to 1914. Here as elsewhere a ruralization of the countryside occurred due to the concentration of industry in the towns. Indeed, for France as a whole, employment in the primary sector of the economy increased from 7,305,000 in 1856 to 8,845,000 by 1906, so that, while insisting upon the significance of migration, it is important not to exaggerate its scale. A sense of historical perspective is vital. There was no *désert français* before the First World War. Depopulation could be said to have occurred only in mountain areas like the Alps, Pyrenees and parts of the Massif Central, and even in those areas the major movements came later.

Most migration took place over short distances, and it is important when considering migration not to lose sight of the remarkable stability of the French population. In 1861, 88.2 per cent of the population lived in the departments in which they had been born. By the 1901 census this was still true of 80.5 per cent. Much movement occurred within the countryside and within departments and went unrecorded. Wherever more fertile land existed close by people tended to move towards it. From upland areas they moved downhill towards the plains. Although large cities did attract people from quite extensive hinterlands, only Paris had a really national appeal, and even this was a development essentially of the second part of the century. Previously most migrants – an estimated 677 per 1000 in 1833 – had come from the north and Massif Central.[36] In many cases migration took place in several steps, spread over a number of generations. In large part this was because potential migrants tended to be better informed about opportunities in places close to their existing homes. In 1911, 26 per cent of the population of Caen were natives of the city and a further 38 per cent had been

born within the department of Calvados. In the Pas-de-Calais, the Marles
mining company recruited most of its labour from villages within a radius of
15–20 kilometres. The improvement of communications did something to
extend the range of information, but the provision of information about alternative destinations did not always overcome the priority accorded to places
already reached by a stream of migrants. From the Ardèche, for example, the
main routes of migration in the second half of the century were towards the
towns of the Rhône valley, and the coal basins of the Gard and Loire; from the
Haute-Loire they were to Lyon and St-Etienne. In some cases daily movements
were possible from village to nearby factory. Miners in the north frequently
retained plots of land, and by 1900 bicycles and special railway tickets enlarged
the area within which it was possible to combine work on the land with that in
the factory, and to become a worker–peasant. Probably due to its low rate of
population increase, France was unique in Europe in the small scale of migration
to other countries. On balance the country experienced a net immigration,
essentially from those countries with which it shared boundaries.

During the nineteenth century French society experienced major structural
changes in terms of industrialization, urbanization, the commercialization of
agriculture, and the extension of urban influences into the countryside.
Increased production of material goods together with a slow growth of population made possible a significant improvement in living standards. The extent to
which this occurred depended in large part, however, upon the social division of
property, upon control of access to scarce resources and ultimately upon the
distribution of social and of political power.

PART TWO

Social Relationships

The first part of this book will have made it obvious that within French society there were major differences between individuals in terms of their incomes, life-styles and standards of living. The purpose of the next four chapters will be to identify the major social groups which together constituted the social system, to discuss the inner characteristics of each group, and to examine the relationships between social groups.

It is clearly impossible to write a history of any society based upon unique individuals. It is necessary instead to talk about the general characteristics of the groups which individuals form and to examine the relationships between these groups. The crucial question, then, is which groups should be given priority? To which groups were individuals conscious of belonging? Clearly the family has some claims. It is the basic unit of socialization. It attracts considerable emotional loyalty. Again, however, practical considerations argue against using it as our basic building block. Certainly, for the examination of extra-local economic, social and political problems, wider social groups have to be considered. Our aim must be to avoid arbitrariness, and the imposition of an artificial schema upon a historical society and to identify groups which had a real existence which was recognized by contemporaries. These must be identifiable, not only in terms of shared characteristics such as levels of income or life-style, but also of a collective awareness of common interests. The social and cultural institutions of nineteenth-century France can only be understood through the ideas and values current at the time.

To a substantial extent social stratification is based upon the distribution of economic resources. This largely determines life-styles, and is a key determinant of the balance of power. But the possession of material resources alone does not determine status within society. Social groups should also be seen as *cultural* groupings – culture being understood in the anthropological sense as a 'manner of living'. Due to this, economic and social status need not necessarily correspond. Effective membership of a social group depends upon acceptance of its particular norms of behaviour and this upon social conformity in, for example, the manner in which income is spent, in terms of occupation, home, area of residence, education, manners, and attitudes. Individuals who share these characteristics are able to accept each other as equals even if they diverge in other matters, such as politics. The existence of such norms has the additional effect of setting up barriers between social groups. In the final analysis social groups must also be defined and their behaviour explained in terms of their relationships with other groups.

3
Elites

Introduction

Power in society is possessed by particular groups by virtue of their control of material resources and the dominant influence this gives them over other social groups. This is exercised not only, or even primarily, through economic relationships but by means of the use of authority on a much broader front through a variety of forms of influence, by means of cultural hegemony and political control. Within every society there exists an élite recognized as such by the possession of certain generally favoured attributes including wealth, life-style, social influence and political power. This élite also serves as a reference point for other social groups. Moreover, it enjoys the advantages of small size and relative cohesion which allow it more effectively to impose itself. Although the symbols of status differ over time and between groups, to an important extent those groups which already possess wealth and high status are able to influence definition of the criteria for according rank within a given social system. Systems of social stratification are in this respect to an important degree self-perpetuating.

The objective of this chapter is an analysis of the evolution of the French social élite in the nineteenth century, a period of substantial economic and social change in which those who combined economic, social and political power in the first half of the century, experienced a significant loss of political power, certainly by the 1880s, while still preserving a major share in economic and social power. The obvious place to begin is with a discussion of membership of this élite using in the first instance the criterion of wealth.

Wealth – the first stage in definition

It makes sense to begin with wealth because, even if wealth itself did not ensure status, it alone permitted the appropriate life-style, without which status suffered. Moreover, statistics exist which, whatever their shortcomings, provide some kind of a basis for the analysis of social hierarchy. Without statistics we could offer nothing more than an impressionistic survey, but it needs to be stressed that in the definition of social groups, statistics are not enough. A social group has existence through a shared way of life and attitudes, rather than common levels of income. The various statistics do not solve the problem of distinguishing the élite group in French society. Analysis of them is simply a first step.

A great deal has been written about the French Revolution as an historical turning-point. In many respects – political, ideological and indeed social – it had vitally important long-term consequences. The political revolution, however, had relatively little effect on the ownership and forms of exploitation of property. Until mid nineteenth century the dominant social group in terms of wealth, prestige and power remained that made up of noble and non-noble landowners. The basic socio-economic structures of the country were to be transformed far more decisively during the period of innovation in communications, in industry and in agriculture beginning around 1840–60. In particular, the process of concentration in industry and finance created new conditions for amassing wealth. The scale of accumulation also changed. Although the absolute wealth of landowners did not decline before the 1870–80s, relative decline began much sooner. The agricultural depression of the last third of the century accelerated this process. The rental value of land has been estimated to have fallen from 2600 million francs in 1879 to 2000 million by 1894, at a time when its capital value was also declining. Land became a less attractive investment. Although development varied greatly between regions, in general agricultural productivity did not increase rapidly enough to offset the decline in prices caused by the transport revolution and increased competition and the rise in costs caused by migration and increased wages. Moreover, landowners were slow to transfer their capital to more lucrative forms of investment. On the basis of wills registered in Paris in 1910, industrialists, merchants and bankers can be seen to have left only 2 per cent of their wealth in the form of land, in sharp contrast with wealthy nobles who, in spite of diversification, still left 30–40 per cent of their wealth in this form. Elsewhere in regions where economic change was less rapid, local élites were even more heavily engaged in landownership. One of the key questions which will concern us is the degree to which this change in the characteristics of wealth-generating property ownership affected social status and power. This requires a more detailed analysis of changing income hierarchies. One thing which is certain (see Table 30) is that on the eve of the First World War France remained an extremely inegalitarian society.

Table 30   *Wealth of deceased, 1911*

Level (in francs)	Number (per cent)	Value (per cent)
1 million and more	0.1	28.0
50,000–1 million	2.6	43.1
Below 50,000	60.3	28.9
No inheritance declared	37.0	0

In spite of the effects of fraud upon the accuracy of the statistics they do give some idea of social inequality. Less than 3 per cent of those who had died left over 70 per cent of the inherited wealth. These men, together with their families and a wider and unquantifiable circle of social acquaintances constituted our social élite. The figures suggest that during the second half of the nineteenth century a progressive concentration of wealth in fewer and fewer hands had occurred. In Paris, for example, whereas in 1820 30 per cent of inherited wealth had been left by 1 per cent of the dead, in 1911 this proportion was accounted for by only 0.4 per cent of the wealthy deceased. In Paris and Lille, both in 1820 and 1911, it was estimated that the gulf between the poorest and richest remained of the order of 1:10,000.[1]

During the First Empire a list of some 70,000 *notables* was drawn up to enable the government to select its officials. This included members of families with recognized local influence, and wealth was clearly a major factor in this. Information survives from 1810 on the professions of 66,735 of these (Table 31).[2] As it is, this list underestimates the significance of landowners within the élite, given that many of those included in other categories drew much, if not most, of their income from landownership. Clearly, however, the élite could not be assimilated with any single socio-professional group. Information on high tax payers in 1840 indicates an important degree of continuity (Table 32).[3]

It is not without significance that of the 377 landowners paying over 5000 francs in direct taxation in 1840, some 238 were nobles and a further seventy-eight had some pretensions to nobility. As late as 1870 this pre-eminence of noble landed wealth survived, although clearly threatened by then by the rising wealth of a group of financiers and industrialists. It is also worth noting the importance of the group of officials. The sons of wealthy families were attracted by the status and power conferred by government service rather than by the relatively low salaries. Their wealth reflected their milieu of origin and not their profession. Wealthy members of the liberal professions were in a similar posi-

Table 31   *First Empire* notables

	per cent
Landowners	24.55
Local administrators	18.12
Senior government officials	15.76
Liberal professions	14.37
Trade and manufacture	10.79
Farmers	8.23
Military	2.35
Clergy	1.23
Total	95.42

Table 32 *Professions of high tax payers, 1840*

Socio-professional group	Total paying 5000 f+ per annum	No. paying 5–6000 f	6–7000 f	7–8000 f	8–10,000 f	10–15,000 f	over 15,000 f
Landowners	377	147	94	41	50	32	13
Senior officials	42	18	13	3	4	4	—
Liberal professions	22	17	2	2	1	—	—
Merchants, bankers	45	10	16	4	9	5	1
Industrialists	26	10	6	3	4	2	1
Total	512	202	131	53	68	43	15

tion. According to the economist Leroy-Beaulieu, by 1885 only around 100 lawyers earned more than 30,000 francs per annum. A social gulf appears to have existed between those who depended upon their professional earnings, and *notables* who also possessed a professional qualification, especially in the law, as part of a gentleman's education. Significantly, a government official or military officer tended to enjoy greater prestige than a businessman of equivalent wealth. The social status conveyed by a particular income also varied geographically. In a mountainous area like the Basses-Alpes, for example, an annual income of 20,000 francs was enough to mark a man off as a person of wealth and status; in more prosperous rural areas, and especially in the cities, this would be regarded as a moderate income. According to Adeline Daumard's analysis of the structure of wealth in Paris in 1820 – based upon the registration of wills – an aristocracy of wealth existed in the capital, leaving over 500,000 francs. These made up 0.3 per cent of the deaths in that year and presumably this group made up a similar proportion of the total Parisian population. 2.4 per cent left over 100,000 francs, a proportion which by 1847 had risen to 3.6 per cent.[4] These were the people whom A. J. Tudesq has labelled the *grands notables* – an élite made up of families with a national reputation.

What kind of people were the very wealthy? Until the middle of the century, with the exception of bankers like the Rothschild or Périer families, most *grands notables* were heavily dependent upon income from rural property. This was even more true of the mass of local *notables*. This was a pre-industrial élite, dominated by landowners and officials. Gradually, and rapidly from the 1850s, leading industrialists accumulated wealth. By 1870 the Schneiders – iron, steel, engineering and coal magnates – had an annual income of 1.5 million francs, almost twice that of the Duc de la Rochefoucauld-Doudeauville, the richest landowner. Indeed the wealthiest landowners, men like the Marquis de Talhouet, the Marquis de Voguë and the Duc d'Audriffet-Pasquier, drew much of their wealth from sources other than land.[5] The balance of wealth had swung to a substantial degree from the landowners to the great financiers and industrialists. Landownership for many of these involved the possession of a château with a park and woods for hunting in a department close to Paris, like Seine-et-Marne. From mid century the Rothschilds at Ferrières, the Périers at Armainvilliers, the Eichtal at La Houssaye adopted the life-style of their aristocratic neighbours the Choiseul at Vaux-le-Vicomte, the Lafayette at La Grange near Rozoy, or the La Tour-du-Pin at Nanteau-sur-Lunain.[6]

At least until the 1870s investment in land offered a secure income, and a decent return on the capital invested. More than this, it provided access to a particular life-style and guaranteed social status. The dream of most business and professional men had continued to be to make enough money to purchase land and adopt the less demanding life of a *rentier*. Investment in loans to the state allowed some diversification once land had been acquired. This offered a secure income, although rates of interest were relatively low in comparison with private loans. The essential aim of most wealthy investors was to gain an income which would allow their families to enjoy the style of life which their place in the social hierarchy seemed to require. Speculative investment was likely to occur using whatever capital remained after the achievement of this essential objective. It was engaged in only with great caution. The fact that wealth tended largely to be inherited served to create traditions of investment and imposed an immobility on investment behaviour.

In spite of the revolution a great deal of property remained in the hands of noble families. They formed an important part of the wealthy élite of nineteenth-century France. Certainly the abolition of seigneurial dues and of tax exemptions, and the confiscation of the property of that 25 per cent of the noble order who became émigrés, reduced their economic power. However, most noble families were able to sit out the difficult years, and others by a variety of means, were able to re-purchase confiscated property, especially after Napoléon's seizure of power in *Brumaire*. Thus, in the Nord nobles lost around 30,400 hectares and re-purchased around 7100; in the Sarthe, they lost around 40,500 hectares but had re-gained almost as much by 1830.[7]

Throughout the century, in comparison with other groups within the élite, nobles continued to express a marked preference for land as a form of investment. To some extent this represented simple habit. Most families had acquired wealth before liquid securities became readily available. More than this, however, preference for land represented the survival of traditional attitudes towards the land as a source of status, and an often idealized patriarchal role in rural society. Even families like the Benoist d'Azy or the Voguë, heavily committed to industrial activity, continued to retain more of their wealth in land than most major industrialists. Often the reluctance to invest in commerce and industry revealed the surviving fear of *dérogeance*, of the loss of status likely to occur from 'degrading', money-making activity. Although traditional noble activities like mining and metallurgy were exempt from such prejudices, the minority of economically active nobles tended to concentrate upon agricultural activity, and through their example and their role in the many flourishing provincial agricultural societies, and the capital they were able to invest, provided an important stimulus to innovation and more intensive cultivation. Most nobles, however, appear to have played a less active role. Much of their income was employed in the re-embellishment or reconstructon of mansions. Many indeed were forced to sell all or part of their property because of debts incurred by such conspicuous consumption.

Investments were gradually diversified. The development of the joint stock company in the last quarter of the century offered a source of income which called for minimum involvement or effort. To some extent patterns of investment varied between regions according to local economic structures and awareness of alternatives. Thus the example of the Marquise d'Aoust, resident in the economically advanced Pas-de-Calais in the 1890s, should not be taken as entirely representative. Her wealth was distributed between bank current account (7.5 per cent), government stock (13 per cent), debenture stocks (36 per cent), shares (30 per cent) – including 5.5 per cent in shares of the Bank of France and the rest in railway shares – furnishings (2 per cent), farm rents (6.5 per cent) and private loans (0.5 per cent).[8] This represented the patterns of investment of a very wealthy, economically inactive individual, concerned to obtain a secure income. More active individuals were often sought after as members of the boards of directors of major companies, especially in transport and assurance, in return for their prestige and influence. The growth of social links with wealthy non-nobles favoured such activity.

The nineteenth-century bourgeoisie should not be conceived of in Marxist terms as a class of factory owners and financiers. These groups grew in importance, but during the earlier part of the century, and particularly in the economically less dynamic regions, there survived a *bourgeoisie d'ancien régime*, numerically more significant and composed essentially of landowners, officials and lawyers. Although distinctions can be made between the structure of noble and non-noble wealth, these should not be exaggerated. Wealthy non-nobles had always been attracted by investment in land, particularly in close proximity to the towns. The mentality of the rich businessman was influenced by the ethos and life-style of the traditional aristocracy, and the purchase of land and a château continued to mark success in business. Thus the sale of *biens nationaux* during the revolution resulted in the transfer of property within the class of wealthy property owners, and throughout the first half of the century wealthy non-nobles continued to purchase aristocratic estates in areas like the rich Beauce plains close to Paris. Among a sample of merchants and manufacturers in the Pas-de-Calais 60 per cent in 1851, 76 per cent in 1878 and 77 per cent in 1896 owned land which had either been inherited or purchased as a means of securing social status.[9] It does, however, appear to have been the case that these bourgeois landowners tended to be more concerned than aristocratic landlords with securing an adequate return on the capital they had invested. It ought also to be stressed that generally land as a portion of the total wealth of such groups declined in significance from the middle of the century.

Most non-noble landowners, just like the nobles they sought to emulate, took only a limited interest in practical farming. Only in those restricted areas in which large scale capitalistic farming developed, especially in the Paris region and Nord did a class of wealthy bourgeois farmers emerge in the countryside. Even in the Beauce they made up only 8 per cent of the active agricultural population.[10] Most large estates were thus divided into small farms which were rented out to as many peasant farmers as possible in order to maximize the returns. This, as we shall see, was a significant factor influencing social relationships in the countryside, especially in those regions with substantial numbers of relatively large estates – the north, in a block stretching from the Paris area to Normandy (Seine-et-Marne, Seine-et-Oise, Seine-Infèrieure, Eure, Calvados), south of Bourgogne, (Nièvre, Saône-et-Loire, Rhône, Allier), and Languedoc (Haute-Garonne, Aude, Hérault), and, to a less marked degree, the region stretching from the north of the Paris basin to the Belgian frontier, that between the Seine and the Loire, south-west Aquitaine and the lower valley of the Rhône (Bouches-de-Rhône and Gard). In contrast large estates were less common in regions of poor soil – Brittany, upland areas, and the east, areas of concentrated habitat in Champagne, Lorraine, Alsace, Dauphiné and Provence.

From the Second Empire purchase of stocks and shares rapidly became more popular among both nobles and non-nobles. For France as a whole the value of liquid assets appears to have exceeded that of fixed assets for the first time between 1890 and 1895. Stocks and shares, which made up 7 per cent of the total value of inheritances declared between 1851 and 1855, constituted 39 per cent of those declared between 1911 and 1915.[11] With the exception of entrepreneurs whose wealth was heavily committed to their own businesses, investors particularly favoured apparently safe investments in railways and the bonds offered by both French and foreign governments. Industrial shares seem to have been regarded with favour only in the years immediately preceding 1914, as industrial concentration both required more capital and produced large and apparently secure companies. The shift away from land was especially evident in the smaller proportion it constituted in the total wealth of the richest families – particularly those directly involved in trade, industry or finance. They were best placed in terms of access to information and professional advice to take advantage of new opportunities, the highest yielding and most secure assets. Their greater wealth made it possible to diversify in order to reduce risks. In Paris in 1911 in the wills of people leaving over 1 million francs stocks and shares made up 20–25 per cent of the total wealth, in comparison with only 8 per cent in the case of people leaving less than 50,000 francs, who were put off by the relatively high price of shares, the lack of information and the fear of risk.

Changing investment habits became evident first of all, as one would expect, in the major financial and industrial centres, above all in Paris. For the industrializing Pas-de-Calais it has been estimated that landowning *rentiers* held only 2.8 per cent of their total wealth in the form of liquid assets in the early 1850s. By 1878 this had risen to 53 per cent, around which figure it stagnated for the rest of the century, because of the uncertainties caused by economic depression. Whereas in the rural Gers in 1905 liquid assets made up only some 26 per cent of private fortunes, they constituted over 70 per cent in the Seine-et-Marne and Rhône. Traditional patterns survived much longer in predominantly agricultural regions, and in the regional centres within them like Bordeaux, although the agricultural depression in the 1870–80s did much to stimulate re-thinking. This and migration from the countryside reduced the attractiveness of land as an investment and also the traditional need for mortgages which had constituted an important means of investing capital. [12] In effect it was the wealthiest families, in the richest regions, who were best placed to take full advantage of the new opportunities for enrichment, and to combine an income derived from investments with the increasingly lucrative opportunities to supplement earnings through professional employment.

These new opportunities brought to the fore a wealthy group of financiers and industrialists. While stressing the significance of the survival of traditional mercantile and small-scale industrial capitalism into the nineteenth century, it is equally important to stress the degree to which concentration and structural change developed from its middle years. In 1906, although 50 per cent of French workers were still employed in establishments with less than five workers, 10.8 per cent were employed in enterprises with over 500 workers (especially in railways, steel and engineering and chemicals rather than textiles) – major enterprises directed by the wealthiest and most influential businessmen and usually constituted as joint stock companies. Many enterprises disappeared, others were able to transform themselves technically and to adapt to changing market conditions. An obvious hierarchy developed among businessmen in terms of the profitability of their enterprises, their incomes and life-styles, with a small group acceding to the social élite.

However, wealth did not always bring corresponding status. In spite of the economic boom during the Second Empire, the proportion of businessmen among the members of the departmental *conseils généraux* hardly changed, remaining around 15 per cent, as in 1840. [13] Successful businessmen continued to mark their achievement by seeking acceptance within a social élite whose life-style in many respects represented the survival of pre-industrial social relations. This is our next problem – to consider the relationship between wealth and social status, to estimate the degree to which an élite, identified so far in terms of the wealth of its members, i.e. as an abstract sociological category, really existed as an active social force. Was there one, or were there several élites in nineteenth-century France?

Élite structures

The question of whether or not an integrated social élite existed is of considerable importance. The degree of integration – of unity – effected the political performance of the élite, and its ability to maintain social stability. Historians have written a great deal about conflict between the various groups we have sought to identify as belonging to the French élite of wealth, particularly between nobles and non-nobles. Stress is inevitably placed on the significance of the French Revolution as a cause of division. Yet, to an important extent a process of fusion between established élites and the *nouveaux riches* had been continually underway during the Ancien Régime. The status of nobility had been the reward for success for many business or professional men, able because of their wealth to purchase ennobling office and land and to enjoy the appropriate life-style. Although the cleavage between noble and commoner had survived, especially due to the efforts of the former to maintain honorific privileges and distinctions, a gulf had also been created between the wealthy and the others within each of the second and third estates. In terms of economic interests, education and culture wealthy nobles and *grand bourgeois* were likely to have more in common than had the rich and the poor noble. The transition from a society based upon orders to one based upon property, wealth and class was already well underway. The revolution had contradictory effects upon this process.

A series of measures between the abolition of the seigneurial system on 4 August 1789 and the Constitution of the Year III established legal equality. However, these also had the effect of establishing an important degree of social and political unity among the nobility. From the rich residents of the mansions in the Faubourg St-Germain in Paris to the impoverished country gentry of Brittany and Languedoc nobles rallied to king and church. The experiences of the revolution, the allegiances chosen or forced upon families and unforgettable memories of the Terror and exile, served to create long-lasting family political traditions. The class of large landowners was thus largely associated with political loyalty to the Ancien Régime, indeed kinship loyalties made it difficult for individuals, even decades after the expulsion of Charles X in 1830, openly to recognize the futility of the Legitimist cause. Other key factors determining political loyalties included religious divisions between Catholics and Protestants in areas of the south, especially in and around Toulouse, Montpellier and Nîmes, which were reawakened by the revolution. In such areas religion proved to be a useful method of mobilizing mass support which heightened the intensity of conflict. In the major administrative and judicial centres of the Ancien Régime and especially the seats of the old *parlements* like Aix or Dijon, members of the liberal professions associated with nobles in support of the Bourbon cause; in ports like Marseille and Bordeaux whose commerce had been destroyed by the wars of the empire, and where the restoration brought prosperity, many merchants did the same. It was not landownership as such that was the basis of the Legitimist alliance, but the complex of ideological options produced by family traditions and the experiences of the revolutionary–empire period.

Thus, regardless of legal changes, the nobility survived the revolution as a status group. It is, however, not easy to decide exactly who the nobility were. Usurpation of titles had always occurred, and although a commission was established during the restoration to prevent this, it was abolished in 1832, and an 1858 decree forbidding usurpation appears to have had little effect. More common was the adoption of the particule (*de*) which gave at least the appearance of nobility. However, the pretension to nobility was more important than the legal validity of titles. Those *bourgeois* families who continued as had their predecessors for centuries to add the particule and the name of a place to their patronyms were determined to adopt the opinions and life-style of their chosen class. Such assimilation was especially likely in regions where the nobility were relatively numerous and socially active, such as the Breton west and in and around Toulouse, Montpellier and Nîmes. Integration of nobles into a wider social élite was delayed in these regions because of their greater retention of social influence. This is one factor which warns against treating the nobility simply as a kind of accidental survival from the Ancien Régime. It remained a group with considerable influence throughout the century, especially before the agricultural depression of the 1870s. One indicator is that even as late as 1869 34.6 per cent of deputies were nobles. In spite of entrepreneurial skills and wealth and a pride in their achievement, many bourgeois families, through their imitation of aristocratic models, admitted an inability to establish a distinctive culture and self-consciousness. For many, the nobility served initially as models for good manners, but also as the source of ideological and hence political leadership, and all the more so as the menace of social revolution replaced aristocratic pretensions as their *bête noire*.

Various indices can be used to measure the degree of integration between noble and non-noble élites, including the pattern of social relationships, intermarriage, cultural and political concensus, and attitudes towards other social groups. Many of these indicators can be grouped together under the general heading of life-style. Clearly there was a 'plutocratic' life-style made possible by great wealth and the desire to make a public affirmation of social status. This was achieved through 'conspicuous consumption' and to a large degree the patterns of expenditure on housing, furnishing and clothing, as well as forms of sociability were based on aristocratic models. The wealthiest non-noble families, such as the Schneider and de Wendel, often after generations of austerity during which profits were re-invested in enterprise, were increasingly unable to resist the temptation to emulate the richest aristocracy as their wealth accumulated. This trend was slowest to develop among the textile *patronat* of the Nord and Alsace. In both these areas intermarriage helped to preserve a distinctive family-based life-style and to limit integration within the wider élite in the period before the Second Empire. The merchants and textile *patronat* of Rouen, in contrast, adopted aristocratic life-styles far more readily, influenced perhaps by the *mores* of the Norman countryside, and, in comparison with their professional colleagues in Lille or Mulhouse, appear to have been far less committed to entrepreneurial activity. For them the château offered confirmation of success and social superiority. Considerable sums of money were spent on constructing or modernizing châteaux in a variety of styles – Louis XIII, Renaissance, neo-Gothic, or Troubadour or more often a mixture of styles – and in order to establish irrefutable links with the past. In the cities, too, housing was a major symbol of social status. The opulent aristocratic mansions and gardens of the Faubourg St-Germain served as a model, and during the Second Empire new mansions like the Hôtel Saccard were constructed in the Parc Monceau. Luxury was increasingly supplemented by comfort with the introduction in the last decades of the century of bathrooms and central heating.

Although there were relatively few members of the élite who did not engage in professional activity during some part of their lives, leisure took up an important part of their time. The use made of this leisure was an important characteristic of the élite. Part of it was spent quietly within the family, especially by women who played the piano, embroidered, painted, read or wrote letters. However, entertaining was important for a family's social standing. This involved both regular dinners and grander receptions and balls. In the countryside, as well as dinners and picnics, and a passion for hunting, membership of the local *salons*, *cercles* (male clubs), and agricultural, learned and philanthropic societies, helped to preserve and to extend social links. Throughout the century the élite was characterized by its dual residence – a mansion or apartment in Paris or, at least before the railways made travelling easier, in some provincial centre such as Toulouse, Caen, Lyon or Rennes – and a château in the countryside. This was particularly true of nobles. An essential part of their life-style was residence in the countryside, at least towards the end of summer and the autumn, for the harvest and to maintain links with 'their' peasants, for hunting, visiting the châteaux of other gentlemen and attending the meetings of local learned and agricultural societies. In the winter those landowning families who could afford to, escaped the discomforts of rural life, moved to their town houses and took part in a cycle of balls, receptions and more intimate *soirées*.

Elite groups were thus characterized by complex forms of social ritual which established the boundary of social acceptability and conversely isolated the participants from the sociability of other groups. Admission to these rituals denoted acceptance into a particular milieu. A lack of invitations signified rejection. Sociability was a key feature of the élite's process of self-definition. Conformity to accepted norms of behaviour was important for continued recognition. In a very real sense, therefore, individual behaviour and patterns of expenditure which involved conspicuous consumption were socially determined and inescapable.

Upbringing and education were of crucial importance in maintaining conformity. Socialization provided the young with a specific cultural identity and values. It defined their future social roles and their expectations as to the behaviour of members of their own social group and that of members of other social groups. Through its distinctiveness their life-style helped to maintain distance between groups and barriers against interlopers – and to exclude those who could no longer afford proper standards. Not only wealth and its material advantages but dress, gestures, language, opinions and beliefs all performed this function. Socialization is inherently conservative in that it communicates and perpetuates culture from one generation to the next. The acceptance of newcomers into such social circles depended on willingness to adopt the established life-style and culture. Like all exclusive groups, they sought to protect their special status by attaching a great deal of importance to the cultural symbols of group membership.

The social season also provided an opportunity for concluding marriage alliances. Significantly, within the nobility, fellow nobles continued to be preferred as spouses. Tudesq found that in a sample of twenty noble families, and of 146 marriages between 1800 and 1860, only eleven involved a non-noble partner.[14] Although a noble family might accept the daughter of a well-off bourgeois household this was conditional upon her accepting the *mores* of her new class. Intermarriage was a crucially important means of maintaining group solidarity. Kinship was especially important among upper-class groups, serving as a means of developing a network of useful contacts. This was true for non-nobles as well as nobles, as can be seen from the examples of the textile *patronats* of Lille–Roubaix–Tourcoing or of Mulhouse, who employed familial resources in order to accumulate both capital and managerial skills, and that of the financial *grande bourgeoisie* of Paris. These were groups which took pride in their origins and economic activity and which to an important degree constituted a closed caste.

However, there were factors that promoted fusion among the wealthy, whether noble or non-noble. These were in part economic – in the general desire to discover secure and profitable investments. By 1840, of the members of the boards of directors of the fifteen largest joint stock companies, 37.7 per cent were bankers and merchants, 10.3 per cent industrialists, 20.4 per cent landowners, 15.7 per cent senior government officials, 10.9 per cent members of the liberal professions. These were men with proven business acumen in some cases, and in others individuals with capital or influence.[15] At least in this sphere – regardless of political allegiances and social status – a community of interest had been created. In economic matters the essential divisions were caused by perceptions of conflict of interest between regions and sectors of the economy, and especially between protectionists and freetraders. This osmosis of interests subsequently only increased as economic structures changed.

Another feature of the changing social structure was the multiplication of jobs requiring a good education. The development of the bureaucracy, like that of the economy, had the effect of bringing together members of the various status groups which composed the élite and who shared an interest in, and a determination to maintain control over the state apparatus. Nobles, in spite of the withdrawal of many of their number from public administration after the 1830 Revolution, continued to subscribe to an ethos of state service, and to be attracted into the administration, army and magistrature. The willingness of the various status groups to collaborate within the administration, and to restrain the expression of their political differences, revealed a shared awareness of belonging to a ruling class threatened from below. The restoration had not involved an attempt to return to 1789, but certainly did try to re-establish the dignity and social power of the old nobility. At court, in government, army and administration, and in society more generally, exclusive policies and attitudes had alienated non-nobles who during the revolution had achieved a consciousness of their own dignity and merit. In spite of the fact that wealthy non-nobles were in general social and political conservatives, they were alienated by a regime which refused to recognize their worth. This was especially marked where Legitimism was strongest and most threatening – in the west and Midi, where the violence of *Chouannerie* and White Terror of 1815 had been greatest. The effect was the promotion of liberal political sentiments and of anti-clericalism among non-noble élites, which culminated in the successful challenge to an increasingly reactionary government in 1830.

The establishment by revolutionary action of the July Monarchy had important effects on élite attitudes and behaviour. It represented a rejection of noble claims to political and social pre-eminence. The extension of the suffrage had the effect of submerging the great landowning nobles within a wider electorate composed simply of men with wealth. Although as individuals many nobles retained considerable local influence, and the ethos of nobility continued to have wide appeal, as a political force the nobility lost much of its importance. Thus, the longer another restoration was postponed, and with the passing of the generations which had attained maturity during the revolutionary period, the more nobles were attracted by conservatism rather than strict dynastic loyalties. Revolution in 1830, with its accompanying social unrest, reminded the wealthy, whatever their politics, of the fragility of the social system, and created anxieties which were to be reinforced in subsequent years by the growth of an urban industrial working class, and above all by the experience of revolution in 1848 and the Paris Commune of 1871.

Although inner tensions survived, lessons were drawn from these experiences, which reinforced the fear of revolution first created in 1789. What mattered above all else was the defence of social order. The expression of diverse political loyalties was subordinated to social necessity. Intermarriage, social life, professional existence, ownership of property, social fears and politics all gradually reinforced the bonds between varous groups within the élite. This can be exemplified by the process through which socially mobile newcomers were integrated into the established élite.

Social mobility

The amount or frequency of social mobility tells us something about the rigidity of class or status systems, and about the extent to which individual opportunity is determined by birth or achievement. It is very difficult either to measure mobility or to decide with any kind of precision what determined its level at any one time. To some extent mobility is implicit within any social system given that some families established within the élite die out, or experience impoverishment, and are replaced. Clearly, however, economic change is another important factor. An expansionary economic situation, particularly if involving structural change in the economy, creates opportunities for enrichment. Migration by individuals towards centres of activity in which opportunity was greatest reveals contemporary awareness of this.

Political change had similar consequences. Under the Ancien Régime access to the élite had been made possible for those with the requisite wealth and culture. The purchase of ennobling office had allowed many aspiring families to set the seal of royal recognition upon their achievements. The revolution and empire, particularly through the disruption and expansion of both the civil bureaucracy and the military, speculation on *biens nationaux*, or on supplying the army, allowed a relatively large number of individuals, mostly of middle-class origin, to rapidly acquire greater wealth and status. Thus, although a significant proportion of senior civil administrators during the First Empire had served in the old royal administration (30.77 per cent), 43.03 per cent appear to have been newcomers.[16]

In the following generations the main opportunities were economic. Wealth and social promotion were acquired through entrepreneurial activity and, as the scale of business grew, particularly in the latter half of the century, through involvement in bureaucratic management. Until mid century – especially in textiles – simple technology meant that only limited amounts of capital were necessary to establish a business and this could be accumulated even by ambitious artisans, such as the Pouyer-Quertier family in the Rouen region, who first set themselves up as 'putting-out' merchants in the domestic system of production. Subsequently, over two or three generations some businesses experienced commercial success and grew through the re-investment of profits. The Motte and Méquillet-Noblot families in the Nord are typical examples. Nevertheless, the growth of competitive pressures forcing technical innovation, which required larger and larger initial investments, tended to restrict this entrepreneurial road to social promotion. Notable instances of individual success could still be found, for example, the former soldier, Thomé-Génot, who set up a factory at Nouzon in 1852 to manufacture parts for railway wagons. By 1880 he employed around 1000 workers. The success of Berliet at Lyon is another case in point. Opportunities continued to exist in new industries producing consumer goods, building materials and a range of specialized products. However, in older established industries like metallurgy and textiles, or in new industries like chemicals or electricity, advanced technology limited access essentially to those with established wealth and/or specialized technical skills. In the cotton industry, by 1848 it cost around 500,000 francs to establish a mill with about 20,000 spindles. By 1860 the cost had risen to 650,000 francs. At the end of the century, in the Nord, an average sized mill with around 10,000 spindles required an initial capital of up to 4 million francs. Costs were even higher in metallurgy, which in the 1860s experienced the rapid introduction of new technology, and especially of Bessemer converters for steel production. Even a medium-sized establishment like the Aciérs at Forges de Firminey, created in 1867, had an initial capital of 20 million francs.

A similar if less marked rise in costs also made social mobility through landownership and farming more difficult. During the prosperous 1850s and 1860s established commercial farmers in the more fertile and advanced regions such as the Paris basin and north were able, due to relatively high productivity and high prices, to accumulate capital which financed further innovation and the construction of such facilities as sugar refineries. However, the growing concentration of farms made it more difficult to gradually acquire small plots and build up a viable unit. A caste of rich noble and non-noble farmers emerged and entry into it became increasingly difficult.

As scale increased enterprises had to search further afield for both capital and managers. This process was restrained by the continued dominance of the family firm and restricted in its social consequences by the limited field of recruitment. The key role of the *grandes écoles* – especially of the *Polytechnique*, *École des Mines* and *Ponts et Chaussées* – in the development of communications, has often been stressed. They produced such eminences as the Talabot brothers and later Albert Sartriaux, for long *chef du service de l'exploitation* of the *Nord* Railway Company. The growing complexity of technology, and the increasing scale of activity, required highly educated managers in larger numbers than could be provided through simple inheritance of functions and access to education within the established *patronat*. To a substantial extent, however, these positions were filled through the extension of recruitment to non-business sections of the élite. Analysis of the directors of major electricity companies during the period 1911–13 has revealed that 73.68 per cent of them came from recognizably upper-class families.[17] Even when men like Berliet and Lumière were able to establish their enterprises on the basis of a relatively simple technology in the 1890s, further expansion depended upon the employment of skilled engineers and scientists and substantial external investment which brought with it the introduction of professional administrators. Individuals trained to become government officials or lawyers, often themselves belonging· to landowning families, possessed the skills, and the professional contacts useful to any large oganization. Gradually, as the scale and importance of economic activity and its rewards increased, members of traditional social groups were able to overcome their prejudices against business activity. Thus, although educational qualifications became an increasingly important means of qualifying for membership of the economic and administrative élites, for most members of French society neither the economic nor the educational opportunities were very great. It largely remained the case that, as Guizot wrote in 1816, the function of secondary education was to supplement 'the superiority of rank and fortune'. Although the correlation was never exact, educational opportunity depended upon social class. Moreover, family links and personal relationships continued to be of fundamental importance in the choice of a career, and in influencing success.

Many social commentators stressed the importance of personal ability and success. It was a fundamental element in middle-class ideology, and yet social mobility cannot be said to have been a major characteristic of French society in the nineteenth century. In terms of the proportion of the population affected, upward mobility was achieved by relatively few. Where it did occur it normally took a step-by-step form, a process spread over generations and subject to numerous reversals. Although individual ability counted for something, inheritance remained the major influence upon the life chances of an individual. Capital and culture were important. Education and establishment in a profession were expensive. Parental wealth made upward mobility easier, and reduced the likelihood of downward movement. According to Christophe Charle's analysis of a sample of members of the business and administrative élites in 1900 only 10 per cent of the former and 12.6 per cent of the latter had lower middle-class or popular family backgrounds,[18] and these newcomers, of course, had succeeded not only because of their intellectual activity and technical competence but due to their ability to conform, and their skill at integrating themselves, socially and culturally into the élite. The renewal of the élite due to economic and social change was thus extremely limited.

Power

One obvious attribute of the social élite I have tried to define was its power. To a very large extent it was conferred by the possession of property and control over the allocation of scarce resources. This largely influenced the form which wider social relationships took. Financiers and bankers controlled the credit system and through this influenced the economic decisions of the mass of entrepreneurs who in their turn took decisions which influenced the employment and wages of workers. Landowners, especially in regions of large estates in the north-east and Paris basin, had a substantial influence upon access to land, and through their tenants upon employment. The wealthy, in general, provided employment through the distribution of work – to groups as diverse as lawyers and domestic servants – and by means of conspicuous consumption to tailors, jewellers, builders, furniture-makers, and decorators both in the villages and market towns close to their châteaux, and in cities like Paris or Toulouse, where they possessed town houses. A network of economic dependencies existed which the revolution hardly affected and which survived throughout the century.

Escape from this tutelage was only possible for those with a degree of economic independence, such as members of the liberal professions with a middle-class, peasant or worker clientele; the wealthy tenant farmers of the Beauce and Brie *vis-à-vis* their absentee landlords; peasant farmers in regions in which the predominant form of landholding was small in scale, like Provence, Bourgogne or the Limousin or, even in regions of large property like the Seine-et-Marne, within limited areas like the Morin and Marne valleys; artisans with skills in short supply and traditional forms of organization which could be used to resist economic pressure. This, however, meant that from the 1848 Revolution onwards élite social and political power appeared to be under continual threat. Moreover, social change gradually weakened established links of dependence. Thus, migration from the countryside, particularly from the 1850s, was of considerable importance in altering the character of social relationships. Even if for many of the people concerned it meant exchanging one form of dependence for another – that of the agricultural labourer for that of the factory worker – it had the almost immediate effect of reducing the power of the traditional rural élite and the longer-term result of increasing the size and more gradually the powers of resistance of the urban working classes.

Population pressure on resources had been a major factor facilitating élite dominance. It created a precarious situation in both town and country under which men competed for a limited amount of work – a process which forced wages down – and also to purchase land or take over the tenancy of farms – which pushed up prices and rents. These were the optimum conditions for economic dependence. From the 1840s the increased tempo of urban industrial development and the creation of employment opportunities which this represented, multiplied the possibilities for escape from oppressive social relationships in the countryside. Even for those who remained, the introduction of more labour-intensive agricultural techniques at a time when migration was reducing the supply of labour not only permitted labourers to ask for higher wages but reduced their dependence upon particular employers. Many landowners complained that paternalistic master–servant relationships were being replaced by more distant employer–employee links based on a simple cash nexus. Workers and peasants in some areas began to reject charity and with it their humiliating subordination. In effect workers were withdrawing from relationships of dependence which had been imposed upon them, but which members of the élite assumed they had freely entered into. As the links of economic dependence were weakened, so the whole socio-cultural system built upon upper-class patronage began to disintegrate more or less rapidly. The high prices and prosperity of the Second Empire allowed many peasants to realize their dream of purchasing land at a time when landowners, discouraged by the rising cost and independence of labour, and attracted themselves by new prospects in the town, were often anxious to sell. The growing absenteeism of landowners and the declining significance of personal relationships with tenants and labourers was an important factor contributing to the erosion of a hierarchical society. Rural élites appear to have found it easier to adapt to economic change than to the alterations in the character of social relationships which resulted. The liberating effects of this period from *c.* 1850 to *c.* 1875 should not be exaggerated, however. The onset of economic depression and the phylloxera crisis, while it had the effect of accelerating the exodus from the countryside, also reduced many peasants to misery and in regions in which large estates survived, like the high quality vine growing areas of the Beaujolais, Bordelais and Bourgogne, they were glad to follow the lead of the local mayor, landowner and wine merchants who organized them in rural *syndicats*. Elsewhere, too, landowners and large farmers reinforced systems of control by means of tied cottages and allotments.

Economic power should be seen as a necessary but not a sufficient means of maintaining social power. In addition, members of the élite were able to exercise a considerable degree of social influence and ideological control. This social power depended upon the will to exert influence and exercise authority, and the degree to which individuals were in a position to create a sense of obligation to themselves. A wide range of social institutions might be employed to facilitate social control by élite groups, including those of religion, education, charity and philanthropy and credit, even when this was not their main characteristic. While economic power influenced access to material resources, control over these social institutions determined access to salvation, to information and to essential or attractive supplements to the basic income derived from labour.

Social influence could be effectively exerted in diverse situations in both town and country, where a wide range of economic and social means of exercising control could be displayed. The survival of sharecropping in the west, south-west and centre can in part be explained by the fact that, although economically less efficient than tenant farming, it allowed close supervision over peasants and still required in many cases the performance of personal services for *notre maître* such as the supply of free carting or dairy products and poultry to the manor house. In areas like the Haute-Garonne landlords and even their children habitually used the intimate *tu* rather than the polite *vous* in addressing *their* peasants – an important symbolic gesture. In this context actual residence by landowners was crucial. Growing absenteeism due to the preference for urban life tended inevitably to weaken such bonds. Sharecropping thus represented an affirmation of social power – resting on an economic base, but more complex and binding than a simple economic relationship – dependent on the survival of interpersonal relationships. Such close bonds of dependence existed most clearly in some of the economically backward and impoverished departments and were often reinforced by debts incurred in order to tide a family over a crisis or to enable it to purchase a plot of land. In some of the poorest areas, however, and the Limousin is a good example, an economically unattractive milieu limited purchases of land by the wealthy and in consequence their numbers and social influence.

Paternalism was a vital characteristic of a hierarchical society. It served to create a sense of obligation towards the donor, as well as to increase his self-esteem and to undermine potential solidarity among the poor. Large industrial enterprises in places like Mulhouse or the northern coalfield provided housing and pensions for their workers, and were in a very real sense adopting traditional modes of control based upon charity in an effort to increase efficiency and to defuse the tensions implicit in the simple, impersonal wage-labour relationships which tended to prevail in the large majority of enterprises which either could not afford the investment in philanthropy or whose owners were disinclined to do so.

Charity was also a key element in élite social ideology. Traditional Catholicism stressed the importance of good works. From pity, and acceptance of the responsibilities of 'social position', much of the leisure time of practising Catholics, and especially of their wives and daughters, was taken up by a variety of charitable activities, under the auspices, for example, from the 1840s of the *Conférence de Saint-Vincent-de-Paul* or through the control by local élites of the activities of hospitals, hospices and the communal *bureaux de bienfaisance*. This represented an acceptance of responsibility towards the poor, but also a rejection of any claims to basic rights that these might present. Charity as a virtue must be voluntary. Public intervention was resisted, therefore, because of the taxation necessary to finance it, and because it threatened both the spontaneity and the interpersonal character of the act of giving. In addition to committed Catholics, much wider sections of the social élite looked upon charity as a means of providing essential aid in periods of economic crisis and of reinforcing the links of dependence between rich and poor at a time when the latter might otherwise be driven into violent protest. According to the director of the Rouen *Société maternelle*, writing in 1854, 'it is essential to establish moral links between the rich and poor which would prevent the latter from giving themselves up . . . to despair and especially to the evil temptations aroused by envy'. Charity was also attractive because it did not represent a permanent and expensive concession. Although it increasingly had to be recognized that the problems of poverty were too great to be solved exclusively by private charity and that in practice growing municipal intervention was unavoidable, effective opposition to the extension of the state's responsibility for social welfare continued.

Social influence was made manifest and reinforced by political power. Its possession needs to be considered at both national and local levels. In national politics the *ère des notables* lasted until the early 1870s. It corresponded to the survival of traditional social structures and habits of behaviour which were only slowly transformed by economic change. It was enshrined in a political system based until 1848 upon a restricted electorate which facilitated the maximum exercise of personal influence. The *notable* was typically an individual whose authority depended on status *within* the local community, and upon the presumption by members of this community that he had the ear of important persons outside that community. His social status, life-style and education were such as to allow him a foot in both the local and the enveloping national society. Conflicts of interest meant this was not always an easy position to maintain. It depended upon the survival of a climate of confidence between particular notables and the mass of the population.

Three types of notables could be identified – at the bottom of the social scale the local (cantonal) notables, well-off peasants, doctors or notaries (often serving as municipal councillors); second, landowners or businessmen, again essentially local notables but wealthier than the first group, with a wider circle of dependants; and third, the range of individuals we have linked to the social élite, i.e. major landowners, bankers, industrialists and merchants, senior military officers and civil administrators, all those who mixed in 'society', who were invited to the prefect's *soirées*, who possessed influence outside the canton, and were in effect regional or even national *notables*, and as such qualified to stand for election to the Chamber of Deputies. Many of them, however, were unwilling to spare the time for politics. The industrial *patronat* of the Nord, for example, before the 1860s, appears to have concerned itself primarily with its economic interests. Subsequently, the desire for greater status and the desire to preserve tariff protection and social order stimulated social and political activism. The type of *notable* varied between regions, to a large extent reflecting their socio-economic structures and the survival throughout the century, especially in rural areas, of community rather than class as a basis for social integration. In the Manche de Tocqueville was repeatedly re-elected deputy from 1839 under both restricted and universal male suffrage due in large part to the interest he showed in the affairs of his constituency, in providing it with a model farm, for example, and through the charitable activities of his wife, but especially because he was believed to be an effective representative of his constituents *vis-à-vis* the administration.

At the national level access to power can most obviously be measured by considering election to legislative bodies. Thomas Beck has provided information on the social status of deputies elected during the restoration and early July Monarchy (Table 33).[19] This was the apogée of power for the traditional landed élite. In the Haute-Garonne, for example, in 1820, 31.2 per cent of the electorate were nobles, as were all sixteen deputies elected in the department during the restoration.[20] The aristocratic and reactionary character of the regime resulted, however, in it being seen as a threat to the revolutionary settlement.

Analyses of election results during the July Monarchy tell us something about the political consequences of the 1830 Revolution in reducing the political status of the nobility within the wider élite. This and the social unrest which accompanied it, however, reminded the wealthy, whatever their politics, of the fragility of the social system, and served to restrain political conflict in the interests of social order. Unfortunately the definitions of status are not quite the same as those used by Beck (Table 34).[21] The change resulted from the reduction of the *cens* – the direct tax qualification for voters – from 300 to 200 francs, and especially the discredit earned by the nobility from its close association with the Bourbons. By 1846, however, the position of the nobility was substantially restored. In that year over a quarter of the deputies elected were Ancien Régime nobles and nearly a fifth had imperial titles.[22] France remained a fundamentally rural society, in which, although change was occurring, traditional élites

Table 33   *Social status of elected deputies (per cent)*

Election of	Titled nobility	Non-titled nobility	Imperial nobility	Near nobility	Bourgeois
1815 (August)	36	9	12	28	15
1816	25	9	18	27	21
1819 partial elections	5	5	32	29	29
1824	39	12	9	25	16
1830	28	10	15	22	25
1830 (October)	13	6	12	24	44
1834	13	6	13	24	45

Table 34   *Social status of deputies (percentage of total)*

Chamber of	Nobility of Ancien Régime	Imperial nobility	More recent nobility	Doubtful nobility	Clearly bourgeois
1827–30	41	10	—	14	35
1831–4	12	12	—	9	66
1837–9	16.2	12	4.2	2.6	65

retained considerable social and political influence. Throughout the July Monarchy, and in spite of its identification by Marx with the interests of big business and especially finance, relatively few businessmen were actually elected (17 per cent of deputies in the Chamber in 1838). Significantly, however, a growing proportion of deputies were acquiring a financial interest in business and certainly the reduction of the voting qualification benefited business and professional men and lesser landowners. The numbers enfranchised rose from 94,600 under the Bourbons to 167,000 in July 1831, and 248,000 in August 1846. Moreover, in cities like Toulouse, the sweeping purge of the administration which followed the revolution contributed to the weakening of the patronage system which nobles had employed to support their influence.

Increasingly, and especially with the advent of universal male suffrage in 1848, elected or bureaucratic office came to be seen as an invaluable supplement to social status as a means of legitimizing authority. Even during the restoration, service in local government which had previously been seen as demeaning began to be viewed as 'politically useful and morally worthy'.[23] In some communities, in areas like the Vendée, former *seigneurs* became mayors. Governments, with only small numbers of professional officials, depended upon local notables to implement policies at local level, and in exchange supported their authority and exercise of patronage. In many areas the conflict between nobles and bourgeois, subdued at national levels after 1830, continued for decades over local power. In a city with parallel élites of landowners and businessmen, like Rouen, from early in the century bitter conflict often occurred between clans and interest groups for control of the municipality. Although the representation of professional groups changed, wealthy élites managed to retain effective control in the face of challenges from more modest social groups throughout the Third Republic.

A growing appreciation of the importance of political power developed as improved communications made the development of a large-scale society possible. The experience of 1848 made obvious the value of a strong repressive state in situations in which informal techniques of social control proved to be inadequate. Thus most members of the élite welcomed, or at least tolerated, Louis-Napoléon Bonaparte's *coup d'état* in 1851. This represented a judgement that the political regime did not matter too much providing social order was preserved. In periods of crisis – in 1848 and especially 1871 – the electorate appears to have turned for leadership towards members of old families. Thus, the 1871 election fought on the war or peace question saw seventy-two departments elect at least one noble. 225 of the 675 deputies were titled nobles.[24] The elections of 1849, 1869 and 1871 appear in general terms to have produced the same patterns, with a tendency for the large towns, and the departments of the east, Rhône valley and south-east, to elect radical, middle-class deputies, while the rural areas of the north, centre, west and south-west favoured the traditional élites. During the Third Republic, however, important changes did occur in the modes by which social élites exercised political power. Although France remained predominantly rural, a marked alteration occurred in the social origins of elected deputies and of governments. In place of wealthy landowners, representatives of the middle classes – typically doctors and lawyers and small businessmen, the so-called *couches nouvelles* – came to the fore, often by taking advantage of the surviving folk memory of seigneurial exploitation and of anti-clericalism and condemning in addition the new 'finance aristocracy'. The advent of universal male suffrage thus, in spite of a time lag, did lead to a substantial reduction in the political representation of those social élites which had previously dominated parliamentary life and government. However, this change did not constitute a threat to the social order. Political decisions were still taken by men with property and privilege and a determination to protect both – symbolized by the successful resistance to the introduction of a progressive income tax until 1914–17. Moreover, through the exercise of influence and a high degree of control over the administrative machine, the wealthy élite was able to retain considerable influence over governmental decisions.

Recruitment into the upper ranks of the administration was, in fact, still largely determined by income, education, family tradition and processes of social co-option. There was remarkably little change in its patterns of recruitment between the 1840s and the turn of the century. Consistently two-thirds to three-quarters of those at the summit of the various administrative hierarchies came from traditional notable families. One can safely assume that administrators, in reaching decisions, were influenced by the attitudes of their social group of origin, and that they in effect constituted a crucial link between the private and public spheres of action of these groups. Within the ranks of the administration the representatives of the various branches of the élite tended to come together, attracted by the social status and power conferred by administrative responsibility.

The decisions taken by civil servants and politicians were subject to the influence of a variety of interest groups, exercised by both formal and, face to face, informal means. The former were especially favoured by economic pressure groups like the *Comité des filateurs de Lille* (1824) and its successors devoted to the preservation of tariff protection; the *Comité des intérêts métallurgiques* (1840) and its better known successor the *Comité des Forges* (1864); by the *Société des agriculteurs de France* (1867) and the agricultural *syndicats* which developed under its influence from the 1880s. Through the provision of co-operative, mutual aid and credit facilities these provided their largely aristocratic leadership with considerable influence in both government circles and over a substantial peasant clientele, especially in the north, south-east and more slowly in the west. Particularly significant was the pressure they were able to develop in favour of agricultural protection during the Great Depression. By such means members of the wealthy élite were able to protect their vital interests, particularly their wealth, and to continue to exert considerable influence despite the apparent loss of political power.

Of even greater importance as an explanation of the retention of so much power in relatively few hands, was the widespread acceptance of traditional values, of ideologies which served to explain and to justify economic and social inequality. The capacity to mould opinion was a key aspect of social power – exercised through education and control over the means of information. This allowed the establishment of a broad concensus on basic social values, which were presented as eternal truths. Consensus was a far more effective conservative force than repressive violence.

A key feature of this normative code was the institution of property. The accepted view was that, 'wealth is no longer a privilege, civil law . . . equal for all has evened everyone up except in terms of intelligence and work. Thus wealth . . . is accessible to all. It has become a moral guarantee, a sign of good conduct . . . a proof of capacity' (*Echo de Rouen*, 21 October 1831). The tax qualification for voting rights, which survived until 1848, could be justified in similar terms. It ensured that only the intelligent were involved in political decisions. As Guizot explained in a speech in 1842, 'the superior classes' were the proper representatives and protectors of the 'inferior classes'. Of even greater importance, property was something which the relatively small élite shared with much larger sections of the community – with the middle classes, peasants and artisans. This provided a means by which a consciousness of interests in common could be developed.

Throughout the century traditional ideals continued to influence social relationships. Rural élites (often at least partly resident in towns) saw a properly ordered society as being based upon a hierarchy of harmonious interests. Society was conceived of in a totalitarian manner as an organic whole, a moral order. Every man had his God-given place in society, and should perform the functions and assume the responsibilities associated with this. Those with wealth, status, education and leisure should naturally provide the leadership. Their superior capacity made this their responsibility, just as it required respect and obedience from the majority of citizens. This sort of attitude was usually strengthened by the belief that the social order was Divinely inspired. Indeed, religious faith was believed to be the only means of controlling the evil inherent in man. Disorder in society was blamed on the declining moral authority of the church and upon the rural exodus and the growth of towns which loosened the natural bonds between men that existed in the small rural community. Although such ideas were strongest among nobles and those of Legitimist political persuasion – for whom they were confirmed by a particular view of history, by a nostalgia for the harmonious society presumed to have existed before 1789, but destroyed by the revolution, in truth by God's punishment for the growth of irreligion – they were to a greater or lesser extent accepted by wide sections of the social élite.

In the developing industrial centres, the directors of modern, large-scale enterprises, sought to re-create the idealized social relationships of the rural community by employing paternalistic measures as a means of controlling their workers. In both economic and social matters their liberalism was characterized above all by its eclecticism. The Catholic textile *patronat* of the Nord, for example, encouraged increased activity by the church in the schools – especially after 1848 – in order to restore moral order. The Protestant entrepreneurs of Mulhouse and the directors of the coal-mining companies of the Nord and Pas-de-Calais engaged in a wide range of philanthropic activities designed to moralize their workers, to reduce their independence and increase their efficiency. This kind of interventionism was typical of large enterprises with capital to spare and which faced a major problem in imposing discipline on large labour forces. Within the context of their own enterprises, their solution was not *laissez-faire* but the adoption of traditional forms of paternalism. In relation to the state, however, they bitterly opposed measures of social reform which might lead to outside interference in their activities.

In spite of major changes in its structure due to industrialization, most members of the social élite came to adhere to a basic set of ideological presuppositions which conferred upon it as a group a certain sense of unity and identity. Liberal critics of the Restoration Monarchy rapidly became first and foremost defenders of social order after 1830, as did many moderate republicans after 1848. The 1835 edition of the *Dictionnaire de l'Académie* defined 'order' as 'tranquillity, police, discipline, subordination'. This was just what the wealthy notable wanted. This is indicative of the way in which élite perceptions of society were worked out in terms of attitudes towards other social groups and, in particular, towards those who threatened the social order. To a large degree they were inspired by fear. Events such as the uprising of silk workers in Lyon in 1831, the 1848 Revolution and the Paris Commune of 1871, revealed the existence of large numbers of desperately poor and discontented people, apparently willing to resort to violent action in support of demands for social reform. According to an editorial in the *Journal des débats* on 8 December 1831, the Lyon revolt,

> has revealed a grave secret, that of the struggle which is taking place within society between those who possess and those who do not. Our society . . . like every other society has its affliction; this affliction is its workers. No production without workers! . . . and with an ever-increasing population of workers, always in need, no peace for Society. Every factory owner lives in his factory like a colonial planter in the middle of his slaves, one against a hundred . . . the barbarians who threaten society are not in the Caucasus or on the Steppes of Tartary; they are in the suburbs of our industrial towns.

The reaction of most notables towards the threat was initially defensive and showed little awareness of the complexity of social problems. They responded with charity and paternalism rather than with reform, or if need be supported the most brutal repression. It tended to be assumed that the main cause of poverty was the worker himself, that every honest worker could be sure of finding work at a reasonable wage; and that misery was the result of laziness, or the expenditure of the family's income on drink and debauchery. The problem appeared to be a moral one and therefore it followed that the only practical solution was also moral. In effect workers tended to be equated with servants and children in need of guidance.

Conclusion

Every social group has a conception of itself and of its place in the world. The great advantage possessed by a social élite is that it is able to exert considerable influence on the outlook of other social groups because it possesses attributes which make it admired (especially property) and also through its influence over the means of information and education. Its ideal was undoubtedly a society in which the masses generally accepted their 'proper' place and were obedient to authority. A few deserving individuals should be allowed to rise in the social scale; others who protested about social conditions should be punished for their perversity. Élites possessed a more or less coherent and nationally shared ideology, especially in respect of their attitudes towards the lower classes. In this they enjoyed a considerable advantage over other social groups whose outlook to a large extent continued to be determined locally. In a very real sense, and in spite of its inner divisions, the social élite existed as a class conscious of itself. This represented a tremendous advantage in its dealings with other groups.

As in any society, behaviour was determined largely by social mechanisms, values and assumptions which were taken for granted. Normally, even though apparent consensus might conceal pragmatic conformity rather than positive acceptance of the social system, no deliberate action needed to be taken to maintain a status quo, which involved the social and political subordination of the mass of the population. Social order was maintained by the adverse reaction of a majority of people to those who appeared to break the rules. This is not to deny the importance of conflict, particularly for local political pre-eminence, both within established élites and with essentially middle-class groups, who demanded a share of power. The latter used the language of 1789, the language of democracy, in an effort to appeal to an increasingly wide section of the population, and to isolate the ruling group. Thus in 1838 the *Journal de Rouen* denounced 'the reign of the new landowning and financial aristocracy'. Similar themes were used throughout the Second Republic and empire and with a renewed vigour during the Third Republic. Yet the aims of middle-class republican politicians were inherently limited. They had a more democratic vision of society than those they sought to replace, but the ideal was still based on property, on respect for many of those values which they shared with the old élite. They played the dangerous game of encouraging mass protest. 1848, the Paris Commune and the rise of the Socialist Party in the closing years of the century provided a terrible warning of the dangers of political agitation and of the need to preserve social order. This served to restrain middle-class critics of the established social order. The coming together of all those who possessed property represented an immense strengthening of the conservative consensus within French society. Thus, even though the élite of wealth might have lost its monopoly of political power, this wealth and its social position continued to be guaranteed by the power of the state.

4

The middle classes

Introduction

In a society characterized by major social inequalities status was accorded to individuals in relation to their membership of a hierarchy of social groups. Among these, contemporaries identified various intermediary groupings which they placed in between the social élite and the *classes populaires*. These middle classes were variously described as the *bourgeoisie*, the *classe moyenne* or *petit bourgeoisie*. They were an extremely diverse body of people, ranging from well-off landowners and manufacturers to self-employed artisans and shop-keepers. The criteria which contemporaries used for placing individuals socially were complicated and varied according to place, social milieu and period. To a substantial extent property and the wealth derived from it were the basic criteria. To be distinguished from the popular classes it was essential to have the means to live in relative comfort, and within the middle classes themselves differences in living standards distinguished various sub-groups. However, wealth alone did not determine rank. It was important to *appear* daily to be part of the social group to which one claimed to belong – through habits of dress, by wearing gloves, for example, speech, manners, accommodation, the employment of domestics, etc., i.e. by the ostentatious observance of particular norms of behaviour. Profession was another key factor. In part it determined income, although only the poorer members of the middle classes depended entirely on earned incomes. Of greater significance was the status conveyed by member-ship of a particular professional group because of the influence, education and life-style its members possessed. The distinctions and prejudices of the Ancien Régime survived into the nineteenth century and with them the stress on the dignity of life commensurate, in particular, with landownership or the liberal professions rather than mercantile or industrial activity. Modern sociological analysis using socio-professional categorization is hardly appropriate in these circumstances. The historian has to be more subtle. Factors such as family background, patterns of sociability, influence, life-style, education and culture all have to be taken into account. In the formation of social groups, individuals with similar backgrounds and life-styles tended to come together because they shared a whole complex of interests, as well as a sentiment of belonging to the same milieu. The choice of profession, of a place to live and especially of a marriage partner, were clear indicators of group membership, reflecting the existence of a sense of belonging, of a shared group psychology. This was reinforced by the exclusive attitudes of members of the social élite determined to keep the middle classes in their place, and the desire of these middle classes to differentiate themselves from groups lower in the social hierarchy.

The actual criteria for defining social status were inevitably affected by changes in the economy and in the scale and forms in which wealth was held. Until the 1840s, certainly, the stress should be placed upon continuity with the eighteenth century. From this period, as economic and demographic structures underwent a more rapid transformation, so status criteria evolved, at first in the minority of more dynamic centres of the economy, and then, by the last third of the century, affecting the most traditional regions. Even then it ought to be stressed that attitudes towards social status changed far more slowly than economic structures.

Structures

Who, more precisely, made up these middle classes? They included traditional elements like landowners, *rentiers*, government officials and practitioners of the liberal professions as well as the majority of entrepreneurs engaged in industry and trade – from factory owners and wholesale merchants to workshop *patrons* and shopkeepers – but not the very wealthiest members of these groups, the aristocrats and the *haute bourgeoisie* who made up a distinctive social élite. Professionally this was an extremely diverse group which in everyday life divided into several distinctive milieux made up of families with similar interests – economic and especially cultural (in the widest meaning of the word). The simplest division we can impose upon them, but one which would have been recognizable to contemporaries, is between middle bourgeoisie (to include most landowners, factory owners, large-scale merchants and members of the liberal professions) and a *bourgeoisie populaire* (to include the mass of workshop owners, shopkeepers, minor government officials and private *employés*).

The approximate hierarchy of wealth at mid century in Lyon (Table 35)[1] is suggested by declarations of inheritance. Our middle bourgeoisie would include essentially categories 3 and 4; the *bourgeosie populaire* category 5. It is worth stressing that the lines of division between social groups were never as clear as Table 35 might suggest. One group faded imperceptibly into the next. That these or similar divisions did, however, exist was ensured by marital endogamy. Like tended to marry like, in large part reflecting the range of day-to-day social contacts. Table 35 illustrates the extreme inequality of wealth within the middle classes. We must stress the importance of other criteria in determining social status, but there can be no doubt that increasingly wealth was regarded as a sign of success, and the status of the wealth-creating professions rose commensurately. Adeline Daumard working on Paris in the 1840s pro-

Table 35   *Social hierarchy in Lyon at mid century*

Category	Inheritance	
1	above 1,000,000f	Very rich landowners – rentiers, bankers.
2	500,000–1,000,000f	Rich landowners – rentiers, industrialists.
3	100,000–500,000f	The most senior government officials, medium landowners – rentiers, wholesale merchants (*négociants*).
4	10,000–100,000f	Liberal professions, medium *négociants*, senior army officers, senior government officials, high clergy.
5	2,000–10,000f	Shopkeepers, small landowners – rentiers, artisans, minor officials.
6	100–2,000f	Workers.

vides a socio-professional breakdown of that city's population (Table 36).[2] She concluded that the middle classes were to be found among the top 36 per cent of the population. A survey of Rouen during the 1880s suggests that the city's population was made up of three broad groups – the propertyless (56 per cent), the *bourgeoisie populaire* (20 per cent), and middle and upper bourgeoisie (24 per cent).[3]

The middle classes were a social group primarily resident in towns and the larger villages. Their numbers and structure in any one place depended upon its functions – administrative, industrial or commercial – and thus varied a great deal. Moreover, while basic structures retained important continuities throughout the century, in the years after 1850 average wealth tended to increase throughout the middle classes and their numbers also rose. For France as a whole by the turn of the century it has been estimated that around 225,000 heads of families and about 1 million people in all (some one in forty of the population) belonged to the upper and middle bourgeosie. This included some 50,000 landowners or *rentiers*, 50,000 members of the liberal professions (including 20,000 doctors, 7000 lawyers, 6000 notaries), 20,000 entrepreneurs in industry and transport, 20,000 wholesale merchants, 20,000 senior government officials,

Table 36   *Socio-professional structure in Paris, 1840s*

Profession	Percentage of total active population
Landowners, rentiers	8
Liberal professions, officials	7
Commercial professions	8
Manufacturing professions	11
Milieux populaires	56
Soldiers	10

25,000 military officers and 20,000 engineers and administrators of private companies (a relatively new group).[4] A further 2.2 million were owners of small businesses. With their families they made up almost 9 million people. These small-scale manufacturers and shopkeepers, together with office workers and *rentiers* (mainly retired – about 500,000 in 1901), made up perhaps 20 per cent of the population of Rouen and 32 per cent of Paris in 1881, and as much as 50 per cent by the beginning of the twentieth century.[5] In many respects they constituted a transition class between the masses and bourgeois society – related to both and yet distinctive. They were close to the mass of workers and peasants in terms of income, and as individuals often originated in these groups, but for this reason they were all the more anxious to distinguish themselves. They were not really bourgeois because of the nature of their work and the mediocrity of their life-style – but they were ambitious to secure social promotion, for themselves (often by means of the purchase of property to secure their old age), and particularly for their sons. These various groups of middle-class people made up a substantial part of the population. They were characterized above all by the ownership of property, and by a range of professional activities.

Socio-professional sub-groups

Landowners

For most of the century investment in land continued to be regarded as secure, profitable and a source of status. In many areas there were alternative forms of investment, but even for the successful businessman social promotion, as during the Ancien Régime, often involved the transfer of family interests from business into the professions and landownership. It was only from the 1870s, due to the dual effects of the agricultural depression on incomes from land, and the greater availability of alternative forms of investment which offered apparent security and higher returns, that land began to be eliminated from the investment portfolios of the mass of provincial bourgeois families.

These landowners might be divided into two groups – a rural bourgeoisie, and an urban bourgeoisie owning land in the countryside. The former included families living on their lands, perhaps taking an interest in agriculture but leaving cultivation of the land to a varying number of tenants or sharecroppers, and also those living in market villages and small towns. The latter included *rentiers* and businessmen with spare cash to invest – millers, merchants, innkeepers, manufacturers – and also professional men such as doctors and notaries, who in spite of their practices remained close to the land. Poor communications which limited access to the larger towns necessitated the dispersal of these practitioners throughout the countryside. They often belonged to families which had a generation or so earlier risen from the ranks of the more prosperous peasants. They were distinguished from the latter more by their education, culture and style of life than by their wealth – particularly by their withdrawal from direct farming and the adoption of a *rentier* life-style.

Their proximity and functions gave them considerable influence over the rural populations, especially in such areas of concentrated habitat as lower Provence or the vine growing areas of Bourgogne and Alsace. In the west, in the Massif Central in particular, modest bourgeois landowners continued to benefit from the survival of the tradition of making payments in kind, in a way absentee landowners could not.

In every generation some families left the countryside and small towns in search of diversion or employment in the cities. But it was only in the last third of the century that the age-old cycle of renewal from among the wealthy peasantry broke down. As rents declined, and, as with better access to the towns, material needs grew more complicated and more expensive, fewer families could afford to live as *rentiers*. The younger generations were encouraged to find urban employment. The value of another major source of indirect income from the land – money-lending (often at usurious rates of interest) – also declined as the price of land fell, and as peasant land-hunger was assuaged by migration and by the creation of alternative sources of credit.

Many landowners had always preferred to live in major towns rather than in the countryside. In the case of the middle-class landowners we are discussing in this chapter, and in comparison with the members of the social élite, their land tended to be in close proximity to their major place of residence. The bourgeoisie of a town like Chartres tended to own much of the land within a radius of about 30 kilometres – individually owning anything from 10 to 50 hectares. It was increasingly evident, however, from the 1850s, as the rate of growth of the towns – especially the larger – accelerated, that more lucrative possibilities for investment in property existed within the towns themselves. This promoted the transfer of capital from the land into urban buildings. In Paris, the process began earlier. Groups like shopkeepers saved in order to become landlords. It was lucrative and increased their local status. During the long economic depression of the last third of the century, incomes from urban property held up better than those from the land (in 1899–1900 the national average net revenue for urban buildings was *c.* 3.7 per cent after deduction of taxes, and 4 per cent in Paris),[6] and was marginally above that for stocks and shares. In Paris, Lyon and Marseille, in particular, the old-style landlords so familiar from the novels of Balzac were however, in economic if not entirely in social terms, pushed back into a marginal position by the development of large-scale investment in building by major property companies, insurance societies and banks from the Second Empire. The small landlord, nevertheless, retained his importance in the poorer quarters of the major cities and in the smaller towns.

Throughout the century these groups of *propriétaires* or *rentiers* (the terms were often interchangeable) constituted a major element within the middle classes, even in industrial centres like Rouen or Lille. They could not be said to have constituted a social class – their incomes, interests and life-styles varied too much – but they did make up a numerically large (an estimated 550,000 heads of families in 1900) and influential force dedicated to property and fundamentally conservative in social attitudes and politics (with numerous individual exceptions). Leisure was one important asset. Often by means of their membership of clubs or *cercles*, or of more informal gatherings in cafés, these people exerted considerable influence on local politics, especially in the numerous small towns. In 1843 there were some 1900 authorized *cercles* with over 120,000 members.[7] In part this was a group made up of the idle, but most had a profession or had retired after accumulating capital for their old age. It was a social category which declined in relative importance during the second part of the century – at Dijon, for example, the number of *propriétaires* and *rentiers* remained practically stable between 1851 and 1891, at a time when the population of the town increased by 103 per cent.[8] Economic depression and the reduction in their incomes increased the dependence of these people upon earned incomes and led to a change both in their professional labels and more fundamentally in their entire life-style.

Liberal professions

The diversity of its functions gave to this group a somewhat heterogeneous appearance. It was made up most notably of lawyers, notaries, doctors, dentists, architects, veterinarians, and *lycée professeurs*. In addition to the different professional interests of say the lawyer and the doctor, within each profession there were hierarchies, in terms of professional status and income. To an important degree, however, members of the liberal professions were aware of a shared culture derived from education, common aspirations for professional success and public recognition and hope of a reasonable income from both professional earnings and investments which would provide material comfort, security and independence. As the century developed members of the various professions became more aware of the value of professional organization to protect their separate and common interests by means of the exercise of control by the group over its members, the establishment of a legal monopoly over certain services, restriction of entry into the profession, and the laying down of standards of practice. This both reflected and intensified the development of an *esprit de corps*.

Due to complex attitudinal changes, to economic development and population growth, and the growing complexity of the social system, the demand for specialized services of various kinds grew throughout the century. The rise in the number of doctors (from 11,254 in 1866 to 20,113 in 1911) can be taken as a case in point.[9] The question of status – both within and between professions – is extremely complicated. To an important extent status depended upon age. The young man who had simply begun to make his way in the world, could expect – with application, patronage and luck – to rise within its internal hierarchy. The actual exercise of a profession did not mean the same thing in the case of a man of wealth and independent means who felt the need to occupy himself (and in this often followed a family tradition) as it did in the case of someone dependent upon his professional earnings. The status of the former was bolstered by his independent position within the broader social hierarchy, and a sense of *noblesse oblige*. In many cases higher education, in the law in particular, was simply the appropriate (and a useful) form of education for a gentleman of property and leisure, and was never intended to lead to professional activity. Among doctors there existed a gulf between the medical aristocracy of professors and great specialists and surgeons, especially those in Paris, and doctors who served the poor in town and country. In this case functions and the characteristics of clientele (social status and ability to pay) were the decisive factors. Although the incomes of doctors in general tended to increase significantly from mid century, these differences survived. Significantly, the status of the medical profession can be seen to have grown even before it applied the scientific discoveries of the last decades of the century. This was in response to the growing demand for medical services as communications networks developed and as new attitudes spread to combat the earlier fatalism of much of the population when faced with disease, and also to the effects of professional pressure group activity.

The status of a profession as a whole reflected to an important extent its patterns of recruitment. 'There were professions to which the sons of good families gravitated and those to which they did not.'[10] The magistrature, for example, was likely to attract *notables* in a way teaching, even in higher education, did not. The traditional status of a legal training attracted the sons of the wealthier bourgeois groups, while those of the lower middle classes tended to be attracted to professions like medicine and especially teaching in which family connections were less important and success more likely. The relatively low prestige of teachers in higher education is indicated by the fact that during the decade 1842–52 around 83 per cent originated in the lower middle classes. Moreover, they were not regarded as good matches for the daughters of bourgeois families. Income, independence and leisure, power (especially in the service of the state), educational requirements and exclusiveness were all relevant factors. So too was the relationship between supply and demand for the services involved. Although the cost of the education necessary for qualification continued to restrict entry, the popularity of careers in the liberal professions tended to result in an oversupply. There were generally too many *avocats* (barristers). In spite of the greater earning capacity of the average notary, the barrister's career had more glamour and social prestige. This was regardless of the key role performed by a notary in the drawing up of legal settlements and as an intermediary in the investment of savings. The cost of purchase of a practice was another limiting factor, however. Around mid century it might cost 15–20,000 francs to buy the cheapest notarial *étude* and up to 700,000 francs for the most lucrative in central Paris. In addition, caution money, varying from 1800 to 50,000 francs had to be deposited with the government.

In a provincial city like Nancy the members of the liberal professions made up a quite distinctive group. In the 1820s the fourteen solicitors (*avoués*), twelve notaries, twenty barristers, twelve doctors, senior government officials in some of the less prestigious posts such as the departmental director of the *Ponts et Chaussées*, and engineers and architects resident in the town, constituted a group active in its intellectual and political life, and frequently resentful of the exclusive attitudes of the élite. For professional reasons they were in close personal contact with a wide cross-section of the population and were able, because of the services they rendered and the prestige they gained, to exert a growing influence which would bear substantial political fruit as the franchise was extended. Newer groups such as company directors, managers and engineers were, in general, assimilated by the older professions. Among these, too, hierarchies developed, based upon qualifications, reputation and earning capacity, but only the most successful, such as the Talabot brothers, involved in finance and railway construction, acceded to the social élite.[11]

Businessmen

For 1896 information exists based on the payment of the *patente* (licence) tax by businessmen. The statistics give some, and even then a simplified, idea of the diversity of economic activity. They include both merchants and manufacturers and the most minute forms of enterprise – the multitude of large and small manufacturies and shops (Table 37).

Entrepreneurs were to be found at various levels in the social hierarchy. A small number of great financiers and major industrialists belonged to the social élite. The remainder made up the numerically greatest part of the bourgeoisie and of the *bourgeoisie populaire*. Early in the century the *négociant* (the wholesale merchant), retained pre-eminence among businessmen. He was often a financier and industrialist as well as a trader. The separation of commercial and industrial activities occurred only gradually. There were relatively few industrial capitalists. Manufacturing production continued to be based essentially upon small workshops with sales controlled and capital provided by merchants. Evidence from Paris for the first half of the century suggests that although upward mobility into this group was possible, the relatively high levels of capital required severely restricted access. In Rouen the major social distinction was between the élite of *négociants* – in this textile town heavily engaged in the trade in raw cotton, cotton thread and cloth – the major industrialists and shipowners closely linked to them, together with a few of the *marchands de gros* involved in the trade in grain, wood, wines and alcohols, and the mass of minor merchants, artisans and shopkeepers. At Nancy in 1836 the *négociants* formed a commercial élite made up of forty-one active and twelve retired members, with its wealth invested in business, urban property and to a lesser extent in land. They were clearly not as wealthy as the social élite of the city made up of aristocratic and *haut bourgeois* landowners. The inner cohesion of this particular group was revealed by intermarriage within it. Most outside marriages tended to establish links with families of equivalent wealth belonging to the liberal professions.[12]

The development of communications and the expansion of commerce occurring from the eighteenth and early nineteenth centuries gradually effected an alteration in the relationship between commerce and industry. Commerce,

Table 37   *Payment of patente, 1896*

Category	Number
Professions linked to agriculture (e.g. grain and cattle dealers, manufacturers of machinery)	69,465 (including 16,504 blacksmiths)
Metallurgy, mines and quarries	24,350
Metal working trades and trade in metal products	14,001 (including 6488 ironmongers)
Manufacture of arms and hunting and fishing equipment	3,057
Saddlery, coach-building	22,177 (including 6265 saddlers and 9352 wheelwrights)
Transport	56,516 (including 23,851 carters with only one cart)
Building industries	80,076 (including 13,935 master-masons)
Chemicals	16,310 (including 7873 retail pharmacists, 1038 paint merchants, 1027 perfumers)
Food industries	341,832 (including 58,087 grocers, 53,135 bakers, 22,304 butchers)
Restauranteurs, innkeepers, hoteliers	371,000
Production of textiles	45,959
Production and sale of clothing	162,000 (including 4061 hairdressers)
Skins and leather	7,418
Furniture and household articles	32,790
Ceramics and glass	21,997
Paper industry	4,083
'Letters, arts and sciences' (publishers, booksellers, photographers, etc.)	18,161
Watchmakers and jewellers	15,350

which had served as the essential stimulant to industry, increasingly took a subordinate place. As mechanization occurred the levels of capital required by industrial entrepreneurs were far greater than those mobilized by the *négociants* and could not be supplied by them, although their role as providers of credit remained significant, particularly for smaller-scale manufacturers. Even in this case, however, during the Second Empire a growing separation between banking and commercial activities was evident, with the emergence of a specialized banking network. The social status of the *négociants* to some extent declined with their economic importance and relative wealth. Merchants of all kinds were also affected by the changes in commercial practices consequent upon improvements in communication. The development of national and international markets for foodstuffs and manufactured goods caused a major *crise d'adaptation*. Many local commercial centres experienced a contraction in their activities as trade was concentrated upon the larger regional metropolis. This was true even of major centres like Toulouse, formerly so important as an entrepôt for regional cereal surpluses, or Orléans, whose *négociants* lost their role as middle men to the merchants of Paris whose agents increasingly organized the dispatch of cereals, wine and alcohol directly to the capital. However, this period of growing demand, rapidly increasing production, and faster circulation of products, remained one in which those who could adapt to new conditions were able to make substantial profits. Another characteristic of the period was the development of manufacturing industry which transformed industrial production from a subsidiary to the central economic activity and with this increased the social status of the manufacturer.

Sociological analysis of the groups involved in industrial production is extremely difficult. Throughout the century modern, dynamic factory industry continued to coexist with small artisanal units. Traditionally most industrial production had been dispersed and small-scale and had required only small initial investment raised by individuals from their savings and the profits of other forms of enterprise, or from family and friends, and increased subsequently by means of the re-investment of profits. According to Markovitch's calculations, at the beginning of the century only 15 per cent of industrial goods were manufactured in factories, the remainder being produced in smaller-scale handicraft workshops. Already by mid century this proportion had risen to some 35 per cent, and the pace of change was accelerating. Factory production was more profitable, due to its organizational and technical advantages and ability to make use of cheap labour. Manufacturers as well as merchants saw their economic position substantially altered as changes in market structures and in technology promoted the concentration of production in many sectors of the economy. Again according to Markovitch, the average employer in manufacturing industry during the period 1860–5 earned annually some 12,500 francs compared with an average of only 4350 francs in handicraft production.[13]

The vast majority of industrial entrepreneurs did not belong to the social élite. The exceptions were mainly those engaged in large-scale financial, mining and metallurgical enterprises. The more prosperous among the others – factory owners – constituted an industrial bourgeoisie, prospering in increasingly competitive circumstances, by means of hard and unremitting work and devotion to business. Typically in textiles the family business predominated, often originating early in the century in a decision by a merchant to invest part of his capital in machinery and buildings. In the first few decades a flexible and low cost response to changing market conditions remained possible using cheap rural labour and/or water power. Increased competition, especially during commercial depressions, imposed the need to increase productivity through further mechanization and the employment of steam power. This substantially increased the costs of entry into the industry and together with intermarriage tended, particularly in the most advanced areas of Mulhouse and Lille, to result in the emergence of a caste of relatively wealthy millowners, some of whose members were able by means of wealth and public service to accede to the social élite. In both of these cases strong religious faith – Protestant in the first case, Catholic in the second – reinforced an ethic of thrift, hard work and loyalty to the family, and an absence of sentimentality. This was useful in a situation in which mechanization required important and repeated changes in the organization of work, and this involved breaking down the productive process into simple repetitive tasks which could be performed by less skilled labour and persuading or forcing workers to accept subordination to the rhythms of the machine. The Parisian entrepreneur Poulot described how in the manufacture of screws, bolts and rivets in the 1860s he introduced machines in order to increase the precision of manufacture, and also to reduce his dependence upon highly skilled workers. He was successful *vis-à-vis* the boltmakers and hammermen, but instead found himself dependent upon the craftsmen who maintained the machines.[14]

According to the industrial censuses in the period 1860–5 there were an estimated 80,000 employers engaged in manufacturing industry with 1,150,000 workers (i.e. about 14.5 per unit), and 1,420,000 employers with 1,600,000 workers in handicraft production (i.e. 1.1 worker per unit). By 1906 there were only around 778,000 employers in total[15] (although comparison is not entirely satisfactory because of differences in the categories used). In textiles alone the number of *patrons* had been reduced by about one-third in this period due to industrial concentration. Nevertheless, even within a single sector like textiles the rapidity of technical development varied between branches of the industry, and so too did levels of capitalization, of profitability, and of wealth. Many enterprises continued to produce for restricted local markets, as in the case of brewing, flour milling, etc., or to create luxury goods on a small scale. Many small businessmen seem to have been unwilling to engage in significant innovation. Their attitudes remained fixed by traditional expectations, and often too by their inability to keep proper accounts.

Paris provides a useful example, both because of its economic importance and the range of information available. The Chamber of Commerce inquiry in 1847 described the city as a centre of small-scale industry producing primarily for local needs. Nine-tenths of *industriels* employed fewer than ten workers. The major industries at this time were clothing, food, building and furniture, although the relatively high cost of labour in the city was producing a growing orientation towards articles of luxury and style. These points are clarified by consideration of Table 38 which shows the value of production and the changing relative importance of industries between 1847 and 1860.[16] Production figures for 1847–8 were undoubtedly affected by economic crisis.

According to the list of *patentes*, the number of small enterprises continued to grow in both the old city and the enlarged area created by the annexation of the suburbs in 1860 (Table 39). The average size of industrial enterprise continued to decline throughout the Second Empire (from an average of one employer for 5.4 workers in 1847 to one employer for 4.8 workers in 1872).[18] Even in the newly annexed suburban areas in which cheaper land had allowed the development of larger-scale production, a mass of small workshops coexisted with factories.

Table 38 *Value of production by industry in Paris, 1847/8–1860*

Industry	Value of Production (in order of importance)	
	1847–8 (in francs)	1860 (in francs)
Clothing	240,950,000 (1)	454,538,100 (2)
Food	226,860,000 (2)	1,087,905,000 (1)
Building	145,412,700 (3)	315,266,480 (4)
Furniture	137,145,250 (4)	200,000,000 (5)
Precious metals	134,830,280 (5)	183,390,550 (6)
Articles de Paris	128,658,780 (6)	334,727,030 (3)
Threads and cloth	105,820,000 (7)	120,000,000 (9)
Heavy metals	103,631,600 (8)	163,852,430 (7)
Chemicals and ceramics	74,550,000 (9)	193,616,350 (5)
Coach building	52,357,180 (10)	93,850,000 (12)
Printing	51,171,870 (11)	94,166,530 (11)
Skins and leather	41,762,965 (12)	100,882,000 (10)
Woodworking	20,482,300 (13)	27,075,320 (13)

Table 39 *Number of commercial and industrial establishments*[17]

1852		1869	
Old Paris	78,237	Old Paris	108,905
Suburbs	13,225	Suburbs	35,756

Although forced out of central Paris by urban renewal and higher rents these enterprises in general needed to remain as close as possible to their clientele. The small-scale entrepreneur was able to survive and even prosper, particularly during the two major phases of economic expansion during the Second Empire and at the beginning of the twentieth century. This was often at the cost of substantial adaptation to new techniques and markets facilitated by the development of small steam-engines and then of gas and electric motors which allowed the introduction of energy consuming machine tools without requiring a substantial increase in the scale of production.

The vast majority of entrepreneurs in the industrial sector remained owners of small businesses employing a limited amount of capital, for the purchase of raw materials and the payment of wages rather than the purchase of equipment. Skilled labour was the major asset. Traditionally the worker had enjoyed a considerable degree of autonomy during the labour process and because of the restrictions which apprenticeship placed upon entry into most trades, the supply of this labour was limited. Relationships between *patron* and worker in this sort of situation were often better than those between the master–artisan and merchants upon whom they frequently depended for credit to purchase raw materials and for the sale of finished products. Even in the building industry major entrepreneurs subcontracted work (*marchandage*) to master-masons who were responsible for the actual direction of labour, although in this case the entrepreneur did tend to provide the large items of equipment like ladders, scaffolds and derricks.

Among small businessmen a hierarchy existed which was related to the skill and artistic level of their trades, to the social status of their clients and to levels of profit and living standards. Often the master–artisan was difficult to distinguish from the worker, particularly in cases where he worked alone, or even from the peasant in rural areas. The numbers and range of artisanal businesses in the countryside varied with density of population and with proximity to market towns. In the countryside of the Pas-de-Calais around mid century it appears that in communes with a population of less than 200 the innkeeper was the only permanent representative of the artisanate, with sometimes a carpenter; in those with a population of 200–500 there were at least a wheelwright, blacksmith, shoemaker, dressmaker, carpenter and innkeeper. Communities with over 500 people enjoyed, in addition, the services of a miller, a grocer, a tailor, mason and cabinet-maker, while those with over 1000 inhabitants included such specialists as nailmakers, rope-makers, watchmakers, etc., i.e. a wide range of artisanal crafts.[19] For at least the first half of the century wide diffusion was possible because of the limited development of large-scale industrial production and of the retail trade. Subsequently development varied. In the south-west of Loir-et-Cher, for example, the intensification of agriculture established new needs in terms of the sale and maintenance of equipment, a greater volume of trade, and increased demand for consumer goods. Moreover, relative isolation from large towns favoured village merchants and artisans so that the number of small businessmen increased more rapidly than the population between 1850 and 1911. In contrast, in the north-east of the department – in the Beauce – a process of ruralization occurred as the number of businesses declined by about a quarter in relation to population.

To a significant extent the self-esteem and social status of the small entrepreneur depended upon the degree of economic independence he enjoyed. This was frequently threatened. In the first place, especially in the larger cities where the scale of demand justified it, and as mass markets developed, a process of division of labour and specialization between workshops occurred. This involved two forms of innovation – the subdivision of tasks between workers in order to increase their productivity and the introduction of individual new techniques such as machine tools or the sewing machine. The furniture, clothing and shoemaking trades appear to have been particularly affected by the production of more or less standardized consumer goods. Thus the first ready-to-wear enterprise was founded in Paris in 1828 and by 1848 ready-made clothing had captured about a third of the Paris market. By the 1890s most small workshops in the clothing trade were entirely dependent upon merchants, major industrialists and department stores. It has been estimated that only a small minority of the workshop *patrons* active in Paris in the second half of the century enjoyed a real economic independence and that their numbers declined as commercial capitalism developed. As a proportion of the active industrial population (not including transport and commerce) they amounted in 1847 to 5.1 per cent; in 1860 to 3 per cent and in 1901 to 1.9 per cent.[20] This dependence imposed upon the workshop *patrons* by the merchants who ordered their goods had important consequences for the organization of work within the *ateliers* and for the employer's relationship with his workers. The latter bitterly resented what they saw as the dilution of their skills. The intensification of competition increased insecurity. More devastating again was the decline from the 1850s of small-scale enterprises in nail-making and ironmongery and of textile enterprises throughout southern France as competition from better-equipped factories in the north and east became more intense. Throughout the countryside and small market towns the last third of the century saw the closure of numerous small mills, as industrial flour milling developed. Thatchers disappeared as tiles and slates became more generally available. Wheelwrights were less in demand as better roads reduced wear and tear on carts. Tailors and shoemakers were unable to compete with factory products available in markets, shops and by mail order. This was symptomatic of the decline of traditional rural society and the imposition of urban patterns of consumption. Even where the numbers of artisans remained relatively stable their activities changed. Existing small businessmen were frequently able to adapt to changing patterns of demand, and new opportunities beckoned. In some cases, like that of light engineering, the new opportunities were often associated with the development of subcontracting for large-scale industry.

Closely linked to the master-artisans in terms of social status were the vast majority of shopkeepers. Traditionally towns and villages had relied upon markets, fairs and pedlars to supply most of the goods they purchased. As communications improved, a new marketing system evolved centred upon the larger population centres which provided a wide range of services to their own residents and to their rural hinterlands. The railway line made even small towns like Bayeux (Calvados) centres of attraction for wide regions. In cities like Toulouse, a large number of specialized small shops were opened to compete with or replace the mercantile entrepôts which had formerly catered for every need. As the towns grew, more and more people became dependent upon purchasing their basic needs; as material conditions improved more and more people wanted to buy luxuries; and so the number of shopkeepers increased. In Paris the number of grocers doubled between 1856 and 1879,[21] and nationally between 1881 and 1910 the number of commercial licences increased by 10 per cent, i.e. by twice as much as the growth in population. Changing dietary habits stimulated a growth in the number of bakers' and butchers' shops. In Paris the number of butchers increased from 299 in 1850 to 1132 in 1860 (including the annexed suburbs) and 1453 by 1868,[22] although for much of the population meat remained a luxury. Alcoholic drinks also became readily available especially as the railways promoted the extension of *vin ordinaire* production in the Midi. This was reflected in the growth in the number of small bars.

Distinguished from the merchant by the fact that they actually served behind a counter, shopkeepers, just like any other professional group were characterized by an internal hierarchy, determined in this case by an individual's earning power and the character of his clientele. In general the jeweller counted for more than the grocer, the grocer with a shop in a smart residential district for more than the grocer serving a clientele of factory workers. Even so, the latter enjoyed greater security and status than the worker. Although their living standards might differ very little, he was a man of property – however small – with 'prospects'. Moreover, through the extension of credit, upon which many workers depended to make ends meet from day to day, and especially during crises, the shopkeeper was a man with a certain influence and power in the community.

Where did this mass of shopkeepers come from? Often from the professions which they displaced. Many of the pedlars chased from the streets by the growth of traffic and police regulations set up shop. In Paris the Auvergnat water carriers, finding in the 1850s and 1860s that demand for their services was declining as more and more houses were connected to the city's water supply, moved into the business of supplying coal or wine. It helped that relatively little capital was needed to start. Workers who wanted to escape from the factory, domestics who had saved their earnings, but especially artisans of all kinds sought to improve their lives by entering the highly competitive and very insecure world of the small shopkeeper. Frequently the shop was the means by which the provincial with some capital, derived perhaps from the sale of family property, installed himself in the city. Success, often mere survival, depended, especially at the beginning, on thrift and a willingness to live in cramped and uncomfortable conditions behind the shop.

Even as the expansion of opportunity for small shopkeepers continued, threats to their position developed, although to only a limited extent during the nineteenth century. The *grand magasin* developed during the Second Empire. Large sums of capital were needed and raised from financiers like the Pereire by men with proven commercial expertise, for example, Boucicaut of the *Bon Marché* or Jaluzot at *Printemps*. This was, however, a phenomenon limited to the major cities with a sufficient concentration of well-off bourgeois, and where the reconstruction of city centres had created major new arteries of circulation and opportunities for people to gather. In comparison with the small shopkeeper the basic principle of business was the rapid rotation of stocks and low profit margins on each item – about 4–5 per cent, compared with the 30–40 per cent of the traditional *boutiquiers*. Quick sales allowed the *grand magasin* to pay suppliers sooner and encouraged the latter to offer discounts. Fixed prices were another feature of these establishments, as were sales to increase business during normally slack periods such as January and February. In 1881 the twelve most important *grands magasins* in Paris employed only 1700 people; by 1913 they had 11,000 employees.[23] From 1875 branches of department stores were also established in provincial centres. This, together with the development of mail order catalogues by, for example, the *Manufacture d'armes et de cycles de St-Etienne*, caused such anxiety among shopkeepers that the government began to manipulate taxes in an effort to satisfy their complaints about unfair competition. Whatever the reality, many shopkeepers felt threatened and along with artisans constituted a relatively discontented *petite bourgeoisie*. By the turn of the century there was talk of a *crise des classes moyennes* seen in the failure of individual businessmen and the more general sense of pressure from large-scale competitors. There was a feeling among small businessmen that they were not obtaining a fair share in the expansion of wealth, and indeed in Paris where small traders and master artisans had possessed 17 per cent of the total wealth in 1820, their share had declined to only 3 per cent by 1911. The average value of their property had increased from 28,600 to 44,000 francs, but this represented an increase of only 65 per cent in comparison with an overall increase in the value of property of 197 per cent.[24] Understandably, this situation caused resentment, partially translated into political terms by the nationalist and anti-semitic movements of the turn of the century.

Office workers

Urbanization had important consequences for the development of commerce. Economic development, together with the growing scale and complexity of government led to the multiplication of another major element of the lower middle classes – namely the office workers and minor officials. At mid century there were fewer than 600,000 public officials (state, departmental and municipal); 700,000 in 1870 and some 1.3 million in 1914. At this time the typical small *chef-lieu d'arrondissement* would have had four officials at the *sous-préfecture*, eight in the schools, twenty in the tax offices, and as many at the *tribunal* and *collège*. If postal, municipal and *ponts et chaussées* officials were included the total would amount to almost 100.[25] Most of the increase was in practice due to the recruitment of school teachers and postmen, i.e. of minor officials, and in 1900 the average wage of the civil servant was only 1490 francs, which was little better than that of a labourer. Substantial recruitment of administrative personnel also occurred on the part of large-scale private enterprise, most notably the railways. These *employés* were a rather disparate group in terms of their education, responsibilities, status, security of employment and earnings, ranging, for example, from office boys, shop assistants and postmen to lawyers' clerks, bank clerks, book-keepers and primary school teachers. These positions offered opportunities for limited social mobility especially to the children of the lower middle classes, of artisanal and peasant families. Although patronage and nepotism continued to influence recruitment and promotion within the public service, competitive recruitment assumed a more important role and together with the growing number of positions available made it increasingly possible for many women as well as men to accede to at least minor positions in the administration, post office and as school teachers.

This wage-earning *petite bourgeoisie* was distinguished from wage-earners in general by the non-manual character of its work, by its dress, education and language, all regarded as marks of distinction. Low salaries and the costs of maintaining appearances often imposed considerable pressure on family budgets. An official inquiry in 1913–14 concluded that although the households of *employés* enjoyed larger incomes than did those of workers, they spent more on accommodation. Significantly, they tended to have fewer children, a sign of a more calculating attitude towards life. Usually office workers and shop assistants, especially in the larger enterprises, were subjected to close supervision and control which must have offended their pride, but although a *Chambre syndicale des employés* was founded as early as 1869 it attracted little support and the strikes it organized among shop assistants were easily broken. It was all too easy to replace people with limited professional skills. Moreover, *employés* tended to identify more closely than did many workers with the interests of their employers and were reluctant to risk the security of employment and pensions which were often a major attraction of their positions. Even the most modest officials and office workers enjoyed a certain social status and some groups, particularly school teachers, exerted considerable social influence. Indeed primary school teachers (about 120,000 in 1910) serve as a useful example of a *petit bourgeois* group providing an important means of upward social mobility.[26] They were a group with a developing *esprit de corps*, conscious of the importance of their functions and anxious from as early as the 1830s, to assert their independence of their traditional superiors – the clergy. Their growing social status was largely determined by increased public appreciation of the practical utility of education.

Social mobility

In general the opportunities for moving up the social hierarchy would appear to have been very limited. Nevertheless the major area of fluidity was the borderline between the working and peasant classes, on the one hand, and the lower middle classes on the other. At the individual level the major determinants to social mobility were ability, hard work, thrift and enterprise. Calculation mixed with luck. Marriage, for example, might be an important factor bringing with it in some cases a dowry or in the case of marriage with a widow, an established business. In many small businesses the practical contribution of the wife in looking after the shop or keeping the accounts was vital. At the societal level, the major determinant of mobility was the degree of expansion and of structural change in the economy, together with the prevailing short-term level of prosperity. Thus opportunities varied considerably over time, between professions and places. At frequent intervals throughout a generally expansive century, crisis and depression served to limit the opportunities for self-improvement and to threaten established groups. Opportunities were also determined by the space left to potential newcomers by existing bourgeois families. Downward mobility however appears to have been relatively rare.

Artisans and shopkeepers benefited from population growth and enlarged markets. Until around 1840, and later in many regions, industrial and commercial development occurred by means of increase in the number of enterprises rather than concentration of production. Professional endogamy had its limits which made it necessary to recruit outsiders, particularly to expanding professions. However, if among the 300 young men from artisanal families conscripted at Nancy in 1836–7 only one in four had taken the profession of their fathers, almost all had remained within the same social milieu, usually entering whichever artisanal trades appeared to offer the best opportunities. Only seven could be said to have shown signs of upward mobility.[27] Remaining within the same milieu – whatever the profession – offered considerable advantages in terms of useful contacts, and various kinds of moral and material support. Subsequently, the growing concentration of economic activity changed the structure of opportunity. It increased the costs of entry into many professions and resulted in a gradual closing of access into expansive sectors like textiles. Nevertheless, artisanal production continued to offer possibilities for social mobility, while opportunities increased in the retail trades and in the services, with the expansion of the liberal professions, the managerial and technical strata and of bureaucracy.

Closely linked to the economic situation, migration was another factor determining levels of social mobility. Certainly a large part of the Parisian bourgeoisie was made up of immigrants from other regions. These were more likely to be attracted to new and developing occupations than members of established families. Immigrants tended to enter the riskiest trades in which failure was common and, partly as a consequence, so were the opportunities. These included the building industry. Often too they were able to serve as intermediaries between Paris and their places of origin. Immigrants from the Yonne frequently set up as wood-merchants; those from Bourgogne or the Midi as wine-merchants; men from eastern France in the cloth trade. Function, area of origin and also religion, as notably in the case of Jewish immigrants, increased the cohesiveness of immigrant groups. Some trades were, however, much less receptive of immigrants – especially those skilled artisanal trades producing *articles de Paris* and fashionable luxuries.

Education also enlarged opportunities. An elementary education made it possible to obtain minor positions within the state bureaucracy, in offices, or as shop assistants, and the more able or lucky subsequently benefited from internal promotion. The institutions of education themselves were vehicles of both status preservation and of social promotion. In the period 1900–14, for example, three-quarters of secondary school teachers had fathers who had not received a secondary education, but who, significantly, had been prepared to accept sacrifices and educate their children. Over three-quarters were recruited among the lower middle classes. Primary education offered less possibilities and generally to men and women of more modest origins. However, the 'popular' origins of primary teachers should not be exaggerated. Even in an area like the Nord – where in the period 1880–1914, 62 per cent of the active population were workers, only 26 per cent of *instituteurs* came from working-class families.[28] Most teachers were *petit bourgeois* in origin, and those who were not, rapidly assumed the attitudes and patterns of behaviour expected of them by their colleagues.

Secondary education was essentially restricted to the established middle classes, and in 1901 only 58,800 boys and 7800 girls attended the various *lycées* and *collèges*. It remained expensive. Even in the 1880s only about 2 per cent of the age-group received *bourses* and these were given mostly to the sons of minor government officials. For a child of humble origin admission to the preparatory classes of the *lycée* and to the school itself involved a cultural uprooting. He was forced to abandon the mode of speech and outlook of his social milieu. Throughout the century the secondary schools tended to stress the non-vocational, and through the humanities to provide a general cultural education. Nevertheless, secondary education opened up a wider vista of opportunity to some members of the lower middle classes, particularly in the less fashionable professions, i.e. in education, in industry and some sectors of government rather than in law, the magistrature or even medicine. A much smaller number of individuals with a *petit bourgeois* (but rarely peasant) background even managed, through access to the *grandes écoles*, to enter the social élite, but prevailing values and a limited range of contacts greatly restricted this kind of movement.

The system of education was in fact designed to provide the training and skills which it was assumed were required by particular social groups, i.e. to replicate social barriers rather than to promote mobility. The apparent social promotion represented by the provision for a child of a higher level of education than its father had received often in fact represented the ratification of the father's success. It was an effort to secure the cultural level thought to be commensurate with the family's new-found material wealth. Parental aspirations were a major determinant of social promotion among the younger generations. In some cases, for example, that of the textile enterprises of the Nord, sons were expected to enter the family business. In other circumstances, especially where economic growth was less dynamic, the traditional route from business into the professions was preferred. At a lower level in society, the options were different. The director of the *Ecole Turgot* in Paris in 1875 reported that workshop *patrons* hoped that their sons would achieve greater status and security by means of office jobs, while an inquiry in the Charente in 1912 indicated that the ambition of small tradesmen was to establish their sons as doctors, engineers or as *lycée* teachers, professions which they considered involved less hard work and brought greater profit and status.[29]

Attaining a social position was one thing, preserving it another. This called for careful investment, the avoidance of waste, and a family planning strategy which prevented excessive dispersal of the family patrimony through dowries and inheritance and which, through investment, equipped the young with the kind of training or education which would allow them to make their way in the world. In general the social promotion of a family took a step by step form spread over two or three generations, and was often interrupted by setbacks due to the economic situation and individual misfortunes or incompetence. Self-made men, examples of spectacular success like the banker Laffitte, the engineering entrepreneur Cail, the Schneider brothers in metallurgy, or Boucicaut, founder of the *Bon Marché*, were often used to justify a social system in which supposedly virtue brought its own reward. They were, in practice, rather rare, especially after the passing of the generation which had benefited from the upheavals of the revolution and empire and the initial phase of industrialization. Inheritance – of wealth or of cultural marks of distinction and social contacts – was clearly of considerable importance in determining an individual's future prospects. At every level of the social hierarchy each generation built upon the achievements of its predecessor. But inheritance also had the effect of reducing the opportunities for newcomers. The further up the social hierarchy one looks, the more rigid social structures appear to have become. Social status was largely reproduced from generation to generation. At the highest levels of the social hierarchy exclusive castes were created, determined to preserve their position, and able to use their wealth and access to economic information to do so. Awareness of this restriction of opportunity together with the constant insecurity experienced by many members of the lower classes created significant tensions within the property owning classes.

Inner divisions

Social stratification can thus be seen both as a source of harmony and of conflict. The existence of groups whose higher status is recognized, admired and aspired to, provides their members with social and cultural authority. Through processes of imitation and of education, the values of the upper classes to a large degree imposed themselves upon the middle classes and even upon peasants and workers. More obvious links of dependence also existed, through the distribution of official posts, and of work to everyone from lawyers to shopkeepers and master artisans. The structure of the middle classes and the relationship between the various groups which composed them, as well as with other social groups, however, varied considerably over time and between places. As well as harmony (apparent or real), mutual suspicions were often evident. The better educated and more cultured groups adopted disdainful attitudes towards 'money-grubbing' shopkeepers and those who worked with their hands. In response, artisans resented the pretensions and apparent idleness of the wealthier business and professional men. Differences of economic interest were also clear. Many small businessmen endured constant insecurity due to competition, lack of credit and fluctuations in the demand for their products. The owners of small- and medium-sized enterprises resented the indifference shown towards them by financiers who controlled discount and interest rates, or the apparent arbitrariness of the wholesale merchants who extended or restricted credit solely to suit their own business interests. They were anxious about the growth of industrial capitalism. Partly associated with this were differences in political interest. 1789 appears to have firmly established a belief in the rule of law, and in equality before the law. On social relationships the prevailing orthodoxy as expressed by Guizot was that, 'inequalities of intellectual capacity as of physical strength . . . exist naturally between men. . . . This inequality is the primary and real source of social inequality' – in short that wealth was the reward for ability and hard work, and conversely that poverty was the inevitable result of moral or intellectual weakness. Even so, many members of the middle classes continued to believe that unjustifiable social and political privileges survived. Until 1848 these were symbolized by the electoral laws which established a tax qualification for the vote and excluded numerous business and professional men, people who were often quite convinced of their personal worthiness and capacity to participate in the political process and, indeed, of the importance of so doing in order to protect their vital interests. Exclusion was an especial blow to the self-esteem of relatively well educated and often politically aware professional men, doctors or lawyers, who saw themselves disenfranchised along with a host of tradesmen. It was one reason, along with the constant squabbles between rival clans for local power, for political conflict at local level. In such a varied world individualism was rampant. At both national and local level, the élites with power were under constant attack from those who felt excluded and who used the language of 1789 to condemn privilege. Throughout the century the same themes, the same vocabulary was employed to isolate the dominant group – the 'bourgeoisie' – from the mass of the 'people' and to denounce its monopoly of power. In practice, rather than an attack on the bourgeoisie this conflict, even after the rise of socialist parties, represented primarily a struggle within the middle class – between those who had succeeded and those who still felt excluded.

Although members of these varied groups had less economic power, and social status, than members of the social élite, they had daily contact with a wide public, which gave them considerable influence. The middle classes thus played key intermediary roles in the transmission of ideas and aspirations of all kinds. The scale of this influence depended upon the local situation – upon the number, prosperity, degree of independence and self-confidence, and cohesion of middle-class groups. In general these groups remained divided internally. They both aspired to secure bourgeois status and sympathized with the critics of a social system within which they seemed condemned to permanent inferiority. Fear of social revolution, of the loss of their superior status *vis-à-vis* workers was, however, an important conservative factor. The middle classes, in spite of their resentment of the social élite, and of considerable internal variations in wealth and culture, shared élite conceptions of a world based upon Property and Order. Their attitudes towards the propertyless frequently combined condescension with contempt. They confused the causes and symptoms of poverty. To blame misery and squalor upon drunkenness and vice was much more satisfying than to explain it in terms of low wages and exploitation. The lower classes were blamed for a failure to exhibit those virtues which the middle classes saw as their own – ability, hard work and thrift. Just like women and children, they were regarded as minors, not entirely capable of rational behaviour. Although sometimes also sharing élite concepts of charity, these middle class groups were usually less willing to assist the poor and more likely to insist that hand-outs encouraged laziness. Just like the élites they resented those proposals for social reform, to be financed out of income tax, made in 1848 and afterwards, seeing them as nothing less than a threat to a civilization based on property.

The growing concentration of large numbers of poor people in the towns heightened this anxiety. In day-to-day terms overcrowding encouraged the rapacious landlord, and the frequent inability of people to pay their rents caused considerable hostility between landlords and tenants, often far more bitter than that between employer and worker. Even so, the increasing scale of industrial production and the growing tensions between workers and their employers, as the latter sought to increase productivity in an increasingly competitive economy, had profound effects upon the psychologies and relationships of the workplace. From the 1840s works like Louis Villermé's *Tableau de l'état physique et moral des ouvriers employés dans les manufactures de coton, de laine et de soie,* revealed a frightening world of poverty and degradation, a brutalized and criminal population apparently on the verge of revolt. Revolution in 1848, and the Paris Commune in 1871 confirmed the worst fears. Widespread discussion of the poor and their problems made the middle classes especially anxious to distinguish themselves by adopting and adapting upper-class norms of dress and speech, and by introducing increased formality into work-place relationships in order to acknowledge the inequality of master and man and the 'social distance' between the two. It became vitally important for many who could hardly afford the cost to keep up appearances. In the textile centre of Armentières (Nord) the first generation of entrepreneurs, active in business from around 1850, appear to have enjoyed relatively intimate relationships with their workers and had often sat on the same benches as them at school. However, the second generation, becoming active from around 1870, adopted very different attitudes. Not only did technical change appear to necessitate greater discipline in the mills, but the growing wealth of the successful entrepreneur had created a massive gulf between his life-style and that of his employees. The chronology of this change – of the adoption of a distinctive bourgeois mentality – varied between places, but it was general in its occurrence.

Politically, members of these social groups had been involved in the struggle to abolish the privileges of nobility in 1789 and 1830 and of the 'finance aristocracy' in 1848. Subsequently they became more concerned to affirm and defend their own superiority. This did not prevent complex internal conflict within the property-owning classes, but the regularly re-awakened conscious-ness of the 'social question' and of the existence of the 'dangerous classes' was sufficient to lead to a substantial closing of ranks. In the last resort, and in spite of inner tensions, the businessman, the professional, the shopkeeper, the school teacher and the clerk generally felt that their interests were best served by the defence of the existing social order and in resisting the threat represented by the growing urban working classes.

5

Peasants

Introduction

As late as the middle of the nineteenth century some three-quarters of the French population was classified as rural, and much of the remainder lived close to the land in small towns and market villages. Rural society had altered very little in spite of the political changes brought about by the revolution, and of the progress made in agriculture since the second half of the eighteenth century. Most of the population, even in close proximity to Paris, remained isolated by poor communications and low levels of functional literacy. The proportion of the population actually employed in agriculture was inevitably less than that made up by the rural population (given the presence in the villages of land-owners, professional men, artisans, etc.). In 1856 the primary sector of the economy (agriculture, forestry, fishing) employed 51.4 per cent of the active population, a share which gradually declined to 49.3 per cent in 1876, 45.3 per cent in 1896, and 43.2 per cent in 1906. These average figures of course conceal major regional variations. Thus in Côtes-du-Nord, even in 1872 the rural population made up 91.6 per cent of the total, while in Pas-de-Calais the agricultural population made up 58.9 per cent of the active population in 1851, but only 26.8 per cent in 1911 – a decline primarily due to the employment offered to agricultural labourers in the developing coalfields. However, in terms of actual numbers of people employed, the active agricultural population continued to increase – from 7,305,000 in 1856 to 7,995,000 in 1876, 8,463,000 in 1896 and 8,845,000 in 1906. There can be no doubt then of the importance of a study of the rural population, even if, as Chapter 1 revealed, the share of agriculture in the total gross national product fell quite substantially.

It would have been possible to have written a chapter about rural society rather than one on the peasantry, but it seemed that a more instructive representation of French society would be achieved by means of an analysis of social groups rather than of contrasting *milieux*. This chapter, therefore, concentrates on the peasants, a social category distinguishable from the rest of the population in terms of the activities and way of life of its members. The peasants' primary function was to cultivate the land, and their essential objective was to provide for family consumption rather than profit-making. The analytical problems are substantial. A complex hierarchy existed both within the peasantry and the enveloping rural society, based essentially upon ownership of land and levels of culture. The difficulties are compounded by the existence of a variety of agrarian systems and modes of organization of rural life. Thus patterns of landowner-ship, social relationships and even levels of culture differed, due in large part to necessary adjustments to environmental conditions, to the contrasting geogra-phy of plain, plateau and mountain, each with its characteristic soils, climate (continental, Atlantic, Mediterranean) and agriculture, its differing levels of productivity and varying population densities. Geographers divide France into over 500 natural regions, making it dangerous to write about the 'peasant' *per se*. Inevitably, economic and social change affected these distinctive communities in varying ways. To the degree to which it is practically possible, peasant life needs to be studied at the level of the individual community, but at the same time it must be remembered that even the most isolated community was part of a wider network of economic, social and political relationships.

During the nineteenth century a series of changes, in particular roads and railways and the development of a more commercial economy, transformed rural life. Closely associated with the development of the physical means of communication were major improvements in the means by which information could be transmitted – by letter post, telegraph, and through the generalization of literacy and access to books and newspapers. It was the communications revolution in all its forms which made the century one of fundamental change. The *social* space within which individuals lived was transformed. It is important to consider how they perceived this change.

Peasants had always enjoyed contacts with the world outside the village, but these had generally remained limited. Although situations had varied, and proximity to major urban centres had encouraged commercial farming, the ideal for most peasants had remained self-sufficiency, in spite of the fact that every family was obliged to sell something – labour or produce – in order to pay taxes and purchase those necessities which could not be produced locally. Normally the range of outside contacts must have been confined within a periphery of something like 25 kilometres, i.e. the distance a man could travel on foot and return home the same day. Marriage partners were selected from within this sort of narrow geographical area. Few, with the significant excep-tion of the temporary migrant, travelled beyond the nearest market town or village and if they did, contact with their place of origin tended to be lost. With the possible exception of the more prosperous and self-confident, peasants in Alsace were, for example, reluctant to visit 'large' towns like Wissembourg or Haguenau, which had populations of 11,000 and 7000 respectively in 1846. In them they encountered the 'authorities' and the well-dressed bourgeoisie, and workers who laughed at their awkwardness. There they risked being cheated by merchants and innkeepers. If one had to visit such a place it was better not to stray from the road that led from the village to the urban market place and directly home again. They felt more at home in the *bourg* or market village with no more than 3000 inhabitants, many of them peasants, and part of the rural world. Only the local rich, the notables, landowners and professional men, retained regular physical and cultural contact with the outside world. They performed the invaluable functions of intermediaries between the village community and the external – especially the official – world. For the most part, news and information was transmitted orally. According to the economist Adolphe Blanqui, writing in 1851, 'village and city represent . . . two completely opposite ways of life', their inhabitants composed of 'two different peoples living in the same land a life so different that they seem foreign to each other'.

The most obvious consequence of the communications revolution was a reduction in the isolation of rural communities and their integration into a national society through processes of commercialization, monetarization and cultural change. From around the 1840s, the intensity and range of external contacts substantially increased and more rapidly than ever before, to an extent which greatly reduced the autonomy of rural communities and increased their dependence upon the growing towns both as markets for their produce and as suppliers of equipment, consumer goods, services and ideas. The town replaced demographic pressure as the vital dynamic force, stimulating change in rural society. Paradoxically, at the same time direct urban investment in landownership, the traditional means of asserting urban hegemony over the countryside, was in marked decline. It was the marketing role of major cities like Paris and Lyon, of ports like Marseille and Le Havre, or of wine-marketing towns like Béziers, which now reinforced urban dominance over the countryside.

The chronology and intensity of change inevitably varied considerably from place to place. Those areas of valley and plain which were privileged in terms of the quality of their communications even before the road and railway building of the nineteenth century, continued in most cases to be favoured by innovation, while, primarily as a consequence of physical geography, areas of plateau and mountain in the Breton peninsula, Massif Central, Alps and Pyrenees, were hardly integrated into the new socio-economic system before the period 1880–1914. Reactions to these changes were inevitably mixed. While improved access to markets initially increased the commercial opportunities of many communities, encouraged increased production and ended the fear of dearth, it also meant heightened competition, which from the late 1860s became a cause of growing anxiety. Rural society experienced a major *crise d'adaptation*. In a very real sense, the traditional rural civilization reached its apogée in the early stages of the transport revolution, in the prosperous 1860s, but this period was followed by a growing sense of crisis as agricultural prices fell and the village artisanate and rural industry declined in the face of urban–industrial competition and because of the new awareness of the inferiority of rural living standards in comparison with those in the towns. This, above all, stimulated migration by both rural notables and the poorer peasants. It had the positive effect of ending rural overpopulation and reducing misery, but together with the diffusion of urban models of behaviour gradually led to the disintegration of traditional rural social structures, and the development of more individualistic value system. Although the chronology of this process and its completeness varied according to the location of particular rural communities in relation to the axes of communication, and the relationships they enjoyed with a network of urban centres in general it could be seen to have occurred between 1840 and the First World War. This chapter will be particularly concerned with life in this period in which the balance within rural communities shifted decisively from continuity to change.

Landownership

Overall structures

Social status in the countryside very much depended upon ownership of land, the means of production and primary source of wealth. Although the precise dividing lines between the various social groups which made up a rural society are difficult to define, the extremes are clear – a small minority of non-peasant landowners owning relatively large areas of land, and a mass of impoverished agricultural labourers. In between a hierarchy of peasant farmers owned and/or tenanted varying areas of land. Although other defining factors will need to be taken into account, particularly culture, an answer to the question of who owned the land, and also how this changed over time, is crucial for an understanding both of social relationships in the countryside and of the way in which rural societies evolved.

The French Revolution had had relatively little effect on the structure of landholding (before it peasants owned 30–40 per cent of the land) and on rural social structures, although of course in many regions it did have marked long-term influences upon social relationships and politics. In most areas land was transferred from the nobility and church to those best able to pay for it, in other words to well-off bourgeois – landowners, lawyers and merchants principally – while many noble families were able to preserve their estates by means of subterfuge or simply lying low. The better-off peasants were often able to acquire more land, particularly where plots were too small (usually former ecclesiastical land), too infertile or too isolated (in the uplands rather than in the plains) to attract men concerned to earn a reasonable return on their investments. The sale of confiscated properties did not cause a substantial subdivision of property and did very little to ease the growing population pressure on the land. Zones dominated by large properties existed in the north of the Paris basin, stretching towards the Belgian frontier; between the Seine and Loire; in south-west Aquitaine; in the lower valley of the Rhône and in Bourgogne – i.e. essentially in areas of plain and rich soil. The presence of large properties was far less marked in the poorer regions (Brittany and upland areas) where soils were inferior and slopes required substantial and unproductive inputs of labour; and in those areas characterized by concentrated habitat (Champagne, Lorraine, Alsace, Dauphiné, Provence). Landholding patterns were closely conditioned by economic structures (of the past as well as the present) and also by the way soil was used. Cattle rearing, in particular, appears to have encouraged concentration, while in contrast vine cultivation allowed the subsistence of a mass of small proprietors on as little as 2 hectares in areas of high quality wine production. It should be stressed, however, that even where land was owned in relatively large units it was usually divided into a number of tenanted farms by landowners who were predominantly *rentiers*, not themselves directly interested in farming the land.

Subsequent changes in structures of landownership were slow, but the trend was clearly towards fragmentation. This is revealed by analysis of the tax statistics, with the average size of a *côte foncière*, i.e. a taxable unit of land, declining from 4.48 hectares in 1826 to 3.5 hectares in 1881, and a slow rise only after 1883 due to the combined effects of migration from the countryside and declining family size (Table 40). This was usually blamed by nineteenth-century economists upon the Napoleonic Civil Code, which required an equalization of the rights of inheritance between the children of the deceased. To some extent they were correct to make this assumption. But it should also be remembered that in many regions older inheritance customs prevailed. The new law was only fully respected in the Midi, where it coincided with the traditions of Roman law. Elsewhere there were countless local customs – in most of the north-east equal division already prevailed; in the Limousin, in much of Brittany and the Alps local custom usually gave preference to a single heir in order to limit the fragmentation of farms, although whoever took over the family farm normally also assumed the burden of providing some compensation to siblings, often through mortgaging the land.

Another major factor was the assessment of investment opportunities by landowners and tenants in particular regions. Thus in the Paris region the technical transformation of farming in the 1830s and 1840s promoted a concentration of both property-ownership and farm units as large landowners bought up medium-sized landholdings. This trend continued until the 1860–80s, by which time in most regions large landowners appear to have started selling land and taking up urban residence. This was especially the case in the south, where,

Table 40 *Number of côtes foncières*

Year	Number	Index
1835	10,893,528	100
1842	11,511,841	105
1858	13,118,723	120
1860	13,293,940*	122
1865	14,027,996	128
1871	13,820,655*	126
1880	14,269,388	130
1884	14,335,733	132

Note: * Territorial changes, *Statistique agricole*, 1882, pp. 251–301

except in areas of developing vine monoculture on the plains of Languedoc, land was a less attractive investment. Even then, the process by which land was transferred to the peasants often remained slow and limited in its effects. In the Pas-de-Calais land in the category of *grande propriété* (i.e. over 50 hectares) declined by only 0.6 per cent between the cadastral survey conducted in the first third of the century and its renewal in 1911; *medium* property (10–40 hectares) declined by 6 per cent, while *petit* (under 10 hectares) increased its share by 5 per cent.[1] In most areas it was the period between the agricultural census of 1852 and that of 1882 which saw the most significant changes, with a national increase in the number of proprietors of around 300,000 (which could be explained, however, entirely by statistical errors in the censuses!) and an increase in the area of land owned by many existing peasant proprietors. These gains appear to have been made mainly at the expense of medium-sized properties whose *rentier* owners were forced mainly into piecemeal sales by the growing cost of living and of production.

The agricultural inquiry of 1892 provides a detailed breakdown of the structure of landholdings, a century after the revolution (Table 41). According to the most reliable information available, that of the administration responsible for collecting the land tax, in 1884 *grandes propriétés* of over 50 hectares made up only 1 per cent of the *côtes foncières*, but these covered 35 per cent of the land area; those of 6–50 hectares covered 39 per cent, and small properties (in this case under 6 hectares) covered 26 per cent. These statistics, which conceal the ownership of a number of *côtes* by a single individual, tend to underestimate the importance of large landowners.★ Clearly, however, the continuous acquisition of land by peasants throughout the century had failed to fundamentally transform rural social structures.

Table 41   *Structure of landholdings, 1892*

Category of exploitation	Total number of exploitations (1000s)	Average area covered (hectares)	Total area (hectares)	Percentage of agricultural land
less than 1 ha	2235	0.59	1,327,300	2.4
1–10 ha	2618	4.29	11,244,700	22.7
10–40 ha	711	20.13	14,313,400	28.9
over 40 ha	139	162.21	22,393,400	46.0
Totals and average	5703	8.65	49,278,800	100

Source: *Statistique agricole*. p. 364.

★ The relationship between the number of landowners and that of *côtes* was officially established in 1851 at 0.63 but with significant regional variations.

Peasant landowners

Table 42 (which includes many non–peasant landowners) reveals that only a minority of landowning families (24.7 per cent in 1862) owned sufficient land to support an independent material existence. This might be achieved on a small intensively cultivated plot of land such as a market garden or vineyard or else upon larger areas devoted to cereals or pasture. However, the majority of peasants depended upon access to resources or opportunities for employment controlled by others. As with all general statements about rural society, these statistics conceal numerous regional variations. The proportions within each category differed from place to place with the character of the farming economy, the cost of land and population density. The proportion of peasant proprietors varied considerably. Small- and medium-sized properties were the dominant (but not exclusive) form of landholding in the east, Midi and the mountains. In an area of relatively advanced market-orientated farming such as the Soissonnais, four groups could be distinguished among the peasants at the beginning of the nineteenth century.[2] First, the class of wealthy capitalist farmers farming over 40 hectares and employing wage labourers – distinguishable from bourgeois landowners because they continued to work the land

Table 42 *Agricultural labour force by status*

| | 1862 | | 1882 | | 1882 as a percentage of 1862 |
	Number (1000s)	Percent-age	Number (1000s)	Percent-age	
Landowners	1813	24.7	2151	31.2	119
Landowners who also rented land	649	8.8	500	7.3	77
Landowners who were also sharecroppers	204	2.8	147	2.1	72
Landowners who were also labourers	1134	15.4	727	10.5	64
Total landowners	3800	51.7	3525	51.1	93
Non-landowners:					
Tenant farmers	387	5.3	468	6.8	121
Sharecroppers	202	2.7	194	2.8	96
Labourers and domestics	2965	40.3	2707	39.2	91
Total non-landowners	3554	48.3	3369	48.8	95
Total employed in agriculture	7354		6894		94

themselves. Second, those with medium-sized farms of 30–40 hectares, who, except at harvest, employed only family labour and usually had little capital to invest. Third, poor peasants owning some land but needing to supplement this by renting additional plots or hiring out their labour. Fourth, the mass of labourers, often owning their own houses and small plots of land, but essentially dependent upon employment by others. The first group, and to a markedly lesser extent the second, possessed wealth and status, a sense of personal achievement and independence. The last, in particular, was characterized by poverty, ignorance and the need to be submissive. Both it, and the third category depended on wealthier neighbours for employment and the loan of plough-teams in exchange for labour service.

The majority of peasants who did not possess enough to secure their economic independence necessarily had recourse to a multiplicity of means of making ends meet. In upland areas in the Alps and Pyrenees, where unoccupied land still existed, the clearance of marginal land on hillsides reached new heights in the 1840s. The alternatives were renting land, exploiting the resources of common lands or forests, working as an agricultural labourer, as an artisan or in rural industry, resorting to seasonal or temporary migration, typically from the uplands to assist with the harvest on the plains, or to the cities to work in such trades as building. These activities made it possible for families to survive in regions where the land was overpopulated, but only the acquisition of a plot of land promised a permanent reduction in the insecurity of life.

Prior to the expansion of the urban economy and the creation of alternative employment opportunities, land remained the essential source of status and security. By means of unremitting effort imposed on the entire family, by stinting on food, clothing and housing, families were able, with luck, to save some money with which to purchase land. This was usually acquired from other peasants in small plots, a factor which together with the subdivision caused by inheritance and the desire, particularly in the south, to gain access to varying types of soil and slope (garden, land for wheat, for olives, vines, for grazing) frequently resulted in the fragmentation of a family's landholding. Thus for 14 million *côtes* in 1880 there were in existence 140 million separate parcels of land. The process of accumulation often took many years, and this together with normal inheritance patterns meant that peasant producers were often quite old (in Pas-de-Calais on the eve of the First World War, only 25 per cent of peasant proprietors had taken over their farms before the age of 40, and over half of the men running their own farms were over 50),[3] which perhaps helps to explain peasant resistance to innovations. Moreover, land was not conceived of as capital but as a means to live.

This land hunger and the competition for the limited amount of land placed on the market pushed prices up to levels which made little economic sense in terms of the potential return on investment. Furthermore, the future of land was often mortgaged, and security of possession subject to fluctuating harvests and market prices. Indebtedness remained a major social problem. In the absence of banks willing to lend to peasants, and given the demand for credit (for example, in the Pas-de-Calais in the single year of 1851, 5 per cent of farmers are estimated to have borrowed in order to purchase land or livestock and seeds, to buy food because of personal crises such as illness or the need to pay a dowry, etc.) usurious rates of interest could be charged by the landowners, merchants and notaries and the wealthier peasants who were willing to make loans (between 4 per cent in Aube and 15 per cent in Corrèze, according to an inquiry in 1850). Many debts went unrecorded, particularly, for example, those owed by a tenant to his landlord following a poor harvest, so it is impossible to estimate accurately the total volume. A bad harvest or paradoxically a superlative crop leading to a glut and a collapse of prices were the cause of great anxiety among debtors. Their debts increased with the inability to pay interest, and with this came the threat of legal expropriation. Moreover, the success of one generation was usually partially obviated by death and the division of property among its heirs. The process of accumulation then commenced all over again.[4]

Change in the structure of landownership began slowly from the 1850s in a period marked by agricultural prosperity, the more rapid development of urban employment opportunities and of migration to the towns which eased the pressure on the land. Price depression and crises such as phylloxera from the later 1870s accelerated this movement. The long cycle of land clearance and parcellation gradually came to an end, although even in a relatively advanced area like the Pas-de-Calais, it only finally ceased around 1880 when the number of very small proprietors began to decline. By the 1890s marginal land was beginning to be abandoned in upland areas, while in the more fertile areas of the north and Paris basin and in the still overpopulated west the migration of the poorest enabled those who remained to enlarge their farms to some extent. These trends can be further illuminated by looking at the evolution of peasant landowners' incomes. Such calculations, however, are complicated by statistical uncertainties and by the heterogeneity of this particular category of the rural population. The problems are obvious in the indexes based on estimates of the real income of farmers working their own land in the various natural regions of the single department of Calvados (Table 43). Within each zone there were marked variations in the capacity of large-, medium- or small-scale peasant farmers to respond to changes in market structures and price levels. In general, the first ten to fifteen years of the Second Empire constituted a major phase of prosperity. Until the 1860s cereal cultivators benefited from rising prices. Subsequently, in more competitive international markets, and as demand for meat and dairy products grew, it was their producers who did best. Throughout, for most small peasant proprietors with less than 5–10 hectares and relatively little to sell, the essential objective remained subsistence.

Such statistics can easily give a misleading impression. Most peasant farmers were not sufficiently adept at book-keeping to distinguish gross and net income. It was the most visible indicator of prosperity – price levels – to which they responded. This response occurred, however, within market structures which from mid century underwent a rapid transformation. For as long as the price fluctuations associated with traditional subsistence crises lasted (i.e. until the

Table 43 *Real income of peasant landowners in Calvados. 1820–1909 (index)*[5]

Year	On the cereal plains	Rearing livestock in the Bessin area	In the Bocage (relatively backward agriculture)
1820	100	100	100
1828			72
1832	110		
1840	124	81	82
1846		98	
1847	161		
1850			123
1851	158		
1852		106	
1862	173	119	187
1871		92	179
1879	137		
1885		139	217
1893	99	112	
1898		130	
1905			232
1909	122	123	210

1850s), most peasant proprietors, because they were unable to produce sufficient food for the subsistence of their families on their own land, were forced at some stage in the year into the market as consumers. In consequence they tended to benefit most in years with large crops and low prices. Only the minority with substantial surpluses to sell profited from the large price rises caused by poor harvests. Subsequently, as productivity increased and consumer spending grew, peasant farmers in general were more and more involved in production for the market. In this situation it was low prices which became the cause of despair. This was even true of the mass of peasants engaged in polycultural farming who only slowly reduced their primary concern to balance production and consumption on the family farm. In the Lyonnais, for example, around 1850 a family consuming 3.5 kg of bread each day, i.e. 1300 kg a year, needed to cultivate 2.50–2.80 hectares of cereals in the uplands and 2 hectares in the plains. Within the context of polyculture and bi-annual rotation this required access to 6–7 hectares of land. By 1860, due to increased productivity, the area needed under wheat had fallen to 2 hectares in the mountains and 1.5 hectares in the plain, and by 1875 to 1.8 hectares and 1.20 hectares respectively, a reduction of 40 per cent in twenty-five years. As well as providing for the subsistence of his family, the typical peasant farmer was thus able to market more of his produce and enjoy an improved standard of living.[6]

Another feature of this period of improvement was the growing social differentiation within rural communities as those peasant-farmers most capable of responding to the expansion of urban markets and competitive pressures began to acquire a distinctive life-style and culture. At Plozévet in Finistère in the 1870s they shared in the hard physical labour but lived in larger houses, slept between sheets, had table-cloths, china plates and cutlery. Their diet was more varied and they dressed better. Frequently such families sought to denote their superior status by securing a secondary education for their sons. This provided further opportunities for upward social mobility. Without seeking to exaggerate the improvement of living standards or to deny the problems caused by the depression, it remained the case that the situation of peasant proprietors significantly improved in the second half of the century. Even the less ambitious still found that the options open to them had widened, with extended opportunities for migration, and those who remained in the countryside enjoyed the possibility of acquiring the land of those who had left.

Tenant farmers

In addition to the peasant proprietors, there were, as the statistics indicate (see p. 149), large numbers of tenant farmers – some holding land on leases of varying length in return for the payment of a fixed rent (*fermiers*), others under sharecropping contracts (*métayers*). Although these tenants in 1892 occupied only 19 and 6 per cent respectively of the total number of farm units (*exploitations*), these covered almost half the cultivated area, their average size (11.71 and 10.70 hectares respectively) being over twice that of those farm units exploited directly by their owners (4.37 hectares) (see Table 44). However, the material advantage of a larger area to cultivate was largely offset in most cases by the need to pay a rental out of their income, and also by the loss of independence which tenancy implied.

Fermage as a form of tenure was especially common in areas of large-scale property ownership in the north and elsewhere on the plains and in the river valleys rather than in the uplands. Substantial variation existed within particular regions, as for example, Table 44 shows for Calvados.[7] The decline in the importance of tenancy was due to the widespread tendency for noble and bourgeois landowners to transfer their capital out of agriculture in the last three decades of the century and the resultant growth of peasant proprietorship.

It is also important to distinguish between types of *fermier*, and most notably

Table 44 *Percentage of land occupied by tenant farmers*

Year	Plain	Bessin	Pays d'Auge	Bocage
1873	65	72	59	51
1882	56	67	52	46
1894–6	53	54	46	43

between the *grands fermiers* renting large farms on the main grain producing plains, and choosing to invest their capital in technical improvement rather than in land purchase (although as the century progressed, often acquiring some land of their own) and the mass of small tenants. The first group included large capitalist farmers in the Nord, Aisne, Pas-de-Calais and the Paris basin, who were among the most technically advanced in the country. In areas like the Brie and Beauce, close to the Paris market, a class of large-scale tenant farmers had developed from early in the eighteenth century. Frequently, the same family occupied a farm for generations and with luck and good judgement was able to prosper. By the middle of the nineteenth century their prosperity had increased their independence *vis-à-vis* the often absentee landowners and, as their education and culture improved, they were anxious to distinguish themselves from the large labour force they employed. In the 1850s it was frequently observed that farm-hands were no longer fed in the farmhouse by the farmer's wife, who had begun to adopt social graces. Living in a solid farmhouse in the middle of 50–150 hectares of good, well-drained land these *fermiers* formed a distinctive social group, estimated in 1859 by the prefect of Seine-et-Marne to include some 2350 families in his department. They, rather than the landowners, had by this date become the socially dominant group, forming part of the rural bourgeoisie rather than the peasantry.

Throughout the century, however, most *fermiers* remained small-scale farmers. They often worked inferior land and lacked the capital to invest in improved techniques. Like peasant proprietors they also were primarily concerned with providing for their families' subsistence, but were under greater pressure to sell their produce in order to pay rents. The payment of rent (estimated at 15 per cent of net revenue in 1892) drained away resources which otherwise might have been employed to improve farms. Low levels of productivity meant that making ends meet was a constant struggle. Poor harvests forced many tenants into the market place as consumers when food prices reached their highest. In periods when prices were low, the lack of stocking facilities and pressing need to pay rents forced them to sell for whatever price they could get. In 1846 in the Pas-de-Calais when prices were high, it was estimated that tenant farmers paid out in rent 20 per cent of the gross income of a hectare of wheat, but in 1849 and 1850, years of low prices, rentals accounted for 34 and 31 per cent respectively.[8]

The conditions laid down in leases varied between places and over time as general economic conditions and relationships between landowners and tenants changed. In areas which remained isolated by poor communications and in which it was difficult for the small tenant with limited commercial opportunities to raise money, part of the rental might be paid in kind – butter, eggs, cheese, poultry – or even labour. In the *bocage* of Calvados in 1851 this made up around 17 per cent of rentals, but on individual farms it might account for as much as 50 per cent.[9] Leases also generally established tenant responsibility for the maintenance of buildings and frequently stipulated that he must farm the land according to established practices and possess sufficient animals and equipment to do so. The length of leases varied. Three years was common, although in the Beauce in the 1840s *grands fermiers* enjoyed relatively long nine to twelve year tenancies, while in Calvados there were long leases for arable farms (nine years), short for pasture (one to three years). There was a widespread feeling that technical innovation was discouraged by short leases and the inadequate compensation allowed for improvements on termination.

For much of the century high rural population densities stimulated competitions for tenancies and maintained rentals at high levels. In the 1860s on the best of land in the Ile-de-France *grands fermiers* paid up to 200–240f per hectare. It was, however, the small tenants who were in the weakest negotiating position *vis-à-vis* landowners, and who because of their lower productivity paid out the larger part of their incomes. From the 1850s rising agricultural prices and higher productivity eased the burden and permitted many former tenants to purchase their own land. Then, particularly from the 1870s, the combination of migration and falling agricultural prices began to reduce the demand for land, and improve the negotiating position of tenants. This can be seen from the movement of rents in lower Normandy:[10]

1820–41	+	5 per cent
1841–88	+	149 per cent
1888–1903	−	30 per cent

In the second period rising prices and productivity made the increase in rents more bearable than it otherwise might have been. It generally took some time for rents to change in response to the movement of agricultural prices, a considerable benefit to the tenant when prices began to rise, and to the landlord when they began to fall (provided of course that the tenant was able to pay his rent). This was not always the case, and landowners were often forced from the 1870s to accept changes in the terms of leases. Even when price levels improved at the turn of the century, reduced demand for farms prevented landlords from substantially raising rents. As a result, between the 1870s and the turn of the century rentals fell by over 50 per cent in Loir-et-Cher, by 38–47 per cent in the Pas-de-Calais, by 29 per cent in lower Normandy, by 15–20 per cent in the Seine-et-Marne.[11] The effect suggested by statistics from the Calvados was to sustain a substantial (if fluctuating) increase in the real incomes of tenant farmers (Table 45).

Table 45 *Index of real incomes of fermiers in Calvados*[12]

Year	Index number	Year	Index number
1820	100	1885	236
1837	21	1892	196
1861	229	1901	324
1870	191	1905	295
1879	245		

Sharecroppers

The distinction between *fermage* and *métayage* was not always clear, especially as tenants frequently paid rents in a mixture of cash and kind. Moreover, share-cropping contracts varied enormously. In general, the landlord provided the land and usually the working capital, cattle and equipment, while the tenant provided the labour of his family and if necessary hired workers. The product of the main crop was usually divided equally between landlord and sharecropper, but there were normally additional obligations – to provide labour for the landowners, to supply poultry, dairy products, vegetables, etc. In general this was the tenure system of regions in which peasants possessed little capital and in which the returns from the land were insufficient to ensure the regular payment of a cash rent. Leases were short, often for a single year, and although families might occupy a farm for generations *métayers* often experienced considerable insecurity. They were also more closely subordinated to their landlords than were cash tenants. The system encouraged the more direct participation by landowners in the supervision of farming. Relationships between the two were often defined by local oral tradition rather than in written documents, and this made them all the easier to revise at the whim of the landowner. The annual settling of accounts with the landowner was a common occasion for dispute, made all the more likely by the illiteracy of many sharecroppers and the lack of accurate accounts. In Emile Guillaumin's account of the life of a sharecropper in the Allier (*La vie d'un simple*), Emile Bertin (born 1823) observed: 'I tried to remember at which fair I had sold animals and at what price. But nobody knew how to write figures, and it was difficult to remember everything in my head, and worse, to count up the figures and work out the exact amount remaining as a profit.'

Nationally 6 per cent of all farms were occupied by sharecroppers in 1892. These farms had an average size of 10.70 hectares and made up 11 per cent of the agricultural land. However, *métayage* was characteristic of particular regions – parts of central France, of the south-west and of the Midi – where it assumed a far greater importance. In areas of vine cultivation in the Lyonnais and Beaujolais it was known as *vigneronnage*. In these areas the landlords owned the land, animals, the winepress and vats, and were responsible for maintaining buildings and paying the land tax. The *vigneron* supplied the labour, carts and farming equipment. He was required to *cultiver en bon père de famille*, that is according to the established practice of the area. Although theoretically left with half the crop, the *vigneron* was dependent upon quick sales to local wine merchants or his landlord because he lacked expensive stocking facilities, and was thus unable to speculate on price movements.

The owners of *métairies* varied from noble families like the Villèle, who in 1847 had thirteen sharecroppers farming 400 hectares in the Lauraguais, to small-town bourgeois with two or three farms. *Métayage* brought not only income but a sense of self-importance, of being the *maître*. It enshrined a particular conception of landownership and an authoritarian paternalism in social relations to which, at least before migration allowed the possibility of escape, peasants had little choice but to submit. Throughout the first half of the nineteenth century and for as long as competition for farms continued, landlords were able to preserve their dominant position. Emile Bertin remembered being turned out of a farm which his family had occupied for over 100 years. As they left with an ox-cart containing their meagre possessions, his father, noticing their former landlord, raised his cap and said, *Bonsoir, notre monsieur*. It was necessary for the poor to be prudent, whatever the circumstances. Conditions were, in fact, particularly harsh in the Allier, where according to the prevailing form of *colonage partiaire*, an agent (*fermier-général*) was frequently interposed between the landowner and sharecropper. He extracted his own share of farm incomes and reduced tenants to a state of utter misery. Not surprisingly, tension between sharecroppers and their *maîtres* was particularly great in this region (Allier, Cher, Indre and part of Côte-d'Or). In 1849, sharecroppers and labourers briefly departed from their usual submissive behaviour and voted for the left, and again at the end of the century this area was a centre of agricultural trades unionism.

The system did offer some advantages to the sharecropper. After a poor harvest his rental declined proportionately, unlike that of the *fermier* who paid a fixed sum. Following a very good harvest the sharecropper, again paying his rent in kind, suffered less from the effects of falling prices. It was nevertheless increasingly criticized. Until the last third of the century landlords enjoyed secure and rising incomes and had little incentive to innovate. Sharecroppers, on the other hand, were left with little capital or incentive to invest. They were generally concerned only with making ends meet from day to day. Regional agricultural societies recommended a change to *fermage*, but landowners were slow to follow this advice. The supporters of the system stressed the moral value of the association between landowner and tenant and the practical value of that between capital and labour, but it was too exploitative for a genuine collaboration to occur, regardless of the efforts of some enlightened landowners.

The decline of sharecropping, particularly from the 1870s, occurred as migration reduced competition for contracts and landowners were forced to accept a reduced share of the produce. The growing opportunities for commercialization increased the desire for cash incomes and stimulated the introduction of *fermage*. While some of those peasants who remained were able to improve their position as tenants, others were able to purchase farms as landlord disinvestment occurred. These new owners, having used their savings to purchase land, then had little to invest in technical improvement, a factor helping to explain the continued relative backwardness of much of southern agriculture.

Agricultural labourers

This was a social group characterized above all by poverty and its dependence upon others for the means of earning a living. As was the case with our other categories of peasant, however, it was far from homogeneous. Some account will have to be taken of the variety of conditions of employment and of living conditions. It is also important to remember that the conditions of the agricultural labourer was often not a permanent one. Many hired out their labour when young, and saved or borrowed in order to purchase or rent land. Others would eventually inherit family farms. Indicative of this was the fact, recorded in the Cher in 1896, that while 93.3 per cent of the agricultural labour force under 25 were labourers, for the age-group 35–55 the proportion fell to 36.3 per cent.[13] This change of status was most likely in those regions dominated by small-scale farming. In the areas of large-scale commercial farming the larger scale and cost of farms mean that there was less likelihood of ever acquiring land, although even on the rich plains of the Paris basin this was not unusual – in the Beauce, for example, in 1851, 20 per cent of labourers owned some property.[14]

A rough hierarchy can be identified among agricultural labourers. There were families with some land and perhaps a house of their own, and who because of this enjoyed greater material security and social independence. In the Brie area of Seine-et-Marne few labourers entirely lacked property. In addition they hired themselves out as shepherds or ploughmen, and in winter as woodcutters or workers in the sugar distilleries. In the Pas-de-Calais this group – called locally *ménagers* and *journaliers-propriétaires* by the census enumerators – in ordinary years enjoyed 'a decent material existence', and even after a poor harvest they suffered less than the landless. Another category was made up of *domestiques* or farm servants hired by the year, and usually for the performance of specialized tasks. They were fed and lodged by the employer and were therefore usually unmarried and completely dependent upon him. Day labourers (*journaliers*) were employed primarily for the harvest and threshing and experienced the greatest insecurity. During these periods of peak demand many seasonal workers were also employed on the larger farms, including peasants from other regions and, prior to the development of modern factory industry, the workers were normally employed in rural manufacture, together with women and children from poor households. Children were able to find employment looking after animals or doing domestic chores from the age of 7 or 8 or even earlier.

It is difficult to accurately estimate the number of agricultural labourers because of changing and inaccurate classification by census enumerators. Thus, although the categories used appear to allow comparison between the censuses of 1852 and 1882, and this suggests a substantial decline of 1.3 million in the number of agricultural labourers (about one-third of the total in 1852, of whom 1 million appear to have left agriculture altogether, while the others became independent peasant proprietors), the decline could well have been grossly exaggerated due to an overestimation of the number of proprietors. On safer ground, according to the 1862 agricultural inquiry there were 2,975,250 agricultural labourers (including those who owned some land), a figure which represented about one-half of the active agricultural labour force. By 1892 the figure had fallen to 2,469,450. According to another count, in 1892 there were 3,420,795 wage-earners in agriculture, of whom 1,832,714 were *domestiques* (including 461,910 servants) and 1,210,081 day labourers, of whom around half owned land. An inquiry in 1906 revealed that 1.3 million farms employed up to five labourers; 45,000 between six and 50; and an exceptional 250 (all in the north) had over 150 workers. There must have been considerable differences in work and social relationships between the large farm with its disciplined work-force and rather distant employer and those farms operated by working peasant-farmers, whose life-styles were similar to those of their labourers and who often only hired workers during the years when their own children were too young to perform heavy physical labour, or during such busy periods as the harvest. Both types of farm, nevertheless, expected hard and unremitting work from those they took on.

As always these national statistics conceal a host of local and regional varia-tions, influenced by such factors as the size of local farms and the density of population. In northern France and the Paris basin there were zones of old-established commercial farming with a large labour force of permanently land-less people almost entirely at the service of capitalist farmers. On the rich cereal plains of the Beauce at mid century the typical large farm of over 50 hectares employed about twelve *domestiques* on a permanent basis, and day labourers whenever they were needed. Some two out of three of the active agricultural population were labourers. Agriculture in the nearby Brie was described as being carried on 'in general on large farms, usually isolated in the centre of 50–100 hectares of land, with some groups of little cottages sheltering the population, entirely agricultural, which hires its labour to the large farmers'. Most of these labourers had little plots of their own, but this did not alter their fundamental social role. The residents of larger communities like that of La Ferté-Gauche also included a large proportion of labourers – in 1848 besides 435 peasant farmers there were 1123 labourers.[15] Similar situations existed in Languedoc–Roussillon in the second half of the century as large-scale vine cultivation developed. Vineyards of over 40 hectares occupied more than 30 per cent of the area under vines by 1892. 56 per cent of the peasantry in the four departments of the Midi were agricultural labourers by this time – substantially above the national average. Their conditions were, however, more diverse than those of labourers in the north. Of some 163,800 individuals, 51,000 were *domestiques* living on the farms, the remaining 120,000 (of whom about 62,780 owned some land) lived in villages and enjoyed the greater independence allowed by life in a larger, socially more diverse, community.[16]

In most regions social structures were less polarized because of the impor-tance of small-scale farming, the numerical significance of peasant proprietors, and the realistic assumption by many labourers that one day they would own or tenant a farm. In the Limousin in 1851, for example, only 8.75 per cent of the active male agricultural labour force were reported to be labourers in the Corrèze; 25.11 per cent in the Creuse and 19.9 per cent in the Haute-Vienne.[17] However, as population densities grew in most regions, prior to the develop-ment of mass migration in the 1850s, more and more peasants came to depend upon hiring out their labour which tended to depress wage levels and reinforce the dependence of labourers upon those who provided them with work. There was a sufficient, and often an excessively large labour force to meet the needs of agriculture. Underemployment was the norm and labourers were frequently reduced to dependence upon charity. In the following decades, in contrast, complaints multiplied about the onset of a shortage of labour which forced farmers to pay higher wages in order to attract and keep labourers. These were no doubt exaggerated, but it does appear to have been the case that the labour supply situation was becoming less overwhelmingly favourable to farmers due to the dual effects of migration and withdrawal from the labour market by those former labourers who were able to acquire land, together with an increasing need for labour because of land-clearance and more intensive cultivation. Thus, in Calvados between 1852 and 1862 at a time when the number of male agricultural labourers had declined by around 9000 (15 per cent) it was estimated that an additional 2000 men (working 300 days a year) were required.[18] Some farmers were more fortunate. In areas in which vine cultivation was spreading like those around Béziers (Hérault) and Narbonne (Aude) growing labour needs were met by the movement of labour from the declining textile industry, and by migration from the mountains of the Ariège, Tarn and Aveyron and, from the 1880s from Spain and Italy.

The actual evolution of wages tends to confirm that the labour market was undergoing significant change. The assessment of wage levels is complicated by the existence of a variety of modes of payment. Frequently payment was made at least partly in kind. This offered the considerable advantage to the farmer of avoiding the disposal of scarce monetary resources. It also, to some extent, protected labourers against massive price rises during subsistence crises. However, this declined in importance with the disappearance of dearth, as the volume of money in circulation grew, as the value of goods for sale increased, and when workers began to demand cash to spend. Even then, however, many workers continued to be fed on the farm – 34 per cent of them in the Pas-de-Calais in 1913.[19] As far as the actual level of wages went, there were variations according to the category of worker, between regions (according to demographic structures, economic conditions, local living standards), between seasons (wages increased during harvest) and years (depending upon the harvest).

The basic determinant of wages was of course the supply of and demand for labour. The general pattern (revealed in Table 46) appears to have been for a significant increase during the First Empire, due to the competing manpower needs of the army, followed by a decline of up to 25 per cent during the restoration, stagnation during the July Monarchy and then a marked rise during the prosperous years of the Second Empire, which slowed subsequently and even declined in some areas in the later 1870s and 1880s, due to the agricultural price depression. In the second half of the century wage levels for female workers tended to increase more rapidly than those for men, partly making up the gulf between the two.

Var	Male	Female
before 1848	1f50–1f75	0f50–0f60
1860	2f25–3f	0f75–1f25

Table 46 *Evolution of nominal wages of day labourers*[20]

Oise	Fed on farm	Unfed	Calvados			
1820–30	0f60		1830–4	1f40	1860	2f06
1830–40	0f75		1835–40	1f50	1861–6	2f10–2f20
1840–60	1f	2f	1841–2	1f60	1867	2f20
1860–75	1f80	2f80	1843–45	1f62	1868	2f33
1875–1900	2f10	3f50	1849–54	1f40	1869	2f40
			1855	1f62	1882	2f60
			1856	1f72	1892	2f36
			1858	1f83	1907	2f67
			1859	1f98	1910	2f82

Corrèze	Fed on farm	Unfed
1852	0f66	1f20
1862	0f98	1f66
1882	1f10	1f81

In general wages tended to be highest where industry made competing demands for labour and in areas of intensive cultivation. Labourers in the Oise benefited from proximity to Paris, those in the Calvados and Var from the development of dairy farming and vineyards respectively. In the Roussillon in the period 1852–62 wages rose by 58 per cent in the vineyards but only by 10 per cent in upland areas.[21] In contrast in the Pas-de-Calais industrial development was partly counter-balanced by the constant influx of Belgian migrants, while in Corrèze unfavourable demographic conditions combined with lack of economic dynamism.

The labourers' negotiating position improved. They were less docile, and expected higher wages and better treatment or else moved on, to another farm or increasingly to the towns which seemed to promise escape from servitude. This position nevertheless remained weak. In many regions, and most notably in Brittany, the decline in the size of the labour force was slow to occur; in the richer areas an effort was made to maximize labour productivity through closer supervison, the introduction of piece-rate payment for such tasks as hoeing and harvesting, and better hand tools and machinery. According to a reply to the 1866 agricultural inquiry from the Soissonnais, reaping machines were not often used, but as long as they were present 'on the farm, in a shed, they make it obvious to the workers that we could do without them'. In addition, to retain skilled workers large farmers increased wage differentials provided allotments and tied cottages at low rents and rewarded fidelity with prizes presented at the agricultural shows. This does not seem to have done much to diminish the irritation of large landowners and farmers who had grown used to a constant supply of apparently devoted labourers waiting deferentially in the market place on hiring days and competing to work for them. In the new situation, both labour discipline and social deference were threatened. They looked back sentimentally to the days when, as the Prefect of Seine-et-Marne wrote, 'the workers only moved according to the will of the rich farmers who employed them'. Their ideal remained that of an organic community, a patriarchal society, a natural order in which everyone knew his place, when in practice paternalistic master–man relationships were being transformed into those of employer and employee more characteristic of a capitalist society.

If the living standards of agricultural labourers remained low in comparison with those of other groups throughout the century this was especially so before mass migration affected labour supply. Even though the labourer engaged in hard physical labour throughout the day-light hours, he was rarely able to escape from poverty and privation, and the constant threat of unemployment due to bad weather or illness. A. de Bourgoing, Prefect of the Nièvre, wrote of this tragic class in 1844 that,

> if tomorrow snow covers the ground, the week will be without a wage. By what miracle will these people without work or savings survive? We can tell you: after having made, at home, the necessary repairs to their tools, these people . . . will pass their days in their beds, squeezed closely together in order to keep warm and eat less. They will voluntarily weaken themselves in order to be able to refuse food to their bodies which do not appear to merit any, since they have remained inactive.

While 'good' workers enjoyed relative security of employment others frequently experienced unemployment, and were likely to suffer from undernourishment which reduced their capacity for work and led to their being denounced for laziness. Obviously living conditions depended a great deal upon family circumstances. Unmarried workers were usually in a much easier situation than those with families, particularly where young children were unable to earn their keep. In the Dijon area in 1848 the annual wage of a labourer would have been no more than 364f. A family of five required at least 708f in order to subsist.[22] It was essential, therefore, that as many members of the family as possible found whatever work was available, and that expenditure be kept to an absolute minimum. Wine and meat were regarded as luxuries. In 1851 in the Pas-de-Calais 64 per cent of agricultural labourers were reported to be in a state of absolute deprivation at their deaths, leaving nothing to their heirs; the fortunate 36 per cent left, on average, property worth 757f made up of a small plot of land and a cottage, tools, a pig or a cow, furniture and clothing.[23] A great deal depended upon local conditions. Within the single department of Loiret, the poorest in 1848 were the day labourers and woodcutters in the Sologne, an area of forest and marsh. They lived in squalor, dressed in rags and ate rye bread and vegetables. In the vine growing valleys of the department or on the cereal plains of the Beauce the worst extremes of misery were usually avoided, but everywhere conditions could deteriorate markedly following a poor harvest when the price of basic foodstuffs rose. The effects of this can be gauged from an index of the cost of living of agricultural labourers in Loir-et-Cher during the long mid century crisis (Table 47).[24] In 1846 and 1847, and again in 1854, at the precise

Table 47   *Cost of living of agricultural labourers, Loir-et-Cher*

1843	100	1849	86
1844	99	1850	86
1845	97	1851	83
1846	112	1852	90
1847	135	1853	98
1848	90	1854	125

moment when prices increased, the amount of work available declined. In such circumstances for many there was often no alternative to begging. This remained endemic in most regions throughout the first half of the century. In Ille-et-Vilaine in 1847 some 90,000 people (16 per cent of the total population) were claimed to be destitute, with some 30,000 forced on to the streets by the inadequacies of public and private charity. Only as it grew less common did begging become a matter of shame.

The gap between industrial and agricultural wages narrowed during the Second Empire, but then widened again at precisely the time when rural populations were becoming better informed about urban life.[25] Unemployment and underemployment, if less likely, remained constant threats due to the decline in opportunities for supplementary employment in rural industry, the elimination of rights of usage on common and private land, and a tendency during the depression for non-essential farm work to be reduced. Even so, by reducing the supply of labour, migration did result in an increase in the employment of those who remained – in the Pas-de-Calais from around 263 days' work per annum in 1852 (relatively high) to 304 in 1913.[26] The essential problem remained that of winter employment when such tasks as hedging, ditching and threshing did not supply sufficient work and even the wages of those who remained in employment were reduced. Harvest work when wages were high and the whole family might find employment and put aside a reserve for the winter, was of crucial importance to a family's budget. Thus, and in spite of improvements in their living conditions, labourers remained desperately poor. In the Pas-de-Calais in 1878, 45 per cent of those who died left something to their heirs, but the evidence suggests that only 5 per cent (leaving goods worth over 2000f) could be said to have lived with any degree of comfort or security.[27] The capacity for hard work was regarded by many as their only virtue – by this they were judged. There were, however, clear signs of a desire for something more in life. There had probably always been disputes over wages, although these had been restrained by adherence to customary levels of payment and by the weak negotiating position of hired labour. The length of the working day had also been a matter of concern, particularly for those labourers who had their own plots of land to cultivate. In spite of this, labourers do not appear to have had a very clear consciousness of their own distinctive interests and this was especially true in areas with small farms in which labourers might hope to become farmers themselves. Social tensions were more apparent on the cereal-growing plains, particularly in periods when family budgets were under pressure from high food prices (and large-scale farmers were making substantial profits), or when efforts were made to reduce wages and increase productivity during the depressed years of the 1870s and 1880s. The sense of dependence, however, continued to restrain the open expression of grievances.

Rural industry

For most of the century agriculture and industry were closely integrated. Artisans like blacksmiths, millers, potters, wheelwrights, masons, shoemakers, tailors, etc., were present everywhere, meeting the day-to-day needs of rural communities. Large-scale manufacture, particularly of textiles, developed in regions with dense underemployed populations, attracted by the prospect of cheap and docile labour. In the Aube hosiery industry in 1848 urban workers were paid 1f50 per day, rural 1f[28] – high quality goods being produced in Troyes, lower quality products by part-time rural stocking makers mainly in the poor agricultural areas of lower Champagne. In Picardy the cotton industry alone employed some 25,000 workers within a radius of 50 km of Saint-Quentin; in the *bocage* areas of the departments of Manche, Orne, Calvados and Mayenne, 28,500 workers operated 12,000 looms producing cotton cloth in the late 1840s, while a further 19,000 worked on linen and flax; in the Rhône, Ardèche and Gard silk was produced by 17,000 workers in 1860 and 13,000 even in 1912.[29] Similar structures long prevailed in the metal-working trades in such diverse areas as the Châtillonnais, Ardennes and Haute-Marne; in the production of cutlery around Thiers; in watchmaking in the mountains of the Doubs during the long winters; and in mining and metallurgy in the Pyrenean foothills of the Ariège. Improved communications, market integration and the development of factory production were to promote the eventual de-industrialization of the countryside in the second half of the nineteenth century. This occurred in two phases – the first and most intense during the 1850s and 1860s, the second in the 1880s. Those who were deprived of their incomes from industry either found full-time employment in the agriculture of the more dynamic regions, in which labour needs were growing, or else migrated to the towns.

Social mobility

The possibilities for social mobility within rural communities were determined primarily by access to land. This was a scarce resource whose possession offered both greater material security and enhanced social status. The opportunities to acquire land were clearly determined by the willingness of its possessors to sell, and by the possession by potential purchasers of the means of payment either through saving or borrowing. Within a competitive land market the ability of peasants to acquire land was greater in regions distant from major urban markets in which competition from non-peasant investors was less likely.

Frequently the creation of a viable *exploitation* was the work of generations. Particular families through a combination of birth control, marriage strategy and sheer good luck, managed to avoid excessive division of their inheritance over two or three generations. Hard physical labour, combined perhaps with small scale trading or money-lending allowed them to accumulate plots of land. In the Pas-de-Calais the opportunities for social promotion appear to have been most substantial during the period of expanding markets and high prices (1851–72), after which they declined, to increase only slowly between 1891 and 1911. Between 1851 and 1911, 35 per cent of agricultural labourers are calculated to have improved their situation, 56 per cent of them within agriculture by becoming farmers, the others by finding more secure and better rewarded employment as gardeners, road workers, etc.

The ambitions of most peasants were determined by their circumstances and socialization. The opportunities for most small peasant proprietors, tenant farmers and labourers were restricted by low incomes which prevented them from acquiring land and if they left the countryside by a lack of the skills which might have secured well-paid urban employment. Social mobility became easier once a family had acquired some resources, but it remained difficult. Thus among a sample of *cultivateurs* in the Pas-de-Calais, between 1851 and 1911, 79 per cent maintained their existing place within the social hierarchy, 10 per cent improved their situation, but 11 per cent experienced some decline. Those who were better-off to begin with, were more likely to be able to improve their situations.[30] For the younger generation, parental income and ambition were the vital determinants of future aspirations. The older generation, which continued to work the land, remained peasants, but if they could afford to, they might send their sons to secondary school, better fitting them for the urban employment opportunities which increasingly provided the major avenues for geographical and social mobility.

The family

Like most other people peasants were first and foremost members of their family of origin, and of the family they had helped to create through marriage. The family was 'The basic social unit, of production and exchange, of holding of land and portable property, of ceremonial activity, and of relations in a wider social order.'[31] Within most families socialization processes together with paternal control of scarce resources helped to maintain the strict control of father over children, and of the older children over the younger. Individuals were not allowed to lose sight of the essential objectives of providing sustenance for the family, acquiring control over land and increasing status within the community. They developed a strong sense of familial solidarity (not always free of tension). In a harsh and insecure world reciprocal help and co-operation appeared to be essential.

Within each family a division of labour was organized in order to achieve a correspondance between the labour it could provide and the resources available. This was largely determined by communal norms, but the size, age and sexual structure of particular families was also crucial. Adaptation over time was essential. There were difficult periods within every family's life-cycle. When children were too young or grandparents too old it might become necessary even for small-scale farmers to hire labour, or for tenants to take on a smaller farm. There was also a clear sexual division of labour. Ploughing, sowing, harvesting and reaping with the heavy scythe, mucking out the stables, cutting down trees (requiring considerable physical effort) were all normally men's work, while housework (including such heavy tasks as drawing water from a well or stream) and care of children, together with a host of tasks around the farmyard, such as milking, butter- and cheese-making, and care of poultry, fell to the women. The ideal *paysanne* needed to be robust rather than beautiful. At peak periods of labour need, most notably at harvest, men and women, young and old, all shared in the heavier tasks. The peasants depicted in Millet's pictures, *Les deux bêcheurs*, *L'homme et la houe* and *La fin de la journée* appear almost dead from fatigue. The poorer the family was, the earlier its children tended to be set to work. Even very young children could be employed to look after livestock or their younger siblings. Where the family farm did not provide enough work to employ the entire family or resources to feed them, then alternative forms of employment had to be found for at least some of its members – as hired labourers, in rural industry or through migration. Where, in their early teens, children were sent to work and to live outside the home this must often have weakened the emotional bonds between them and the rest of the family.

Household structures were determined by economic and technical needs, and by cultural factors (in particular inheritance). Nationally at any one time there was a large majority of nuclear (two generation) families, but there was always a significant minority of extended (three generation) families. The existence of such extended families obviously depended upon mortality and fertility rates. The quality of life within them depended a great deal upon whether or not the older generation remained capable of contributing to the economic life of the family, and upon the locus of decision-making. Where a young couple had moved in with parents (usually the groom's) the need for a division of roles between his mother and wife was a frequent cause of strife. Where local inheritance custom favoured a single heir, and the size of the holding provided sufficient work, unmarried siblings might also remain within the family home. At its most extreme, in a limited number of cases in the Bourbonnais and Limousin, until the last third of the century, extended families made up of parents plus a number of married children with their families, continued to hold large farms. Although the practical significance of kinship bonds varied between regions, in general recognition of obligations was restricted to siblings and to first cousins, those most likely to provide reciprocal aid in case of crisis.

How did the division of responsibilities within the family affect human relationships? The evidence of nineteenth-century folklorists appears to reveal considerable prejudice against women. In the Corrèze, or example, they always walked some distance behind the men. In the Manche, in Berry and Maine the men employed the familiar *tu* form in addressing their wives and children, while they used the more respectful *vous* to him. It seems also that outside marriage women enjoyed little status, the unmarried being treated as little better than servants, even by their own families. To what extent, however, were these bourgeois intellectuals led astray by judgements based upon norms typical of urban middle-class society? The problem is to determine how peasants themselves perceived of familial relationships.

Without doubt the contribution made by the wife to the family economy was of vital importance, her role complementing that of the man, and her dominance of the domestic sphere unchallenged. It seems probable also that inequality between the sexes was more apparent outside the household than within. Certainly peasant proverbs, particularly those of northern France, suggest that the extent of female subordination has often been exaggerated, and that customs, such as that which required women to stand to serve meals to their menfolk might be seen as part of the division of labour. Even so, we should not entirely discount the mass of evidence which suggests that women were regarded and treated as physically and intellectually inferior to men.

Similarly, authoritarian paternal control over children remained a reality, relaxed only among the poorest, whose children were forced to find employment away from home, and more widely as the responsibility for socialization was partly assumed by the schools, and as migration by the younger generations became more common. Otherwise their upbringing taught children to accept subordination, often until the moment when, on the death of their father, they inherited a share in the family's land. Control over inheritance was one of the means by which familial solidarity could be maintained. The forms of inheritance were determined by law, custom and family strategy.

In many regions – especially in the south – in spite of the Napoleonic Code, inheritance customs were preserved which favoured one heir (usually, but not always, the eldest) over his siblings and so helped to preserve the viability of a family's farm. The favoured heir might – if the family had enough land – be permitted to marry and to associate himself in a subordinate manner with his father during the latter's lifetime. When he ultimately assumed ownership it was likely that he would be burdened by the need to compensate siblings. Particular problems then ensued where these were unable to find alternative employment (especially in upland areas like the Lozère, Cantal or Aveyron) and where they were in consequence unable to establish independent households of their own. Unmarried siblings might, therefore, continue to work for the favoured brother on the family farm. In such situations celibacy rates were relatively high.

Almost inevitably this control of the access to family resources by a father and then by a favoured son which determined the marriageability of siblings often promoted bitter internal rivalry. Disputes were also likely when fathers became physically unable to work. In such situations agreements were commonly reached which allowed the younger generation use of the land in return for a promise to provide for their parents. The maintenance of unproductive dependants frequently caused tension. Only migration and a falling birth rate would reduce these strains implicit in the inheritance process by easing pressure on scarce land resources.

For as long as high rural population densities were maintained, marriage remained a matter of vital interest both to the families of the bride and groom and to the wider community. This was because it affected the distribution of the land, the vital scarce resource. The seriousness of the transaction was exemplified by the dowry, the subject of a contract legalized by a notary. This represented a compensation, both to the bride for the loss of her rights to the property of her family of origin, and to her new family for the additional claims made upon its resources. Its disappearance in the closing decades of the century was indicative of a major change in attitudes, brought about in large part by the easing of population pressure on resources and increased geographical mobility which reduced individual dependence upon familial resources and allowed greater freedom in the selection of marriage partners.

Marriage established an alliance between two families. It was accompanied by ceremonies which announced this and which also provided an occasion for recognizing obligations and reaffirming wider bonds of friendship, as well as simply having a good time. People who normally lived quite frugally sang, danced, ate and drank to excess. Families were frequently impoverished by the cost of weddings. Subsequently they would be faced with the problem of reciprocating in the exchange of gifts. For all these reasons it was important to the entire household that its members should not marry 'beneath themselves'. This would not only waste its investment, but demean the status of the family and affect the prospects of as yet unmarried members. The choice of partners was thus too serious to be left entirely to the whims of young people. In Eugène Le Roy's novel, *Le Moulin de Frau*, the son, Yrieix, who wanted to marry a girl without a dowry was warned that 'For someone who would himself not have a great deal, to take a girl with nothing meant misery when children came. In life people cannot always follow their own desires.' Inevitably the young, in considering marriage partners, were conditioned by family interests and by the normal pattern of behaviour in the community. The *Creusois* mason–peasant Martin Nadaud accepted the arrangement made by his parents that he should marry a girl he had never met but who would bring into the family a dowry of 3000f, payable in 400f instalments, together with furniture, linen, six sheep and their lambs. In the more or less deliberate determination of a marriage strategy, family attitudes were shaped by the amount of property possessed, and by the number and sex of children. Its property needed to be used so as to establish the best possible conditions for the younger generation. Even when the families involved were poor and propertyless it was still important to choose carefully. Haunted as such people were by the prospect of destitution, it was vital to find a partner who was physically fit and capable of hard work.

In general, then, a bride was selected from a family which was close to that of the groom's both socially and geographically. Geographical endogamy was especially common in the isolated communities of Brittany, the Massif Central, Alps and Pyrenees. In the canton of Le Bleymard (Lozère), for example, in the decade 1811–20 nearly one-third of marriages united couples living less than 1 kilometre apart. Very few had been separated by more than 20 kilometres. This pattern had not substantially altered by the 1890s.[32] When girls brought land as part of their dowry it was important that this should be nearby, although to some extent the church's ban on consanguinous marriage (especially between relatives to the fourth degree) ensured that young people had to look outside their villages to find an unrelated spouse. On the plains the zone within which regular social contacts existed and from which marriage partners were selected was somewhat wider. Taking a sample of twenty-five cantons in the Pas-de-Calais in 1851, 9 per cent of marriage partners came from the same commune, 41 from the same canton, 22 from the same *arrondissement*, 15 from the same department, and only 13 per cent from outside it.[33] It appears as if in general young people made their own choice of a marriage partner, but that this generally had to meet with family approval. If families exerted pressure upon their members to adopt particular forms of behaviour, this was in large part because the reputation of the family depended upon conforming to established communal norms, and upon this reputation depended its integration within a network of economic and social relationships.

Communities

Structures

Most of the rural population in the first part of the century continued to live in small and relatively isolated 'face-to-face' communities, each within its own particular physical environment and marked by cultural peculiarities. They were socialized within these communities. This isolation, and the dependence upon neighbours it implied, moreover, created a very strong sense of local identity. Although relationships within the community were clearly influenced by differences in wealth, in the degree of control over scarce resources and in status, social tensions were normally muted by a sense of mutual dependence, by the solidarities of age and sex and of profession. For as long as their isolation survived, rural communities had complex socio-professional structures. Besides peasants, the inhabitants of the larger centres (the market *bourgs* and small towns) included landowners, officials and members of the liberal professions. These were the representatives of social groups with a national consciousness and culture, whose wealth and behaviour were of considerable significance to the community, who frequently represented its interests in the external world, but who, because they were so firmly situated in this other world, were not entirely part of the local community. Every community also had its artisans -- blacksmiths, carpenters, masons, shoemakers, *sabotiers*, weavers, tailors, millers, etc., many of whom worked on the land for at least part of the year. These two groups – peasants and artisans – had a great deal in common. They occupied the same geographical space and participated in the same processes of social interaction. Their living conditions were similar. They suffered from a similarly restricted range of marital opportunities. They lived in the same educational, linguistic and cultural universe. They had access to limited opportunities for social advancement and geographical mobility. In a very real sense they constituted a community which included most, although usually not all, the local residents, and which in spite of economic and status divisions possessed a sense of identity sufficient to distinguish its members from those of other communities. Suspicion of outsiders was constant. These might seek a share in the community's scarce resources through the purchase of land or through a marriage which would additionally deprive a member of the community of a suitable partner. The poor among them were likely to beg without any intention of ever reciprocating. Strong local loyalties often led to quarrels between the youths of neighbouring villages, which further reinforced internal cohesion.

Although experiencing a more or less continuous process of change due to internal demographic pressures and also increasingly because of closer relationships with the external (urban) world due to the development of state centralization, education and commerce, for most of the century rural communities managed to preserve their vitality. Generalization is, however, difficult. The chronology and characteristics of change varied with contrasting physical environments and differences in initial social structures. Geographically the differences were as marked as those between the northern plains and the plateaux and uplands of the Massif Central or alpine foothills. Climatically, environments varied between the temperate north, the continental interior, and the Mediterranean south. All these factors affected life-style, habitat structures, economic activity and social relationships. The characteristics of social intercourse were to an important degree defined by their intensity. Habitat structures were crucial determinants of this.

At the risk of oversimplification, two basic types of settlement structure can be identified. On the plains of the Paris basin, of the north and east (areas of open field), of the Garonne basin, Rhône valley and the Mediterranean coastlands, populations usually lived in concentrated settlements, relatively open to the external world, although significant variations occurred within these regions, as in the Ile-de-France between the concentrated *habitat* typical to the north of Paris and the more dispersed structures in the Hurepoix and Brie. At its most extreme in lower Languedoc centuries old defence needs had been one cause of the concentration of population in large 'urbanized' villages (with 1500–5000 inhabitants), with their buildings crowded together and frequent occasions for meeting. In the north communal solidarity was maintained by the collective restraints of the open field systems which survived in spite of the Constituent

Assembly's proclamation of individual freedom. This proclamation and the law of 10 June 1793 authorizing the subdivision of common land were only gradually applied. With similar sociological effects, if in very different contexts, in the south and upland areas communal possession of substantial areas of land suitable for pasture and forests or the need for collective action to preserve earth walls and terracing, helped to preserve a sense of shared interests, particularly where these rights, vital to the survival of the traditional economy, were threatened.

In sharp contrast to these areas of concentrated habitat were those with dispersed populations – reflecting in part the gradual expansion of population into zones with inferior soils – in the *bocage* areas of the west and the Massif Central with their enclosed fields and populations dispersed in farms and hamlets, and isolated by a network of hedges and country lanes. Such dispersal (particularly in upland areas), tended to reduce the occasions for meeting and for collective activity, and to minimize the sense of shared interest within the population of an area, while maximizing that of the family or of the inhabitants of particular hamlets. In 1872 over half of the rural population lived in such dispersed settlements. Their isolation should not be exaggerated, however. There were occasions on which wider gatherings were essential; for work on large farms, for reciprocal aid during harvest, at the mills or forge, and most notably in the market place and at church. These provided focal points for the inhabitants of otherwise isolated farms and hamlets and, in the case of the church, reasons for processions and pilgrimages which were the open expression of a collective solidarity based upon the parish.

Interrelationships

It was within the bounds of the concentrated village, or the parish, that norms of behaviour were defined. In most small communities cohesion and order were maintained through informal social controls – gossip, criticism, ostracism, insult and ridicule – and if necessary by a variety of sanctions. Everyone was known to everyone else. Families were concerned to preserve a good reputation, to gain respect within the community and also to maintain the system of interdependency (for work, charity, etc.) upon which most to some degree depended. Family and community opinion combined to induce conformity to established norms of behaviour and to limit transgressions. Individual dissidents tended to be viewed as a challenge to the stability of the entire social group. Public opinion was formulated through various mechanisms. The church, in the person of its parish clergy, was one of the more important. It provided occasions for the affirmation of the community's existence and identity. In addition to *fêtes* held in honour of the village's patron saint, there was an annual cycle linked to major events in the religious calendar, including carnival in the week preceding Lent (and especially the three days leading up to Shrove Tuesday (*Mardi Gras*)), Easter Monday, the feast days of Our Lady on 15 August and 8 September and of Saint John on 24 June, and the period from

Christmas Day until Epiphany, and to the agricultural year and especially harvest. In general these were organized by the young unmarrieds – those in their late teens and early 20s. In many villages the tradition of nominating a 'King of the Young' (*roi de la jeunesse*) to direct the proceedings survived until mid century. These religious festivals provided an occasion for celebration and feasting, an interval in a normally frugal existence. Also closely linked to the church, at least in their origins, were the various devotional and charitable confraternities which assembled to provide a respectable burial for the dead and assistance to the living. The church constantly struggled to control these various forms of popular sociability and to resist their secularization. Dances such as the *bourrée* or *farandole*, a mixture of procession, singing and dancing, to the sound of a flute or bagpipes, which combined elements of a pagan fertility ritual with the celebration of a saint's day were naturally suspect.

This kind of folkloric activity, which varied in detail between villages, retained its vitality into the late decades of the century. However, more secularized forms of entertainment increasingly provided alternative means of expressing communal solidarity. Urban models of song and dance, came to exert an ever-growing influence. With the exception of Sunday mass, most of the more mundane social gatherings were anyway secular in intent. These were likely to occur at the blacksmith's which offered warmth and shelter, on the village square, and for women at the well or wash-place (*lavoir*) or simply on the doorstep. Female sociability, however, tended to be more closely linked to work and to the church than that of men. Collectively these were the means by which news was exchanged and which allowed the survival of rich oral traditions with their tales of giants and witches, of famous criminals and of princely heroes (including the great Napoleon). Particularly important in most areas was the *veillée*, a gathering of perhaps twenty or thirty people, usually of both sexes, in a house or barn for the multiple purpose of work (repairing tools, sewing, etc.), songs, games, stories and courtship, which took place from the autumn (following the ploughing) until around Easter. These had the added advantage of allowing economies in heating and lighting. Other gatherings of family and neighbours took place to celebrate the so-called 'rites of passage' – baptism, first communion, marriage and death, the major turning points in an individual's life – and served as occasions for the re-affirmation of social bonds through the exchange of gifts, compliments or respect. Other important elements in popular (male) sociability, which grew in importance with prosperity, were the *café* and the *chambrée* (associations of artisans and/or peasants, modelled on the bourgeois *cercle* or club). The latter, with its rules, democratic organization and mutual aid functions was especially suspect to the authorities anxious about the spread of alcoholism and particularly the privacy and potential for seditious discussions which it provided. It became particularly common in Provence. In other areas similar functions were performed by a variety of groups including musical societies, archery and bowling associations.

Beyond the community, links with the populations of wider geographical areas were maintained through the market and fair which had vital social as well as economic functions. On the market place and in nearby cafés men from different communities met and exchanged information which they later passed on in their own villages. The market place was thus an important place of contact with the external world – and a key element in the communications system through which new ideas were diffused. Through it varous cultural zones were interlinked and elements of the élite culture slowly seeped into the countryside, influencing first of all those artisans and peasants resident in the marketing centres themselves, where the close proximity of the bourgeoisie made inter-social imitation more rapid and more intense. The spread of new attitudes towards such diverse matters as politics or education, or new fashions in farming or dress was also facilitated by the movements of migratory workers and of conscripts, although perceptions of places and people temporarily encountered were frequently rather distorted.

Within an under-policed society sanctions were sometimes necessary to maintain respect for community norms and to limit the occasions for conflict and violence. An intense concern with property rights was one frequent cause of quarrels in cases, for example, where animals strayed into a field or a plough went over property boundaries. Transgressions were remembered for genera-tions. The honour of a family and its social status required it to react to injury (imagined or real) by denigrating its rivals, by means of oral or physical violence, and in extreme cases through recourse to law. Conflict usually occur-red between individuals and families of roughly equal rank, rather than between rich and poor. The dependence of the latter was too deeply rooted. Interpersonal violence, however, does appear to have become generally less acceptable from at least the eighteenth century. Socially unacceptable behaviour might be sanc-tioned by means of the *charivari* which involved banging pots and pans, the singing of derisory songs, etc.; or by daubing excrement on the doors of the offenders' homes. This occurred most commonly in cases of moral transgres-sion such as adultery or marriages which offended accepted norms, as when widows or widowers showed unseemly haste in remarrying, or a man from another village married into the community. In both these cases the control of property was at stake. Nagging wives, the harsh treatment of dependants, theft or drunkenness could be similarly punished. In the south if individuals refused to recognize the judgement of the *charivari* they might subsequently be paraded on a donkey during carnival seated facing its hind-quarters, or even burnt in effigy. In such fashion moral and civil order might be maintained and the necessity of involving the authorities, i.e. outsiders, in the policing of the community was restricted to exceptional circumstances. Frequently, too, the songs and processions of carnival were used to convey political messages, providing a useful guise for political protest.

Increasingly, however, as the better-off members of communities were drawn into the economic and social relationships of the outside world they became less attached to traditional practices. Population growth in the early part of the century and the opportunities for commercialization stimulated more intense, and competitive exploitation of the land. Individualism and familism weakened commitment to the collectivity, and led to the gradual dissolution of the traditional rural society in a process which began at varying dates, depending upon the efficiency of communication networks and the degree of integration of particular communities into the wider society. Migration from the countryside further contributed to change in the character of many rural communities, resulting in a loss of cohesion and of dynamism as a disproportionate number of the younger inhabitants left. This all represented a major change in peasant perceptions of the physical and social environment.

Mentalités

The difficulty of obtaining evidence about popular culture has already been stressed. To a very large extent we rely upon urban or urbanized intellectuals or the often equally uncomprehending condescension of folklorists anxious to catalogue the remains of a rapidly disappearing civilization. Their basic visions varied between the conservative ideal of the amiable rustic threatened by urban *mores*, to the brutalized beings presented by Balzac, Zola or the artists Courbet and Millet. These descriptions frequently need to be re-interpreted.

The relative isolation of the first fifty to seventy years of the century had ensured the survival of often extremely localized linguistic usages, including specialized words and phrases, particular forms of pronunciation, as well as distinctive languages (Flemish, Breton, German, Basque, Catalan, Langue d'Oc – for a further discussion of language, see p. 349, of folkloric practices, and ways of producing material objects (buildings, furniture, tools) which varied from village to village. These practices represented the distinctiveness and helped create a sense of unity within each community. However, and in spite of the countless variations in detail, they also reveal that peasants everywhere shared the same fundamental attitudes. In effect culture involved the ritualization of behaviour and of social relationships through language, through a code of politeness, by means of proverbs and the particular rituals of local festivals. The richness of popular art, furniture and clothing suggest that the traditional rural culture reached its apogee in the twenty or thirty years of prosperity which followed the mid century crisis, although the loss of vitality *vis-à-vis* urban culture, which heralded rapid subsequent decline, was already evident.

Until this period rural life had involved a continual struggle with nature to provide for family subsistence. Community and culture provided discipline and reassurance in often harsh circumstances, helping the rural population to cope with the anxieties which continually beset them, above all fear of hunger, of sickness, of old age, of fire, of rabid dogs and the agonizing death from hydrophobia, and in upland areas of the wolves* who in harsh winters like that

---

* These continued to decline in number – in 1883 1316 bounties were paid on wolves killed, in 1900 only 115.

of 1848–9 howled around the houses at night. Less corporeal forms also caused fear, notably the spirits and phantoms which haunted the countryside at night. Magical beliefs both reassured and increased anxiety. There were sorcerers and witches who cast evil spells on neighbours and their animals, and others from whom assistance might be requested. Wise-folk were, through their empirical knowledge of plants and minerals able to provide medicaments which, for much of the century, were quite as likely to provide cures as those of the professional doctors and *pharmaciens*. This undoubtedly reinforced their prestige.

Religious beliefs (see Chapter 7 for a fuller discussion) were an important part of the value system of every community, even if the character and intensity of religious faith varied. Religion offered a view of the world and a set of rules (both moral and social) to abide by. Thus religion and morality were intimately linked. Religion also held out the comforting hope of life everlasting. Nevertheless, traditional peasant beliefs tended to focus on the practical utility of religion in the present. For as long as men in their daily lives felt subject to the overwhelming forces of nature, prayer and pilgrimage had an instrumental value – that of requesting divine intercession.

It is important to stress the dichotomy between popular religion and that of the theologian. In effect peasant religion contained two elements – the first institutional and imposed by the church through its organization and teaching, and concern to eliminate sin; the second exhibiting practical concerns and associated with communal sociability and celebration and often pre-Christian in its origins. Poorly educated populations often had a very limited understanding of the church's teaching. Their main concern was to propitiate divine forces and especially that fearsome God of retribution described by the priests. Ritual practices, a mixture of magic and religion, helped to allay fears and reduce feelings of helplessness. Prayer or votive offerings within a church or at a holy place, such as a well or spring, might prevent misfortune, cure the sick, or at least ease the anguish of the dying. The cholera epidemics of the 1830s and 1850s were met with prayer to Saint Roch, the traditional guardian against plague and by appeals for intercession through processions and the planting of crosses and calvaries. The saints had a key role in popular religion as intercessors between Man and God. This was also the role of the parish priest, who could easily be regarded as some sort of magician, conversant as he was with a tongue (Latin) which no one else understood, and daily practising in his church a series of complicated gestures and rituals. In the 1840s the church bells were still rung to ward off storms in some 486 of the 500 parishes in the Gers, indicating the overwhelming concern with the harvest and fecundity.

Popular fears were perpetuated both through day-to-day experiences and a sense of history – an oral tradition which in highly selective fashion recorded past events such as the subsistence crisis of 1817 when people in some areas had eaten grass and weeds. Memories of the past were concerned with events of unusual importance and particularly with their negative local effects. The recent and the distant past were rarely distinguished. Years were recalled by their most important characteristics – the year of the snow, that of the floods, that of the bumper harvest. Events like the revolution were remembered alongside those of centuries earlier and their chronology inextricably confused. People's sense of time was governed by the seasons, by the church's liturgy and by its bells, especially the morning and evening *Angelus*. People worked by the day, not by the hour. Their behaviour was governed by the accumulated wisdom of the community, preserved in the form of proverbs, which ensured that most situations had their precedents. The entire mode of thought was empirical, linked to the accumulation of a mass of undifferentiated facts and rumours interpreted in a manner which conformed to existing presuppositions.

Religious, and cultural life more generally, developed in precise sociological milieux. The more deeply enrooted it was, the more fully it satisfied the daily needs of the people. However, judgements about the intensity of faith are difficult to make. To a substantial degree variations in religious behaviour in the first half of the nineteenth century need to be related to the style of post-tridentine reform from the sixteenth century in particular diocese, to the training of the clergy, their missionary activities and the forms of devotion they encouraged. In the department of Loiret, for example, traditional beliefs were generally strongest in the west and south where most of the population attended church on Sundays (save during harvest) and regularly made their confessions. This was the area which before the revolution had been part of the diocese of Auxerre. Unlike neighbouring Orléans it had largely escaped the moral rigour of the Jansenist priests who had alienated so many laymen. These were, moreover, areas isolated from new ideas by poor communications. The main determinant factors appear to have been the strength of religious tradition and the social pressures exerted in its favour, i.e. pressures inducing conformity. The influence of the revolution also needs to be taken into account. The persecution of the church had resulted in a polarization of attitudes between those individuals and families, communities and regions for which religion was a matter of vital interest and those for which loyalty to the church was not a primary concern. A whole complex of historical factors thus has to be taken into account along with geographical, economic, social and political structures. In areas of dispersed settlement in the Massif Central (Aveyron, Cantal, and Haute-Loire) and in the west (Brittany, Vendée, Mayenne, and parts of Normandy) the relative intensity of religious practice lends support to the notion that the church and its priests constituted the central focal point for the surrounding area, the basis of its culture and view of the world and its source of protection. Support for the church by local élites was also of significance. Thus, in much of the Limousin, which was too poor to sustain a class of wealthy nobles, the influence of the clergy appears to have suffered greatly from the lack of powerful supporters. Rural populations in these areas were characterized by a 'superstitious' religiosity which was combined with anti-clericalism. The latter was also a characteristic of many areas in which small peasant proprietors had been integrated at a relatively early date (often centuries before) into commercial circuits and enjoyed regular links with urban centres and an alternative culture. Vine cultivators were an obvious example.

Disaffection might also have resulted from clerical attacks on impiety, super-stition or vice, and the efforts made through the confessional and pulpit to condemn contraception, dancing and drinking and the failure to observe the sabbath. The posing of embarrassing personal questions in the confessional was resented and often led to a divorce between the clergy and the faithful which was the first step towards non-attendance. If they wanted to retain their influence it was often advisable for priests to tolerate those forms of behaviour which were acceptable in secular society. Relationships between priests and parishioners were best when the former lived up to the expectations of the latter. They were expected to be moral paragons, and even legitimate requests for fees or com-munal expenditure on the upkeep of churches and presbyteries were likely to be met with accusations of avarice.

The major reason for the rapid decline in the influence of the church, particu-larly in the second half of the century, must, however, be sought in changing perceptions of the environment. This involved a decline in the popular sense of helplessness as improvements in food supply occurred, as epidemics became less frequent and less threatening and elementary learning, which provided simple scientific explanations of rain, drought, health and sickness, became more widespread. Many people became less dependent upon the forms of moral and material support which the church had always offered. Furthermore, economic opportunity and a growing desire for a better life in the here and now reduced the attractiveness of heavenly rewards. In the last third of the century, too, a host of new forms of association and entertainment effectively challenged the church's role as the centre of social life. More than ever, church attendance became a matter for women and children (representing the household) and at best very occasionally for men. Significantly, in Millet's painting 'Angelus' (1855–7) the man does not pray, but twists his hat between his fingers, waiting for his wife to complete her prayers. Respect for the rites of passage remained fairly general – birth, marriage, and death continued to be celebrated both from religious motives and from a sense of conformity – but even in isolated upland communities the vitality of religious live declined as migration drained away their populations.

Education, as a factor changing popular mentalities, also needs to be consi-dered in some detail. The essential object of the 1833 Education Law had been to civilize the masses. They were to be integrated into the national community through the diffusion of the basic skills of literacy and of a new moral outlook. The process took generations. Even in 1860 the village schoolmaster at Boyer in the Lyon region, not untypically described the local peasants as 'gross, un-civil, ridiculous, brutal in their dealings and day-to-day relationships, noisy, rowdy in gatherings, imbued with the most absurd prejudices which transmit them-selves from generation to generation'. This was a measure of the task described by one of his colleagues, as being to 'moralize' at least the younger generation, and 'to initiate them into a new life'. Progress was usually associated with that of the other means of communication. In Bourgogne at mid century the typical community with a high level of literacy was nucleated, situated on open plains or in an area of vine cultivation, with good roads and a significant number of artisans and small traders (setting an example); while the community with a low level was almost exclusively agricultural, living in dispersed hamlets or isolated farms, and handicapped by poor soils, inadequate roads and low levels of commercialization, with much of the land owned by absentee landowners and occupied by sharecroppers.

Improved literacy often left marked differences between the generations. The progress of the young was slowed by the hostility and lack of interest of the old. Only in the second half of the century, as the generations educated in the 1830s and 1840s reached maturity, did this decline. By the 1870s virtually all boys and most girls attended school, although no doubt many left with low levels of attainment. Improvements in living standards which reduced parents' dependence on the work of their children, and an appreciation of the utilitarian value of learning also contributed to changes in attitudes.

For some considerable time the printed literature available to the poor remained compatible with the traditional popular culture. The mass production of popular images (particularly at Epinal where 17 million prints were produced during the Second Empire alone), of *canards* or news-sheets, of the little volumes of the *bibliothèque bleue*, and almanacs (about 9 million per annum by 1848), all generally sold by pedlars, provided the illiterate or semi-literate with practical advice, works of piety and sensational stories of saints and heroic princes. Only from the 1860s did cheap newspapers (like the *Petit Journal*) and changing literacy standards drive out the traditional folk tales and replace them with a new vision of the world and an interest in national events – often just as sensationalized. Thus cultural isolation continued to limit access to new ideas. Its decline was gradual and took longest in the geographically more isolated areas, but everywhere the process accelerated from the 1840–50s as village communities became integrated to a greater extent than ever before into a developing urban–industrial society. Local custom, the local culture, tended to lose its internal dynamic and to respond more and more to external influences. In this process the role of 'innovators' should be noted. They tended to be influential members of local communities with a foot in the outside world, normally the more prosperous and better educated. In the Béziers area, just to take one example, a combination of factors – political activity during the Second Republic, the rapid development of vine cultivation and the wine trade, the establishment of railways, population movements, conscription, increased literacy, *francization*, and the development of the mass media – combined to induce change. Mental habits tend, however, to change more slowly than economic and social structures, so that it would be a mistake to directly correlate the two, just as it would be an error to minimize the complexity of the process, or even in this period to exaggerate its rapidity. Nevertheless, the period 1840/50–1920/40 saw an irreversible decline in traditional culture. In the past, particular aspects of this culture had declined – under the pressure of the counter-reformation, for example – but for the first time rural societies did not generate alternatives. The growing use of French was one key indicator of change. In many areas (see

Chapter 8), even at mid century, the language of daily life was not French. And within broad linguistic regions (including those using French) words and pronunciation often varied considerably between villages, greatly reinforcing both their homogeneity and particularism. This situation changed by stages, slowly at first and then ever more rapidly, with an intervening bi-lingual period, in which peasants adopted French words and came to understand French even before they could speak it, coming before more or less complete Frenchification. The growing adoption of French was evident even before the generalization of primary education and was a largely spontaneous development. It was linked to increased mobility and a growing range of contacts with the outside world which created an awareness of the practical advantages of speaking the most widely used of the national languages, particularly in dealings with merchants and officials.★ Thus, in lower Brittany French spread from the south and east and from the coast and larger towns into the interior. The *instituteur*, however, served to massively reinforce this trend and to encourage the development of linguistic uniformity. Increasingly the local language came to be regarded with contempt as the language of the ignorant. Its use was relegated to private occasions and day-to-day work-place situations. 'Important' matters, like politics, were the preserve of French. This decline in the social prestige of the language had important linguistic consequences – the simplification of syntax, and impoverishment of vocabulary due to borrowings from French. The efforts of groups of intellectuals to preserve the purity of the 'old' language and its written forms had little impact in the case of *langue d'oc* or even Basque, Catalan and Breton. More important were the efforts of the church whose priests often continued to preach in a local language as part of their effort to communicate with a mass audience, and to protect traditional culture against contamination by 'immoral' urban influences. The contraction in the sphere of use was also of socio-psychological significance. It reflected the intensified feelings of social inferiority among minority linguistic groups.

Other significant manifestations of new attitudes included the gradual disappearance of the *veillée*, a key element in the preservation of oral tradition. This was replaced both by more private family-centred forms of sociability and by the male orientated *cabaret*. The *charivari*, previously so important in communal discipline, always suspect to the authorities, but never more so than in an age of growing political activity, lost much of its functional value as policing improved and it was disowned by the more 'respectable' members of local communities, Thus all manner of traditional activities were rejected as old-fashioned or childish. In this the schools with their emphasis on 'good' manners and 'civilized' behaviour were important. Other traditions disappeared almost in the course of things. The mechanization of threshing and harvesting, for example, caused the suppression of work-teams and of their festivities; migration removed many of the young people who had organized and been the life

★ The use of French in official documents had been required by the ordinance of Villers-Cotterèts in 1539.

and soul of the folkloric activities, while those who remained tended to become more independent of the community by virtue, for example, of the mobility offered in the 1890s by the bicycle.

Songs and dances made popular in the towns came to replace the traditional music of the countryside. Religion, which had offered explanations of natural phenomena and a means of controlling them, lost much of its utilitarian value as improved techniques made agriculture less susceptible to climate, as the fear of famine disappeared, and science offered alternative explanations and better medical care. In effect a way of life was disappearing due to a complex of pressures which shattered the previous relative stability of material life and of village social structures, which destroyed much of the context which had given meaning to the traditional culture. In a changing world new institutions were required. New forms of voluntary association were established, based in local society, but responding to new definitions of its needs derived from the external world by the local bourgeoisie. These included the various musical societies and sporting clubs developing from the 1860s with rules and regulations intended to moralize leisure and inculcate patriotic virtues, the associations intended to support local schools (e.g. the *Sociétés des amis de l'instruction* of the 1880s), and the local political organizations which developed from the 1870s. All contributed to the integration of the rural population and particularly of the young into the national society.

The timing of this process varied, largely in relation to the degree of development of communications. In the Aude musical societies were organized first of all in the major towns – Carcassonne and Narbonne – and then spread, initially to the larger *bourgs* and villages along the main roads with a significant proportion of non-agricultural inhabitants and then into the zones of commercial wine production. In contrast, cultural change was much slower in isolated upland regions such as the Lodèvois and Montagne noire in Hérault where industrial decline, the survival of a traditional pastoral economy, and migration combined to reduce the pressure for innovation. More generally the rapid increase in relations with the external world would not entirely replace the orientation of the peasant towards his immediate community and environment. To an important extent pre-industrial values continued to influence behaviour.

Social relationships

While insisting upon the importance of community, and of relationships based upon inter-dependence within it, it should also be obvious that these were very often unequal in character. Control over the land, and employment opportunities were the bases of economic and social power. The subordinate status of much of the rural population was particularly evident in the first half of the century, when high population densities forced the poor to compete for access to land and work, and in approximately half of the country in which large landowners predominated. Submissive behaviour was expected. The tenant farmer or labourer who insisted upon his rights was likely to find himself blacklisted. These factors created a sense of dependence and of inferiority which was intensified by the cultural superiority enjoyed by men with wealth and education who were able to give advice and support to peasants in their relationships with the external world and perform representative functions as *conseiller-généraux* or mayors.

In perhaps a quarter of the countryside – in some parts of the Paris basin, in Berry, Bourbonnais, parts of Languedoc and Provence, in the Comtat and along the southern and eastern borders of the Massif Central and in the Breton west – traditional social relationships prevailed for which large landowners sought moral justification through paternalism. They strengthened their influence by responding positively to traditional expectations concerning their behaviour, and respecting a normative order which required that the poor were given work, which recognized their right to glean in the fields following the harvest, and rights of usage in private and communal forests, and provided charity in case of need. To a large degree this ethos was maintained by the residence of large numbers of landowners and the personal contacts established with dependents. The model remained that of the noble living among 'his' peasants and in close alliance with the parish priest. In the west, in particular, religion provided the dominant ideology, with the clergy employing the myth of the *chouannerie* of 1794–6 as a means of stressing the unity of landlord and peasant against disorder, immorality and irreligion. The *curé* served as an intermediary between rich and poor – preaching submission and collecting and distributing charity. Where the influence of the clergy was less strong deferential behaviour might conceal bitter social hostility. In the Allier, where sharecroppers were subjected to particularly intense exploitation, they were normally submissive, but none the less bitterly resented their situation. In Le Roy's novel *Jacquou le Croquant*, set near Perigueux in the Dordogne, peasants were afraid to talk about politics:

> afraid of the nobles, as wealthy as they had been under the old King; afraid of the clergy who brought rain and fine weather to the countryside; of the notaries to whom they were in debt; of the mayors who represented the government; and of the *bourgeois* who take legal action against those they call 'badheads' and ruin them. The sharecroppers were afraid of their masters, the labourers of their employers, the artisans of the bourgeois who gave them work.

The poor were 'prudent' and although protest was rarely entirely absent, they generally felt obliged to respect existing relationships of dependence in the hope of gaining some advantage.

In another quarter of the countryside, in the technically most advanced agricultural regions of the north and most of the Paris basin, social relationships were also authoritarian, but traditional paternalism had long been in decline due to landlord absenteeism and the development of a 'cash nexus' between the large-scale tenant farmers, who dominated society, and the mass of small peasants and labourers. The contrast between rich and poor tended to become all the greater as involvement in commercial agriculture developed. Very gradually, and especially after mid century, traditional forms of paternalism declined everywhere. Growing absenteeism on the part of the landowners reduced personal contacts, while market pressures, and from the 1870s declining revenue from the land, stimulated the development of more commercial relationships between landowners, their tenants and labourers. Deference declined as more peasants were able to acquire land and a spirit of independence was stimulated by political debate, and above all by migration which provided the opportunity for escape from harsh social relationships and improved the negotiating position and material conditions of those who remained.

In the remaining half of the countryside, in spite of significant structural variations, social relationships tended to be more egalitarian. Where most of the land was owned by small proprietors, and where there were relatively few large landowners or agricultural labourers influence in rural communities tended to be exercised primarily by the moderately well-off peasants, and representatives of the professional classes. This was the case in Alsace, where a foreign nobility had largely been displaced by the revolution. It also occurred generally throughout the east, in much of the Midi, in mountain areas, and in a variety of small regions within zones otherwise dominated by large landowners, for example, the *bocage* areas of Calvados which were in marked contrast to the richer agricultural *plaine*, where wealthy nobles predominated. The existence of a real peasant 'democracy' seems to have depended in most cases on a relatively concentrated habitat structure, which facilitated intense patterns of sociability and informal organization. Frequently, however, the developing sense of independence from traditional social élites was counter-balanced by a growing consciousness of subjection to the impersonal forces of the market.

Protest

The causes of social tension were numerous, particularly in the first half of the century as popular pressure on resources became more intense. They included old memories of feudal exploitation and the latent fear, waning as time passed, that seignorial dues might be re-established; competition for land and disagreements over rights of usage on commons or in private forests; and disputes over conditions of employment. Even where a sense of grievance existed, however, it did not usually lead to protest, much less to violence. Discontent was normally attenuated by a very real sense of interdependence within the community and by an inability on the part of the poor to conceive of alternatives to the existing social system. Peasant politicization developed only slowly in response to the widening of the suffrage, increased literacy and the extension of governmental activity. In certain circumstances, nevertheless, protest might occur, particularly where community members were able to identify the apparent cause of their grievances, whether this be an individual, group or institution, and to justify action by appealing to established custom, against a threat to the existing 'moral order'. This was especially likely to be the case along the expanding frontier of economic commercialization and state intervention, and in response to innovations which appeared to threaten livelihoods and subsistence, rather than in the older-established zones of commercial farming close to major cities. Even then, some kind of often fortuitous precipitating incident was necessary before disorders actually occurred. Furthermore, while a past history of successful protest might encourage action, the experience of failure and administrative repression inevitably discouraged subsequent action. Even so, the merest threat of disorder was often sufficient to secure compliance, and in most villages there existed a traditional repertoire of actions which could be taken in crisis situations. These included both individual 'delinquent' behaviour and collective action involving everything from ostracism, verbal threats and those contained in *placards*, symbolic acts such as hanging in effigy, to the actual destruction of property by means of arson, cattle-maiming, crowd action and (although less frequently) physical violence against persons. In relatively isolated 'closed' communities, such pressures for conformity could be extremely effective.

The most important cause of protest until the 1850s was misery, normally endemic in the overpopulated countryside, but regularly intensified by the effects of poor harvests on food prices. Severe crises occurred in 1817, 1829, 1846–7, 1853 and 1855. The scale of price rises varied considerably between localities, but at Evreux (Eure), for example, between July 1845 (normal price) and April 1847 (cyclical high) the price of wheat rose from 17f50 per hectolitre to 39f. Slow and expensive communications ensured that prices varied considerably between regions because of the cost of transporting foodstuffs from areas of surplus to those of deficit. Dearth increased the tension between those with food to sell and the rural poor, who were forced to buy in the market place. For some – large landowners, the wealthier peasants, and merchants – a poor harvest was an opportunity for profitable speculation. Others, unable to produce enough food to meet the needs of their families, or to find sufficient work because of the small harvest, suffered from hunger and heightened anxiety. Panic buying and speculation pushed up prices far beyond the level that the local shortfall in the harvest would have suggested likely. Whether or not disturbances actually occurred depended upon such factors as local food resources and the nature of commercial activity, on socio-professional structures and the intensity of misery, and also upon the quality of social relationships within communities. Disorder was most likely to occur at markets or on the roads leading to them, as people sought to secure food at prices they could afford, justifying their activities in terms of a basic human right to sustenance at a 'just' price. Figure 16 suggests that areas dependent on a cereals monoculture, and those not normally producing sufficient foodstuffs to meet local demand and therefore reliant upon the former, and especially those most recently integrated into commercial circuits and not yet used to seeing a proportion of the local harvests taken away by merchants supplying the cities, were likely to experience disorders. Paradoxically, some of the more isolated regions in which a technically backward

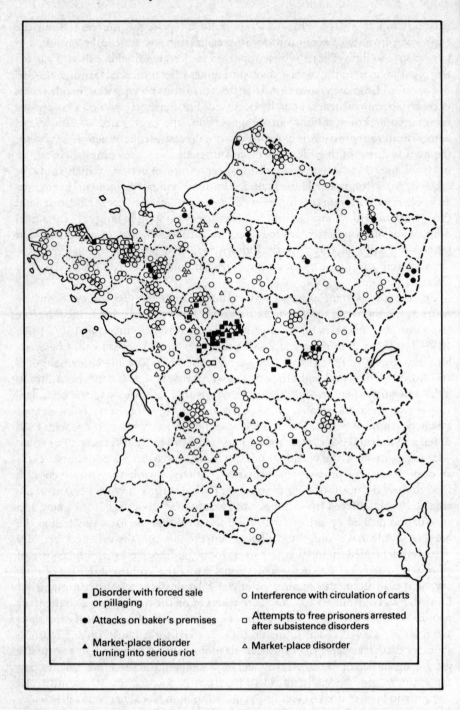

Figure 16   *Subsistence disorders 1846–7*

subsistence agriculture predominated saw relatively few disorders. They were less dependent upon commerce and had recourse to alternative forms of nutrition such as potatoes, rye or chestnuts. An abundant harvest brought its own problems. It provided food in plenty, but depressed prices, which could cause severe problems for those who needed cash to pay taxes or the interest on debts. In Loir-et-Cher, for example, wheat prices in 1850 were 59 per cent below the high levels of 1847, while wine prices fell by 69 per cent between 1845 and 1849.[35] It was the succession of crises between 1846 and 1851, in which dearth was followed by glut, which made the mid century crisis so severe.

Other causes of tension and protest included disputes over rights of access to common land* and (especially in northern areas of open field) to private land following harvest – particularly to graze animals on the stubble (*vaine pâture*) and to glean. Traditional rights of usage, which served to guarantee at least some access to land even for the poorest, conflicted with the growing individualism and desire to maximize income of both landlords and the wealthier peasants. The socially and politically dominant groups in communities were also increasingly anxious to sell or lease common land as a means of limiting the rise in local taxation and of financing the widespread improvement of roads and the construction of schools, etc. Such differences of interest and the divisions they caused were often extremely complex. Large-scale stock-breeders and poor peasants with a cow or two or some pigs might favour traditional rights of usage on common land, while the poorest with no animals to graze might prefer its division into private plots. However, in many areas, as population pressure grew, peasants were increasingly likely to resist threats to even the least significant source of subsistence. Following the 1830 and 1848 Revolutions – as the authority of the state temporarily declined – there were widespread instances of protest against enclosure, or restrictions on access to common land, and above all to the forests. This was in reaction to the law of 1827 which, seeking to prevent degradation of the woodlands which were still the primary source of heat and energy for the towns and industry, imposed severe hardships on the poor, especially in upland areas of the Alps, Pyrenees, Jura and Vosges where the forests provided not only wood for heating and construction but pasture and compost and were an integral and indispensable part of traditional agricultural systems. In response in the Pyrenean foothills of the Ariège in 1829–30 groups of men dressed as women and with blackened faces (the *demoiselles*), armed with sticks and guns, drove out the woodcutters and charcoal burners and the forest guards employed by the iron-masters, who had repeatedly fined people for collecting firewood or pasturing their animals. They took part in a vast *charivari* and deliberately devastated plantations as a means of 'punishing' their owners. Balzac's *Les Paysans* provides eloquent and accurate testimony to similar social hatreds aroused in parts of the Yonne.

---

* A law of 10 June 1793 had permitted division or sale of common land, but only with the consent of two-thirds of the inhabitants of the commune aged over 25 and having rights of usage.

The political crises of 1830 and 1848 also encouraged protest against taxation, and, particularly in vine cultivating areas, against the drink tax with its inquisitorial methods of collection, and the municipal *octroi*. Both were felt to depress sales. At Castres, for example, early in March 1848 crowds burned the tax records and pillaged the house of the tax collector. In 1848 peasant discontent was intensified by an ill-advised increase of 45 per cent in the land tax. This caused a series of incidents between May 1848 and the spring of 1849, particularly in the south-west. Peasants in the Guéret area of the Creuse actually marched on the town to protest and also to secure the release of four recalcitrant tax payers, arrested by the *gendarmerie*. Hostility towards the towns as centres of government was reinforced by the residence in them of landowners and usurers. Thus in Alsace in 1848 hostility to Jewish money-lenders and cattle dealers led to serious anti-semitic manifestations.

Characteristically these disorders did not involve an attack on the social order but on the abuse of established relationships. They were a call for justice. Significant changes in the forms of popular protest were, however, evident from the 1850s, partly as the result of widespread politicization during the Second Republic, but particularly due to the amelioration or disappearance of the crises which previously had been the main cause of protest. The communications revolution and transformation of agricultural marketing systems considerably attenuated cyclical and regional price fluctuations and effectively eliminated the subsistence crises which had been the cause of misery and protest since time immemorial. Moreover, as economic structures changed, a poor harvest was less likely to result in a generalized economic crisis with its devastating combination of high food prices and widespread unemployment. In most regions the last subsistence disorders occurred some time between 1853 and 1857. Moreover, the growth of urban employment opportunities increasingly stimulated migration from the countryside, easing the pressure on its resources (including woodlands), extending property ownership among those who remained, and making generally acceptable those measures taken to restrict collective rights which had previously caused so much tension. The effects of these economic changes were reinforced by improved education, more effective policing, and the creation of alternative institutionalized forms of protest, i.e. by the development of means of socialization which discouraged violent protest and promoted the more effective integration of rural communities into the national society.

Peasants and politics

It is not easy to generalize about the place of peasants in politics. Once again, regional variations in behaviour abound, but the role of peasants might be described as insignificant, once the initial stimulus and/or threat of the revolution had passed, until 1830, modest between 1830 and 1848, but then crucial following the introduction of manhood suffrage in 1848. Subsequently, although awareness of political issues remained limited in the countryside, politicians took far more interest in peasants.

For most peasants, and for much of the century, politics must have appeared irrelevant and interest was episodic. Narrow horizons and the problems of making ends meet inevitably restricted day-to-day concerns. In such a situation social tensions, even protest, could coexist with a profound spirit of conformism. For politics to become of importance to the peasant it first had to appear relevant. It was the growth of commerce, of state activity, and of urban influences which impinged ever more frequently on life in even the most isolated communities, that stimulated a growth in interest and encouraged less passive attitudes. The essential result was to induce a low level of political participation in return for promised material inducements – roads, schools, lower taxes, tariff protection, etc. – with occasionally more intense activity in an effort to secure public policies favourable to what were perceived to be essential socio-economic interests. The best government was the one which appeared to ensure prosperity. According to the *sous-préfet* at Falaise (Calvados) in 1872, 'The countryside . . . will accept the Republic as it accepts every government, without much love or much hate. As long as public order is maintained and foodstuffs sell well, its sentiments will not change.' Attention must also be paid to the role of new cultural intermediaries – professional men, artisans and the better-educated peasants – with physical and cultural contacts in the world outside the village. They were able to relate the immediate problems of peasant life to political ideologies, to explain and translate political ideas into the familiar language of the *cabaret*, the *chambrée* and the market square. In terms of the chronology of politicization and its regional variations it would seem likely that the rural population of the economically more advanced areas, with better communications and continual links to the towns, would show an interest in politics (whether in support of left or right) at an earlier date that those of the more isolated and economically backward areas. Literacy had a further stimulating effect. However, the local significance of particular issues and internal village social structures and relationships caused much greater diversity in politicization processes than a straightforward diffusion theory would allow. As a result, economically 'backward' societies often appeared relatively 'advanced' in political matters.

The essential characteristics of the national political context were not established by peasants. Their involvement in politics varied over time in relation to changes in political institutions and the extent to which their local interests were affected by issues and events external to the village. Certainly, from 1789 the events of the revolution and empire had attracted sustained interest and concern. The experience was frequently traumatic. The abolition of the seigneurial system, the introduction of requisitioning and conscription, the issues of war and peace, were all of considerable importance for life in even the most isolated community. At its most extreme this resulted in a series of protest movements but not in a sustained interest in political ideology or organization. New oral traditions were nevertheless created. Particular families and communities became identified, both in their own minds and in those of their neighbours, with political labels, due to their association with one side or the other in disputes over the sale of confiscated clerical or émigré land, or over the Civil Constitution of the clergy in the 1790s. It was inevitable that these associations, however much they lacked real ideological content, would influence subsequent political behaviour.

However, until 1848 a restricted franchise and political repression did much to restrict further politicization. It was only with the 1830 Revolution that participation in political debate had once again widened. The event itself, and the political uncertainty which followed it, encouraged agitation and protest. Subsequently, the 1831 law on municipal elections, which introduced a less restrictive franchise than that for national elections, brought 10–15 per cent of the population, including some artisans, shopkeepers and the better-off peasants into the local political arena, and provoked a gradual extension of interest in the relationship between local needs and aspirations and national politics. Through local elections a wider public became familiar with political labels, which were given meaning at village level by the personalities of the contenders for local power. A diffuse politicization occurred. The scale of this development is difficult to measure. Maurice Agulhon charted it through the growing mutual contamination of politics and folklore. Thus, the *charivari* was increasingly likely to be mounted against a political adversary, or the *farandole* (danced to the rhythm of a drum) involve the display of effigies of the defeated Charles X or of the new king, Louis-Philippe, rather than the effigy of a saint. Certainly administrative reports insisted on the increased politicization of day-to-day discussion in *chambrées* and bar-rooms.

The 1848 Revolution, again due to the initial post-revolutionary 'liberty', but particularly because of the introduction of universal male suffrage, and the length and intensity of the succeeding period of political conflict, saw a major extension of interest in politics. Peasant reactions to the republic varied considerably. In many areas during this phase of transition to modern politics traditional means of expressing grievances through threats, songs or riot remained common. Indeed, in the immediate aftermath of the proclamation of republican liberty widespread protest occurred intended to resolve all manner of disputes over such matters as rights of usage in forests and taxation. In contrast, memories of the first revolution, of the Terror and the supposed threat to established property rights from the *partageux* (especially in areas close to major cities), often encouraged support for traditional élites. The rural population was alienated by the fiscal policies of the new republic, especially its 45 per cent increase in the land tax, and blamed it for the continuing economic crisis. Most peasants were attracted to Bonapartism with its promises of social order and prosperity. Even so, from the end of 1848 substantial support was mobilized by *démocrate-socialiste* militants, particularly in central France and the south-east. They attempted to attract peasant voters by linking their economic grievances to national politics. Particularly effective was the promise of lower taxes and cheap credit to help peasants to purchase land and to escape from the clutches of the usurers. When the prospect of such reforms and the almost utopian dream of a new world to follow the 1852 elections, represented by Pierre Dupont's popular song *La République des paysans*, were threatened by political repression, including the passage of a restrictive electoral law in May 1850, radical republican militants continued their agitation underground, often employing folkloric activities or local forms of sociability to disguise the activities of political secret societies. This repression culminated in Louis-Napoléon's *coup d'état* in December 1851, to which some peasants responded by participating in a series of uncoordinated and short-lived insurrections – in the south-east, parts of the Drôme, Ardèche, Hérault, Gard and Var, in the south-west in Gers, and Lot-et-Garonne, and in central France in Nièvre, Yonne and Allier. The major problem for the historian is to determine why peasants in these areas, and other areas in which revolts did not occur, were more predisposed to accept radical ideas than others. These were regions in general characterized by economic backwardness and growing population pressure on resources and where the commercial activities developed to provide additional resources (silk, wine, olive oil, cork, forest, rural industry) and to take advantage of the availability of cheap labour, had been adversely affected by overproduction and generally depressed economic conditions. The rural populations in these areas were by no means the most miserable. They were distinguished by their integration into (depressed) commercial circuits and by their close contacts with urban centres of political agitation. Usually they belonged to socially quite complex communities with a high proportion of artisans and landowning peasants, and had the means of escaping from dependence upon the wealthy. Other common features included concentrated habitat structures which facilitated contacts between peasants and members of other social groups, particularly the bourgeois and artisans who provided leadership, and the absence of strong clerical influence. The *coup d'état* was the culmination of a long period of political repression supported by traditionally conservative social élites and by the clergy. This had had the effect of pushing the rural population in some areas back into old forms of violent protest based upon an ethos of communal solidarity, and away from the institutionalized electoral forms which the introduction of universal male suffrage had seemed to herald. In December 1851, on the ringing of the *tocsin*, and to the sound of the municipal drums, entire communities took up arms (farm tools, National Guard muskets and hunting guns), disarmed the local 'rich' and marched on the nearest town to take over authority, often in spite of the hesitancy of bourgeois leaders. It was difficult for individuals to stand out against the apparent unanimity of the community and to ignore the taunts and threats which greeted such behaviour. In most rural areas, however, the vast majority of peasants had no interest in a republic which they identified with economic crisis and political unrest, and were positively attracted by Louis-Napoléon's promises of firm government, social order and prosperity.

Political repression following the *coup d'état* and during the authoritarian empire slowed the process of politicization. Nevertheless regular elections were held, and the habit of voting was maintained until the attributes of a liberal parliamentary system were restored in the late 1860s. Throughout the empire most peasant voters supported the official candidates nominated by the government, generally from among the ranks of regional social élites. The cult of Napoléon was a potent factor in this. The myth appealed to patriotism and the desire for strong government and prosperity after the long mid century crisis. Indeed, electoral manipulation was unnecessary in most areas, often doing more harm than good. More significantly, the regime appeared to satisfy the real interests of much of the rural population. In spite of some difficulties it was fortunate in coinciding with an upturn in the economic cycle. Most peasants were able to live better because agricultural prices were relatively high and so were wages, the latter partly due to migration, which also had the effect of removing the more dissatisfied elements from the countryside. Access to property became easier. Official propaganda laid claim to the credit for prosperity and a series of government measures (roads, railways, schools) appeared to confirm this. In a very real sense the roots of a conscious and long-lasting peasant conservatism were laid during the Second Empire.

In some areas, however, support for Bonaparte was based on hostility to traditional élites, their social power and monarchist sympathies. This fear of a return to the *temps des rois* and hostility towards both the counter-revolutionary aristocrats and the clergy, and the urban bourgeoisie of lawyers, merchants and money-lenders, was most marked in central France. It was democratic and egalitarian, but often also anti-parliamentary. Indeed, most peasants continued to see parliamentary debate as an irrelevance. Nevertheless their growing prosperity and the greater independence this ensured made it easier to express resentment of age-old exploitation. It also facilitated, in the 1860s, the revival of rural republicanism, in some, but not all, of its earlier centres of strength and particularly in the Rhône–Saône valley, along the coasts of Provence and Languedoc, in the Garonne valley, and to a much less significant extent in the Paris basin.

After the collapse of the empire in 1870 peasant voters seem above all to have desired a return to peace and order, and to normality. To achieve the first objective most voted in February 1871 for the conservative and monarchist advocates of bringing the war to an end. Subsequently, as a means of ensuring stability they tended to oppose the extremes of both left and right and to support moderate republicans, a process which forced many conservatives to adopt republican labels. Peasants demanded from the new regime precisely what they had wanted from that of the emperor. According to the Prefect of the Creuse in 1877 this was 'stability, economic recovery, prosperity, and public works' – the last to secure full employment for the migrant masons from his department, who worked in Paris and Lyon. In regions like the Limousin a vote for the republic could also be seen as a reaffirmation of independence *vis-à-vis* the old élites. More generally, the increased absenteeism of the large landowners, the sale of their land as rentals fell during the depression, the continuing rise of an élite of bourgeois professionals and well-off peasants, and the growing influence of the republican administration all contributed to a reduction in traditional social influences.

During the 1870s farm incomes generally continued to rise, but from the end of the decade a sense of crisis rapidly developed, caused by changing market structures, rising costs and falling prices, and the phylloxera epidemic which devastated the vines. Protection against imports appeared to many to be the solution, and farmers were encouraged to look to the state for assistance. Governments were denounced for their failure to provide tariff protection, for high taxes and the lack of cheap credit; the railway companies were accused of assisting import penetration by means of low long-distance freight rates; merchants and intermediaries of all kinds were condemned for exploiting the peasant; while in the countryside itself social tensions increased with growing awareness of the conflicting interests of landlords and tenants, employers and their labourers. In this situation, more than ever before, politics appeared relevant. All sections of the agricultural community agreed on the need for protection. The size of the rural electorate and threatening conservative electoral successes in rural areas probably made governmental action inevitable and a series of laws re-establishing higher levels of tariff protection were introduced in 1881, 1885, 1887, 1892 and 1894. In some areas continued economic difficulties and social tension nevertheless encouraged peasants to vote for socialists rather than 'radical' or moderate republican electoral candidates (especially in Var, Isère and Allier), and six of the 103 socialist deputies elected in 1914 appear to have been peasants. Even so, the representation of peasant interests in parliament and through pressure group activities remained essentially in the hands of non-peasant landowners and professional men.

Thus the *Société des Agriculteurs de France*, founded in 1867 to represent the interests of the large landowners, encouraged its members to create *syndicats* to provide technical information, fertilizer, credit, etc., for their own benefit and as a means of extending their social influence. Following the 1884 law on associations it established a federal body – the *Union central des syndicats des Agriculteurs de France* with headquarters in Paris in the Rue d'Athènes. By 1914 this had 5000 associated *syndicats* with over a million members organized into provincial associations, such as the *Union du Sud-Est* covering ten departments around Lyon (130,000 members by 1912 out of 800,000 agricultural households in the area covered), and the *Fédération agricole du Nord*, which by 1914 included 264 *syndicats* with 10,000 members in the southern parts of the Nord and in Pas-de-Calais. These were nominally non-political, but in practice acted to preserve traditional social relationships by stressing the common interests of all those engaged in agriculture. The development of a paternalistic syndicalism dominated by aristocrats and *grand bourgeois* and involving the rural clergy facilitated a significant recovery of leadership by these groups, although at the local level well-off peasants played active roles. In spite of the fact that in the west the *syndicats* were slow to emerge, presumably because local landowners were relatively satisfied with their ability to exert social control, these groups were inevitably strongest in clerical regions in which paternalism remained acceptable. In such areas intensification of church–state conflict over the laicization of education in the 1900s further encouraged mobilization. Elsewhere the movement was countered by the establishment of *syndicats* with overtly republican sympathies and a federal organization with headquarters in the Boulevard Saint-Germain, set up initially by professional men and merchants from market towns such as Chartres, and the wealthy farmers in the rich countryside around Arras. This was influential in the Paris basin and enjoyed the support of the official *services agricoles*.

Both the conservative and republican *syndicats* had in common their determination to reinforce existing social structures. More democratic in their internal relationships and in this reflecting distinctive local patterns of sociability were the co-operatives, developing around the turn of the century among *vignerons* in the Midi and cheese producers in the Jura and Haute-Savoie. Such relatively independent peasant organizations were slow to develop, their growth hindered by the lack of leisure and individualism of the peasant–proprietor.

Organization was also slow to develop among agricultural labourers, particularly in regions with large farms like northern France, where they were too isolated and culturally deprived to take effective action. Exceptions included marginal groups such as workers in market gardens in the Paris region and especially those with traditions of protest such as forestry workers in central France (Allier, Yonne, Nièvre, Cher, Loir-et-Cher) who organized and then went on strike in 1891–2 and then again at various times between 1899 and 1903. By 1912 the *Fédération national des bûcherons* included 170 *syndicats*. In the Allier in 1904–5 sharecroppers merged thirty-seven *syndicats* with 1800 members into a *Fédération des travailleurs de la terre*. From 1891 workers in the vineyards of the Midi (especially on large *domaines* around Béziers) also began to organize and by 1903 were able to establish a *Fédération des travailleurs agricoles*, which had at its peak 15,000 dues-paying members. The essential weakness of these movements is revealed by the fact that nationally in 1914 only some 2 per cent of agricultural workers were organized.

The most significant movements of popular political protest in rural areas during the Third Republic occurred in 1907 in Languedoc–Roussillon (Aude, Gard, Hérault, Pyrénées-Orientales) and in 1911 in Marne and Aube. Both were caused by overproduction resulting in low wine prices. For four consecutive years many peasants had worked at a loss and were ultimately faced with the prospect of the seizure of their land to pay debts at a time when its value was anyway rapidly depreciating. Moreover, labourers had experienced wage reductions of 25–30 per cent and increased unemployment. In the Midi the movement began with a gathering of 600 peasants at Bize (Aude) on 21 March 1907, followed by demonstrations by 80,000 at Narbonne, 120,000 at Béziers, 170,000 at Perpignan, and 220,000 at Carcassonne in May and culminating in estimated gatherings of 300,000 at Nîmes, and 500,000 at Montpellier early in June. These were followed by the resignation of municipal councils and the proclamation of a tax strike. The government responded initially with repression, leading to a series of incidents in which six civilians were killed at

Narbonne, the *Préfecture* was burned at Perpignan, rioting occurred at Montpellier and sympathetic troops mutinied at Agde, and then by concessions on the payment of overdue taxes and a law to prevent the falsification of wine. Prices, however, only really recovered after a poor harvest in 1910 and this was only temporary, given the basic saturation of the market.

Clearly peasants had learned to look to the state for assistance, and given their weight within the electorate had enjoyed a certain degree of success, evident particularly in tariff legislation, and the development of rural communications and schooling networks. Politics had in these terms acquired relevance. The various administrations of the Third Republic had been sufficiently responsive to rural interests to secure widespread support for the institutions of the moderate republic. Not surprisingly politics in itself therefore provides a crucial key to an understanding of peasant political behaviour. Historians have in addition frequently attempted to explain political options in relation to socio-economic structures. Areas in which the predominant form of property was the smallholding, especially where vine cultivation was practised, have been associated with a radical politics. The point does have some validity. Property ownership provided the means of independence and the wine trade created a continuous link with the external world. Unfortunately such neat explanations often do not work. In the first place areas with similar socio-economic characteristics frequently took up different political options. Thus in Bourgogne, during the Second Republic, the population of the relatively egalitarian, peasant-dominated communities in the south of Saône-et-Loire were more likely to support *démocrate-socialistes* than were those with similar social structures in northern Côte-d'Or. In the former population densities were higher, and parcellation of land greater. There were marginally more large landowners and above all the lack of extensive common land made the material situation of small peasants that much more precarious. Acceptance of radical ideas appears to have depended above all on pre-existing social tensions and was especially likely to occur where large and small property coexisted and competition for resources was intense rather than where one or the other form was predominant. In the latter – in the Brionne area and southern Chârollais – small farmers enjoyed relative prosperity through cattle-fattening and remained politically quiescent. Vine cultivators in the Midi and east-central France, in the zones of *vin ordinaire* production plagued by unstable market conditions and taxes and blaming governments for both, were much more likely to vote for the left than peasant *vignerons* in areas of higher quality wine production in the Loire valley, Gironde or Champagne.

Similarly, the existence of large-scale landownership has been correlated with conservative political behaviour by peasants. Landownership involves control over scarce resources and is potentially a source of power and influence. In the west, and especially Vendée, Maine and Anjou, sharecropping and the social relations built upon it tended to result in support for conservative politicians. Rejection of radical ideas seems to have been linked with the ability of traditional élites to maintain social control through charity, pressure, and the use of integrative ideologies, which affirmed the community of interests between rich and poor in support of the church and property. In the absence of such paternalism the sharecroppers of the Allier and neighbouring departments voted in protest against the excessive demands of often absentee landlords and their agents, and against their dependence upon usurers. There, and in Bourbonnais, Limousin and Périgord a centuries' old tradition of hostility towards their *seigneurs* fuelled peasant radicalism and led to the development of democratic politics in economically and culturally 'backward' regions. Thus in the Morvan, the western part of Saône-et-Loire, a miserable and mostly illiterate population responded positively to the *démocrate-socialistes* during the Second Republic. At the same time in the north-west of the department, in the Autun and Epinac regions, social tensions were alleviated by the presence of paternalistic landowners.

The characteristics of property structures and of economic activity are clearly relevant to explanations of political behaviour, but a complex of other causal factors needs to be taken into account. Habitat structures have served as another major explanatory factor. Along with communications networks, settlement patterns clearly served as crucial determinants of the capacity for organization and the availability of information. In Provence concentrated habitat and an active social life based on such institutions as the *chambrée*, enabled democratic politicians to work more effectively. However, access to ideas does not in itself determine which of the various political options will be taken up. Conversely, dispersed settlement and poor communications might, as in the Breton west, reinforce the importance of the social roles performed by the clergy and landowners. This was not the case, however, in areas of dispersed settlement in the Limousin due to the absence of large landowners and the limited influence of the clergy. In many hamlets migrant labourers working in Paris and Lyon were the source of new ideas.

The traditional keys to electoral sociology thus do not work very well. Explanations of peasant politics require recognition of a complex multiplicity of factors operating at community level. The significance not only of structures but of events and the particular circumstances of time and place have to be accounted for. Religion was especially important. The revolution had politicized religious antagonism, and where the faith remained strong (particularly it appears in the geographically more isolated regions where monetarization of the economy was less advanced and aspirations less materialistic), and especially where dispersal of habitat increased the social role of the church, political conservatism was greatly reinforced. Thus in the west Catholicism was decisive in reinforcing the notion of a partnership between rich and poor on the land, in common worship and against materialism, Protestantism (particularly in the south-west), liberalism, socialism and revolution. In those regions in which his functions gave him status and influence, the parish priest was thus an important agent of politicization – in a conservative sense.

At most times, and in most villages, only a small minority were interested in the ideas and institutions of politics. These tended to be regarded as the province of local notables. For most of the population the relevance of politics was occasional and fleeting, but silence should not be taken to mean apathy. When governmental decisions threatened to directly affect their lives and livelihoods peasants were likely to take an interest. In situations such as those created by the 1830 and 1848 Revolutions and during discussion of protectionist duties in the 1880s, and particularly as the habit of voting and awareness of political issues gradually developed, rural populations were increasingly likely to take an interest in the views of the political activists who served as cultural brokers, i.e. usually landlords and their agents, priests and the inhabitants of nearby market centres (professional men, merchants, shopkeepers and artisans). The latter group, frequently challenging old élites for local authority, were far more likely to serve as the agents of democratic propaganda than the former. Thus in Eugène Le Roy's novel, it was the republican miller Nogaret and the tailor Lagarthe who read newspapers and commented on the news to local peasants. Only gradually did peasants themselves move beyond the various forms of 'democratic patronage' and assume leadership roles at village level. This occurred briefly, in some areas and among the younger generations, during the period of *démocrate-socialiste* organization from 1849 to 1851, and more generally from the 1880s under the impact of economic difficulties.

An interest in politics was diffused essentially through local social relationships, but what was the nature of the links between village politics and the ideology of national politics? In many cases behind the party labels there occurred primarily a struggle for local influence, between rival groups made up of notable families, their associates and dependents; and between rival villages. Often the political options taken up by these groups were related to the stands taken by their ancestors at previous moments of crisis in say 1793 or 1815, or to enmities inherited from conflict between Catholics and Protestants, clericals and anti-clericals. Politics was usually personalized by people unused to abstraction. The issues of national politics were given meaning through being related to local issues, certainly for as long as the economic and social well-being of most families appeared entirely dependent upon local forces and decisions. A more widespread and sustained interest in political life grew during such exceptional periods as the Second Republic, when social tensions were heightened in reaction to the increasingly interventionist capacity of the state, due to the changing scale of politics, because of improved communications and of cultural integration into the national society and in response to the development of organized parties in the closing decades of the century.

Conclusion

The nineteenth century saw major changes in rural society: economic – due to better communications, changes in market structures and increased productivity; social – due especially to migration, to the relaxation of population pressure on resources and improved living conditions, and the lifting of the age-old fear of famine; political – due to the gradual intensification of the links between community and state, to the widening of the franchise and gradual politicization of the popular consciousness. In each of these spheres I have tried to trace alterations in the balance between continuity and change, and to stress the importance of variations between regions. In general the years around the middle of the century were a clear turning point, but even then social structures and attitudes do not appear to have changed as rapidly as economic. The passing of generations appears to have been a necessary prelude. Nevertheless, on the eve of the First World War the countryside was a very different place in which to live than it had been in 1815. The rural world had lost its independence, and had become economically and culturally far more dependent upon the towns and cities which in France as elsewhere had grown so rapidly in a century of change.

6

Urban working classes

Introduction

Industrial development in France during the nineteenth century occurred gradually, and yet with more rapidity than ever before, and with effects which varied between social groups and regions. The shift of labour away from primary production towards manufacturing, commerce and the services, and the growing concentration of productive activity, had important consequences for working conditions, living standards and social relationships. One major problem for the historian is how to convey the experience of being a worker. Contemporary accounts of working-class life were mainly written by people from a different class and culture, who were often interested in describing extremes of misery, drunkenness or political agitation. The relatively few workers who attempted to describe their experiences, as did Martin Nadaud in his *Mémoires de Léonard, ancien garçon maçon*, came very largely from the élite of skilled workers. This should not, however, lead us to underestimate the variety of the working-class experience. Workers lived and worked in a range of different social and economic milieux, varying with the size and social complexity of their place of settlement, the type of industrial employment, the scale of production, and the pressure for innovation. Major differences in experience and in perception were likely between generations, occupational groups and places.

Structures

Statistics on the industrial labour force are very uncertain, particularly for the early periods, but it does appear to have expanded quite rapidly from around 1.9 million in 1803–12, to 3.5 million in 1833–40, with the rate of increase subsequently slowing to reach 4.2 million in 1866, and then stagnating at around 4.5 million between 1876 and 1891, rising to 5.6 million in 1896 and to 6.7 million in 1913.[1] Figure 17 indicates where this industrial population lived.

In 1860–5, if a distinction is made between manufacturing industry and handicrafts production, the first category included 80,000 employers with 1,150,000 workers, i.e. an average of 14.5 workers per enterprise, and the latter

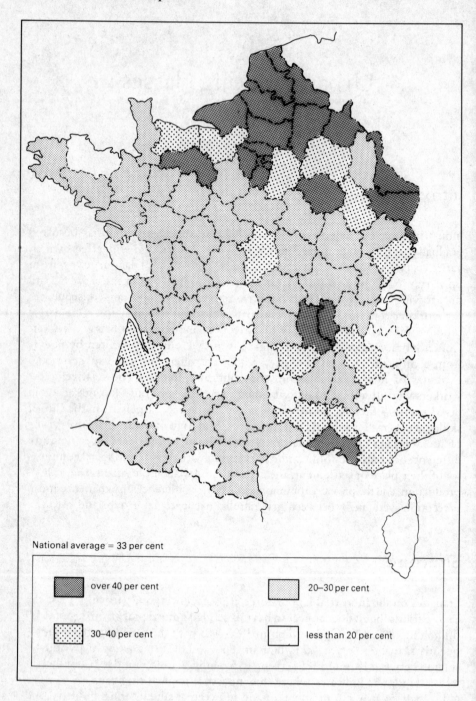

Figure 17 *Percentage of the active departmental population employed in industry 1910–12*

1,420,000 employers with 1,600,000 employees, i.e. 1.1 workers per establishment.[2] In 1906 in terms of their place of employment industrial workers were divided as follows:[3]

28 per cent worked at home
32 per cent in establishments with 1–10 employees
12 per cent in establishments with 10–50 employees
28 per cent in establishments with more than 50 employees.

Numerous variations in economic structures, the diversity of professional life and of local social structures, of wages and living conditions and cultural peculiarities helped to create a multiplicity of experiences. Georges Duveau, in his *La vie ouvrière en France sous le Second Empire*, distinguished four types of worker. First, those dispersed throughout the countryside. These were occupied at a variety of tasks but especially textiles. The domestic weavers and sugar-refinery workers of the Picardy plains, and those in the mines and water-powered textile mills in the valleys of the Vosges were isolated in the countryside, and able to work on the land as well as in industry. They were worker–peasants, sharing the life-style and mentalities of the rural population among whom they lived. Second, workers living in medium-sized towns such as Orléans or Montereau, centres with diverse activities, such as flour milling, distilling, tanning, brick-making, and a range of artisanal crafts, and with no large-scale concentrated enterprises; third, the worker in a small town dominated by a single enterprise – typically the metallurgical centres of Thann, Guebwiller and Mulhouse in Alsace; and last, the workers of the major urban centres, and especially Paris and Lyon, characterized by extreme diversity in their employment. They included the employees of the major engineering shops of Cail at Grenelle, or Gouin at Vaugirard and Batignolles with their 1000–2000 workers and wide range of skills, but also large numbers of skilled artisans employed in small workshops, and a mass of unskilled labourers working on the roads, the quays alongside the river, or in the markets. In Paris, in particular, the production of consumer goods using artisanal techniques remained predominant. The Chamber of Commerce inquiry of 1860 revealed that in the capital the textile and clothing trades were the most important single employer of labour with 78,377 workers, followed by the building industry with 71,242. In such large centres occupational structures might vary between *quartiers*. In Lyon in 1866, the Croix-Rousse was dominated by silk workers, and the area of La Guillotière by workers in such new industries as chemicals, engineering and especially metallurgy.

Among workers there existed a professional hierarchy within which the fundamental distinction was between the skilled with corporate traditions and some form of craft organization, and the mass of unskilled labourers. The relatively strong position of the skilled in the labour market was clear from wage differentials and the differences in living standards and life-style which preserved forms of social segregation among workers. In the Paris building industry, for example, it was possible to distinguish the fully qualified *compagnons-maçons* from the *limousins* who laid foundations and erected walls, and the mass of labourers, who mixed and carried mortar and stones to the masons. In the Limoges porcelain workshops there were more than a dozen categories of labour in 1855, from the decorator who considered himself to be an artist to the labourers who filled and emptied the kilns. Their wages varied between 1500 francs per annum and 1f40 per day, and there appears to have been very little sense of solidarity between them.

According to an inquiry conducted in 1891–7 wage levels varied between the 1f per day paid to female labourers in the chemical industry in the provinces to the 12f per day paid to a male foreman in the Parisian engineering industry. Some industries, like chemicals and textiles, employed especially large propor-tions of miserably paid workers, while others, like metallurgy, tended to pay relatively high wages. However, even in the new factories hierarchical struc-tures rapidly evolved – in textiles, for example, with unskilled labourers, semi-skilled machine-minders, and skilled technicians responsible for mainten-ance of the equipment or engaged in supervisory activities. In addition to the diversity of occupational structures developing both within and between groups of workers they continued to be divided by differences of language, manners and customs. In the last resort the only factors which appear to have given the working classes some degree of unity were the poverty and insecurity which the vast majority shared. In Lille in 1908, 87 per cent of workers still died without leaving any significant material possessions. It was this, together with a growing willingness to take some form of action in an effort to protect or improve their tenuous material position which during the nineteenth century gradually led to the development of a common consciousness among these diverse groups.

Artisans

The strength of artisans within the labour market was based upon their posses-sion of scarce skills, their own tools, relatively high levels of literacy and a capacity for organization which allowed them a considerable degree of control over recruitment into their trades through the training of apprentices, and a large degree of autonomy in the organization of labour and work rhythms in their workshops. As a result they enjoyed relative job security and high wages, and a strong sense of craft solidarity. Often this was shared with employers (*patrons*) who were frequently former workers themselves, and worked along-side their journeymen. However, the significance of the basic difference of interest with an employer engaged in an often highly competitive business and determined that his efforts should be financially rewarded and his social status recognized, should not be minimized.

During the nineteenth century urban artisans were affected by a complex of technological and organizational changes which by devaluing some skills and threatening others created general feelings of insecurity. These strains were the consequence of growing competitive pressures imposed upon the small master craftsmen by the development of large-scale industry and the growing dependence of small producers upon the middlemen who provided credit for the purchase of raw materials and organized the sale of finished goods. Even before the advent of mechanization work processes were being reorganized to facilitate the further division and intensification of labour. In the building industry this took the form of *marchandage*, a process of labour subcontracting, which resulted in wage reductions and the employment of less highly skilled labour from among the many migrants desperately searching for work. In order to maintain their competitiveness, the owners of small workshops were also forced to increase the productivity of their employees by means of gradual technical innovation. In tailoring, this took the form of the sewing machine. As early as the late 1840s in the Parisian tailoring trade, the 3000 master tailors faced competition from 200 *confectionneurs* organizing the production of ready-to-wear clothing.[4] The latter employed mostly women, often working in their homes, to supply the growing market for cheaper consumer goods. In shoemaking nails and rivets were substituted for stitching. The mechanical saw transformed cabinet-making, and in metal-working the introduction of machine tools had by the 1860s reduced such processes as putting a thread on bolts to a simple mechanical activity. In the Lyon silk trade the cost of more expensive machinery – some versions of the Jacquard loom cost up to 4000 francs – led to a gradual concentration of production.[5] Those master-craftsmen who acquired such equipment were often only able to do so because of loans from silk wholesalers which not only caused financial difficulties, but also increased their dependence upon particular merchants. A process of commercial and financial concentration was underway. Although workshop *patrons* and their workers frequently collaborated to resist merchant pressure, not only in defence of their incomes but also of conceptions of good workmanship and quality, the longer-term effect was to cause tensions and conflict between master and man as they struggled for control of the workplace. For numerous groups of artisans their status as craftsmen, their incomes and living conditions were all under threat; a great deal was at stake. Frequently the possibility of change hung like the sword of Damocles over the heads of groups like typographers, aware as they were in the 1860s, of efforts to develop an effective typesetting machine.

The ability of artisans to resist change obviously depended on the development of the market for the goods they produced, and also upon their own organizational capacities and their perception of the problems they faced, i.e. upon what they felt was happening to them. To an important degree the growing division of labour broke down traditional solidarities by increasing specialisation and facilitated increased employer control over the labour force. Artisans, however, as we shall see (p. 228), were better able than any other group in the labour force to resist the pressures associated with the development of industrial capitalism, and were able, in so doing, to exert considerable influence upon the behaviour of other groups within the industrial labour force.

Domestic workers

While highly skilled work tended to remain urban based, entrepreneurs had for centuries made use of underemployed rural labour in manufacturing, particularly in textiles. Relatively isolated in the countryside, as much peasants as workers, and not entirely dependent upon their industrial earnings, they were easily subordinated to their employers' demands. More than any other single group these were the workers who were to be displaced by the machine. From the 1830s and especially as communications networks improved, the development of mechanical production heralded the long decline of domestic weaving and the progressive de-industrialization of the countryside. The family economy of the domestic weaver underwent a long crisis intensified by depressions in 1846–8, the 1860s and especially from 1882 to 1895. In the Lyon region hand-looms in the silk industry still numbered 115,000 in 1873, and there were 60,000 as late as 1905, before the final collapse.[6] But as their incomes from manufacturing were reduced or eliminated many families were forced to endure working days of up to 16–18 hours and degrading living conditions, and finally to migrate. The establishment of factories in some rural areas, including sugar refineries in the north and Paris region, could do little to stem the flow.

In an increasingly competitive economy manufacturers tended to appreciate the advantages of concentrating production in factories in order, among other reasons, to improve the supervision of labour, its productivity and the quality of the finished product. The migration of women into the cities did, however, increase the attractiveness, particularly in the clothing trades, of another alternative – urban domestic labour. This 'sweated' labour enabled workers, in theory at least, to determine their own work-rate, but in practice low piece rates and division of labour enforced long hours of work at boring, repetitive tasks. By 1904 there were around 800,000 domestic workers of various kinds (80,000 in Paris), of whom 86 per cent were women.[7]

Industrial workers

In the earlier stages of the industrialization process employers often faced considerable difficulties in recruiting and training labour. The new setting of the factory, its scale and the need to impose disciplined work rhythms upon the labour force caused major problems. The first generation of workers in most enterprises were recruited from the surrounding countryside and frequently continued to combine industrial employment with working a small plot of land. The pattern was different in areas which already had manufacturing traditions and where former rural artisans and out-workers had experience of industrial work rhythms. Thus in the 1820s in the textile mills of Darnétal in Normandy 58 per cent of the fathers of spinners had been domestic weavers,[8] 50 per cent of the first generation of factory workers were natives of the commune, 20 per cent came from nearby Rouen or its suburbs, and 10 per cent from other parts of the

Normandy textile region. Occupational continuities remained strong, due to transfers from declining to developing sectors of textiles. The second generation was largely recruited among the families, or on the recommendation of workers already employed in the mills. Similarly, in the mining areas of the north, at least until the 1880s, recruitment was based on a relatively limited region in the Artois and Cambrèsis. Migrants, even if changing occupations, at least had the sentiment of remaining within their own *pays*. To an important extent the subsequent growth of the labour force was self-generating, due to exceptionally high birth rates and the movement of labour from old to new pits – especially in the Pas-de-Calais in the 1870s.

In metallurgy, new works established early in the century at Châtillon-sur-Seine (Côte-d'Or), at Hayange (Moselle), and Le Creusot (Saône-et-Loire) took on mainly local workers experienced in iron-working, together with key personnel brought over from Britain and whose presence and high wages caused considerable resentment. At Fourchambault (Nièvre), in an area without such traditions, recruitment, particularly of skilled labour was far more difficult. At Alès (Gard) it was necessary to attempt to find workers in areas as distant as the Nord and Belgium. Enterprises frequently competed with each other for skilled labour. In Paris engineering works, such as that of Cail at Grenelle, were initially able to recruit from among the traditional artisanal metal-working trades, but growth created problems and by 1859 only 12 per cent of workers were natives of Paris or of the Seine department. Most of the others were attracted by higher wages and greater job security from provincial metallurgical centres. In terms of their higher level of skill, negotiating position in the labour market and higher wages, their pride in their work and sense of dignity, skilled workers in the expanding metallurgical industry resembled the traditional artisanate. Although they had less control over the process of production, they frequently proved capable of resisting pressure from employers. For the employer, the increased scale of production did not necessarily facilitate close control over the labour force. The situation was, however, very different for other categories of less skilled labour, even within the same establishment. They could easily be replaced with former agricultural labourers from the Paris region, or migrants from the densely populated regions of Flanders and Brittany, men hardened to low wages and harsh discipline.

From the entrepreneur's perspective, relatively expensive machinery needed to be fully employed, so workers had to be persuaded to become aware of the value of time and to work to the rhythm of the machine – to adopt new patterns of work and leisure. Rural work routines, or even those of the putting-out system were not adequate. Forms of collective discipline had to be imposed to limit absenteeism and to stimulate increases in both the regularity and the intensity of work. Draconian factory regulations were created with these ends in mind, introducing sanctions for absenteeism, lateness, poor quality of work, for talking, singing and smoking, 'quarrelling, rudeness, scurrilous language, indecent behaviour',[9] or insubordination, and to ensure respect for the authority of employers and their foremen. A new social organization of production evolved – allowing closer control over the labour force. In the mines at Carmaux (Tarn), for example, absenteeism during or following *fête* days was punishable by a fine of 3 francs in 1859, at a time when the average daily wage was only around 1f90. Even this was insufficient, for in 1862 bonuses were offered to workers to encourage regular attendance, in 1867 to foremen to encourage them to persuade miners to come to work regularly, and in 1868 the fine had to be increased to 5 francs. The problem in this case was to reduce the commitment of miners to the plots of land which many still cultivated, and to the customs of the rural communities they inhabited. Only the reorganization of shifts from 1871 which effectively reduced the time available for secondary occupations finally increased the energy miners retained for work underground and reduced absenteeism.[10] Mechanization itself was in part designed to increase control over workers, as for example in textiles in the case of the introduction of the self-acting loom in Paris in the 1820s, and in Lodève (Hérault) in the 1840s.[11] It undermined the workers' monopoly of skills and facilitated efforts to standardize quality, increase productivity and restrain wage demands. Although frequent disputes occurred over the control of machinery, in time the machine imposed its own rhythm upon the workforce.

Systems of discipline changed over time and varied between factories. There was always considerably diversity. In the earlier phases of industrialization, and in the smaller establishments, face-to-face relationships between an entrepreneur and his workers might survive, creating the basis for mutual understanding and trust. Where workers were encouraged to recruit their own assistants, as initially in textiles and mining, this absolved the entrepreneurs of considerable responsibilities for the recruitment, paying and supervision of labour. Increasingly, however, and particularly in the larger enterprises, more impersonal techniques of management were introduced. These included the employment of foremen distinguishable by their wages, dress and social aspirations, formal sets of rules, fines (according to an inquiry conducted between 1893 and 1897 in Paris 6 per cent of establishments employing 13 per cent of workers, and in the provinces 22 per cent of establishments with 47 per cent of workers still used fines to maintain discipline – and this particularly in the larger enterprises),[12] and a variety of wage systems.

For employers wages were above all a cost of production and although they might be increased as a means of stimulating productivity or attracting scarce skilled labour, there was a constant incentive to maintain them at the lowest possible level. Systems of payment varied over time, and between factories or tasks. Metallurgical, chemical and textile factories in the Nord, for example, tended to pay by the day; in rural textiles or coal-mining piece-rates predominated. In general, employers preferred some form of piece-rate in order to minimize the need for supervision and to encourage hard work. At Le Creusot in the 1850s, the introduction of piece-rates together with a bonus system had the effect of doubling production in some workshops, while wages overall increased by only 50–60 per cent. Piece-rates were calculated to increase the intensity of work. Thus in the coal-mines at Rive-de-Gier (Loire) in 1851 miners complained that new piece-rates required them to cut 126 hectolitres of coal instead of 105 in order to earn 3f95 a day.[13] In building, wages were kept down by a system of labour subcontracting, in which the various *marchandeurs* who organized teams of workers bid against each other. In mining and metallurgy collective responsibility and productivity were frequently stimulated by means of the payment not of individuals but of an *équipe*, although some mining companies preferred individual piece-rates as a means of encouraging effort and reducing cohesion among the miners.

The ability of employers to maintain wages at low levels depended a great deal upon the supply and demand for particular categories of labour. For the least skilled trades continued in-migration enabled a high degree of exploitation. 'Dilution' of the labour force could have similar consequences. In textiles and the clothing trades, in particular, a large proportion of the workforce was made up of women, regarded as relatively docile and traditionally paid something like half the male wage. Moreover, competitive pressures, especially in depressed periods like 1846–7 or the 1890s, encouraged employers to further reduce wage costs. They frequently met with resistance. In the Lyon silk industry, where piece-rates had been continually reduced since the beginning of the century, major revolts occurred in 1831 and 1834. But if these movements of resistance had some success they also stimulated a transfer of the lowest quality silk weaving into rural areas so that cost-cutting could continue.

The main disadvantage of these procedures was that they were a frequent cause of disputes. In large enterprises during the closing decades of the century this realization led to a reversion to hourly wages. These were preferred by most workers because they eliminated the uncertainty and pressure imposed by piece-rates. The change was combined, however, with closer supervision, and early in this century bonus systems were introduced which rewarded production in excess of a carefully defined norm. This was linked to the slow spread, from the 1880s, of rationalized management techniques involving cost accounting as well as further technical change. It encouraged the further division of labour and use of such procedures as time and motion studies as part of the second industrial revolution in metallurgy, electricity and the automobile industry. This kind of sophistication remained rare before 1914. Far more significant were a variety of other forms of control extending beyond the factory gates, and which served to reinforce the authority of the employer.

One characteristic of the industrial entrepreneur, whatever the scale of his activity, was the will to preserve his authority, and an often intransigent refusal to negotiate on any matter which might appear to threaten this. It was usually believed that concessions would be seen as a sign of weakness and only encourage further demands. This explains the bitterness of many labour disputes. Moreover, if force of circumstances obliged employers to make concessions this was usually accompanied by a determination to revoke them as soon as possible. For those enterprises which could afford the outlay, paternalistic measures were greatly preferred. They did not involve concessions to workers as of right, but were voluntary and dependent upon the goodwill of employers. Most common was the encouragement of mutual aid societies funded by the employers by means of compulsory worker contributions, but housing and gardens, pensions, company shops, food subsidies in periods of high prices, medical care, churches, crèches and schools and leisure facilities might also be provided. These were particularly common where large enterprises developed at a distance from major population settlements and were thus obliged to provide housing for workers and to create what were in effect company towns. Such measures developed on a significant scale from the period 1840–60, first in textiles, engineering and watchmaking in Alsace and the Franche-Comté, and subsequently spreading into mining and metallurgy. By 1867, 800 model houses, many with vegetable gardens, had been built at Mulhouse, providing accommodation for some 6000 people. These not only improved living standards and reduced the waste of energy involved in walking long distances to work, but served as a means by which the conjugal family – as the basis of moral order – was supported. In practice, they helped a limited number of better paid, skilled workers in *grande industrie*. However, there can be little doubt that many workers welcomed at least some of these measures. In the absence of state provision, pensions which promised at least a modicum of security in old age must have been valued, even though the ability of companies to withhold them provided an important means by which they could exercise pressure, as did the possibility of dismissing workers and evicting them from company-owned housing at the same time. This was especially effective in influencing the behaviour of older family men rather than the young and bachelors, and provided an important means of dividing the workforce.

These measures were aimed at increasing the stability of the labour force, stimulating its devotion to the enterprise and reducing the likelihood of workers joining unions or going on strike. Employers were also stimulated by a Christian sense of responsibility and a desire to improve the moral standards of the labour force and impose upon it a sense of responsibility and order. It was thus regarded as particularly important to educate the young, normally in schools staffed by the religious orders. From 1872 the Anzin mining company insisted on employing only literate workers. At Le Creusot, too, the importance of education was emphasized. The company's schools produced a supply of skilled labour and also provided a means of upward mobility in its service. A. P. Deseilligny, director of the works in the 1860s, saw religious education as the essential means of avoiding the 'moral dangers' of work in a large industrial agglomeration. The essential value of religion had been stressed by the Baron de Gérando in 1830 – only through faith would 'each be content with his fate', and this was the basis of 'social order'. At Armentières (Nord) even at the turn of the century, textile employers still imposed an obligation to attend mass on Sunday. At its most extreme the association between the church and employer paternalism created the *usines-internats* of the silk industry, like that founded by Claude-Joseph Bonnet at Jujurieure in the Bugey which employed and lodged in dormitories 400 young girls whose every move – both in and out of work – was closely supervised by nuns. In 1872 an estimated 40,000 girls worked in similar establishments – many of them saving their wages to provide dowries.

Inevitably measures which resulted in a loss of personal liberty were resented. As early as 1866 in the Loire coal basin and 1870 at Le Creusot and at Lens in the northern coalfield, this led to demands for autonomous mutual aid funds controlled by workers' representatives rather than the employers. Yet in spite of the occasional protests paternalism worked. It increased the dependence of the labour force and divided it through the creation of privileged groups. Complaints were seen as instances of 'ingratitude' and were followed by harsh repression. Although generally the worker was regarded as intellectually and morally inferior, when wages and conditions were in question it was asserted that in law he was free and independent and capable of negotiating his own contract. Moreover, if unwilling to accept the authority of his employer, he could look for work elsewhere.

This authoritarian attitude was far more evident in the large, technically complicated establishments in which systematic control appeared to be an essential element of the productive system, than in artisanal workshops. It was, however, increasingly mitigated by the development of feelings of solidarity and of organization among workers, beginning with the more skilled. In spite of considerable resistance by employers, the risk of disruption or of losing skilled workers gradually forced compromises. The railway companies accepted unions from the 1890s, Schneider at Le Creusot in 1899, Renault in 1912. Many others continued to resist. It depended upon the state of the labour market and of the economy in general, as well as upon assessments of relative strength. An indefinite and shifting area of toleration came into existence, frequently re-defined, especially when employers judged that the pretensions of labour were becoming excessive. In such a situation selective dismissals were resorted to. It was assumed that most workers were fundamentally 'loyal'. The fear engendered by the prospect of dismissal, more than any other measure, helped to preserve a spirit of submission among the mass of workers.

When strikes did occur, they were frequently met with a total refusal to make concessions under pressure. At the same time, efforts were made to break the strike by persuading some at least of the workforce to return, by the employment of 'black-legs', and various measures of intimidation including blacklisting and lockouts, usually with the support of government officials. The effectiveness of such activities was frequently increased by collaboration between local employers, as in the case of *Union des fabricants de porcelaine de Limoges* created following a strike in 1869. Particularly in the years immediately preceding the war there was a clear stiffening of resistance on the part of major companies with the development of company unions, major lock-outs and massive dismissals (e.g. 1500 at Le Creusot in 1899, 400 at Renault in 1913).

The constant effort to increase labour productivity had complicated effects upon workers' negotiating positions. The introduction of machinery, while diminishing the value of some skills, reinforced the negotiating position of other groups of key workers. The effects were thus often contradictory, and in practice life in factories must often have been very different from the impression given by the printed sets of rules which frequently alone survive as evidence. The inculcation of new values, however, occurred not only within the factory but throughout society and affected home life and leisure as well as work, as a variety of agencies, including most notably the schools, combined to more effectively socialize the working classes.

Workers in services

Domestics
Although until 1896 the census lacked precision, it appears that the number of domestic servants grew until around 1880, and then slowly fell. On the eve of the First World War there were still close to 1 million, including some 200,000 in Paris, making up 11 per cent of the population. A growing proportion of the group were women – about 70 per cent in 1851 and 80 per cent in 1901. Domestic servants were the largest group of working women. They were in general isolated, as few households had more than one or two domestics, and entirely dependent upon their employers. Their lives were governed by rules of etiquette which maintained social distance and forced the domestic to hide her own thoughts and feelings, to learn to obey and at least in appearance to identify with the interests of her 'family'. In spite of this, they enjoyed low status, were poorly paid (25f30 a month plus keep in Paris in 1900) and often lived in very poor conditions with no legal protection. Situations varied according to the wealth and personal inclinations of employers, but generally domestics were lodged in cramped rooms without adequate light or ventilation under the *mansard* roofs of apartment blocks in the larger towns. They worked for 15–18 hours a day in many cases, were poorly fed and were frequently prey to tuberculosis. The physical effort of carrying water, washing clothes by hand and cleaning was considerable – and to this there were often added difficult responsibilities for the care of children. The important role of servants in the upbringing of middle- and upper-class children should not be ignored. Even so, many girls chose domestic service in preference to work in the factories or fields. For most, service was simply a stage in their lives – a prelude to marriage. It provided a means of integration into the urban world and permitted them to accumulate some small savings.

Shop and office workers
The changing structure of the economy and society stimulated a substantial growth in employment opportunities for clerks, secretaries (from the 1880s), typists and shop assistants – positions which required a modicum of education but not a high level of skill, and which were not very well paid. Secretarial and clerical jobs appear to have attracted men and women with a better education and from a higher social milieu than did those for shop assistants. For the latter, the commercial revolution and the creation of the *grand magasin* in the major cities (from the mid 1850s) created a new range of employment. In Paris at the

end of the century there were thirty-eight stores each employing more than 100 people, and seven *grands magasins* each with over 1000. In 1910, and taking into account only the shop assistants and clerks, the Bon Marché employed 4500, la Samaritaine 2500, the Louvre 3500, Printemps 1350, Galeries Lafayette 2700, Bazar de l'Hôtel de Ville 1200. Before 1914 the majority of these were men. Bon Marché employed, for example, only 1350 women in essentially subordinate functions. In general wages were low, hours long and discipline harsh. In Paris around 1900 shop assistants could earn 50–60 francs per month plus commission, with the hope of an increase to 150–200 francs after several years of service.[14] People entering such employment appear to have been particularly concerned to secure 'respectable' positions which would distinguish them from industrial workers. Subjectively they were not part of the working classes.

Social mobility

Social mobility is a complex phenomenon which is difficult to measure. It appears to have been small in scale and gradual in nature. Neither the economic nor the educational structures provided much opportunity. Thus in Lille in 1908, 90 per cent of the sons of workers were themselves workers. It also seems clear that the working-class children who made the most of educational opportunities were drawn from the milieu of the skilled artisan rather than the machine-minder or labourer. For many a skilled worker social ambitions were realized not through self-improvement but at the cost of material sacrifice in order to finance children's education. Often resources were of necessity concentrated on one child (probably the youngest) whose success would symbolize that of his parents and for whose future his siblings were also expected to make sacrifices. However, the *fact* that upwards mobility was perceived to be possible by some workers at least, and even when this was usually within the working class itself, by moving from unskilled to skilled employment, or by acquiring a little house, clearly influenced attitudes towards the social system as a whole. As for the more ambitious – according to the printing worker Martin Bernard, writing in 1848, 'In general workers conceive of their emancipation in only one manner, and that is to become a *bourgeois*, that is to say to become the owner of a workshop and the tools of the trade.' Those who sought one of the growing number of office jobs (in 1866 there were ten office workers to 240 industrial workers, by 1904 ten to 145), a foreman's post, or who set up their own small businesses have received a bad press from many historians who have implicitly condemned their willingness to imitate the dress, manners and speech of the bourgeoisie. Similarly, to many of their fellow workers, those with ambitions appeared to want to rise above themselves. Even so, anxious to improve their own working and living conditions and those of their families, they had little choice but to accept norms of behaviour established by their employers and customers. Nevertheless, awareness of opportunities for self-improvement and the diverse attitudes it bred inevitably had the effect of reducing solidarity among workers. However, while ambition promoted acceptance of the existing social system, failure might well breed resentment.

Working conditions

Conditions in the new factories, because of their very novelty, aroused far more interest than had those in the often cramped and unhygienic workshops. Medical observers were struck by the high temperatures, humidity and clouds of dust typical of the early textile mills, and the scrophula and tuberculosis which seemed to be the frequent result of hard work in such conditions. It was not simply that working conditions remained generally mediocre, but that workers spent too long in an unhealthy environment, engaged in work which was often too demanding given the poor quality of their diets. Another striking feature of the factory was the noise made by the machinery, and the pulleys and transmission belts that linked it to the steam engines, which, as late as 1907, and in spite of the growing use of electricity, still supplied 70 per cent of industrial power. The situation was especially bad in the smaller enterprises which often used converted buildings. Gradually, however, conditions improved as these were replaced by purpose-built structures with larger dimensions, better suited to the installation of machinery. In particular, efforts were made to reduce the physical effort of labour and to improve ventilation. Initially, manufacturers appear to have set working hours in order to maximize the use of machinery without considering the actual effects upon production. However, in 1841 the Alsatian textile entrepreneur Gros found that by reducing the working day by half an hour he was able to secure an increase in production of 4 per cent. During the 1840s a number of large enterprises followed his lead, reducing the working day from 13 to 12 or even 11 hours. The 1860s appear to have been another period of significant improvement. This was not a response to worker pressure, but depended upon employers' estimates of the most effective means of raising productivity. This kind of awareness was, however, slow to spread.

The length of the working day, according to an official inquiry conducted between 1893 and 1897 in *grande* and *moyenne industrie*, is displayed in Table 48. The working day was shortest for skilled workers in industries like printing (*c.* 10 hours) or mining (8–10 hours). It was longest in textiles and clothing and particularly in domestic production. In small-scale artisanal and especially sweated industries days of 12–14 hours were still not uncommon. Piece-work was an effective means of encouraging long hours of work. The tradition of Sunday rest appears to have survived in most sectors, although it did come under pressure in textiles and especially domestic piece-rate production. By 1893, 93 per cent of workers were free on Sundays. Even so, Renault employees still worked a 60 hour week in 1904 and this rose to 72 hours in 1914,[15] in spite of legislation in 1902 and 1904 which sought to reduce the length of the working day to 10 hours. Moreover, paid holidays were still in the future.

Table 48 *The length of the working day, 1893–7*

Length of working day	Enterprises in Department of Seine (per cent)	Enterprises in other departments (per cent)
8 hours	2	3.5
8½–9 hours	1	16
9½–10 hours	59	29
10½–11 hours	30	31
12 hours	8	20
Over 12 hours		0.5

Long hours spent in factories packed with unguarded machinery inevitably led to numerous accidents. In a report presented to the *Congrès de l'hygiène* in 1907 and dealing with the year 1905 the following causes of accidents were recorded:

Causes	Per cent	Causes	Per cent
Hot or corrosive materials	5.8	By carts, carriages	8.1
Machine tools	8.4	Hand tools	8.2
Cave-ins, falling objects	14.5	Diverse causes	16.4
Fall by worker	17.3	Unknown	0.6
Lifting heavy weights	20.5		

Serious injuries were often caused by attempts to clean moving machinery in response to pressure from employers to maintain production and to the workers' own financial needs especially where piece-rate payment prevailed. Clothing or hair was caught in drive shafts, belts or fly-wheels, fingers were crushed in the metal teeth of machine gearings. Undoubtedly, dangerous working conditions in factories and mines imposed severe physical and psychological strain on workers and upon their families. An accident rate of 18.05 per cent was recorded for engine drivers of the Nord railway company between 1868 and 1873, and for their firemen one of 28.72 per cent. These were mainly due to falls from engines, burns, or being crushed between moving locomotives and other rolling stock or structures.[16] Miners were constantly threatened by falls, fire, gas and floods. Again, the risks were increased by piece-rate systems of payment which encouraged risk-taking. Employers normally blamed such incidents upon worker carelessness, and not until 1898 was a law voted providing minimal compensation for accidents at work.

In addition to accidents, industrial employment was a factor contributing to the incidence of a variety of diseases and ailments. Professional pathologies emerge. Dust in the atmosphere in small workshops or in textile mills – especially bad in linen and jute weaving – was a major cause of respiratory diseases (bronchitis and tuberculosis). Engine drivers, necessarily alert, on their feet for considerable periods of time, and living an irregular life, suffered from a variety of ocular and nervous complaints, from circulatory disorders and those of the digestion. Coal-miners were unlikely to be able to work at the coal face much beyond the age of 40 because of the direct (silicosis) and indirect (cardiac arrest) effects of dust. Chemicals of various kinds also had adverse consequences – the sulphuric acid and caustic solutions used in textile dyes, for example, caused skin disorders. Between 1872 and 1877 some 3244 cases of lead poisoning were treated in hospitals, mostly involving workers in paint manufacture.[17] Sheer physical exhaustion together with the effects of poor diet and living conditions frequently led to premature aging, even if in general these conditions did tend to improve, especially from the 1860s.

The employment of women and children was frequently condemned. According to an inquiry into *grande industrie* conducted between 1839 and 1844, adult males made up 65 per cent of the labour force, women 23 per cent and children under 16 years of age 12 per cent. Yet children had always worked as soon as they were able in rural society. Their lack of skill and physical strength limited the range of industrial occupations in which they could be gainfully employed. Thus, in metallurgy their employment was minimal. However, for some jobs they were ideal. In textile spinning, for example, they could slide under machines in order to tie together threads which had snapped. In Alsace in the 1830s children began to perform this kind of function from between the ages of 6 and 12. In the mining community of Anzin (Nord) in the 1860s, 50 per cent of the boys found work assisting adult miners, but only 12 per cent of the girls. Their other advantage was cheapness. A child could expect to earn no more than one-third of the adult male wage. On the other hand, while he might gradually be able to acquire skills, his productivity was usually low, and as industrial equipment became more complicated and expensive employers appear to have become less interested in the employment of children. Moreover, in the second half of the century as real incomes improved parents became less dependent upon the earnings of young children. Their attitudes towards primary education also changed, so that even before the 1882 law making attendance compulsory a large majority of children were already regularly attending school, although they were still expected to leave at around the age of 12. Legislation on child labour also had some effect. The law of 22 March 1841, which applied only to establishments with more than twenty workers, banned the employment of the under 8s, limited the working day of the 8 to 12 year olds to 8 hours per day, and that of the 12 to 16 year olds to 12 hours. It also required the under 12s to attend school. It was some time before its provisions were observed. Employers resented any kind of interference in their affairs and were afraid that limitations on the hours children could work might have effects on the organization of adult labour. Furthermore, voluntary inspectors were frequently anxious both to avoid offending employers and to deprive poor families of a source of income. The legislation was, however, symptomatic of changing attitudes towards the employment of young children and helped to reinforce these.

Similarly, in the case of women. The early nineteenth century did not see an increase in female participation in the labour force. What was new was the scale of employment outside the home, particularly in the textiles industries in which formerly a large proportion of production had been based upon family workshops. Cotton, wool and then silk were successively affected. According to the 1866 census, women made up 30 per cent of the active industrial population (40 per cent of agricultural labour), with their numbers tending to increase because of demographic stagnation and labour shortage. 73 per cent of this female labour was, however, absorbed by textiles (51 per cent of the labour force), and clothing (87 per cent). Between 1866 and 1911 the number of women employed in industry grew from 1,269,700 to 2,192,500, although by this date employment in shops and offices had been added to domestic service as alternatives (in 1906 women made up 39 per cent of workers in the tertiary sector). Even so (as Table 49 shows), the nature of women's work remained overwhelmingly traditional and largely outside the factory. The opportunities open to women were limited. Custom, male prejudice and educational deficiencies all tended to restrict them to poorly rewarded occupations. Employers believed that women were more amenable to discipline as well as cheaper than men. However, to some extent technical progress altered the range of jobs to which women were recruited. The introduction of the power loom reduced the opportunities in domestic textile manufacture, but at the same time by limiting the strength and skill needed it allowed the replacement of male workers and increased employment in factory work. In contrast, the development of the sewing machine allowed a substantial expansion of domestic work towards the turn of the century – by 1906 there were around 800,000 domestic workers, 86 per cent of them women.[18] Textiles and clothing were exceptional. In other trades male predominance survived. Few women worked in the new heavy industries. Even at the end of the century, and in the burgeoning tertiary sector women were largely restricted to low status jobs as counter assistants and typists. The reserve army of labour identified by Marx was in practice to a large degree made up of women.

Largely as a result of this concentration of women in relatively unskilled and low productivity occupations they were poorly paid in comparison with men. In 1872 the average wage of the female worker was calculated to have represented 45 per cent (1f50:2f35) of that of her male counterpart and in 1911, 47 per

Table 49   *Employment of women in 1906*

Category	Per cent
Employers	12.2
Domestic workers	35.9
Office workers	7.9
Industrial workers	25.1
Servants	17.4
Unemployed	1.5

cent (2f29:4f81). More generally, however, it seems to have been assumed that a woman was only worth half the wage paid to a man. This was justified in part by the assumption that a man's wage was the basic source of family income, the woman's only a more or less temporary supplement. In practice women's wages were so low that it was extremely difficult for a women to subsist without the support of a husband or family. Indeed, poverty forced many women into prostitution. Men, as individuals or as members of trades unions, appear to have viewed women in employment with a great deal of suspicion. As competitors in the labour market they might be used by employers to force down wages. More fundamentally it was generally felt that women's work in factories was somehow unnatural, this being linked to assumptions about male physical and intellectual superiority. The mill, in particular was regarded as no place for a married woman. The gossip, singing, and the comradeship among women workers, together with their use of derision to resist factory discipline were all suspect due to their apparent vulgarity.

The structure of female employment was determined partly by the demand for labour, i.e. the opportunities for work. These varied considerably between industrial centres. Textile towns were at one extreme, coal-mining communities at the other. In the latter male wages were relatively high and the opportunities for women to work more limited. Those who found employment worked mainly from their homes, as laundresses or dress-makers, for example. In other non-textile towns women worked mainly in the clothing industry, food production, in domestic service, as laundresses, as small traders, etc. The supply of labour reflected individual family structures and the degree of dependence upon women's earnings. In most cases women worked from necessity. In the 1860s in the woollens centre of Roubaix (Nord) male textile workers earned between 2f20 and 2f60 per day, women between 1f50 and 1f80.[19] For a family of five with young children and expenses of 22–24f per week, it was essential for the mother to work until the children began to earn. The need to work was frequently the cause of personal tragedies. The practice of contraception appears to have been comparatively rare until the beginning of this century, so back-street abortions were common. These, the fact that pregnant women remained at work until just before they gave birth and returned to work long before children were weaned, resulted in still-born babies, high infant mortality and gynaecological problems. Significantly, the 1892 law which restricted women's working hours and the 1909 and 1913 laws providing for maternity leave were inspired by a patriotic desire to increase the population by reducing infantile mortality. More generally, and although most working-class women gained experience of paid employment at some time during their lives, the ideal appears to have been that women should cease work outside the home following marriage or at least after the birth of the first child. Thus, even in Roubaix in 1872, 81 per cent of unmarried women over 15 years of age worked, but only 17 per cent of married women. Nationally in 1906, in the non-agricultural labour force 40.8 per cent of single women over 16 years of age worked, and 20.2 per cent of those who were married.[20]

Living standards

Living standards were determined by a complex of general economic factors, including levels of employment, wages, the cost of living, together with an individual's age, sex, skill and family size. There was thus great variation between individuals and families, over time and between places. The historian's task is to provide some appreciation of the variation and of the 'reality' of everyday life.

The essential source of income was wages. The quality of the information available is poor, but calculations for Paris indicate that wages rose between 1800 and 1816 or even 1825–6 and then stagnated or declined until the middle of the century. Thus, in the Parisian luxury trades, cabinet-makers earned about 3f50 per day throughout the period 1830–47, typographers, jewellers, watch makers 4f, bakers 3f50, and skilled engineering workers 4f50. The earnings of workers in the textiles and clothing industries tended to fall, as did those of foundry workers (from 5f to 4f50) and of shoemakers (from 3f50 to 3f). Only workers in the building and related industries appear to have enjoyed small increases – carpenters, for example, from 3f50 to 3f75, masons from 3f50 to 4f. Then during the Second Empire wage levels returned to those of the 1810s, before gradually increasing to higher levels. In the metal-working trades and in furniture production, for example, they had almost doubled by 1906–11.[21]. Although complex variations between trades and fluctuations over time render the construction of a general index extremely problematic, similar trends have been noted in the provinces. The development of industrial capitalism certainly favoured improvements in wage levels, although the gulf between the incomes of the wealthy and those of the working masses remained as great as ever.

Wage levels were influenced by a variety of factors, including the levels of prosperity of particular industries, prices and the cost of living in particular places (higher in Paris than in the provinces), and especially the state of the market for particular categories of labour. There is need to stress the variety of circumstances and the importance of wage differentials between workers. On the railways, locomotive drivers, who were required to satisfy high standards of safety and regularity, were paid 7–8f per day by 1881, as much as the best remunerated Parisian artisans. However, if for the period 1892–1910 the remuneration of engine drivers is accorded the index number 100, the average wage of firemen should be given index number 61, that of railway workshop-men 49, that of guards 47, of signalmen 32.[22] Similar differences occurred in mining and metallurgy and to a lesser extent textiles. As a result, calculations of average wages conceal as much as they reveal. In 1848, in the urban sector of the silk industry, in which the most skilled labour was concentrated, a male weaver earned 2–2f50 per day; in the countryside his less highly skilled counterpart made up to 50 per cent less.[23]. In 1910 metallurgical workers at St-Chamond (Loire) earned 8f50, 5–5f50 and 3f50 per day, depending upon whether they were skilled foundrymen (34.6 per cent), semi-skilled forgers and adjusters (37.8 per cent) or unskilled labourers (27.6 per cent).[24]

Nominal wages were, of course, only one determinant of real incomes – the cost of living was the other. Expenditure patterns are difficult to summarize. They obviously varied according to family circumstances. However, according to surveys among workers in the Nord in the 1840s, the better-off spent 51–56 per cent of their incomes on food and drink, the poorer 70–80 per cent; then, perhaps 6–12 per cent on rent; 13–21 per cent for clothing; 8–12 per cent for heating, lighting and furniture, and whatever remained on medical care, recreation, etc. Little remained to save for a rainy day.[25] For most of the century the price of foodstuffs and particularly that of bread remained the key influence. Prior to the commercial revolution of the 1850–60s a poor cereals harvest and the increased prices which resulted had marked effects upon popular living standards. The late 1840s, when nominal wages were steady but the cost of living rose substantially, saw the tragic culmination of a long period, beginning around 1822, of declining, or at best stagnating living standards. Subsequently the cost of living fluctuated far less widely. Between 1856 and 1871 wages rose more rapidly than prices and real incomes improved. The situation was even better in the succeeding period because until 1882, while wage levels continued to rise, the cost of living actually fell. Subsequently, although the cost of living continued to decline, this was less marked and accompanied by a slowing in the rate of increase of wages. Then, in marked contrast, in the period 1905–13, real income tended to decline because prices rose more rapidly than wages.[26] The broad picture is then one of almost constant improvement in real incomes and consequently in living conditions during the second half of the century due to economic growth, the increased demand for industrial labour and the more favourable bargaining position this established for workers *vis-à-vis* their employers. One should not forget, however, that this change was very gradual and, even by 1914, amounted to an increase of only around 25 per cent in real incomes and from a low base. Moreover, the improvement was frequently interrupted by short-term fluctuations in the cost of living.

The experience of individual families varied considerably but almost all endured particularly intense periods of difficulty before young children started earning, due to sickness or unemployment, when food prices rose, and especially as earning capacity tended to decline with age (from about 40), as it did in most professions. For most families life, even at the best of times, must have involved a constant struggle to make ends meet. Poverty was a source of strain and tension and successfully coping with it required emotional and physical strength. All too often men sought refuge and relief from domestic squalor and overcrowding in the *cabaret*. Their drinking added to budgetary problems and frequently resulted in drunken brutality. A great burden was placed on many wives. They were responsible for managing the family budget in addition to all their other duties. Families were judged by their ability to pay their way, by their cleanliness and good conduct. It is difficult for us to comprehend the effort involved in keeping clean when water had to be carried long distances, and up stairs from taps or wells, when clothes had to be boiled and stirred in order to use as little expensive soap as possible, and then dried in cramped apartments or overcrowded courtyards, and in constantly repairing and altering clothes in order to pass them down or exchange them with neighbours. In spite of constant physical effort within the home, and frequently at work, women tended to deprive themselves of food in order to feed their husbands and children. They submitted to the sexual demands of their husbands and to the repeated pregnancies and the gynaecological problems which often resulted. When they were first married, and especially if they both still worked, a husband and wife could live reasonably well. This period, however, was normally a short one. The arrival of children prevented wives from earning and increased the cost of living. The burden was relieved a little when adolescents found work and in the period prior to their establishing families of their own. But then came old age and for those without families to support them this could be a tragedy.

The harshness of life could be alleviated in a variety of ways. For example, a garden in which to cultivate at least some food was very important. The size of the family was a vital factor. Inability to conceive, or deliberate contraception meant better living standards. More generally, the interrelated improvements in real incomes, in diet and health, and the reduction in the incidence of illness and premature death, all contributed to an alleviation of conditions from the 1850s. But improvement was not incompatible with the survival of widespread poverty. Furthermore, the lack of security remained a basic problem of working-class life. Even the majority of the highly skilled and best paid were unable to escape this entirely, which explains the attraction of employment in such relatively protected spheres as military arsenals and naval dockyards which paid low wages but provided secure employment, free medication and even pensions. Many workers, however, earned at best only enough to subsist from day to day. Poor trading conditions forced employers to lay-off workers or to impose short time or wage reductions. Dismissals were of course usually selective, affecting especially the least skilled, the undisciplined, bachelors and strangers, a process which served to accentuate the normal divisions between workers. As a group domestic and rural workers were particularly easy to lay-off. Raw materials were simply no longer distributed. Factory workers received some protection from the desire of employers to continue to meet overhead costs and to limit the possibilities of violent protest by workers in urban concentrations. Security of employment thus probably increased with growth of factories.

In the 1890s and 1900s the normal level of unemployment was estimated at around 3–400,000 – perhaps 3–3.5 per cent of the industrial labour force[27] – although union officials claimed that this was a gross underestimation. This was increased by economic crises. In the first part of the century these were in general shorter, more intense and more frequent than they were to be after the 1850s. In the building trades – a barometer of economic activity – serious crises occurred in 1826–7, from 1830 to 1835, 1840–3, 1847–51, from 1856 to 1858, 1873–5, 1882–5, 1892–4. Many building workers traditionally went to the place de Grève in Paris in search of work. The Limousin mason, Martin Nadaud, described it in 1835 as covered with emaciated men, clothed in rags, begging soup from soldiers in nearby barracks. The influx of seasonal and temporary workers from the provinces tended to create an oversupply of labour. To crises should be added the effects of technological unemployment and of seasonal unemployment especially serious in building, in the clothing trades and industries producing luxury goods. The Lyon silk industry was peculiarly susceptible to trade cycles and changes in fashion, so that even in the best years around forty-five days were lost.

The long mid century crisis with its complex of economic and political causes was particularly severe in its effects. In the industrial Nord in 1846, 191,600 people (1:5.9 inhabitants), and in 1847, 268,100 (1:4.2) were in receipt of public assistance. It should be noted that this ignores those too proud to ask, or those earning more than a basic minimum wage, insufficient to provide even a modicum of comfort for a family. During the admittedly exceptional circumstances following the 1848 Revolution, the Paris Chamber of Commerce estimated that most industries had dismissed 50–75 per cent of their workers – and this following the especially intense crisis of 1846–7. It is easy to understand the importance attached to the 'right to work' demanded in this revolutionary year. The depression of 1882–6 was estimated to have increased unemployment to 10 per cent, but with much higher proportions in some industries (20 per cent in metallurgy) or regions (200,000 unemployed in Paris in spring, 1883). Moreover, at any time illness or an accident threatened loss of earnings and possibly the cost of medical care. Savings were rapidly exhausted. Indeed an inquiry in 1892 revealed that of 1000 Parisian working-class households, 871 saved nothing.[28] The pawn-shop and credit from shopkeepers were important standbys. They could not be relied upon for long, but many families were unable to escape from the burden of debt. Assistance to the unemployed took the form of charity and municipal work relief. These were always inadequate and were increasingly regarded as degrading, an attitude which added to the nightmare of being without work, from which suicide was a not infrequent means of escape. Provision for old age was similarly inadequate. In 1850 the state had established a savings bank to encourage workers to provide for their old age (*Caisse des retraites pour la vieillesse*), but its depositors were mainly middle class, attracted by a relatively high rate of interest (5 per cent in the 1860s). There were also some private societies like the *Prévoyants de l'Avenir* (1880), but most workers who felt able and willing to save did so as members of mutual aid societies which provided pensions rarely exceeding 100 francs per annum. Some occupational pension schemes were established primarily for government employees, but in the later decades they expanded to cover a growing number of workers in large-scale mining, metallurgy and railway enterprises. Even in 1898, however, an official inquiry revealed that only 3.7 per cent of the employed labour force of 2,656,674 covered by government factory inspectors received pensions. Inevitably the old tried to work for as long as they were able, and then relied on their children, if they had any. This dependence frequently caused financial strain and tension between the generations.

Poverty is not easy to analyse. There is no absolute level of subsistence below which people are poor. To an important degree it is a state of relative deprivation and has to be considered in relation to evolving standards of living, i.e. to changing norms. The rise in real wages from the 1850s and especially in the last quarter of the century increased consumer spending and allowed the development of new material aspirations -- better food, more comfortable accommodation, and new clothing (encouraged by the growth of advertising and ready-to-wear products). Clothing is an interesting example of the complex influences on patterns of expenditure. Workers, as a sign of a desire to escape from their conditions, became increasingly desirous of dressing like bourgeois during their periods of leisure. Diet provides another key indicator of change. Again, generalization is difficult. However, it appears that standards of nutrition – in Paris certainly – declined between *c.* 1820 and 1850. During these years the price of bread continued to serve as the basic determinant of living standards. The rioting which accompanied increases in prices after poor harvests was symptomatic of this dependence. Subsequently, slow improvement occurred as bread prices were stabilized, and gradual dietary diversification occurred (meat, dairy produce, vegetables) as real incomes increased. This improvement was not without its set-backs, particularly during the depression of the 1880s and 1890s when annual meat consumption per capita in Paris fell from around 80 kilogrammes in 1883–6 to about 70 by 1911.[29] Paradoxically urban workers normally enjoyed a better diet than did the mass of peasants because the commerce in foodstuffs was focused on urban centres. Even so, few ate a nutritionally balanced diet, and most continued to subsist on a monotonous fare of bread, potatoes, soups and vegetables, with a little meat once or twice a week. Much depended upon income and family size. Role within the family was also important. Men engaged in hard physical labour tended to receive a lion's share of available food in order to keep up their strength, women to stint themselves to provide for their husbands and children. A diet with too much starch and fat and lacking in calcium and vitamins was a major cause of deficiency diseases such as rickets and scrofula; it impeded the physical development of the young and could result in the permanent state of imperfect health which so many workers and their families endured. Other common physical illnesses such as gastro-enteritis provided evidence of the frequent adulteration of food, of low standards of hygiene in its storage and preparation (especially meat), and also of the poor facilities for cooking in most homes, and the limited culinary skills of many working women.

The need to spend a large proportion of income on food left relatively little to meet the costs of accommodation. According to the *Statistique générale de la France* in 1910 rent took between one-tenth and one-fifth of a worker's income in Paris. Conditions were generally appalling, especially in some of the older cities in which growing populations were squeezed into existing buildings with inadequate sanitary facilities. Poorly constructed tenement blocks existed side by side with workshops and factories in an environment polluted by noise, smoke and filth. Overcrowding was a major cause of poor hygiene. There was an overpowering smell from people who rarely washed. Their dirty bodies and filthy living conditions provided ideal breeding grounds for numerous parasites. Constant close proximity stimulated psychological tensions within and between families. This and the lack of comfort – furniture was minimal, typically including beds, table and chairs, a stove and some ornaments – reduced the attractions of home and family and men, in particular, often sought refuge in the bar. Life would become more home-centred only as living conditions slowly improved.

Urban renewal, especially from the 1850s, if it removed the worst slums, could barely keep pace with the growth of the population. The development of suburbs and cheap urban transport at the turn of the century allowed workers to live at a distance from their work without exhausting themselves by walking to and fro and thus substantially improved the situation. Even then, however, convenience and habit and the need to avoid unnecessary expenditure encouraged families to take up residence close to their places of work. Only where land was cheap in the suburbs and in smaller urban centres were a significant proportion of workers able to own their own houses and enjoy access to a garden and to the nearby countryside. To be free from the burden of rent was a considerable attraction, but in 1865 it cost 1600–2000 francs to build a house in the mining town of Carmaux and few were able or willing to commit themselves to borrowing such relatively large sums.

The shortcomings of diet, of working and living conditions, and of the general environment inevitably resulted in poor standards of health. These problems were brought to the attention of public opinion and governments from the 1840s by the work of influential critics like Villermé. Normal physiological misery made many workers susceptible to a whole range of endemic illnesses such as bronchitis, pneumonia, tuberculosis, typhoid, gastro-enteritis, to skin diseases, and to major epidemics of which cholera was the most notable. There can be little doubt that the reputation of some of the growing urban centres as *mangeurs des hommes* was justified. Infant mortality rates were, as we have seen, especially high among working-class children. Yet the picture was not entirely black. The contrast so often drawn by conservative critics of the industrial system with the healthy countryside tended to minimize the miseries of rural life and conditions did become better. Information on exemptions from military service shows that by the late 1850s, and especially the 1880s average height had increased and the likelihood of physical ailments declined. This was due to the combined effects of growing real incomes, and better standards of public hygiene and of medicine.

Better health did something to reduce the insecurity of working-class life – and at the turn of the century the state began to make efforts to improve assistance during periods of personal crisis. As part of a deliberate governmetal effort to win over the workers, in 1891 a *Conseil supérieur du travail* was created to advise on social problems and an *Office du travail* to gather information. In 1899 the former was reformed so that in addition to nominated members, one-third of its membership was elected by trades unions and one-third by employers. In

1894 the principle of compulsory assurance against sickness and old age was accepted in the case of miners; in 1898 a law provided for (inadequate) compensation for workers injured in accidents. In 1905 a not very effective law established pension rights for some 10 million people – a privilege previously enjoyed only by limited numbers of state employees and the more valued employees of some large paternalistic enterprises like the railway companies. National standards were also imposed upon the poorly funded communal *bureaux de bienfaisance* which had previously provided poor relief. Further reform was impossible, however, without adequate funding and parliamentary opposition to the introduction of income tax made this impossible before the First World War.

Family and community

In determining the characteristics of working-class communities an examination of the geographical origins of workers and the balance between settled inhabitants and newcomers is a matter of some significance. The extent to which the labour force was recruited from established families or from recent migrants varied considerably over time and between both professions and places. In general the importance of newcomers tended to increase until the 1870s. In 1866, 61 per cent of the inhabitants of Paris had been born in the provinces – mainly in the Paris basin, north and east, although the range of attraction was expanding, especially in the centre and west – and 6 per cent abroad. The attraction was primarily higher wages and better employment prospects.[30] In the textile centre of Reims, as late as 1881 over two-thirds of the population had been born outside the town – 23,500 in the surrounding department of the Marne, 36,000 in other parts of France and 6000 abroad.[31] In general, migrants tended to be relegated to the dirtiest, most poorly paid jobs because of their lack of skills, and as a result were forced into slum housing. In Marseille in 1846, for example, 52 per cent of skilled workers were natives of the city, but only 26 per cent of unskilled. In Paris, similarly it was very difficult for newcomers to find work in the traditional skilled trades. The jewellers of the third *arrondissement* were 53 per cent Parisian.[32] This was a skilled trade with a high degree of occupational inheritance. There were, however, some skilled professions with their own currents of migration. Thus in the 1850s, the engineering works of Gouin and Cail at La Grenelle encouraged the migration of skilled workers from the metallurgical centres of Le Creusot, Fourchambault and Decazeville, and the sinking of new pits in the Pas-de-Calais in the 1870s attracted recruits from the mining communities of the Nord. In these cases in periods of economic expansion the demand for skilled labour far exceeded local supply.

Historians and sociologists have long debated the question of whether rapid urbanization led to the disruption of social life, to *anomie* and to social disorganization. Clearly the transition from rural to urban life, or even the less uprooting move from one town or *quartier* of a city to another, required major and difficult adjustments. Life in squalid overcrowded housing, unemployment, uncertainty about where the next meal was coming from, clearly provoked tension and strife. Slum areas in the major cities were characterized by a barely suppressed climate of violence in which quarrels within families and between neighbours, especially over noise and drunken behaviour, were common, and screams and torrents of abuse part of daily life. Groups like miners, masons and labourers employed at hard, manual labour, fortified by strong drink and proud of their physical strength, appear to have been particularly irritable. For many poor women, often clothing workers or domestics (the latter group especially susceptible to sexual exploitation), prostitution was often the only means of alleviating hardship. Their misery produced an apparently inexhaustible supply of women to meet the demands of mostly unattached males in the growing urban centres. Criminal acts were common. Moreover, many of them were never reported or discovered by the police – sexual abuse within families, assaults upon or thefts from people who were too afraid of their assailants or else too much in awe of the police and justice to report their problems. The concentration of the poorest in particular streets or *quartiers*, and the neglect of children by their hard-pressed parents, while they received much of their education on the streets alongside their peers, further weakened social controls.

The cities both provided greater opportunities for crime and a more impersonal social milieu in which the values and informal sanctions of the small rural community were less effective. Until the 1870s, moreover, there was a clear relationship between bread prices and theft. This was the sort of situation which created bougeois anxiety about 'the vile multitude' (Thiers) or 'the savages' (Balzac). These characterizations provide evidence of a widespread sense of disgust combined with fear of people who were dirty, frequently deformed and maimed, and who dressed and spoke differently. There was a tendency to confuse the marginal, semi-criminal groups of beggars, rag-pickers and street-hawkers (estimated to number around 30,000 in Paris in the 1820s),[33] with the 'labouring classes' in general. Gradually the expansion of employment opportunities, the disappearance of dearth, and the development of more stable, personal relationships reduced the levels of violence due to frustration, the pressure on women to prostitute themselves, and the number of crimes caused by the desperation, so typical of the rapidly growing city. At the same time, however, crimes against property tended to increase as new material needs were aroused.

Even when conditions were at their worst, the situation of newcomers was nevertheless frequently eased by the tendency for chain migration to occur as members of a family or community, or inhabitants of a particular region followed each other and settled in close proximity. Many migrants found working conditions similar to those in their places of origin. Often, as in the case of former rural weavers, they moved to work in nearby textiles factories in places like Rouen or Lodève from the 1820s, or Armentières in the 1840s and

1850s. In these cases they not only engaged in similar work, but because of the short distance of movement remained within a familiar cultural milieu. The possession of skills, in particular, promoted rapid integration into the new community through professional contacts and because relatively high incomes allowed active sociability and intermarriage. Even when families had diverse origins and occupations, as residence became more stable so reciprocal systems of rights and obligations developed within kinship and neighbourhood groups which offered the nuclear family limited protection during periods of sickness or unemployment. Within one or two generations a distinctive working-class community emerged, particularly in the mono-industrial centres of metallurgy or coal-mining, and in predominantly working-class suburbs. Newcomers to these relatively settled communities subsequently sought to reduce their isolation by accepting prevailing behavioural norms. It is obvious, therefore, that in order to understand the working classes it is essential to consider the interrelationships between work, family and community which determined daily life.

Evidence of growing social stability can also be found in demographic statistics which reveal the transition from an initial situation in which the availability of work promoted an influx of young migrants, and led to early marriage and high birth rates; towards one in which a more calculating attitude towards family life developed especially in the last third of the century as infant mortality declined, the opportunities for child labour were reduced, living standards improved and aspirations for a better life were generated. This is the pattern suggested by birth rate statistics from the coal and glass producing centre of Carmaux in the Tarn, from the northern mining community at Anzin, and the textile centre of Roubaix (Table 50).[34] The trends are similar, although the chronology differs due to varying age and social structures, the pace of industrial development and of migration, and community *mores*. All the evidence is that major changes occurred in working-class value systems. Within the family greater material prosperity served to reduce marital tension, although without altering the prevailing division of roles. Thus the status of the husband reflected

Table 50 *Birth rate (percentages)*

Year	Carmaux	Anzin	Roubaix
1851	37.2	38.4	
1861	40	37.2	42.8
1866		32.8	44.8
1872	37.3	33.0	42.2
1876		33.0	42.4
1881	37	28.7	39.0
1891		26.9	36.4
1896		22.9	32.5
1901		27.5	29.9
1906		26.5	27.0

the degree of dependence upon him as breadwinner. Providing he properly fulfilled this role his household responsibilities were negligible. This was the sphere of the wife. A family enjoyed status within the community to the extent to which husbands were able to provide 'properly' for their dependants, and wives were seen to be good managers of their family budgets, and took proper care of their spouses and children. This division of labour within the family provided the basic structure within which children were socialized, i.e. in which boys and girls learned about the values of the community and appropriate forms of behaviour. These lessons were often enforced by the imposition of harsh discipline. Within the home mothers and daughters worked together and often developed particularly close relationships. Girls learned to knit and sew, to clean and take care of younger children, but were not entirely prepared for their future lives. It appears that mothers rarely talked to their daughters about sex, so that they remained sexually ignorant and often became pregnant and were forced to marry in order to preserve their own honour and that of their family. Similarly, boys learned about work and were introduced to the male culture by their fathers – often, as in the case of miners, going out to work alongside them as soon as they were able. Even in an economically more complicated setting – like that of Lyon – at mid century, more than half of the workers had taken up the same trade as their fathers, and one in three married the daughter of a worker in the same trade.[35]

The factory system was often condemned for weakening the bonds of occupational solidarity and especially for its disruptive effects on family life. However, the family largely preserved its socializing functions and in the absence of developed welfare facilities, continued to play a key role as a budgetary unit, and in supporting its individual members in times of distress, during the many crises which punctuated working-class life. Even where the emotional ties between couples suffered from the stress of poverty, a strong sense of obligation was likely to survive. There was, however, only a narrow safety margin. Many families drowned during the constant struggle to keep their heads above water. Harsh conditions inevitably caused irritation. One or other parent might give up the struggle and seek solace in drink; children might resist the demands for family solidarity. The result was usually greater misery and unhappiness. Yet in spite of the worst fears of bourgeois moralists, the family survived and even became stronger. The proportion of illegitimate children born in Paris, for example, fell from 26.9 per cent in 1852–6 to 25.78 per cent in 1869,[36] in part because more couples actually married rather than just living together. As the entry of children into the industrial labour force began to be delayed, the family inevitably became more home and child centred.

The family is, however, only one part of the social network within which individuals grow up. The nature of relationships within the local community are also of fundamental importance. The cultural isolation and geographical segregation of working-class communities in particular *quartiers* (the 10th, 11th, 19th and 20th *arrondissements* of Paris after Haussmann's reconstruction), in the spreading suburbs of major cities (Villeurbanne, La Guillotière, and Vaise in

Lyon), or new mining or metallurgical settlements, served to reinforce the importance of a range of mutual ties based on work, neighbourliness and leisure activities – and to promote a sense of solidarity. In part this was the consequence of children escaping from over crowded housing and spending much of their time together on the streets. Peer group participation was crucial in the socialization process. It was because women met regularly at shops or when they fetched water or washed clothes, or gossiped on doorsteps, or looked after each other's children. It was due to the regular meetings of men on the street or in cafés. The existence of a shared living space – symbolized by intermarriage between families – served to strengthen the bonds established by common economic interests and problems. These were reinforced further by collective action in the form of the bread riot or strike. It required perhaps a generation to create, and the result was an urban village with solidarities and also fissures similar to those of the rural community.

The fissures were in part the product of the inner hierarchy of the working classes. Relatively well-off artisans cultivated the values of thrift, sobriety, independence and respectability. Although within the community they might well have friends and relatives in far less favourable circumstances, there was always an awareness of the differences of status between them. In the ironworks at Fourchambault, the second generation of skilled workers tended to withdraw from the popular sociability of the *cabaret*, and to save in order to purchase a home or a field.[37] Perceptions of the opportunities available to individuals and families varied considerably.

Except in the major cities, workers had little interest in events outside their own locality, and even in the cities the same was true of much of the population. Linguistic particularism helped to maintain this isolation for at least the first half of the century in Marseille, and for longer in regions like Alsace. If the aristocracy and *grande* and *moyenne bourgeoisie* existed as national classes with some sort of shared ideology and self-consciousness, the same could not be said of the working classes. The stress ought to be upon diversity, although as the study of popular culture and of organizational activity indicates, a growing sense of unity was slowly being created. In part this was the product of the growing residential and social segregation which left workers to their own devices. It was also an aspect of broader patterns of cultural development, part of a complex urbanization process which involved the constant change and recreation of aspects of the popular culture. To a degree this constituted the autonomous development of a properly working-class culture, but subject to significant external influences on the part of the bourgeoisie and of the state.

Periodization is difficult. The initial phase was destructive rather than creative. It occurred first of all in Paris, and subsequently in the major provincial centres. Migration increased the cultural heterogeneity of the population, while the lengthening of working hours and the subjection of women and children to factory discipline, especially in the 1830s and 1840s, left little time for leisure. Even the artisan was threatened as the division of labour and intensification of work processes destroyed traditional habits and an old technical culture.

Moreover, the search for greater social status encouraged the younger men, including many worker militants to reject features of the traditional culture, including Christianity, or popular literature, in favour of a more 'scientific' and bourgeois learning. Nevertheless, a genuinely working-class culture did emerge from the 1840–60s, influenced by tradition but recognizably different from the pre-industrial urban culture. It was centred upon the work-place, inevitably given long working hours, and upon the *cabaret*. It was at its strongest – almost forming a distinct sub-culture – among geographically and/or socially isolated groups like miners.

Alcohol was a means of reviving flagging energies and a source of comfort especially important for those whose work exposed them to the elements. More than this, the *cabaret* provided warmth, light and company, and a place of escape from overcrowded homes. It reinforced the male comradeship of the work-place and neighbourhood, just as gossiping in the streets or on doorsteps reinforced links between women. In Lille in 1830 there was one *cabaret* per 137 inhabitants; by 1850 this had increased to one per eighty. Police reports constantly complained about drunkenness and violence, especially at weekends. Middle-class reformers took up their complaints. It was psychologically easier for them to explain poverty in terms of the moral inadequacy of the working classes than through the shortcomings of the social system. But more than a place for drinking, the *cabaret* was a meeting place. It was a centre for games (of cards or dice), for discussion and for reading newspapers. Only slowly as economic conditions improved did the habit of drinking appear to decline and family sociability increase. According to the economist Leroy-Beaulieu the *cabaret* was 'the workers' church' and symbolized their detachment from religion (see also p. 299).

The reasons for this detachment were varied. They ranged from simple exhaustion after a long working week, to resentment of the efforts of the clergy to interfere in their private lives (especially by influencing women through the confessional and children in school, and by denunciations of 'immoral' acts like dancing or drinking), and the identification of the clergy with the established social order. Sermons on the duty of resignation to one's miserable lot in return for hope of reward in the hereafter in the shape of life everlasting were often resented. It was hardly surprising that in the 1840s the Parisian workers' newspaper, *L'Atelier*, criticized the church for its domination by the state and by the rich. It still hoped at this time for an alliance between religion and democracy. 1848 was to destroy such optimism. Even then religion still provided consolation and church attendance an interlude in many a monotonous existence. The clergy and religious laymen were a source of charity and advice – although this often seemed calculated to humiliate the recipient. Most workers, especially those living in small communities or employed in dangerous occupations, like miners, continued to respect at least the 'rites of passage', to baptize their children, and to ensure that they took their first communion and were married in church. They were finally buried by a priest. Although regular attendance at mass, especially by men, might have declined, the major steps in life were thus marked by religious ceremonies. Upbringing and education made Christianity an important source of reference – part of a common culture, although priests frequently complained that workers' had little knowledge of the church's teaching and that their faith had degenerated into simple superstition. In determining workers' attitudes towards the church a great deal depended upon the social and cultural context within which they lived, and in the case of migrants that of their region of origin. The rural hinterlands of towns like Limoges and Orléans were themselves substantially deChristianized. Elsewhere, especially in southern industrial centres like Lodève, at least until the middle of the century, religious mutual benefit associations like the *confréries* of penitents retained a certain vigour, although the process of secularization and the creation of independent working-class organizations and meeting places was already well underway. As Belleville became the most working-class *quartier* of Paris, so in the 1870s and 1880s a marked increase in indifference to religion occurred. By 1883–1903, 38.7 per cent of burials were non-religious.[38] The experience of the Paris Commune appears to have been one factor in this case, but above all it was the creation of an overwhelmingly working-class milieu concerned primarily with making ends meet, i.e. with the material rather than the spiritual. The church proved incapable of integrating newcomers, and also increasingly had to compete with alternative, secular institutions – such as the ubiquitous *cabaret*.

The significance of this institution was increased by the shelter it provided to a variety of voluntary associations – mutual aid societies, musical groups, trades unions and political groups which in periods of repression were protected from informers by the exclusiveness of the neighbourhood café. Sometimes these groups were able to use a back room and acquire many of the attributes of a private club – with rules and regulations in imitation of those of the bourgeois *cercle*. This was symptomatic of a process of cultural imitation, through the diffusion of ideas down the social hierarchy, facilitated by the everyday contacts between urban social groups. It reflected the ambivalent attitude of many workers towards bourgeois culture. The more ambitious sought to acquire its forms in order to fulfil their social aspirations, but more generally the development of primary education resulted in the growing integration of workers into the wider national community.

Working-class culture would remain oral to an important degree due to poor standards of literacy. As the historian Michelet wrote to Béranger in 1848, 'the masses do not know how to read, and do not want to read because it is tiring for a man who is not used to it'. This partly explains the popularity of Béranger's own political and patriotic songs. Nevertheless, better education and mass literacy increasingly contributed to a process of cultural integration which provided an important means by which the socially and politically dominant groups were able to sustain themselves. The use of Occitan by workers in Toulouse or the major social contrasts which marked the use of language in Paris during the earlier half of the century largely disappeared afterwards. This process was reinforced by the growing commercialization of leisure especially in the big cities, where with the development of cheap mass transport from the 1880s the *quartier* began to lose its individuality and become integrated into the city with its theatres, café-concerts, and ultimately cinemas. Mass circulation newspapers like *Le Petit Journal* and *Le Petit Parisien*, launched in 1863, each with a daily circulation of around a million by 1900, which concentrated on crime, tragedy and 'human interest' stories, further contributed to the standardization of language and thought.

Protest

The existence of information in police reports and the press has tended to attract historians to the study of working-class organization and protest. Inaction, in contrast, draws very little attention. It needs to the stressed, therefore, that protest or sustained trades union and political activity normally attracted only a relatively small proportion of workers and that the exceptional circumstances in which large numbers of people were mobilized could not be sustained. The obvious question which follows is, why did workers normally tolerate their often appalling living conditions and inferior place in society?

'Deference' could be one answer, i.e. the more or less willing acceptance of the existing social and moral order. Indeed, the absence of obvious alternatives, the prospect of loss of employment or police repression directed against 'militants', religious convictions which favoured resignation, the philanthropic activities of employers, the workings of the educational system, all contributed to the development of an inferiority complex and feelings of dependence on employers and on the 'rich' for work, help and advice. For most people, and for most of the time, wisdom involved accommodation rather than conflict. Protest was limited to the expression of grievances among friends in the privacy of the work-place or bar-room. Deference might, however, conceal more complicated attitudes, including resentment of dependence and even the development of alternative values, leading to the emergence of a counter-culture not necessarily opposed to, but nevertheless distinct from that of the dominant social groups. It should not be forgotten either that the poor also favoured order and security, both the social order which maintained employment and limited violence and the comfortable sense of belonging to a particular social group. Often they were reasonably content with their lot, and from the 1850s could enjoy rising living standards and limited personal advancement. On the other hand, non-participation in protest, in trades union, or political activity, cannot be taken to denote satisfaction with the status quo. Inactivity might conceal latent discontent.

A range of possible means existed for expressing this discontent. The heterogeneity of the working classes ensured considerable variety. Decisions as to whether or not to protest and on the form protest should take were influenced by experience, culture, the structure of working-class groups, their economic situation, relationships with other social groups, assessment of the likelihood of success, fear of repression, etc. The strike has often been taken to be the working-class form of protest *par excellence*. This is an oversimplification. Until the 1850s the most significant forms of working-class protest were probably those directed, particularly by women, against the grain merchants and bakers whom they blamed for the high cost of bread. For as long as the traditional subsistence crisis survived, the major factor determining workers' living standards remained the fluctuating cost of basic foodstuffs. The large increases in the price of bread which followed poor harvests had devastating effects on family budgets, at the same time as the generalized economic crisis led to wage reductions and unemployment. Subsequently, this type of demonstration almost disappeared although the cost of living continued to influence worker action. In particular, inflationary pressure between 1851 and 1876, and 1900 and 1910 encouraged demands for wage increases and indeed complaints concerning food prices led in August 1911 to serious disorders in the mining and metallurgical areas of the Nord (which spread into the north-east, east, centre and Brittany). These renewed 'subsistence' disorders were, however, insignificant in comparison with those of 1846–7. That they were concerned with the price of dairy products rather than bread reveals how popular expectations had altered. The disappearance of massive cyclical fluctuations in the price of food meant that wages became the essential determinant of living standards, and that action to protect or improve living standards was now more likely than before to be directed at the employer.

Even then, however, there were alternative forms of action, which often made striking unnecessary. The strike was normally an action of last resort which most workers – and especially the unskilled with low earnings, no savings and limited negotiating strength – were anxious to avoid. The threat of loss of earnings, or dismissal, was not to be taken lightly. Thus, following a series of strikes by Parisian craftsmen in the 1860s, the delegates of the precision instrument-makers reported that, 'we do not desire [strikes] because they demand resources that we can produce only at the price of cruel sacrifices, and which are never justified by the results obtained, even admitting that complete success were to crown our efforts'. Negotiations with employers were preferred. If these were rejected or failed, there was still a series of possible actions which stopped short of a strike. These obviously included the threat to strike, often made by posting anonymous *placards* on the doors of workshops or employers' homes. In the period before 1864 when strikes were illegal, boycotts of particular workshops could be organized, particularly by artisans, with men simply leaving one by one, or else productivity might be reduced by absenteeism, or a go-slow (enforced if necessary by means of the verbal abuse or physical beating of overzealous workers), raw materials could be wasted and machinery sabotaged. Information about these less dramatic, but traditional, means of exerting pressure is less likely to be found in the police archives. Strikes are only part of the picture of worker protest, but they can be counted, although even then far more probably occurred than were ever reported. Tilly and Shorter's calculations reveal that between 1830 and 1880 the number of strikes per year fluctuated at a relatively low level, without any marked tendency to increase, although there were short-lived periods of relatively intense activity particularly following the 1830 and 1848 Revolutions. It is likely that the relatively slow rate of industrial development served to ease the strains and to limit the occasions for strife. Over time the number of strikes rose as groups of workers evolved strategies to help them cope with the new problems of factory employment, but it was only in the early 1880s that a substantial and sustained increase in the number of strikes occurred.[39]

The levels of strike activity were influenced by changes in government policy, and by changing socio-economic structures and the effects these had on working conditions, standards of living and group consciousness. It certainly appears as if mechanization and the concentration of industrial activity were important factors leading to an increase in the number of strikes. In the period 1871–90, while 29 per cent of strikes occurred in enterprises employing fewer than fifty people, these (according to the 1896 census) made up 98 per cent of the total number of enterprises. In contrast 71 per cent of strikes took place in enterprises with more than fifty workers which made up only 1.3 per cent of the total number of enterprises.[40] Efforts have also been made to analyse the links between strike activity and economic cycles, and reveal that there are no simple correlations. The cycles themselves were complex. In 1846–7 when textile workers at Roubaix (Nord) were experiencing an intense depression, miners at nearby Anzin were able to take advantage of a high level of demand for coal. Much depended upon how particular employers and groups of workers perceived their situation. In general, and especially in large enterprises, employers adopted rather authoritarian attitudes towards their workers. This inhibited the development of negotiating procedures which might have made the use of the strike weapon unnecessary. Employer attitudes did, however, vary in relation to the economic situation. They were far more likely to make concessions if trade was prosperous and they risked losing orders in case of a prolonged strike. Conversely, during a depression they were more likely to resist workers' demands in order to preserve already slim profit margins.

Workers were aware of this and to some extent calculated their own strategies accordingly. They were able to judge employers' profitability from levels of stocks, the demand for labour, etc. Requests for wage increases which might or might not need to be supported by strike action were much more likely in prosperous than in depressed years. The *procureur-général* at Lyon in 1833 explained a wave of strikes involving metal-workers at Oullins, coal-miners at Rive-de-Gier, and masons at St-Etienne by pointing out that, 'The worker who realises that he is needed becomes demanding.' The same was to be true during the Second Empire, in 1855, 1865 and 1869–70. In contrast 1867 and 1868 were years in which harvests were poor and food prices high, and the economy was less buoyant. Employers in *grande industrie* were anxious to rationalize production and increase productivity, and were less tolerant of strikes. In these years, in spite of increased discontent, workers found their resources and capacity to sustain a strike diminishing. The nature of strikes altered. A much higher proportion were defensive as opposed to offensive strikes (46 per cent in 1867, 36 per cent in 1868),[41] i.e. attempts to oppose the reductions in wages and employment by means of which employers sought to reduce their costs. There was also a higher failure rate. Following such periods of depression there was often a tendency for the number of strikes to increase again, as the economic situation improved and workers made an effort to restore previous wage levels. Thus at Montceau (Saône-et-Loire) miners reacted to the wage cuts of 1896–7 in the early years of the following decade. Nationally the strike waves between 1899 and 1901, which involved miners, steel-workers, dockers and sailors, were on an unprecedented scale with 1,200,000 days lost in 1898, 3,500,000 in 1899 and 3,760,000 in 1900.

The legal and political environments were clearly significant factors. Thus the period of political instability, new aspirations and relaxation of police repression which followed the 1830 Revolution saw the first major strike wave of the nineteenth century – with a peak of seventy-two recorded strikes in 1833. Of the fifty-five which can be identified thirteen occurred in Paris, nine in Lyon, four in Le Havre and three each in Lille and St-Etienne. Nineteen occurred in the textile industries, and the others mainly in the printing, woodworking and the building trades.[42] Another peak occurred in 1840 partly as a product of republican agitation, especially among Parisian artisans. This encouraged strikes by tanners, bakers, building workers, waggon-makers and metal-workers, involving in all 20–30,000 men. The 1848 Revolution similarly stimulated organization, protest and strikes, as did the re-awakening of political agitation during the Liberal Empire. Conversely, political repression was part of the explanation for the relative rarity of strikes between 1850 and 1861. Until the law of 25 May 1864, strikes remained illegal, although they occurred in spite of the risks. Even with the passing of this legislation which legalized *coalition*, i.e. the existence of 'temporary groups formed to co-ordinate strikes', trades unions were still banned and intimidation of non-strikers brought rapid police action. It nevertheless encouraged workers to make demands and discouraged employer resistance. A wave of strikes occurred in Paris in the autumn of 1864 and spring of 1865, and spread to craftsmen in other regions. The prosperous economic situation provided further initial encouragement, but even the onset of depression did not prevent strikes throughout 1867–8. In 1869 and 1870 their number and scale again increased, especially among textile workers in the Mulhouse area, coal-miners in the St-Etienne region, and steel-workers at Le Creusot and Fourchambault. Most of the strikes in this last period were at least partially successful, an experience which stimulated wider acceptance of the strike tactic. Less notable political crises also had their effects. In the spring of 1893, 635 strikes involving 170,000 workers occurred (compared with an annual average of 157 and 47,000 between 1871 and 1892). This was the first major wave of strikes since 1870 and can be associated with a series of political *affaires*, including the Panama scandal, the closure of the Paris *Bourse du Travail* and May Day riots. Again in 1899–1900 the appointment of the independent socialist Millerand to the Waldeck–Rousseau cabinet raised hopes of imminent social reform which helped to promote major strikes. In 1906 strikes were precipitated by the Courrières (Pas-de-Calais) mine disaster in March in which 1200 miners were killed in a gas explosion. In protest against inadequate safety measures 61,000 miners went on strike in the north, and the movement spread to other mining basins and then by process of imitation to other groups of workers – in the north to involve dockers at Dunkirk and engineering workers at Lille; in the Lyon area workers in metallurgy and textiles; in the Mediterranean coastal departments building workers; and in Paris 126,000 workers in the woodworking and metal industries, including for the first time a substantial number in the automobile industry.[43]

Edward Shorter and Charles Tilly have produced statistics which provide us with a clearer idea of who actually came out on strike (Table 51). The involvement of semi- and unskilled workers in modern industrial establishments was slow to develop, reflecting weak negotiating positions and also the slowness with which industrial structures themselves changed. As their participation grew, particularly in the period 1890–1914, so by definition did the average size of strikes, which had previously involved relatively small numbers of workers

Table 51   *The share of strikes by industrial sector, 1830–1914, as percentages of the period's total (absolute number of strikes in parentheses)*

Industrial sector	1830–47 (%)	(No.)	1850–89 (%)	(No.)	1890–1914 (%)	(No.)
Agriculture – fish – forest	1	(3)	—	(1)	4	(823)
Mining	3	(10)	12	(42)	3	(679)
Quarrying	3	(8)	—		2	(392)
Food industries	3	(8)	2	(9)	3	(567)
Chemicals	1	(3)	1	(2)	2	(497)
Printing – paper	8	(26)	6	(21)	3	(629)
Leather – hides	3	(8)	13	(48)	5	(989)
Textiles	35	(107)	21	(75)	24	(4,720)
Smelting	1	(2)	—	(1)	1	(264)
Metal-working	6	(20)	23	(82)	12	(2,278)
Wood industries	15	(45)	11	(41)	7	(1,448)
Building materials – ceramics	6	(18)	6	(20)	4	(843)
Construction	16	(49)	4	(15)	19	(3,675)
Transport	1	(3)	1	(4)	9	(1,762)
Tertiary	—		—		1	(220)
Total	102	(310)	100	(361)	99	(19,786)

Source: Based on E. Shorter and C. Tilly, *Strikes in France, 1830–1968* (Cambridge University Press 1974), p. 195.

Table 52 *Percentage of strikers within industry, 1871–90*

Mines and quarries	2.82	Chemicals	0.47
Textiles (production of cloth)	2.27	Glass, bricks, pottery	0.47
Woodworking	0.97	Transport	0.45
Construction	0.95	Food industries	0.23
Skins and leather	0.78	Printing and paper	0.20
Metal-working	0.71	Clothing	0.16

due to the small scale of enterprises, the dispersal of workshops, and the lack of organization among workers. Michelle Perrot has gone one step further in preparing an index of the propensity to strike during the period 1871–90, i.e. a calculation comparing the numbers of strikers in particular industries with the total numbers employed in them (Table 52).[44]

These broad categories conceal as much as they reveal. Within them, labour militancy essentially emerged from the traditional artisanal world with its pride in craft solidarity, and long experience of organization and protest. At least until the 1890s skilled craftsmen in the major urban centres were the most active groups. Miners were one major exception to this. The constant anxiety created by dangerous working conditions, frequent conflict over piece-rates, hours of work and discipline helped to create a solidarity made all the more effective by strong bonds of community. Among the textile trades it was the most skilled, those engaged in preparing new materials, and weavers, rather than spinners, who were more likely to strike. Significantly there was a low propensity to strike in the clothing trades because of the growing competition from domestic workers. Thus low wages, social deprivation, the absence of a sense of commitment to a particular trade or community, all reduced the capacity for collective action, except in its simplest forms, i.e. in short-lived, angry and often violent agitation when employers threatened already desperately difficult situations. Women were in a special position. As semi- or unskilled labour their propensity to strike was low. Moreover, they were often only temporarily engaged in the labour force and lacked commitment to efforts to improve conditions, while male colleagues, regarding women as competitors, were usually unwilling to support them.

It took time to establish the sense of solidarity which was a prerequisite for industrial protest. In the southern woollen industry in the first part of the century, strikes were more likely at Castres and Lodève, both old established centres with semi-artisanal traditions which survived into the period of mechanization, than at Mazamet, a new industrial town. In the northern mining area, strikes were more likely at Anzin, which had developed from the eighteenth century, than in newer mining regions such as Alais. In growing industries like building and engineering strike activity tended to increase because of the influence of artisanal groups within the residential community, or of artisans from the traditional trades employed at highly skilled work in the factory. In general, strike activity seems to have been more likely in mixed artisan–industrial locations rather than in predominantly industrial towns. Due to this, to the significance of community as well as of craft traditions, such activity was relatively concentrated geographically. Large areas were almost untouched, and although strikes became more common by 1914, they were still essentially limited to the Nord, Normandy, upper Alsace, the Nantes area, Lyon region, Mediterranean coast and Paris. The big city (Brest, Nantes, St-Nazaire, Rouen, Le Havre, Lyon, Limoges, Bordeaux, Marseille, Paris and its suburbs) was the typical location, with some dispersal due to the mines and cotton mills of the Nord and the mills of Alsace. Once a tradition of successful strike activity had been established, repeated strikes occurred in these locations.

The median duration of strikes during the July Monarchy was only 3.8 days. This can be explained both by the rapid success of some strikes, especially those involving skilled workers, and also the quick collapse of many strikes due to the lack of effective formal organization. Strike funds were always limited, but especially so in depressed economic circumstances. Indeed, the situation was only marginally altered when unions were formed. Their strike funds were normally very limited. Typically, in the 1900s the local union of the metallurgical workers at Le Chambon-Feugerolles (Loire) was able to provide 40 per cent of their members' weekly wages in the case of brief stoppages, but only 6–7 per cent during the long strikes of 1910–11.[45] The prospect of a lengthy strike, ending perhaps in dismissals was a nightmare for most workers, when the loss of even a day's wages was a cause of grave anxiety.

Michelle Perrot's analysis of the causes of 1997 strikes between 1871 and 1890 concludes that wages were a cause of 74 per cent; a shorter working day of 13 per cent; relations with foremen, questions of discipline, etc., of 12 per cent; and discontent with working conditions and pensions of a minimal 1.6 per cent.[46] It seems likely that strike objectives had changed very little over the century. Analysis by profession makes it clear that if differences of interest existed, e.g. miners being far more likely to strike over dangerous working conditions than other groups and unskilled workers to make simple and more limited demands, the basic pattern was unaltered. The vast majority of workers who went on strike even in the 1900s do not appear to have been motivated by the grand statements of principle made at union and socialist party congresses. They were far more concerned with the realities of their everyday existence, and indeed often seemed to be pleading rather than making demands. There is, however, a problem: that of knowing whether strikers had objectives other than their stated grievances – demands they were afraid to make, or simply found difficult to formulate. On some occasions questions of wages might well have had some sort of symbolic importance in the minds of strikers, representing a challenge to the employer, even to the social order, as well as a statement of material needs. Thus, in the relative freedom of April 1848, striking miners at St-Etienne, while asking for wage increases also protested about the 'monopoly' position of the *Compagnie des Mines de la Loire*, and the increased economic and social power given to the mine-owners through association in a powerful company.

Most strikes about wages involved relatively skilled men who sought to protect their living standards. They usually explained their action in terms of their inability to assure the necessities of life to their families, and in relation to the value of the work they performed. Frequently strikes also expressed dissatisfaction with the way in which resources were distributed, most commonly between wages and profits, particularly in periods when employers were clearly making substantial profits (for miners the rising price of coal was a sure sign of this and was used, for example, to justify a strike at Anzin in October 1866), but also between workers. Lyon silk-workers in 1831, and cabinet-makers and carpenters in Paris in 1833 complained about differences in wage rates between workshops and demanded standardization through the establishment of an agreed *tariff*, both on grounds of equity and in order to prevent undercutting. In May 1866 the carpenters of Orléans went on strike for an extra 10 centimes an hour in order to gain the same wage of 45 centimes per hour paid to carpenters at Blois. Craftsmen wanted both equal pay for equal work and also the preservation of differentials according to skills. Such demands for a tariff were repeated on numerous occasions. Once agreed, they were regarded as having the force of a contract by workers, and a breach of the agreement could easily lead to a strike.

In addition to efforts to increase wages, defensive strikes were frequently called in opposition to reductions, normally when trade was depressed. Thus a major strike by shoemakers in Paris in 1833 was in response to a meeting of employers which had decided on a general reduction in wages. Such strikes frequently involved poorly paid, unskilled workers who found it difficult to conceive how they might make ends meet when their wages were reduced. In a depressed year like 1867, 46 per cent of strikes appear to have been defensive. They were normally short lived. Groups like the textile workers or miners, who typically took this kind of action, possessed only a limited capacity for resistance in the face of employers' determination to reduce their costs of production. Other workers, from fear of unemployment, or the survival of a sentiment of common interest with the employer, avoided strikes during periods of depression, although once recovery occurred they might strike in an effort to restore their wage levels. This was the main cause of major strikes by coal-miners at Montceau and Le Creusot in May 1899, at St-Etienne in September and at Carmaux in February 1900.

The length of the working day was less significant as a cause of strikes, although its importance did gradually increase. During the strike waves of the 1830s in Paris, craftsmen paid at piece-rates were not interested in a reduction of their working day which would have substantially reduced their earnings. Significantly, in 1848 shorter hours were demanded as part of the more general aspiration for a better world and this ambition survived. Thus in Lyon between 1851 and 1860 there were eight strikes in favour of a reduction in hours worked (11.8 per cent of the total), and from 1861 to 1870 twenty-four (29.1 per cent).[47] In the Mulhouse region in April 1870 the 10 hour day was a major cause of strikes involving 12–15,000 textile workers. This was a period when wages and real incomes were increasing rapidly, and workers were dominated less by the need to make ends meet. As a petition in favour of a 10-hour day signed by 400 workers in the railway workshops expressed the feeling in May 1870, 'An hour for us is enormous; it is life, it is liberty, it is study and the development of intelligence.' For most workers a reduction in hours meant above all more leisure. By the first decade of this century the demand for an 8 hour day was increasingly being heard. Employers resented these attempts to interfere with the organization of the work process and their control over it even more than requests for wage increases.

Working conditions were another cause of disputes, most notably in mining because of the danger. In 1857, for example, strikes occurred at Ronchamp (Haute-Saône) following the deaths of eight miners in January and a further two in explosions in March. These were blamed upon poor ventilation, seen as symptomatic of the company's negligence. Far more substantial strikes took place in the northern coalfield following the death in March 1906 of about 1200 miners at Courrières. As mechanization progressed and employers sought to increase their control over work-place routines, disputes about questions of discipline and control became more common. Within the traditional crafts interference with established working practices was resisted, especially from the 1840s by cabinet-makers, shoemakers and tailors reacting to attempts to dilute their skills. The reorganization of working practices also led to major strikes in mines and factories. In 1847 at Anzin (Nord) this was in response to the company's plan to replace the large numbers of youths employed in underground haulage with ponies; at Roubaix (Nord) in 1867 to employer's demands that weavers care for two looms, instead of one. In the 1880s it was the growing use of electricity for power and light which encouraged employers to further reorganize production, and in the period 1885–9, 12 per cent of all strikes, and in 1910–14, 25 per cent involved disputes over working practices. Within factories protests also occurred about regulations and the levying of fines or against particularly unsympathetic foremen or engineers. By 1907 regulations and fines were a central issue, a cause of seventy-eight strikes involving 20,000 workers in 277 factories.[48] Closely linked to these strikes were efforts to secure employers' recognition of workers' rights to negotiate and to organize, and resistance to company paternalism. The latter was usually an objective of second generation workers – as in the case of efforts to secure control over pension funds by miners in the Loire basin in 1866 and at Lens (Pas-de-Calais) in 1870, as well as by metallurgists at Le Creusot in the same year. This was dangerous ground to stand on because employers were likely to resist firmly any challenge to their authority.

The course of a strike tended to vary according to its participants and a range of economic, technical, demographic and historical factors. Basic distinctions might be made between the massive tumultuous strikes of miners, the short-lived and often violent movements by textile workers and the calmer, more calculated action of metallurgical workers and most skilled artisans. The decision to strike might be taken in the heat of the moment, particularly by unskilled workers with little organizational experience, but, in general, it was something not decided upon lightly. It usually followed a period of agitated and anxious discussion, and action might well be postponed until after the winter months. The onset of better weather reduced the need for heating, warm clothing and proper food. Skilled workers, in particular, adopted a calculating attitude and attempted to avoid striking during a depression which reduced the employers' ability to make concessions.

Strikes required at least minimal forms of organization. Even at their most spontaneous as in the textile trades, in response to news of a wage-cut during an economic depression, some kind of prior agreement was necessary. The initiative for action normally came from a small minority of workers, respected for their strength, their skills or their eloquence. Among Parisian artisans in the 1830s such a group would visit or deposit circulars at other workshops, listing grievances and calling a meeting at a café frequented by members of the trade. Thus, even in a period when trades unions were illegal organization could easily be improvised, as it was by the Lyon silk weavers whose repeated strikes were part of the process of negotiation of wage tariffs. During the Second Empire, for example, those producing *tulle* (a mixture of silk and cotton thread) struck in May 1855, June and September–October 1864, April–May 1865 and again, although only partially, in 1866 and 1867. Nevertheless, the absence of some form of more permanent organization was a major handicap, particularly when it came to negotiating with employers, maintaining solidarity among strikers or implementing an agreement.

At its beginning a strike must have felt like a holiday. In place of subordination and often humiliation the worker was affirming his own rights and dignity. The onset of hunger might be briefly postponed by calling a strike immediately after pay day. There was often, particularly after the 1864 law legalizing strikes, an air of a fête as processions of workers went from factory to factory, shouting and singing and calling on their comrades to join them. At Le Creusot on 13 and 15 July 1899, 5–7000 striking workers and their families marched, singing the *Marseillaise*, shouting *Vive la République* and accompanied by carts carrying *tableaux*. The first represented the workers before the strike – in chains and flogged by their foremen – the second contained only the 'fattest' and best dressed participants. These adopted poses of idleness and represented the *patronat*, those whose economic and political authority was being challenged. Subsequently, daily meetings were held and there were frequent processions with bands and flags in an effort to maintain the strikers' enthusiasm. However, as the strike wore on and the prospect of defeat grew, initial exaltation and confidence gave way to depression and within families to tension, as wives became increasingly anxious about their ability to make ends meet.

Violence was rare in strikes – in Perrot's sample, some 21 per cent were involved 'incidents', usually minor in character[49] and directed against non-strikers. The 'blackleg' had to be taught a lesson for threatening the livelihood of other workers. The success of every strike depended upon maintaining solidarity and both verbal abuse and physical assault might be employed to this end with particular effect in the self-contained mining or textiles communities. On occasion, however, pent-up frustrations were relieved in more substantial incidents, indicative of the intensity of social tension. Frequently women were involved – 37 per cent of the strikes in which females participated resulted in 'incidents'. These mostly involved textiles workers or miners and the mobilization of entire communities. Typically workers threw stones through the windows of factories or their employers' homes. At Roubaix early in 1867 woollen workers faced unemployment, or at best reductions in working hours and wage rates, with the prospect of a 30–40 per cent loss of income, at a time when food prices were rising. The employers' demand that weavers accept the British practice of working two looms instead of one was seen as a further and major threat to employment. It led, on 16 March, to a strike during which workers smashed equipment in four factories as well as furnishings in the homes of their employers. Similarly bitter were the strikes in the northern coalfield, following the Courrières mine disaster in March 1906. This was blamed on the inadequacy of safety precautions and violence aginst property, non-strikers and police was common during a prolonged two-month strike.

Luddism, as in the case of the Roubaix affair, was not blind violence but represented an effort to prevent the employer from destroying customary practices at the expense of the worker. Workers in many trades were anxious about mechanization. It threatened jobs. In 1833 Parisian printers claimed that each mechanical press displaced sixteen workers. Most artisans also felt that it destroyed the artistic quality of their work. More than anything else, perhaps, mechanization intensified the sentiment of exploitation and of subordination to the employer. The machine intensified his control over the work-place. Often machine-breaking was a stage in a process which involved warnings to employers delivered by anonymous placards, sabotage, or in the case of the better organized artisanal trades, the placing of an *interdit* on a particular workshop forbidding workers to work there. However, one should not exaggerate the scale of resistance to mechanization. There were only fifteen recorded cases of machine-breaking between 1815 and 1847, together with fifteen more attempts. Much depended upon the economic situation, and upon particular craft traditions. The most serious incidents appear to have been concentrated in the years 1787–9 (mechanization of cotton spinning), 1816–19 (mechanization of woollens, particularly the introduction of the cropping machine in the Midi), 1829–33 (Parisian artisans), 1840, 1847–8 (woollen and silk weavers in the south-east and Champagne; Parisian artisans) in which economic and political crises frequently coincided. 1848 was especially serious, with factories destroyed by fire in Lyon, Strasbourg, Reims, Elbeuf, Romilly and Lodève. In more prosperous periods innovation was less threatening to jobs and was more easily accepted. The workers most likely to be involved in luddism were those engaged in the preparatory and finishing stages of textiles production, printing workers, workers in the clothing trades (tailors and hatters), and in the woodworking industries – men and women who feared that their skills were about to be made redundant. There was little resistance to innovation in the new heavy engineering and metallurgical industries – among the machine-builders.

It is difficult to estimate how successful the various forms of workers protest might have been in securing concessions from employers. In the artisanal trades employers were often divided in their response. During the 1833 Parisian tailors' strike, for example, 150 *patrons*, including the most important clothing houses, established a committee to co-ordinate resistance. Others among the 1500 employers, especially the smaller and presumably weaker houses, were willing to negotiate and to make concessions. Success was not uncommon, particularly in periods of prosperity like the 1860s, when employers were reluctant to lose opportunities for profit. It also depended on the strikers' organization and financial capacity for resistance, and upon the intensity of repression. In the same decade the 1864 law legalizing coalitions was seen by employers as proof of government sympathy for workers. Overall it has been estimated that during the period 1864 to 1914, 56.6 per cent of strikes involving 64 per cent of the total number of strikers enjoyed some degree of success, while 44 per cent involving 36 per cent failed to achieve their objectives.[50] Success encouraged further action, failure left bitterness together with a reluctance to risk another defeat. Determined employer resistance, as at Le Creusot in January 1870, soon led to cold and hunger and to a growing desire for a return to work, particularly among married men with children. The eventual return was followed by the dismissal and blacklisting of workers prominent in the strike movement. It left deep scars and hostility both between workers and employers and among workers. The failure of a strike by miners at Montceau-les-Mines (Saône-et-Loire) in 1878 so demoralized the mass of workers that they were unwilling to contemplate further action until 1899. Similarly, at the Le Creusot steelworks the spectacular development of union membership (6000 in October) and of strike activity in 1899 was followed by a lock-out, selective re-employment and the collapse of the union.

Solidarity between workers was necessarily limited by differences of interest and of experience, and by the lack of effective co-ordinating organization to supplement informal associations. It varied between places and according to the general economic and political circumstances of the moment. Thus, apparent government sympathy in the 1860s appears to have encouraged collaboration among Parisian artisans. Sentiments of solidarity were further increased as groups of workers became aware of interests in common. Solidarity was more easily maintained within trades. This was evident in the wave of strikes which occurred between 1868 and 1870, when iron- and steel-workers left work at Lyon, St-Etienne and Vienne in April–June 1870, and then silk-workers at Lyon and throughout the lower Dauphiné in April and May. Similarly, in the northern coalfield strikes frequently spread in imitative fashion from one mine to another. However, the geographical scale of activity was usually more limited. In these cases processes of imitation operated on a regional basis, but strikes were usually local in character, a fact typified by the refusal, in 1844, of miners at St-Etienne to support those at Rive-de-Gier 20 kilometres away. In 1846, unsurprisingly, the same happened in reverse. At the same time contacts between the miners of the north and those of the Loire basin were almost nonexistent. Workers were divided by geography, and by sectional interests. In particular, there was usually little solidarity between skilled workers anxious to preserve their distinctive status and wage differentials and the unskilled masses, and far less between French and foreign workers – Belgians in the north, Italians in the Mediterranean area. They were seen only as competitors, taking the bread out of the mouths of French families.

Workers' organizations

Modern workers' organizations, in the form of trades unions, were slow to develop in France. To a large degree this was because they were illegal before 1884, but also because there were alternatives. This is evident from the ability of workers to organize strikes. Much of this organization was of course secret, informal and ephemeral, and difficult for the historian to trace. The bar-room was the most obvious informal agency of association. Particular trades had their regular meeting places where men gathered to socialize, discuss their work and exchanged information about job opportunities. There were numerous continuities with the pre-revolutionary period. Masons and building workers in search of work continued to gather on the *Place de Grève* in Paris, and painters, glaziers and locksmiths on the *Quai de Gesvres*. Such gatherings offered excellent opportunities for the organization of collective action. These traditional solidarities and the craft-consciousness which survived the disappearance of the Ancien Régime guild structures were reinforced by work-place and neighbourhood links. Embodied within these groups was the assumption that on occasion the common interests, which were frequently uppermost in relationships between master and man, were outweighed by differences which made putting pressure upon employers the most appropriate form of action.

This could also be achieved through *compagnonnage* forms of organization. These were craftsmen's associations which, although illegal, were often tolerated and had survived the revolution and empire to enjoy a revival in the 1820s. They were important in the building trades and among such diverse groups as cutlers, nailers, forge-workers, blacksmiths, hatters, turners, coopers, tanners, wheelwrights, harness-makers, bakers, some skilled textile workers and shoemakers, and in different forms among stevedores in some ports (notably Marseille). Artisans owned allegiance to three different orders (*devoirs*) – the *Enfants de Père Soubise*, the *Enfants de Maître Jacques*, and the *Enfants de Salomon*. Each of these included several different trades, and each had its own vocabulary and rituals. Their revival was never as complete in Paris – where earlier repression had been particularly intense – as in such provincial centres as Lyon, Bordeaux, Nantes, Orléans and in the south. Nevertheless, the various *devoirs*, through their rituals – initiation ceremonies, assemblies, processions on patron saints' days when the *compagnons* wearing top hats and carrying canes decorated with ribbons marched to church, banquets, ceremonies of greeting and parting, and funerals – helped to maintain the craftsman's sense of dignity and unity. They also served the more practical purpose of providing a means by which the recruitment of apprentices could be controlled and of exercising pressure on employers, particularly through the traditional tactic of the *interdit*, i.e. the banning of employment in a particular workshop. Even though the active members were usually young, unmarried men engaged in the *Tour de France* as a means of gaining professional experience and for whom the *compagnonnage* provided lodging, contacts and work, it also retained the loyalties of older men and could serve as a centre for collective action. Its effectiveness as a workers' organization was, however, greatly reduced by the exclusive craft-orientated ideals of its members as well as by the internal ranks and distinctions and the often bitter hostilities between rival *devoirs*. Efforts were made to increase unity. Dissident younger aspirants for membership who rejected the strict internal hierarchy favoured by the older, more traditionalist craftsmen organized a congress at Bordeaux in 1822 and at Toulon in 1830, a short-lived *Société de l'Union des Travailleurs du Tour de France*. The cabinet-maker, Agricole Perdiguier, in his *Livre du Compagnonnage* (1839) searched for a compromise between reform and tradition. This enjoyed some success, revealed in the collaboration between craftsmen belonging to the two main rival *devoirs* – the *Enfants de Père Soubise* and the *Enfants de Salomon* – in strikes in Paris during the July Monarchy (1830: locksmiths and blacksmiths; 1832, 1833 and 1845: carpenters). However, as the economy changed and the labour market expanded and control over job placement became more difficult, *compagnonnage* lost one of its major sources of strength. Newer, more appropriate forms of organization were established. Moreover, potential supporters were alienated by the violent brawls which occurred, particularly between stone-cutters and carpenters belonging to rival *devoirs*. The disappearance of such brawls from the late 1840s signified both the emergence of greater solidarity between workers and the rapid decline of the traditional *compagnonnage*. It retained some significance in the building trades, where technical change was slow, but by the end of the century membership had slumped to 8–10,000.[51]

A further reason for the decline of *compagnonnage* was the development of an alternative and more attractive form of association. This, the mutual aid society (*société de secours mutuel*), had its origins in the religious confraternities of the Ancien Régime. In the early decades of the century societies were often still named after patron saints, although in practice they were increasingly secularized. Less common than *compagnonnage* in the 1820s, by the 1840s they had become the most likely form of association between workers. In return for the monthly payment of dues, members and their families received assistance in case of sickness, retirement or death. Typically, though and reflecting the moral earnestness of many skilled workers, assistance to those sick because of alcoholism or venereal disease was normally forbidden. Although the *devoirs* had also offered assistance to members, the mutual aid society had the advantage of a local base and wider membership. It was free of the arcane rituals, strict hierarchy and divisions of the *compagnonnage*. In the absence of state welfare facilities the assurance these societies provided proved very attractive to those who could afford the dues. Their value was recognized by a law of 15 July 1850 and a decree of 26 March 1852, which offered legal status and financial advantages to societies which registered, agreed to accept a degree of official supervision and promised not to provide aid to the unemployed because this might assist workers on strike. Significantly, in 1869 some two-thirds of societies, with around a half of the total membership, remained unregistered, indicative of a desire to keep their distance from the régime. According to official reports in 1852 there were 2438 mutual aid societies (of which forty-five had been founded in the eighteenth century, 114 between 1800 and 1814, 337 from 1814–30, 1088 during the July Monarchy, and 653 since February 1848). By 1869 there were nearly 6000 societies with close to 1 million members, including around 500,000 unskilled manual workers.[52]

In practice the character of these societies varied considerably. Many had an intermittent existence. They were too small and lacked a proper actuarial basis. At best they provided inadequate levels of assistance. Some, especially in cities like Toulouse with traditionalist Catholic élites, served as a means by which wealthy honorary members could exercise charity; some were primarily devotional groups closely supervised by the clergy; many were social clubs; others restricted themselves to mutual aid activities; while others again served as a front for trades union activity, and caused frequent concern to the authorities. Thus the *Société de St-Claude*, formed by Marseille tanners in 1821, and with around 100 official members in 1854 seems to have managed to control clandestine organizations. The Parisian *Société philanthropique des ouvriers tailleurs* actually grew out of the strike movements of the early 1830s. The same was to be true of the Lyon tailors' *mutuel* founded in 1864 and that of the masons (1865). Such societies provided useful cover for the collection of strike funds and a semi-permanent organization capable of supervising the implementation of agreements with employers.

In many cases mutual aid societies developed from and reinforced existing craft solidarities. Of the 138 societies known to exist in Paris in June 1822 only eleven had a mixed membership. Of the others, twenty-six were composed of printing workers; nineteen of stevedores, porters and dockworkers; thirteen of textile and clothing workers; eleven of jewellers, goldsmiths and watchmakers; nine of building workers; five of woodworkers and five of leather-workers. Most remained small, which limited their effectiveness as a means of putting pressure on employers, although later in the century some large societies developed. Thus, the Parisian *Société de secours mutuel des ouvriers boulangers* (bakery workers), the largest in the capital, had 5361 members in 1869. In return for monthly dues of 2f50 it provided 2f per day in sickness benefits for the first ninety days of illness and 1f25 for the next ninety. It also offered a pension at 65 and acted as an employment agency. The *Caisse fraternelle de prévoyance des mineurs de la Loire*, founded by twenty-five miners in June 1866, had 5000 members two years later. The hazards faced by miners no doubt encouraged membership, as did the desire to escape from the paternalism of the mining companies' own mutual aid funds. In this case, involvement in the 1869 strikes led to police repression and collapse.[53] These associations responded to the practical need of workers to do something to protect their families. Less exclusive than *compagnonnages*, although again restricted largely to skilled, relatively well-paid workers, they were of some significance in the development of workers' organizations and of a sense of solidarity.

Producers' co-operatives were a parallel development from the early 1830s. They were initially intended to be a means of lending support to striking workers and of putting additional pressure upon their employers. In November 1833, however, the Parisian *Société des tailleurs* announced its intention to establish a co-operative for unemployed workers which would have a permanent existence. Shoemakers and cabinet-makers declared similar intentions. At this stage workers do not seem to have conceived of the principle of association as a means of securing long-term social reform. It was essentially a means of alleviating the difficulties caused by strikes and trade recession. As such it was an attractive idea to skilled artisans employed in small workshops. More grandiose ideas were rapidly popularized among militants – in the workers' newspaper *L'Atelier* in the 1840s, for example, on the basis of ideas borrowed largely from the Christian Socialist Buchez. These involved a gradual collectivization of production and emancipation from the wage system. It was easy for skilled craftsmen to consider the employer as a useless parasite. A producers' co-operative absolved from the need to provide the capitalist with profit would be capable of rapidly accumulating capital, which could be used to finance expansion and the establishment of new co-operatives until entire industries were collectivized. Such notions exercised a particular fascination among artisans for decades.

The 1848 Revolution aroused great hopes. The Provisional government encouraged producers' associations and established the Luxembourg Commission to discuss social reform. Throughout France some 299 co-operatives were established, although most quickly disappeared with the onset of political repression, because of adverse economic conditions, managerial inadequacies and especially lack of capital and of credit. An attempt in November 1849 by 104 co-operatives to establish an *Union des Associations* to organize mutual credit failed. Survival was only possible where socialist ideals were abandoned and the associations were run on normal commercial principles. By 1863 only fourteen remained. A revival, however, occurred in the 1860s. By 1868 there were fifty-three producers' associations in Paris and fifty-three in the provinces, including nineteen at Lyon. Although only very small numbers of workers were actually involved, particularly bronze-founders, engineering- and building-workers, producers' co-operatives do appear to have been the subject of widespread discussion. Thus in 1867 delegates from 120 Parisian trades approved of association as a means of eliminating capitalism. This stimulated often bitter disputes over whether or not to accept official aid, the government having established a *caisse impériale* with 500,000f as a means of diverting workers from revolutionary aims. By the 1880s, however, repeated failure appears to have largely discredited the notion of the producers' co-operative. Increasingly, strikes and political action were the favoured means of action of militant workers. In 1895 there were only 174 producers' associations with about 4700 worker members and 6800 employees. In contrast consumers' co-operatives, with far more limited objectives, offered practical advantages and slowly increased in popularity. In Lyon a chain of twenty-five foodshops was established between January 1849 and the end of 1851 by the *Travailleurs réunis*. Closed by the police because of their socialist sympathies, the movement developed again in the 1860s and had around 4000 members by 1868. Throughout France consumers' co-operatives had 200,000 members by 1895, growing to almost 1 million by 1914. In 1906 they included 1016 grocers and 651 bakeries.

The capacity of workers to organize was of course to a large degree dependent upon the attitude of the authorities. The *Loi Le Chapelier* of May–June 1791 and the Penal Code required government authorization for associations and this was not given where these were believed likely to act in restraint of individual enterprise. Thus for most of the century worker organizations existed at best on the margins of the law and were subject to frequent acts of repression. It was clear even so that artisans especially were aware of the value of organization as a means of protecting their interests and were making efforts to create more effective forms. At a local level awareness of a common interest in improving wages or conditions often stimulated efforts to establish informal committees which could negotiate with employers, and if necessary organize collective action, including strikes. Such organizations were usually short lived, but might subsist as a means of policing agreements reached with employers, as was the case with Parisian printing workers in 1833. At the same time the tailors' representatives declared that 'without organization there is only weakness and misery'.

Stimulated by the post-revolutionary political situation and more immediately by economic recovery, the period from September 1833 to the beginning of 1834 saw large numbers of strikes and efforts to create organizations in which such figures as the Parisian tailors' leader, Grignon, and the shoemaker, Efrahem, both influenced by radical republican ideas, played leading roles. The preamble to the statutes of a proposed shoemakers' co-operative, written by Efrahem, stressed the need to create a unitary organization both within and between trades, as a means of exerting pressure on employers. The authorities were especially concerned by the development of links between the organized groups of tailors and shoemakers in Paris and those in provincial centres. The tailors appear to have created a network of associations, usually in the form of mutual aid societies, throughout western France. Again, in February 1837, in spite of years of repression, it was discovered that striking workers at La Rochelle were receiving financial support from tailors in Nantes, Bordeaux and Rochefort. Even though such organizational efforts were ephemeral and limited to particular localities and trades, lessons were gradually learned and traditions established. Thus in 1845 in Paris, carpenters agreed to subordinate the differences betweeen their rival *compagnonnages* and to establish a united strike organization with an elected commission. In the same year in Marseille, prior to approaching their employers, the shoemakers created an association composed of thirty-six sections, with an executive of twelve members. Workers' delegates agreed to demand a single wage scale, and control over the engagement of new employees. When these demands were rejected a strike was called and a producers' co-operative was established both to provide work and place added pressure on employers. As this stage the authorities arrested the strike leaders and the association collapsed, but a network of *compagnonnage* and mutual aid societies survived to serve as an organizational base until the time would be ripe – in 1869 – to establish a union (*chambre syndicale*). In other cases – such as that of the miners of St-Etienne – it was the freedom briefly created by the February Revolution in 1848 which encouraged a first attempt to create a permanent trades union organization financed by regular payment of dues.

The closing years of the Second Empire, when the government again relaxed its grip, legalizing strikes in 1864 and declaring in March 1868 that it would tolerate *chambres syndicales*, was another period of organizational innovation. This was often inspired by the desire of skilled and well-paid workers, particularly those in the larger cities with their organizational traditions, to defend their position *vis-à-vis* their employers during a period of accelerating change in technology and work-place organization. Their goal was to protect their relatively privileged economic position rather than to support social revolution. Indeed the craft consciousness which was so important in promoting organization among traditional artisanal groups was also an exclusive force directed at other workers. In the late 1860s, for example, the Parisian tailors excluded unskilled workers employed in the mechanized branch of the clothing industry from their union, and the building workers refused to admit the *terrassiers*, who did the less skilled work of constructing foundations. Estimates of union membership in Paris in the 1860s confirm this exclusiveness and also make the weakness of organized labour clear, although it ought to be remembered that these militants were far more influential than their numbers might suggest (Table 53). Thus by July 1870 an estimated 65,000 Parisian workers (around 13 per cent of the labour force) belonged to unions. A similar movement in Lyon was stimulated by growing contacts with Parisian workers, particularly following the dispatch of workers' delegates to the London Universal Exposition in 1862. A 'union' established between June and July 1869 organized strikes by steel and engineering workers in favour of a 10 hour day, the success of which encouraged activity in other trades. In Limoges at the beginning of 1870, first the skilled porcelain workers and subsequently cabinet-makers and tapestry-makers formed *chambres syndicales* and in April, by which time fifteen separate unions existed, they were able to agree on the setting up of a federation to co-ordinate activity. Although the leaders of this movement appear to have been anxious to avoid a repetition of the unsuccessful strikes of 1864, they did not escape official persecution in the difficult years following the Paris Commune in 1871, and its timid imitation at Limoges. It was not until 1877 that militant activity recommenced, so that by 1884, when unions were finally

Table 53   *Percentage of workers unionized in selected occupations in Paris, 1862–July 1870*[54]

| | No. in occupation | | No. in | Percentage unionized | |
| | Men and | | | Men and | |
Occupation	women	Men	union	women	Men
Building trades	71,242	67,680	377	0.53	0.56
Carpenters	4,971	4,971	160	3.22	3.22
Shoemakers	18,082	11,910	700	3.87	5.88
Upholsterers	3,394	1,805	240	7.07	13.30
Bookbinders	2,238	979	179	8.00	18.28
Bakers	4,489	3,314	365	8.13	11.01
Leather-workers	6,597	5,842	625	9.47	10.70
Tailors	10,232	6,849	1,111	10.86	16.22
Organ and piano makers	3,554	3,554	480	13.51	13.51
Jewellers (*bijoutiers*)	7,685	5,942	1,600	20.82	26.93
Tanners	1,283	1,283	300	23.38	23.38
Housepainters	6,031	6,031	1,400	23.21	23.21
Tinsmiths	1,403	1,340	366	26.09	27.31
Mechanics	8,415	8,415	2,750	32.68	32.68
Typographers	5,716	5,308	2,077	36.34	39.13
Hat-makers	3,265	2,114	1,319	40.40	62.39
Bronze-workers	4,452	4,245	3,701	83.13	87.18
Paris	500,000		65,928		

legalized, sixty already existed, although these had only 989 members. This was a pitifully small number, even compared with membership of the mutual aid societies (twenty-seven with 3495 members), and serves to highlight the continuing weakness of working-class organization.

In Paris itself, in spite of the mass arrests and massacres which accompanied the repression of the commune, efforts to reconstitute workers' organizations were evident as early as January 1872 in the printing and jewellery trades. By October 1872 fifty-five unions had reorganized themselves. Ten years later the police reported that there were 206 unions in the city. By 1881–2 unionization varied between 32 per cent for cabinet-makers and 17 per cent for tailors to less than 5 per cent for joiners and carpenters.[55] It was in this period that the sporadic organizational development of earlier years became more sustained and unions became the pre-eminent form of working-class organization. In recognition of this and in an attempt to integrate the working classes into the new republic, unions were finally legalized in 1884 although important restrictions on their activities survived. This official favour encouraged a substantial growth in membership, particularly in the periods 1888–94 and 1898–1906, stimulated by the strike waves of 1893 and 1899–1900, which occurred in favourable economic and political circumstances and thus were relatively successful, and were followed by a series of ameliorative government laws and decrees. The number of trades unionists grew from around 139,000 in 1890 to 400,000 in 1893, 750,000 in 1905 and 1,025,000 in 1913, but even this figure included only about 10 per cent of French industrial workers, compared with 26 per cent in Britain.[56] Moreover they were divided between over 5000 local unions with extremely unstable memberships that increased in periods of prosperity when unions were in a relatively strong negotiating position, but fell rapidly during depressions.

Although the proportion of union members was much higher in some professions, for example, miners, printing- and metal-workers, railwaymen, and also in some regions (particularly Paris and Lyon), it remained the case that in most manufacturing establishments the workforce remained non-unionized (Table 54). In part this was because the unions themselves were not particularly attractive. Most were local in character and not very well organized. They rarely offered significant benefits and members proved reluctant to pay their dues and to attend meetings. In some cases, after 1884, rival organizations competed for members. In the case of the railwaymen there was the *Fédération des chauffeurs mécaniciens* (1884) and the more combative *Syndicat national* (1889), but both

Table 54   *Union members per 100 active population by industry*

Industry	1884–97 (average)
Tobacco–matches	55
Mining	12
Ceramics	6
Textiles	3
Printing–paper	9
Food industries	2
Leather–hides	4
Garments	1
Building materials and construction	4
Wood	2
Metals	4
Chemicals	4
Glass	11
Mining–manufacturing	3
Post–telephone–telegraph	0
Utilities (*éclairage*)	44
Railways	18
Transport	9
Ports–docks	1
Proletarian tertiary	8

Source: Edward Shorter and Charles Tilly, *Strikes in France, 1830–1968* (Cambridge University Press 1974), p. 151.

were largely ignored by the railway companies which actively discouraged membership. Indeed, many employers chose to ignore the 1884 law and refused to tolerate union membership. There was no union activity in the Anzin coal-mines for fourteen years following the defeat of a fifty-six day long strike in 1884, which was followed by a thousand dismissals. In Paris and the north some employers encouraged efforts to establish Catholic unions, which offered attractive mutual benefits but failed because workers believed the church to be too closely associated with the employing classes; others, like the Le Creusot mining and metallurgical company in 1899 and the industrialist Japy in the Montbéliard region in the 1900s, attempted to set up company unions as a means of controlling their more compliant workers and following the large-scale dismissal of militants.

The years from the 1880s were, however, notable for efforts to co-ordinate the activities of local unions and to establish national federations. At local level the *Bourse du Travail* was created as a means of providing information about jobs and social, cultural and educational facilities, and of co-ordinating the activities of the various unions. By 1892 there were fourteen, and in 1914, 143 serving 2199 unions with 500,000 members. Often they were given material support by politically radical town councils, although disputes over objectives were frequent. Federal organization was created first in skilled trades with a tradition of extra-local links, such as the hatters (1880), printing workers (1881), furniture and building workers (1882), and subsequently among workers in large-scale industry: the miners and steel-workers (1883), railwaymen (1890), in textiles (1891), and among office workers (1902). In general these new organizations and the *Confédération générale du travail* (CGT) to which many of them were to affiliate, still represented the more highly skilled trades. In spite of the rhetoric, craft loyalties continued to triumph over working-class solidarity.

The objective of federation between workers' organizations had been proposed frequently enough, for example by the delegates of the various trades meeting as the *Comité central des ouvriers du département de la Seine* in 1848, and again in the late 1860s by the delegates of the Parisian and Lyonnais crafts elected initially for the London Exposition and by members of the International, who succeeded in creating a *Chambre fédérale des sociétés ouvrières*, which in 1868 represented some forty Parisian trades. The concept of a national federation was discussed at a congress in Marseille in 1879, but it was only after a further two decades of quarrelling, particularly about whether or not this body should involve itself in politics, that, in 1895, at a congress held in Limoges the CGT was established by agreement between twenty-eight craft federations, eighteen *bourses du travail* and twenty-six local unions representing in all around 300,000 of the then total of 420,000 members of trades unions. Through its congresses and its press (*Le Voix du Peuple* (1900) and *La Bataille syndicaliste* (1911)) the CGT came to exert considerable influence, and this in spite of the limits placed upon its authority by a constitution designed to preserve the autonomy of its constituent organizations, and a membership made up of fewer than 3 per cent of the industrial labour force (200,000) in 1906 and still less than 10 per cent in 1912

(400,000), although at this date it included about half of unionized workers. It remained the only organization representing French workers, and as such could at times arouse interest even among normally apathetic non-unionists.

The views it expressed were, however, as often as not unrepresentative of the members of its affiliated groups, much less of the large majority of non-unionized workers. Its congresses, which gave rights of representation to unions regardless of size, tended to overrepresent the outlook of the smaller, more militant groups. Thus its dominant ideology, especially in the first decade of the twentieth century, was revolutionary syndicalism. It was assumed that workers would achieve growing class consciousness through their daily struggles against the employers, landlords and shopkeepers who exploited them. This would culminate in a general strike during which the army, recruited from among the people, would refuse to engage in repression. In this situation capitalism and the state which supported it would both collapse. Often revolutionary rhetoric appeared to matter more than the hard work of building support for the unions through the improvement of their organizations and the benefits they offered. Yvetot, editor of the *Voix du Peuple*, Pouget, the head of the *bourse* section of the CGT, and Delasalle, secretary of the general strike committee, insisted upon the need for electoral abstention, industrial sabotage and anti-patriotism, and were ignored by the vast majority of the rank and file. This led to growing divisions within the CGT as groups like the printing workers in the *Fédération du Livre*, the textile workers, and subsequently the powerful *Fédération des Mineurs* rejected this all or nothing outlook, especially after the failure of the May Day strike in 1906. In 1909 they even established their own reformist *Comité d'Union syndicaliste* with a separate journal (*Action ouvrière*).

Was this symptomatic of the failure of a specifically working-class consciousness to develop? A clear answer is difficult to give. Solidarities did slowly develop in spite of the diversity of the workers' experience, but until the turn of the century this was essentially at a local level. Moreover, it remained unfocused. The gradual character of French industrialization, the geographical dispersal of workers, the high proportion of recent migrants, variation in working and living conditions and in the possibilities for self-improvement, meant that people's perception of what was happening to them and of the society in which they lived, varied enormously. Social antagonisms were restrained in most communities by the lack of hard and fast boundaries between groups, while the weakness of trades unions and socialist political organization further reduced the likelihood that a working-class consciousness with revolutionary political implications would develop. In spite of this historians of the socialist movement manage to leave the impression that a revolutionary movement was developing and are apparently supported in this by the political turbulence of nineteenth century France. Perhaps it is time, therefore, to examine the role of workers in politics.

Workers and politics

The development of a distinctive and widely shared working-class political consciousness was a slow affair. During the restoration police reports from Paris repeatedly insisted upon the lack of interest in politics of those whose all-consuming concern was with making a living. The misery and strife of the revolution and the repression and wars of the empire had created a widespread desire for order, or at the very least had promoted habits of circumspection. Significantly, the songs of the period revealed the persistence of a Napoleonic legend, but few signs of interest in republican or revolutionary ideas. The minority of literate artisans with an interest in public affairs, informed themselves by reading the liberal press and adopted as heroes such moderate liberals as Casimir Périer, Jacques Laffitte and especially General Lafayette. Political ideas seeped down the social hierarchy from the articulate professional classes and journalists, through the lower middle classes to the workers with whom they were in daily contact. *Quartiers* like the Faubourg St-Antoine in Paris were places in which the various social milieux mixed and ideas spread, while the social distance between employers and artisans in small-scale manufacture in cities like Paris and Lyon was rarely great enough to promote strong sentiments of separate interest and hostility.

The July Revolution of 1830 brought popular quiescence to an end. It mobilized large numbers of people and forms of political expression which had no recognized place within a political system based upon a restricted suffrage. In 1830 popular politics was reborn and it was to survive in spite of considerable efforts to smother it. Although they had not initiated the movement against the Bourbon Monarchy and were in general satisfied with having raised the moderate liberals into positions of power, Parisian workers certainly felt that they were owed something. The praise heaped upon them in the press and by spokesmen of the new regime for defending 'liberty' encouraged demonstrations and the presentation in August–September 1830 of demands for a ban on *marchandage*, increased wages, uniform wage tariffs , and a shorter working day. For many workers liberty meant freedom from the scourge of unemployment and expensive bread. Subsequently, in the economically depressed years of 1831 and 1832, this agitation declined. Indeed on 14 July 1831 hundreds of workers from the Faubourg St-Antoine in Paris actually set upon republican workers and students celebrating the anniversary of the fall of the Bastille and demanded an end to the political agitation which was affecting business confidence and causing unemployment. In contrast, in Lyon in November 1831, the authorities, to the horror of respectable opinion, actually lost control of the city to workers fighting under the slogan *Vivre en travaillant ou mourir en combattant* (live working or die fighting). This followed the decision by Périer, the Minister of the Interior, to condemn a declaration by the local prefect in favour of a wage tariff for silk workers. More generally, disappointment at the increasingly obvious conservatism of the new regime helped to increase the audience for republican militants. Social tension grew. The economic upturn of 1833 encouraged strikes, and from early 1834 bourgeois republican groups like the *Société des Droits de l'Homme*, dissatisfied with the outcome of the July Revolution, sought to attract the support of workers by linking the promise of social reform to further revolution. This movement seems to have attracted artisans from trades without strong *compagnonnage* organization, or otherwise the young who were not fully integrated into traditional associations. They were energetic and idealistic and anxious to secure opportunities for collective self-improvement. Numerically, however, they made up only a small minority, even among Parisian workers, and interest was soon reduced by the intensification of governmental repression (most notably the 1834 law banning associations), which effectively ended the long period of agitation stimulated by the July Revolution.

Nevertheless, the experiences of contact with the young radicals of organizations such as the *Droits de l'Homme* had important consequences for the intellectual development of worker–militants. In the face of an uncomprehending response from a government for which 'liberty' meant *laissez-faire* discouragement was inevitable, but a widespread sense of betrayal survived, together with a desire for greater political and social equality. The decade of social peace which followed the 1834 law did not prevent the slow penetration of socialist and republican ideas. The ideal of association by means of producers' co-operatives developed by St-Simon, Fourier and their followers (particularly Buchez and later Blanc, Cabet and Proudhon) promised a legal and peaceful means of transforming social relationships and also an apparently practical means of protecting job autonomy and avoiding unemployment. As repression eased in the 1840s, socialist ideas were diffused through workers' newspapers, such as *La Ruche populaire* (1839–45) and *L'Atelier* (1840–50), and socialist tracts, most notably Cabet's *Voyage en Icarie*, Blanc's *Organisation du Travail* (both 1839) and Proudhon's *Qu'est-ce-que la propriété?* (1840). Through the glorification of labour as the source of all wealth this literature informed discussion in the workshops and *cabarets* and heightened both the self-confidence and aspirations of those who became familiar with at least its basic themes. It also appears to have created a false optimism concerning the ease with which social reform might occur. Although the idea of revolution had not disappeared and the exploitative features of the existing economic system were bitterly condemned, there appears to have been a widespread belief in the possibility of creating by peaceful means, through an appeal to reason and human generosity, a society based upon universal fraternity. This debate also reaffirmed the link between social reform and the republic. Thus, the establishment of the Second Republic in February 1848 seemed to promise the dawn of a new era.

According to *L'Atelier*, 'The goal of the February Revolution is social reform' and on 25 February, the day following its establishment, the new Provisional Government appeared to accept this by recognizing 'the right to work'. The national workshops set up by the government as a means of providing work relief for the large numbers left unemployed were taken by workers to be the first stage in the creation of a network of producers' associations and as a permanent means of providing security from unemployment. Moreover, under the presidency of Blanc, supported by a genuine worker, Albert, both of whom were members of the new government, a *Commission du Gouvernement pour les travailleurs* was set up at the Luxembourg Palace to study workers' problems and propose further reforms. The revolution, to the success of which workers had contributed so much, was followed by political democratization and an intense debate in the press, political clubs and everywhere people met, on the future shape of society. The new freedom also encouraged more immediate pressure on both employers and government. All the demands of earlier years re-emerged in a sudden rush. Some such as the shorter working day and a ban on *marchandage* were recognized by the government, others were conceded by employers all over France. According to the worker François, 'The advent of the Republic amazingly increased the stature of human being within a few days; everybody knew his rights and asserted them. Exploitation was no longer possible; because the exploited were no longer afraid, nor patient.' Workers were aware of their power and sang:

> Hats off before the cap
> On your knees in front of the Worker.

Organization was also stimulated, most notably in Paris. The delegates selected by the various trades to meet with the Luxembourg Commission established a *Central Committee of the workers of the Department of the Seine* in an effort to co-ordinate their activities and to secure the nomination of candidates for the elections to be held in April 1848 with, for the first time, universal male suffrage.

In other areas, particularly in the south, artisans had been divided in their loyalties during the restoration and the July Monarchy between popular royalism and republicanism. In cities like Nîmes, Toulouse or Marseille the use of patronage by local notables within the context of a traditional, religiously orientated culture was for some time an effective means of influencing political sentiments, just as later patronage by republican notables was to be one of the means by which republicanism spread. The eventual breakdown of popular royalism from the 1830–40s was linked to a decline in the economic and thus the social power of the local nobility and clergy, i.e. of their ability and also willingness to provide employment (especially through the production of luxury consumer goods) and charity, and also to a growing rejection by workers of the deferential behaviour traditionally expected from them. This was made easier by the development of industry outside the limits of the old city centres, in which relationships with middle-class employers was far less paternalistic than had been those with old élites. Moreover, the influx of migrants into the new suburbs and the development of relatively independent working-class social networks led to the decline of the old cultural nexus. The experience of 1848 in many places accelerated the destruction of traditional loyalties. Republican ideals of popular sovereignty were more appealing than anything the monarchists had to offer, and this remained so, even if, particularly after the experience of brutal repression of workers' protest by a moderate republican government in 1848, middle-class republicans were regarded with suspicion by many workers.

In effect the era of hope was to be short lived. Support for the workers' cause was limited – even among workers themselves – particularly outside the major cities. Political reaction was inevitable following the election in April 1848 of a socially conservative Constituent Assembly afraid of disorder and social revolution. The subsequent decision in June to close the Paris national workshops, the insurrection which resulted and its brutal repression, signified the end of dreams of equality and social harmony. In spite of the long period of repression which ensued, the experience of 1848 had done much to accelerate the process of politicization, already underway among traditionally combative groups of craftsmen.

This period of repression culminated in the coup d'état of December 1851 and the establishment of the authoritarian empire. Throughout the 1850s political activity was extremely restrained. Workers in most areas appear to have remained favourable to republican ideas and hostile to the empire, although at particular moments, such as in 1859 during French military intervention in Italy, patriotism might induce more positive attitudes. Outside the major cities, and for most of the time, indifference was probably the most characteristic attitude. This turned into hostility where government representatives intervened to prevent and repress strikes, as they did at Le Creusot in 1858. However, workers in the countryside and small towns often, just like the rural populations among whom they lived, expressed sympathy for the regime. Indeed, in the early 1830s Parisian artisans had often associated loyalty to the Bonapartist legend with republicanism. Even during the insurrection in June 1848 shouts of *Vive Napoléon!* were heard from the insurgents. Both political traditions contained elements of anti-clericalism, patriotism and popular sovereignty and in December 1848 Louis-Napoléon Bonaparte had been able to take advantage of this in his presidential election campaign. In this election and in others, even in the closing years of the Second Empire, workers in mining communities like Anzin and textile areas like Mulhouse were able to reject the advice of their employers, who were hostile to the Bonapartist regime, and express their independence by voting for the empire, although by this time in the major cities there were few signs of the survival of a popular Bonapartism. Official efforts to win over working-class militants had, in fact, enjoyed little success. These efforts had initially taken the form of patronage for a delegation of workers (183 from Paris and sixty from Lyon) sent to the London Universal Exposition in 1862, together with the subsequent publication of their reports (which in spite of official censorship remained highly critical of the economic and social system). But, as the Parisian bronze-worker Tolain had written in 1861, 'When the initiative comes from on high, it inspires little confidence amongst workers. . . . The only way is to say to us : You're free, organize yourselves, attend to your own problems.' A more ambitious attempt to integrate workers, through the legalization of strikes in 1864 and the toleration of workers' associations, soon created major problems for the regime.

The more general liberalization of the 1860s encouraged both political agitation and waves of strikes. In Paris, in particular, numerous opposition newspapers and the frequent public meetings held between June 1868 and May 1870 (933 – involving an estimated 15–25,000 participants) exposed a new generation of workers to republican and socialist ideas. The Workers' International, first established in France in 1865 but in 1869 reorganized and radicalized by new, more influential leaders such as Varlin and Malon in Paris, Richard in Lyon and Bastelica in Marseille, contributed to this activity in the major cities, and also, by 1870, in the textile regions around Rouen, Reims, Troyes, in the Lille–Roubaix–Tourcoing complex and in the east around Mulhouse, although not in the zones of mining and metallurgical development. Accurate assessment of its influence is impossible because both its supporters and the police and conservative opinion all exaggerated the scale of its activities. Clearly, however, widespread politicization occurred during this agitated period. In April 1870 strike posters at Le Creusot included the words *Vive la République*. Economic and political motives for protest were inextricably mixed where, as in this case, government support for employers was clear, even if political ideas usually remained extremely vague.

One effect of this renewal of political activity was that in Paris in the last two years of the empire there must have been a public meeting somewhere almost every evening. Often these were initiated as a form of 'popular university' by well-intentioned economists, Catholics and social reformers, but discussion in them rapidly became more radical as worker–militants demanded consideration of issues which concerned them. This and the often turbulent proceedings, replicated in bars and on street corners, was a growing cause of alarm both to the authorities and to many of the more moderate republicans, who began to feel that the movement was getting out of hand. The absence of an organized republican party made it impossible for them to control it, while the militant workers who were involved in this agitation were extremely suspicious of middle-class republicans after what they regarded as the betrayal of 1848. Even in the 1840s writers in the newspaper *L'Atelier* had insisted that the liberation of the working class must be the creative act of the workers themselves, and had frequently expressed misgivings about the representation of workers by middle-class politicians who could not hope to fully understand their problems. The delegates of the Parisian artisanal corporations had actually selected working-class candidates for the April 1848 elections, only to see them easily defeated by better-known bourgeois candidates. Again, the 1864 'Manifesto of the Sixty' had rejected bourgeois dominance of the republican movement, but when the bronze-worker Tolain stood for election in Paris as a worker-candidate he obtained only 395 votes. Even worker–militants tended to remain impressed by and dependent upon the organizational and oratorical skills of bourgeois politicians. This is part of the explanation of the continuing strain between revolutionary and reformist approaches to social reform. The extreme brutality of the repression of the Paris Commune in 1871, following upon that of the June Insurrection of 1848, however, persuaded many socially conscious workers to abandon dreams of the harmonious creation of a better world through co-operation. The experience of the Third Republic under both 'opportunist' and 'radical' leadership only confirmed this disillusionment. It encouraged the development of a commitment to revolutionary socialism, although paradoxically its proponents were to remain dedicated to the defence of republican institutions and of the political liberties they guaranteed.

In October 1876, soon after the decisive republican electoral victory, a *Congrès ouvrier de France* was held in Paris and attended by the delegates of skilled workers from the capital and thirty-seven provincial towns. Middle-class delegates were deliberately excluded on the grounds that only genuine workers, fully aware of the problems of their fellows, could effectively represent them. The preferred form of organization for these militants remained the producers' co-operative, associated with trades unions, but already and more obviously at subsequent congresses held in Lyon in 1878 and in Marseille in 1879 some delegates were clearly in favour of the establishment of a worker–socialist party. In 1877 in *L'Egalité* Jules Guesde attacked the supporters of co-operation and called for political organization and agitation as a prelude to eventual revolution. In October the *Parti ouvrier* was established, but the National Congress at Le Havre in November 1880 revealed bitter divisions among militant workers. The majority of delegates, mainly from the Parisian luxury trades and smaller provincial towns remained committed to co-operative association; a minority from the less skilled Parisian trades such as shoemakers, tailors, engineering workers and masons, together with some of the delegates of the larger provincial cities, accepted the importance of political activity and the objective of revolution as the means of taking over control of the state. In the Nord and Pas-de-Calais, where support for Guesde was greatest, this came primarily from textile workers rather than the more moderate miners. These divisions were further complicated by differences between Guesde, influenced by Marx, and his son-in-law Lafargue, who wanted to establish a centralized party with a revolutionary programme, and those like Brousse and Malon, who stood for greater democracy and recognized the need to work for immediate reforms within the existing social system at both municipal and national level, in order to achieve whatever was possible (*possibilists*).

Historians have paid a great deal of attention to these and subsequent splits and factional squabbles (*Parti ouvrier français* – Guesde; *Fédération des Travailleurs socialistes* – Brousse; *Comité révolutionnaire central* – Vaillant; *Parti ouvrier socialiste révolutionnaire* – Allemand). They have frequently seemed to assume that workers in general shared a consuming interest in the frequent debates on ideology and organization. In reality most workers were primarily concerned with their own material welfare, and while a minority were, as a last resort, willing to protest about what they regarded as abuses of their situation they were unwilling or unable to challenge the fundamental values of the existing social system. Even within these socialist organizations, at a local level ideological differences were frequently ignored. Their greatest significance perhaps was to make socialism unattractive to large numbers of potential recruits. For these, in the 1890s, the unions and *Bourses du Travail*, the ideas of revolutionary syndicalism and the dreams of a general strike often proved more attractive. Nevertheless, growing support for political socialism was evident. This was clear at municipal level, especially from 1892, when socialist majorities were elected in some sixty communes, including the important towns of Toulon, Roubaix, Montluçon and Narbonne, and nationally with the election to parliament in 1893 of thirty-seven socialists. By 1896 socialist municipalities dominated some 150 communes and were able to encourage the activities of unions and *Bourses*, and to increase expenditure on social welfare. They were, however, prevented by law and prefectoral financial supervision, from engaging in ambitious projects of municipal socialism.

In response to the experience of collaboration at local level and to an awareness of the weakening effects of sectarian division, around the turn of the century both unions and political groups began to take an increased interest in the discussion of unity. In 1901 the reformist socialists established the *Parti socialiste français* led by Jaurès. At the same time the revolutionaries formed the *Parti socialiste de France – Union socialiste révolutionnaire* led by Guesde and Vaillant. The two amalgamated in 1905 and established the *Section française de l'Internationale ouvrier* (SFIO). The price of compromise was a rejection of participation in coalition governments alongside bourgeois republicans and a loose organizational structure which allowed the sixty-five regional federations to retain considerable autonomy. On its foundation the SFIO had 36,000 members. By 1914 this had grown to over 90,000. The circulation of its newspaper *L'Humanité* (founded by Jaurès in 1904), with its dry intellectual style, rose to only 12,000. It proved unable to compete with the mass circulation press.

Historians have displayed considerable ingenuity in explaining the development of support for trades unions and socialism, but less in considering the other crucial aspects of the same problem – why so many workers remained indifferent or hostile to both, and why no more than half of all workers were prepared to vote socialist. Part of the explanation rests in the existence of political alternatives. The development of communications, the introduction of universal male suffrage and the growing respect for political liberties had all served to encourage increased interest in politics. The development of more formal political organization both during the early part of 1848 and more permanently in the 1880–90s, however, had the effect of reinforcing the leadership roles of middle-class intellectuals. Whereas repression enforced the localization of political activity and its use of everyday social institutions like the café, formal political activity called for the skills of the bureaucrat and the public speaker. The radicals were particularly successful in claiming to represent the best interests of workers especially in the period from the end of the Second Empire to the development of distinctive workers' organizations at the close of the century. In the Parisian working-class *quartier* of Belleville, for example, Gambetta's campaign in defence of the republic in the 1870s was sufficient to ensure him the support of 61.4 per cent of the registered voters in the 1870 election, compared with the 8.2 per cent which went to the worker–candidate Donnay; and this in spite of complaints concerning Gambetta's unwillingness to commit himself to social reform.

Other elements in the explanation include the fact that in spite of growing politicization many workers remained, for most of the time, indifferent to politics and outwardly deferential towards those members of local communities whose superior status was generally recognized and made obvious by their dress, manners and speech. They were socialized within their families, neighbourhoods, schools and work-places, in a manner which induced a sense of personal inferiority to and dependence upon other social groups. In the Nord in 1867 and 1869 textile workers appear to have meekly followed the advice of their employers and protested against the regime of free trade, which appeared to threaten their livelihoods. In the 1890s, even in the industrial communes of the Paris region – in St-Denis, for example, the commune with the highest proportion of wage-earners in France – support for socialism was slow to develop. Only in 1912 did the socialists finally capture the municipality there and in Puteaux, the centre of the new motor industry.

Conversely, even if levels of union and socialist party membership remained low throughout the century, it does not necessarily follow that this was because non-members rejected the aims of union activity. Solidarity and organizational capacity were limited by the heterogeneity and geographical dispersal of the industrial labour force, many of whom were recent migrants from rural areas, while others only slowly emerged from a closed universe in which unions and politics appeared to have very little relevance. Difficulties of communication should not be forgotten. For much of the century the cost of travel or of posting letters restricted mobility; and low levels of functional literacy, together with cultural and linguistic differences hindered contacts. In practice, therefore, there was an important time-lag between the beginnings of industrialization and the development of a sense of common interest and of organizational activity among groups of workers. As more permanent communities were created, which served to reinforce work-place bonds and to offset differences in skill levels and culture, a growing sense of working-class consciousness slowly became evident. This was particularly true in the years after 1890, due both to the activities of unions and the emergence of new aspirations as living conditions improved.

Signs of such a development had been evident much earlier, in the description by militants like Grignon in the 1830s of the workers as 'the most numerous and useful class of society' (a theme frequently repeated), suffering from poverty and oppression due to the blind egoism of the rich – of the new bourgeois aristocracy. This was a vision of society derived in large part from the more radical bourgeois republicans who identified the monarchy with the rule of the idle, privileged classes. It was not the mass of employers they attacked, but the *grand bourgeois* – the financiers, bankers, great merchants and industrialists closely identified with the July Monarchy. By the 1840s, however, at least in the case of the influential Parisian workers' newspaper, *L'Atelier*, a polarized view of a society based upon class rather than trade solidarities had begun to emerge.

Even without becoming socially or politically very aware many workers remained antagonistic towards a system which kept them in poverty. In a city like Lyon, the 1830 Revolution followed by the uprisings of 1831 and 1834 and then the 1848 Revolution helped to maintain aspirations for something better. In both practical terms – as a means of avoiding the scourge of unemployment – and more idealistically – as an affirmation of the dignity of labour – it is easy to comprehend the appeal for a guaranteed 'right to work' so popular in 1848 and again in the discussions of the Parisian clubs in the closing years of the Second Empire. After the brutal repression of such hopes in June 1848 it is also easy to comprehend the belief of the future Communard Varlin in March 1870 that, 'We will never achieve any social reform if the old state is not destroyed.' Repeated confrontation between representatives of the state and worker–militants inevitably politicized the consciousness and stimulated support for political revolution. The role of the state and the evolution of the legal and political framework were clearly of some importance in determining the chronology and nature of working-class politicization. The enforcement of repressive legislation not only led to the arrest of strikers and political agitators, but more significantly had a general deterent effect and helped to establish a sense of political powerlessness among workers. The development of more positive policies and, in particular, the creation of a system for mass primary education gave the state a major role in socialization and especially in the diffusion of ideas which legitimized the existing social system. This was reinforced by the control over the means of mass communication exercised by members of the dominant social groups. There ensued a deliberate effort to 'moralize' and 'civilize' workers and peasants, an effort to integrate them into a national culture through the destruction of their own particularistic subcultures and the imposition of supposedly universal values. Education, religion, politics – all in their various ways – served this purpose; helping to limit discontent and to channel protest into forms which were more or less acceptable to the social and political élites. The experience of familial upbringing, of school, of military service and work, of relationships with other social groups, all served to impose a sense of discipline, and of dependence – patterns of belief and behaviour which were often accepted quite unconsciously and which limited the likelihood of protest and of social revolution. Part Three will analyse aspects of this process of socialization.

PART THREE

Social Institutions

A social history which concentrated exclusively upon social groups would hardly be adequate. Account must also be taken of the institutions whose existence and activities impinged upon people's lives. The most significant of these were the churches, most notably the Roman Catholic Church, the schools and the state. The first two, in addition to their overt religious and educational objectives, provided means for the transmission of broader ideologies constructed by those who exercised control over them. Similarly the state was far from being the socially neutral institution described by conservative political theorists. Together these three bodies provided complex and pervasive means by which members of socially and geographically diverse groups were socialized, and integrated into an ordered and increasingly stable social and political system.

7

Religion

Religious life has to be examined at a number of levels: in relation to the structure and teachings of established churches; at the level of the parish in which clergy and people interrelate; and most difficult of all, in terms of the beliefs of the population.

The Roman Catholic Church

According to the official census of 1872, of a population of 36 million, 35,387,703 were Roman Catholics, under 600,000 Protestants, 50,000 Jews and 80,000 freethinkers. Although, as will become evident, these statistics have many shortcomings, they justify the emphasis placed in this chapter upon analysis of the Roman Catholic Church as an institution and upon the relationships of its clergy with the wider society.

Parish clergy

The revolution had been a disaster for the church. Between 1790 and 1802 recruitment of priests had been virtually suspended. Subsequently, it averaged only 350–500 per annum during the empire, so that in 1814 there were only 35,952 priests in France, half of the number in 1789, and of these almost 11,000 were over 60. Of some 23,000 churches, 3345 had no priest. During the restoration, encouraged by increased stipends and obvious government favour, and by the development of the network of church schools and seminaries the number of ordinations constantly increased, from 918 in 1815 to 2357 in 1830; reducing the percentage of sexagenarians from 42 per cent to 32 per cent. By 1830 there were 4655 more clergy than in 1814, in spite of high mortality among the many aged priests. Subsequently, the number of ordinands declined, falling to 1095 by 1845. This in part reflected a deterioration of state–church relationships. However, between 1845 and 1851 there was some recovery, with the average annual number of ordinations rising to 1295 and then stabilizing at around 1310 between 1852 and 1860. Indeed, throughout the Second Empire, encouraged by government assistance and active recruitment the overall numbers of clergy continued to increase, although some concern was already being expressed about the rising average age of priests (in the diocese of Montpellier 6.3 per cent of priests were over 60 in 1850, but 27.3 per cent by 1880), and from some dioceses about the declining social status of ordinands. Even so, by 1869 the number of priests was 39 per cent above the 1830 figure, although the population had risen by only 17 per cent. In 1870 the maximum figure for the century was attained, with 56,500 priests, and not only had their numbers increased, but they were an altogether more dynamic force than in 1814 – more youthful and more combative, and controlling a dense institutional network of churches, schools, charities and lay organizations.

From this point there began a long period of decline. This can be related to increasingly more rapid socio-economic change, affecting the status of the church within society, and reducing the attractiveness of the priesthood. One significant factor in this was the development of attractive alternative career opportunities, most notably in teaching. From a peak of 1753 ordinations in 1868, the number stagnated at around 1550 per annum until disestablishment in 1905, after which, due to the loss of status and income, a rapid decline occurred from 1580 ordinations in 1904 to 1014 in 1909 and 704 in 1914.[1]

To a greater extent than in the previous century the priesthood was recruited from among the lower classes. A church stripped of most of its wealth and much of its influence by the revolution and providing in 1850 a stipend of around 350f for assistant priests and 850–1500f for parish priests (together with income from pew rents and fees), had ceased to offer an attractive career to the sons of the nobility or well-off bourgeoisie. Overwhelmingly, the fathers of priests were peasants, artisans or shopkeepers, and they had been attracted in part by the greater security and status promised by the priestly function (Table 55). The nature of the recruitment depended in large part on socio-economic structures

Table 55   *Socio-professional origins of the clergy in the diocese of Luçon (in per cent)*[2]

Category	1791 (very incomplete)	1873–82
Liberal professions, large-scale merchants and industrialists	41.7	2.4
Artisans, small traders	30.1	45.7
Peasant farmers	21.7	37.2
Workers, clerks minor officials, agricultural labourers	6.5	14.7
Total number of priests	263	210

and inevitably varied between diocese. In that of Rouen, during the July Monarchy, 38 per cent of the parish clergy were of peasant origin, another 11 per cent were the sons of agricultural labourers and domestic weavers, 2 per cent of sailors, 2.5 per cent of domestic servants, 6.6 per cent of clerical employees, and almost as many of urban workers, 25 per cent were the sons of shopkeepers and artisans, 4.5 per cent came from the wealthy commercial, senior government official, liberal profession categories, and 3 per cent from the milieu of landowners and *rentiers*. By 1890–1914, the proportion recruited from peasant families had fallen by 50 per cent, that from those of domestic servants and especially clerks had increased (the latter to 22 per cent), and those from an urban-worker background (usually described as deChristianized) had grown to 13 per cent. The intake from the bourgeois professions had also increased, indicative of a greater religiosity in these social groups.[3] Clearly the wealthiest and poorest groups in society were underrepresented. The absence of the latter was not, however, necessarily regarded as cause for concern. Monseigneur Bouvier, Bishop of Le Mans, in a circular to his parish clergy in 1846, insisted that youths from the poorest classes should not be encouraged in their vocations because their families could not afford to support them in their studies. He also felt that the misery they had experienced all too often engendered vice and prevented the development of altruism and lofty ideals.

This partial democratization of recruitment was mirrored to some degree in appointments to bishoprics. During the restoration the royal administration once again favoured nobles, as it had before the revolution. 82 per cent of the bishops appointed were nobles. During the July Monarchy this declined to 13 per cent and between 1848 and 1870 to 10 per cent. The result was that by 1871, 53.3 per cent of bishops came from the lower classes (including thirty-four from peasant families, eighteen sons of artisans, two of workers, fifteen of clerks and eight of shopkeepers), 12 per cent from noble families, and 33 per cent from a bourgeoisie of large-scale merchants, the higher ranks of the administration, the liberal professions and well-off landowners.[4] This was a structure which reflected both overall recruitment to the priesthood and deliberate government policy to promote men of intellect whatever their social background. It remained true, however, that a cultural gulf existed between the bishops (and also clergy in key administrative and educational positions) who either came from wealthy backgrounds or at least had received the benefit of a higher education, and the mass of parish priests.

The ability of the church to recruit priests varied considerably between regions. The number of vocations was influenced by a complex of factors, including the intensity of local religious belief, the existence of church schools which encouraged youths to enter the seminaries, and almost coincidental factors such as one or two charismatic parish priests, or families anxious to *faire un prêtre*. The scale of recruitment could thus vary considerably, even within areas with apparently similar levels of faith. Especially in the earlier part of the century, regions were differentiated by levels of literacy and income which helped to determine the size of the base from which recruitment occurred.

Factors such as local models of social mobility, and celibacy rates, are also relevant. In the second part of the century vocations appear to have been especially common in rural areas with high population densities and limited opportunities for social mobility, rather than in the more dynamic economic regions. As a result, the diocese of Montpellier depended on neighbouring mountain dioceses (Viviers, Rodez, Mende) to provide it with a sufficient number of priests. The geography of recruitment was complex, suggesting a need to analyse cultural zones quite small in scale. In the Vendée ordinations per 100,000 of population in the period 1878–97 varied between eighty-five in the Haut-Bocage and twenty-six in the plains.[5] In general, however, recruitment was relatively easy in the west, in Flanders, the Franche-Comté, Massif Central and parts of the Midi, regions in which populations remained devoted to their priests and in which the prestige, influence and material life of the latter was assured. It was in them that the religious network was most rapidly reconstructed after the revolution. The plethora of priests in the diocese of Rennes is indicative (Table 56).[6] Recruitment was much more difficult in parts of central France, in Bourgogne and especially in Champagne and the Paris region. Indeed by the 1880s the number of ordinations was regarded as sufficient to meet local needs in only twenty-five departments. In other regions the church experienced severe difficulty because of the low density of its network of priests and the tendency of areas with surplus clergy to export to them the least competent.

In areas of strong recruitment, and in spite of the process of urbanization, the majority of new priests tended to come from the countryside. Elsewhere, in dioceses such as Orléans or Limoges, where much of the rural population was rather indifferent to religion, most of the priests came from the towns, and in insufficient numbers. The significance of geographical variations in recruitment becomes clearer when the relationship between priests and population is considered. For the diocese of Paris (i.e., the department of the Seine) the dual consequence of low levels of recruitment and high immigration caused severe pastoral problems (Table 57).[7] The situation was much better in a diocese like that of Albi, where in 1850 there was one priest for every 514 inhabitants, a situation which improved continuously to attain 1:395 by 1900.[8]

At a national level, the most favourable situation was achieved by 1875 with one priest for every 639 inhabitants (compared with 1:818 in 1815).[9] At diocesan level it was not simply the number of priests which mattered, but their distribution. A rigid parishional structure existed. Every community wanted its own

Table 56 *Parish clergy in the diocese of Rennes*

	Curés	Recteurs	Vicaires	Teachers	Charity	Regulars
Year IX	43	300	156	9	10	153
1850	43	333	328	42	30	28
1900	60	324	588	100	105	98

Table 57 *Diocese of Paris*

Year	Population	Index no.	No. of priests	Index no.	Average no. of inhabitants per priest
1802	629,908	100	375	100	1,680
1836	1,097,078	184	408	109	2,689
1861	1,953,660	310	661	176	2,956
1886	2,961,089	470	770	205	3,845
1914	4,154,042	659	925	246	4,491

priest, and at a time when urbanization was increasing, this resulted in a maldistribution. Already in 1856 Monseigneur Darboy's inquiries had revealed that there was only one priest per 4000 inhabitants in the Montmartre district of Paris, and 1:5000 in Belleville.[10] By 1906, in the 12th and 20th *arrondissements* parishes with a population of 50,000 served by five priests were normal. Inevitably the clergy's pastoral efforts reached only part of the population.

The religious orders

The religious orders had been banned during the revolution. Bonaparte had tolerated the female congregations and a small number of male orders, primarily because of their value in teaching and nursing. Even during the restoration it had taken time to devise a satisfactory legal base for their existence due to the persistence of both Gallican and philosophical prejudices. However, legislation in 1817 and 1825 allowed the government to authorize orders of nuns, and in a favourable social and political climate these rapidly expanded. There were 12,400 nuns in 1815, 25,000 in 1830, 40,000 in 1851, 98,200 in 1861 and 128,000 in 1877, at which level their numbers stagnated until 1940.[11] Additionally, alongside the regular orders, in departments marked by male emigration and high female celibacy rates, particularly in the Massif Central, Brittany and Normandy, young girls too poor or insufficiently educated to become nuns, took vows of celibacy and served in the so-called *tiers-ordres*. They remained in their villages, assisting the parish priest and caring for the sick. In 1853 in Haute-Loire there were an estimated 1200 of these *beatés*.[12] Subsequently their numbers declined as the regular teaching and nursing orders expanded, and as opportunities for female emigration grew. However, in the conditions of rural isolation so common in the early nineteenth century, especially in zones of dispersed habitat, they had proved a significant factor in the preservation of popular religiosity.

The growth of the female orders resulted not only in a feminization of the personnel of the church but inevitably affected its sensibility. Most bishops saw them as vital to the work of reChristianization. The ideal was a group of nuns in every parish, able to influence the women in particular, and through them the younger generation. Throughout the century the care of the sick and aged, the distribution of charity, and the education of girls remained very much in the hands of the religious orders, and generally served to ensure their popularity and to encourage vocations. In areas like the Breton west the nuns were everywhere, venerated by the female populations whose piety they encouraged, respected for their dedication and the low cost of the education and the medical care they provided, in spite of the growing criticism of their competence by the lay teachers and doctors with whom they competed. The Second Empire, which brought a further relaxation of legal controls (decree–law of 31 January 1852), and which coincided with and encouraged a renewed religious revival in some social groups, saw particularly rapid expansion. From the 1870s, however, the number of female vocations slowly began to decline, due to various factors, including the fall in birth rate, changing parental attitudes, alternative employment opportunities for women, and the growing secularization of attitudes and institutions.

The male orders were far less popular than those of nuns. Even their legal position for long remained unclear. Most orders were simply tolerated. Nevertheless they also prospered, and the number of monks grew from 9136 in 1856 to 17,676 in 1861, 30,286 in 1877 and 37,000 in 1901.[13] The largest single group was the teaching order of *Frères des écoles chrétiennes*, while the most notorious were orders such as the Redemptorists, Capucines, Carmelites, Dominicans and particularly Jesuits (prohibited from teaching even under the restoration, but with 2658 brothers in 1870),[14] suspect because of the influence they were presumed to exercise and the wealth they accumulated as teachers, preachers and confessors to the bourgeoisie and aristocracy. Indeed, during the Second Empire the regime moved from initial toleration to discrimination against the male orders in the 1860s in an attempt to prevent their further expansion. Growing anti-clericalism during the Third Republic led to legislation in 1901, initially intended to increase state controls, but harshly implemented by Prime Minister Combes (a former seminarist). The religious corporations (male and female) were required to apply to parliament for authorization, and if they refused to do so or this was not granted (as was usually the case) they were dissolved and their corporate property sold. The teaching orders were given ten years to withdraw from their functions. These measures significantly reduced, but far from destroyed their influence.

Pastoral care

The training provided for future priests seems to be the appropriate place to begin an analysis of their pastoral work. The local clergy took great pride in encouraging likely candidates for the priesthood, in providing them with the first rudiments of a religious education, in persuading parents to allow their sons to attend first the *petit seminaire* for some seven years and subsequently the seminary proper for three to five years. At all stages in their training young men appear to have had impressed upon them the shortness of human life, man's relative insignificance, and the importance of God's judgement in determining whether an earthly existence was to be followed by eternal damnation or celestial bliss. According to the Abbé Mérault, director of the seminary at Orléans in the 1820s, the priest should encourage 'a religion which consoles, but which at the same time provides a salutory warning to the sinner'. In general, candidates for the priesthood appear to have been imbued with a very pessimistic view of human nature.

The education provided in the seminaries was characterized by an unimaginative routine within an authoritarian environment. The directors themselves appear to have been selected because of their piety rather than intellect. Teaching concentrated upon simple theology, morality and the liturgy. Hatred of the revolution, which had attempted to deny the truths of religious faith and to destroy the fabric of the church, contributed to an exaggerated suspicion of all modern ideas. At no stage in the training of the future priest (or indeed during his future career) was personal initiative or curiosity encouraged. Nevertheless, some improvement did occur, especially from the late 1820s and 1830s, following the initial effort to fill the gaps in the ranks caused by the revolution. The establishment in Paris by Monseigneur Affre in 1845 of an institution for advanced religious studies – the *Ecole des Carmes* – was a small sign of a growing awareness of the need to improve the quality of religious study. Such developments, however, had only limited effects on the quality of intellectual debate within the church, or on the capacity of churchmen to defend Christian beliefs, which were increasingly under attack. Theologians continued to insist upon the fundamental truth of the Bible, written, according to Pope Leo XIII in 1893, 'under the inspiration of the Holy Ghost'. Monseigneur Dupanloup refuted Renan's attack on the divinity of Christ simply by reference to various biblical prophecies; the Abbé Dessailly proved that Jonah could have lived inside a whale because toads had lived for thousands of years inside stones. Given their poor general education, only a minority of priests were interested in theological ideas anyway, although some achieved local fame as *érudits*, especially through their parish histories. More notable were the efforts made in the seminaries and among the established parish clergy to improve the quality of pastoral care by means of increasingly frequent conferences and spiritual retreats.

In practice the individual priest was subject to the constraints of a strictly hierarchical organisation. The Napoleonic *Concordat* had increased the authority of bishops over the parish clergy. In the absence of ecclesiastical tribunals, bishops tended to decide themselves on disciplinary questions, often making use of the right to move the regular clergy at will, which now applied to all save the 10 per cent who, as *curés* of parishes, enjoyed irremovable status. The vast majority of priests remained assistants for life, lacking security and status and often engaging in bitter competition for the vacant posts of *curé*. At the same time the independence of bishops *vis-à-vis* Rome had been strengthened. Governments were anxious both to reinforce the authority of the bishops, whom they largely appointed, and to reduce interference in French affairs by the Papacy.

In these circumstances an energetic bishop could exercise considerable influence – for good or ill. The bishops of the nineteenth century were rarely absent from their diocese, and the quality of diocesan administration and its supervisory capacity (through the vicars-general) was greatly improved. In practice the bishops were inevitably a varied lot. During the restoration 82 per cent of new appointees were nobles, including representatives of such notable families as the Clermont-Tonnerre, Talleyrand-Périgord and Clausel de Montals. Most of these were old men, who dreamed of reviving the eighteenth-century church and were unable to provide the kind of leadership required in changed circumstances. With the advent of the July Monarchy, in a very different political situation, which in itself hardly encouraged nobles to enter the church, it became deliberate government policy to appoint commoners to vacant sees. For successive governments the choice of amenable bishops was of considerable importance, especially in regions like the west, in which their social and political influence was quite considerable. The character of the episcopacy was determined, however, more by the training and the functions exercised before preferment than by social origins. Of 167 bishops created between 1870 and 1883, seventy-nine had been trained in seminaries controlled by the order of Saint-Sulpice, and had been taught to adopt a reserved and moderate attitude in relations with the civil authorities. Only eighteen had served previously as parish priests, twenty-three had risen through work in the various diocesan administrations, and ninety-two from teaching in seminaries or faculties of theology.[15] Although sometimes men of humility, their natural pride in their educational and social attainments tended to create a gulf between them and their parish clergy and to develop a taste for authority. They were most unwilling to condone any sign of insubordination. Movements such as that associated wth Lamennais, Montalembert and the journal *L'Avenir*, which in the 1830s promoted such notions as the separation of church and state, liberty of speech and association, and increased assistance to the poor, were quickly condemned. Bishops were nevertheless obliged to take some account of the views of their parish clergy, and the appointment of an energetic bishop like Parisis to Arras in 1851, which was followed by regular visitations and often humiliating criticism of local customs and the pastoral work of the clergy, was bitterly resented.

The essential objective of the priests' pastoral work was to secure participation by the largest possible number of people in the spiritual life of the church, and to persuade them to observe its moral teaching in their everyday life. For the clergy faith was the supreme end. Revealed religion provided the only effective guarantee of morality, and only Catholics could be genuinely moral. Through confession the priest served as the confidant, counsellor and judge of his flock. Monseigneur de Ségur, in a well-known work (*La Confession*) published in 1862, advised Catholics that, 'the priest has not only the right but the rigorous duty to teach you in general and in detail what you ought to do and what you ought to avoid'. Success depended upon the abilities and energy of the individual priest, upon the practical difficulties he faced (for example, a large parish and poor roads made pastoral work more difficult), and the receptiveness of parishioners. The ideal was to provide a framework of teaching, practice and devotion within which people could live out their lives. The objective must be to achieve domination over them. In practical terms this meant receiving confession, celebrating mass, administering the sacraments, preparing children for their first communion (a crucial stage in their religious education), visiting the flock (especially the sick and poor, whose links to the church might be reinforced by the distribution of charity), arbitrating in their disputes, seeking to attract worshippers, and to give evidence of their devotion by ensuring that the fabric of the local church was protected and embellished. In the diocese of Rennes, for example, in the more prosperous second part of the century half the communes reconstructed their churches and presbyteries and provided them with the sacred objects, ornaments and furnishings which they had frequently lacked since the revolution – for moral and ideological reasons as well as to make up for long neglect. In addition, the good priest should set an example through his behaviour, avoid excessive familiarity with his parishioners, and prepare himself in the solitude of his presbytery through meditation, prayer and study. In spite of sometimes well-publicized exceptions, the morals of the clergy were normally irreproachable, helping to justify the view they held of themselves as the moral guardians of the population. Indeed, it was all too likely, given the role of the priest as intermediary between Man and God, the authority derived directly from Christ, and the protective role he assumed in relation to his parishioners, that many priests should develop an intolerant and even arrogant attitude towards lay people. According to the *Semaine religieuse*, published in the diocese of Albi in 1882, 'in the priest there is something above man. . . . To venerate the priest is to come closer to God and to render Him glory'. Taken from his family at an early age, given an intensely theological education, required to distance himself from his flock and their daily concerns, the priest was all too likely to become socially and culturally isolated.

Within the parish, preaching was a key means of implementing moral guardianship. The spoken or written word assumed clear pride of place over the traditional iconography used in the decoration of churches as a means of conveying the message. Through it the dogmas, defined and codified by the Council of Trent in 1545, were received by the nineteenth century, and it was these, supported by the authority of the church, rather than personal judgements based upon a reading of the scriptures, which defined the proper relationship between layman and priest. Sermons obviously varied according to the abilities of individual priests and the character of their congregations. Effective communication with the mass of the population required that they were clear and simple and often in *patois* (in spite of the hostility of the *Université*), although in urban areas there was a tendency to address sermons to the cultural élites of a parish, employing a rhetorical style and allusions which were often meaningless to the less well-educated. Pierre Loti in his *Le Roman d'un Enfant* (1890) describes the agonising boredom of listening to the stereotyped messages in sermons delivered week after week in unctious manner by an inept and pompous parish priest. Their content seems to have undergone a significant change over the years. In the earlier part of the century most priests preached a religion of fear, threatening transgressors with God's Judgement and eternal damnation, and stressing the importance of daily prayer and meditation, eternal self-vigilance, mortification of the senses and frequent confession. The catechism of the diocese of Orléans asked, 'What punishment will God impose upon those who violate His commandments?', and answered, 'He will often punish them in this life, and make them burn eternally in the next.' With the Day of Judgement in prospect only religion could curb human lust and greed. Man's primary obligation was to fulfil his religious duties. The vanities of this transitory existence were nothing compared with death and the Last Judgement. Secular concerns should be strictly subordinated to the interests of religion. The essential lesson here was that Man should accept the Divine Plan. Moreover, he should be satisfied with the place in society which God, in his wisdom, had granted him. In this respect the message was socially very conservative. Moreover, individual or collective misfortunes could easily be seen as God's punishment. Events such as the revolution, the cholera epidemic of 1832, or military defeat in 1870 were presented as Divine warnings of the need for moral reform. From around mid century, however, it seems that the 'Cruel God' of the Old Testament began to give place to evocations of the loving Christ of the New Testament (the 'Sweet Jesus, Divine Jesus, Good Jesus, Tender Jesus' of the hymn) and of the Virgin Mary ('beloved Mother, Sweet Hope').

The reputation of the church, however, continued to suffer from the obsession of many of its priests with a routine dominated by the formal observance of ritual. At most they sought to attract the wayward through religious pomp and the spectacle of missions and pilgrimages rather than by creating a sense of personal devotion. Even the work of catechizing the young, which was crucial to religious revival, often involved little more than children learning the catechism by heart with little explanation by the priest.

To reinforce the work of the parish priests missions were organized by such groups as the *Missionaires de France*, founded in 1814, the Jesuits or in the Midi the *Oblets de Marie* as well as by diocesan societies. They were particularly active during the restoration when they enjoyed the full co-operation of the civil and military authorities anxious to repair the 'damage' of the revolution. Their activities involved the public affirmation of faith, by means of processions, the singing of hymns to popular tunes, and preaching in a campaign, which might last for three weeks and culminated in the erection of a cross. Often they enjoyed spectacular success. In May 1821 in Montpellier a procession of 20,000 people, including 6000 young girls dressed in white, choirs, the *confréries* of penitents, local officials, soldiers and National Guards, was watched by another 40,000 spectators as it proceeded to where a cross was to be erected. The drama sometimes promoted an almost hysterical collective affirmation of faith. However, the effects usually tended to be short-lived, and the personnel available too few for the effort to be repeated regularly. After the 1830 Revolution the ceremonies became far less dramatic. They were revived, however, on a large scale again during the Second Empire, in the 1870s and around the turn of the century when their lessons were reinforced by a large circulation religious press which included diocesan *Semaines religieuses* and simple, moralizing novels, such as those published as early as 1827 in the Nord by the *Bibliothèque des bons livres*, with heroes who tended to be workers resigned to their condition, and villains who were Protestants, Jews, atheists, lay school teachers, Jacobins and ungrateful children.

The parish clergy was also supported in their work by a variety of lay associations. Efforts were made to reconstitute such traditional groups as the *confréries* of penitents, so common, particularly in the south, before the revolution. While these continued to participate in devotional activities and particularly the funerals of their members, for many priests they had become too secular in their interests. Bitter complaints were frequently made about the drinking bouts which followed funerals. In the 1850s in the Pas-de-Calais, a region of traditional devotion, it was felt necessary to regularize thirty-five and to suppress thirty-eight. As a consequence of this dissatisfaction a complex of new associations was developed with the primary objectives of intensifying the religious character of everyday life, and protecting the faithful against evil influences. Within these associations, while associating laymen with their pastoral work, the clergy sought to ensure that their own predominant role was unchallenged. In the diocese of Limoges in the 1860s and 1870s these new groups included the *Oeuvre des douze apôtres* to encourage ecclesiastical vocations; the *Oeuvre de Saint-François-de-Sales* to struggle against Protestantism; the *Oeuvre des bons-livres* to provide a moralizing literature; the *Oeuvre de dimanche* to oppose Sunday work; the *Apostolat de la prière* consecrated to the Sacred Heart, which in 1878 distributed in Limoges and its hinterland 7000 large engravings of the Sacred Heart of Jesus and the Virgin Mary, over 30,000 Sacred Heart scapularies, 2000 small Bibles and a periodical, the *Petit messager du coeur de Marie*; the charitable *conférence de Saint-Vincent-de-Paul*; and the Catholic mutual aid societies organized under the aegis of Saint-Joseph. An effort was being made to provide a form of association for each category of the population. In this particular diocese these efforts to renew popular piety appear to have been a devastating failure. Elsewhere – in the north and west for example – greater success was enjoyed. In 1861 in the parish of Maure in Ille-et-Vilaine, for example, of 1400 inhabitants 700 belonged to the confraternity of the Rosary, and 1300 to that of the *Scapularie*. There were also two sections of the *Adorators of the Holy Sacrament*. Few adults escaped from the network of devotion.[16]

This constant effort to intensify and to control the religious life of the population was manifested in various other ways. Since the Council of Trent, the church had sought to purify the faith and to eliminate superstition and paganism. This had often led to tension between the two religious cultures, that of the priest and that of the masses. Jansenism and the enlightened rationality of the eighteenth century had intensified these trends. The dividing line between religion and superstition, however, was not always easily definable, and at parish level priests frequently found it necessary to tolerate magico-religious practices of which they did not necessarily approve. Prayers of intercession for better weather, and to Saint-Roch for protection against cholera appear to have been regarded as quite proper. There was more doubt concerning local pilgrimages to saints' shrines, to holy wells whose waters supposedly had curative properties, or to stones with mysterious shapes and trees with strange silhouettes, especially where these were accompanied by dancing and drinking. However, during the nineteenth century, under the impact of Romanticism, and the development of ultramontane ideas, the attitude of the clergy towards popular religious practices became rather more subtle. As a result the gulf between élite and popular devotions was reduced, and the church was able to respond more effectively to the spiritual needs of the masses.

The most dramatic manifestations of these trends were the mass pilgrimages (taking advantage of the new railways) organized to Lourdes and La Salette – places blessed by the appearance of the Virgin Mary and subsequent miracles. The church promoted a renewal of the Marial devotions which already possessed such strong roots, particularly through the declaration of the Immaculate Conception by the Pope in 1854. The miraculous appearance of the Virgin to Bernadette at Lourdes in 1858 during which She declared, 'I am the Immaculate Conception', seemed to confirm the truth of the church's theological position, and could be taken to be proof of Christ's blessing. There were thus strong pressures on bishops and investigatory commissions to accept that a divine intervention had occurred. The encouragement of such 'devotions' stimulated an intense, emotional faith, an effective counter to the false pride of rationalism. It was encouraged by the distribution of cheap literature and medals and statues mass-produced by new technology. To some extent this development occurred at the expense of traditional devotion to local saints, but efforts were also made to encourage the cult of the saints and the veneration of holy relics as further means of stimulating popular piety wherever the official representatives of the church felt confident that they could control such manifestations.

These efforts to stimulate faith and organize the faithful were also a response to growing clerical anxiety concerning the rise of 'materialism'. This was condemned because it interfered with the performance of man's fundamental obligation to worship God. Peasants and workers were frequently castigated for the 'egotistical' hunger for land and money which led them to neglect church attendance. Popular leisure time activities were also condemned in part because the clergy had little formal control over them. The Bishop of Arras insisted in 1852 that his priests refuse absolution to young people who frequented bars and evening dances. The hostility of the church to the *cabaret*, the *veillée*, 'evil' books, the *charivari*, carnival processions, gatherings at fairs and markets, dancing, etc., moreover, enjoyed the support of 'respectable' citizens and the authorities. The church was able to participate in a wider, conservative alliance, devoted to the restoration of 'moral order'. It also enjoyed the satisfaction of being able to blame the decline in its influence upon the moral weakness of laymen rather than upon its own shortcomings. However, this could be counterproductive. It alienated many of those it was directed against. This was especially true of interference in sexual matters – the sins of the flesh which haunted priests. Published guides for confessors stressed a wife's duty to submit to her husband's 'libidinous needs', but also suggested that priests should encourage restraint. Furthermore, the practice of contraception was a growing cause of concern. Through its practice 'man defies providence'. It was assumed that sexual relationships should have no other objective than procreation. The 'weaker sex' was in need of protection. In order to achieve this and to prevent sexual promiscuity the clergy systematically sought to separate the sexes at school, and to condemn the stimulation of carnal lust by such activities as dancing. Through the pious wife and mother the entire family might enjoy the benefits of Christian life. She was the hope of the future.

In general, however, the clergy did not look to the future with any great optimism. They looked back to a mythical Ancien Régime as an age of gold. This prevented them from coming to terms with the world in which they lived and adopting a critical view of their own activities. Their reactions to social change were essentially protective and reactionary. They complained incessantly about the evils of their times and presented religion as the only cure for a sick society. Industrialization and urbanization were perceived of as threats to the immutable relationships of traditional rural civilization. Although frequently aware of and concerned about social problems, their theological training and general outlook led them to explain these in essentially moral terms, and in consequence to propose primarily moral solutions – love of God, obedience to His commandments, charity on the part of the rich, resignation on the part of the poor during their transitory existence on Earth. Primarily they sought to protect the Good from contamination by Evil. They adopted an essentially Manichean outlook on society, which engendered a ghetto mentality and made it all the more difficult to come to terms with the decline in the influence of the church.

Among the lower and younger clergy, in particular, *ultramontane* sympathies developed, especially between about 1840 and 1870, as priests increasingly looked to Rome to protect them against their own authoritarian bishops and to end the subservience to the state on which Napoleon had insisted in the 1802 *Concordat*. Submission to the Pope was a means of increasing the confidence of priests fighting trends towards secularization. Influential writers such as Lamennais in his *De la religion considerée dans ses rapports avec l'ordre politique et civil* (1825), and later Louis Veuillot in the newspaper *L'Univers* (from 1843), and the Assumptionist order in *La Croix* (1883) and its imitators, insisted that the Papacy was the guardian of the word of God. The theological basis for their outlook was expressed by Monseigneur Pie, Bishop of Poitiers (1849–80) in the statement 'Christ must reign also upon earth.' This could be assured only through the extension of the influence of the church in the spheres of both private and public morality. In his encyclical *Quanta Cura* (1864), Pius IX vehemently condemned the limits placed upon the authority of the church over civil society, including the Gallican liberties of the church in France, and all modern freedoms. It was accompanied by a *Syllabus* listing some eighteen major errors of the times. By 1870–83 only twelve of the 167 French bishops still appear to have had reservations concerning this extreme position,[17] while the lower clergy was even more enthusiastic in its support. The apparent determination on the part of the church to restore the practices of the 'centuries of faith' inevitably led it into conflict with the state and the proponents of scientific and libertarian ideas. Thus in 1875 the *Semaine religieuse* of the diocese of Albi, calling for support for the establishment of a Catholic university, promised that it would combat the teaching of 'geology which undermines the Bible; the theory of the man-monkey; linguistics, which combats the Scriptures; history, which is re-written against Christianity'.

Protestants and Jews

The presence of religious minorities was another cause of disquiet for the Roman Catholic clergy. Nominally, at least, they were in a position of overwhelming strength. In 1815 there were some 500,000 Protestants in France, around half of whom were Lutheran, living mainly in Alsace and in the Doubs and Haute-Saône, and the others mainly Calvinists belonging to the *Église Réformée de France* and dispersed over some forty departments, but with compact minorities in the Drôme, Ardèche, Gard, Lozère, Tarn, Torn-et-Garonne and Deux-Sèvres and small groups in the Montbéliard (Doubs) and Paris regions, in Seine-Inférieure and Alsace. Like the Catholics they were experiencing considerable spiritual ferment. Pietistic elements were reacting against the rationalism of the eighteenth century and reasserting the doctrines of the Reformation – the Bible as God's Word revealed, and the utter sinfulness of man. Their most consuming objective remained, however, the preservation of their separate identity. Within an overwhelmingly Catholic society they sought to secure this by means of a rigid social segregation in their own urban *quartiers* and villages and the maintenance of their own schools and charitable and voluntary organizations. The rarity of mixed marriages suggests a high degree of success, particularly in areas where they were relatively strong numerically, such as the *arrondissements* of Alais and Vigan in the Gard. There memories of the renewal of persecution during the White Terror in 1815, when their churches had been pillaged and around eighty Protestants had been murdered, remained fresh for much of the century. The survival of an intense sense of identity could be seen in repeated efforts to oppose the pretensions of Catholic extremists and to assume local political power in co-operation with those political regimes which appeared most likely to respect religious liberty, i.e. the July Monarchy, liberal empire and republic, even to the extent of accepting the laicization of the 1000 Protestant schools in the 1880s.

By 1851 there were about 565,000 Calvinists and 270,000 Lutherans in France. According to the 1872 census, however, the overall number had fallen to 580,000, due primarily to the weakening of the Lutheran community by the loss of Alsace-Lorraine. It remained primarily rural, but with sizeable churches in particular *quartiers* of Nîmes, Bordeaux, Le Havre and Paris. In Nîmes between 1870 and 1905, where Protestants made up around 25 per cent of the population, about 29 per cent of them were lower middle class (compared with 19.5 per cent among the Catholic community), 21 per cent were *employés de commerce* (compared with 7.5 per cent), and 21 per cent workers (compared with 45 per cent).[18] For whatever reasons Protestants were especially active in manufacture and commerce and tended to favour their co-religionists in making appointments to the better jobs.

There were also sizeable Jewish communities in France, made up in 1815 of some 60,000 people divided into two main groups. In the south in the Comtat-Venaissin, there were the descendants of Jews who had once enjoyed the protection of the Papacy at Avignon. These remained mainly artisans, while members of other communities at Bayonne and Bordeaux were mainly engaged in trade. These southerners had assimilated more fully into French society than had the members of the other major group living in Alsace (about 14,000 people dispersed in over 200 communities). Professionally they were mainly pedlars, money-lenders, cattle-dealers and aroused anti-semitic feeling because of their reputation as usurers. By the end of the century a substantial redistribution had occurred. Of some 71,000 Jews counted by the Consistory, 45,000 were resident in Paris. These constituted a heterogeneous group. Many, especially those with bourgeois professions, were largely assimilated. This was in marked contrast to the new (uncounted) immigrants, driven from eastern Europe by persecution, many of whom settled in Paris around the Place de la Bastille and in the Marais, working as tailors, shoemakers and furriers, and isolated by their poverty and Yiddish language. Their presence and distinctive appearance, was one factor giving new life to the traditional current of anti-semitism associated with what the Catholic press and especially *La Croix* referred to as, 'the question of Christ'. The old accusations of usury also received new force due to attacks from both left and the extreme right directed at the Jewish bankers, described in 1845 by the Fourierist Toussaint as the *rois de l'époque*. From the 1880s and subsequently in association with the Dreyfus affair anti-semitism became a key element in the growth of right-wing nationalism. Drumont's *La France juive*, published in two massive volumes in 1886–7, ran into 127 editions in two years. His newspaper, *La Libre Parole*, had a circulation of 500,000 in the late 1890s. It combined the Catholic myth of the harmonious middle ages and hatred of the revolution, with a social Catholic desire for a new economic order.

The church and society

Moral order

To an important degree the clergy, because of their fear of social change, respect for the God-given social hierarchy, and dependence upon the financial and moral support of national and local élites, served as guarantors of the existing social system. They were instrumental in various ways, from social teaching to the respect so publicly accorded to the wealthy by priests, through precedence in public processions and in the giving of communion, seating arrangements in churches and the greater splendour of the marriages and burials over which they officiated for those who could afford ostentatious display. Even bishops, although they might resent the fact, usually felt bound to respect the wishes of influential notables, such as in the 1870s the industrialist Kolb-Bernard in the diocese of Cambrai, the banker Thomasset at Lyon, or the Duc d'Aumale in Beauvais. In particular, co-operation between the clergy and nuns and Catholic laymen in the work of poor relief, of hospital care and education, was both the visible, everyday manifestation of Christian charity, and a vital means by which the church preserved its influence.

Traditionally the church had insisted that the wealthy had responsibilities towards their less fortunate bretheren. The concept of charity summed up clerical attitudes towards society. Through Christian resignation to their suffer-ings the poor gained hope of Eternal Salvation, while assistance to the poor, freely given, offered the prospect of Divine Reward to the rich. The philan-thropic activities of the wealthy both supported the pastoral work of the parish clergy and reinforced their own social influence. Charity was in fact central to the ideology of both traditional landed élites and indeed of many large indus-trialists. It helped to justify their wealth and facilitated social control by promot-ing dependence and deference. It obviated the need for social reform, and for state intervention in welfare which would have threatened individual 'freedom' and increased taxation. The writings of influential Catholics like Monseigneur Dupanloup reveal how close theologians came to accepting the ideals of a pure economic liberalism. Even the exceptions, 'social Catholics' like Villeneuve-Bargemont (*Traité d'économie politique*, 1834), Frédéric Ozanam and Armand de Melun, who condemned the English model of social development and the inordinate greed which led to excessive mechanization, overproduction, unem-ployment and low wages went no further than to propose the restoration of the corporations of the Ancien Régime, and in practice limited their activities to a paternalism which differed hardly at all from that of the proponets of charity pure and simple. Most clerical authors continued to assimilate workers with domestics and to conceive of labour relations in master–servant terms. To the poor they offered above all 'hope everlasting'. The clergy affirmed the moral superiority of poverty, simplicity and humility in the eyes of God. Even a relatively concerned bishop like Monseigneur Giraud of Cambrai held to the view that work was 'God's punishment for the sins of Adam' and ought to be accepted with resignation. Following the 1848 Revolution even his criticisms of employers' greed became more circumspect. The efforts of workers to improve their situation by means of organization, strikes and political protest were unreservedly condemned as evincing materialistic envy. The church was interested primarily in the preservation of a social and ideological order within which it assumed souls were most likely to be saved. Thus criticism of the existing social system could be seen as blasphemous. According to Monseigneur Astros of Toulouse, socialism was 'impious, senseless, savage, barbaric'. It threatened to 'annihilate the family', to destroy 'law, justice and morality'. Only religion would promote harmonious social relations.

The most important of the many associations developed by laymen was the *Société de Saint-Vincent-de-Paul* (1833), which by the end of 1848 had 282 local groups with between 8000 and 10,000 members, and by 1861, at its peak, 1549 with around 100,000 members. This success of an organization suspect because of the clerical and legitimist sympathies of its members led to restrictive government measures and a loss of momentum, so that although growth was resumed after 1870, in 1903 there were still only 1526 branches. The *Société* in Angers was fairly typical. In 1842 it disposed of 12,000f, and assisted 300 families materially and spiritually through the circulation of books and religious instruction of children. Other associations included the *Société de Saint-Joseph* aimed at adolescents (1836), and the *Société pour l'amélioration et l'encouragement des publications populaires* (1850), one of a number of groups which sought to publish and distribute cheap, edifying literature such as *The Cabinet Maker or the Fruits of Good Conduct* (1864), and lives of the saints, and the *Oeuvre des Cercles* whose foundation was stimulated by the shock of the Paris Commune. This was intended to be a club for workers. It was too paternalistic to be attractive to many. More successful was the *Association Catholique de la Jeunesse française* (1886, reformed 1896), a youth movement which by 1905 had 14,000 groups with 60,000 members. [19]

As a means of reaching the masses Catholic involvement in education was of far greater significance. Education was conceived of in terms of the needs of religion, as a means of catechizing the young. It was the essential means of restoring the influence of the church. According to the Archbishop of Toulouse, the young were the 'unique' hope of the church after the revolutionary crisis which had spread general corruption. In his letter, *Quum non sine*, in 1864, Pius IX merely reiterated the established view that 'in the schools, religious education must take first place . . . and dominate to such an extent that other knowledge should appear to be provided as an extra'. The church would never be satisfied with anything less than total control.

The appointment of Monseigneur Frayssinous as *Grand Master of the Université* during the restoration signified government support for the desire of the church to restore its predominance. Parish clergy were encouraged to supervise lay teachers (*Ordonnance* of 1824). Efforts were made to educate the children of the élite through the establishment of secondary schools controlled by the religious orders, and those of the masses mainly by means of the provision of teachers for municipal institutions. The major limiting factor was the lack of personnel. Subsequently, the increase in the number of schools controlled by members of the teaching orders (and especially the *Institut des Ecoles Chrétienne*) was most substantial (not surprisingly) in some of those regions in which church attendance was highest, particularly in the west, i.e. where demand for religious education was greatest. The degree of clerical control therefore tended to increasingly vary between regions. Within the social élites and government, clerical ambitions enjoyed considerable support. The major education laws of 1833 and 1850 both reaffirmed the importance for society of moral and religious education, the latter in direct response to the fear caused among conservatives by the 1848 Revolution. Article I of the implementing regulations published in August 1851, stressed that, 'the principal duty of the teacher is to give a religious education to children'. The law increased the supervisory powers of priests over primary schools and by reducing the qualifications required by members of the teaching orders helped correct the problem of a shortage of personnel. For municipal councils the presence of members of the teaching orders in schools saved money and where nuns were involved also improved the provision of assistance to the poor. Significantly, and in spite of clerical pressure, this law left the system of secondary education, catering for a small élite, virtually untouched. It was after all, the masses who represented the danger. At this stage the secular and the religious authorities agreed that the political subversion and irreligion which threatened them were closely related and that both were caused by immorality. The masses needed protection from such demoralizing forces as the *cabaret*, and subversive ideas. Without this religious influence, the school itself might become the generator of revolution through increasing literacy.

By the beginning of the Third Republic about 25 per cent of boys in primary schools and 60 per cent of girls were taught by members of the religious orders. The difference was due to the easier recruitment of nuns and to the widespread parental feeling that the virtues of the good wife and mother were more effectively taught by the religious orders. 70,000 pupils attended clerical secondary schools, compared with 116,000 in lay schools. Already, however, during the Second Empire, ministers had expressed anxiety about excessive clerical influence over the minds of the young, while both parents and municipal councils had frequently expressed unease about the quality of the education provided and resentment over clerical criticism of lay teachers. The hardening of the church's doctrinal position stimulated growing opposition to its claims and considerable anxiety among the increasingly well-trained and professionally aware lay teachers, even when as generally seems to have been the case, they were practising Catholics themselves. The opposition gradually grew stronger. In 1879 the Paris municipal council decided to exclude the *frères* from public schools. In the same year Jules Ferry introduced legislation to remove the clergy from supervisory bodies; in 1886 it was determined to replace monks and nuns in public schools as rapidly as possible. These moves culminated in the 1901 law designed to limit the growth of the religious orders by requiring prior authorization, but interpreted by Combes in the most extreme sense as permitting the suppression of all non-authorized congregations and the closure of about 3000 of their schools. The congregations were required to abandon their teaching functions within ten years. As a result, between 1905 and 1914 the number of children attending Roman Catholic primary schools fell by a third and secondary schools by a quarter. This struggle to control education involved the church in increasingly bitter political conflict.

Politics

There were four main phases of clerical political activity – the end of the empire and beginning of the restoration, immediately after the 1830 Revolution (1830–4), from 1859 in reaction to the government's Italian policy, and from the early 1880s. Throughout the century, the collective consciousness of the church remained marked by the experiences of the revolution. This had clearly been a major blow, although prior signs of disaffection were conveniently forgotten. The very existence of the church had been threatened, its property confiscated and the pastoral work of the clergy interrupted, in many areas for as much as ten years. The *Concordat* of 1801 had allowed the reorganization of the church, and throughout the century it enjoyed considerable financial and practical support from the state, but at the cost of concessions in respect of the appointment of bishops and limitations on its freedom of action, which were increasingly felt to be excessive. 1789 thus served as a major historical reference point, around which a traditionalist, Manichean ideology and martyrology was constructed. An idyllic myth of the Ancien Régime was created and all social ills were identified with the revolution – 'a revolt against Providence'. For traditionalists like de Maistre and Bonald, writing during the restoration, God had punished France for the growth of individualism and materialism, which had been stimulated by the Protestant Reformation and the Enlightenment. Yet out of disaster arose hope. God's warning should encourage men to seek salvation. The advice of Monseigneur Beauregard, Bishop of Orléans, in 1823 was to 'love God [and] serve the King'. Indeed it followed from this earlier experience of 'pure evil' that the safeguarding of the interests of the church was subsequently associated with the preservation of the existing social and political order. Succeeding regimes would be judged in terms of the support they were prepared to give to the church. Nineteenth-century clericalism was both a defensive reaction to the revolution and an offensive effort to secure as much influence as possible, with governmental support whenever this was forthcoming, and through the creation of a Catholic counter-society in less favourable circumstances. This latter tactic was to be particularly effective in such regions as the Breton interior where, in defence of religion and on the basis of the *chouan* tradition of resistance to the demands of the centralizing state, an alliance of nobles and peasants could be maintained.

The restoration appeared as nothing less than providential and helped to create an eschatological perspective, which for most of the century led legitimists to believe in the possibility of further restoration. Although, to the disappointment of many priests, the *Concordat* was retained, the regime was clearly much more favourable to the interests of the church than had been its predecessor. Indeed, to the restored monarch the church appeared to be an institution of fundamental importance. The regime appointed as bishops, priests noted for their political loyalty and mostly nobles; a law of November 1815 banned Sunday work and re-established public religious processions together with the obligation to decorate houses along their routes. It encouraged the work of

material reconstruction and widespread missionary activity. The clergy
responded with prayers begging God to forgive the nation for the sacrilege and
crimes of the revolution, and through such public manifestations as the service
in 1814 in expiation for the murder of Louis XVI, the coronation of Charles X at
Reims and the Jubilee processions of 1825, which spectacularly affirmed the
alliance of throne and altar. Of the coronation, the Bishop of Orléans wrote,
'kings are the Images of God on earth. It is their mission to give us laws'. The
clergy in general felt bound to support the regime, sometimes to excess, with
virulent attacks on liberals and the possessors of former church property, and
indeed anyone who opposed their pretensions. During the election campaign of
1827 the Bishop of Nancy, de Forbin Janson, ordered his clergy to refuse
absolution to readers of liberal newspapers.

This close identification of the church with the restoration monarchy was the
cause of the anti-clerical demonstrations which followed the July Revolution in
1830. In spite of grave misgivings, however, the Papacy and bishopric were
soon convinced that the best way forward was through co-operation with an
obviously conservative regime. Although they realized that the new government was far less sympathetic towards their ideals than the old, and often
maintained an attitude of reserve towards it, the mass of the clergy were
unwilling to compromise the future of the church by supporting the deposed
monarch, even if in clerical areas of the west and Midi legitimists were able to
use religious festivals to publicly display their political sentiments. The only
major cause of contention was to be the debate over secondary education in the
1840s, when, under the impulsion of Montalembert and Louis Veuillot, the
editor of the clerical newspaper, *L'Univers*, a committee was established to
demand freedom for the church to establish its own secondary schools.
Significantly, its leading figures were at pains to make it clear that their political
opposition was motivated by the interests of the church rather than legitimist
sympathies.

The lack of any sentimental attraction to the July Monarchy did make it
easier, however, for the clergy to accept the republic in 1848. They were then
quickly alienated by signs of radicalism in political life and the threat of educational reform, and when these were paralleled by revolution in Rome itself,
turned into ardent supporters of counter-revolution. 1848 was undoubtedly a
major turning point. For an eminent liberal Catholic like Montalembert it
brought to an end efforts to seek a compromise 'between the Church and
modern principles'. The church welcomed the bloody repression of the June
Insurrection in Paris. In clerical areas it used its political influence, greatly
reinforced by the establishment of universal male suffrage, to good effect. It
welcomed, although it was not satisfied by, the new education law (*loi Falloux*
of March 1850), which sought to moralize the masses by increasing the role of
the clergy in primary teaching. According to Monseigneur Menjaud, Bishop of
Nancy, the lesson of 1848 was that 'fear of God is the basis of social order'. The
alternatives represented by democracy and socialism would bring anarchy. The
conservative and usually legitimist social and political attitudes of the vast

majority of the clergy in the crisis years between the February Revolution and Louis-Napoléon's coup in December 1851 (presented by Monseigneur Régnier, Archbishop of Cambrai as the intervention of 'Divine Providence') and the growing involvement of the clergy in municipal and national politics, were major stimulii to anti-clericalism.

In the short-term, though, and throughout the 1850s the church benefited considerably from its close association with the Second Empire. For the first time since 1830, the alliance of church and state was marked by numerous public ceremonies. Thus the Archbishop of Rennes, Brossays-Saint-Marc, surrounded by 800 priests received the emperor on the steps of his cathedral in August 1858 and hailed him as 'The monarch most devoted to the work of civilization and the progress of the Papacy since Saint-Louis.' The clergy enjoyed freedoms of association denied to laymen, state subsidies were substantially increased, and the church encouraged to extend its role in public education. The *Concordat* and the restrictions it imposed upon the independence of the church were nevertheless maintained. In practice the alliance between state and church was always conditional, each seeking to use the other. Thus from 1859 the initial support for the Bonapartist regime turned to bitter opposition in many cases, and a realignment with legitimism because of the regime's Italian policy.

Napoleon III had wished to both secure the independence of Italy and to preserve the temporal power of the Pope. The clergy were more aware of the threat to Rome posed by Italian nationalism. Even moderate Gallican bishops condemned government policy. In a pastoral letter in December 1859 the Bishop of Pau insisted that 'to the Vicar of Jesus Christ is owed a double kingdom – a spiritual or supernatural on the one hand, and on the other, a temporal or human. The temporal kingdom is to ensure the independence of the divine ministry and to facilitate its exercise. The sovereign pontiff must have an independent domain. . . . a free state where he must reign and be accountable to God alone'. The more extreme, such as Monseigneur Pie, Bishop of Poitiers, condemned the regime for associating with 'the party of the Anti-Christ, of heresy and of Revolution' against that of 'Jesus Christ and the Church'. Opposition to the government on these grounds had little mass support. Government policy posed no obvious threat to popular religious practice, and even in clerical areas like the west, its military victories increased its prestige. However, it did further stimulate a group consciousness among the clergy and increased intervention in elections in alliance with Catholic social élites.

The Emperor and his ministers had already been concerned about the growth of clericalism even before the Roman crisis. They now sought to make it clear that the government would not tolerate what was regarded as excessive political interference by the clergy. Action was taken against the central organization of the charitable *Société de Saint-Vincent-de-Paul* and the ultramontane newspaper *L'Univers*, and, of far greater significance, the *Concordat* was interpreted in an increasingly restrictive fashion to obstruct, for example, publication of Papal pronouncements in France. Most important of all, measures were introduced to encourage lay education at the expense of the religious congregations. Throughout the empire the continued growth of ultramontane influence within the church had, however, served to reduce the capacity of the state to effectively control the clergy through the Episcopate. The generally enthusiastic reception by the clergy of the publication of the Syllabus of Errors in 1864 was indicative of their new more aggressive and intolerant spirit of independence. Even so, in the closing stages of the empire the reawakening of republican and anti-clerical agitation encouraged state and church to return to a conservative alliance, dedicated to the preservation of the existing social order.

Military defeat in 1870 and the Paris Commune in 1871 were both interpreted by churchmen as signs of Divine disfavour. Dupanloup, Bishop of Orléans, insisted that it was 'atheistical socialism which burned Paris' and drew the lesson that 'this is how God reminds those people who forget Him'. The remedy, just as in 1848, was a return to a moral order in which the church should play a leading role in alliance with other conservatives. As Monseigneur Duquesnay, Bishop of Limoges, warned them in 1875, the church might well be the first victim of revolution, but they would be next. The only answer for ultramontane bishops like Pie was the restoration of both the legitimate monarch in France and of the Pope to his temporal possessions, and for most of the 1870s the former at least appeared likely. This last reaffirmation of the alliance between the conservative state and the church again reinforced anti-clericalism and the determination of republicans to eventually laicize the schools as a means of spreading enlightenment, the ideals of democracy and patriotism and of protecting the republic.

Their accession to power from 1878 was followed by reprisals at local and national level. In Béziers the annual *Corpus Christi* procession was banned in 1879, street names were laicized, and in June 1881 a column in the Place Saint-Félix, dedicated to the Immaculate Conception and other religious emblems, were destroyed. The government's decision in 1878 to commemorate the centenary of the death of Voltaire and to celebrate 14 July as a national holiday from 1880 inevitably caused great offence to Catholics. More threatening again was the legislation on the laicization of education presented to parliament by Jules Ferry in March 1879; the introduction of obligatory education in March 1882, which was seen as interference with the rights of fathers, and the independence of the family; and the law of 13 October 1886 which required the replacement of monks in public schools by laymen within five years. The concept of a lay school, neutral in matters of faith, was utterly repugnant to most priests. Laicization was entirely contrary to the church's ideal of clerical domination, and of religion as the basic inspiration of life. This attack on the church and Catholic schools, in some regions at least, mobilized support for the clergy in its resistance to the republic.

Both republicans and Catholics in effect accepted the validity of the republican educationalist Macé's statement that 'he who controls the school, controls the World'. This explains the bitterness of their conflict. The former, committed to egalitarian ideals and to a secular morality, the latter striving for the moral regeneration of society through Christianity. The battle over the schools from 1878 was frequently bitter. In the Tarn in 1882 the 'moderate' Bishop de Maret reminded his parish clergy that some of the textbooks used in lay schools were included in the Papal index of works which should not be read by Catholics. He insisted that teachers using these works, or parents allowing their children to read them, should be refused the sacraments, and that the children involved should not be admitted to their first Communion – a vital rite of passage involving recognition of adulthood in most communities. This forced many parents to send their children to religious schools, but also created considerable animosity.

In spite of Pope Leo XIII's efforts to encourage *Ralliement*, i.e. acceptance of the republic, as a means of reducing the danger of political–religious conflict, the clergy remained suspicious of and frequently hostile to a republic which appeared to be a threat to their vital interests. As the Archbishop of Rennes pointed out in 1891 it was a 'sin' to vote for men who were not resolute in defence of the 'interests of religion'. This attitude can be seen in efforts to establish Catholic counter-societies, based upon the châteaux, the factory, on 'free' schools, *confréries*, patronages and pilgrimages or agricultural *syndicats* which enjoyed considerable success in the south-east of the Massif Central, in the west and much of Flanders. From the 1890s, in contrast, efforts to establish a Christian democratic movement, particularly by Marc Sagnier and the *Sillon* movement and by the Abbé Lemire in rural Flanders, which represented an attempt to attract the poor back into the church while avoiding traditional paternalism, failed, in large part because of the hostility of the church hierarchy to movements which demanded justice instead of charity. At its most virulent, clerical hostility to the regime was represented by the press of the Assumptionist Order – in *La Croix* and *Le Pèlerin*. These blamed the problems of the church upon plots by Jews and freemasons. Their fanaticism, especially during the Dreyfus affair, aroused suspicion of the religious orders in general and led to the 1901 law which stipulated that, unlike other associations, they required legal permission to exist and that without this their members were not permitted to teach. Following a succession of increasingly restrictive administrative decrees the law of 7 July 1904 suppressed all teaching by the congregations, and finally, in 1905, legislation for the separation of church and state was promulgated. The church ceased to enjoy a privileged status. Although it was allowed to use its presbyteries and churches, a great deal of its property was confiscated. The clergy would no longer be paid by the state. In February 1906 resistance to official efforts to carry out inventories of church property occurred in some twenty departments, above all in those isolated areas in which the church played an important part in community social life. The church, however, had clearly lost the political battle and, as we shall see, the way in which it had fought had greatly increased disaffection and outright hostility towards both the institution and its faith.

In the short term, these measures and the loss of status which resulted led to a considerable reduction in the church's access to the young, and in the number of ordinations. In the longer term the ending of the *Concordat* gave it increased freedom of action, although this did nothing to arrest the continuing decline in church attendance.

Religious geography

The religious sociologist, Le Bras, identified five types of attitude towards the church. These were: the seasonal conformists, who from family custom observed the major rites of passage (baptism, first communion, marriage and burial); regular observants who frequently attended church for Sunday mass and Easter communion; the devout, who participated in communion and a variety of religious duties and pious activities more regularly; those who rarely, if ever, attended church, but whose outlook was impregnated with the religious attitudes of the society in which they lived, by the all-pervasive presence of religion in daily life, speech and sentiment; and finally those who had definitely broken all links with the church. This provides a starting point for an attempt to measure the intensity of belief, but many problems remain. As Le Bras insisted, religious practices can only be understood within particular social contexts, and account will have to be taken of variations in the nature of belief between social and cultural groups, geographical regions and over time.

A variety of statistical indicators can be employed, including figures for attendance at Sunday mass, observance of the canon law injunction to receive Easter communion, preceded by confession, respect for the instruction that infants be baptized with the shortest possible delay, the prevalence of religious weddings and burials – abandonment of the latter might be seen as a sign of extreme deChristianization and was rare, because few were prepared to abandon the last sacrament and hope of life everlasting, as well as less direct (and even less reliable) indicators, such as recruitment of the clergy, the visual evidence from altar pieces, statues, funerary monuments and church restoration and construction, respect for the church's moral teaching revealed by low levels of illegitimacy and of contraception, Sunday observance, and attitudes towards lay education and towards politics. Essentially this is information about the accomplishment (or not) of the ritual acts required by the clergy. Many of the statistics which are derived from such sources are, however, nothing more than estimates of the number of nominal Catholics and tell us little about the content or quality of individual belief. This might vary between an intense personal faith and the wooden accomplishment of ritual gestures where community pressures enforced regular attendance at church. Certainly this information tells us little about the beliefs of the large and growing numbers who rarely, if ever, attended church services.

The information we have makes it clear that the character and intensity of religious belief varied considerably between regions, and that certainly by the middle of the nineteenth century, i.e. even before the repercussions of substantial socio-economic change were felt, large regions were already disaffected (in terms of attendance at church), especially those areas between Beauvais and La Rochelle, including the Paris basin and centre, and from Calvados and the Pays-de-Bray to Bourgogne. However, the general tendency for religious practice to decline was geographically far from uniform and this gradual process of so-called 'deChristian-ization' was interrupted by contrary movements of 'reChristianization'. The religious state of many diocese by the middle of the nineteenth century was the product of a long decline, increasingly aggravated by new social factors. In many places this had probably commenced in the Middle Ages and only pressure by the authorities had preserved appearances. Elsewhere, though, the long post-Tridentine missionary activity had restored the situation.

Disaffection had long been evident in the larger towns, where the social pressures for conformity were more relaxed. In Provence, for example, from the 1760s last wills and testaments had revealed a growing disinclination among urban notables to leave money for religious purposes. In contrast, at the end of the eighteenth century probably 95 per cent of the rural population received Easter communion. The decline of religious practice was both gradual, and associated with broader changes in society which affected people's outlook on life and on death, and sudden, due particularly to the effect of major political crises. The latter, although of considerable significance, were nevertheless causal factors of essentially secondary importance which tended to amplify developments already underway. Even so, the successive relaxation of social and administrative constraints in favour of the church, particularly after 1789, and the long interruption of religious practice in regions like the south of the Paris basin, where the official campaign of deChristianization in the Year II enjoyed wide support, and in the northern Massif Central and Rhône valley, broke the habit of attendance for many who were not highly motivated. Subsequently, the integrating network of parishes, charitable institutions, and confraternities was never fully restored. The *curé* of Bohas (Ain) in the 1820s was one who registered his despair when the inhabitants of this mountainous com-mune remained unimpressed by 'the greatest truths, the truths the most terrible of religion'. A sense of alienation was likely to develop between priests and parishioners, reinforced by the practice of punishing the least competent clergy by sending them to the most difficult parishes. Moreover, in the earlier decades of the century, to solve the crisis of recruitment, too many unsuitable candidates had been admitted to the priesthood. These men with doubtful vocations, yet vowed to perpetual celibacy, were especially likely to be implicated in the relatively small number (but often well-publicized) cases of outrages against moral decency by priests. Elsewhere, as in much of Brittany, communities had united to protect their priests against the revolutionary authorities, creating a tradition which lasted beyond the nineteenth century. The revolution thus accentuated existing social and geographical loyalties and linked them to politi-cal options with important long-term consequences for political and for religi-ous life. The 1830 and 1848 Revolutions and the *Ordre moral* regime of 1871–6 would further accelerate such polarization.

From around mid century, however, more fundamental processes of social change, involving the 'modernization' of French society, had vital effects. Improved communications, better education and the spread of French, universal male suffrage, migration, conscription, agricultural innovation and the disappearance of the fear of dearth were causes of a major cultural revolution which in many areas appears to have caused a further substantial decline in religious practice from the 1860s and 1870s. The church was slow to adapt to these changes. The Christian message appeared to have been prepared for a different world. In a rapidly changing society the eternal truths it offered had less appeal, the framework for social activity it had provided became less important due to the spread of the ubiquitous café and the creation of voluntary associations. The teaching and transmission of tradition became a function of the schools and with laicization from the 1880s church and school frequently ceased to provide mutual support. Moreover, through its association with conservative social groups and politics and due to the authoritarian attitude of many of its priests, their inability to divorce spiritual and temporal matters, and their constant complaints about 'impiety', 'vice' and 'materialism' as living standards improved, the church attracted criticism from all those who were attracted by intellectual, social and political change. This included political radicals, but also many people who were made to feel uncomfortable by the clergy because they felt obliged to work on Sundays to make ends meet, or sought to ensure a more comfortable life by restricting the size of their families. Questions in the confessional about the most intimate details of private life appear to have been bitterly resented and to have led many men (the principal agents in the practice of *coitus interruptus*) to refuse to confess. This rendered then 'unfit' to receive the Holy Sacrament at Easter. As a result, in some areas the number of men at Sunday mass might be much higher than those attending the most important service of the year at Easter. In the diocese of Orléans, as early as 1850, only 3.8 per cent of men over 20 were Easter communicants, while by the 1880s in a socialist dominated town like Narbonne the number was only 9 per cent and in both cases these minorities were the objects of considerable sarcasm from other men – promoting a new anti-religious conformism.[20] These low levels of attendance were very discouraging for the clergy.

Historians have tended to concentrate on 'deChristianization', but at the same time there were important signs of religious renaissance associated with the post-revolutionary reconstruction of the fabric of the church, the return to religion of traditional élites after the revolutionary trauma, and the growing success enjoyed by the clergy in using public ceremony and pilgrimage as a means of appealing to mass emotions. These efforts gradually bore fruit, so that in many areas religious practice was more widespread at mid century than it had been twenty or thirty years earlier. The Second Empire was another period of militant evangelization, apparent in the numerous new churches, mission crosses and statues of the Virgin. At the very least this activity arrested the process of decline, although in many areas this revival was cut short by the controversy in the 1860s over the Roman question and the Papal Syllabus of Errors, both of which seemed to reveal a church dangerously out of touch with modern society.

If the faithful were less numerous, they were often more fervent and, due to more widespread literacy, better informed about the teachings of the church, especially where education was provided by the teaching orders. *L'ignorance crasse*, so frequently reported early in the century, was relatively uncommon by the 1850s. An historic compromise became possible as popular superstition declined and an increasingly ultramontane church became more attuned to popular devotions. To an important degree the pastoral activity of the church succeeded in consolidating Christian life, especially among women. This development was reinforced by social crises, by the anxiety caused by the cholera epidemics in 1831–2, 1849 and 1854 which reawakened devotion to Saint-Roch, protector against plague, by revolution in 1830 and 1848, and by war and the Paris Commune in 1870–1. It is significant that the effort to restore the church's influence enjoyed its greatest success in areas like western France and in Flanders where there were already relatively high levels of practice and social structures and the clerical organization capable of supporting sustained pastoral activity, rather than in dioceses like Orléans in which indifference continued to prevail and where missions were as likely to stimulate hostility as support. The problem of encouraging a return to the church in the zones of 'indifference' as opposed to the *bons pays* proved insuperable. It is also quite likely that the clergy exaggerated their successes. In Marseille they took comfort from crowded churches and the incessant activity required to minister to their parishioners. Certainly there the numbers attending Sunday mass appear to have grown – from about 57,000 in 1825, to 73,000 in 1841, and 86,358 in 1862 – but this was a constantly declining proportion of a rapidly increasing population,[21] and the proportion of Easter communicants fell from 47 per cent of the eligible population in 1841 to 16 per cent in 1901, although the absolute number grew. Generally the euphoria of the early restoration, of the 1850s and the early 1870s when social élites and the state again appeared to be prepared to support the church, soon turned to pessimism.

It should be clear that there are no simple explanations of religious behaviour. The most effective approach is to consider religion in relation to the structures and *genre de vie* of particular regional societies. Even then it is unwise to draw straightforward correlations between levels of religious practice and such factors as socio-professional structures, literacy levels, or living standards. Numerous differences existed within regions, and often between neighbouring parishes. This complexity is illustrated by a study of the department of Pas-de-Calais,[22] a region with high overall levels of religious practice, but which can be divided into nine distinctive *pays*, which suggests that probably the key explanatory factor is historical and internal to the history of the church. The strength of religious faith in the nineteenth century was determined by the effectiveness of the church's pastoral effort in that and in previous centuries, and by its capacity to integrate itself into the regional culture. In spite of the revolution, eighteenth-century religious structures in this area survived well into the next century. Only in the largest towns, and especially from the middle years of the century as a result of socio-economic change undermining local cultures, did major distinctions between social groups begin to become evident.

Nationally, throughout the nineteenth century the regions of most intense faith (as Figure 18 makes clear) were on the frontiers or in mountain areas in the north-west, north-east, east (from the Vosges to the Basses-Alpes), south-west, east and south-east of the Massif Central (Ardèche, Aveyron, Cantal, Haute-Loire). Areas of indifference were on the plains of the Paris basin, western fringes of the Massif Central, the Charentes and parts of the Rhône–Saône corridor and coastal regions in the south. The tendency in almost all regions, especially from the 1860–70s, was, however, towards a reduction in the influence of the clergy and a decline in religious practice. A variety of milieux appear to have been favourable to the maintenance of high levels of religious practice and clerical influence. This was especially likely in societies with hierarchical structures and where influential élites, whether landowners or manufacturers, supported the church. Such *sociétés d'encadrement* were typical of eastern Brittany, Anjou, Vendée and Poitou. Furthermore, in upland zones, in much of Brittany and the north-west geographical isolation and enforced familial solidarity helped to preserve traditional hierarchies and to reduce the inward flow of new ideas to challenge established norms of behaviour. Thus in *bocage* areas of the *arrondissements* of Laval and Château-Gontier (Mayenne), the western part of the Sarthe, in most of Brittany, western parts of Normandy, and the southern Massif Central, with their dispersed settlements, fields enclosed by ditches and high hedges and poor rural roads, the church served as the major focus for community life. The social predominance of the clergy was far clearer than in *non-bocage* areas in the same regions. We should not slip into a geographical determinism, however. In apparently similar *bocage* zones of Bourgogne around Charolles and Autun, the clergy had far less influence. Normally the historian has to search for a complex of explanatory factors. Again, while many of the areas in which traditional religious behaviour was preserved were characterized by linguistic particularism, especially the survival of Breton, Basque, Catalan or German dialects which reinforced physical isolation, in the department of the Nord, high levels of religious practice characterized not only the Flemish speaking areas in the *arrondissements* of Dunkirk and Hazebrouck, but also French language areas around Lille and other urban centres. Moreover, loyalty to the church in the Nord and Pas-de-Calais was characteristic of areas with good communications, concentrated habitat and precocious industrial development, usually presented as preconditions for rapid deChristianization. Here the ultramontane clergy of the nineteenth century were able to build upon the structures and missionary activities of the Counter-Reformation, and particularly in the northern Pas-de-Calais (unlike the south where peasant property was more important) were able to benefit from the support of landowning notables. Elsewhere in France, in the south-east, in parts of Gard and Tarn, and in the north-east, traditions of religious conflict due to the rivalry between Catholics and Protestants helped to maintain solidarity and religious enthusiasm within distinctive communities. In the same way the revolution had served to

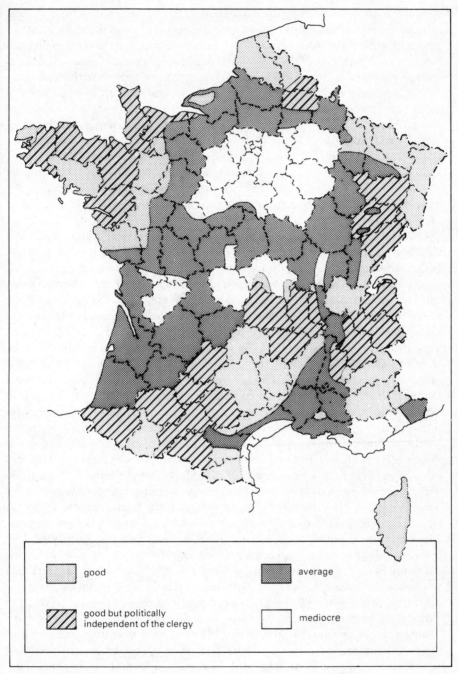

Figure 18 *Religious vitality of the dioceses of France, c. 1880*
Source: *After G. Cholvy, Y.-M. Hilaire*, Histoire religieuse de la France
Privat 1985

integrate individuals within particular ideological communities. This was most obvious in the *Chouan* ethos of the west, which united rural populations under the leadership of their priests and nobles and in resistance to the centralizing and secularizing tendencies of the state. Such situations, especially where combined with physical and cultural isolation and traditionalism, promoted the leadership role of the clergy and resulted in massive church attendance. These bastions of the faith flourished because the high number of vocations for the priesthood and the activities of Catholic laymen permitted the maintenance of churches, schools and voluntary associations and the preservation of a distinctively Catholic culture, even where the traditional oral culture was giving way to a more literate civilization. Indeed, throughout France the primary objective of the developing system of primary schools was to moralize and civilize the population, and for most of the century this mission involved the inculcation of religious ideas and close co-operation with the church.

Other milieux were less favourable to the preservation of religious life, and although the breach with the church was rarely total and the 'rites of passage' continued to be observed, only a minority of their populations attended church regularly. In such regions the parish priest was expected to restrict himself to his spiritual duties (narrowly defined) and to avoid interference in the day-to-day life of the community. These included areas in which missionary activity had been less intense or less effective in the eighteenth century; in which anti-clericalism had developed, as in the Charentes, in the seventeenth and eighteenth centuries as a reaction to the forced conversion of Protestants or, as in the diocese of Auxerre, to puritanical Jansenist pressure on popular customs (although formerly Jansenist regions in Lorraine remained faithful); and areas in which, prior to the revolution, monastic communities had been major landowners. Partly as a result of the latter a marked contrast existed between the northern Vendée, an area of *bocage*, and the southern areas of plain and *marais* which were both less isolated and marked by an anti-clericalism which had developed in reaction to the wealth of the abbeys and the burden of the tithe. The absence of powerful landowning élites was an important permissive factor. The Limousin with its poor soils had proved relatively unattractive to aristocratic and bourgeois investors. The clergy thus suffered from a lack of support. Moreover, rural populations, characterized for much of the century by low levels of education and culture, were unresponsive to missionary activities. They provided few priests themselves and saw the parish clergy as outsiders who they continued to identify with the exactions of the Ancien Régime. Similarly, in the generally religious department of the Tarn in the 1860s, the main areas of relatively low practice were around Gaillac and Castelnau-Montmirail where small-scale vine cultivation predominated, and forested zones in the extreme north-west with poor soils populated by impoverished woodcutters, isolated from the care of the church. In both the clergy lacked the support of large landowners which they enjoyed in other parts of the department. Again in another region of *fidelité*, the department of the Nord, it was the populations of the inland areas of the Cambrésis and southern Hainaut with the largest proportion of small peasant proprietors, many of whom had acquired the property of the old abbeys, which were the most suspicious of the clergy.

More generally, religious practice tended to be relatively low on the plains, in the river valleys and close to major cities, in the hinterland of Paris, in the dioceses of Evreux, Beauvais, Meaux and Orléans for example, i.e. wherever the development of communications and of commerce, and the mobility of population facilitated the spread of ideas and the establishment of alternative value systems, and the creation of conditions for greater independence from traditional familial and social pressures. This could be conceived of as part of the process of urbanization in which the growing interdependence of town and country ensured that processes of cultural change in the urban areas inevitably influenced belief systems in increasingly wide rural areas. Gradually even the more religious areas were affected by these processes of socio-economic change. Improved communications, increasingly competitive markets, falling agricultural prices and the decline in their rentals reduced the capacity of large landowners to maintain paternalistic relationships with a mass of quasi-dependents and to lend support to the clergy. The traditional agrarian order was upset. Many landowners sold land to peasants, who were thus able both to improve their material situation and to increase their social status and their independence of the *maîtres*, whose charity they had often bitterly resented without daring to complain. There was also the alternative of migration to the lowlands or cities in search of a better life. For many young people in backward regions like the Gévaudan poor living conditions became intolerable once escape was a practical possibility. In such circumstances religion no longer offered sufficient consolation. The exodus of mostly young people from so many rural communities, especially during the last third of the century, inevitably had destructive effects upon the vitality of social and religious relationships in their communities of origin.

It should not be forgotten, however, that the cities (especially Paris, Lyon, Marseille and Toulouse) were also the location of bishoprics, centres of religious organization, bases for the activity of missionary and teaching orders. In regions with low overall levels of religious practice, such as the dioceses of Limoges and Paris, the cities frequently had higher (although still low) rates of religious participation than the surrounding rural areas. It remained the case, however, that it was within the towns that the dominance of natural, divine forces first became less apparent and that secular preoccupations increased. In them social pressures for religious conformity were less intense and anti-clerical sentiments could develop. In effect most towns were influenced by processes of cultural change sooner than their rural hinterlands. In Saône-et-Loire in the 1840s around 47 per cent of those entitled to receive Easter communion took it in the towns, compared with 67.3 per cent in rural communes; in Côte-d'Or overall levels of participation were lower, at 37.7 and 45 per cent respectively.[23] In both departments it was the towns and rural areas along the most active lines of communications which were the most detached. Similarly, within the devout diocese of Rennes, the city itself and the various other minor urban centres stood out with what were, for the region, low levels of practice, although in most other regions they would have been considered exceptionally high. Thus pastoral visits in the 1890s revealed 30–40 per cent male participation in Easter communion at Rennes and Fougères, 40–50 per cent at St-Malo, St-Servan and Vitré, and 50–60 per cent at Redon. In contrast, male participation fell below 85 per cent in only forty-six of 348 rural communes.[24] Again, in the faithful diocese of Arras it was the towns and their bad influence on the surrounding countryside which concerned the clergy. Significant variations in religious practice could be observed, however, between towns, and this was not so much in relation to their size or social structures as to the characteristics of the cultural regions to which they belonged. Within the single diocese of Montpellier in 1852, 42 per cent of babies were baptized within three days of birth at Béziers, a centre of the wine trade, compared with 58 per cent at Marseille and 75 per cent at the woollens town of Lodève.[25]

The survival of a traditional religious culture in an urban setting depended to a large degree upon the cultural characteristics of its hinterland, and levels of inmigration. At Marseille, for example, the church's teachings on infant baptism were generally respected between 1806 and 1847, with about 75 per cent of babies being baptized within three days of birth. Subsequently this proportion declined, at first gradually (to 58 per cent in 1852), then more rapidly in the 1870s and 1880s.[26] This reflected the growing heterogeneity of the city as its socio-economic structures were transformed, and migration occurred from a wider and more diverse circle of cultural regions and created a population difficult to integrate into the life of the church, and for many of whom religious practice had little bearing on daily life. Similar situations prevailed in other rapidly growing cities. In Paris, Lille, Lyon and St-Etienne marked contrasts could be drawn between the old city centres with their established parish structures and more settled populations, and the newer suburbs where populations were poorly integrated into the church's parish organization.

In Paris the situation of the church was made particularly difficult by the predominance until late in the nineteenth century of inmigration from the already deChristianized area of the Paris basin. This combined with social class differences to establish a marked contrast between the western and eastern *arrondissements* of the city, with the worst situation in the *banlieu*. There, according to an inquiry in 1898 only in seven parishes to the south of the city with relatively high middle-class populations did more than 15 per cent of those entitled take Easter communion. The lowest rates were in the north-east at Romainville (0.9 per cent), Aubervilliers (1.0 per cent), Rosny-sur-Bois (1.2 per cent).[27] This suggests that the attempt to define the relationships between particular milieux and religiosity must be extended and given more precision by means of analysis of the religious experience of particular social groups.

The characteristics of religious belief

Social élites

Religious ideals were fundamental to the outlook of members of the social élite. Moreover, support from the clergy and beliefs shared with many members of other social groups were a vital means of extending conservative influence throughout society. There were, however, corresponding disadvantages. The association of the church with conservative politics was a major cause of growing hostility from members of the middle and lower middle classes anxious to share in political power.

Members of the nobility are usually described as passing from an eighteenth-century scepticism towards a more sincerely held religious faith as part of the search for individual certainty and social security after the revolution. Certainly the earlier faith in progress had been shattered and respect for religion, even when individuals did not practise it, came to constitute a vital element in noble 'class consciousness', and the conservative ideal of an alliance between 'throne and altar'. Given that man was inherently evil, only God could curb his material passions. Conversely, authority and hierarchy were essential to morality and to ensure respect for God's word. In practical terms conservative notables, in return for the promotion of good works, benefited from the support of the clergy. Although they tended to behave rather condescendingly towards the often poorly educated parish priests, once manhood suffrage had been established they came to depend upon the clergy for political influence.

The *grande bourgeoisie* appears to have been more divided in its attitudes, favouring a more Gallican and liberal Catholicism. Even the proponents of a sort of Voltairian anti-clericalism usually appreciated the socially conservative character of the church's pastoral work. Following the 1848 Revolution notorious sceptics, such as Adolphe Thiers, could, in the discussion of the 1850 education law, press for an extension of the role of the religious orders in the education of the masses. Noble and non-noble élites came increasingly to share a common conservative ideology which saw religion as the primary 'obstacle to disorder and anarchy' (*Mémorial de Rouen*, 21 March 1845). In the Senate in May 1868 Sainte-Beuve would criticize this 'singular disposition of French high society to make use of religion as a means of political action'. But in this he was isolated. An increasingly radical Catholicism appealing to the emotions and intransigently opposed to modern ideas attracted those whose commitment to traditional values had previously manifested itself in monarchist politics. Analysis of the content of the edifying works produced by publishers like Mame at Tours reveals the development of a profoundly Manichean outlook. Society was divided in two. The *good* were represented by such categories as practising Catholics, contented peasants, frugal and submissive workers, God's clergy, the worthy poor, the pious and resigned wife, wealthy paternalists and the opponents of revolution. These would be rewarded by God. To them were opposed the *wicked*: Protestants, Jews, freemasons, unbelievers, the unworthy rich, freethinkers, *la femme coquette*, republicans, revolutionaries, socialists, those who did not observe the sabbath, disloyal, lazy and debauched workers (the three categories being inseparable), lay teachers, townsmen and especially Parisians – all likely to meet with eternal damnation.

Throughout the nineteenth century religion and politics were inextricably confused, and yet we should not be too cynical. Conservatives themselves seem not to have suspected that their attitudes might have been conditioned by their social situation and material interests. Religious beliefs were frequently sincerely and profoundly held and as the century progressed this became increasingly so, primarily due to the influence of the womenfolk, who invariably received a religious education, upon the younger generations, and additionally to the increased provision of secondary education by the religious orders. It also reflected the continuous process by which individuals with social pretensions to join Parisian high society, or the aristocratic coteries found in many provincial towns sought to imitate the behaviour and adopt the values of traditional élites. Although religious vocations were comparatively rare among males, a minority at least were constantly active in parish affairs, and most regularly set a good example by ostentatiously participating in church services. Faith impelled action to assist the less fortunate. Charitable measures, according to the Montpellier *Société de persévérance*, allowed, 'the propagation of religious instruction, the sentiments of piety and the spirit of subordination in the inferior classes' (1820) and served to strengthen what the Lille industrialist Kolb-Bernard described as the union of 'our brothers and ourselves under the eyes of God'.

The middle classes

The movement of the *grande bourgeoisie* towards acceptance of conservative social and political values tended to enlarge the gulf between it and some sections of the middle and lower middle classes. In other cases religion promoted greater unity. The analytical problem is again one of diversity. Individuals and families varied considerably in their attitudes towards the church with the predominant view being determined by the characteristics of the local environment and the nature of the pressures for conformity there established. Thus, they were particularly likely to attend church regularly in such deeply religious areas as Brittany. The most prominent participants were the more traditional bourgeois groups, composed of government officials, army officers and magistrates, often from landed families, together with their clientele of old-established merchants, tradesmen and artisans. In the large towns an important and, particularly following the long mid century crisis, a growing fraction of the professional classes seem to have come to appreciate the spiritual and moral support provided by religion for themselves or at least for their wives, daughters and employees. Often, too, they were attracted by the opportunities offered by the church and philanthropic activity for making useful contacts. Protestant businessmen in Mulhouse and their Catholic counterparts in Lille significantly appear to have shared a Christian-inspired world-view which stressed the virtues of hard work and thrift in a fashion similar to that defined by Weber as the 'Protestant ethic'. In response to the anxious situation caused by revolution in 1848, by defeat in 1870, and the Paris commune in 1871, many people turned to prayer from a sense of impotence and guilt and in the belief that these disasters represented Divine Punishment. Large crowds gathered for public prayer at such shrines as Lourdes, Auray, Chartres and Paray-le-Mondial. Middle-class Catholics, who would have felt uncomfortable at the local shrines associated with popular religion, found spiritual relief in the Marial devotions officially sanctioned by the church.

Peasants

The poor rarely described their faith, and this makes it extremely difficult to gain insight into the religious beliefs of the masses and to assess the degree to which the major social and economic changes of the century affected people's perceptions of their world and their religious sensibilities. Another problem is that of analysing the relationship between what might be called the ecclesiastical dimension of people's religious experiences, i.e. teachings and a liturgy designed largely by and for the social élites and derived from church attendance, the orthodox teachings of the clergy, and lessons in school; and the spontaneous element contained in the oral traditions of numerous distinct communities. These were two forms of piety which often came into conflict, but which also frequently influenced each other. Especially significant in this respect was the process by which the church came to compromise with popular beliefs and became better able in the latter part of the century to impose its own cultural domination upon the faithful.

Popular religion as a dynamic and substantially independent system of beliefs reached its apogée during the first half of the nineteenth century. It experienced a revival during the revolution when the activities of the clergy and the schools as the proponents of the competing clerical system were disrupted. The resurgence of pagan–Christian religiosity which this allowed was a cause of considerable anguish among the clergy. The Bishop of Fréjus, Monseigneur Richery, invited, in 1823, missionaries to 'reawaken the spirit of faith that is almost extinguished in the souls of the people under our care'.

Traditional rural life was subject to the forces of nature to a far greater extent than we can imagine. Life appeared to be a constant struggle, in which men were subject to forces they conceived of in supernatural terms. In the absence of scientific explanations the course of the seasons, the success or failure of crops, illness or disease in man or beast, or death from a multiplicity of natural causes were understood to be the designs of a supernatural being, of a God who intervened constantly in human history. This attitude did not lead necessarily to fatalism. It provided not only consolation in the face of disaster but also a means of understanding, frequently enshrined in the proverbs which were an important source of guidance within the oral tradition, and in the calendar of saints' days which corresponded to the rhythm of nature and influenced decisions on when to plant or harvest and told the peasant when his rent was due. Religious belief also provided a means of action. God could be appealed to in a variety of ways involving both personal prayer and a complex of ritual acts. In the light of this outlook it was more logical to appeal to God than to a doctor, whose remedies, moreover, were both expensive and, for most of the century, of doubtful efficacy. Religion was in effect rooted in the problems of daily life and, as an instrumental force, attracted the mass of the population.

To some extent the church provided a structure for these beliefs, above all through the catechism (learned by heart at the age of 11 or 12 in preparation for the first communion) and the teaching associated with it, and subsequently by means of the mass and such practices as the veneration of the crucifix and holy images and the burning of candles. These were essential to the development of a routine, followed unquestioningly by most of its practitioners throughout their lives. However, the great mass of illiterate or semi-literate peasants appear to have remained remarkably ignorant of the basic precepts of Catholic teaching. Their limited education and practical outlook allowed little place for abstract religious ideas, although the extension of the primary school network allowed, at least until 1877, a substantial effort to inculcate religious and moralizing ideas and resulted in the introduction of a limited doctrinal content and greater logical sense into popular beliefs. Popular faith remained based less on Jesus Christ than on the God of the Old Testament – Creator and Avenger – a deism which took on Catholic forms because this was the only formal religion they knew, but which did not necessarily imply a commitment to the institutional church or to its priests. According to the harsh judgement of the *curé* of La Selle-en-Hermois in the diocese of Orléans in 1850, his flock displayed,

> certain habits, which have nothing to do with religion. They recite the formulae of prayer, but they do not pray; they attend Mass, but they never listen; they believe in a God, whom they fashion themselves; they pray to God fervently when they are ill, when they believe they are bewitched, when their animals are sick; they ask God for temporal goods but never for spiritual ones. They pray for the dead, but only from habit and custom; and among the prayers for the dead they prefer those which give most glory to the living.

The rural population was attracted to religion by its utility, and to the church above all by the external forms of religious practice, by *les grands offices* on Palm Sunday, Easter, Pentecost, All Souls and Christmas, by processions and pilgrimages rather than the confessional, although belief in a future life and in divine judgement made ultimate confession prior to the last sacrament supremely important. The *maison de Dieu* additionally served as a meeting place, especially in areas of dispersed habitat, and its priests sanctified the major steps in family live. Baptism guaranteed access to paradise for infants whose early death was quite likely, while first communion marked the beginning of adult life, and marriage the creation of a new family. Death had to be carefully prepared for, and solemnized by the church's liturgy. It was succeeded by a veritable cult of the dead, especially marked in central France and the west, where on All Souls' day families gathered around the tombs of their ancestors in order both to commune with them and to pray for them. Major events of the life of a community were similarly marked, by an annual fête during which the village celebrated its continued existence and expressed gratitude to its patron saint by carrying his statue in procession and rejoicing. This conveniently combined an act of religious dedication with a major occasion for dancing, feasting and for escaping from the endless daily routine. Occasional conformity even in the most deChristianized regions was maintained by fear of eternal damnation and the need to conciliate the Divine Power as a form of assurance.

The influence of the priest depended a great deal on judgements as to his efficacy as an intermediary between man and God. Most village priests were forced to compromise with the beliefs of their parishioners if they were to retain any influence over them. The practice of religion remained rooted in custom, and was credited with magical powers, as part of a system of beliefs which allowed for the existence of wise-men and women, ghosts and werewolves. The priest was frequently accredited as the most powerful of sorcerers, a man whom it was prudent not to alienate. The inextricable mixture of Christian and pagan belief not only reflected a profound ignorance of religious dogma, but was compatible with extremely low levels of religious practice, and anti-clericalism. In addition to the priest it was the Virgin Mary and a multitude of saints (often unknown outside a particular locality and unrecognized by the church) who provided the means of communication with God. These were personages more accessible spiritually and materially than God himself, and who, to the dismay of many priests, were often seen not as intercessors but as themselves the practitioners of magical acts. Appeals were made to them by means of prayer, procession and pilgrimage, by individuals or groups of parishioners headed by their priest, carrying crosses and banners and singing hymns as they processed to such holy places as churches or chapels, the wayside crosses so common in areas like Flanders, to wells and springs associated with miraculous cures, to stones with strange shapes or trees with mysterious silhouettes. These were associated with the legend of a particular *bon saint* like Saint-Roch, the traditional source of protection against the plague, whose cult was revived by fear of cholera. At Montpellier in 1856 a week of processions marked the arrival of a relic of the saint (a bone from his leg). Such processions during epidemics might, in practice, spread contagion, but at least they offered spiritual and psychological relief.

A rich variety of saints could be appealed to, depending on the place and according to the illness. In the twenty-six parishes of the diocese of Blois, for example, twenty-three different saints were invoked against fever in the middle of the century, and others for more specific complaints – Saint Mame against the colic, Sainte Apolline or Saint Laurent against toothache, Saint Cloud in case of boils, Saint Léonard to assist with childbirth, Saint Criard when babies cried at night, Saint Yves against diseases affecting sheep. Saint Eloi protected the horses indispensable for work on the large farms of the Nord. Thus on

1 December, the saint's day, the animals were blessed and rested. A vital element in the appeal to any saint was the ritual gestures necessary to invoke assistance. These included fasting, bathing the afflicted parts of the body, drinking water, lengthy marches, long periods spent kneeling in prayer, along with particular prayers and liturgies, and subsequently the presentation of an *ex-voto* – often a ribbon draped over the shrine – as an expression of gratitude to the saint. Frequently soil or grains of stone from a venerated shrine or, increasingly, religious medals, were carried away in the hope that they would offer continued protection when worn as amulets. Over time a hierarchy of pilgrimages evolved in relation to the miracles reputed to have occurred in particular places. In Brittany, for example, these included pilgrimages to Notre-Dame-de-Tout-Remède at Rumengol or Notre-Dame-de-Bon-Secours at Guingamp. At such places chapels were constructed, allowing the local clergy to play a more prominent role in organizing and controlling these popular manifestations.

The line of division between superstition and true religion was difficult even for the church hierarchy to draw. Sermons insisted upon the omnipotence of the Divine Being and upon the need to fear God and to conciliate Him. While constantly warning about the dangers of superstition, bishops at the same time accepted the validity of such traditional practices as praying for rain and ringing of the church bells to ward off thunder storms. The clergy led the series of processions in spring and summer – on Saint Mark's day in April, on the Feast of the Rogation in May when the fields were blessed, on Holy Day in June and throughout the summer in processions devoted to the Holy Sacrament – which interceded for a successful harvest. In an episcopal circular requesting prayers for an end to a period of heavy rainfall, the Bishop of Bayeux in 1879 significanctly recommended that priests should ensure that parishioners understood 'that the prayers we address to God would be superstitious and ineffective if we did not begin by humiliating ourselves before His majesty, by recognising His sovereignty and our dependence, in observing faithfully the laws He has imposed on us'.

Frequent conflict nevertheless occurred between priests, anxious to eliminate practices they regarded as superstitious, and parishioners unwilling to risk abandoning apparently efficacious rites or pilgrimages. To an important extent the development of the Marial cult, encouraged by the clergy, bridged this gulf between popular and clerical religiosity, by satisfying the need for a deep emotional experience and facilitating closer control over mass movements. There was a risk that it would fail to correspond to any living local current of piety and might disorientate and diminish the faith of many traditional believers. But in general this development had considerable appeal. When on 19 September 1846 the Virgin appeared to children at La Salette in the Isère, she criticized prevailing standards of religious and moral behaviour and warned of catastrophes if improvement did not occur. In the middle of a severe economic crisis this served not only as a warning but also gave hope. God could be mollified. Moreover, the railway soon made great national pilgrimages possible. In the last decade of the century an estimated 500,000 pilgrims a year visited

Lourdes, often in search of the cures and comfort the medical profession remained unable to provide. Industrialization made it possible for every home to possess religious statuettes and lithographs and for every individual to wear sacred medals, all of which served to remind the faithful of the power of prayer, and often helped to create a shrine, a place of daily pilgrimage within the home itself. In a typical pamphlet illustrating the appearance of the Virgin at La Salette, the final illustration contained four heavenly figures – an angel sheathing his sword, another dropping grain to earth, and Mary kneeling before Christ in supplication. The caption reinforced the pictorial message: 'Mary presenting the prayers of humble and repentant hearts to the Master.'

By the closing decades of the century, however, even in such areas of relatively intense faith as rural Flanders, popular devotion appears to have undergone marked decline in deferred response to the major changes which had occurred in people's mental universe, all of which had contributed to reducing the sense of helplessness, subordination to natural forces, or of insecurity in which most of the population had lived. Traditional practices sometimes simply became unnecessary. Better ploughing, the increased use of fertilisers, improved veterinary care and the better breeding of animals must have made it seem a little pointless to continue to put branches of consecrated boxwood in the corner of fields to ensure a good harvest, or in the cowshed to ward off disease. Prayers to the *bons saints* like Saint-Viatre in the Sologne became irrelevant as the marshes were drained, quinine became available and malaria disappeared. Such practices lost their utilitarian value and were abandoned. Moreover, those seasonal rites which survived often lost their original meaning, and became forms of entertainment or games for children. Popular religion also fell prey to the commercialization of agriculture which increased the opportunities for profit taking and promoted a greater individualism and materialism (seen, for example, in the spreading practice of birth control in spite of clerical prohibitions), and to migration which reduced the vitality of village life and revealed the growing interest of its younger inhabitants in urban life and *mores*.

Urban workers

The declining hold of religion on urban workers was more clearly perceived by observers, particularly in those cities – Paris above all – that were experiencing rapid economic modernization and population growth, and where the traditional social relationships and culture were in decline. However, relationships between town and the country and within and between social groups need to be considered in each particular case, and inevitably there are exceptions to the basic trends. In the 1880s, within the single department of the Tarn, the miners and glass workers of Carmaux and the leather-workers of Graulhet were largely anti-clerical, the former partly in reaction against the company-founded church and schools which had come to be regarded as one more symbol of oppression, while the woollen workers of Mazamet, a region still relatively isolated and inward-looking, were clerical partly in opposition to a Protestant *patronat*. In Marseille until the late 1850s the fishermen (aware perhaps of the 'perils of the sea') and the old corporation of stevedores remained faithful to their religious traditions. In the latter case the attack by the *Compagnie des docks* on restrictive practices in the 1850s led to a decline in the prestige of their corportion and to an influx of newcomers into a formerly relatively closed social group. One consequence, revealed by declining religious practice, was the weakening of its cultural unity. More generally, in the industrial parishes of the rapidly growing Mediterranean city, like St-Maurant, St-Lazare, St-Adrien and La Capelette, by the 1850s only around 8.5 per cent of men received Easter communion, although the substantial participation in the eight-day cycle of processions held annually in each parish to celebrate its *Fête Dieu* revealed a more widespread religiosity among workers.

This paradox could also be seen in the custom by which mutual aid societies, incorporated patron saints' names into their titles, held masses on these saints' days and participated *en masse* in the funerals of their members. However, it was increasingly evident that even when such titles were used, the decision had declining religious significance. Even in towns with high levels of religious practice like Rennes, a traditional artisanal group like the cabinet-makers, while claiming in the 1848 inquiry into working conditions that they 'asked for nothing better than to live according to Christ's laws', nevertheless expressed considerable irritation with the clergy's attitudes towards the poor and appeared to be on the verge of moving outside the church's cultural universe. In contrast the more sedentary and less literate domestic weavers seem to have continued to attend church regularly. Even in Lille, again normally regarded as a relatively religious city, while the 'rites of passage' were still observed as in the surrounding countryside, and everyone shared a diffuse religiosity, relatively few workers attended church regularly. The aptly named Father Coeurdacier, a missionary active in Lille, estimated in 1855 that of the 50–55,000 workers in the city only 1500–2000 could be expected to take Easter communion. The majority appear to have been indifferent to the church's message, save on such occasions as the 1866 cholera epidemic, when huge crowds processed through the miserable streets of the suburb of Wazemmes in front of houses decorated with garlands, with candles illuminating their windows.

For many workers, their relatively few hours of leisure were too precious to be spent in church. For others, sheer exhaustion or Sunday work bred spiritual apathy. Their overwhelming concern had to be to make ends meet. The church offered moral guidance, spiritual consolation and charity, but usually in forms which humiliated the recipient. Even in a city like Montpellier, where social changes were not as rapid as in major industrializing centres, Archbishop Le Courtier felt obliged to warn his clergy in 1868 that workers regarded charity as degrading. The workers' increased sense of their own dignity did not develop everywhere to the same degree or at the same time, but was widespread due to the reduction in the numbers of desperately poor people as material conditions improved, and also reflecting the declining ability and desire of traditional élites to maintain old patron–client relationships. Thus, whereas in pre-industrial cities like Toulouse or Nîmes, popular devotion to the Church and monarchy had been widespread as late as the 1840s, by the 1850s this had all but disappeared along with the economic and social patronage upon which it had been based.

There was also growing resentment of clerical attempts to impose middle-class values on workers whose day-to-day lives and problems were very different. Such practices as 'concubinage' which was often a means of avoiding the expense of marriage and frequently a prelude to an eventual legal union, were all too easily condemned out of hand by the clergy. Workers were also made to feel ill at ease in church by sermons they could not understand, by their inability to dress 'properly' and their displacement to the back of the nave behind their 'betters' who could afford the pew rents that were often levied. They could expect little sympathy from priests who frequently reminded them from the pulpit that poverty was inevitable, that protest against misery was a sin and that only the meek, resigned to their condition, could expect Heavenly Reward. Among the clergy the views expressed by Perret de Fontenaille in 1826 remained common – that 'the duties of servants and workers towards their masters and mistresses are the same as those of children towards their father and mother. They owe them respect and obedience, honesty, love and fidelity'.

In Paris, in particular, the anti-clerical campaigns of the revolution appear to have had long-term effects which were reinforced by the continued influence of middle-class intellectuals and the intellectual ferment of the secret societies, friendly societies and trades unions. The religious sentimentalism of the Christian Socialists of the 1830s–1840s did little to counteract this. The church had only too clearly identified itself with the rich and with political reaction. Furthermore, in many rapidly growing urban parishes the clergy were simply unable to provide adequate pastoral care and lost contact with many of their nominal parishioners. The attitudes of the large proportion of these who were recent immigrants were in no small degree conditioned by the situation in their region of origin. Immigrants to Paris and Limoges mainly came from deChristianized rural hinterlands. However, even when migrants originated in areas with high levels of religious practice, in their new urban environment the parish community had much less cohesion, and customary devotions had lost their practical significance. Numerous alternative meeting places to the church existed, and there was little point in praying for the harvest.

The situation was different in the smaller towns and industrial villages, again provided that migrants came from rural areas in which the levels of practice remained high. The inhabitants of small industrial communities tended to retain close links with rural life, as was the case even in the 1890s in the Pas-de-Calais coalfield around Béthune and Vimy. Although miners might not themselves normally go to church, save perhaps to celebrate Sainte-Barbe their patron saint, they ensured that their children were baptized, received first communion and the brief period of instruction which preceded it, and were themselves desperately anxious to secure the ministrations of the priest on their death beds.

Above all, perhaps, they were anxious to provide for 'proper' funerals, indicative of a cult of death which might be associated with the dangerous nature of their work. In such *locales* much also depended on the identification of local *notables* for or against the church. In company towns like Le Creusot and in many coal-mining communities churches were constructed and chaplains were employed as a means of preserving moral order and labour discipline. At Montceau-les-Mines, although it was permissible not to attend church, all hope of promotion or of assistance in time of distress disappeared as a result. In the Pas-de-Calais the period of initial coalfield development, 1850–75, has been described as the 'Golden Age' of paternalism. The first generation of miners seem to have appreciated its advantages. Subsequently, however, resentment at company interference in every aspect of their lives developed. This was to prove especially counter-productive when the advent of the anti-clerical republic in the late 1870s generated hope of emancipation among miners. This decline in attachment to the church began sooner in the older-established Nord coalfield. Lazarist missionaries at Fresne were already complaining in 1876 of empty churches on Easter Sunday, and regarded Marcoing, where 30 per cent of the population attended, as a good village. By the eve of the First World War miners – although still observing the rites of passage – had largely abandoned a church they identified with their employers, and had created a rich social world of their own with its clubs, *cabarets* and festivals. The same was true of other categories of industrial worker in the same region. At Maubeuge, a metallurgical centre, participation in the missions declined from 70 per cent in 1869 to 15 per cent in 1913.[28]

Women and religion

In addition to geographical and social variations in religious behaviour, the major differences between the sexes have to be considered. Many men believed religious practice to be an important source of support for the 'feeble' sex, a means of preserving female morality. Even anti-clericals tended to favour the image of *la jeune fille chrétienne*. This sort of attitude ensured that the religious orders played a major part in the education of girls, and this in turn helped to stimulate their participation in religious activities as well as that of the children for whose upbringing they were largely responsible. Conversely men often viewed religion as a threat to their own independence. They particularly resented clerical interference in questions of personal morality. Such divergent attitudes between the sexes could have been a potential cause of tension within the family, but this was largely sublimated within sexual role playing. The male represented the family in the everyday world of work, male sociability and politics; the female in the more spiritual confines of the Church, where by means of prayer she served to protect her entire family. This is not to deny, however, that in some deChristianized communities women did not share male indifference or resentment of 'excessive' clerical influence in their 'private' lives – a concept which itself illustrates the declining role of the priest. At Montpellier in 1866 Easter communion was received by 10,000 females – only 50 per cent of those eligible to do so (only 14 per cent of males took part).[29] In those regions where levels of practice were highest, virtually every woman regularly attended mass, while in the regions of relative indifference women, together with their children, provided the vast majority of worshippers. The disparity in behaviour between men and women was, however, especially great in those regions with low levels of practice. Thus, in the Loiret in 1868 women made up 81.6 per cent of the Easter communicants and men only 18.4 per cent.[30]

In addition to its important role in their spiritual life, the church provided women with the major focus of sociability in what were (especially in the south) male-orientated communities. In effect the church was the only place outside the home and work-place which was normally allowed to women. A growing number of pious associations were established, particularly for young girls. In the diocese of Montpellier during the first half of the century these included the *Confréries des Enfants de Marie Immaculée*, linked to the order of the *Filles de la Charité* and intended to provide a means of prolonging the influence they had established at school. The Marial cult, developing rapidly in the second half of the century, was both cause and effect of the growing feminization of Catholicism. The Virgin Mary served as a model of the virtuous woman for generations of young girls, symbolizing ideals of maternity and virginity. For older women there was the *Congrégation des Mères Chrétiennes*, founded in 1850, whose members among other things promised to prevent their daughters from going to dances. Amongst upper-class women, besides church attendance, charitable work served multiple functions – a reason for going outside their homes, for meeting friends, for humanitarian work, and for establishing their social status. For the women of the Lille bourgeoisie, life was dominated by the spiritual teaching of the church, by regular (daily) attendance at mass, and meetings of the various lay associations; for women more generally in both town and country, religious life formed the basis of a distinctive subculture.

Anti-clericalism

Anti-clericalism has attracted fewer historians. Nevertheless, an attempt must be made to explain such an important development. It was promoted by particular milieux and currents of ideas. These included attitudes towards the revolution and subsequent clerical support for political conservatism, local competition for social and political influence in which clerical attempts to interfere in community affairs were often bitterly resented, rationalist ideals derived from the Enlightenment and described by the clergy as *Voltairianisme*, in which religious belief was largely supplanted by a faith in human progress, and at a more intimate level rejection of the right of the clergy to intervene in personal relationships and particularly those between husband and wife or to condemn out of hand so many popular activities and ideas. Anti-clericalism did not usually imply atheism. It represented an attack on the institutions of the church and it was often accompanied by the expression of a desire for a return to some form of primitive Christianity. This was evident in the 1830s and 1840s among Christian Socialists like J.-P. Buchez and the contributors to the Parisian artisans' newspaper *L'Atelier*. Nevertheless, supporters of the church tended to regard anti-clericalism as a manifestation of atheism. They did not take kindly to such attacks as that in the *Echo du Nord* on the 'senile vanity' of Pius IX (10 March 1870). A polarization of views occurred as increasingly aggressive radical republican anti-clericals clashed with equally intransigent supporters of the church, particularly after 1848 and during the Third Republic.

From the anti-clerical side this polarization can be seen in the development of an alternative philosophy, a rationalist dogma and an almost mystical faith in progress and in the emancipation of man through science and education, which constrasted with what was seen as the obscurantism of clerical teaching, the growing anti-liberalism and superstition of the ultramontane revival and the demand for submission to the judgement of the Pope enshrined in the *Syllabus* of 1864 and the encyclical *Quanta Cura*. Certainly by the late 1860s intellectuals like Renan, Taine and Sainte-Beuve were clearly orientated against Catholicism, joining such illustrious representatives of the older generation as Hugo, Michelet and Sand. Increasingly too, their anti-clericalism was devoid of the earlier expression of sympathy for Christian beliefs. Religion as such, rather than simply the church, was associated with obscurantism.

The appeals of anti-clericalism, however, went far beyond bourgeois intellectuals. There was a large potential audience for such views, particularly in the towns and in those rural areas in which religious practice was weakening and nonconformity had become socially permissible. It is difficult to characterize beliefs in social terms, but it does appear that a division existed between a clerical bourgeoisie, likely to include both traditional landowning elements and state officials as well as successful merchants and factory owners and an anti-clerical bourgeoisie, more likely to include 'newer' elements – members of the liberal professions, small businessmen and artisans. Members of the middle and lower middle classes who resented the authority of established social élites were critical of the church as a manifestation of traditional society. Doctors frequently condemned the obscurantism of those parish priests who supported the ministrations of the nuns who continued to care for the poor, employing remedies rejected by professional men. There was widespread condemnation of the *bouffonnerie* at such shrines as La Salette and Lourdes, described by a contributor to the *Journal de Rouen* (25 September 1864) as an 'insult to the progress of Science and an outrage to Human Reason'. Significantly, A. Corbon, the owner of a small engineering workshop and author of *Le Secret du Peuple de Paris* (1863), expressed his resentment at the clergy's stress on the insignificance of life on Earth and his indignation that work, in which he took so much pride, should summarily be dismissed as punishment for original sin.

Many of these critics condemned the church's apparent collusion with every reactionary movement and its identification with the Ancien Régime. In the small towns of such diverse regions as Loiret or Hérault, the struggle for local power between the middle classes and traditional élites enjoying clerical support continued throughout the century. They were supported by peasants who continued to fear the restoration of the tithe for decades after the revolution, and, by the possessors of former church land whose families had come under pressure to make restitution during both the Thermidorean reaction and the restoration. Workers resented the church's identification with their employers. Members of most social groups resented the clergys' will to dominate, their demands for payment for services rendered (especially funerals), and their constant interference in the affairs of individuals, their families (especially through the confessional) and communities (in disputes over the expense of re-roofing the local church, or for control over the local school), their intervention in elections (particularly after the establishment of universal male suffrage in 1848) and constant efforts to 'moralize' and control popular religious practices and collective celebrations such as carnival. Great pleasure was taken in cases of clerical immorality and failures to live up to evangelical virtues. The moral failings of a small minority of the clergy were used as a means of ridiculing the clerical order. In short, the clergy were frequently resented for their apparent arrogance and greed — as a rhyme popular in Lille in the 1840s expressed it:

> Aussi bien à pauv'qu'à riche
> On n'fait rien pou rien à l'Egliche;
> Quand un prêt'di un oremus
> I faut qu'i sot payé tout juss.

This groundswell of 'spontaneous' anti-clericalism was very different from the intellectual anti-clericalism of the middle classes that was voiced in numerous meeting places — in *cercles*, masonic lodges, and bars — and which influenced a minority of educated workers and peasants, the latter particularly in regions where small property and growing commercialization predominated, and with it the growing social independence and aspirations for material prosperity which were frequently condemned by priests obsessed with the dangers of social change, materialism and birth control.

Anti-clericalism remained closely associated with political conflict. During the restoration, belief in the Congregation, a vast secret society whose supposed object was to destroy the constitution and create a theocracy, and hostility towards the ever-active Missions provoked considerable tension, and after the accession of Charles X in 1825 this led to the mass diffusion of anti-clerical propaganda. According to the popular poet Béranger, the missionaries were the 'commercial travellers' of the Jesuit Order which symbolized the clerical threat. The 1830 Revolution was accompanied by considerable anti-clerical agitation, including the sacking of seminaries at St-Omer, Auxerre and Metz, the removal of mission crosses at Poitiers, Niort, St-Maixent and Chalon-sur-Saône, the expulsion of Bishop Forbin-Janson from Nancy, and in February 1831 the sacking of the church of St-Germain-l'Auxerrois in Paris because its clergy had dared to hold a memorial service for the Duc de Berry. The continued close association of the church with political conservatism made it appear as a major obstacle to political and social reform. Thus anti-clericalism characterized an increasingly republican opposition to monarchy. Just as the 1848 Revolution accelerated the return to the church of many conservatives, repression, welcomed by the clergy, encouraged the development of a more virulent anti-clericalism among republicans. In regions like the Biterrois and Minervois in the Hérault, where peasants had dreamed of a better life with the creation of a *République démocratique et sociale* following the 1852 elections, church support for Louis-Napoléon's *coup d'état* largely destroyed the effects of the previous half century's evangelization.

In the long run the church lost enormous credit through its opportunistic, if hardly surprising, alliance with anti-republican forces during the Second Republic. The theme of the *sans-culotte Jésus*, popular since 1789, with its message of justice hostile to the rich appears to have almost entirely disappeared. Moreover, as the government of the Second Empire, initially anxious to establish a close alliance with the church, became increasingly concerned about clerical pretensions, especially in the sphere of education, it began, in the 1860s, both to resist these and to tolerate the expression of an often virulent anti-clericalism in the mass circulation press. For republicans, too, control over the education of the younger generations was of crucial importance. A reduction in the influence of the church seemed essential to the future of democracy. This outlook was fundamental to the debate on laicization in the 1880s, and was reinforced in the late 1890s by the reactionary and anti-semitic activities of Catholic laymen and the Assumptionist Order during the Dreyfus Affair. This anti-clericalism represented both a philosophical stance against clerical obscurantism and a political tactic around which the Left, divided on economic and social questions, could unite. Religion, it was felt, ought to be purely a private matter and the church should restrict itself simply to spiritual matters. In contrast, for the clergy and many devout Catholics the laicization of society and the establishment of schools neutral in matters of faith was incomprehensible and intolerable. This was a dialogue of the deaf between the proponents of two conflicting visions of the world, the one based upon 'divine' revelation the other on reason and science. This dispute, and its implications for education, was a fundamental political issue during the Third Republic culminating in the disestablishment of the church in 1905 and the final replacement of a religious by a secular ideology as the official basis of social order.

8
Education

Introduction

The crucial importance of the study of education can best be appreciated in terms of the school's role, alongside the family, in the communication process which gives form and meaning to social life. The purpose of this chapter is to consider the development of a key social institution by examining the development of school networks, of pedagogical practice and of attitudes towards education within evolving and varied social and geographical contexts.

The educational system developed within limits set by the interplay between the objectives of governments, the practical efforts to realize these and the attitudes of children and of their parents. From the point of view of legislators, the primary purpose of education was socialization – the transmission of the values of the social élite to both the younger generations of that élite and to outsiders, in the hope of establishing social concensus and of securing the willing collaboration of subordinate social groups. This would limit the risk of social unrest and the need for repressive activity by state agencies.

There were, in practice, two educational systems in France. For those who could afford it, the secondary schools, together with the elementary classes attached to them and in some cases higher education, created a distinctive culture which identified them as members of the propertied classes, both to other members of these classes and to outsiders – in the latter respect helping to preserve a 'social distance' between members of different social groups. In utilitarian terms, an education of the right sort was a means of entry into prestigious, well-paid positions in the administration, the liberal professions and business. In these various respects, education was a source of social power. The vast majority of children were restricted, however, if they received an education at all, to the primary schools. These had more limited objectives, essentially to provide elementary instruction. Adolphe Thiers wrote in 1848 that, 'To read, write and count, that is all that is necessary to learn; the rest is superfluous.' From a belief that inequality was inevitable, it followed that children ought to be taught only what was fitting for the role in life into which they had been born. This served to restrict social mobility and to reinforce class barriers. Only those with exceptional ability and/or luck were able to overcome their educational handicap and to improve their social status. Furthermore, as

Guizot instructed the teachers in 1833, moral education should inculcate a basic sense of loyalty to the existing political regime and respect for authority and social order. Similarly, in his influential work on the *Forces productives et commerciales de la France* (1823) the Baron Dupin concentrated not on any supposed utilitarian, economic value the schools might have, but on their role in 'inspiring amongst the young love of our laws, respect and devotion for our princes, the need for public order, the sage habits of deference towards the magistrates'. In this respect the teachers' mission was a civilizing one directed against ignorance but also idleness, drunkenness and crime, lack of cleanliness and envy of the rich. The schools were also to serve as the agents of the centralizing state. By means of uniform instruction, employing the French language, diverse local communities were to be more effectively integrated into the national whole.

At least until the 1880s, morality was judged to be inseparable from religion. Significantly, both Catholics and most of their bourgeois anti-clerical critics tended to assume that social problems like crime and poverty would be solved by the moral reform of mankind rather than practical measures of social reform. In this respect, the civil morality with which the Third Republic sought to replace religion was little different in spite of the democratic idealism of its proponents, save in the greater emphasis placed upon patriotism. Little had changed by the early twentieth century. Certainly the basic division between *l'école des notables* and *l'école du peuple* survived, and was subject to only ineffective criticism. The complaint voiced in *Le Socialiste* (13 December 1906) that primary education was no more than 'a training for subordination' was not entirely without foundation. Its basic functions remained moralization and the preservation of the established order, rather than the initiation of economic and social change. That the main aim of primary education was socialization should not be taken to imply an absence of debate among social and political élites over the means employed and the ends desired. In particular, rivalry developed between the church, the traditional provider of education, and the state as it assumed a wider range of functions. More significant were the ideological differences – varying concepts (religious and secular) of the ideal society – reflected in the major political divisions of the century. As it was generally agreed that education was a powerful means of social control, there was inevitably an intense battle to control it.

Primary education

The creation of a school network

The rate and chronology of growth of the school network is shown in Table 58. Some of this growth was a statistical illusion, due to more efficient accounting procedures. It appears, however, that the increase in the number of schools was particularly rapid during the restoration and July Monarchy, with renewed periods of rapid growth during the Second Empire and from 1876 to 1886.

Table 58 *Number of primary schools of all types in France (to nearest 100)*[1]

Year	Number	Annual compound growth rate (per cent)
1813	23,000 (estimate)	4.6
1821	33,500 (estimate)	
1829	36,200 (estimate)	1.0
1832	42,100	5.2
1833	45,000 (estimate)	6.9
1840	55,300	1.6
1850	60,600	0.2
1863	68,800	1.0
1872	70,200	0.3
1882	75,600	0.9
1891	81,200	0.3
1901	83,700	0.3

While not wishing to deny the importance of legislation and governmental pressure, the fact that the Guizot law of 1833 was introduced in the middle of a period of rapid growth suggests that legislation responded to a growing demand for education as well as stimulating it. As will become clear, though, attitudes towards education were not everywhere the same. The development of schools and of literacy was the product of a complex interplay between government policy and differing levels of local demand and initiative, with governments frequently finding it difficult to secure implementation of policy.

Prior to the revolution, the organization, financing and direction of schools remained to a very large degree a function of the church, inspired by the ideals of Catholic renewal formulated during the seventeenth-century Counter-Reformation. Everywhere primary education was thoroughly religious in content. The teacher, if not a *frère* was an auxiliary of the priest. It is also clear that the towns were best provided with schools, while in rural areas the density of school networks varied greatly, although by the end of the eighteenth century most villages in the north (Flanders, Picardy, Artois and Normandy) and in the east (Alsace, Lorraine, Champagne, Bourgogne, and Franche-Comté) possessed schools, as did those in some other areas, for example, Aunis and Saintonge in the west, Béarn in the south-west, the Vivarais and Cevennes in the south, and the Dauphinois uplands in the south-west. On the other hand, the west and south of the Paris basin, Aquitaine and Provence, most of the Massif Central and Brittany had relatively few schools. Many of these rural schools, moreover, lacked permanence and provided only partial instruction – usually limited to reading.

The revolution had essentially destructive effects on the primary schools precisely because of their association with the church and the belief of revolutionaries like Talleyrand, Condorcet, Rabaut-St-Etienne and Barère that education could be used to enlighten and to 'regenerate' the nation. The dissolution of the teaching orders and the loss of their endowments was balanced by legislation which proclaimed 'free, compulsory and lay education', but which in practice remained ineffective due to the lack of money and teachers and more pressing priorities. An inquiry in the Year II into the application of this legislation which required a school in every commune, revealed that in the 400 (of 557) districts which replied only 6831 officially recognized schools existed, where there should have been 23,125. However, the ideals were to remain the goal of committed republicans throughout the following century. More immediately, during the conservative Thermidorean period of the republic these ambitious objectives were abandoned. The Directory and empire subsequently left primary education to private and local initiatives, and from 1804 permitted the re-establishment of the religious orders. Thus, gradually, and in response to local demand, the school networks of the Ancien Régime were re-established so that, according to the (probably over-optimistic) official *Exposé de la Situation de l'Empire* of 1813, there were 31,000 primary schools with 900,000 pupils. The central administration showed little interest in this process, concentrating instead on establishing the administrative structures of future close control through the foundation of the Imperial *Université*.

During the restoration governments were anxious to encourage the expansion of the school system and to ensure that order, morality and religion were properly taught within it. An ordinance of 19 February 1816 required every commune to make provision for the education of its children and insisted that the very poor should receive free instruction. The number of communes with schools is estimated to have risen from 17,000 (in 44,000 communes) in 1817 to 24,000 in 1820.[2] But in practice this owed little to the efforts of the central administration, as no sanctions were taken against communes which failed to comply. Administrative control was reinforced characteristically through the requirement that budding teachers acquire both a certificate of good morality and a *brevet de capacité*. After appointment they were to be subject to inspection by local *notables* including the parish priest. Subsequently, the assassination of the Duc de Berry in 1820 led to even closer surveillance of the schools and reinforcement of the insistence that religious education should be the basis of all teaching. This culminated in the ordinance of 8 April 1824 which transferred responsibility for authorizing teachers from the *Université*'s regional *rectors* to the bishops. Although this was reversed in April 1828, following the election of a more liberal chamber, the influence of the church remained predominant. Even so, during this period of close co-operation between state and church, churchmen frequently expressed their dissatisfaction with anything less than an educational monopoly. Thus, the *Frères des écoles chrétiennes* were unwilling to accept the obligation of priests to obtain the *brevet* as this implied recognition of the authority of the state over the church, while efforts by the *Société pour l'instruction élémentaire* to reduce the problems caused by lack of money and teachers through the promotion of low cost monitorial methods of teaching, were obstructed by the church because of the liberal credentials of many of its supporters. In spite of initial government encouragement (until 1821) the number of such schools fell from 1500 in 1821 to 258 in 1827.[3]

The 1830 Revolution was followed by the Guizot law of 28 June 1833. This, arguably the most important educational legislation of the century, resulted from the growing governmental appreciation of the value of control over education and led to *effective* state interventions, in contrast with earlier legislation when prefects were given powers of enforcement. It might have been expected to herald a reaction against clerical dominance, but the new regime seemed more concerned to reach an accommodation with the church – in spite of suspicion of its political proclivities. As Guizot insisted, 'It is essential that popular education be given and received in a religious atmosphere. . . . Religion is not a study or an exercise to which one assigns a time and place; it is a faith, a law, which must make itself felt constantly and everywhere.' The main provisions of the law were the requirements that every commune in France should maintain an elementary school and provide a minimum stipend of 200f to its teacher as well as free education to *indigents*, whose families could not afford to pay the *contribution scolaire*. The teachers could either be laymen or members of the teaching congregations, the schools public or private. As a result competition for control of local schools was to be a divisive factor in many communities for the rest of the century. Indeed, in Lille and other towns in the Nord efforts by the more liberal town councils elected after the July Revolution to replace the teaching orders with laymen aroused bitter Catholic hostility. The Catholic response was to establish private schools. The clergy doubted the efficacy of the religious instruction provided by lay *instituteurs*, however well-meaning. In general the extension of Catholic teaching was restrained only by the number of teachers available and the role of the church in the extension of literacy was a considerable one.

Although existing teachers, however poorly qualified, were to remain in their posts, the law sought to raise standards by requiring the establishment of an *école normale* to train teachers in every department. Provision was also made for closer supervision by government inspectors (especially by the ordinance of 26 February 1835) and by committees of local worthies including, but no longer dominated by clerics. However, many of the clergy continued to hold the traditional concept of the teacher as an assistant to the parish priest, which conflicted with the growing desire for professional status and independence on the part of teachers. An inspector's report from the Oise in 1839 warned that rivalry was inevitable: 'the priest, very much aware of his position of superiority, expects a submission which differs very little from that of the obedience required from a valet; the other, who is far from considering himself as such, revolts and finds refuge in his position as a teacher'.

The effects of the law varied. In the economically more advanced departments like the Nord relatively few new schools needed to be established, although much needed to be done to improve the quality of education; in areas of religious rivalry, like the Gard, too, there were relatively large numbers of schools. Elsewhere rapid and effective implementation depended upon the wealth of a commune – its income from local taxation, ownership of common land, etc. – and the attitudes of influential local notables, as well as upon cultural factors. In Calvados, where substantial increases in the number of schools and in attendance (of 22 per cent) had already occurred during the restoration, the major breakthrough occurred in the 1830–40s when the number of schools increased by 23 per cent and of pupils by 54 per cent.[4] Poverty and indifference combined to obstruct enforcement, especially in isolated and economically stagnant areas. In Ille-et-Vilaine 55 per cent of communes had to be taxed *ex officio* by the prefect in order to raise the necessary funds to equip and/or construct a school, and in the *arrondissement* of Redon this rose to 90 per cent.[5] In this area teaching orders such as the *Frères de Ploërmel* were favoured both from religious notives and because they cost less to maintain, although successive prefects were to express concern that so much influence over the younger generation should remain in the hands of the church. Nevertheless rapid progress was achieved. In the Nièvre, another backward area, only eighty-six communes (of 319) had schools in 1831; by 1840 the number had risen to 197, although it took until 1859 for provision in every commune (287 schools, some shared).[6] The gradual provision of state subsidies to poor communes was a factor of some significance. Nationally in 1833, 11,438 of the 38,148 communes had been without boys' schools; by the end of 1840 the number had fallen to 4196.[7]

Another potentially important piece of legislation in this period was the 1841 law on child labour. As well as limiting the hours worked by children it required that those under 12 working in factories be provided with instruction either at midday or in the evening. The time allowed was insufficient and the children often too tired to benefit; moreover, the law was not effectively enforced. It did represent, however, a growing awareness of the problems of urban/industrial development, and increasing anxiety about some of the potential social consequences.

The 1848 Revolution seemed to confirm conservatives' worst fears. Moreover, in its aftermath, republicans appeared prepared to use education to destabilize the social system. Carnot, the education minister in the Provisional Government, inspired by a faith in education as a means of emancipation, proposed to make schooling both free and obligatory. He also suggested that worthy boys from poor families be assisted to attend the *lycées*. Equally threatening were proposed steps towards the laicization of education, by replacing the catechism with civic instruction and in Paris through curtailing the clergy's right to inspect local schools. Furthermore, Carnot encouraged *instituteurs* to propagate republican ideals and to support republican electoral candidates in the first elections held under universal male suffrage in April 1848, and indeed many teachers enthusiastically supported a regime which seemed to promise a marked improvement in their status. Carnot, however, fell from power before his education bill was presented to the Constituent Assembly. Despite this, the activities he had encouraged left conservatives with a grossly exaggerated, yet deep-seated fear of the subversive potential of both school teachers and the literacy they promoted in this new era of mass politics. This contrasted with the more optimistic view of education as a means of moralizing the people, which had prevailed in the 1830s.

As a result, the conservative assembly elected in May 1849 voted in favour of a law presented by a Minister of Education of very different political complexion, the Legitimist Comte de Falloux, and Carnot's proposals for free and obligatory education were quickly abandoned. The leading figure in the extra-parliamentary commission nominated by the minister to prepare legislation, and unanimously elected president by its members, was the 'liberal' politician Adolphe Thiers. At its first meeting he set the tone for its work by insisting that, 'Today when violent communism threatens society, it is essential that education calls the religious sentiment to its aid in a common war, to repulse the Barbarians.' He asked that the clergy be made 'all-powerful' in the primary schools, and justified the reversal of his previous hostility to the church by his fear of social revolution. Only the clergy could 'propagate the philosophy which teaches man that he is here to suffer'. Victor Cousin, a leading figure in the *Université* during the July Monarchy, further insisted that where lay teachers were retained they should learn to submit to the parish priest. Even if the sincerity of their commitment to religion might be in doubt, Thiers and Cousin agreed with the leading Catholic layman, their colleague on the commission, the Comte de Montalembert, on the need 'to establish respect for property among those who are not property owners' by inspiring in them a belief in God – 'not the vague God of the Ecclectics . . . but the God of the Catechism, the God . . . who inflicts eternal punishment on thieves'.

A clear atmosphere of panic emerges from a reading of the commission's discussions. Its proposals were justified in parliament by Beugnot as essential for the defence of 'religion, morality, the most precious interests [of society] its holy and eternal laws . . . . the most elementary notions of truth, of justice and of law, without which no human association could exist for a single day'. The commission's proposals became law on 15 March 1850. The implementing regulations of 17 August 1851 were unambiguous. According to the first article, 'the principal duty of the teacher is to give a religious education to the children, and to inscribe on their souls the sentiment of their duties towards God'. Their mission was to form the characters of the pupils rather than to transmit intellectual knowledge. They were, furthermore, to instruct by good example and to avoid cafés, bars and situations that might threaten their personal dignity (including *tutoiement*). In effect they were to be isolated from their communities. To ensure compliance, they were to be more closely supervised and the role of the priest in this was enlarged. Indeed, for most of the Second Republic there were purges of lay teachers suspected of republican sympathies. The stick was accompanied, however, by the carrot in the form of higher salaries. Other regulations required that the *écoles normales* reduce the intellectual content of teacher training to the minimum possible in order to avoid the creation of an overeducated, *déclassé* body of teachers, dissatisfied with their social status. In addition, extension of the religious teaching orders was to be encouraged by requiring from members of the clergy who intended to teach only minimal qualifications and in the case of nuns, simply a letter of obedience to their superiors, rather than a *brevet de capacité*. This allowed a substantial increase in the number of church schools and their extension from existing areas of strength in Brittany (where in 1850 in Côtes-du-Nord, Morbihan and Ille-et-Vilaine they controlled 33, 21 and 19.3 per cent of schools respectively) and the Rhône area where their strength was in the departments of Loire, Rhône, Vaucluse, Ardèche and Haute-Loire (46.6, 18, 14.5, 13 and 11.6 per cent), and (in the case of girls' schools) in the east.[8] The strength of the teaching orders was, however, far from sufficient to satisfy Thier's dream of a priest in every school.

The principles of this law were in fact much the same as those enshrined in the *loi Guizot* in 1833, but in a situation of political and social crisis they were more vigorously affirmed. Even so, only thirty bishops approved of the law, while fifty felt that it did not sufficiently meet the church's desire to control primary education. Few seem to have agreed with Bishop Dupanloup of Orléans who accepted that those *instituteurs* who remained generally performed their duties satisfactorily and were properly subservient to the clergy. Most clerics saw education as a potentially rival spiritual force which ought as far as possible to be subject to control by the church as the fount of all truth.

The Falloux Law and the general political climate it symbolized had significant effects (including the revocation of around 4000 teachers, i.e. one in nine, in a sustained purge of 'subversives' between 1848 and 1859).[9] In this period the state appears to have accorded low priority to education. Expenditure from central funds stagnated. Until 1860 it was kept below the 6,131,391 francs spent in 1852. However, the ministers responsible, first Fortoul and then from 1856 Rouland, both assumed that paternalistic social control was the essential means of preserving social order. The clergy was solidly entrenched throughout the educational system and exercised considerable influence through its bishops, parish clergy and influential laymen. Whereas in 1850, 15 per cent of boys and 45 per cent of girls in both public and private primary schools had been taught by clerics, in 1863 the proportions had risen to 22 and 54 per cent respectively, while, in addition, much had been done to reinforce the religious ethos of teaching by laymen.[10] During the first 'authoritarian' decade of the Second Empire, the church continued to strengthen its position in the schools, and to such a degree as to cause growing anxiety among government officials, who were worried by the increase in the potential political influence of the clergy. This concern was considerably heightened when the alliance between church and state began to break down because of Napoléon III's support for the unification of Italy and the threat this posed to the Papal states.

As early as 1856 Rouland had refused to authorize new male religious orders. However, between 1852 and 1859, 923 new female associations had been recognized. The continued expansion of these bodies was the essential means of extending direct Catholic control over education. In the 1860s a more restrictive policy was also adopted towards the female orders. This followed Rouland's insistence, in April 1860, upon the need to combat ultramontane tendencies within the church, pointing out that 'we would be seriously weakened from the point of view of universal suffrage if primary education in its entirety passed into the hands of congregations who depend more on Rome than on France'. Subsequently an 1854 law, which transferred the right to appoint teachers from the academic rectors to prefects, was used to limit the influx of clerics into the schools, although in principle municipal councils retained the right to choose between a lay or a clerical teacher. The consequences of this change of policy can be judged from the fact that whereas between 1850 and 1853 47 per cent of new public primary schools for boys and 60 per cent of those for girls had been entrusted to the religious orders, the corresponding figures for the 1863–9 period were only 5 and 33 per cent respectively.[11] At the same time, school building was encouraged – in Paris expenditure rose from 1.7 milion francs in 1859 to over 5 million by 1866. This new policy culminated in the appointment of Duruy as Minister of Education in 1863 – a liberal and anti-clerical enjoying the emperor's personal support, but otherwise isolated in the government as the opposition to his proposal to introduce free and compulsory education reveals. Even the introduction in 1867 of subsidies to communes to encourage them to provide free education, was bitterly condemned by Catholics, especially in regions in which the church maintained private schools in competition with municipal institutions. Although since 1848 the church had managed to strengthen its position in primary education substantially, it did so at the cost of arousing considerable suspicion among lay teachers who increasingly felt threatened, intellectuals who condemned what they saw as growing Catholic obscurantism, and all those who resented the church's close identification with political reaction. The immoderation and intolerance of Catholic spokesmen increased anti-clerical feeling. Opinions about education were clearly becoming polarized, and to a large extent along political lines. This could be seen in the foundation of the *Ligue de l'Enseignement* in 1866. This was intended to support the extension and improvement of educational facilities but by supporting lay teachers it inevitably attracted Catholic criticism, which drove the more moderate members from its ranks.

These developments could be seen as foreshadowing the much greater laicization of the Third Republic. Initially, however, the conservative regime established following the Franco-Prussian War and the Paris Commune reverted to the policy of a close alliance of church and state in defence of 'moral order', so that it was not until 1878–9 that clerical influence in the schools reached its peak, when 22.4 per cent of *école communales* were directed by clerics. The proportion was considerably higher in areas of strong religious faith – 26.09 per cent of public schools in the Nord for example (345 of 1322 schools), and 63 per cent (of 573) private schools.[12] Here, as elsewhere, the effect was maximized by concentrating upon the larger towns; in 1860, 88 per cent of pupils in Roubaix, 85 per cent in Elbeuf, 63 per cent in Lyon, Rouen and St-Etienne were taught by priests. The overall effect was that whereas in 1850, 28.7 per cent of 3,222,000 primary school pupils (boys and girls) had been taught by clerics, by 1875 this had risen to 40.4 per cent of a total of 4,620,000 (with much higher proportions

Table 59 *Proportion of pupils taught by clerics*

Year	Percentage of schools directed	Boys Percentage of school-age children attending them	Percentage of schools directed	Girls Percentage of school-age children attending them
1850	5.0	16.3	41.6	44.2
1867	9.9	20.7	52.3	55.2
1896	9.5	18.6	42.0	53.4

in departments like the Loire, Rhône, Ardèche, Finistère and Côtes-du-Nord). The clerical share was, however, much lower in the Paris basin, centre-west, Champagne and Bourgogne. Table 59 shows the proportion of schools directed by the clergy and of the children they taught, and the way these evolved.[13]

The debate on education was to be a central feature of political life during the Third Republic. Jean Macé's statement that, 'he who controls the school, controls the world' appears to have been accepted by both republicans and Roman Catholics and largely explains the bitterness of their struggle. It seemed to republicans like Jules Ferry that the future of democracy could only be assured by reducing the influence of 'clericalism' over the young. A modern, lay, free and obligatory education would ensure the 'liberation' of the population from ignorance and oppression, increase equality of opportunity, reduce class divisions and provide a means of demonstrating the rationality and justice of the newly established republican order. National unity and strength could be promoted through the inculcation of civic virtue. This was not simply a question of practical politics, but for many republicans represented a sincere 'love of humanity'. However, in introducing change in the educational system, republicans were to meet with considerable resistance. Even in 1882 in the *Revue des Deux Mondes*, G. Valbert could express conservative fears that the schools would provide the poor with, 'superficial and half digested knowledge, confused ideas on a thousand things . . . disgust or contempt for the condition into which they were born, ridiculous pretensions, unrealistic ambitions', and oppose free education on the grounds that the 'sacrifice' imposed on families by the payment of fees increased their appreciation of education; and obligation as an attack on paternal rights and responsibilities, on the independence of the family and, given children's earning power, on its financial viability. In particular, the prospect of an *école sans Dieu* horrified Catholics. Laicization was viewed as an attack on Truth and Morality. Thus, in many areas it had the effect of creating a conservative party determined to preserve its schools.

The consolidation of the republican parliamentary majority in the late 1870s was followed by a series of measures, including the law of 16 June 1881, which made education in the public primary schools free, and also required all teachers to possess the *brevet*. Shortly afterwards, the law of 28 March 1882 made

education compulsory and heralded its laicization. The teaching of the catechism was to be replaced by 'moral and civic' education in public schools. From
1883 as a means of increasing the density of the school network, every village or
hamlet with more than twenty children of school age was required to maintain a
public school. Substantial subsidies and loans were provided to finance the
construction and repair of school buildings (311 million francs and 231 million
francs in 1878 and 1885 respectively), while the normal educational budget rose
in the same period from 53,640,714 to 133,671,671 francs. Thus if, in terms of
the basic provision of schools, the key legislative act was the 1833 law, the
Second Empire and Third Republic were important for increasing the density of
the school network and encouraging increased attendance. The proportion of
total expenditure on education provided by the state reflected this growing
commitment. It reached 22.7 per cent in 1834, fell to 14.2 per cent by 1866, and
then increased again to 67.2 per cent by 1896.[14] The last figure reflected, in
particular, the decision taken in 1889 that public school teachers should be paid
(and more fully controlled) by the state rather than the municipality. It was a
measure which increased the teachers' freedom from local pressure and further
reinforced their status.

Provision for the laicization of the teaching staff in *écoles communales* for boys
within five years was finally made by a law of 30 October 1886. In the case of
girls' schools no time limit was stipulated for the replacement of nuns. This was
to follow resignation or death. In many areas, Catholics were able to circumvent
the law by establishing private schools. Nevertheless, even in relatively religious areas like the Nord, between 1879–80 and 1899–1900 the proportion of the
school population attending schools with members of the religious orders on
their staff (public and private) fell from 24.7 per cent to 18.8 per cent in the case
of boys, and from 62.4 to 45.2 per cent in that of girls, although the Nord
continued to have a higher proportion of boys' schools staffed by clerics than
any other department (783 with 144,030 pupils in 1893).[15] In the Breton
department of Ille-et-Vilaine, a more determined defence of religious schools
occurred. There, in the same period, the proportion of boys in clerical schools
fell from 49.8 to 39.5 per cent and of girls from 86.3 to 80.4 per cent. It appears
that children from poor families were particularly likely to be sent to state rather
than the new private schools in order to avoid payment of fees. Thus, in Lille the
Frères found their clientèle limited increasingly to boys from artisanal and lower
middle-class families. Geographically, Catholic schools were gradually pushed
back into the areas of most intense religious faith – in the Nord into industrial
Flanders (and especially the Flemish speaking zones), and in Ille-et-Vilaine into
the Vitré region of the old diocese of Saint Malo.[16]

Further secularization measures were postponed when, during the period of
Ralliement, politicians of the centre-right and centre-left combined to defend
their republic against the radical and socialist threat. However, partly as a result
of the Dreyfus Affair, and in reaction against the anti-semitic and anti-
republican excesses of the extreme right, the Waldeck–Rousseau government in
1899 and particularly the Combes administration of 1902 again sought to

combat clerical influence. The latter interpreted a 1901 law on associations in an extreme fashion and required the immediate dissolution of unauthorized religious congregations and as a result the closure of several thousand schools. In spite of recourse to such measures as the 'secularization' of clerics in order to circumvent this measure, and of increased reliance on devout lay teachers, this was a major blow to Catholic education. Private (mainly Catholic) primary schools educated around a third of all pupils in 1886–7, but only a fifth by 1912–13. However, these are indicative of a great determination among both the clergy and Catholic laymen to preserve religious schools. The implementation of anti-clerical legislation in areas in which the church retained considerable influence was fraught with difficulties. Parents could be threatened with refusal of the sacraments if they failed to send their children to private Catholic schools. Where these did not exist, sincerely religious lay teachers could often be persuaded, or if necessary coerced, into providing a traditional religious instruction. Parents were encouraged to ensure that items placed on the church's *index* of forbidden books, which included many school textbooks, were not used by public school teachers. This affected history books, in particular, given the radically different conceptions of the causes, significance and consequences of 1789. In 1909, the episcopate condemned twelve of the most popular history textbooks, while J. Gueraud's *Histoire partiale, Histoire vraie* (36th edition, 1914), which pointed out the 'errors' of republican history, was to be found in many presbyteries. The position of the *instituteur* could otherwise, in some regions, be rendered almost insupportable by the hostility of the clergy and Catholic laymen.

The education of girls

The major legislative acts explicitly sought to cater for the education of boys. The development of instruction for girls was almost incidental in the first instance, although subsequently the various provisions were extended to girls by legislation which recognized their special needs, as these were then perceived. Thus, the law of 23 June 1836 simply extended the provisions of the Guizot law to girls. Although both state and church agreed on the moral value of sexual segregation, the lack of teachers and money at this time made it impossible to insist upon the maintenance of separate girls' schools. The Falloux Law stipulated in 1850 that communes with over 800 inhabitants *ought* to have a separate school for girls, but accepted lack of resources as a reasonable excuse for inaction. Only in 1867 was the establishment of separate schools for girls made compulsory. Nevertheless, in an area of strong religious faith such as the Pas-de-Calais, the number of schools for girls had already increased from 289 to 585 between 1850 and 1876, by which date 67.8 per cent of the teachers were nuns.[17]

The instruction given was to a large degree based upon particular conceptions of womanhood, and on the functions of women within the family and community. For most of the century the dominant model was that of *la jeune fille chrétienne*, an idealization of the Virgin Mary, pious and modest. Thus, as the *Conseil Général* of the Nord insisted in 1842, 'the important thing for a village girl is that she knows how to sew, read, write and reckon, that she has a firm grasp of religious education and has a perfect understanding of all those manual skills which might be useful to her'. The education of girls was normally regarded as far less important than that of boys, and throughout the century female literacy rates were much lower than those for men, although the difference continually narrowed. In 1847, 40 per cent of girls of school age did not attend school (about 1.1 million), and in some areas, especially in the centre and west, the proportions were much higher, reaching 79.4 per cent in Indre, 80 per cent in Vienne and Cher, 81 per cent in Finistère, 87 per cent in Nièvre and 89 per cent in Haute-Vienne. Whereas for boys the essential quantitative increase in attendance came before 1850, for girls it came after.[18]

The empire and restoration had seen considerable efforts by the church to rebuild the female religious orders, and in some areas they rapidly acquired a quasi-monopoly over girls' education. In the west, for example, this period saw the establishment of such local teaching orders as the *Soeurs de Saint-Gildas-de-Bois*, the *Filles de la Sagesse*, the *Soeurs de la Providence* of St Brieuc and the *Soeurs Adoratrices de la Justice de Dieu* of Rille-Sougres. The continued expansion of these orders and the widespread belief that girls had need of a religious education ensured that by 1870 three-fifths of girls were taught by sisters belonging to some 500 congregations. This continuing expansion was encouraged by allowing nuns to teach even when they did not possess the qualifications required of lay teachers (the *brevet*). By 1863 the sisters controlled 8061 public schools (5998 lay) and 5571 private schools (7637 lay).[19] The proportion of girls they taught was even greater due to their concentration in the largest centres of population. Even this underestimates the influence of the teaching orders, for many lay *institutrice* were trained by them in such establishments as the *Cours normal des dames du Bon Sauveur*, established at Albi in 1838 and which controlled teacher training in the Tarn until 1889.

The church constantly remained determined to increase its control over the education of girls as a means of ensuring the piety of future generations. Moreover, the establishment of the religious orders in their schools was doubly advantageous to communities. The sisters assisted the parish clergy, and cared for the poor and sick as well as teaching. Conservative notables saw their presence as a guarantee of moral and social order. According to a school inspector at Lille in 1853, 'it is by means of girls rather than boys that the dissolute morals of our manufacturing populations will be reformed'. In reaction republicans, although often sharing the same basic beliefs in women's intellectual and moral inferiority, were increasingly determined to establish lay education. As Michelet pointed out in his *Du Pretre, de la Femme, de la Famille* (1845), 'our wives and daughters are brought up and governed by our enemies. . . . The enemies of the modern spirit of liberty and of the future'.

The existence of a school network was obviously a prerequisite for the continued development of education, but was not in itself enough to ensure widespread attendance.

School attendance

School attendance was determined by a variety of factors, including obviously the provision of schools and judgements at the level of the individual family as to the practical utility of education. The attitudes of the family generally reflected those of the social milieu to which it belonged, its enveloping cultural environment. The statistical information available on school attendance is, however, highly misleading. It is impossible to be certain to what extent actual attendance corresponded to the numbers of pupils registered. In Paris in 1866 the official figures claimed that 90 per cent of children of school age were at school. Gréard, the senior school inspector, estimated that as many as 29 per cent of the appropriate age group did not actually attend school. Furthermore, absenteeism continued to substantially reduce the effectiveness of schooling, although attendance did gradually become more regular, so that in the later periods registration and actual attendance corresponded more closely. Bearing this in mind, Table 60 gives estimates of attendance for the age group 5–15.[20] They suggest that a return to pre 1789 levels of attendance was achieved during the 1820s.

The main obstacles to attendance were poverty and the attitudes it engendered. For large numbers of peasant farmers and unskilled workers in town and countryside what was taught in school had little apparent relevance to the practical concerns of life. In some areas, this cultural isolation was reinforced by an inability to speak French, the language of education. In such situations there appeared little point in paying school fees or in managing without children's

Table 60   *Primary school attendance, 1817–1912 (in thousands)*

Date	Total number of pupils	. . . of which boys
1817	866	
1829	1358	969
1832	1939	1203
1840	2897	1657
1850	3322	1794
1861	4286	
1872	4722	2445
1876–7	4716	2400
1881–2	5341	2708
1886–7	5526	2789
1911–12	5628	

labour or earnings. Martin Nadaud remembered how his father, who had worked as a mason in Paris, and was thus aware of the wider opportunities in life, and ambitious for his son, was opposed in his desire to send the child to school by his wife, who needed his help in the fields, and by his grandfather who pointed out, 'neither my brothers, nor you, nor me, have learned our letters and we've managed to eat all the same'. Education could easily be regarded as a luxury, intended for others. The well-informed republican politician, Jules Simon, in a book on *L'Ecole* published in 1865 made a similar point: 'general rule: the less one knows, the less one wants to know . . . in a poor commune, where no-one conceives, can conceive or even dreams of a better life; where, from father to son, they live from routine manual labour, in the most profound ignorance, without thinking of the future . . . there usually exists little interest, and indeed contempt for learning'. Poverty encouraged a short-term utilitarianism and the more numerous the poor, the less likely they were to develop a sense of dissatisfaction with their condition. It took time after the opening of a school for widespread appreciation of the social utility of literacy to develop. Other significant factors included the sheer inaccessibility of schools, especially in upland areas and regions of dispersed habitat, and during bad weather, although this should not be exaggerated in an age when people were used to walking long distances.

These practical obstacles gradually declined in importance. Even before free elementary education was introduced by the law of 16 June 1881 a large number of free places were provided. The *Frères des écoles chrétiennes* insisted upon this as a condition of their opening a school. The Guizot law had required that indigents at least be relieved of the burden, and some large towns with a significant income from the *octroi* were able to entirely abolish fees. Opponents of free education argued that people only appreciated what they had to pay for and objected to paying increased local taxes, but the number of free places gradually increased – from 29 per cent in 1833 to 57 per cent in 1875[21] – though with significant regional variations, and particularly rapidly during Duruy's term as minister in the 1860s.

More important than fees as a reason for non-attendance was the frequent dependence of parents upon children's earnings. Attendance was very much influenced by the extent to which local economies provided employment opportunities for children. The availability of such work (especially in textiles and agriculture) influenced decisions as to whether to send children to school at all, on the number of years they might attend and the regularity of their attendance. The 1841 law restricting child labour (which only applied to factories) was ineffective due to the indifference and hostility of both employers and workers. It was the combination of a decline in the demand for child labour, the improvement in living standards and a more positive attitude towards education which secured generalized enrolment in schools, even before the 1882 law introducing compulsory attendance.

Who did attend, and how regularly? As we have stressed, schools became important to people when what they taught appeared relevant – for artisans as a means of increasing their technical competence, for many others as a means of improving their social status particularly as a host of minor clerical positions were created, for peasants increasingly involved in the market, as a means of keeping accounts. Legislators might be primarily concerned with the moralizing objectives of primary education, but potential recipients were more interested in its instrumental functions. Socio-economic status was the crucial variable. Poverty was a disincentive. Generally those who possessed property or skills tended to adopt less fatalistic attitudes. They might reasonably expect their offspring to benefit from education. The children's achievements in the classroom became a matter of pride. Conversely the uneducated gradually came to feel a sense of shame. More positive attitudes towards education spread down the social hierarchy from the old élites in the seventeenth century to the merchants, shopkeepers, artisans, and well-off farmers in the eighteenth, and finally to the mass of workers and peasants in the nineteenth century. Geographically these spread outwards from the economically more advanced regions into the more backward, and within regions from the urban centres into the countryside. The improvement of communications, the development of commerce, the widening of horizons, stimulated by the interest in politics, through travel, and universal conscription, together with the improved quality of education itself, all contributed to a changing outlook, and to the intensification of these processes of cultural imitation.

Another major problem was the regularity of attendance. In the countryside attendance declined markedly from around Easter until the late autumn, as the weather improved and work in the fields became more demanding. Children could look after animals and help with the various harvests. The situation was particularly serious in areas in which rural industries provided additional work for children in winter. Thus many children only went to school for some three to four months in winter. Frequently they resented even this. The Breton, P. J. Hélias, remembered that, 'the worst thing for country children was to spend fine days indoors to learn things that had nothing to do with our daily life, when real men's work went on outside'. In industrial centres, too, either due to the availability of work, or because children were kept at home to assist with domestic chores, or else because parents simply did not understand the importance of punctuality and regular attendance, absenteeism reduced the effectiveness of schooling. In Lille in 1852 one-third of the pupils on the schools rolls attended only irregularly.[22] Although absenteeism continued to be significant in the poorer (e.g. 20 per cent in the 13th *arrondissement* of Paris in 1894) or in the more isolated areas, the enforcement of new legislation, the arrangement of holidays largely to meet the needs of agriculture, and in particular changing parental attitudes, led to its gradual reduction. Whereas in 1833 the number of children attending in the summer had been only one-half of those in winter, by 1850 the proportion had risen to two-thirds, by 1876–7 (i.e. before legislation on obligatory attendance) to 79 per cent, and in the 1880s to four-fifths[23] – indicative of a profound socio-cultural transformation.

The number of years during which children went to school was also gradually extended. In most regions education began at the age of 6 or 7 and continued until 10 or 12, when attendance at church for the first communion served as the traditional rite of passage marking the end of childhood. Except in some of the most backward areas, the periods of most rapid growth in attendance pre-dated the introduction of compulsory education for children between 6 and 13 in 1882. This legislation was intended, however, to increase regularity as well as to prolong the period of attendance. Its enforcement was made easier by a law of 2 November 1892 which forbade employment in industry, though not in agriculture, until a child had obtained the *certificat d'études primaires*, introduced in 1882, which thus served as a new rite of passage. The increasingly positive attitudes of parents towards the schools were also the product of improvements in the quality of the education they provided.

Teachers and teaching methods

Judgements about the quality of education are not easy to make. They require information concerning the recruitment of teachers, their training and about what actually went on in the classrooms. Prior to the establishment of the *écoles normales*, primary school teachers varied considerably both in terms of their own educational backgrounds and their capacity to teach. Mediocrity was widespread. The only qualifications required by the 1816 law were a certificate of good conduct from the local *curé* together with a certificate affirming that its possessor was capable of teaching. This was not difficult to obtain given prevailing low standards. The profession for long remained unattractive as a means of earning a living and in the early years of the century tended to attract underemployed peasants and artisans, ex-priests, demobilized soldiers, etc., unable to find alternative employment. In the south these included itinerant teachers from the Briançonnais in the Alps who hired themselves out for the winter at the autumn fairs in Lower Provence wearing as a sign of their trade a hat with one, two or three feathers denoting their willingness to teach simply reading, reading and writing, or these plus arithmetic. This was a particular form of migratory seasonal labour. Even in 1863 there were only 3500 applications for 1224 places in *écoles normales* and in 1880 only 5279 for 1554.[24] The attractiveness of the teaching profession gradually increased due to the improvement of conditions of service and of training. The numbers of teachers grew in response to an ever-expanding demand (Table 61).

Table 61 *Number of primary school teachers*[25]

Year	Number	Year	Number	Year	Number
1837	59,735	1872	110,238	1891–2	147,000
1840	63,409	1876–7	110,709	1896–7	152,000
1843	75,535	1881–2	124,965	1906–7	159,000
1863	108,799	1886–7	136,819	1911–12	158,000

Generally student teachers entering the *écoles normales* came from modest families for whom the teaching profession represented a social promotion, but who could nevertheless afford the cost of their training. The teaching profession was attractive as a means of escaping conscription, hard manual labour, and of gaining a secure income. The more able, after more or less brief periods in the classroom, were often able to find better rewarded employment in offices, although it is perhaps indicative of a growing sense of professional commitment that annual turnover rates did decline and stabilized at around 6 per cent by the 1860s.[26] Students were thus drawn mainly from the ranks of skilled workers, the lower middle classes, and moderately well-off peasants. In the earlier part of the century peasants predominated, but subsequently the social range of recruitment widened. Statistics exist for only some departments, for example, in the Vosges between 1862 and 1892, of 567 students 61 per cent were of peasant origin, 28 per cent came from families of artisans and shopkeepers; in the Manche in 1883–4, 53 per cent of *normaliens* were the sons of peasants (only 26.1 per cent by 1910–14), 28.2 per cent of artisans and shopkeepers (10.2 per cent) and 3.4 per cent of workers and clerks (34.3 per cent); in the Nord between 1893 and 1914, 10 per cent of pupils were of peasant origin, 15.2 per cent sons of wage-earners and the same proportion came from the *artisanate*, 10.8 per cent were the sons of shopkeepers, 20.9 per cent of clerks and minor officials, and 19 per cent of school teachers.[27] By the early twentieth century, *écoles normales* in the major urban centres, and especially the Paris area, tended to recruit higher proportions of their students from among the better-off social groups due in part to their higher cultural standards.

There was considerable and growing rivalry between lay and religious teachers throughout the century. Although, or perhaps because, both the *écoles normales* and the *noviciats* of the teaching orders tended to recruit from among the same social groups, and until the 1880s the training of laymen included a considerable element of religious instruction, the two groups competed for influence and posts, and particularly for the better rewarded positions in urban schools. Central to the growth of hostility on the part of lay *instituteurs* towards their clerical counterparts were questions of salary and status. To an important extent salaries rose with the status of the school teacher. For male teachers the 1833 law established a minimum and extremely low basic salary of 200 francs plus lodging and the income from fees (5 per cent of this income was to be paid into a pension fund). Women teachers were lucky if they earned half as much. Prior to the *loi Falloux* which established a minimum of 600 francs (thus attempting to buy the loyalty of a profession subject to considerable political repression), salaries were frequently so low – particularly in the countryside – as to require many teachers to supplement their incomes. The most common means of doing so included accepting the traditional role of assistant to the parish priest, or the increasingly important position of secretary to the mayor, a function which had the additional advantage of increasing the importance and prestige of the teacher in the community. In 1832 fifty-eight of the 201 *instituteurs* in three *arrondissements* of the Creuse had supplementary occupations

– nineteen were farmers, eight sacristans, three tobacconists, three traders, three lawyers' clerks, two bakers, one innkeeper, one café proprietor, one black-smith, one roofer, one surveyor, and three *secrétaires de la mairie*.[28] Conditions improved significantly in the 1850s and 1860s and discontent declined. Even so, in a sample of 5940 essays on the means of improving primary education submitted to the Minister of Education in 1860, 80 per cent still complained of low pay.[29] At this time most male teachers in the countryside were paid 600 to 800 francs annually, plus free lodging worth 50–70 francs, which compared unfavourably with the wages of unskilled labourers in the towns who earned about 675 francs and clerks with 795–1080 francs.[30] In 1863 women teachers in public schools were paid on average 480 francs, but they were increasingly excluded from the larger urban schools, in which both basic salaries and the income from fees were higher, by the expansion of the religious orders.

Table 62 gives statistics on public schools in Calvados in 1870. These provide some idea both of the continued prevalence of low incomes and of the hierarchy within the profession.[31] Salaries were again increased in the 1880s, and in spite of continued mediocrity this helped confirm the general withdrawal from supplementary activities now clearly regarded as demeaning by *écoles normales* trained teachers, although not from the politically sensitive post of *secrétaire de la mairie*. In order to increase their status and set an example to the lower classes, teachers were also encouraged to maintain middle-class standards of dress and behaviour. High moral standards were imposed upon them by the authorities, by the expectations of parents, and by their own desire for respectability. This self-discipline was an essential attribute of the successful teacher. Together with their superior education it did have the effect, however, of setting them apart and of isolating them socially. Nevertheless, the prestige of the *instituteur* slowly increased.

The detailed inquiry which preceded the 1833 law had emphasized the need to improve the quality of teaching. Although teacher training centres for both

Table 62   *Teachers and their salaries, Calvados 1870*

Salary	No. of men teachers	No. of women teachers
Less than 400 francs	—	118
Less than 500 francs	—	101
Less than 600 francs	44	68
Less than 700 francs	185	40
Less than 800 francs	71	37
Less than 900 francs	47	17
Less than 1000 francs	33	15
Less than 1100 francs	21	—
Less than 1200 francs	24	7
Less than 1500 francs	16	4
Less than 2000 francs	17	—

laymen and clerics had been established during the restoration, largely due to local initiatives, most teachers had learned their trade simply by helping in schools. The 1833 law required that an *école normale* be established in every department. From fourteen in 1830 their numbers rose to seventy-four by 1837. Gradually teachers trained in these colleges replaced their untrained predecessors – by 1846, 9200 of some 40,000 teachers were *école normale* trained. By 1869 there were seventy-six *écoles normales* for men and eleven for women, and by 1887 ninety and eighty-one respectively – the last figure indicative of the growth of interest in the education of girls culminating in the 1879 law which required departments to maintain an *école normale d'institutrices*. The task of the *écoles normales* was to provide professional training, but also to civilize and moralize student teachers. They achieved this in extremely austere and authoritarian conditions. For two years (from 1851) young men of 17 or 18 prepared for the basic teaching qualification (the *brevet simple*), following a programme which emphasized the three Rs, but with some science and maths, French, history and geography, and which laid considerable stress on religious morality. The *écoles normales*, according to the Minister of Education Salvandy, writing in 1838, were to provide 'the modest knowledge' which was all that primary teachers required. Students were subjected to a conservative and religious indoctrination and where necessary were shown how to dress with dignity, employ polite table manners and develop personal hygiene. They were taught to respect the existing social and cultural order and made aware of their subordinate place within it. In spite of the narrowness of the curriculum, by the 1840s conservatives were already anxious about what they saw as the over-education of teachers. It was felt that this might render them dissatisfied with their lot. The radical politics of a minority of teachers in 1848 appeared to confirm their worst fears. Closure of the *écoles normales* was seriously discussed and actually occurred in eight cases, but generally an intensification of the moral and religious supervision of pupil teachers was felt to be sufficient. This was especially strict in the small number of *écoles normales d'institutrices*, the first of which had been established in 1838 at Argentan (Orne) under the direction of the order of *Dames religieuses de l'éducation chrétienne*. Only from the 1860s did some relaxation of this strict discipline occur. At the same time the syllabus, restricted by regulation on 24 March 1851, was again extended. Furthermore, the organization of regular conferences and the existence of a specialized professional press increasingly allowed qualified teachers to improve their pedagogical skills and stimulated a growing professional *esprit de corps*.

It is far easier to write a history of education based upon legislation and administrative instructions than upon actual classroom practice. Some of the constraints upon teachers, such as irregular pupil attendance, have already been noted. Financial restrictions were also a continuing problem, resulting in a shortage of properly constructed schools, of school furniture and of such basic equipment as books. Certainly in the early years of the century educational programmes appear to have been extremely rudimentary. In 1840 the regulations established for primary schools in the Seine Inférieure and Eure contained mainly religious prescriptions. Thus Article One required a crucifix in every classroom; Articles Three and Four prayer four times a day, with in addition a special prayer for the King on Wednesdays and Saturdays; Article Eleven invited teachers to divide the time remaining after religious instruction between reading, writing and counting. Particularly before the 1833 law which created an effective state inspectorate, many teachers, especially in rural schools, continued to disassociate the teaching of reading, writing and arithmetic. The last two involved complex manipulative operations, required quills which needed constant sharpening, and expensive paper. Only the growing provision of slates, and of sufficiently cheap steel pen-nibs and paper (1840s) eased these practical problems. Until then many children learned only to read, often imperfectly, using whatever texts their parents could provide – usually religious works like the Catechism and the various lives of Jesus or the saints. Rather than fulfil the programmes laid down in official regulations, teachers often felt under a greater obligation to satisfy parental demands and were obliged to make do as best they could with inadequate resources.

Except in the towns, classes were normally large and mixed in age, ability and frequency of attendance. Teaching in such conditions was invariably difficult. The *Société pour l'instruction élémentaire*, founded in 1815, had encouraged the use of the Lancastrian (mutual) method of teaching through intermediary monitors, in an attempt to compensate for the shortage of teachers. This development had been bitterly opposed by the church, partly in an effort to maintain its own dominance over education but also on the grounds that an adequate education required close supervision by teachers. It was maintained, in particular, that moral and religious instruction would suffer without this. The 'mutual' method spread to relatively few schools (4.4 per cent of the total in 1834). Despite this it did stimulate debate and encourage the practice of group teaching to replace the individual method which had been commonly practised by untrained teachers who had never learned to direct a class, and because pupils had not been provided with a common text. It had meant that individual pupils received relatively little instruction and suffered from acute boredom, a feeling compounded by the prevalence of learning by rote, with little effort at explanation by teachers. In the countryside, in particular, in the early decades of the century, education generally remained rudimentary. Certainly good teachers were to be found, especially in the towns where their services were most appreciated and better remunerated. There, too, the *Frères des écoles chrétiennes* and the other teaching orders which provided their members with a serious training were concentrated, although in comparison with their male counterparts the nuns were usually concerned less with their teaching functions than with care of the sick and the provision of moral guidance for young girls.

The Guizot law of 1833 at least provided for increasing numbers of *écoles normales*, proper inspection and supervision and the establishment of an official *Manuel générale de l'instruction publique* to guide teachers. This represented the beginning of efforts to impose a systematic pedagogy upon the schools – based at elementary level on 'reading, writing, the elements of the French language and of arithmetic, the legal system of weights and measures', and at the higher level of the *écoles primaires supérieures* for a small minority of pupils, 'the elements of geometry and its practical application, especially linear drawing and surveying, notions of the physical and natural sciences applicable to daily life, singing, history and geography, and especially that of France' (Article One). It continued to insist, however, that the principle duty of the teacher was to provide religious instruction. Thus, as the means of achieving another basic objective, the propagation of literacy, it was stipulated in the *Statut des écoles primaires* of 25 April 1834 that the texts used should 'constantly tend to penetrate the souls of pupils with the sentiments and principles which are the safeguard of good morality and which are proper to inspire fear and love of God'. The teaching orders saw their main purpose as being to provide instruction in the Catechism which was a passport to first communion, but in every school the day was to begin and end with prayer. Verses from the Holy Scriptures were to be learned, and a simple fundamentalist religious faith inculcated.

As a means of encouraging simultaneous teaching and of avoiding the excessive waste of time due to the individual method, it was now required that every pupil in a particular class should use the same textbooks, although this could only gradually be implemented because of its cost, and remained impossible in small rural schools with mixed-age classes. Nevertheless, the requirement did encourage the preparation and publication of new texts and brought to an end the practice of making use of whatever books happened to be available, almost regardless of suitability. These might include, according to a report from the Haute-Vienne in 1864, anything from *Télémaque*, the *Iliade* and the Psalms to the *Imitation de Christ* and especially the *Devoirs d'un Chrétien*. Another feature of schools in the early part of the century that slowly declined was the tradition of teaching children first to read, then to write and finally to count. Parents frequently claimed themselves to be satisfied once some proficiency in the first skill had been achieved, especially as fees were often fixed according to the number of subjects taught. Whatever the continued shortcomings, the quality of education gradually improved. A revolution in teaching methods began around the middle of the century, involving for example, in the teaching of reading, the use of phonetic spelling and of primers with basic words and simple sentence structures more attuned to the learning ability of young children than the old manuals. Even then, however, the primers most favoured appear to have been those which provided examples of the dismal end of children who failed to live in imitation of Jesus Christ. Their content and style can have done little to stimulate a taste for reading. By the 1870s further improvement had occurred. While textbooks were still designed to provide a moral lesson and to prepare children for an adult life, they were at least increasingly written for children and addressed their message in a more interesting story form; writing became less ornamental; teaching less mechanical; while the improvement in teaching methods saved time and allowed an enlargement of the curriculum. There were still major problems. All too frequently lessons were learned by heart, and handwriting, to which considerable importance was attached, was limited to formal exercises, the copying of passages with rarely any attempt to encourage composition and individual creativity. History and geography, according to *L'Education* in March 1851, was no more than 'an indigestible mass of names and dates'. They were only made obligatory by Duruy in 1867 and subsequently began to benefit from a supply of reasonably adequate maps and books. In these circumstances, extreme boredom and large classes often caused disciplinary problems for teachers. Many of them used frequent and severe forms of punishment – humiliation and beatings – in a desperate effort to retain the attention of their pupils, and also to inculcate the virtues of self-discipline.

To a large degree the improvement in teaching methods was due to the growing supply of trained teachers from the *écoles normales*. Their efforts were supplemented by those of an inspectorate which insisted upon the need for timetables and the written preparation of lessons as a means of enforcing stricter control, the development of regular *conférences pédagogiques* at the local level, and the publication of a specialized professional press. Significantly, whereas the *frères* had previously been regarded as the best teachers available, criticism of their methods and especially those of the female orders became increasingly common with school inspectors bemoaning the lack of effective control over these institutions.

Improvement in the quality of teaching also required the provision of well-built and properly equipped schools. Communes were reluctant to spend the money. Making do with whatever was available was all too common, and resulted in classrooms which were often damp, badly ventilated and heated, equipped with rudimentary furniture and overcrowded with dirty, smelly children, covered in vermin. Increasingly, the state felt compelled to provide subsidies for poor communities, and to enforce strict controls over the design and construction of new schools.

Although a series of laws and of implementing decrees defined the general principles of the system of primary education, there was surprisingly little debate in government circles before the 1880s. While central government encouraged the inspectorate to impose greater uniformity on the system, ministers and senior civil servants took little interest in pedagogical methods, leaving far more room for diversity than a reading of the regulations might suggest. The fundamental concern of government throughout the century remained the moralizing character of education, that is, its socially conservative functions. In this respect the main significance of the establishment of the Third Republic was the gradual laicization of moral teaching. In the state schools religion gave way to civic instruction with an increasingly pronounced emphasis on patriotism, exemplified by Bruno's famous *Tour de France par deux enfants* (209 editions between 1877 and 1891), which introduced millions of children to the regions of France and its national heroes, insisting upon the natural beauty of the land and the social harmony which prevailed among its citizens, describing a France of artisans and peasants from which industrial workers were strangely absent and social conflict had disappeared once the egalitarian, progressive republic had finally been established. Its message was that it was the duty of all citizens to be prepared to defend this happy land. The main role of the teacher was to impose the culture and ethics of the dominant social group upon children, basing their teaching upon the ideals of self-discipline, honesty, thrift, the avoidance of vice, respect for the family, hard work, cleanliness, politeness and grateful acceptance of the established social order which was the best of all possible worlds. Teaching encouraged passivity, obedience and conformity, virtues imposed upon the teachers themselves by their training and the authority of school directors and inspectors in what was an extremely hierarchical profession. The adhesion of a small minority of teachers to *syndicats* in the 1900s, while a sign of widespread discontent, had little effect on the instruction they provided.

Literacy

How successful were the schools in promoting basic literacy? The statistical information available has serious shortcomings. For the early nineteenth century we still have to rely upon analysis of signatures in marriage registers. In many cases these might simply represent the desire to achieve a limited skill for a special occasion. Information gleaned from the registers nevertheless indicates that whereas 32 per cent of men and 48 per cent of women were unable to sign in 1855, these figures fell to 1.6 and 2.7 per cent respectively by 1913. Statistics also exist concerning illiteracy rates among conscripts (Table 63). These sources, of course, provide information only about the *relatively* well-educated younger generations. For society as a whole illiteracy rates must have been substantially higher. Throughout the century illiteracy was always much higher among the older age-groups, born too early to benefit from the improvement of educational provision and changes in attitudes towards schooling. They do, however, combine to suggest that the centuries old process of increasing literacy markedly accelerated in the nineteenth century, particularly among women who had previously suffered from the belief that education mattered less for girls. The gap between the sexes narrowed considerably, although according to the 1901 census, while 16 per cent of males over 20 were illiterate, this was true of 24 per cent of females.[32]

Table 63   *Illiteracy among conscripts (percentage of total)*

1831–5	47.4
1836–40	43.7
1841–5	40.0
1846–50	36.0
1851–5	34.1
1856–60	31.1
1861–5	27.0
1866–8	21.4
1871–5	17.9

The various measurements of literacy based upon school attendance, the ability to sign a marriage register, a conscript's response to questions by the local mayor or the head of a family's reply to census questions, reveal important qualitative variations. Although they claimed to be literate, many young men coming before the military commissions at the age of 20 had forgotten a great deal since leaving school eight or ten years before. Without frequent practice the capacity to read and write, often learned by rote with little enthusiasm, was easily lost. Functional literacy must have been much lower than official literacy levels. Estimates vary, but the 1865 *Statistique de l'enseignement primaire* concluded that 16.4 per cent of those who attended school left unable to read and write, or able to read only, while the Education Minister Duruy claimed that a further 19 per cent possessed such limited learning that they would soon forget it. Thus, over one-third of those leaving school were functionally illiterate, and how many others would become so in following decades? In 1863 Jules Simon estimated that among adults aged 30 to 60 not one man in ten nor one woman in twenty were able to write a letter or read a book. It was figures like these which encouraged the authorities to make efforts to improve the regularity of pupil attendance and teaching methods. Together with more positive social attitudes this resulted in improvements in standards of literacy which meant that most school-leavers from the 1880s were able to write a more or less correct French and at least manage to read the popular press. But even in 1914, when the official military records indicated that only 1.92 per cent of conscripts were illiterate, further investigation led to the claim that 35 per cent had an, 'education which is nil or inadequate'.

Attention must also be paid to the considerable regional variations in literacy levels revealed in Figures 19–23. It continued to be possible, as it had since the seventeenth century, to make a distinction between the relatively advanced north and east and the backward Atlantic façade, the centre and south, with the two regions roughly separated by a line drawn from St-Malo to Lake Geneva (although substantial variations always existed even within departments). At its most extreme, in 1827–31 a gulf existed between the Doubs where 83.2 per cent of conscripts were able at least to read, and the Corrèze where the figure was only 14.9 per cent. Gradually, however, the backward areas caught up. Progress was especially rapid in the south-east (the Rhône corridor and Alps), slower in the south-west, and slowest in Brittany and the centre (Berry, Limousin), and even at higher levels of development and in spite of a narrowing of the gap these areas continued to have relatively high levels of illiteracy. Thus between 1871 and 1875, whereas to the north of the St-Malo–Geneva line it was only in the Nord (of thirty-one departments) that fewer than 70 per cent of those being married were unable to sign the register, and in twenty-one departments over 90 per cent signed; to the south of the line, only six of the fifty-nine departments had rates above 80 per cent and these were all on the upper Rhône or in the northern Alps. Most backward were clearly the departments of the south-west, of the centre and of Brittany, such as Corrèze, Haute-Vienne, Indre, Cher, Allier, Morbihan and Finistère. Obligatory education was to have its most

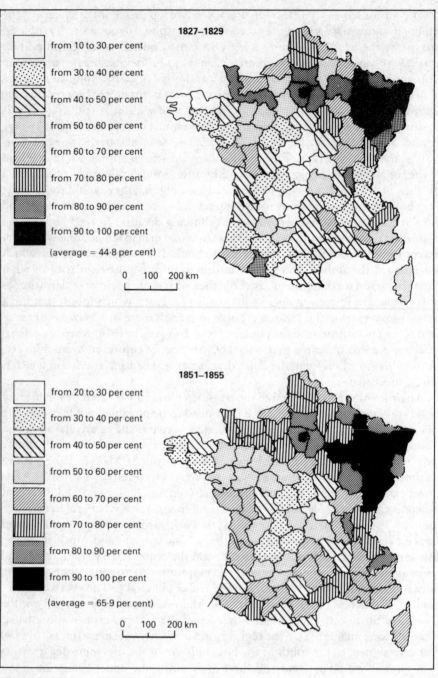

Figures 19—23 *The progress of literacy among conscripts: percentage able to read and write 1827–1913*
  Source: *After G. Dupeux*, Atlas historique de la France   *Colin 1966*

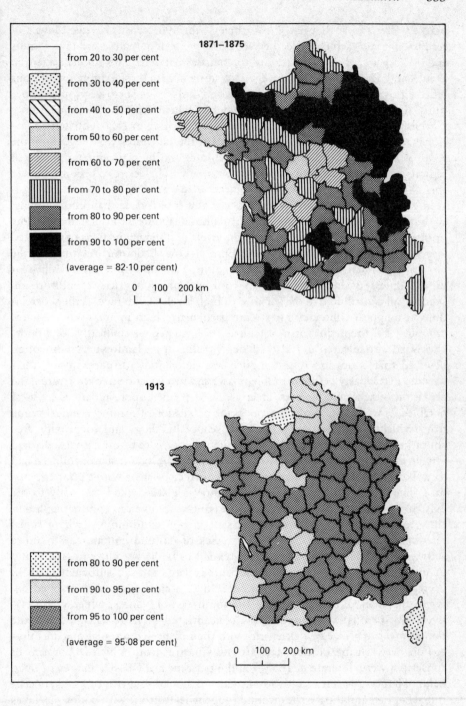

1871–1875

from 20 to 30 per cent
from 30 to 40 per cent
from 40 to 50 per cent
from 50 to 60 per cent
from 60 to 70 per cent
from 70 to 80 per cent
from 80 to 90 per cent
from 90 to 100 per cent

(average = 82·10 per cent)

0   100   200 km

1913

from 80 to 90 per cent
from 90 to 95 per cent
from 95 to 100 per cent

(average = 95·08 per cent)

0   100   200 km

marked effects in such areas. Nevertheless, the 1901 census revealed levels of
residual illiteracy which varied between 2.05 per cent of males over 15 in Doubs
and 34.05 per cent in Corrèze, and for females between 3.08 per cent again in
Doubs and 47.13 per cent in Ariège. To some degree these regional variations
reflected the density of the school network, but it was socio-economic structures and the mentalities they engendered which largely determined how
schools were perceived. Thus Charles Dupin, writing in 1826, equated educational advance with economic development. Literacy rates were highest in the
areas of open field, of commercial agriculture and high productivity, and in
regions in which industrialization was occurring. The desire to become literate
spread, to a large degree, with the market economy.

In general, literacy levels were lower in the countryside than in the towns,
with small-scale peasant farmers and agricultural labourers the least literate. The
presence of the latter explained the high levels of illiteracy in areas of advanced
large-scale farming such as Cher and Eure-et-Loir. Economic retardation, the
poverty of much of the population, cultural isolation and the inability or
unwillingness of local notables to commit communes to expenditure on
schools, all contributed to the survival of high levels of illiteracy. Other correlations also appear. Illiteracy rates were particularly high in areas where sharecropping was the major form of tenure. Its existence was indicative of a poor,
backward agriculture, and also of dependence upon landowners who often
believed that education might induce less deferential attitudes among their
tenants. Particularly before the Guizot law, and to a lesser degree afterwards, the
provision of schooling and its effectiveness depended upon initiatives by local
notables, as well as upon such factors as the possession of common land, revenue
from which might be used to finance school building, and to provide free
education, etc. Regions of dispersed habitat, of *bocage*, of forest, also usually had
low literacy rates, partly because of isolation and the long distance children had
to walk to school, mainly because these tended to be areas with a poor agriculture. The progress of literacy in the countryside was linked especially to the
existence of a less dependent 'middle' peasantry involved in commerce, living
close together in less exclusively peasant village communities where social
relations were relatively intense, processes of cultural contamination more
active, and access to school easier. It tended to be higher close to towns and
major commercial routes, than in the more isolated and self-sufficient areas. In
Loire-Inférieure, for example, from the 1850s a clear contrast developed between the vine-cultivating areas to the south-east of Nantes, which were relatively prosperous with populations concentrated in large villages, and the
poorer areas of *bocage* or marshland with their dispersed populations; in Eure-
et-Loir between the Beauce plain around Chartres from which 28 per cent of
conscripts were illiterate in 1835–7 and 4 per cent in 1878–82, an area of open
field, of large-scale cereal cultivation, with a rich market agriculture and concentrated habitat, and the Perche (around Nogent-le-Rotrou) with poor soils, lakes
and forests, small farms engaged in semi-subsistence production and a population living in small hamlets, with illiteracy rates of 56 and 11 per cent in the same

periods.[33] In Bourgogne similar contrasts can be drawn between the areas of open fields predominating in the department of Côte-d'Or and those of *bocage* in Saône-et-Loire, i.e. in the Morvan, Autunais and Charolais which geographically belonged to the Massif Central. It was the combination of all these adverse factors – poor soils, small sharecropped farms, dispersed habitat and extreme poverty, as in the Allier – which resulted in the highest rates of illiteracy. However, and again indicating the difficulties of generalization, the persistence of rural industry in areas of open field, for example in the Nord and Pas-de-Calais, into the second half of the century, tended to reduce school attendance as did cultural isolation regardless of habitat structures. The Norman *bocage* which had been long involved in the cattle trade had high literacy rates in spite of dispersed habitat, as did those zones of the otherwise backward Limousin which regularly provided temporary migrant labour for the Paris and Lyon building trades. The significance of other factors including religion and language also cannot be ignored. A southern department like the Gard had literacy rates above the national average largely because of the stimulus afforded to educational activities by Catholic–Protestant rivalry. Within the Massif Central the effects of the Counter-Reformation in the Rouergue, the Velay and Lozère created traditions of literacy far stronger than those of the Limousin. There are thus no simple explanations beyond perhaps the fact that commercialization and prosperity could usually be correlated with high levels of literacy.

Towns, as centres of economic and administrative activity, generally had higher literacy rates than rural areas, although the character of their rural hinterlands and the literacy rates of in-migrants obviously affected these. This partly explains the 37.6 per cent illiteracy measured in Limoges in 1872, even though this was much lower than the 66.3 per cent in rural Haute-Vienne. In even more backward Finistère there was a marked contrast between illiteracy rates, averaging 27.8 per cent in the four largest towns and 69.8 per cent in the countryside.[34] Distinctions can also be drawn between towns in relation to their socio-professional structures. Literacy rates were lower in the rapidly developing industrial centres than in traditional administrative and marketing centres. In Saône-et-Loire in 1846, illiteracy was around 54 per cent in the former, compared with 21 per cent in the latter.[35] The directors of the Le Creusot ironworks which recruited many of its workers in the particularly backward *bocage* area of Saône-et-Loire claimed that the rapid establishment of schools was essential to civilize a population described by a school inspector in 1833 as 'ignorant, savage, turbulent, corrupt', and gradually the positive policy of the employers in this case, together with the usual processes of cultural imitation took effect. Moreover, the initial period of uncontrolled and rapid industrialization was followed by a decline in the demand for child labour as technical change occurred and by declining dependence upon the contributions children made to family budgets as living standards improved.

There was also considerable variation within towns between professional groups. Thus artisans and skilled workers more generally were, from early in the century, largely literate, while among the unskilled literacy was only gradually attained. In Paris the Chamber of Commerce inquiry of 1847–8 revealed that 87 per cent of males could read and write, with the highest literacy rates being attained by artisans in printing (97 per cent), in the precious metal and jewellery trade (96 per cent) and those producing the various *articles de Paris* (95 per cent). Conversely rates were much lower in the building trades – little over 50 per cent according to the 1860 inquiry – and lower again among the unskilled. By 1868 among Parisian conscripts only 3 per cent of skilled artisans were recorded as illiterate, 7 per cent of workers from the clothing trades, 10 per cent of building workers and 20 per cent of labourers, with illiteracy especially high in the main centres of immigration, the 11th, 12th, 13th, 19th and 20th *arrondissements* which had 10–14 per cent illiteracy.[36] In Mulhouse in the 1840s only 7 per cent of the engineering and printing workers were illiterate, but almost 50 per cent of textile workers and labourers. At St-Etienne in 1848, 50 per cent of all workers were literate, but less than 10 per cent of miners – probably due to the influx of recent immigrants from the countryside.[37] Generational differences become particularly marked in such situations.

Literacy did not necessarily increase in linear fashion. Early industrializaton tended to depress rates. Thus in the north the development of factory industry offered unskilled labour from an early age and had damaging consequences on school attendance. Literacy rates in the developing industrial centres were also affected by the influx of rural poor in search of work. In Lille in 1859 an estimated 60 per cent of workers employed in small workshops were literate, but only 33 per cent of those in *grande industrie*. Textile workers and miners had particularly low rates.[38] In such circumstances valuable efforts were made to supplement and reinforce the work of the primary schools through the establishment both of pre-school training and of evening classes and libraries. The *salles d'asiles* functioned to look after children between the ages of 2 and 7, and to allow their mothers to work. According to a circular authorized by Guizot in July 1833, which established official supervision, they were intended to inculcate the 'habits of order, discipline, and regular occupation that are a beginning of morality'. Many were indeed religious foundations and saw their work as an aspect of charitable activity, their main concern being to catechize their charges at the earliest possible moment. In Lille, a textile centre with numerous working women, the first was established in 1835, and by 1847 there were six caring for 1169 children. Nationally their numbers rose from 261 in 1837 with 29,514 children to 1861 with 124,287 children in 1848.[39] Most communes, however, were reluctant to invest scarce financial resorces. Even where *salles d'asile* existed, they usually took in too many children to provide them with proper instruction and firm discipline was necessary to maintain order. Perhaps their most important contribution was to improve standards of hygiene by insisting that children had clean hands and faces. The *écoles maternelles*, which were established from 1881 as successors to the *asiles*, also tried to ensure that children had a weekly bath and lice-free hair. There were, however, relatively few of them – in 1900 only one-quarter of the children in the relevant age-group attended – and generally working mothers with young children depended upon relatives, neighbours and unofficial *garderies* or child-minders.

Evening classes were founded initially by religious philanthropists in the large cities and industrial centres and combined the functions of Christian schools and youth clubs. They tended to attract mainly literate, skilled workers (Table 64). Only during the Second Empire did the government, disturbed by the large numbers of illiterate conscripts, actively encourage *instituteurs* to open evening classes (circular of 11 July 1865). Although these official statistics record a substantial increase in attendance, success was frequently short-lived. Even so, the effort was revived in the 1880s. These classes tended to attract young people who had attended school, but who had not achieved complete functional literacy or who had subsequently forgotten their lessons, rather than those who had never attended school at all. For many young conscripts the regimental schools established (but not very systematically) from 1818 were more effective. It has been estimated that in them over 1,150,000 learned at least the rudiments of reading between 1844 and 1869.[41] In the larger towns there were also evening classes which offered opportunities for self-improvement with training in technical drawing or book-keeping, but it required considerable dedication to attend these after a long working day.

Another means of extending mass literacy and of attempting to ensure that education succeeded as a means of social control was through the development of libraries. It was important to prevent the newly educated from reading subversive or corrupting literature. In this respect, especially after the 1848 Revolution, libraries for the masses may be linked with censorship. Various initiatives were taken, including the Catholic *patronages* and the parishional libraries founded from the 1830s, the *Bibliothèque populaire* movement of the 1860s inspired by Jean Macé among others, and the official efforts from 1862 to create popular libraries in the *écoles communales* (14,395 with 1,239,165 books by the end of 1869).[42] Creating a 'taste for reading' was the major obstacle. Religious texts, works of political economy, popular science and history attracted few readers. More successful in this respect were the illustrated journals developed on a commercial basis in the 1860s and catering for a public with

Table 64 *Attendance at evening classes*[40]

Year	Men	Women
1837	36,964	
1843	90,451	4,613
1850	73,800	7,003
1863	115,673	9,974
1866	747,002	82,553
1869	678,753	114,616
1872	539,978	101,616
1876–7		105,710

developed reading skills, such as the *Musée des Familles* and *Magasin pittoresque*. Private associations such as the *Société Franklin* and *Ligue de l'Enseignement* appear to have been more attuned to popular taste and provided novels and exotic travel books as well as more serious literature, but always with the same basic aim of diverting the reading public towards utilitarian and edifying literature and protecting it from corruption. Most readers, however, preferred the entertainment offered by the cheap mass circulation press, by such newspapers as the *Petit Journal* (1863) with its lurid headlines and exciting and simply written serials.

Technical training

To avoid threatening the élitist character of secondary education, the Guizot law of 1833 had sought to provide a practical French-based education for the lower middle classes, which would have the effect, as Victor Cousin insisted in parliament, of limiting the number of socially unsuitable pupils attending the *lycées*, pupils who frequently developed unrealistic ambitions and ended up *déclassé* and dissatisfied. Towns with over 6000 inhabitants were to establish *écoles primaires supérieures* which would provide a few years additional instruction beyond the primary stage in French, arithmetic, geometry, technical drawing, book-keeping, geography and commercial law. In commercial and industrial centres, especially where flexible courses suited to local needs were developed this measure enjoyed some success. Elsewhere the schools were frequently starved of resources. Their numbers increased from forty-five in 1834 to 455 in 1840, with 15,285 pupils.[43] The standard of education they offered was often low, but their abolition in 1850 was due primarily to the conservative view that the people were being over-educated. In 1881, partly in response to the demand for suitably qualified personnel for the growing number of technical and administrative posts, and partly to head off Catholic initiatives, they were re-established. Their subsequent popularity was ensured primarily because of the enlarged range of employment opportunities to which they offered access and also because instruction was free.

Otherwise there were only limited opportunities for technical training to meet the needs of the developing industrial economy. The three *Ecoles des arts et métiers* (at Châlons-sur-Marne 1806, Angers 1815, Aix-en-Provence 1843) and the *Ecole Turgot* provided a training in scientific and commercial subjects, for a mainly lower middle-class clientèle seeking employment as draughtsmen, designers and foremen. In 1865 an *Ecole normale spéciale* was established at Cluny to train technical teachers, but their subjects continued to enjoy little status. Even in 1910 there were no more than 50,000 pupils receiving some form of technical education.[44] Otherwise this was left to private initiatives. Entrepreneurs in major industrial centres like Le Creusot and Mulhouse provided facilities to train their own personnel. However, the training provided in these large modern enterprises does not appear to have compensated fully for the decline of traditional forms of apprenticeship. In Paris, in spite of increasing population, the number of apprenticeships clearly stagnated. In 1848 there were 19,114 for a labour force of 342,530 workers; in 1860 still only 19,742.[45] This decline was in part due to the availability of relatively well paid jobs for young people and the cost of an apprenticeship in terms of lost earnings, and in part to the erosion of craft skills caused by the intensification of division of labour across the range of traditional skilled crafts. By the end of the century, however, shortages of skilled labour were causing concern, particularly because much of the training provided was designed to meet the needs of artisanal manufactures or of the first rather than of the second industrial revolution, indicative of the difficulty of providing the appropriate technical training in a period of rapid economic change.

Primary education and social mobility

For all the reasons considered, it is clear that by the turn of the century the major social and geographical variations in basic literacy had been substantially reduced but what did these educational opportunities fit children to do? For most they did not lead to social promotion. Secondary education remained closed to the vast majority. However, especially in the last third of the century, the pace of economic development was such that the proportions able to move into more skilled jobs within the working class, or even into white-collar employment, were sufficient to lend some justification to the republican ideology in its stress upon equality of opportunity. At Lille between 1873–5 and 1908–10 the working class declined from 47 to 37.7 per cent of the population, while the *classes moyennes* of artisans and shopkeepers rose from 14.2 to 18.9 per cent, and that of clerks and minor officials from 7.5 to 10.3 per cent.[46] Economic expansion and structural changes in society were creating new opportunities, although these varied between the more dynamic areas and such economically backward regions as Brittany. However, most children were conditioned by their families' experience to have low expectations and limited ambitions. Not surprisingly, individuals with a lower middle-class background whose parents were more likely to appreciate the opportunities provided by schooling had better chances of upward mobility than those of worker or peasant origin. Furthermore, in spite of the achievement of high levels of basic literacy, marked cultural differences continued to exist between social groups. Indeed the development of almost universal literacy made qualitative differences all the more important as a mark of distinction.

Secondary education
Schools

The educational system was the product of decisions taken by those with political power. Its structure reflected their fundamental attitudes towards social relationships. The primary education provided for the masses was unambiguously designed to keep them in their place in society. Conversely secondary education was made available as a privilege to only small numbers. It was a means by which access to the social élite was controlled and also provided forms of self-identification for that élite. In 1809 an estimated 51,085 children attended both public and private secondary schools; by 1854 the number had risen to 119,560; by 1910, following a period of more gradual growth in the second half of the century, to 176,796. The broad pattern of evolution can be seen from calculation of enrolment rates (Table 65).[47]

In spite of temporary disruptions the discontinuities caused by the revolution should not be exaggerated. There were 348 *collèges* in 1789, and in 1812, 337 *collèges communaux* and thirty-six *lycées*.[48] Estimates vary, but it is doubtful if overall the number of pupils had been substantially reduced. The revolution had entrusted the *collèges* of the Ancien Régime to the municipal authorities (15 April 1791). Subsequently some of these were transformed into *écoles centrales* in 1795, and an ambitious but unrealistic programme of education proposed, to include mathematics, physics and the moral and political sciences. The establishment of *lycées* by the law of 1 May 1802, recognized practical realities, and especially the shortage of qualified teachers. It resulted in a return to the traditions of classical education and accepted the existence of private schools while imposing prefectoral controls upon them. Subsequently the decree of 17 March 1808 founded the *Université* as the supervisory agency, its basic objective being the provision of a uniform education for the reconstituted social élite. However, as part of the compromise with the church it was allowed to establish seminaries under episcopal control as a means of educating not only boys intending to take holy orders, but others whose parents desired to ensure them a wholly Catholic instruction. These were so successful that new legislation had to be introduced in 1811 to limit their number to one per department in order to maintain the vitality of the *lycées*. Legislation in 1815 and 1820 which required the *baccalauréat* for entry into the liberal professions, the *grandes écoles* and senior state adminis-

Table 65   *Secondary education, 1809–1910*

Year	Enrolment rate (per 10,000 school-age children)	Number of pupils (per 10,000 total population)
1809	167	17
1820	162	16
1830	209	21
1854	375	33
1876	483	41
1884	478	42
1898	500	42
1910	470	38

trative posts had a similar objective. During the restoration the modern and scientific element in teaching programmes was further reduced to the advantage of Latin and Rhetoric, and Catholic influence within the *Université* strengthened, but its basic structures and objectives were untouched. Indeed, after a brief interval, entry into the *petits seminaires* was again restricted (16 June 1820).

The July Monarchy was less sympathetic towards the church which as a result attempted to build an independent system of secondary instruction. An organized campaign in favour of the 'freedom of education' developed in the 1840s to which some concessions were made by the *loi Falloux* in 1850. In the wake of another revolution even former opponents of the church like Thiers were prepared to concede a larger role to it. The law stipulated that any man over 25 with the *baccalauréat* and five years' teaching experience was entitled to open a secondary school and that municipalities could turn over their *collèges* to private associations while continuing to subsidize them. Moreover, *petits seminaires* were again allowed to take in day boys who did not intend to become priests. This was particularly significant in religious regions like Flanders, where a substantial demand for a Catholic education existed. The number of boys attending *lycées* and municipal *collèges* significantly declined. In the Gard the *lycée* at Nîmes had 423 pupils in 1843 but only 311 in 1853, while the number of pupils attending the school directed by the Assumptionist Order rose from forty to 202.[50] This extension of Catholic secondary education was inevitably limited, however, by the shortage of suitably qualified teachers. The 1850 law also sought to decentralize the administration of education. A *Conseil supérieur de l'instruction publique* was established together with departmental academic academies whose rectors were to be closely supervised by a council of *notables*. This reform was, however, short-lived. Centralized control was reintroduced in 1854 by a regime which clearly felt that the education of the future élites was too important a matter to be left to local initiative, and that a shared educational experience was essential to the political cohesion of the governing class. In the 1860s, therefore, efforts were made to prevent unauthorized orders (particularly the Jesuits) from opening schools, and expenditure on secondary schools was increased. By 1875 there were seventy-seven *lycées* and 251 municipal *collèges* compared with 935 private schools, of which 278 were directed by ecclesiastics. Of the 65,668 pupils attending state schools, 32,630 attended the more prestigious and expensive *lycées* and 33,038 local *collèges*; 43,009 attended lay private

Table 66 *Attendance at secondary schools in 1842*[49]

Type of school	Number of schools	Number of pupils
Lycées	46	18,697
Municipal *collèges*	312	26,584
Private schools	1016	43,195
Petits seminaires	127	*c.* 20,000

schools and 34,897 ecclesiastical schools, with in addition 23,000 pupils at *petits seminaires*. The trend now, however, was for a growing number and proportion of pupils to attend state rather than private schools. Their numbers increased from 59,764 in 1861 to 71,594 by 1868. This would be reversed temporarily in the 1870s, but the main effect of the Catholic reaction then was to stimulate a more intense anti-clericalism, leading to the expulsion of unauthorized congregations in 1880, but which many Catholic schools were able to survive by means of a variety of legal fictions. By 1914, even so, there were 119 *lycées* together with 220 *collèges communaux*.[51]

Attendance

Who actually attended these institutions of secondary education? Clearly those who could afford to pay the fees and manage without the earnings of their children, and those who saw some advantage for their children or for the entire family group, through enhanced career prospects and social status. In 1842 about 1.2 per cent of children aged between 8 and 17 were in receipt of some form (public or private) of secondary education (*c*. 1.5 per cent if the *petits seminaires* are included). The proportion of the age group attending rose slowly to 1.7 per cent in 1854, 2.2 per cent in 1868, 2.4 per cent in 1876 and 1887, and 2.5 per cent in 1898. The primary schools provided no preparation for and no access to secondary education. Children intended for the latter attended the preparatory classes associated with particular secondary schools. High tuition fees were a major discriminatory factor, which reinforced the feeling among the poor, in the unlikely event of them considering the possibility, that secondary education was irrelevant to their lives. In 1864 the cost of tuition in secondary schools varied between 50 and 100 francs per annum for day pupils, but where residence was necessary (and at this time the limited number of schools ensured that many pupils were boarders – 60 per cent in *lycées*), the cost was 650–740 francs. Financial assistance was provided in only a few cases. In the *lycées* and royal *collèges* the proportion of students in receipt of *bourses* fell from 43 per cent in 1810 to 16.6 per cent in 1830, 11 per cent in 1850, 7 per cent in 1880, rising to only 10 per cent in 1890. The proportion in communal *collèges* was 0.5 per cent in 1830 and 4.1 per cent in 1882. Moreover, these were awarded not on intellectual merit, but mainly to the sons of army officers and government officials (60 per cent of the total in 1890).[52]

In the 1860s something like 2 per cent of secondary school pupils were the sons of unskilled rural or urban workers. The lower middle classes were more likely to be attracted. Around one-third of pupils were the sons of well-off peasants, artisans and shopkeepers. In absolute terms, however, this apparent democratization was not very significant. Only a minute proportion of these particular social groups attended. This did little to alter the fundamentally élitist character of secondary education, and even in the 1900s discussions of reform brought forward very few proponents of radical change (Table 67).

Table 67 *Occupations of the fathers of secondary school pupils (in percentage terms) in 1865*[53]

Professionals	18.6
Landowners	17.0
Businessmen	13.1
Civil servants	11.3
Peasant farmers	12.3
Petit bourgeois	27.7 (shopkeepers made up 14.3, artisans 6.1)
Size of sample	12,603

Many of those who enrolled did not complete their secondary studies, either because their families had never intended that they should stay the whole course because of its lack of practical utility, or else because they failed the *baccalauréat* (39–46 per cent did in the years 1840–1900), although the numbers passing gradually rose from 3068 in 1820 to 7225 in 1909 (from 1 to 2.4 per cent of 19-year-old males), largely due to an increase in the number of science *bacheliers* from 119 in 1850 to 2570 in 1909.[54] The virtues of a secondary education were most clearly obvious to government officials, members of the liberal professions and the more successful businessmen and landowners – all concerned to provide their sons with careers which would help them to preserve their social status. The *baccalauréat* was the essential means of entry into the professions and higher administration, although not necessarily into the business élites. Not surprisingly the proportions of children entering the secondary schools tended to be highest in the major urban centres with their complex of economic, commercial and administrative activities, with the social élites preferring the *lycées* (particularly those of Paris) or the more prestigious Catholic *collèges*, while the municipal *collèges* tended to be the preserve of the middle and lower middle classes.

The public provision of secondary education for girls developed much more slowly than for boys. The field was initially left open to the religious orders and to private *pensionnats* which offered not only the facilities for study, but also for close supervision of young bourgeois ladies. There are no national statistics dealing with these, but, for example, in the department of the Seine in 1846 there were 246 *pensionnats* and lay boarding schools with 13,487 pupils and twenty-eight convents with 1600 pupils.[55] Subsequently efforts were to be made to improve the education of the bourgeoise as a means of reducing what was conceived to be an intellectual divorce between men and women and in order to make the latter more fitting companions for their husbands. Duruy's *cours secondaires*, however, met with sustained conservative and clerical opposition, and were short-lived. Only the republican decision in 1880 to provide full-scale secondary education for girls, the establishment of an *école normale* at Sèvres in 1881 to train teachers, together with the concurrent expansion of employment opportunities for middle-class girls in offices and teaching radically transformed the situation. Starting with only 300 pupils in 1880, by 1913 the *lycées* and *collèges* had 19,700 pupils, while a further 37,800 attended the much less advanced *écoles primaires supérieures* where they received an education which was increasingly similar to that given to boys.[56]

To what did secondary education lead? Although patterns of opportunity reflected regional economic and social structures, individual ambition was essentially determined by family culture and aspirations. Thus the sons of the traditional upper classes – landowners, officials, liberal professions – together with those of the new commercial and industrial classes were drawn towards training in the law as a means of entry not only into the legal profession but also into government service. Less prestigious (and less crowded) professions like medicine tended to attract those with a slightly lower social status. Social and economic change forced many families previously dependent upon *rentes* or the income from land to use the educational system to secure access for their sons to the *grandes écoles* and to well rewarded and respectable careers. Successful businessmen used the same means to reinforce the status of their families. These processes facilitated horizontal rather than vertical mobility. Children with a lower middle-class or well-off peasant background tended to have more limited ambitions (remaining in the family business, obtaining minor government posts, or those in medicine, teaching, etc.). Only a very small minority possessed the intellectual ability and the will to strive for something more. Even so, during the first half of the century an over-supply of professional men caused discontent among those whose aspirations were disappointed. This was subsequently reduced through the expansion of opportunities in private enterprise and government service. The social élite both protected its exclusiveness by limiting access to secondary education and renewed itself (necessarily for both demographic and socio-economic reasons) by a limited process of assimilation. The result was to severely restrict changes in the existing social structure.

Secondary school teachers

By 1842, 3744 teachers were employed in the public system of *lycées* and *collèges*. Judging by their social origins this was one means of securing upward social mobility (Table 68). A small minority, due to their social origins and intellect, were able to move on and achieve positions of eminence. Guizot and Victor Cousin are good examples. Most were socially insecure and culturally conservative. They were poorly paid in comparison with other professional men, and their choice of marriage partners indicates that they were not regarded as a good catch by bourgeois families. Conditions were at their best in the major Parisian *lycées* and there was always considerable competition for such prestigious posts. Success depended upon cultivating the good opinion of superiors and people with influence.

By the 1900s the numbers and status of secondary teachers had grown as part of the general development of education. There were around 5000 *lycée* teachers

Table 68   *Social origins for public secondary school teachers*[57]

	1842	1842–52	1877
Landowners and liberal professions	13.2	15	11.5
Merchants, *employés*	12.2	15	16.5
Farmers	16.4	10	13
Artisans	26.4	25	15
Soldiers	4	8.6	6
Officials	3	6.4	10
Teachers	6.8	18	27.5

with a further 4000 in *collèges*, and they included some 1900 women. The profession was still a means of social promotion. 75 per cent of their fathers had received no secondary education themselves, 56.4 per cent were of lower middle-class origin, 9.5 per cent working class, 17.4 per cent peasant. Only 14 per cent had a solid middle bourgeois background.[58] The greater status they enjoyed can be seen in the more active roles they performed in provincial society, through local learned societies and political committees. The quality of the education they provided, however, varied considerably. It was frequently poor in the small provincial *collèges*, which attracted the least well qualified and ambitious staff, were poorly equipped, and where individual initiative was discouraged. If a better education was usually offered in a *lycée*, there was still growing criticism of teaching methods which demanded an effort of memory rather than a critical understanding and of the growing dominance of preparation for examination throughout the entire syllabus.

The syllabus

Although one should not exaggerate the homogeneity of a system which included both public and private institutions, as well as great Parisian *lycées* and poorly staffed, small town *collèges*, the basic classical syllabus which dominated all forms of secondary education for most of the century was an inheritance from the Jesuit and Oratorian colleges of the Ancien Régime. Its survival represented the widespread attraction of an élitist culture and the strength of opposition to enlarging the place within the curriculum occupied by more 'modern' subjects. It was argued on pedagogical grounds that the classics were the best way to cultivate a pupil's reasoning ability and quickness of mind, and his ability to express himself clearly in both written and oral forms. Even if Latin was often learned by rote without much reflection, it was believed to add quality to thought and elevation of style to the vernacular. Furthermore, reading the great classical writers was seen as a means of cultivating the moral senses. The greatest strength of the traditional education was assumed to be its *vertu formatrice*. It moulded the *honnête homme*, capable of entering bourgeois society and of feeling at ease in it. From Latin men went on to law and from rhetoric to polite salon discussion and public speaking. In a very real sense, secondary education was designed to prepare the future *notable* for his professional and public life. Less explicit was the concern that a diminution in the classical content of education would attract socially undesirable elements into the schools and add to the 'excess of educated men' which it was believed existed. For these reasons, the syllabus of 25 August 1840 announced by Victor Cousin as Minister of Public Instruction in Thier's ministry reinforced the position of the classics. Between the ages of 11 and 16 Latin was to dominate the curriculum, together with some French, Greek, history, geography and philosophy between the ages of 13 and 15. The study of mathematics and sciences was largely postponed until the ages of 17 and 18, by which time many students had already left school. This was an act of consolidation on the part of the ruling élite, an attempt to maintain its cultural homogeneity and an effort to ensure social stability. According to the Marquis de Belbeuf, in a prize-giving speech at the Rouen *lycée* in 1866, 'in a country where the political edifice rests on universal suffrage . . . power is reserved to those who a strong classical education has raised above their fellow men'. This outlook was not without appeal to prospective newcomers to the élite. Many members of the developing middle classes continued to look for personal satisfaction and social status on the basis of essentially pre-industrial values. They wanted their sons to be provided with the forms of education which marked the gentleman, rather than the vocational instruction suitable for such socially inferior activities as commerce. Thus for most of the century there was only a limited demand for specialized skills, particulary since the traditional classical education served as the means of entry into the administration, professions, and the *grandes écoles*. The whole system was, in fact, increasingly geared to prepare students for success in the examinations which were the means of entry into these professions and institutions, rather than towards economic activity.

This was as true of the Catholic as of the public schools. Catholics throughout the century made great efforts to establish, extend and latterly to preserve an independent system of secondary schools. A major campaign was mounted with this intention from 1843, with teachers in the *lycées* attacked in one pamphlet because they were 'philosophers, deists, disciples and adversaries of the revolution, Jews, Protestants, renegade and faithful Catholics all mixed together and enjoying the same status'. Substantial concessions were made to Catholic pressures in 1850 by the *loi Falloux*, with the result that during the 1850s Catholic schools expanded rapidly, especially in the Paris basin, in the Nord, Pas-de-Calais, and Somme, in Brittany, the south-west, the Rhône valley and Massif Central, before the situation stabilized with their share of pupils reaching around 24 per cent in 1865. The *Université* was, however, through its continuing control over the *baccalauréat* and other state examinations, able to maintain considerable indirect control over what was taught in private schools.

The status and quality of education offered in these Catholic schools inevitably varied. At one end of the spectrum there were schools like the Jesuit *collège* at Brugelette (in Belgium) or the Assumptionist *collège* at Nîmes, which catered for the social exclusivism of the traditional élites and for those who imitated them like the rich textile *patronat* of the Nord. These maintained their exclusiveness by charging high fees. At the other end of the spectrum were the *petits seminaires* which offered a relatively cheap education to a mainly lower middle-class and well-off peasant clientele. In general, Catholic secondary schools, while appealing to a genuine desire for religious instruction and close moral supervision (involving frequently an obsessive anxiety about sexuality), cultivated a certain *snobisme* among the socially ambitious. They enjoyed sufficient success to cause considerable and growing anxiety from the late 1850s among officials of the *Université* aware that the sons of many state officials who were likely themselves to become bureaucrats or army officers were being educated by clerical teachers hostile to the empire. In the 1880s the animosity of the governing republicans towards these schools was all the greater. The increasingly bitter debate which developed was not about whether secondary education should be élitist. Both sides agreed that it ought to be. It was to some extent about the composition of the élite, but more particularly about the sort of education this élite should enjoy.

In practice, the secondary schools helped to perpetuate traditional values and attitudes. Proposals for curriculum reform met with strong resistance on both pedagogical and ideological grounds. The preservation of the existing social system appeared to be a matter of crucial significance to most members of the social élite. The syllabus was, nevertheless, subject to growing criticism. Anxiety was expressed about the lack of scientific education before the age of 17. The developing economy needed better-trained personnel. As early as 1829 Vatimesnil had authorized 'preparatory courses for the industrial and commercial professions', but in 1842 these were being taken by only 1191 pupils and in the municipal *collèges* rather than in the *lycées*. It was also felt that too many young men were being prepared for the liberal professions. 1848 revealed the danger apparently posed by unemployed intellectuals. Thus, in 1852 *bifurcation* was introduced, so that at the age of 14 pupils were able to choose between a literary or scientific *baccalauréat*. The latter, however, had little appeal to families conditioned to believe that the traditional classical training ensured social status and was suppressed in 1864. Significantly, during the Second Empire it was evident that even successful businessmen among, for example, the Mulhouse textile *patronat* were anxious to secure a classical in place of a technical education for their children in order to reinforce their status. It also took time to overcome the innate conservatism of educational administrators and teachers. Duruy's less ambitious *enseignement spécial*, introduced in 1865, enjoyed greater success. It provided for a four year programme based on French, modern languages, history and geography (of France, rather than of ancient Rome) and the applied sciences, intended according to an official circular, for the sons of the 'merchant, industrialist or farmer'. It catered for those with more limited social ambitions. It was successful in part because it was modern and promised to be more prestigious than a technically orientated education (laboratories, anyway, hardly existed). In practical terms it gave access to the lower ranks of the administration, and to such professions as primary teaching and to courses for veterinary surgeons and pharmacists. By 1876, 22,708 pupils were enrolled. Efforts were subsequently made to increase its appeal, in part by increasing its literary and philosophical content. In 1891 it finally achieved full *baccalauréat* status as 'modern education'. As a result, whereas between 1865 and 1880, 68 per cent of secondary pupils had taken classical courses and 32 per cent modern, by 1899 parity had been achieved.[59] However, nothing had occurred to alter the élitist character of secondary education.

Higher education

Until the 1880s only the prestigious *grandes écoles* including the *Ecole Polytechnique*, *Ecole des mines*, *Ecole des ponts et chaussées*, the *Ecole normale* and the military schools together with the faculties of law and medicine actually had students; those of science and letters functioned essentially to administer the *baccalauréat*, and to provide public lectures, although the foundation of the *Ecole pratique des hautes études* in 1868, to encourage research, was one sign of changing attitudes (Table 69). Subsequently, following defeat by Germany in 1870, the introduction of university courses in the arts and sciences was promoted by republican governments anxious to improve the intellectual capacity of the élite and influenced by academics belonging to the *Société pour l'étude des questions d'eneignement supérieur*, which included such influential public figures as the historians Lavisse and Monod, jurists like Boutmy (the founder of the *Ecole libre des sciences politiques*), and scientists like Pasteur and Berthelot. At the same time the facilities for medical and legal training were improved and adequate buildings provided in Paris, Lille, Lyon and Bordeaux. The law of 10 July 1896 created fifteen universities (one per academy), although the number of university teachers remained small – rising from 503 in 1880 to 1048 in 1909[60] – as did the number of students. This reflected the limited demand for a university-trained personnel, and the very obvious fact that if secondary education was élitist then that obtained at university was inevitably much more so.

Table 69   *University students (by faculties)*

Year	Law	Science	Letters	Medicine	Pharmacy	Total	No. of whom were women
1866–70	5,200	—	—	4,322		9,552	
1888	5,152	1,335	2,358	8,658		17,503	
1900–1	10,152	3,910	3,723	8,627	3,347	29,759	942
1910–11	17,292	6,096	6,237	9,933	1,632	41,190	3,954

Nevertheless, this period saw the creation of the modern university with its faculty engaged in the interdependent activities of teaching and research. The initial stimulus during the Second Empire was a growing belief in governmental, and to a lesser degree entrepreneurial, circles in science as the essential means of modernization. This resulted in the commitment of resources in order to avoid falling behind in the international 'science race'. Military failure added to the sense of urgency, although rapid expansion, the growing complexity and expense of scientific research, and the establishment of specialized research institutes, inevitably raised problems of funding, and only in 1901 did the state accept a permanent commitment and transfer part of its profits from the lucrative betting monopoly into scientific research.

A constant of government policy throughout these years was an obsession with applied research. The universities and research institutes were frequently criticized for an excessive interest in pure research. However, fruitful collaboration did develop, most notably between the faculties of science of Paris, Lille, Nancy and later Grenoble, and regional industry and agriculture, and indeed for university researchers this was a vital means of attracting both local funding and students. The major failing appears to have been that of businessmen, who, save in the newest industries in which scientists had a creative role from the beginning, such as chemicals and electricity, either lacked the resources or were simply unwilling to invest in research and development.

Significance of the development of education

Linguistic change

The development of school networks had complex effects on attitudes and social relationships. Some of these have already been considered, but attention needs to be given to changes in linguistic usage, and the interrelationships between increased literacy and the development of the mass media. According to the inquiry conducted by the Abbé Grégoire at the end of the eighteenth century, French was spoken exclusively in fifteen departments and by some 3 million people; over 16 million others were bilingual, although of these 6 million could not speak French properly; while some 6 million people were entirely unable to speak French. The national language was dominant in most towns, but the situation was very different in the countryside. The inquiry revealed that France played host to seven linguistic groups. The major two were French in the north and *occitan* in the south, but in addition Flemish was spoken in the north, Breton in the west, Basque in the south-west, Catalan in the south-east, and German in the east, together with some thirty different *patois* (defined by Grégoire as degenerate forms of French). For a complex of reasons, the use of French became far more common over the next century, although the statistics remained little more than rough estimates. An official inquiry in 1863 revealed that of 4,018,427 school children, 448,328 (11 per cent) spoke no

French, and a further 1,490,269 (37 per cent) while able to speak and understand some French, could not write it.[61] This lack of French was, of course, much more common in the older age-groups.

The spread of the language was already a centuries' old process. To a large degree it reflected the political dominance of the north. Thus, its use was required for official business by the Ordonnance of Villers-Cotterèts in 1539. More generally diffusion occurred from town to country and along the main routes, as part of a process of economic and political integration; and down the social hierarchy as part of a process of administrative and political integration and of cultural imitation. As Grégoire's inquiry makes clear, political imperatives during the revolution awakened considerable interest in the language issue. In 1791 Talleyrand had condemned the 'mass of corrupted dialects, the last remains of feudalism'. Minority languages were criticized as both uncivilized and as counter-revolutionary. The spread of French was insisted upon in the interests of equality and national unity. The 'linguistic terrorism' which ensued was, however, less effective in spreading the use of French than the movements of people caused by the wars of the period. This combination of factors stimulated a growing sense of being French and a desire to speak the national language. Nevertheless, the use of French spread only gradually until it became possible to use the developing school network to forward this *mission civilisatrice*. Salvandy, in a ministerial circular to *instituteurs* in 1838, insisted on the need to 'purge all pronunciations and languages which recall times when the same education and the same language were not common to all Frenchmen'. Even then progress was initially slow because, except in Flanders and Alsace where major European languages were in use and the spoken language supported by a written culture, it took time to attract the non-French speakers to school. Even when this happened, teachers either found it difficult to communicate with them (and pedagogical texts assumed a knowledge of French) or else were forced to make compromises, and if they were able and did not find it beneath their dignity, to employ dialect in the classroom themselves. During the Second Empire the campaign against minority languages became more intense. In Alsace, even German, which had escaped the ban on the use of dialect, was reduced to 35 minutes a day by the 1853 regulations. This was the essential means, according to the academic rector, of 'completing Louis XIV's conquest'. In order to achieve such objectives, coercion was frequently employed against children who used the wrong language at school. They were forced to wear a token, such as a *sabot* in Brittany, around their necks until they could report another child for failing to speak French. Every effort was employed to persuade children, and through them their parents, that speaking in Breton was a sign of ignorance. Indeed, Pierre-Jakez Hélias remembers how Breton speakers were regarded as simpletons by officials and town dwellers. It was pointed out that French was not only superior in itself, but potentially far more useful. Increasingly children throughout the country, provided with more or less standardized lessons, came to accept common values, a shared sense of identity – heightened in the case of men by the experience of military service. There were few attempts to resist the spread of French and these were centred essentially on the clergy, for some of whom local languages were a means of resistance to modern ideas. According to the priest of Plénée-Jugon (Côtes-du-Nord) in 1868, a 'language is the expression of the human soul, and the human soul is the image of God'. In Lorraine, where German speakers were only a small minority, as in the Meurthe, the church co-operated in the imposition of French. In contrast in Moselle, because German speakers were more numerous, it was felt that similar actions would isolate the clergy from their flocks and obstruct the presentation of the Christian message. Similarly, and in spite of long-standing official pressure the catechism was still taught in Flemish in forty-three northern communes of the Nord in 1900.[62]

The real strength of the various languages and dialects was that they expressed the needs of everyday life within the family, the community and the church – something personal and local – and expressed a strong sense of identity which the increased use of French would gravely weaken. They survived for as long as they were useful as means of communication, and in social situations in which the use of French – the language of the schoolroom and officialdom – would have appeared unnatural. This resistance lasted longest where the local language was genuinely distinct from the *langue d'oil* forms of French, and where isolation limited the occasions for using French. It helped to preserve a genuinely independent and dynamic peasant culture in the Breton interior and upland areas of the Massif Central, for example, throughout the century. The decisive moment of decline can often be linked to the traumatic experience of 1914–18. In these areas, at the risk of over-simplification, the old language declined first in the towns, then in the *bourgs* – the rural marketing centres – and finally in the surrounding countryside. It survived in daily use longest among the poor, the older generations and women, i.e. those least influenced by schooling.

However, the *rapprochement* between dialect and national French and the decline of other languages was not due simply to the development of better communications and of schooling, but to an increasing desire among the older generations, as links with the national society intensified, that their children acquire French as a source of status and as a possible means of promotion. As Pierre-Jakez Hélias was told by his grandfather, 'With French you can go everywhere. With only Breton you are tied on a short rope, like a cow to her post. You have to graze around your tether. And the meadow grass is never plentiful.' Gradually the balance between French and non-French speakers changed within communities. In Bourgogne this appears to have occurred from the 1830s; in the Toulouse area, *occitan* remained in general use even in the towns until the 1830s, although most of the population were able at least to understand French. By the mid 1850s French had become the usual language of the towns, but not of the surrounding countryside. Normally this process involved a bilingual stage in which first the local language and then French assumed primacy. During this stage the vocabulary of the former was impoverished (becoming pidginized) as more and more words were borrowed from French. At the same time French came to be spoken and written with increasing fluency.

By the last third of the century the use of the local language was increasingly restricted to private, 'unimportant' situations. Increasingly, too, a generation gap developed. Parents often felt obliged to avoid speaking *patois* in front of their children and adopted a passive, disparaging, self-demeaning attitude towards their own language and culture. In these various stages the lead was usually given by the wealthier, better educated social groups in the community; those whose business and official responsibilities associated them with the world outside and for whom knowledge of French was essential. French became the language of the *messieurs* whose social domination was increased by their role as linguistic intermediaries between the community and the exterior. Thus language denoted status. Gradually they refused to speak anything but French. The Lille bourgeoisie abandoned Picard *patois* from the early nineteenth century. As the number of French speakers increased they sought to preserve their superior status through grammatical correctness and the ability to 'turn a phrase'. The loss of élite support meant that languages like Breton and Provençal ceased to be written, and their oral forms became debased. Efforts by groups of poets and intellectuals, like the Félibrige movement in Provence who from 1854 attempted to revive and purify the language and to recreate its literature – to establish standard grammatical forms – had little success. The purified language was incomprehensible to the masses and they preferred to learn to read and write in French.

The acquisition of a language involves a complex of cultural references and means of perception. The spread of the French language was a key means of socio-cultural integration, whereas *patois* had served as a source of identity and unity for particular communities, but a cause of isolation from the outside. Acquiring literacy in French had other important consequences. With the exceptions of Flemish and German speaking areas, most non-French speaking departments had relatively high illiteracy rates due to the concordance of poverty, their local cultures and resistance to French cultural influences. The lack of a literate culture had significant socio-psychological consequences. It seems to have made it difficult to express logical relationships and complicated explanations. Ideas appear to have been accumulated in empirical fashion, facts and rumours undifferentiated. The abnormal was particularly difficult to absorb, given the lack of points of reference. The difficulty of abstraction was only partly compensated for by a vocabulary rich in words useful in particular situations, as, for example, for various type of tools, of soils and climatic conditions. The importance of gesticulation frequently revealed the limits of verbal expression. Emotions and especially anger tended to be revealed more often physically then than now. This was true even in Paris as late as the 1840s, as the French of the masses was increasingly corrupted by the *patois* of migrants and a peculiar *argot* developed. The extension of literacy through the schools was thus the crucial means by which information would be distributed and assimilated and the dominant influence of social and political élites more fully asserted.

Development of the mass media

Traditional popular literature had been didactic and moralizing, inculcating basic religious ideas, notions of correct behaviour and respect for established social hierarchies. Lives of the saints, legends and tales of chivalry illustrated the virtues of justice, loyalty and courage. Other works catered for a growing interest in history and public events through romantic and mythical accounts of the lives of great figures like Napoleon and descriptions of such events as the conquest of Algiers in 1830. These little books and almanacs produced for a predominantly illiterate audience in Breton, langue d'oc, or Catalan, as well as French – were organized in short chapters, to be read slowly and aloud at gatherings such as the *veillée*, by people who had received only a basic elementary education. They were badly printed, on poor quality paper and cost very little. They were supplemented, particularly from the 1830s, by popular prints, of which some 17 million are estimated to have appeared during the Second Empire alone. Published in most regional centres and especially in Paris, Rouen, Limoges, Troyes, Epinal and Tours, books and prints were distributed throughout the countryside by pedlars. The eventual decline in their popularity, first in the towns, and much more slowly in the countryside – the publication of almanacs in Limoges, for example, went through a last surge of prosperity in the late 1870s – reflected changes in taste due to a higher standard of education and the availability of better produced, modern newspapers and books.

Before the 1860s newspapers had been reserved essentially to the well-off bourgeois – by their cost, style and contents – although as the authorities frequently complained, especially in the aftermath of the 1848 Revolution, the poorer members of the community had access to the press in cafés. The development of a more modern mass media was linked to a complex of factors, including technical developments such as the introduction of the rotary press and of distribution by rail, cultural factors, and especially the advance of literacy and changes in public taste, political decisions to relax the controls over publishing, socio-economic factors which resulted in changes in real income and in purchasing power (see Table 70), and the efforts of the newspaper owners themselves to attract readers by means of a simplified and standardized literary style, serials, illustrations and sensationalist stories. This was an evolution which began with Emile de Girardin's *La Presse* in 1836 – a serious political paper which sought to enlarge its revenue by means of a relatively low cost and large circulation and through advertising, and which advanced another stage with the appearance of Polydor Milaud's *Petit Journal* in 1863. This sold at 5 centimes and attracted a mass public by providing political news, but primarily because it provided a form of escapism in a similar way to the traditional popular literature. At the end of 1869 its circulation was substantially increased (to 467,000) by its journalists' exploitation of the notorious murders at Pantin. Crime, tragedy and 'human interest' stories sold newspapers.

By the 1860s, the cheap press was destroying the pedlars' trade, first in the towns, and more gradually in the countryside. It took time for newspaper

Table 70   *Declining real cost of Parisian newspapers for labourers in the provinces (Index 100 = 1910)*[63]

1795	821	1851	288
1834	576	1871	224
1836	281	1889	131
		1910	100

reading to become a regular habit. Nevertheless, the progressive relaxation of the censorship laws, temporarily in 1848 and then more permanently in 1868 and 1881, together with the major political events of the period, increased the number of newspapers and their circulation. By July 1880 the sixty Parisian dailies had a combined circulation of 1,947,000, of which 583,000 was accounted for by the *Petit Journal*. By 1910 the number of newspapers published in the capital had risen to seventy with a circulation of 4,937,000, of which the largest (1,400,000) was accounted for by the *Petit Parisien*. The 'quality' press by then accounted for at most one-third of total circulation. An audience also developed for provincial newspapers. The numbers published increased from the 1820s, although on a small-scale in many country towns. Circulation was slow to develop. Thus in Corrèze as late as 1865, only around 3000 daily newspapers were sold, which represented only about 9 per 1000 inhabitants. This provincial press really came into its own with the development of mass circulation dailies from the 1870s. Newspapers like the *Progrès* of Lyon or the *Dépêche* of Toulouse, typically published in the major regional capitals, were normally the only newspapers with which even the small minority of regular rural newspaper readers had any contact, although of course this minority was significant beyond its numbers in influencing public opinion. The circulation of provincial dailies appears to have reached 250,000 by 1868, 500,000 by 1875, 1 million by 1885 and 4 million by 1914, out of a total daily press circulation which rose from 1.5 to 12.5 million between 1875 and 1914.[64] Whereas initially the provincial press obtained its national and international news by means of reprinting articles from the Parisian press, from the 1850s use of the telegraph and of news agencies (especially Havas), allowed them to be as up to date.

Another feature of the period was the development of more specialized periodicals to supplement the old-established literary journals like the *Revue des Deux Mondes* (1829) and fashion journals for bourgeois women like *La Mode* (1829, 9500 subscribers in 1858). These were both influential and commercially successful, but had been directed at a limited market. Efforts were subsequently made to appeal to both wider numbers and a variety of specialized audiences by means, for example, of Emile de Girardin's didactic *Journal des Connaissances Utiles* (1832), illustrated magazines like *L'Illustration* (1843), religious weeklies like the Assumptionist fathers' *Le Pelerin*, collections of popular stories, such as *Lectures pour tous* and *Les Veillées des Chaumières*, and by the turn of the century the sporting press, for example *L'Auto*.

In spite of reductions in printing costs which led to a fall in the cost of books in 18° format from 7–9f at the beginning of the century, to 3f50 in 1838 and 0.90–1f in the 1890s, books remained luxuries for most of the population, even when their schooling had left them with the inclination to read, and they had the time and the energy. The growth of the middle classes and of skilled labour, however, ensured that from around mid century a large readership existed for the novels of Georges Sand, Erckmann-Chatrian and especially Eugene Sue's *Mystères de Paris* (1843) and *Juif Errant* (1844–5). In many respects the latter replicated the traditional popular culture – Rudolphe in the *Mystères* stood as the redresser of wrong and the symbol of good. Publication in serial form – at about 20 centimes each episode – both spread the cost and built up an audience. Distribution circuits were also improved, although outside the major cities shops selling books had little to offer. Efforts were also made, especially by Catholic publishing houses (such as Editions Mame at Tours), to produce cheap, moralizing works particularly for the young. The most successful of these series was Hachette's (founded in 1840) *Bibliothèque Rose*, which included the Comtesse de Ségur's best-selling novels (the first edition of *Les Malheurs de Sophie* sold 680,880 copies). The best of these captured the imagination of children by introducing them to a world not their own. They also successfully inculcated the values of a bourgeois society. Jules Verne's success was equally due to his creation of *un univers d'évasion*. The appearance of such works reflected the widespread desire among educationalists and politicians to ensure that the newly literate were provided with morally and politically safe reading material, an attitude seen also in the movement to develop or establish libraries stocked with carefully selected books.

The press, and particularly the newspaper press, played a major role in influencing public opinion, providing information and subjects for debate – but of course on an extremely selective basis. Newspapers with identifiable political views normally preached to the converted. These 'serious' objectives were, moreover, fulfilled primarily by the relatively expensive and linguistically complicated newspapers designed for a well-educated readership. Newspapers critical of the existing social system were, especially before 1881, frequently subject to prosecution. Subsequently, in competition with the new mass media they had little popular appeal. Most members of the lower middle classes, workers and peasants, if they read newspapers at all, wanted to be entertained. The free market proved more effective than government repression in restricting the influence of the radical press. As a result the evolution of the press served to strengthen social and political conservatism. In addition it promoted social integration. The more rapid transmission of information about events, the descriptions of fashion and behaviour in the major cities, served to promote ideological, cultural and material imitation and growing cultural centralization. It promoted a closer sense of association between the members of diverse social groups, more effectively linked town and country, and accelerated the decline in the independence and dynamism of traditional popular culture.

Conclusions

Education was clearly far more than a means of transmitting literacy, skills and knowledge. In the process it also diffused political and social ideologies which served as an effective means of social integration and facilitated the imposition of the values of the dominant social groups upon the rest of society. This is not to deny that these values were adapted to the situation of each social group, that a tension existed between local values and those imposed from above, or even that counter-cultures might develop in partial rejection of those diffused by educa-tion and the media. Historians have too often confused the aims of education with their fulfilment. School was, after all, only one influence among many in a child's life. Familial and peer group influences were other important factors, as also, although to a much less significant extent, were such institutions as the *Bourses du Travail* which attempted to encourage workers' self-education, and to create the orgnizational base for a more independent working-class culture. It does, however, appear that those institutions whose major function was to prepare the young to assume a subordinate position in the existing social system, enjoyed a considerable degree of success, and that institutions like the family or community which might have served as a means of resistance were themselves unable to escape from a growing sense of dependence upon the state. Thus a process of cultural integration, and of political centralization was achieved, and through it the domination of bourgeois language and modes of thought. Schooling introduced the young to the geography and history of France, and systematically inculcated a sense of belonging and the need for a patriotic response in times of crisis. According to Ernest Lavisse, whose *Histoire de France* provided a widely imitated model, 'if the pupil does not become a citizen aware of his duties and a soldier who loves his rifle, the teacher will have wasted his time'. The success of this process from the point of view of the dominant élites was revealed by the *Union sacrée* of 1914, surely proof of the existence of a fundamental cultural consensus.

9

In conclusion: state and society

This is a book about 'modernization' as a social process in nineteenth-century France. In it I have sought to examine the impact of a complex of changes upon the living standards, day-to-day experience and social relationships of the various groups which made up French society. Much of what happened over the course of the century was for the better, resulting in greater material prosperity, the reduction of physiological misery, and of insecurity, higher levels of literacy, the disappearance of traditional forms of protest and the provision of institutionalized means for expressing grievances. Nevertheless, in the shorter term the transition from a predominantly agricultural and rural society towards an urban–industrial system was not without its problems. These included most obviously the threat or reality of technological unemployment, and urban poverty. Initially and before migration was able to relieve the strain, social tensions in the countryside were also intensified by the combination of population pressure on resources and the expansion of commercialization, at the same time as the potential for conflict grew in the overcrowded cities. The threat to social order was at its most intense precisely during the period of transition towards an urban–industrial society and liberal–democratic political system.

In this situation the capacity of the various social groups to exercise power within the wider society depended upon their possession of scarce material resources which, on the one hand, gave them access to the leisure and culture necessary for active participation in politics and administration, and, on the other, through control of access to land, to credit, and to employment allowed them to influence members of other social groups. Moreover, there can be no doubt, given its varied responsibilities, that the state was a key social institution. An analysis of the way in which it functioned is essential for an understanding of the nature of authority and the exercise of power in society – of power in its various forms, including the ability to inflict punishment, to offer rewards and to instil values or beliefs. This chapter therefore will seek to answer such questions as, who ruled? In whose interests? How? And with what effect? It involves an inquiry into the nature of the French state in the nineteenth century.

Historically the French state was the product of a long evolution, but it was during the period of revolution and empire that the institutions of the modern centralized state were largely created. In its beginnings the revolution had involved a reaction against excessive centralization, but the exigencies of war and internal disorder soon forced a reversal and the creation of new state organizations. The restoration of the French monarchy in 1815 brought to an end a long period of revolution and war. The accession of Louis XVIII, by the Grace of God, King of France, appears to have been generally received with a sense of relief, above all for this reason. It promised to bring an end to conscription, heavy taxation, the destruction of trade, to unemployment and misery, to defeat and the presence of foreign armies. There was relatively little enthusiasm for the Bourbons, but in 1815 at least they meant the end of Napoléon. Moreover, Louis XVIII was realistic enough to accept the need for compromise in the political settlement which followed the restoration. The Constitutional Charter, which had been discussed with representatives of the Senate and Chamber in 1814, accepted many of the fundamental principles of 1789: liberty, equality, and rights of property. These were to be guaranteed by the independence of judges and the jury system, and by a two-chamber parliament – an Upper House composed of peers, initially named by the king but subsequently hereditary, together with a Chamber of Deputies to be elected by males over 30 years of age and paying 300 francs in direct taxation, for which only men over 40 and paying 1000 francs in tax were to be eligible. In 1817, 90,000 were able to vote and some 1652 were entitled to stand for election. It was the responsibility of the king to convoke the two chambers each year. He was given the power to dissolve an unsatisfactory Chamber of Deputies, but in this case was required to convoke a new one within three months. The charter in effect provided for a strong executive. Ministers were responsible to the king, whose person was declared to be sacred and inviolable. The monarch was to be commander of the armed forces, had the sole right to make war and peace, the right of appointment to all official positions and the responsibility for implementing laws through administrative orders.

The most significant constitutional restriction on royal power was the right of the chamber to refuse to sanction taxation. The desire to preserve strong government was thus combined with the recognition of the political rights of the wealthy – those with the independence, the leisure for meditation, and the vital stake in the country which was supposed to ensure both a sense of responsibility and moderation in political debate – and by the exclusion of the masses from political life. Prominent among this new political élite were many old noble families. Nobles had often sat out the revolution quietly at home. Others had been able, particularly in the west, centre and south, by a variety of means, to regain property confiscated when they had emigrated. Many of these were to share in an indemnity of 1 milliard francs in 1825. Among the 381 deputies elected in 1816, 176 were nobles. Enjoying royal patronage, they were to assume a prominent position in the higher administration and the church. The nobility thus continued, in spite of its losses during the revolution, to exercise substantial economic, social and political power. The electoral system, however, gave recognition not to the rights of the *noble* as such, but to those of the *notable* – a social category defined earlier by the constitutions of the Years VIII and X. Political rights then, as in 1815, were granted to the wealthy. The legal privileges of the nobility had been destroyed by the revolution, and were replaced by those accorded to men of wealth. In a predominantly rural society, the wealthy were by profession often administrators and lawyers, but primarily they were landowners. Prior to the revolution successful non-nobles had been able to secure social recognition through ennoblement. This was no longer necessary, but the character of the social and political élite was hardly changed. It was simply that men who would once have purchased ennobling office were now no longer required to do so. A more stable and increasingly self-confident bourgeoisie was in the making.

The largest category of bourgeois was that of landowners, particularly in the economically less developed regions, but even in major commercial centres like Rouen and Marseille the successful merchant or manufacturer invested much of his income in land. Business was only a temporary phase. The instability of the revolutionary and imperial period and the availability of confiscated church and émigré property for purchase had intensified this traditional practice. Paris was perhaps exceptional in possessing a more stable business class composed of successful bankers and major merchants. There, and among the textile manufacturers of the Nord and Haut-Rhin a new capitalist élite was being established. The legal establishment of a class of *notables* did not entirely destroy past distinctions. Old social tensions were made all the more bitter by the revolution, and in some regions – Brittany and the Midi in particular – by the personal and political vengeance exacted against former republicans or Bonapartists and against Protestants after the Hundred Days. This initial anarchy was followed by a more systematic purge of disloyal or insufficiently zealous elements from the administration and army, and by a substantial reduction in the size of the latter from its wartime establishment. Perhaps 50–80,000 officials (a third to a quarter of the total) were dismissed. Ordinary tribunals together with special courts prosecuted some 8000 individuals on essentially political charges. For some time restoration turned to counter-revolution, awakening fears about personal liberty and the security of possession of former *biens nationaux* and arousing doubts about the new regime's moderation and willingness to compromise. The social exclusiveness of many nobles and the favours accorded to them by the government contributed to the creation of suspicion and tensions which in the long run were roots of political instability.

The growth of a liberal opposition determined to ensure that ministers were responsible to parliament as well as to the king – reflecting an increasing lack of confidence in the royal government – led to a major constitutional crisis in 1830, and to an ill-judged move by Charles X and his ministers to reaffirm monarchical authority by means of ordinances limiting public rights of discussion and defining the electorate in a more restricted manner. The development of this and other crises was illustrative of two basic points: first, that subjects had certain (evolving) expectations of rulers. Continued recognition of the legitimacy of particular kings depended in large part on their ability to satisfy these expectations. Second, that the power of any ruler was diminished by the need to delegate to subordinates upon whose capacity and willingness to co-operate he depended. In the aftermath of the 1830 Revolution the leaders of the liberal parliamentary majority – Laffitte, Périer, Dupin, Bérard, Guizot, Constant, Thiers, Broglie, Lafayette, Sébastiani, Laborde and Delessert – anxious to avoid an interregnum which might allow the emergence of more radical forms of republican protest, or else a movement in the provinces in support of the deposed king, were also determined to prevent a re-establishment of royal absolutism. The charter was to become a right of the nation, not a gift of the crown; the possibility that the head of the government might again take advantage of emergency powers was strictly limited, and the responsibilities of parliament in such matters as the initiation of legislation (formerly reserved to the crown) greatly enlarged. In spite of efforts by the new king to maintain his authority, particularly in questions of foreign policy, there was a much greater awareness of its practical limits.

The changing conception of the nature of government can be seen from revised perceptions of the role of ministers. During the restoration and especially the reign of Charles X, ministers were seen essentially as servants of the king, functionaries rather than politicians, while during the July Monarchy, of sixty ministers, only four were not already members of parliament (twenty peers, thirty-six deputies) and the exceptions found it necessary to become parliamentarians at the first opportunity. An apparent contradiction of this trend was, however, the fact that thirty-six of these ministers were by profession state officials.[1] Office holders continued to dominate governments.

The extension of voting rights to men paying 200 francs in direct taxation had the effect of roughly doubling the electorate to *c.* 200,000 by 1840. The continued narrowness and conditional character of support for the July Monarchy was made clear, however, by the desertion of many of its erstwhile supporters and by the revolution of February 1848, following a period of intense economic and social crisis during which the image of the regime was further tarnished by electoral manipulation and accusations of corruption in high places. This revolution was succeeded by the introduction of universal male suffrage and an experiment in democratic government. Paradoxically, the social composition of the Constituent Assembly elected in April was not markedly different from the parliaments of the July Monarchy, and it proved to be particularly anxious to ensure strong government, especially in the aftermath of the Parisian insurrection in June. Its constitution provided for the election of a head of the executive with substantial powers and led in December to the successful candidature of Louis-Napoléon Bonaparte, a 'Prince–President', who soon revealed his determination to make maximum use of this authority. On 31 October 1849 a ministry composed of leading parliamentarians was replaced by a team clearly dependent upon Bonaparte – an affirmation of presidential government which can be seen as a major step towards the re-establishment of the empire.

The constitution of 14 January 1852, introducing a period of extraordinary and repressive government by decree following Louis-Napoléon's *coup d'état*, was based on that of the Year VIII with the vital addition of universal male suffrage, but with the practical significance of this limited by political censorship and repression. It required little amendment to serve as the constitution of the empire. In its essentials it provided for the responsibility of ministers (on an individual, not a collective, basis) to the president (in office for two years); and subsequently to the emperor, who alone might initiate laws; for a *Conseil d'Etat* (its forty to fifty members were senior state officials) to prepare and discuss proposals for legislation, which were then to be presented to a *Corps législatif* elected by universal male suffrage (but meeting for only some three months each year and convoked, adjourned and dissolved almost at will by the emperor), and a senate made up of members nominated for life (and richly endowed) by the emperor, which was to interpret the constitution and to be consulted in case of proposed changes. These assemblies were not constitutional checks on authoritarian government, but rather functional parts of that government. The only real power exercised by parliament was through the examination and vote of the budget and it was some years before it began to make use of this. The president was responsible not to parliament, but to the Sovereign People, which would exercise its rights by means of periodical plebiscites which only the president could call.

Increasingly, however, as their fear of revolution declined, it again became evident that government required the co-operation of traditional élites, and that concessions would have to be made to their elected representatives in the *Corps législatif* in order to secure this. Napoléon III, unlike his predecessors, was prepared to adapt his regime to changing political conditions. Nevertheless, while he appears to have always intended to liberalize the political system once the threat of social disorder had declined, Napoléon had not intended to return to a parliamentary regime, so that the constitutional amendments of the 1860s and the new constitution of 1870 while increasing the role of the *Corps législatif* in the formulation and discussion of legislation, preserved considerable prerogative powers for the emperor, particularly in the spheres of foreign policy and military affairs, and in the last resort his right to appeal to the people over the head of parliament through the plebiscitary process.

The military disasters of 1870 cut the empire short. Elections fought in an atmosphere of great anxiety, with resumption of the war a real possibility, led to the election of an assembly with a monarchist majority. Although the royalist factions could not agree on the details of another Bourbon restoration, they would at least accept the establishment of a politically repressive, conservative republic, committed to peace and order, objectives symbolized initially by the presence of Thiers as *Président du Conseil* and by the crushing of the Paris Commune. The constitution of 1875 established a parliamentary regime with the clear statement that 'ministers are collectively responsible to the Chambers'. After the use made of them by Louis-Napoléon, the executive powers of the presidency were severely limited. The president was to be elected by parliament in the hope that he would have very little authority against it. The right to appoint a prime minister gave him potential power, but President MacMahon's attempt in May 1877 to establish a government which did not have a parliamentary majority made the limits to this clear.

Until at least the late 1870s, whatever its constitutional character, the gov-

Table 71 *Professions of fathers of 320 ministers (1871–1914)*[2]

		Percentage in active male population (1851 census)	Percentage among ministers' fathers
Sector IA	Workers, farmers, clerks	78	6.5
Sector IB	Primary teachers, public officials, master artisans	10.4	9.7
Sector II	Property-owning petty bourgeoisie	5.2	10
Sector III	Professional bourgeoisie	1.8 (maximum)	37.8
Sector IV	Senior state officials	0.1 (maximum)	8.4
Sector V	Landowners	5.1	25.9

ernmental machine was dominated by landowners and *hautes fonctionnaires*, wealthy nobles and non-nobles, with smaller contingents of financiers and lawyers. Only subsequently, as a recent study of members of cabinets between 1870 and 1914 indicates (Table 71), did a gradual democratization of recruitment occur with two decisive moments of change. The first came in 1887 following the electoral success of the Opportunist Republicans, and the second in 1902 with the election victory of the radicals. Even then change was limited. The trend was for the sons of bourgeois professional families to replace those of large landowners and capitalistic entrepreneurs and for a marked professionalization of politics to occur. The former were less wealthy, but still very comfortably off – 42 per cent of them were involved in the legal professions (indicative of the advantages conferred by knowledge of the law, practice in public speaking, and the benefits of a legal career for political notoriety), and some were co-opted by major enterprises anxious to promote links with government (in the 1900s, for example, Paul Doumer and Joseph Caillaux). To some extent a shared culture and a commitment to private property provided an important unifying factor between groups III, IV, and V. Nevertheless, it is worth stressing the existence of a growing social gulf between the politically dominant group and the socio-economic élite, a development which had the advantage however of creating an illusion of social democratization which republican ministers sought to reinforce by the language of their appeals for justice and equality.

It was in this period, too, that the social origins of parliamentary deputies began to change – a slow democratization of political personnel occurred with an influx of *moyenne bourgeois* and especially members of the liberal professions to replace traditional notables and particularly landowners. Even so, parliament remained dominated by well-off bourgeois. In 1893 88 per cent were of *grande* or *moyenne bourgeois* origin. Only the radical electoral victory in 1902 brought a more substantial influx of lower middle-class personnel, reflecting the establishment of modern political parties and a mass politics, and even then there were barely thirty deputies with peasant or working-class origins. The great majority of deputies were property owners, many of them using politics not only as a means of access to political power but to find new opportunities to increase their incomes. They proved to be major barriers to economic and social change thoughout the Third Republic. Furthermore with the conservatism of the lower house was reinforced by that of a senate elected by representatives of the communes and thus designed to represent in particular rural interests. Senators were primarily retired deputies and civil servants, and consistently obstructed proposals for income tax, old-age pensions, the improvement of factory conditions, etc. Thus, in spite of the changing social characteristics of parliament and the fact that political power no longer coincided with economic power, the interests of the old social élite were safeguarded, along with those of the new political élite. This situation was reinforced by the recruitment of senior civil servants. Even in 1900 between two-thirds and three-quarters of a sample of 548 individuals at the head of various administrative hierarchies continued to be drawn from aristocratic or wealthy bourgeois families, and only 10.7 per cent from the lower middle and popular classes.[3] Marginal change had occurred since mid century, partly for political reasons, partly because of the sheer expansion of the civil service, but also because members of the old élites had been attracted towards more lucrative employment in private enterprise.

It should not simply be assumed that the state acted as an instrument of class domination. As we have seen, political divisions were frequently evident within the social and political élites and state agencies did not always act in a fashion which élite groups saw as favourable to their interests. Nevertheless, it does seem that the state usually acted in a broadly conservative manner in order to maintain 'order' and to preserve existing social and economic relationships. The social origins of ministers and senior civil servants alone would seem to confirm that the state could not have been politically or socially neutral.

Prior to 1848 political participation had been restricted to a relatively small group drawn mainly from among the social élite, which was able to make use of the state and its various agencies as a means of regulating social and political disputes. Then and later, politically dominant groups sought to establish the legitimacy of government policy, to negate critical actions and ideologies and to increase the capacity of the state for effective social management in order to avoid the need for coercion. To do so they insisted upon the universality of the 'rule of law' and 'law and order'. It should be borne in mind, however, that the state, because it was actively involved in social conflict, and of the social origins of its personnel, could not be seen as an impartial actor. As a last resort, the prospect of the employment of physical violence by state agencies served as a powerful deterrent to all those forms of behaviour, from crime to political protest, which might be seen as a threat to the established order. In an under-policed society the army played a fundamental and essentially conservative role – as an agency for internal policing. Throughout the century the basic principle of behaviour of its officers and men was obedience to hierarchical superiors. The army became the instrument of whichever government existed, with a pronounced sympathy – derived in part from a professional concern with discipline – for strong regimes which guaranteed social order.

In 1830, 1848 and 1871 the power of deterrence failed; social tension could no longer be contained. The combination of generalized economic and social crises in the first two cases, disagreement within the social élite about access to power, and the peculiar circumstances of war in the last case, together with a crisis of confidence within governmental circles, led to revolution. Successive chapters have examined these crises from the perspective of the various social groups to show how social élites were able to safeguard their privileged position through a mixture of concessions which had the gradual effect of extending political enfranchisement, and of brutal repression.

Political repression was always present, but its more extreme forms were essentially short-term reactions to real or supposed dangers, holding operations, while measures were taken by government to promote the establishment of a new social consensus in favour of stability and social order as the essential means of safeguarding property rights, and the preconditions for economic prosperity. Crucially important in securing this concensus was the extension of voting rights to virtually the whole male population from 1848, which although initially seen by conservatives as a threat to the established social system, would eventually have the opposite effect by institutionalizing protest and reinforcing political stability; together with the development of more effective means of socialization employing both religious, and then increasingly a secular, ideology transmitted through the schools.

The establishment of 'popular sovereignty', of equality before the law, and the myth of equality of opportunity, in a society experiencing economic expansion, created the preconditions for bourgeois liberal democracy in which private property was to be respected as the symbol of success and the basis of individual freedom and in which in consequence inequality was to be enshrined. As a result, socialist criticism was effectively marginalized within a democratic and pluralistic political culture. The ease with which military mobilization occurred in 1914 was evidence of the degree to which, in spite of social divisions, a sense of national community had been created based upon overwhelming acceptance of such values as manhood suffrage and parliamentary democracy, and a shared belief in the superiority of French civilization and the moral responsibility to defend *la patrie*. By these means the era of revolution was brought to an end.

Notes and references

Chapter 1   The economy: continuity and change

1   F. Caron, *An Economic History of Modern France* (1979), p. 12.
2   J. C. Toutain, 'Les Transports en France', *Economie et société* (1967).
3   M. Lévy-Leboyer, 'Capital investment and economic growth in France, 1820–1930', *Cambridge Economic History of Europe* (1978), p. 252.
4   M. Morineau, *Les Faux-semblants d'un démarrage économique: agriculture et démographie en France au 18ᵉ siècle* (1970), p. 24.
5   J. C. Toutain, 'Le Produit de l'agriculture française de 1700 à 1958', *Economie et société* (1961), pp. 13–14; Caron, *Economic History*, p. 24.
6   Toutain, 'Produit', pp. 98–9.
7   M. Agulhon, G. Désert and R. Specklin, *Histoire de la France rurale* (1976), p. 241.
8   ibid., p. 37.
9   ibid., p 398; J. Lhomme, 'La Crise agricole à la fin du 19ᵉ siècle en France', *Revue Economique* (1970), pp. 527–8.
10 Caron, *Economic History*, p. 33.
11 M. Lévy-Leboyer, 'La croissance économique en France au XIXᵉ siècle', *Annales ESC* (1968), p. 794.
12 Caron, *Ecomomic History*, p. 93.
13 H. D. Clout (ed.), *Themes in the Historical Geography of France* (1977), p. 450.
14 Caron, *Economic History*, p. 137.
15 T. J. Markovitch, 'Le Revenu industriel et artisanal sous la Monarchie de Juillet et le Second Empire', *Economie et société* (1967), pp. 79–84.
16 Caron, *Economic History*. p. 163f.
17 J. Bouvier, F. Furet and M. Gillet, *Le Mouvement du profit en France au XIXᵉ siècle* (1965), p. 270; Lévy-Leboyer, 'La croissance', p. 788; F. Crouzet, 'Encore la croissance économique française au 19ᵉ siècle', *Revue du Nord* (1972), p. 272.
18 Caron, *Economic History*, pp. 148–9.

Chapter 2   The demographic indicators

1   A. Armengaud, *La Population française au XIXᵉ siècle* (1971), p. 115.
2   R. H. Hubscher, *L'Agriculture et la société rurale dans le Pas-de-Calais du milieu du 19ᵉ siècle à 1914*, Doctorat d'Etat, Université de Paris IV (1978), p. 1381.
3   A. Husson, *Les Consommations de Paris* (1856), p. 39.

4   ibid., p. 36; R. Price, 'Poor relief and social crisis in mid-nineteenth century France', *European Studies Review* (1983), *passim*; J. Singer-Kéral, *Le coût de la vie à Paris de 1840 à 1954* (1961), p. 129.

5   *La Parisien chez lui au 19ᵉ siècle* (1976), p. 91.

6   L. Gaillard, *La Vie ouvrière et les mouvements ouvriers à Marseille de 1848 à 1879*, Doctorat d'Etat, Aix-en-Provence (1972), vol. I, pp. 48–9.

7   J. C. Toutain, 'La Consommation alimentaire en France de 1789 à 1964', *Economie et société* (1971).

8   F. Braudel and E. Labrousse (eds.), *Histoire économique et sociale de la France*, vol. 3/1 (1979), p. 50.

9   Hubscher, *L'Agriculture*, p. 376.

10   J. Gaillard, *Paris, la ville (1852–1870)*, Doctorat d'Etat, Université de Paris X (1974), p. 72.

11   See, for example, D. H. Pinkney, *Napoleon III and the Rebuilding of Paris* (1958), p. 105f.; M. Daumas *et al.*, *Evolution de la géographie industrielle de Paris et sa proche banlieue au 19ᵉ siècle* (1976), pp. 307, 529; A. Daumard, 'Quelques remarques sur le logement des parisiens au 19ᵉ siècle', *Annales de démographie historique* (1975), p. 60.

12   L. Chevalier (ed.), *Le Choléra. La première. La première epidémie du XIXᵉ siècle* (1958), p. 67.

13   A. Armengaud, *Les Populations de l'est-acquitain au début de l'époque contemporaine* (1961), pp. 204–5.

14   J.-P. Goubert, 'Eaux publiques et démographie historique dans la France urbaine du 19ᵉ siècle: le cas de Rennes', *Annales de démographie historique* (1975), pp. 118–19.

15   J. Gaillard, *Paris, la ville*, p. 321; L. Girard, *Nouvelle histoire de Paris: la Deuxième République et le Second Empire* (1981), p. 88; J. Léonard, *La France médicale au 19ᵉ siècle* (1978), p. 14; G. Jacquemet, *Belleville au 19ᵉ siècle. Du faubourg à la ville*, Doctorat d'Etat, Université de Paris IV (1979), p. 922.

16   L. Gaillard, *La Vie ouvrière*, vol. II, p. 359.

17   L. Chevalier, 'Towards a history of population', in D. V. Glass and D. E. C. Eversley (eds.), *Population in History* (1965), p. 692.

18   P. Ariès, *Histoire des populations françaises et de leurs attitudes devant la vie depuis le XVIIIᵉ siècle*, (1948), p. 232.

19   J. Bourgeois-Pichat, 'The general development of the population of France since the eighteenth century', in Glass and Eversley (eds.), *Population in History*, p. 487.

20   J.-P. Chaline, *La Bourgeoisie rouennaise au 19ᵉ siècle*, Doctorat d'Etat, Université de Paris IV (1979), p. 292.

21   A. Lesaege-Dugied, 'La mortalité infantile dans le départment du Nord de 1815 à 1914', in M. Gillet (ed), *L'Homme, la vie et la mort dans le Nord au 19ᵉ siècle* (Lille 1972), p. 114; G. Sussman, 'The end of the wet-nursing business in France, 1876–1914', *Journal of Family History* (1977), p. 254.

22   A. Corbin, *Archaïsme et Modernité en Limousin au XIXᵉ siècle*, vol. I (1975), p. 520.

23   Armengaud, *La Population française*, p. 15.

24   ibid., p. 11f.

25   M. Ségalen, *Nuptialité et alliance. Le choix du conjoint dans une commune de l'Eure* (1972), pp. 78–9.

26   L. A. Tilly and J. W. Scott, *Women, Work and Family* (1978), pp. 124, 196.

27   A. Armengaud, 'Industrialisation et démographie dans la France du XIXᵉ siècle', in *L'Industrialisation en Europe au 19ᵉ siècle* (1972), pp. 193–4.

28 J. Dupâquier, 'Problémes démographiques de la France napoléonienne', *Revue d'histoire moderne et contemporaine* (1970), p. 350.
29 G. Désert, 'La Dépeuplement des campagnes bas-normands pendant la première moitié du 19ᵉ siècle', in *Sur la population française au 18ᵉ et 19ᵉ siècles. Hommage à Marcel Reinhard* (1973), p. 213; A. Armengaud, *La Population française*, pp. 49–50.
30 A. Armengaud, *La Population française*, p. 113.
31 ibid., p. 74.
32 A. F. Weber, *The Growth of Cities in the Nineteenth Century*, (Ithaca, NY 1963), p. 71.
33 A. Chatelain, *Les migrants temporaires en France de 1800 à 1914* (Lille 1977), p. 42.
34 Based upon Armengaud, *La Population française*, p. 71.
35 Hubscher, *L'Agriculture*, p. 1165.
36 L. Chevalier, *La formation de la population parisienne au XIXᵉ siècle* (1950), p. 164.

Chapter 3   Elites

1   F. Braudel and E. Labrousse (eds.), *Histoire économique et sociale de la France*, vol. 4/1 (1979), pp. 368, 416–19, 424.
2   L. Bergeron, G. Chaussinand-Nogaret, 'Les *Masses de granit*. Cent mille notables du Premier Empire', in H. Watelet and J.-C. Dubé (eds.), *Rencontres de l'historiographie française avec l'histoire sociale* (Ottawa 1978), p. 43.
3   A. J. Tudesq, *Les grands notables en France (1840–1849): Etude historique d'une psychologie sociale*, vol. I (1964), p. 429.
4   A. Daumard, *La bourgeoisie parisienne de 1814 à 1848* (1963), pp. 64–5.
5   Tudesq, *Les grands notables*, vol. I, p. 429.
6   P. Bernard, *Economie et sociologie de la Seine-et-Marne (1850–1950)* (1953), p. 170; T. Zeldin, 'France', in D. Spring (ed.), *European Landed Elites in the Nineteenth Century* (1977), pp. 33–4.
7   R. Forster, 'The survival of the nobility during the French revolution', *Past and Present* (1967), pp. 77–8.
8   R. H. Hubscher, *L'Agriculture et la société dans le Pas-de-Calais du milieu du 19ᵉ siècle à 1914*, Doctorat d'Etat, Universite de Paris IV (1978), p. 1578.
9   ibid., p. 1584.
10 J. C. Farcy, *Agriculture et société rurale en Beauce pendant la première moitié du 19ᵉ siècle*, Thèse de 3ᵉ cycle Université de Paris X, p. 394.
11 J. Bouvier, 'Le mouvement d'une civilisation nouvelle', in G. Duby (ed.), *Histoire de la France*, vol. III (1972), p. 55.
12 A. Daumard, 'La Fortune mobilière en France selon les milieux sociaux (XIXᵉ–XXᴱ siècles)', *Revue d'histoire économique et sociale* (1966), p. 385.
13 L. Girard, A. Prost and R. Gossez, *Les conseillers généraux en 1870* (1967), p. 415.
14 A. J. Tudesq, 'Les survivances de l'Ancien Régime: la noblesse dans la société française de la première moitié du XIXᵉ siècle', in D. Roche and E. Labrousse (eds.), *Ordres et classes* (1973), pp. 206–7.
15 Tudesq, *Les grands notables*, vol. I, p. 425.
16 Bergeron, Chaussinand-Nogaret, 'Les *Masses de granit*', p. 40.
17 P. Lanthier, 'Les dirigeants des grandes enterprises électriques en France, 1911–1973', in M. Lévy-Leboyer (ed.), *Le Patronat de la seconde industrialisation* (1979), p. 104.

18 C. Charle, 'Les Milieux d'affaires dans la structure de la classe dominante vers 1900', *Actes de la recherche en sciences sociales* (1978), p. 86.

19 T. D. Beck, '*French Legislators 1800–1834: a Study in Quantitative History*' (1974), p. 147.

20 D. Higgs, *Ultraroyalism in Toulouse* (1973), p. 88.

21 L. Girard *et al., La Chambre des Députés en 1837–1839* . . . (1976), p. 19; P.-B. Higonnet, 'La composition de la Chambre des Députés de 1827 à 1831', *Revue Historique* (1968), pp. 369, 376.

22 Higonnet, 'La Composition', p. 369.

23 Higgs, *Ultraroyalism*, p. 99.

24 J. Bécanuer, 'Noblesse et représentation parlementaire (1871–1968)', *Revue française de science politique* (1973), p. 976.

Chapter 4   The middle classes

1 A. Aboucaya, *Les Structures sociales et économiques de l'agglomération lyonnaise à la veille de la Révolution de 1848* (1963), p. 19.

2 A. Daumard, *La Bourgeoisie parisienne de 1815 à 1848* (1963), p. 14.

3 J. P. Chaline, *La Bourgeoisie de Rouen: une élite urbaine au XIXe siècle* (1982), p. 127.

4 J.-B. Duroselle, *La France et les français, 1900–1914* (1972), p. 79.

5 ibid, p. 84.

6 F. Braudel and E. Labrousse (eds.), *Histoire économique et sociale de la France*, vol. 4/1 (1979), p. 405.

7 M. Agulhon, *Le Cercle dans la France bourgeoise, 1810–1848* (1977), p. 40.

8 P. Gonnet, *La Société dijonnaise au 19e siècle*, Doctorat d'Etat, Paris-Sorbonne (1974), pp. 1112–3.

9 T. Zeldin, *France 1848–1945*, vol. 1 (1973), p. 37.

10 G. Weisz, 'The politics of medical professionalisation in France, 1845–48', *Journal of Social History* (1978–9), p. 3.

11 O. Voilliard, *Recherches sur une bourgeoisie urbaine: Nancy au 19e siècle (1815–1871)*, Doctorat d'Etat, Université de Strasbourg (1976), pp. 57–8.

12 Chaline, *La Bourgeoisie rouennaise*, pp. 113–15, and Voilliard *Recherches*, pp. 57–88.

13 T. J. Markovitch, 'L'industrie française de 1789 à 1964', *Cahiers de l'ISEA* (1966), pp. 85–6.

14 A. Cottereau, 'Introduction', in D. Poulot, *Le Sublime ou le travailleur comme il est en 1870 et ce qu'il peut être* (1979), pp. 46–7.

15 Markovitch, 'L'industrie française', p. 87; Duroselle, *La France*, p. 85.

16 J. Gaillard, *Paris, la ville*, p. 376.

17 ibid.

18 ibid., p. 433.

19 R. H. Hubscher, *L'Agriculture et la société dans le Pas-de-Calais du milieu du 19e siècle à 1914*, Doctorat d'Etat, Université de Paris IV (1978), p. 263.

20 Cottereau, 'Introduction', p. 46.

21 Zeldin, *France*, p. 107.

22 Braudel and Labrousse, *Histoire économique et sociale*, vol. 4/1, p. 403.

23 ibid., p. 402.

24 ibid., p. 423.
25 P. Sorlin, *La société française: 1840–1914* (1969), p. 91.
26 Duroselle, *La France*, p. 128.
27 Voilliard, *Recherches sur une bourgeoisie urbaine*, p. 76.
28 Duroselle, *La France*, pp. 128–30; F. Muel, 'Les instituteurs, les paysans et l'ordre républicain', *Actes de la recherche en sciences sociales* (1977), p. 40; P. V. Meyers, 'Professionalization and societal change: rural teachers in nineteenth century France', *Journal of Social History* (1975–6), p. 553.
29 Braudel and Labrousse, *Histoire économique et social*, vol. 4/1, p. 431.

Chapter 5   Peasants

1 R. H. Hubscher, *L'Agriculture et la société dans le Pas-de-Calais du milieu du 19ᵉ siècle à 1914*, Doctorat d'Etat, Université de Paris IV (1978), p. 1240.
2 G. Postel-Vinay, *La Rente foncière dans le capitalisme agricole* (1974), p. 36.
3 Hubscher, *L'Agriculture*, p. 295.
4 A. Gueslin, *Les Origines du crédit agricole (1840–1914)* (Nancy 1978), p. 389.
5 G. Désert, *Une Société rurale au 19ᵉ siècle: les paysans du Calvados, 1815–1895*, vol. III (Lille 1975), pp. 1014, 1018, 1045.
6 G. Garrier, *Paysans du Beaujolais et du Lyonnais, 1800–1970*, vol. I (Grenoble 1973), p. 388.
7 Désert, *Une Société rurale*, vol. III, p. 1092.
8 Hubscher, *L'Agriculture*, p. 937.
9 Désert, *Une Société rurale*, vol. I, p. 244.
10 ibid., vol. III, p. 965.
11 M. Agulhon, G. Désert and R. Specklin, *Histoire de la France rurale*, vol. III (1976), p. 402; P. Brunet, *Structures agraires et économie rurale des plateaux tertiaires entre la Seine et l'Oise* (Caen 1960), p. 370.
12 Désert, *Une Société rurale*, vol. III, p. 1045.
13 C. Pennetier, *Le Socialisme dans les départements ruraux français: l'exemple du Cher (1850–1921)*, Thèse de 3ᵉ cycle, Université de Paris I (1979), pp. 60–1.
14 J.-C. Farcy, *Agriculture et société rurale en Beauce pendant la première moitié du 19ᵉ siècle*, Thèse de 3ᵉ cycle, Université de Paris X, p. 110.
15 A. Chatelain, 'Une classe rurale au milieu du XIXᵉ siècle: les ouvriers agricoles de Seine-et-Marne', *Bulletin de la société d'études historiques de la région parisienne* (1953), p. 12.
16 J. Sagnes, 'Le Mouvement de 1907 en Languedoc–Roussillon: de la révolte viticole à la révolte régionale', *Le Mouvement social* (1978), p. 6.
17 A. Corbin, *Archaïsme et modernité en Limousin au XIXᵉ siècle*, vol. I (1975), p. 263.
18 Agulhon *et al.*, *Histoire de la France rurale*, vol. III, p. 551.
19 Hubscher, *L'Agriculture*, p. 965.
20 Based on Désert, *Une Société rurale*, annexe 43; Brunet, *Structures agraires*, p. 371; Hubscher, *L'Agriculture*, p. 978; Corbin, *Archaisme*, vol. II, p. 1035.
21 G. Gavignaud, *La Propriété en Roussillon. Structures et conjonctures agraires aux 18ᵉ et 20ᵉ siècles*, Doctorat d'Etat, Université de Paris I (1980), p. 580.
22 P. Leveque, *La Bourgogne de la Monarchie de Juillet au Second Empire*, Doctorat d'Etat, Université de Paris I (1976), pp. 562–3.

23   Hubscher, *L'Agriculture*, p. 1511.

24   G. Dupeux, 'Aspects agricoles . . . Le département du Loir-et-Cher', in E. Labrousse (ed.), *Aspects de la crise et de la dépression de l'économie française au milieu du XIXe siècle, 1846–51* (1956), p. 80.

25   Désert, *Une Société rurale*, vol. III, p. 922.

26   Hubscher, *L'Agriculture*, p. 1341.

27   ibid., pp. 1515–21.

28   C. Heywood, 'The rural hosiery industry of the Lower Champagne region, 1750–1850', *Textile History* (1976), p. 96.

29   P. Bozon, *La Vie rurale en Vivarais* (1963), pp. 144, 440.

30   Hubscher, *L'Agriculture*, pp. 1399–1400.

31   F. C. Gamst, *Peasants in Complex Society* (1974), p. 51.

32   E. Weber, *Peasants into Frenchmen. The Modernisation of Rural France, 1870–1914* (1976), p. 28.

33   Hubscher, *L'Agriculture*, p. 28.

34   For a fuller development see R. Price, *The Modernization of Rural France. Communications networks and agricultural market structures in nineteenth-century France* (1983), chs. 4–6.

35   G. Dupeux, *Aspects de l'histoire sociale et politique du Loir-et-Cher* (1962), p. 315.

Chapter 6   Working classes

1   J. C. Toutain, 'La Population de 1700 à 1959', *Cahiers de l'ISEA* (1963), Table 17.

2   T. J. Markovitch, 'Le Revenu industriel et artisanal sous la Monarchie de Juillet et le Second Empire', *Economie et Société* (1967), p. 87.

3   F. Braudel and E. Labrousse (eds.), *Histoire économique et sociale de la France*, vol. 3/1 (1979), p. 465.

4   R. Gossez, *Les Ouvriers de Paris* (1967), pp. 160–1.

5   L. S. Strumingher, 'The artisan family: traditions and transition in nineteenth century Lyon', *Journal of Family History* (1977), p. 215.

6   M. Perrot, 'Une Naissance difficile: la formation de la classe ouvrière lyonnaise', *Annales ESC* (1978), p. 831.

7   Braudel and Labrousse (eds.), *Histoire économique et sociale*, vol. 4, p. 466.

8   W. M. Reddy, 'The textile trade and the language of the crowd at Rouen, 1752–1871', *Past and Present* (1977), p. 78.

9   M. Perrot, 'The three ages of industrial discipline in nineteenth century France', in J. M. Merriman (ed.), *Consciousness and Class Experience in Nineteenth Century Europe* (1979), p. 158.

10   R. Trempé, *Les mineurs de Carmaux, 1848–1914*, vol. I (1971), pp. 205–10, 248–9.

11   M. Perrot, 'Les Ouvriers et les machines en France dans la première moitié du 19e siècle', in L. Murard and P. Zylberman (eds.), *Le Soldat du travail. Guerre, fascisme et taylorisme* (1978), p. 350.

12   Braudel and Labrousse (eds.), *Histoire économique et sociale*, vol. 4, p. 470.

13   R. Gossez, 'Une grève de mineurs à l'avènement de Napoléon III', *Mines* (1955), p. 505.

14   C. Lesselier, 'Employées de grands magasins à Paris (Avant 1914)', *Le Mouvement Social* (1978), pp. 109–10.

15 Braudel and Labrousse (eds.), *Histoire économique et sociale*, vol. 4, p. 471–2.

16 F. Caron, 'Essai d'analyse historique d'une psychologie du travail. Les mécaniciens et chauffeurs de locomotives du réseau du Nord de 1850 à 1910', *Le Mouvement Social* (1965), p. 9.

17 C. Jacquemet, *Belleville au 19ᵉ siècle. Du Faubourg à la ville* (1984), p. 919.

18 A. Martin-Fugier, 'Les domestiques en France au 19ᵉsiècle', *Le Mouvement Social* (1978), p. 164.

19 L. A. Tilly, 'Structure de l'emploi, travail des femmes et changement démographique dans deux villes industrielles: Anzin et Roubaix, 1872–1906', ibid., pp. 45–6.

20 ibid., p. 41.

21 J. Rougerie, 'Remarques sur l'histoire des salaires à Paris au 19ᵉ siècle', *Le Mouvement Social* (1968), pp. 74–8, 87–8.

22 Caron, 'Essai', p. 18.

23 Y. Lequin, *La Formation de la classe ouvrière régionale: les ouvriers de la région lyonnaise (1848–1914)*, vol. II (Lyon 1977), p. 47.

24 M. P. Hanagan, 'Artisans and industrial workers: work structure, technological change and worker militancy in three French towns, 1870–1914', Ph.D thesis, University of Michigan (1976), pp. 243–4.

25 A. Lasserre, *La Situation des ouvriers de l'industrie textile dans la région lilloise sous la Monarchie de Juillet* (Lausanne 1962), p. 124.

26 J. Lhomme, 'Le Pouvoir d'achat de l'ouvrier français au cours d'un siècle, 1840–1940', *Le Mouvement Social* (1968), p. 45; Rougerie, 'Remarques sur l'histoire des salaires', p. 78.

27 Braudel and Labrousse (eds.), *Histoire économique et sociale*, vol. 4, p. 484.

28 Jacquemet, *Belleville*, p. 1183.

29 Rougerie, 'Remarques sur l'histoire des salaires', pp. 95–6.

30 A. Plessis, *De la fête impériale au mur des fédérés, 1852–71* (1973), p. 158.

31 M. Crubellier, *Histoire culturelle de la France* (1974), p. 149.

32 Lequin, *La Formation de la classe ouvrière*, vol. I, p. 211.

33 G. de Bertier de Sauvigny, *Nouvelle histoire de Paris. La Restauration* (1977), p. 269.

34 Trempé, *Les mineurs*, vol. I, p. 313.

35 L. A. Tilly and J. W. Scott, *Women, Work and Family* (1978), pp. 99–100; T. Leleu, 'Scènes de la vie quotidienne: les femmes de la vallée de la Lys (1870–1920)', *Revue du Nord* (1981), pp. 643–5.

36 J. Gaillard, *Paris, la ville (1852–1870)* (1970), p. 223.

37 G. Thuillier, *Aspects de l'économie nivernaise au XIXᵉ siècle* (1966), p. 293.

38 Jacquemet, *Belleville*, p. 919.

39 E. Shorter and C. Tilly, *Strikes in France, 1830–1968* (1974), pp. 48, 108; Braudel and Labrousse (eds.), *Histoire économique et sociale*, vol. 4, p. 519.

40 M. Perrot, 'Grèves, grévistes et conjoncture', *Le Mouvement Social* (1968), p. 116.

41 M. Perrot, *Les ouvriers en grève. France, 1871–1890*, vol. I (1974), p. 76.

42 Shorter and Tilly, *Strikes*, p. 107.

43 ibid., p. 120.

44 Perrot, *Les ouvriers en grève*, vol. I, pp. 350–1.

45 M. P. Hanagan, 'The logic of solidarity. Social structure in Le Chambon-Feugerolles', *Journal of Urban History* (1976–7), p. 418.

46 Perrot, *Les ouvriers en grève*, vol. I, p. 75.

47 Lequin, *La Formation de la classe ouvrière*, vol. II, p. 59; see also Perrot, *Les ouvriers en grève*, vol. I, p. 75.

48   Shorter and Tilly, *Strikes*, pp. 66–7.
49   Perrot, *Les ouvriers en grève*, vol. I, p. 319.
50   Perrot, 'Grèves', p. 117.
51   See W. H. Sewell jr, *Work and Revolution in France. The Language of Labor from the Old Regime to 1848* (1980), p. 66f.
52   H. Hatzfeld, *Du paupérisme à la sécurité sociale, 1850–1940* (1971), p. 199; Zeldin, *France 1848–1945* (1973), vol. I, p. 660.
53   Lequin, *La Formation de la classe ouvrière*, vol. II, pp. 191–5.
54   D. Willbach, 'Work and its satisfactions: origins of the French labor movement, 1864–70', Ph.D. thesis, University of Michigan (1977), p. 10.
55   Jacquemet, *Belleville*, p. 1293.
56   Braudel and Labrousse (eds.), *Histoire économique et sociale*, vol. 4, p. 523.

Chapter 7   Religion

1   E. Weber, *Peasants into Frenchmen. The Modernization of Rural France, 1870–1914* (1976), p. 371: G. de Bertier de Sauvigny, *La Restauration* (1955), pp. 306–8.
2   F. Boulard, *Matériaux pour l'histoire religieuse du peuple français, XIXᵉ–XXᵉ siécles.*, vol. I (1982), p. 135.
3   N.-J. Chaline, 'Le recrutement du clergé dans le diocèse de Rouen au 19ᵉ siècle', *Revue d'histoire économique et sociale* (1971), p. 397.
4   J. Gadille, *La Pensée et l'action politique des évêques français au début de la 3ᵉ République* (1967), p. 26.
5   Boulard, *Matériaux*, p. 131.
6   M. Lagrée, 'L'Age de remise en cause (1840–1970). Eglise et pouvoirs', in J. Delumeau, *Le Diocèse de Rennes* (1979), p. 240.
7   Y. Daniel, *L'équipement paroissial d'un diocèse urbain: Paris (1802–1956)* (1957), p. 130.
8   J. Faury, *Cléricalisme et anticléricalisme dans le Tarn* (Toulouse 1980), p. 286.
9   G. Cholvy, 'Société, genres de vie et mentalité dans les campagnes françaises de 1815 à 1880', *Information historique* (1973), p. 159.
10   L. Girard, *Nouvelle histoire de Paris. La deuxième République et le Second Empire* (1981), p. 278.
11   G. Cholvy and Y.-M. Hilaire, *Histoire religieuse de la France contemporaine, 1800–1880* (Toulouse 1985), p. 39f. – in 1789 there had been only *c*. 35,000.
12   J. Maurain, *La Politique ecclésiastique du Second Empire de 1852 à 1869* (1930), p. 296.
13   T. Zeldin, *France, 1848–1945*, vol. II (1977), p. 1010. In the late eighteenth century there had been around 70,000.
14   Maurain, *La Politique ecclésiastique*, p. 118.
15   Gadille, *La Pensée*, pp. 26–7.
16   M. Lagrée, *Aspects de la vie religieuse en Ille-et-Vilaine (1815–1848)*, Thèse de 3ᵉ cycle. Rennes (1974), p. 408.
17   J. McManners, *Church and State in France, 1870–1914* (1972), p. 55.
18   J.-D. Roque, 'Positions et tendances politiques des Protestants nimois au 19ᵉ siècle', *Droit et gauche de 1789 à nos jours* (Montpellier 1975), pp. 199–205.
19   Maurain, *La Politique ecclésiastique*, p. 555; McManners, *Church and State*, p. 89.

20 G. Cholvy, 'Bîterrois et Narbonnais. Mutations économiques et évolution des mentalités à l'époque contemporaine', in G. Cholvy, *Economie et société en Languedoc–Roussillon de 1789 à nos jours* (Montpellier 1978), p. 427.

21 F. Charpin, *Pratique religieuse et formation d'une grande ville. Le geste du baptême et sa signification en sociologie religieuse (Marseille, 1806–1958)* (1964), p. 164.

22 Y.-M. Hilaire, *Une Chrétienté au XIXᵉ siècle: Le diocèse d'Arras de 1840 à 1914*, vol. II (Lille 1977), pp. 34–5.

23 P. Leveque, *Société en crise. La Bourgogne de la Monarchie de Juillet au Second Empire*, 2 vols. (1983), p. 730.

24 M. Lagrée, *Aspects de la vie religieuse*, pp. 148–9.

25 C. Cholvy, *Religion et société au 19ᵉ siècle. Le diocèse de Montpellier*, 2 vols. (Lille 1973), p. 571.

26 Charpin, *Pratique religieuse*, p. 50.

27 Boulard, *Matériaux*, p. 65.

28 Y.-M. Hilaire,. *La Vie religieuse des populations du diocèse d'Arras, 1840–1914*, Doctorat d'Etat, Université de Paris IV (1976), p. 1056.

29 Cholvy, *Religion et société*, p. 1454.

30 C. Marcilhacy, *Le diocèse d'Orléans sous l'épiscopat de Mgr. Dupanloup, 1849–1879* (1962), p. 314.

Chapter 8 Education

1 R. Grew, P. J. Harrigan and J. Whitney, 'The availability of schooling in nineteenth century France', *Journal of Interdisciplinary History* (1983), p. 31.

2 M. Gontard, *L'Enseignement primaire en France de la Révolution à la loi Guizot* (n.d.), pp. 139, 262.

3 M. Crubellier, *L'Enfance et la jeunesse dans la société française, 1800–1950* (1979), pp. 81–2.

4 G. Désert, *Une Société rurale au 19ᵉ siècle: les paysans du Calvados, 1815–1895*, vol. I (Lille 1975), p. 358.

5 R. Gildea, *Education in Provincial France, 1800–1914* (1983), p. 94.

6 S. Narjoux-Waquet, 'Une région-charnière. L'arrondissement de Clamecy et l'évolution de l'enseignement primaire (1832–60)', *Annales de Bourgogne* (1979), pp. 236–7.

7 M. Gontard, *Les Écoles primaires de la France bourgeoise (1833–1878)* (Toulouse n.d.), p. 19.

8 F. Furet and J. Ozouf, *Lire et écrire*, vol. I (1977), pp. 302–3.

9 P. Gerbod, 'Les épurations dans l'enseignement public de la Restauration à la 4ᵉ République (1815–1946)', in P. Gerbod *et al.*, *Les Epurations administratives, 19ᵉ et 20ᵉ siècles* (Geneva 1977), p. 91.

10 R. D. Anderson, *Education in France, 1848–70* (1975), p. 112.

11 ibid., p. 111.

12 P. Pierrard (ed.), *Les Diocèses de Cambrai et de Lille* (1978), p. 241.

13 Furet and Ozouf, *Lire et écrire*, vol. I, p. 304.

14 ibid., p. 272.

15 Pierrard (ed.), *Les Diocèses*, p. 268.

16 Gildea, *Education*, p. 130.

17 Y.-M. Hilaire, *La Vie religieuse des populations du diocèse d'Arras, 1840–1914*, Doctorat d'Etat, Université de Paris IV (1976), p. 702.
18 Gontard, *Les Écoles primaires*, p. 26.
19 Hilaire, *La Vie religieuse*, p. 702.
20 A. Prost, *Histoire de l'enseignement en France, 1800–1967* (1968), pp. 108, 294.
21 ibid.
22 P. Pierrard, *La vie ouvrière à Lille sous le Second Empire* (1965), p. 314.
23 Crubellier, *L'Enfance*, p. 234; Prost, *Histoire de l'enseignement*, p. 61.
24 P. V. Meyers, 'Professionalization and societal change: rural teachers in nineteenth century France', *Journal of Social History* (1975–6), p. 553.
25 Prost, *Histoire de l'enseignement*, p. 61.
26 Gontard, *Les Écoles primaires*, p. 140.
27 Meyers, 'Professionalization and societal change', p. 553; J.-B. Duroselle, *La France at les Français, 1900–14* (1972), p. 130.
28 Gildea, *Education*, pp. 128, 147; A. Corbin, *Archaïsme et modernité en Limousin au 19ᵉ siècle*, vol. I (1975), p. 341.
29 C. R. Day, 'The rustic man: the rural schoolmaster in nineteenth century France', *Comparative Studies in Society and History* (1983), pp. 36–7.
30 Meyers, 'Professionalization and societal change', p. 553.
31 G. Désert, 'Alphabétisation et scolarisation dans le Grand-Ouest au XIXᵉ siècle', in D. Baker and P. Harrigan (eds.), *The Making of Frenchmen* (1980).
32 Furet and Ozouf, *Lire et écrire*, vol. I, p. 58.
33 G. Cholvy, 'Société, genres de vie et mentalité dans les campagnes françaises de 1815 à 1880', *Information historique* (1973), p. 163.
34 Furet and Ozouf, *Lire et écrire*, vol. I, pp. 187–8, 266.
35 ibid., pp. 175–7.
36 ibid., p. 261; Girard, *Nouvelle histoire de Paris*, p. 285.
37 Y. Lequin, *La Formation de la classe ouvrière régionale: les ouvriers de la région lyonnaise (1848–1914)*, vol. II (Lyon 1977), p. 108.
38 Gildea, *Education*, p. 230.
39 Prost, *Histoire de l'enseignement*, p. 22.
40 Furet and Ozouf, *Lire et écrire*, vol. I, p. 299.
41 ibid., p. 297.
42 Anderson, *Education in France*, p. 147.
43 Gontard, *Les Écoles primaires*, p. 19.
44 F. Braudel and E. Labrousse (eds.), *Histoire économique et sociale de la France*, vol. 4 (1979), p. 476.
45 Crubellier, *L'Enfance*, pp. 137–8.
46 F.-P. Codaccioni, *De l'inégalité sociale dans une grande ville industrielle: Le drame de Lille de 1850 à 1914* (Lille 1976), pp. 126, 141, 360.
47 P. Gerbod, 'The baccalaureate and its role in the recruitment and formation of French elites in the nineteenth century', in J. Howarth and P. Cerny (eds.), *Elites in France* (1981), p. 147.
48 D. Julia and P. Pressly, 'La population scolaire en 1789', *Annales ESC* (1975), p. 1546.
49 Anderson, *Education in France*, p. 20.
50 Gildea, *Education*, p. 80.
51 J. Rohr, *Victor Duruy, Ministre de Napoléon III. Essai sur la politique de l'instruction publique au temps de l'empire libéral* (1967), p. 67; Crubellier, *L'Enfance*, p. 126.

52   F. K. Ringer, *Education and Society in Modern Europe* (1979), p. 133; Crubellier, *L'Enfance*, p. 144; P. J. Harrigan, *Mobility, Elites and Education in French Society of the Second Empire* (Waterloo, Ontario 1980), pp. 8–9; Gerbod, 'The baccalaureate', p. 47.

53   Based on P. J. Harrigan, 'The social origins, ambitions and occupations of secondary students in France during the Second Empire', in L. Stone (ed.), *Schooling and Society* (1976), p. 210; and R. D. Anderson, 'New light on French secondary education in the nineteenth century', *Social History* (1982), pp. 150–1.

54   Gerbod, 'The baccalaureate', pp. 48–9.

55   Anderson, *Education in France*, p. 20.

56   Crubellier, *L'Enfance*, p. 284; Braudel and Lebrousse (eds.), *Histoire économique et sociale de la France*, vol. 4, p. 112.

57   Prost, *Histoire de l'enseignement*, p. 76.

58   Duroselle, *La France*, p. 128.

59   Crubellier, *L'Enfance*, pp. 258, 261.

60   Duroselle, *La France*, p. 125.

61   Gildea, *Education*, p. 133.

62   G. Weber, *Peasants into Frenchmen. The Modernization of Rural France, 1870–1914* (1976), p. 67.

63   C. Bellanger *et al.*, *Histoire générale de la presse française*, vol. III (1972), p. 141.

64   ibid., p. 137.

Chapter 9   In conclusion: state and society

1   C.-H. Pouthas, 'Les ministères de Louis-Philippe', *Revue d'histoire moderne et contemporaine* (1954), p. 102.

2   J. Estèbe, *Les Ministres de la République* (1982), p. 22.

3   C. Charle, 'Le recrutement des hauts fonctionnaires en 1901', *Annales ESC* (1980), pp. 181–3.

Select bibliography

(Place of publication London or Paris unless otherwise stated).

General

M. Agulhon (ed.), *Histoire de la France urbaine*, vol. IV, *La ville de l'âge industriel* (1983).

M. Agulhon, G. Désert and R. Specklin, *Histoire de la France rurale*, vol. III (1976).

J. Bouvier, F. Furet and M. Gillet, *Le Mouvement du profit en France au 19ᵉ siècle* (1965).

F. Braudel and E. Labrousse, *Histoire économique et sociale de la France*, vols. 3/1 and 4/1 (1973–9).

S. Chassagne, 'L'Histoire de villes: Une opération de renovation historiographique?', in M. Garden (ed.), *Villes et campagnes* (Lyon 1977).

A. Daumard, 'La Fortune mobilière en France selon les milieux sociaux (XIXᵉ–XXᵉ siècles)', *Revue d'histoire économique et sociale* (1966).

A. Daumard, 'L'Evolution des structures sociales en France à l'époque de l'industrialisation', *Revue historique* (1972).

A. Daumard (ed.), *Les Fortunes françaises au 19ᵉ siècle* (1973).

A. Daumard, 'Le Peuple dans la société française à l'époque romantique' *Romantisme* (1975–6).

G. Duby (ed.), *Histoire de la France* vol. III, *Les temps nouveaux de 1852 à nos jours* (1972).

G. Dupeux, *La Société française, 1789–1960;* (1960)

J.-B. Duroselle, *La France et les Français, 1900–14* (1972).

E. Labrousse (ed.), *Aspects de la crise et de la dépression de l'économie française au milieu du XIXᵉ siècle, 1846–51* (1956).

Y. Lequin (ed.), *Histoire des Français XIX–XXᵉ siècles*, 3 vols., 1983–4.

R. Magraw, *France, 1815–1914. The Bourgeois Century* (1983).

J. M. Merriman (ed.), *French Cities in the Nineteenth Century* (1982).

D. H. Pinkney, *Decisive Years in France, 1840–47* (1986).

W. M. Reddy, *The Rise of Market Culture. The Textile Trade and French Society, 1750–1900* (1984).

P. Sorlin, *La Société française: 1840–1914* (1969).

J. Vidalenc, *La Société française de 1815 à 1848*, 2 vols. (1969–72).

T. Zeldin, *France, 1848–1945*, 2 vols. (1973–7).

Regional studies

C. Aboucaya, *Les Structures sociales et économiques de l'agglomération lyonnaise à la veille de la révolution de 1848* (1963).

E. B. Ackerman, *Village on the Seine. Tradition and Change in Bonnières, 1815–1914* (1978).

M. Agulhon, *La vie sociale en Provence intérieure au lendemain de la Révolution* (1970).

M. Agulhon, *The Republic in the Village. The People of the Var from the French Revolution to the Second Republic* (1982).

A. Armengaud, *Les Populations de l'est-Aquitain au début de l'époque contemporaine* (1961).

J. Bastié, *La Croissance de la banlieue parisienne* (1964).

P. Bernard, *Economie et sociologie de la Seine-et-Marne, 1850–1950* (1953).

G. de Bertier de Sauvigny, *Nouvelle histoire de Paris. La Restauration, 1815–1830* (1977).

M. Chevalier, *La Vie humaine dans les pyrénées ariègeoises* (1956).

G. Cholvy, 'Biterrois et narbonnais. Mutations économiques et évolution des mentalités à l'époque contemporaine', *Economie et société en Languedoc-Roussillon de 1789 à nos jours* (Montpellier 1978).

G. Cholvy, 'Histoire contemporaine en pays d'Oc', *Annales ESC* (1978).

E. Constant, *Le Département du Var sous le Second Empire et au début de la 3ᵉ République*, Doctorat ès lettres, Université de Provence-Aix (1977).

A. Corbin, *Archaïsme et modernité en Limousin au 19ᵉ siècle*, 2 vols. (1975).

M. Daumas *et al.*, *Evolution de la géographie industrielle de Paris et sa proche banlieue au 19ᵉ siècle* (1976).

G. Désert, 'Structures sociales dans le villes bas-normandes au 19ᵉ siècle', *Conjoncture économique. Structures sociales. Hommage à Ernest Labrousse* (1974).

G. Dupeux, *Aspects de l'histoire sociale et politique du Loir-et-Cher* (1962).

R. Fruit, *La Croissance économique du pays de St.-Amand (Nord), 1668–1914* (1963).

J. Gaillard, *Paris, la ville (1852–70)* (1977).

L. Girard, *Nouvelle histoire de Paris. La deuxième république et le second empire* (1981).

P. Gonnet, *La Société dijonnaise au 19ᵉ siècle. Esquisse de l'évolution économique, sociale et politique d'un milieu urbain contemporain (1815–90)*, Doctorat d'Etat, Université de Paris IV (1974).

P. Goujon, *Le Vignoble de Saône-et-Loire au 19ᵉ siècle (1815–70)* (Lyon 1974).

G. Jacquemet, *Belleville au 19ᵉ siècle. Du faubourg à la ville* (1984).

M.-M. Kahan-Rabecq, *L'Alsace économique et sociale sous le règne de Louis-Philippe*, vol. I (1939).

P. Léon, *La Naissance de la grande industrie en Dauphiné (fin du XVIIᵉ siècle-1869)*, 2 vols. (1954).

P. Léon. *Géographie de la fortune et structures sociales à Lyon au 19ᵉ sièle* (Lyon 1975).

P. Leuilliot, *L'Alsace au début du 19ᵉ siècle, 1815–30*, 2 vols. (1959).

P. Leveque, *Société en crise. La Bourgogne de la Monarchie de Juillet au Second Empire*, 2 vols. (1983).

J. Merley, *La Haute-Loire de la fin de l'Ancien Régime aux début de la 3ᵉ République*, 2 vols. (Le Puy 1975).

J. M. Merriman, *The Red City. Limoges and the French Nineteenth Century* (1986).

J. Raymond, *Histoire économique, sociale et politique du département de la Haute-Savoie de 1875 à 1939*, Doctorat d'Etat, Université de Paris I (1978).

J. Renard, *Les Evolutions contemporaines de la vie rurale dans la région nantaise* (Les Sables d'Olonne 1975).

M. Rochefort, *L'Organisation urbaine de l'Alsace* (Gap 1960).

P. Seignour, *La Vie économique du Vaucluse de 1815 à 1848* (Aix-en-Provence 1957).

G. Thuillier, *Aspects de l'économie nivernaise au XIXe siècle* (1966).

G. Thuillier, *Pour une histoire du quotidien au 19e siècle en Nivernais* (1977).

J. Vidalenc, *Le Département de l'Eure sous la monarchie constitutionnelle (1814–48)* (1952).

P. Vieille, 'Formes de Productione, institutions et culture en Provence. La rupture de la première moitié du 19e siècle', *L'Homme et la Société* (1976).

P. Vigier, *La Seconde république dans la région alpine*, 2 vols. (1963).

The economy

A. Armengaud, P. Léon *et al.*, *Industrialisation et démographie dans la France du 19e siècle* (1970).

P. Bairoch, 'Commerce extérieur et développement économique. Quelques enseignements de l'éxpérience libre-échangiste de la France au 19e siècle', *Revue économique* (1970).

J. Bouvier, *Naissance d'une banque: le Crédit lyonnais* (1968).

J. Bouvier, 'L'économie – les crises économiques. Problèmatiques des crises économiques du 19e siècle et analyses historiques: le cas de France', in J. le Goff and P. Nora (eds.), *Faire de l'histoire*, vol. 2 (1974).

F. Caron, 'Les commandes des compagnies de chemin de fer en France, 1850–1914', *Revue d'histoire de la sidérurgie* (1962).

F. Caron, *Histoire de l'exploitation d'un grand réseau: la compagnie du chemin de fer du Nord, 1846–1937* (1973).

F. Caron, 'Remarques sur la croissance bourguignonne principalement au 19e siècle', *Annales de Bourgogne* (1977).

F. Caron, *An Economic History of Modern France* (1979).

E. C. Carter, R. Forster and J. N. Moody (eds.), *Enterprises and Entrepreneurs in Nineteenth- and Twentieth-Century France* (1976).

P. Cayez, *Crises et croissance de l'industrie lyonnaise, 1850–1900* (1980).

J.-M. Chaplain, *La Chambre des tisseurs. Louviers: cité drapière, 1680–1840* (Seyssel, 1984).

S. Chassagne, 'La formation des entrepreneurs à la période de l'industrialisation', *Entreprises et entrepreneurs* (1984).

H. D. Clout (ed.), *Themes in the Historical Geography of France* (1977).

H. D. Clout, *Agriculture in France on the Eve of the Railway Age* (1980).

H. D. Clout, *The Land of France, 1815–1914* (1983).

N. F. R. Crofts, 'Economic growth in France and Britain, 1830–1910: a review of the evidence', *Journal of Economic History* (1984).

F. Crouzet, 'Essai de construction d'un indice annuel de la production industrielle française au 19e siècle', *Annales ESC* (1970).

F. Crouzet, 'Encore la croissance économique française au 19e siècle', *Revue du Nord* (1972).

P. Deyon (ed.), 'Aux origines de la révolution industrielle. Industrie rurale et fabriques', *Revue du Nord* (1979).

C. Fohlen, *L'Industrie textile aux temps du Second Empire* (1956).

C. Fohlen, 'Charbon et révolution industrielle en France', in L. Trenard (ed.), *Charbon et sciences humaines* (1966).

C. Fohlen, 'Entrepreneurship and management in France in the nineteenth century', *The Cambridge Economic History of Europe*, vol. II, part I (1978).

B. Gille, *Recherches sur la formation de la grande enterprise capitaliste, 1814–48* (1959).

B. Gille, *La sidérurgie française au 19ᵉ siècle* (Geneva 1968).

B. Gille, *La banque en France au 19ᵉ siècle* (Geneva 1978).

B. Gille, *Les origines de la grande industrie métallurgique en France* (n.d.).

M. Gillet, *Les Charbonnages du Nord de la France au 19ᵉ siècle* (1973).

G. W. Grantham, 'Scale and organisation in French farming, 1840–80', in W. N. Parker and E. L. Jones (eds.), *European Peasants and their Markets* (1975).

G. W. Grantham, 'The diffusion of the new husbandry in Northern France, 1815–1940', *Journal of Economic History* (1978).

C. Heywood, 'The rural hosiery industry of the Lower Champagne region, 1750–1850', *Textile History* (1976).

C. Heywood, 'The rôle of the peasantry in French industrialisation', *Economic History Review* (1981).

R. Larrère *et al.*, 'Reboisement des montagnes et systèmes agraires', *Revue forestière française* (1982).

A. Lefebvre-Teillard, *La Société anonyme au XIXᵉ siècle* (1985).

M. Lévy-Leboyer, 'La croissance économique en France au 19ᵉ siècle', *Annales ESC* (1968)

M. Lévy-Leboyer (ed.), *Le patronat de la seconde industrialisation* (1979).

J. Lhomme, 'La crise agricole à la fin du 19ᵉ siécle en France: essai d'interpretation économique et sociale', *Revue Economique* (1970).

T. J. Markovitch, 'L'Industrie française de 1789 à 1964', *Cahiers de l'ISEA* (1965).

T. J. Markovitch, 'Les cycles industriels en France', *Le Mouvement Social* (1968).

J. Merley, *L'industrie en Haute-Loire de la fin de la Monarchie de Juillet aux début de la 3ᵉ République* (Lyon 1972).

M. Morineau, *Les faux-semblants d'un démarrage économique: agriculture et démographie en France au 18ᵉ siècle* (1970).

J. Mulliez, 'Du blé "mal nécessaire": reflexions sur les progrès de l'agriculture de 1750 à 1850', *Revue d'histoire moderne et contemporaine* (1979).

P. O'Brien and C. Keyder, *Economic Growth in Britain and France, 1780–1914* (1978).

J. Pautard, *Les Disparités régionales dans la croissance de l'agriculture française* (1965).

R. Price, *An Economic History of Modern France, 1730–1914* (1981).

R. Price, *The Modernization of Rural France: Communications networks and agricultural market structures in nineteenth-century France* (1983).

D. Renouard, *Les Transports de marchandises par fer, route et eau depuis 1850* (1960).

R. Roehl, 'French industrialisation: a reconsideration', *Explorations in Economic History* (1976).

M. S. Smith, *Tariff Reform in France, 1860–1900: The Politics of Economic Interest* (1980).

J.-C. Toutain, 'Le produit de l'agriculture française de 1700 à 1958', *Cahiers de l'ISEA* (1961).

J. Vial, *L'industrialisation de la sidérurgie française, 1814–64* (1967).

Demographic indicators

P. Ariès, *Histoire des populations françaises et de leurs attitudes devant la vie depuis le XVIIIᵉ siècle* (1948).

A. Armengaud, *La Population française au 19ᵉ siècle* (1971).

H. Bergues *et al., La Prévention des naissances dans la famille* (1960).

P. Bourdelais and J.-V. Raulot, 'La Marche du choléra en France: 1832 et 1854', *Annales ESC* (1978).

A. Chatelain, *Les Migrants témporaires en France de 1800 à 1914*, 2 vols. (Lille 1977).

L. Chevalier, *La Formation de la population parisienne au 19ᵉ siècle* (1950).

L. Chevalier (ed.), *Le Choléra* (1958).

L. Chevalier, *Laboring Classes and Dangerous Classes in Paris during the first half of the Nineteenth Century* (1973).

W. Coleman, *Death is a Social Disease. Public Health and Political Economy in Early Industrial France* (1982).

A. Corbin, *Les Filles de noce. Misère sexuelle et prostitution (19ᵉ–20ᵉ siècles)* (1978).

A. Corbin, *Le Miasme et la jonquille* (1982).

A. Daumard, 'Quelques remarques sur le logement des parisiens au 19ᵉ siècle', *Annales de démographie historique* (1975).

G. Désert, 'Le Dépeuplement des campagnes bas-normandes pendant la première moitié du 19ᵉ siècle', *Sur la population française au 18ᵉ et 19ᵉ siècles. Hommage à Marcel Reinhard* (1973).

G. Désert, 'Viande et poisson dans l'alimentation des Français au milieu du 19ᵉ siècle', *Annales ESC* (1975).

G. Désert, *Les Archives hospitalières* (Caen 1977).

G. Désert, 'Le Coût de la santé en Normandie', *Cahiers d'histoire* (1984).

G. Dupeux, 'La Croissance urbaine en France au 19ᵉ siècle', *Revue d'histoire économique et sociale* (1974).

T. Fillaux, 'Alcoolisation et comportements alcooliques en Bretagne au 19ᵉ siècle', *Annales de Bretagne* (1983).

R. Fuchs, *Abandoned Children. Foundlings and Child Welfare in Nineteenth Century France*, (Albany, NY 1984).

L. Girard, *La Politique des travaux publics du Second Empire* (1952).

J.-P. Goubert, 'Equipement hydraulique et pratiques sanitaires dans la France du XIXᵉ siècle' *Etudes rurales* (1984).

J.-P. Goubert, *La Conquête de l'eau* (1986).

R. H. Guerrand, *Les Origines du logement social en France* (1967).

H. Hatzfeld, *Du Paupérisme à la sécurité sociale, 1850–1940* (1971).

G. Jacquemet, 'Urbanisme parisien: la bataille du tout-à-l'égout à la fin du 19ᵉ siècle', *Revue d'histoire moderne et contemporaine* (1979).

A. Lesaege-Dugied, 'La Mortalité infantile dans le département du Nord de 1815 à 1914', in M. Gillet (ed.), *L'Homme, la vie et la mort dans le Nord au 19ᵉ siècle* (Lille 1972).

P. Merlin (ed.), *L'Exode rurale* (1971).

L. Murard and L. Zylberman (eds.), *L'Haleine des faubourgs. Ville, habitat et santé au 19ᵉ siècle* (1978).

P. Pierrard, 'Habitat ouvrier et démographie à Lille au 19ᵉ siècle', *Annales de démographie historique* (1975).

J. Pitié, *Exode rural et migrations intèrieures en France* (Poitiers 1971).

C. H. Pouthas, *La Population française pendant la première moitié du XIXᵉ siècle* (1956).

R. Price, 'Poor relief and social crisis in mid-nineteenth century France', *European Studies Review* (1983).

F. Raison-Jourde, *La colonie auvergnate de Paris au 19ᵉ siècle* (1976).

C. Rollet, 'Allaitement, mise en nourrice, et mentalité en France: 1832 et 1854', *Annales ESC* (1978).

W. Sewell, *Structure and Mobility. The Men and Women of Marseille, 1820–70* (1985).

A. L. Shapiro, *Housing the Poor of Paris, 1850–1902* (1985).

J. Singer-Kérel, *Le Coût de la vie à Paris de 1840 à 1954* (1961).

G. Thuillier, 'Pour une histoire régionale de l'eau en nivernais au XIXe siècle', *Annales ESC* (1968).

G. Thuillier, 'Pour une histoire de l'hygiene corporelle aux 19e et 20e siècles', *Annales de démographie historique* (1975).

J.-C. Toutain, 'La Consommation alimentaire en France de 1789 à 1962', *Economie et société* (1971).

J. Vidalenc, 'La Crise des subsistances de 1817 dans la Seine-Inférieure', *Actes du 93e Congrès national des sociétés savantes* (1968).

E. van de Walle, *The Female Population of France in the Nineteenth Century* (1974).

E. van de Walle, 'Alone in Europe: the French fertility decline until 1850', in C. Tilly (ed.), *Historical Studies in Changing Fertility* (1978).

D. R. Weir 'Life under pressure: France and England, 1670–1870', *Journal of Economic History* (1984).

Elites

J. Bécanuer, 'Noblesse et représentation parlementaire (1871–1968)', *Revue française de science politique* (1973).

L. Bergeron, *Les Capitalistes en France (1780–1914)* (1978).

J.-P. Chaline, *Les Bourgeois de Rouen: une élite urbaine au XIXe siècle* (1982).

C. Charle, 'Les Milieux d'affaires dans la structure de la classe dominante vers 1900', *Actes de la recherche en sciences sociales* (1978).

G. Chaussinand-Nogaret, *Une Histoire des élites* (1975).

J.-G. Daigle, *La Culture en partage. Grenoble et son élite au milieu du 19e siècle* (Grenoble 1977).

A. Daumard, 'Les fondements de la société bourgeoise en France au 19e siècle', in D. Roche and E. Labrousse (eds.), *Ordres et classes* (1967).

A. Daumard, 'L'oisiveté aristocratique et bourgeoise en France au XIXe siècle: privilège ou malédiction?' in A. Daumard (ed.), *Oisiveté et loisirs dans les sociétés occidentales au XIXe siècle* (Abbeville 1983).

M. Denis, 'Reconquête ou défensive: les stratégies de la noblesse de l'Ouest au 19e siècle', in S. Köpeczi and E. H. Balász (eds.), *Noblesse française. Noblesse Hongroise, 16e–19e siècles* (1981).

R. Forster, 'The survival of the nobility during the French revolution', *Past and Present* (1967).

R. Forster, 'The French revolution and the new elite, 1800–1850', in J. Pelenski (ed.), *The American and European Revolutions, 1776–1848* (Iowa City 1980).

P. Gerbod, 'The baccalaureate and its role in the recruitment of French elites in the nineteenth century', in J. Howarth and P. Cerny (eds.), *Elites in France* (1981).

R. Gibson, 'The nobility in nineteenth century France', in J. Howarth and P. Cerny (eds.), *Elites in France* (1981).

L. Girard, A. Prost and R. Gossez, *Les conseillers généraux en 1870* (1967).

A. Guillemin, 'Patrimoine foncier et pouvoir nobiliaire: la noblesse de la Manche sous la Monarchie de Juillet', *Etudes rurales* (1976).

D. Higgs, 'Politics and landownership among the French nobility after the revolution', *European Studies Review* (1971).

D. Higgs, *Ultraroyalism in Toulouse* (1973).

J. Lambert-Dansette, 'Le patronat du Nord,. Sa période triomphante (1830–80)', *Bulletin de la Société d'histoire moderne* (1971–2).

M. Lévy-Leboyer (ed.), *Le Patronat de la seconde industrialisation* (1979).

R. R. Locke, *French Legitimists and the Politics of Moral Order in the Early Third Republic* (1974).

B. Smith, *Ladies of the Leisure Class: Bourgeoises of Northern France in the Nineteenth Century* (1981).

M. S. Smith, 'Thoughts on the evolution of the French capitalist community in the 19th century', *Journal of European Economic History* (1978).

M. Soutadé-Rouger, 'Les notables en France sous la Restauration (1815–30)', *Revue d'histoire économique et sociale* (1960).

R. Trempé, 'Analyse du comportement des administrateurs de la Société des mines de Carmaux vis-à-vis les mineurs', *Le Mouvement Social* (1963).

A.-J. Tudesq, 'La bourgeoisie du Nord au milieu de la Monarchie de Juillet', *Revue du Nord* (1959).

A.-J. Tudesq, *Les Grands notables en France (1840–49): étude historique d'une psychologie sociale*, 2 vols. (1964).

A.-J. Tudesq, 'Les survivances de l'Ancien Régime. La noblesse dans la société française de la première moitié du 19ᵉ siècle', in D. Roche and E. Labrousse (eds.), *Ordres et classes* (1967).

A.-J. Tudesq, 'Les structures sociales du régime censitaire', *Conjoncture économique. Structures sociales. Hommage à Ernest Labrousse* (1974).

T. Zeldin, 'France', in D. Spring (ed.), *European Landed Elites in the Nineteenth Century* (1977).

Middle classes

A. Daumard, *La bourgeoisie parisienne de 1815 à 1848* (1963).

C. Fohlen, *L'industrie textile au temps du Second Empire* (1956).

H. G. Haupt, 'The petite bourgeoisie in France' 1850–1914', in G. Crossick and H. G. Haupt (eds.), *Shopkeepers and Master Artisans in Nineteenth Century Europe* (1984).

J. Lambert Dansette, *Origines et évolution d'une bourgeoisie: Quelques familles du patronat textile de Lille-Armentières (1789–1914)* (Lille 1954).

J. Léonard, 'L'Example d'une catégorie socio-professionnelle au 19ᵉ siècle: les médecins français', in D. Roche and E. Labrousse (eds.), *Ordres et classes* (1967).

J. Léonard, *Les Médecins de l'Ouest au 19ᵉ siècle* (Lille 1976).

P. N. Stearns, *Paths to Authority. The Middle Class and the Industrial Labour Force in France, 1820–48* (1978).

G. Weiz, 'The politics of medical professionalisation in France, 1845–48', *Journal of Social History* (1978–9).

Peasants

M. Agulhon and M. Bodigull (eds.), *Les Associations au village* (Le Paradou 1981).

J.-M. Augustin, 'Le Métayage au pays d'Emile Guillaumin avant 1914', *Etudes d'Histoire du droit de l'époque contemporaine* (1985).

F. Baby, *La Guerre des demoiselles en Ariège* (Montbel, Ariège, 1972).

P. Barral, 'Aspects régionaux de l'agrarisme française avant 1930', *Le Mouvement social* (1969).

J. Bastier, 'Les Paysans de Balzac et l'histoire du droit rural', *Revue d'histoire moderne et contemporaine* (1978).

E. Bougeatre, *La Vie rurale dans le mantois et le vexin au 19ᵉ siècle* (Meulan 1971).

P. Bozon, *La Vie rurale en Viverais* (1963).

R. Brunet, *Les Campagnes toulousain. Etude géographique* (Toulouse 1965).

A. Burguière, *Bretons de Plozévet* (1975).

M. Burns, *Rural Society and French Politics. Boulangism and the Dreyfus Affair, 1886–1900* (1984).

F. Chauvaud, 'L'Usure au XIXᵉ siècle; le fléau des campagnes', *Etudes rurales* (1984).

G. Cholvy, 'Société, genres de vie et mentalités dans les campagnes françaises de 1815 à 1880', *Information historique* (1974).

G. Désert, 'Les Paysans du Calvados au 19ᵉ siècle', *Annales de Normandie* (1971).

G. Désert, *Une société rurale au 19ᵉ siècle. Les paysans du Calvados, 1815–95*, 3 vols. (Lille 1975).

D. Fabre and J. Lacroix, *La Vie quotidienne des paysans du Languedoc au 19ᵉ siècle* (1973).

J.-C. Farcy, 'Les Archives judiciaires et l'histoire rurale: l'example de la Beauce au 19ᵉ siècle', *Revue historique* (1973).

J.-C., Farcy, 'Rural artisans in the Beauce during the nineteenth century', in G. Crossick and H. G. Haupt (eds.), *Shopkeepers and Master Artisans in Nineteenth Century Europe* (1984).

A. Fel, *Les Hautes terres du Massif Central. Tradition paysanne et économie agricole* (1962).

J.-L. Flandrin, *Les Amours paysannes. Amour et sexualité dans les campagnes de l'ancienne France (16–19ᵉ siècles)* (1975).

G. Garrier, *Paysans du Beaujolais et du Lyonnais, 1800–1970*, 2 vols. (Grenoble 1973).

P. Goujon, 'Associations et vie associative dans les campagnes au 19ᵉ siècle: le cas du vignoble de Saône-et-Loire', *Cahiers d'histoire* (1981).

R. H. Hubscher, *L'Agriculture et la société rurale dans le Pas-de-Calais du milieu du 19ᵉ siècle à 1914*, Doctorat d'Etat, Université de Paris IV (1978).

P. Jones, 'Common rights and agrarian individualism in the southern Massif Central, 1750–1880', in G. Lewis and C. Lucas (eds.), *Beyond the Terror. Essays in French Regional and Social History* (1983).

P. Jones, *Politics and Rural Society. The Southern Massif Central, c. 1750–1880* (1985).

E. Juillard, *La Vie rurale dans la plaine de Basse-Alsace: essai de géographie sociale* (1953).

R. Laurent, *Les Vignerons de la Côte-d'Or au XIXᵉ siècle* (1958).

R. Livet, *Habitat rural et structures agraires en Basse-Provence* (Aix-en-Provence 1962).

P. McPhee, 'Popular culture, symbolism and rural radicalism in nineteenth century France', *Journal of Peasant Studies* (1978).

T. Margadant, *French Peasants in Revolt: The Insurrection of 1851* (1979).

J.-L. Mayaud, *Les Paysans du Doubs au temps de Courbet* (1979).

R. Price, *The Modernization of Rural France* (1983).

J. Sagnes, 'Le Mouvement de 1907 en Languedoc–Roussillon: de la révolte viticole à la révolte régionale', *Le mouvement social* (1978).

M. Segalen, *Mari et femme dans la société paysanne* (1980).

B. Singer, *Village notables in Nineteenth Century France. Priests, Mayors, Schoolmasters* (Albany, NY 1983).

P. Vigier, 'Les Troubles forestiers du premier 19e siècle français', *Revue forestière française* (1980).

E. Weber, *Peasants into Frenchmen. The Modernisation of Rural France, 1870–1914* (1976).

E. Weber, 'Comment la politique vint aux paysans: A second look at peasant politicisation', *American Historical Review* (1982).

Working classes

J.-P. Aguet, *Les Grèves sous la Monarchie de Juillet* (Geneva, 1954).

M. Agulhon, *Une Ville ouvrière au temps du socialisme utopique. Toulon de 1815 à 1851* (1970).

M. Agulhon, 'Working class and sociability in France before 1848', in P. Thane, G. Crossick and R. Floud (eds.), *The Power of the Past* (1984).

A. Aminzade, *Class, Politics and Early Industrial Capitalism. A Study of Mid-Nineteenth Century Toulouse, France* (1981).

L. Berlanstein, *The Working People of Paris, 1871–1914* (1985).

F. Caron, 'Essai d'analyse historique d'une psychologie du travail. Les mécaniciens et chauffeurs de locomotion du réseau du Nord de 1850 à 1910', *Le Mouvement social* (1965).

F. Chavot, 'Les Sociétés de secours mutuels sous le Second Empire', *Cahiers d'histoire de l'Institut Maurice Thorez* (1977).

E. Coornaert, *Les Compagnonnages en France* (1966).

J.-P. Courtheaux, 'Naissance d'une conscience de classe dans le prolétariat textile du Nord, 1830–70', *Revue Economique* (1957).

A. Cuvillier, *Un Journal d'ouvriers: L'Atelier, 1840–50* (1954).

F. Demier, 'Les Ouvriers de Rouen parlent à un économiste en juillet 1848', *Le Mouvement social* (1982).

G. Duveau, *La Vie ouvrière en France sous le Second Empire* (1946).

A. Faure, 'Mouvements populaires et mouvement ouvrier à Paris (1830–34)', *Le Mouvement social* (1974).

J. Gaillard, 'Les Usines Cail et les ouvriers métallurgistes de Grenelle', *Le Mouvement social* (1961).

R. Gossez, *Les Ouvriers de Paris* (1967).

P. Guiral and G. Thuillier, *La Vie quotidienne des domestiques en France au 19e siècle* (1978).

M. P. Hanagan, 'The logic of solidarity. Social structures in Le Chambon-Feugerolles', *Journal of Urban History* (1976–7).

C. Heywood, 'The market for child labour in nineteenth century France', *History* (1980).

P. Hilden, 'Class and gender: conflicting components of women's behaviour in the textile mills of Lille, Roubaix and Tourcoing, 1880–1914', *Historical Journal* (1984).

C. H. Johnson, *Utopian Communism in France. Cabet and the Icarians, 1839–51* (1974).

C. H. Johnson, 'Economic changes and artisan discontent: the tailors' history, 1800–48', in R. Price (ed.), *Revolution and Reaction. 1848 and the Second French Republic* (1975).

C. H. Johnson, 'Patterns of proletarianisation: Parisian tailors and Lodéve woollens workers', in J. M. Merriman (ed.), *Consciousness and Class Experience in Nineteenth Century Europe* (1979).

T. Judt, 'The French labour movement in the nineteenth century', in T. Judt (ed.), *Marxism and the French Left* (1986).

J. Julliard, 'La C.G.T. devant la guerre (1900–1914)', *Le Mouvement social* (1964).

S. L. Kaplan, C. J. Koepp (eds), *Work in France* (1986).

A. Kriegel, 'Patrie ou révolution: le mouvement ouvrier français devant la guerre (Juillet–août, 1914)', *Revue d'histoire économique et sociale* (1965).

A. Lasserre, *La Situation des ouvriers de l'industrie textile dans la region lilloise sous la Monarchie de Juillet* (Lausanne 1952).

B. Legendre, 'La Crise d'un prolétariat: les ouvriers de Fougères au début au 20ᵉ siècle', *La Mouvement social* (1977).

T. Leleu, 'Scènes de la vie quotidienne: les femmes de la vallée de la Lys (1870–1920)', *Revue de Nord* (1981).

Y. Lequin, *La Formation de la classe ouvrière régionale: les ouvriers de la région lyonnaise (1848–1914)*, 2 vols. (Lyon 1977).

Y. Lequin, 'Labour in the French economy since the revolution', *The Cambridge Economic History of Europe*, vol. VII, part I (1978).

J. Lhomme, 'Le pouvoir d'achat de l'ouvrier français au cours d'un siècle, 1840–1940', *Le Mouvement social* (1968).

F. L'Huillier, *La Lutte ouvrière à la fin du Second Empire* (1957).

Y. Marec, *Pauvres et philanthropes à Rouen au 19ᵉ siècle* (Rouen 1981).

B. H. Moss, 'Parisian producers associations (1830–51): the socialism of skilled workers', in R. Price (ed.), *Revolution and Reaction. 1848 and the Second French Republic* (1975).

B. H. Moss, *The Origins of the French Labor Movement. The Socialism of Skilled Workers* (1976).

L. Murard and P. Zyberman, *Le Petit travailleur infatigable ou le prolétaire régénéré. Villes-usines, habitat et intimités au 19ᵉ siècle* (Fontenay-sous-Bois 1976).

M. Perrot, 'La Presse syndicale des ouvriers mineurs, (1880–1914)', *Le Mouvement social* (1963).

M. Perrot, 'Grèves, grévistes et conjoncture', *Le Mouvement social* (1968).

M. Perrot, *Les Ouvriers en grève. France 1871–90*, 2 vols. (1974).

M. Perrot, 'Le Militant face à la grève dans la mine et la métallurgie au 19ᵉ siècle', *Le Mouvement social* (1977).

M. Perrot, 'Une Naissance difficile: la formation de la classe ouvrière lyonnaise', *Annales ESC* (1978).

M. Perrot (ed.), 'De la nourrice à l'employée. Travaux de femmes dans la France du 19ᵉ siècle', *Le Mouvement social* (1978).

M. Perrot, 'Les Ouvriers et les machines en France dans la première moitié du 19ᵉ siècle', in L. Murard and P. Zylberman (eds.), *Le Soldat du travail. Guerre, fascisme et taylorisme* (1978).

M. Perrot, 'The three ages of industrial discipline in nineteenth century France', in J. M. Merriman (ed.), *Consciousness and Class Experience in Nineteenth Century Europe* (1979).

M. Perrot, 'La classe ouvrière française au temps de Jaurès', in M. Rebérioux (ed.), *Jaurès et la classe ouvrière* (1981).

M. Perrot, 'De la manufacture à l'usine en miettes', *Le Mouvement social* (1983).

P. Pierrard, *La Vie ouvrière à Lille sous le Second Empire* (1965).

P. Ponsot, 'Organisation et action dans le mouvement ouvrier. Réflexion sur le cas de Montceau-les-Mines au tournant du 19ᵉ et du 20ᵉ siècles', *Le Mouvement social* (1977).

J. Rancière. 'The myth of the artisan', *International Labor and Working Class History* (1983).

J. Rougerie, 'Remarques sur l'histoire des salaires à Paris au 19ᵉ siècle', *Le Mouvement social* (1968).

J. W. Scott, *The Glassworkers of Carmaux* (1974).

J. W. Scott, 'Men and women in the Parisian garment trades; discussion of family and work in the 1830s and 1840s', in P. Thane, G. Crossick and R. Floud (eds.), *The Power of the Past* (1984).

W. H. Sewell, 'La Classe ouvrière de Marseille sous la seconde république: structure sociale et comportement politique', *Le Mouvement social* (1971).

W. H. Sewell, *Work and Revolution in France. The Language of Labor from the Old Regime to 1848* (1980).

W. H. Sewell, 'La confraternité des prolétaires; Conscience de classe sous la Monarchie de Juillet', *Annales ESC* (1981).

G. J. Sheridan, *The Social and Economic Foundations of Association among the Silk Weavers of Lyon, 1852–70*, 2 vols. (New York 1981).

E. Shorter and C. Tilly, *Strikes in France, 1830–1968* (1974).

L. S. Strumingher, *Women and the Making of the Working Class: Lyon, 1830–70* (1979).

L. A. Tilly and J. W. Scott, *Women, Work and Family* (1978).

R. Trempé, *Les Mineurs de Carmaux, 1848–1914*, 2 vols. (1971).

R. Trempé, 'Travail à la mine et vieillissement des mineurs au XIXᵉ siècle', *Le Mouvement social* (1983).

Church

F. Bédarida and J. Maitron (eds.), *Christianisme et monde ouvrier* (1975).

F. Boulard (ed.), *Matériaux pour l'histoire religieuse du peuple français XIX–XXᵉ siècles*, vol. I (1982).

P. Boutry, *Prêtres et paroisses au pays du curé d'Ars* (1986).

N. J. Chaline, 'Pratique et vie religieuse en Haute-Normandie aux 19ᵉ et 20ᵉ siècles', in P. Chaunu (ed.), *Mentalités religieuses dans la France de l'Ouest* (Caen 1976).

G. Cholvy, *Religion et société au 19ᵉ siècle. Le diocèse de Montpellier*, 2 vols. (Lille 1973).

G. Cholvy, 'Réalités de la religion populaire dans la France contemporaine', in B. Plongeron (ed.), *La religion populaire* (1976).

G. Cholvy, ' "Du Dieu terrible au Dieu d'amour": Une évolution dans la sensibilité religieuse au XIXᵉ siècle', *Actes du 109ᵉ Congrès national des sociétés savantes* (Dijon 1984).

G. Cholvy and Y.-M. Hilaire, *Histoire religieuse de la France contemporaine* (Toulouse 1985).

G. Désert, 'Ruraux, religion et clergé dans le diocèse de Bayeux au 19ᵉ siècle', P. Chaunu (ed.), *Mentalités religieuses dans la France de l'ouest* (Caen 1977).

G. Dubosq, B. Plongeron and D. Robert (eds.), *La Religion populaire* (1979).

J.-B. Duroselle, *Les Débuts du catholicisme social en France, 1822–1870* (1951).

M. Faugeres, *La Reconstruction Catholique dans l'ouest après la révolution. Le diocèse de Nantes sous la monarchie censitaire* (Fontenay-le-Comte 1964).

J. Faury, *Cléricalisme et anticléricalisme dans le Tarn* (Toulouse 1980).

J. Gadille, *La Pensée et l'action politique des évêques français au début de la 3e République* (1967).

Y.-M. Hilaire, 'La Pratique religieuse en France de 1815 à 1878', *Information historique* (1963).

Y.-M. Hilaire, 'L'Eglise dans le monde rural. Le XIXe siècle', *Recherche sociale* (1971).

Y.-M. Hilaire, 'Responsables et agents de la catéchèse en France au XIXe siècle', *Actes du 109e Congrès national des sociétés savantes* (Dijon 1984).

Y.-M. Hilaire, *La vie religieuse des populations du diocèse d'Arras, 1840–1914*, Doctorat d'Etat, Université de Paris IV (1976).

F. A. Isambert, *Christianisme et classe ouvrière* (1961).

A. T. Kselman, 'Miracles and prophecies: popular religion and the church in nineteenth century France', Ph.D. thesis, University of Michigan (1978).

M. Lagrée, *Mentalités, religion et histoire en Haute Bretagne* (1977).

C. Langlois, *Le Catholicisme au féminin. Les congrégations françaises à supérieure générale au XIXe siècle* (1984).

M. Launay, *Le Diocèse de Nantes sous le Second Empire*, 2 vols. (Nantes 1983).

R. Luneau, 'Monde rural et christianisation', *Archives de sciences sociales des religions* (1977).

J. McManners, *Church and State in France, 1870–1914* (1972).

C. Marcilhacy, *Le Diocèse d'.Orléans sous l'épiscopat de Mgr. Dupanloup, 1849–79* (1962).

C. Marcilhacy, *Le Diocèse d'Orléans au milieu du XIXe siècle* (1964).

J. Maurain, *La Politique ecclésiastique du Second Empire de 1852 à 1869* (1930).

P. Pierrard, *La Vie quotidienne du prêtre français au XIXe siècle, 1801–1905* (1986).

C. Savart, *Les Catholiques en France au XIXe siècle. Le témoignage du livre religieux* (1985).

E. Sevrin, *Les Missions religieuses en France sous la Restauration*, 2 vols. (St-Mandé 1948).

M. H. Vicaire, 'Les Ouvriers parisiens en face du Catholicisme de 1830 à 1870', *Revue Suisse d'histoire* (1951).

T. Zeldin (ed.), *Conflicts in French Society* (1970).

Education

M. Agulhon, 'Le Probléme de la culture populaire en France autour de 1848', *Romantisme* (1975–6).

R. Anderson, *Education in France, 1848–70* (1975).

D. N. Baker and P. J. Harrigan (eds.), *The Making of Frenchmen: Current Directions in the History of Education in France* (Waterloo, Ontario 1980).

J. Beauroy, *et al.* (eds.), *Popular Culture in France* (Saratoga, California 1976).

C. Bellanger *et al.*, *Histoire générale de la presse française*, vols. II and III (1972).

M. Crubellier, *L'Enfance et la jeunesse dans la société française, 1800–1950* (1979).

J.-J. Darmon, *Le Colportage de librairie en France sous le Second Empire* (1972).

Y. Fumate, 'La Socialisation des filles au 19e siècle', *Revue française de pédagogie* (1980).

F. Furet and J. Ozouf, 'Literacy and industrialisation: the case of the Département du Nord in France', *Journal of European Economic History* (1976).

F. Furet and J. Ozouf, *Lire et écrire*, 2 vols. (1977).

P. Gerbod, *La Condition universitaire en France au 19e siècle* (1965).

R. Gildea, *Education in Provincial France, 1800–1914* (1983).

P. Giolito, *Histoire de l'enseignement primaire au 19ᵉ siècle*, vol. II, *Les méthodes d'enseignement* (1984).

M. Gontard, *L'Enseignement secondaire en France, 1750.–1850* (Aix-en-Provence 1984).

M. Gontard, *Les Ecoles primaires de la France bourgeoise (1833–1878)* (Toulouse n.d.).

M. Gontard, *L'Enseignement primaire en France de la Révolution à la loi Guizot* (n.d.).

P. J. Harrigan, 'Secondary education and the professions in France during the Second Empire', *Comparative Studies in Society and history* (1975).

P. J. Harrigan, 'The social origins, ambitions and occupations of secondary students in France during the Second Empire', in L. Stone (ed.), *Schooling and Society* (1976).

P. J. Harrigan, *Mobility, Elites and Education in French Society of the Second Empire*, (Waterloo, Ontario 1980).

M. F. Lévy, *De mères en filles. L'éducation des Françaises, 1850–80* (1984).

P. V. Meyer, 'Professionalisation and societal change: rural teachers in nineteenth century France', *Journal of Social History* (1975–6).

F. Muel, 'Les Instituteurs, les paysans et l'ordre républicain', *Actes de la recherche en sciences sociales* (1977).

J. Ozouf, *Nous les maîtres d'école* (1967).

J. and M. Ozouf, 'Le Thème du patriotisme dans les manuels primeurs', *Le Mouvement social* (1964).

A. Prost, *L'Enseignement en France, 1800–1967* (1968).

N. Richter, *Les Bibliothèques populaires* (1978).

H.-C. Rulon and P. Friot, *Un siècle de pédagogie dans les écoles primaires (1820–1940)* (1962).

L. S. Strumingher, *What were Little Girls and Boys Made of? Primary Education in Rural France, 1830–80* (Albany, NY 1983).

R. Thabault, *Education and Change in a Village Community: Mazières-en-Gâtine, 1848–1914* (1971).

P. Zind, *L'Enseignement religieux dans l'instruction primaire publique en France de 1850 à 1873* (Lyon 1971).

State

J. Aubert *et al.*, *Les Préfets en France (1800–1940)* (Geneva 1978).

J. Aubert *et al.*, *L'Etat et sa police en France (1789–1914)* (Geneva 1979).

T. D. Beck, *French Legislators, 1830–34* (1974).

P. Chalmin, *L'Officier français de 1815–1870* (1957).

C. Charle, *Les Hauts fonctionnaires en France au 19ᵉ siècle* (1980).

C. Charle, 'Le recrutement des hauts fonctionnaires en 1901', *Annales ESC* (1980).

B. Le Clèrc, V. Wright, *Les Préfets du Second Empire* (1973).

J. Estèbe, *Les Ministres de la République, 1871–1914* (1982).

L. Fougère *et al.*, *Histoire de l'administration française depuis 1800* (Geneva 1975).

P. Gerbod *et al.*, *Les Epurations administratives, 19ᵉ et 20ᵉ siècles* (Geneva 1977).

J. M. House, 'Civil–military relations in Paris, 1848', in R. Price (ed.), *Revolution and Reaction. 1848 and the Second French Republic* (1975).

H. C. Payne, *The Police State of Louis Napoleon Bonaparte, 1851–60* (Seattle 1966).

R. Price, *The French Second Republic. A Social History* (1972).

R. Price, 'Techniques of repression. The control of popular protest in mid-nineteenth century France', *Historical Journal* (1982).

J. F. Stone, *The Search for Social Peace. Reform Legislation in France, 1890–1914* (Albany NY 1985).

R. Tombs, *The War against Paris, 1871* (1981).

Index

189, 291, 335; renewal 35, 55, 57–8,
84, 220
urban transport 58, 87, 220, 228
urbanization, processes and
problems 42, 51, 55, 84–91, 117,
221–3, 225, 264, 273, 287–8, 291–2,
299, 301, 357

vaine pâture 185
Vaillant, E. 255–6
Vanne, river 60
Var (dépt) 160–1, 189, 191, 295
Varlin, E. 254, 258
Vatimesnil, H. de 347
Vaucluse (dépt) 27, 314
vegetables, cultivation and consumption
of 10, 21, 53–4
veillée 172, 179, 272, 353
Vendée (dépt) 23, 88, 115, 176, 193,
264, 290
venereal disease 64, 241
Verne, J. 355
veterinarians 126
Veuillot, L. 273, 280
Vienne (dépt) 319
Vienne-Haute (dépt) 73, 159, 291, 319,
328, 331, 335
Vienne (Isère) 239
Vienne, river 61
village social structures 133, 143, 159,
169
Villèle family 156
Villeneuve-Bargemont, A. de 276
Villermé, L. R. 69, 142, 220
Vimy (Pas-de-Calais) 301
vine cultivation 9, 12, 17–21, 26–7, 39,
53, 85, 87, 90, 111, 147–8, 156,
159–62, 176, 178, 185–6, 192–3, 290,
334
violence 173, 183, 216, 222, 226, 237–8,
241
Vitré (Ille-et-Vilaine) 292

Viviers (Ardèche) 264
Voguë, Marquis de 98–9
voluntary associations 180
Vosges (dépt) 24, 38, 185, 259, 324
Vraiville (Eure) 76

women's: education 294, 302, 343–4,
351; religion 302–3, 319; status 78,
80–1, 224, 319, 343; wages 75;
work 33, 74–5, 77–8, 89, 136, 200–2,
205–9, 212–14, 216–17, 219, 223–5,
265–6, 343–4
wood consumption 38, 185
working classes 197–258; family
life 82, 221–4; living
conditions 199, 206, 208, 215–21,
229, 250, 257; organization 199–201,
206–7, 225, 227, 231, 233–7, 239–49,
252; politics 200, 218, 227, 243–5,
248–58; protest 205, 207, 217, 225,
228–39; property ownership 52, 91,
217, 220, 225; recruitment 89–91,
202–4, 221–3; relationships with other
social groups 142, 200–1, 203, 208,
218, 222, 225–7, 237–9, 242–3, 245,
249–50, 252, 254–7, 299–300, 302;
religion 299–302; social
mobility 135, 137, 206, 208–9,
225–7, 302, 324, 338–9, 342, 345;
structures 197–210, 212–14, 217,
225–6; women 33, 77–8, 200–2,
205–8, 212–13
working conditions 49, 62, 69, 131–2,
134, 142, 199–201, 203–5, 207–8,
210–14, 236, 238; hours 50, 202, 208,
210, 212, 234–6, 245, 250, 252
Workshops, National 251–3, 258

Yonne (dépt) 138, 185, 189, 192, 290

Zola, E. 174